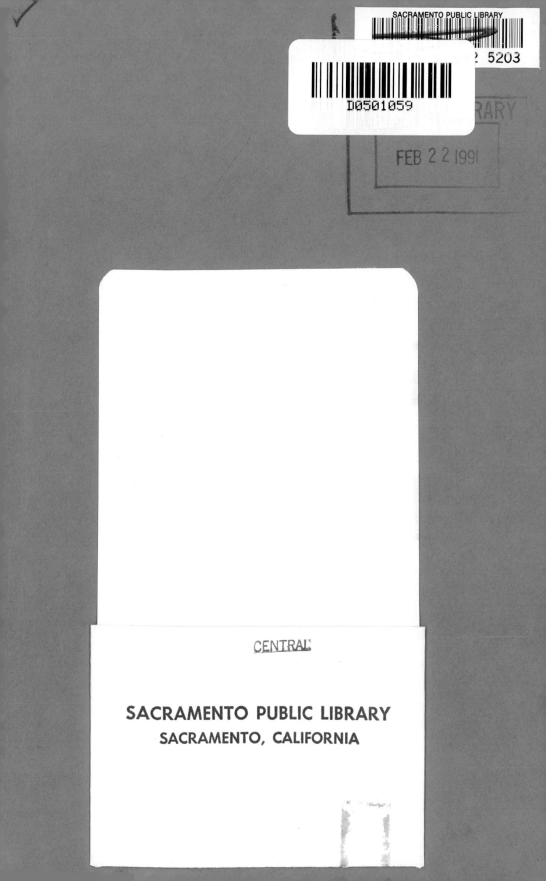

Lafayette in the Age of
the American Revolution

Marie-Joseph-Paul-Yves-Roch-Gilbert du Motier, marquis de Lafayette

Lafayette in the Age of the American Revolution

SELECTED LETTERS AND PAPERS, 1776–1790

Volume I · December 7, 1776–March 30, 1778

STANLEY J. IDZERDA, *Editor*

ROGER E. SMITH, *Associate Editor*

Linda J. Pike *and* Mary Ann Quinn,
Assistant Editors

CORNELL UNIVERSITY PRESS

ITHACA AND LONDON

First published 1977 by Cornell University Press.
Published in the United Kingdom by Cornell University Press Ltd., 2-4 Brook Street, London W1Y 1AA.

International Standard Book Number 0-8014-1031-2
Library of Congress Catalog Card Number 76-50268
Printed in the United States of America by Vail-Ballou Press, Inc.
Librarians: Library of Congress cataloging information appears on the last page of the book.

IN MEMORY OF
LOUIS R. GOTTSCHALK

THE PAPERS OF THE MARQUIS DE LAFAYETTE

*Sponsored by the Cornell University Libraries
and the National Historical Publications
and Records Commission*

ADVISORY BOARD

E. Marie Benabou, *Université de Paris I*
Yves-Marie Bercé, *Archives de France*
Louis Bergeron, *Ecole Pratique des Hautes Etudes*
Herbert Dieckmann, *Cornell University*
Durand Echeverria, *Brown University*
C. Herbert Finch, *Cornell University*
Jacques Godechot, *Université de Toulouse*
Louis R. Gottschalk,* *University of Chicago*
Michael G. Kammen, *Cornell University*
Steven L. Kaplan, *Cornell University*
J. Gormly Miller, *Cornell University*
Mary Beth Norton, *Cornell University*
Robert R. Palmer, *Yale University*
George W. Pierson, *Yale University*
Howard C. Rice, Jr., *Princeton University*
Fred Somkin, *Cornell University*
Chantal de Tourtier-Bonazzi, *Archives Nationales*

HONORARY MEMBERS

Theodore Besterman *
Comte René de Chambrun

Arthur H. Dean
Mary Marden Dean

* Deceased.

ACKNOWLEDGMENTS

Any contemporary editorial project is made possible only with the help and support of many persons, institutions, and organizations; we, the editors of the Papers of the Marquis de Lafayette, are extremely grateful for the courtesies and assistance we have received from the archives, repositories, and libraries that have been the source of the documents we use in this volume.

Of particular value have been the personal aid and counsel we have received from the editors and the editorial staffs working with the papers of other eighteenth-century figures: the Papers of Thomas Jefferson, the Adams Family Papers, the Papers of George Washington, the Papers of James Madison, the Papers of Nathanael Greene, the Papers of Benjamin Franklin, and the Papers of Henry Laurens.

Especially notable for the extensive personal services rendered to us during our visits have been the staffs of the Skillman Library of Lafayette College, the South Carolina Historical Society, the New-York Historical Society, the New York Public Library, the Pierpont Morgan Library, the Connecticut Historical Society, the Yale University Library, the Rhode Island Historical Society, the National Archives, the Manuscript Division of the Library of Congress, the Public Record Office in London and in Ashridge, Hertfordshire, and the Bibliothèque Nationale and the Archives Nationales in Paris.

We are also grateful for generous assistance given us by the staffs of the New Hampshire Historical Society, the Houghton Library at Harvard University, the State Papers Office of the State of Vermont, the Maryland Historical Society, and the Frick Art Reference Library.

Many archives, libraries, and individuals gave us permission to reproduce the material in this volume, as credited in the provenance note to each document. We are most grateful to them.

Financial support has come from the beginning from the National Historical Publications and Records Commission and from the Cornell University Libraries. Without such continuing support, neither the collection and collation of Lafayette's papers in the United States, the production of the guide to those papers (*Lafayette: A Guide to the Letters, Documents, and Manuscripts in the United States*, edited by Louis Gottschalk, Phyllis S. Pestieau, and Linda J. Pike [Ithaca: Cornell University Press, 1975]), nor this first volume of selected letters and documents would have been possible. Additional grants have been awarded to the project by the National Endowment for the Humanities, the Gebhard-Gourgaud Foundation, and the Rockefeller Foundation.

It was Arthur H. Dean's vision and generosity that were responsible for bringing the major collection of Lafayette manuscripts to Cornell more than a decade ago; at many stages of the project Mr. Dean has provided encouragement, ideas, and guarantees for the future of the project which were indispensable. Louis Gottschalk's directorship of the Lafayette project until 1974 assured that his lifetime of Lafayette scholarship and his gentle and thoughtful guidance would give a firm foundation to the editorial labors that followed his. Phyllis S. Pestieau served as assistant editor until 1975 and continued her valuable services to the project in European archives during her leave of absence. We also express our appreciation to Joseph L. Narun, who compiled the index, and to all those other persons who have assisted us in our editorial tasks: Mara Silvers, Flo Smith, Katy Gottschalk, Gail Dixon, and Linda Andersen. Peg and Jim Johns and Gerry Idzerda generously helped us with proofreading. And to Mme Chantal de Tourtier-Bonazzi, conservateur aux Archives Privées in the Archives Nationales, we owe more than we can say for her diplomacy, her unstinted spirit of cooperation, her advocacy, and her friendship as she shared with us the concern to uncover the vital documents we needed to complete this volume.

Finally, we must express our heartfelt thanks to the directors and staffs of the National Historical Publications and Records Commission and the Cornell University Libraries. These persons went far beyond the call of institutional or corporate requirements in their involvement with, assistance to, and support for the editorial labors on this volume. Their expertise, their patience, and their good humor as they provided humane and thoughtful colleagueship are among the daily rewards of being part of the Lafayette editorial staff. Whatever good qualities this volume may have must be the first measure of our gratitude to them.

STANLEY J. IDZERDA

Ithaca, New York

CONTENTS

PART III. VALLEY FORGE

DECEMBER 3, 1777–JANUARY 22, 1778   167

ILLUSTRATIONS

MAPS

INTRODUCTION

This is the first volume in a documentary chronicle of the Marquis de Lafayette's participation in the American Revolution, from 1776, when he signed an agreement to serve as a major general in the Continental army, to 1790, when he devoted his full attention to the revolution in his own country.

Much of the material for this edition is taken from Lafayette's own collection of manuscripts, which was not accessible until Arthur H. and Mary Marden Dean presented it to Cornell University in 1963. Many items from that collection were published in 1837, three years after Lafayette's death, as *Mémoires, correspondance et manuscrits du Général Lafayette, publiés par sa famille.* For a century and a half that edition has been accepted as the main source of information about Lafayette and one of the basic sources for the study of the American Revolution.

In preparing a new edition of Lafayette's papers, we have discovered that the texts of many of the letters presented in *Mémoires* are significantly different from those of the manuscripts. In the printed versions, spelling and punctuation have been regularized, some words and phrases have been added, and many words, sentences, and even whole paragraphs have been silently omitted. Now we are able to publish, for the first time, the complete texts as they appear in the manuscripts.

An additional cache of Lafayette papers was discovered in 1955, at the Château de La Grange, Lafayette's home after the French Revolution. Some of that material deals with the period of the American Revolution, and Lafayette's descendant the Comte de Chambrun has made it available for inclusion in our volumes.

To these reconstituted papers we have added letters written by Lafayette which are now in public and private collections, many letters written to Lafayette, some letters about him, and several extracts from journals and memoirs dealing with events in which he participated. Many of these documents are published here for the first time.

With so much new material at hand, some earlier appraisals of Lafayette's motives and actions and some judgments about events in which he was a participant or which he observed will require revision. These documents may even help us to understand why Lafayette has remained a central figure in the American memory.

II

During the years covered by these volumes, Marie-Joseph-Paul-Yves-Roch-Gilbert du Motier, marquis de Lafayette, was the best known foreigner serving the American cause. As a field officer he fought at Brandywine, Gloucester, and Monmouth, and he held important commands at Albany, Barren Hill, and Rhode Island. His last military assignment in America was as commander of the Continental forces in Virginia during the spring and summer of 1781, until he was joined by the allied armies before Yorktown. Lafayette proved himself as a field commander and won the confidence of his commander in chief, his fellow officers, and his men.

Lafayette also had a significant part in the creation and maintenance of the French alliance. During his service in America, from 1777 to 1782 (and while on leave in France in 1779), he maintained an extensive correspondence with family, friends, and officials in both France and America. In France he was the steady representative of the American cause; he reported American prospects, strengths, and needs, and he proposed ways in which the French government could increase its support for the "insurgents." In America he was the principal advocate of the alliance; he reassured the Americans about the capacities and intentions of the French, and the French about those of the Americans; he soothed wounded sensibilities on both sides; and he supported Washington's proposals for the military coordination that ultimately won the war.

After Yorktown, Lafayette returned to France and assisted the American commissioners in the peace negotiations, and from 1783 to 1790 he devoted a great deal of time to developing commercial concessions in Europe for his adopted country. When Jefferson was sent to France in 1784, he continued a warm friendship with Lafayette which had begun during the Virginia campaign, and he noted that, during his term as minister, he often only "held the nail" while Lafayette "wielded the hammer" for American interests.

When Lafayette first espoused the American cause, he described the American independence movement as a unique opportunity to distinguish himself and to learn his profession as a soldier. Even before he reached America, however, he began to think about the principles that inspired the American patriots, and the moment he landed he was won over by American republican habits and ideas. When he returned to France he was not only a military hero, he had become the European embodiment of the American experiment, and he began to work for liberal causes he may never even have dreamed of before he went to America: the abolition of slavery, the emancipation of French Protestants and Jews, and the establishment of constitutional government in France.

In 1783 Lafayette had an engraving made of the American Declaration of Independence. He placed it in one side of a double frame, leaving the other side empty for a French declaration of rights. At the very beginning of the French Revolution he drafted such a declaration, inspired by the Declaration of Independence and the proposed American Bill of Rights. He submitted his draft to the new National Assembly, which incorporated most of it in the basic text of the Revolution: the Declaration of the Rights of Man and the Citizen.

In 1790 he thought it only fitting to have Thomas Paine carry the key of the Bastille to President Washington. In an accompanying letter Lafayette explained that as commander of the Paris National Guard he had ordered the demolition of the "fortress of despotism," and that the key was "a tribute which I owe as a son to my adoptive father . . . as a Missionary of Liberty to its Patriarch."

When Lafayette visited ten of the thirteen states in 1784, he sensed that he occupied an unusual position in his second country. "Our marquis," as he was called, had the affection and esteem of every section of America; he was one of the few truly national figures at a time when local loyalties prevailed. His national stature enabled him to use every public and private occasion to speak bluntly of the necessity for a stronger union, if the country he called "the hope of the world" was not to be picked off piecemeal by European powers. He was very proud of his dual citizenship and conscious of the different roles he played as he represented the hopes and expectations of a new political era in each of his countries.

All of these ideas and experiences will emerge in these volumes in Lafayette's correspondence with an extraordinary range of persons involved in the fate of revolutionary America: with Louis XVI's ministers, ambassadors, generals, and admirals, and with nearly every important political, military, and naval figure in the United States. Lafayette was one of the indefatigable letter writers of the eighteenth century, and he made many fast friends. The publication of these letters and, on occasion, some contemporary testimony about Lafayette provides a richly textured and vivid account of the ambitions, sacrifices, failures, and successes that Lafayette shared with a galaxy of Americans and Frenchmen who considered him an "efficacious and essential servant" of the American cause.

The publication of Lafayette's papers for the period 1776–1790 gives a picture of the first years of the new nation which the papers of few other persons can provide. They give the American Revolution a wide, thorough, and intimate coverage, and reveal the strains and the binding ties of the French alliance from a point of view unmatched in the papers of any other participant; for Lafayette's dual loyalty and his influence with leaders on both sides of the Atlantic had no parallel. Finally, the record of his continuing advocacy of American interests after the revolutionary war and of his transmission and adaptation of American principles to his native country provides a significant perspective on the relationship between the American and French revolutions. An extensive selection from Lafayette's papers can help us to understand his personality and his contribution for their own sakes, and provide some insight into the reasons for his prominence in our collective consciousness for two centuries: the names of only Washington, Jefferson, and Franklin appear more frequently on the American landscape. "The emblem of liberty," he was called, and "the hero of two worlds." These are time-worn metaphors for Franco-American friendship, based upon the common appreciation of Lafayette's services in the cause of liberty in America.

III

The documents in these volumes have been chosen to reveal Lafayette's personality and motives, and his impact upon the people and events of his time, as well as their effect upon him. No secondary source can offer the particularity and concreteness of these documents, or match the elements of mystery and ambiguity to be found in them. We have attempted to be terse and succinct in our annotation, because these documents, by their very nature, must in large measure be their own justification.

Yet for readers of these documents who are unfamiliar with the rhetoric of the eighteenth century, certain themes and concepts, though they implicitly color every page, may be obscure or misleading because the language in which they are expressed is quite ordinary. Among these key concepts are glory, honor, and liberty. For the leading participants of the American Revolution, these words and their cluster of related concepts were powerful ideas that provided motivation for or barriers to action, and the values they expressed were so deep-seated that they were taken for granted.

Lafayette used these words often, and, with minor personal variations, they had the same range and depth of meaning for him as they did for his American friends. During his first week in America, Lafayette remarked that he was pleased to find an "affinity" between American ideas and his own. His constant talk of a desire for glory and his concern for honor were easy for his American hosts to accept and understand, because they believed that all gentlemen (the term most American leaders would have readily applied to themselves) were motivated by such concepts. For them, glory and honor were closely linked to fame, renown, reputation, consideration, and esteem. If we add to these concepts a concern for the approbation of posterity, we have nearly the entire lexicon of the personal value system shared by the leaders of western Europe and America at the end of the eighteenth century.

These key words had their opposites. When one disagreed with or disliked a man, the reason often given was that he had not cleaved to honor or glory; rather, he had fallen prey to ambition. Ambition in such a person derived from either pride or vanity: if from pride, then the goal was power; if from vanity, then the goal was popularity. Power was to be feared and popularity was contemptible. Both were the dreadful fruits of ambition, and the final reward of the ambitious scoundrel was to be execrated by posterity.

When Lafayette accuses others of ambition in these letters, the twentieth-century reader may believe he can discern something very much like ambition in Lafayette himself, but such a judgment misses the point of the eighteenth-century distinction between ambition and the desire for glory. When an individual attempted to advance his private interest, or that of his party or faction (read "cabal" or "conspiracy" when the stakes were high), then he was accused of ambition, vanity, or pride. When, on the other hand, an individual sought eminence as a leader for the common weal, that aim not only purified ambition but transmuted it to the desire for glory or the fulfillment of the requirements of reputation and honor. Most men of Lafayette's generation were confident they could make that distinction in regard to themselves and those around them.

Because of the currency of this value system, members of Congress, as well as Washington and his officers, could empathize with Lafayette's constant importunities for a command—preferably a dangerous one—in order to earn the glory he sought, in the cause of liberty. An understanding of the value system also puts into perspective the rhetorical overkill brought to bear upon the "Conway Cabal" by Lafayette and his American friends. A cabal was by definition a scheme

of ambitious men, and what was particularly heinous about this cabal
was that it would satisfy the schemers' ambition at the cost of General
Washington's glory and reputation. The Conway Cabal appears to
many historians to have been an inconsequential phantom, but it was
very real to the actors in the drama, and more than one appeal to the
dueling code made up the last act.

In an early letter back to Europe, Lafayette wrote, "Here only two
sovereigns are cherished and idolized: Glory and Liberty." What did
Lafayette mean by "liberty"? The historians who comment upon Lafayette's use of the word usually choose one of two explanations. At
one extreme are those who hold that when Lafayette used the
word "liberty" in 1777 he hardly could have known what he was talking about. In his ingenuous desire to please, he merely parroted language he heard other men use. To believe that Lafayette knew what
liberty meant, or that he meant what he said, these historians contend,
is to accept the legend of precocious liberalism which he wished to
believe about himself, as when he wrote in 1799, "With the enthusiasm of religion, the rapture of love, the conviction of geometry: that
is how I have always loved liberty." At the other extreme are those
who hold that Lafayette was an unusual French nobleman who ran
counter to the political principles that prevailed in monarchical
France, a farsighted precursor of the French Revolution who simply
confirmed his natural libertarian principles with his services in
America.

Neither of these interpretations accurately describes Lafayette's position. When Lafayette and other European aristocrats used the word
"liberty" in 1777, they meant freedom from arbitrary, despotic, or tyrannical government. The European aristocrat knew that it was his
duty to oppose a king who aspired to unchecked rule, or a government that would diminish the "liberties" of the realm. A commitment
to liberty—that is, a fierce defense of personal liberty and an opposition to tyranny—was the common heritage of the European nobility.
It was also the heritage of the leaders of the American Revolution,
who fought against the "absolute Tyranny" and "absolute Despotism"
of which the Declaration of Independence speaks. It was both natural
and ordinary for a man of Lafayette's station to fight on behalf of liberty.

When Lafayette spoke of liberty in 1777, he did not mean political
democracy; neither did most of the Americans with whom he con-
sorted daily. What was revolutionary about the American experience
in the years 1776–1790 was that liberty came to mean something
more. Freedom developed from liberty—freedom as Hannah Arendt
defines it, the opportunity to participate in and shape the public

realm. That the Americans would finally settle upon a radically new form of government, which might be called a democratic republic, was not foreseen by many persons who fought for liberty during the early years of the American Revolution. But that Lafayette's understanding of liberty developed apace we may be sure. He was a quick study.

EDITORIAL METHOD

Lafayette, like most of the leaders of the American Revolution, believed it was important to leave a detailed documentary record of his public life for posterity. During the last decades of his life he corresponded with many historians, made lists of corrections for the early histories of the Revolution, wrote several personal memoirs, and prepared his papers for publication.

Only a small part of Lafayette's papers survived the French Revolution. He left them in France when he fled from the Terror, and all that was saved was a memoir about his first trip to America written in 1779, a bundle of letters to his wife, a letter book of copies she had made of them, and a few letters to his father-in-law. Lafayette was able to reconstitute part of his correspondence by persuading Bushrod Washington, George Washington's nephew, to return the letters Lafayette had written to the commander in chief, and by obtaining copies of the letters preserved in the French ministerial archives, as well as a few copies of letters saved by American recipients.

These were the papers from which a selection was made for publication in *Mémoires, correspondance et manuscrits du Général Lafayette, publiés par sa famille*. The family edited them at La Grange, where the papers remained for many years. Sometime during the nineteenth century the papers were transferred to Chavaniac, Lafayette's ancestral château in Auvergne. In 1913 all of the papers except Lafayette's letters to Washington were acquired by the Parisian dealer Dieudonné-Elie Fabius. In 1963 his widow sold a large portion of them to Mr. and Mrs. Arthur H. Dean, who presented them to Cornell University. Nearly all of Lafayette's letters to Washington were acquired by Mrs. John Hubbard, who presented them to Lafayette College.

When the Lafayette papers presented by the Deans had been catalogued, the Cornell University Libraries and the National Historical Publications and Records Commission sponsored a project to identify all the other Lafayette materials in the United States, which resulted in the publication of *Lafayette: A Guide to the Letters, Documents, and Manuscripts in the United States*. Mme Chantal de Tourtier-Bonazzi has published a companion volume for Lafayette materials in the public archives of France, *Lafayette: Documents conservés en France* (Paris: Archives Nationales, 1976). A selection from the Lafayette papers identified by these two projects will be printed in these volumes.

SELECTION

Nearly three thousand first- and second-party Lafayette documents are available to us for the period 1776–1790. We shall publish about three-fifths of them in these volumes. The choice of documents depends upon the exigencies of space and the desire to avoid undue repetition. We intend to provide material sufficient to illuminate the events in which Lafayette participated, his motives and character, and those of the people with whom he lived and worked. The selections include first-party material: letters and documents written by Lafayette himself, including the memoir he wrote in 1779; second-party material: letters and documents addressed to Lafayette; and some third-party material: contemporary letters, journals, and documents that contain information about Lafayette. Much of the third-party material is extracted from longer documents; we have reproduced only the portions relevant to Lafayette. In such cases, the letter *E* is placed as a superscript after the title of the document.

TRANSCRIPTION

In our transcription of English-language manuscripts we retain the original spelling. If it is unusual enough to cause confusion, the modern spelling follows in brackets. Punctuation is retained as found, except for dashes at the ends of sentences, which are replaced by periods. A minimum of additional punctuation is supplied, when necessary, for clarity. When the writer's punctuation is unclear, we follow modern usage. Original capitalization is also retained, except that each sentence is made to begin with a capital letter, and names of persons and places are silently capitalized. Abbreviations are not spelled out unless they are not readily recognizable; contractions are retained. When the manuscript has been damaged or contains an illegible passage, if no more than four letters are missing, we supply them silently. If more than four letters or entire words are missing, we supply them in brackets, with a question mark within the brackets if the conjecture is doubtful. Gaps that cannot be filled in are explained in brackets in the text; for example, [*illegible*], [*torn*]. The writer's interlineations or marginal notes are incorporated into the text without comment. Slips of the pen are silently corrected. Words underlined once by the writer are printed in italics. Signatures are printed in large and small capitals. Addresses, endorsements, and docketing are not transcribed unless they are contextually significant, in which case they are included in the provenance note.

The greatest problems arise in the materials that were altered in preparation for the publication of Lafayette, *Mémoires:* Lafayette's Memoir of 1779 and his letters to his family and to George Washington. Many changes have been made in these manuscripts in pencil and nineteenth-century ink. Words, sentences, and even paragraphs have been scribbled over or marked for deletion with slashes or brackets, and words and phrases have been added in the margins and between the lines in Lafayette's nineteenth-century hand. It is likely that he made or approved all the changes, because copies of the letters and memoir which Lafayette sent to Jared Sparks in 1829 conform to the text of the amended manuscripts. Most of the changes Lafayette indicated were incorporated in the texts printed in *Mémoires.* A comparison of the printed texts with the amended manuscripts reveals further changes, but these alterations follow the pattern Lafayette established. The majority of the changes are purely stylistic, and we disregard them. We have attempted to print the text as Lafayette first wrote it. When a significant passage has been deleted on the manuscript or omitted from Lafayette, *Mémoires,* we print it in angle brackets. All other significant changes are explained in the notes.

TRANSLATIONS

No translators' apologies or rationales have ever been convincing to those who can read the language that is being translated. At the same time these documents, untranslated, would be either a closed book or very poorly understood by too many readers who might otherwise find them interesting and useful. The letter *T* is placed as a superscript after the title of every translated document. The French texts of all the translated documents are printed in the Appendix.

ANNOTATION AND INDEX

Notes to the text follow each document; the first note gives the provenance and other necessary information about the document and is unnumbered. The numbered notes provide clarification, information, and explanation of materials in the text. In our annotation we have tried to take into account the pattern of Lafayette's life and thought, and the fact that the best commentary on his letters usually is to be found in the other documents. This is particularly true of the Memoir of 1779, which is presented serially at the beginning of each of the parts in the volume; if a subject mentioned in the memoir is clarified in another document in the volume, we do not annotate the memoir. When we cite documents that are printed in our volume, we identify them by title and date only. The source citation is given for all other items mentioned in our notes.

All proper names are identified in the Index; people and places are given space in the annotation only when the information is immediately required for an understanding of the text.

GUIDE TO EDITORIAL APPARATUS

DNA   National Archives and Records Service
InU   Indiana University, Lilly Library
MdHi   Maryland Historical Society
MH   Harvard University, Houghton Library
MHi   Massachusetts Historical Society
MiU   University of Michigan, William L. Clements Library
NcD   Duke University Library
NcFayM   Methodist College, Davis Library
NhHi   New Hampshire Historical Society
NHi   New-York Historical Society
NIC   Cornell University Libraries
NjMoW   Morristown National Historical Park, U.S. Department of the In-
            terior, National Park Service
NN   New York Public Library, Manuscripts and Archives Division;
            Astor, Lenox, and Tilden Foundations
NNPM   The Pierpont Morgan Library
PEL   Lafayette College, David Bishop Skillman Library
PHC   Haverford College Library
PHi   Historical Society of Pennsylvania
PPAmP   American Philosophical Society Library
PPRF   The Philip H. & A. S. W. Rosenbach Foundation
ScHi   South Carolina Historical Society
ViHi   Virginia Historical Society
VtSS   Vermont, Secretary of State, State Papers Office
VtU   University of Vermont, Guy W. Bailey Library

Foreign repositories:

ADG   Archives Départementales de la Gironde, Bordeaux
ALG   Archives de La Grange
AN   Archives Nationales, Paris
BN   Bibliothèque Nationale, Paris
PRO   Public Record Office, London

LAFAYETTE MANUSCRIPTS: AUTOBIOGRAPHICAL NOTES I–VII

In conjunction with the preparation of his papers for publication, Lafayette composed several memoirs and historiographical works. We have titled those that relate to the period 1776–1790 "Autobiographical Notes" and have numbered them for easy reference. We have treated the Memoir of 1779 separately because it will be printed in full in our first two volumes. It is described on p. 12.

Autobiographical Notes I: autobiographical materials copied for Jared Sparks, ca. 1828–1829 (MH: Sparks MSS 86, fols. 1–254; used by permission of the Houghton Library, Harvard University). Copy in French and English, in a secretary's hand, of materials Lafayette had collected for his memoirs. They include a copy of the amended Memoir of 1779 with Lafayette's notes, letters written during the American Revolution, a memoir of the Virginia campaign of 1781, letters from prison during the French Revolution, and a memoir on the American Revolution entitled "3ème Cahier contenant des Observations sur la guerre de la Révolution américaine, & particulièrement sur le Général Lafayette." This "3ème Cahier," which contains some corrections in Lafayette's hand, was sent to Jared Sparks on November 20, 1829. Much of the material in Sparks MSS 86 is printed in Lafayette, *Mémoires,* where the "3ème Cahier" is designated "Manuscrit no. 1."

Autobiographical Notes II: "Observations sur quelques parties de l'Histoire Américaine par un ami du Gal. Lafayette" (DLC: Peter Force Collection, series 8 D, item 127). Portions of the manuscript are printed in Lafayette, *Mémoires,* vols. 1 and 2, where it is designated "Manuscrit no. 2." Copy, in French, in the hand of Félix Pontonnier, Lafayette's secretary; 54 pp. Written ca. 1809–1812. A historiographical work, commenting on and correcting histories of the American Revolution by William Gordon and David Ramsay, and biographies of Washington by John Marshall and David Ramsay. Discusses events in which Lafayette took part from 1776 to 1789. The manuscript is transcribed, translated, and annotated in Jane Lohrer Cates, "Observations sur quelques parties de l'histoire américaine, par un ami du Général Lafayette" (unpublished Ph.D. dissertation, University of Chicago, 1946).

Autobiographical Notes III: untitled (NIC: Dean Collection); begins: "Vous me demandez, ma chère amie quelques détails sur ma famille. . . ." Copy, in French, in the hand of Virginie de Lasteyrie, Lafayette's daughter, with some corrections in his hand; 8 pp. Written after 1811. Gives details of Lafayette's ancestry, childhood, education, and marriage.

Autobiographical Notes IV: untitled (NIC: Dean Collection); begins: "C'est dans l'automne de 1776 lorsque la déclaration d'Indépendance parvint en Europe. . . ." Copy, in French, in the hand of Félix Pontonnier; 5 pp. Written ca. 1800–1812. A justificatory piece, dating Lafayette's devotion to the American cause from the autumn of 1776, and his relationship with Canada from the winter of 1777–1778, apparently in response to an unidentified newspaper article.

Autobiographical Notes V: untitled notes, taken by Jared Sparks in conversation with Lafayette at La Grange, November 1828 (MH: Sparks MSS 32, 1:96–212; used by permission of Houghton Library, Harvard University). In English, in Sparks's hand; 116 pp. A series of topical notes on Lafayette's American experiences with sketches of other persons involved. Notes specifically intended to supplement the Memoir of 1779 are found on pp. 150–197. The manuscript covers events from 1774 to 1786, and was used in the preparation of Sparks, *Writings of Washington,* 5:445–456.

Autobiographical Notes VI: untitled fragment (DLC: Papers of Alexander Hamilton, vol. 84). Lafayette's answers to eight queries about participants in the American Revolution and events in which both Hamilton and Lafayette were involved. In English, in an unidentified hand; 20 pp. Portions quoted in

John Church Hamilton, *Life of Alexander Hamilton*, vol. 1 (New York, 1834), where it is referred to as "Manuscript Memoir of General La Fayette." Probably written ca. 1824–1825, in part from manuscripts Lafayette had composed earlier.

Autobiographical Notes VII: undated letter (to César de Latour-Maubourg?) containing notes for the preparation of Lafayette's memoirs (NIC: Dean Collection). In French, in Lafayette's hand, written in the third person; 4 pp. Probably written ca. 1800–1806. The letter was apparently sent with many copies of letters Lafayette had written during and after the French Revolution. The letter suggests various persons who may have still other letters that might be copied. Lafayette suggests an outline for an arrangement of his American and French correspondence and editorial guidelines for an edition of his memoirs.

SHORT TITLES

Barrière, *Bibliothèque:* Jean-François Barrière and Mathurin de Lescure, eds., *Bibliothèque des mémoires relatifs à l'histoire de France pendant le 18ème siècle,* 37 vols. (Paris, 1853–1881).

Burnett, *Letters of Congress:* Edmund C. Burnett, ed., *Letters of Members of the Continental Congress,* 8 vols. (Washington, D.C.: Carnegie Institution of Washington, 1921–1936).

Chittenden Papers: John A. Williams, ed., *Public Papers of Governor Thomas Chittenden,* vol. 17 of *State Papers of Vermont* (Montpelier, 1969).

Clinton Papers: Hugh Hastings, ed., *Public Papers of George Clinton, First Governor of New York, 1777–1795,* 10 vols. (New York and Albany, 1899–1914).

Correspondence of John Laurens: William Gilmore Simms, ed., *Memoir and Correspondence of Colonel John Laurens* (New York, 1867).

Deane Papers: Charles Isham, ed., *The Deane Papers,* vols. 19–23 of *Collections of the New-York Historical Society* (New York, 1887–1891).

Doniol, *Histoire:* Jean-Henri Doniol, *Histoire de la participation de la France à l'établissement des Etats-Unis d'Amérique,* 5 vols. (Paris, 1884–1892).

Fitzpatrick, *Writings of Washington:* John C. Fitzpatrick, ed., *The Writings of George Washington,* 39 vols. (Washington, D.C.: U.S. Government Printing Office, 1931–1944).

Ford, "Defences of Philadelphia": Worthington C. Ford, "The Defences of Philadelphia in 1777," *Pennsylvania Magazine,* vols. 18–21 (1894–1897), passim.

Freeman, *Washington:* Douglas Southall Freeman, *George Washington: A Biography,* 7 vols. (New York: Scribner, 1948–1957).

Gottschalk, *Lafayette Comes to America:* Louis Gottschalk, *Lafayette Comes to America* (Chicago: University of Chicago Press, 1935).

Gottschalk, *Lafayette Joins the American Army:* Louis Gottschalk, *Lafayette Joins the American Army* (Chicago: University of Chicago Press, 1937).

Gottschalk, *Letters of Lafayette:* Louis Gottschalk, ed., *The Letters of Lafayette to Washington, 1777–1799* (New York: privately published, 1944).

Henkels, *Confidential Correspondence of Robert Morris:* Stan V. Henkels, ed., *Catalogue No. 1183: The Confidential Correspondence of Robert Morris* (Philadelphia [1917]).

JCC: Worthington C. Ford, ed., *Journals of the Continental Congress, 1774–1789,* 34 vols. (Washington, D.C.: U.S. Government Printing Office, 1904–1937).

Kapp, *Kalb:* Friedrich Kapp, *The Life of John Kalb, Major-General in the Revolutionary Army* (New York, 1884).

Knollenberg, *Washington and the Revolution:* Bernhard Knollenberg, *Washington and the Revolution, a Reappraisal: Gates, Conway and the Continental Congress* (1940; reprint ed., Hamden, Conn.: Archon Books, 1968).

Lafayette, *Mémoires: Mémoires, correspondance et manuscrits du Général Lafayette, publiés par sa famille,* 6 vols. (Paris, 1837–1838). Letters written in English are translated into French.

Lafayette, *Memoirs* (London): *Memoirs, Correspondence and Manuscripts of General Lafayette, Published by His Family,* 3 vols. (London, 1837). Letters written in French are translated into English.

Lafayette, *Memoirs* (New York): *Memoirs, Correspondence and Manuscripts of General Lafayette, Published by His Family* (New York, 1837). Same as vol. 1 of the London edition, with some additional letters.

Lasseray, *Français:* André Lasseray, *Les Français sous les treize étoiles,* 2 vols. (Mâcon: Imprimerie Protat Frères, 1935).

Maurois, *Adrienne:* André Maurois, *Adrienne, ou la vie de Mme de La Fayette* (Paris: Hachette, 1960).

New Hampshire State Papers: Isaac A. Hammond, ed., *Rolls and Documents Relating to Soldiers in the Revolutionary War,* vol. 17 of *State Papers of New Hampshire* (Manchester, 1889).

Peckham, *Battle Casualties:* Howard H. Peckham, ed., *The Toll of Independence: Engagements & Battle Casualties of the American Revolution* (Chicago: University of Chicago Press, 1974).

Pennsylvania Magazine: Pennsylvania Magazine of History and Biography.

Rossie, *Politics of Command:* Jonathan G. Rossie, *The Politics of Command in the American Revolution* (Syracuse, N.Y.: Syracuse University Press, 1975).

Segretain, ed., "Journal par Du Rousseau de Fayolle": L. Segretain, ed., "Journal d'une campagne en Amérique par Du Rousseau de Fayolle," *Bulletin de la Société des Antiquaires de l'Ouest,* 25 (1901):1–48.

Sparks, *Writings of Washington:* Jared Sparks, ed., *The Writings of George Washington,* 12 vols. (Boston, 1834–1837).

Stevens, *Facsimiles:* Benjamin F. Stevens, *Facsimiles of Manuscripts in European Archives Relating to America, 1773–1783,* 25 vols. (London, 1889–1898).

Sullivan Papers: Otis G. Hammond, ed., *Letters and Papers of Major-General John Sullivan,* 3 vols. (Concord: New Hampshire Historical Society, 1930–1939).

Ward, *War of the Revolution:* Christopher Ward, *The War of the Revolution,* ed. John R. Alden, 2 vols. (New York: Macmillan, 1952).

Wharton, *Diplomatic Correspondence:* Francis Wharton, ed., *The Revolutionary Diplomatic Correspondence of the United States,* 6 vols. (Washington, D.C., 1889).

CHRONOLOGICAL OUTLINE

(Italics indicate major historical events in which Lafayette did not participate.)

1757
  September 6. Born at Chavaniac, in Auvergne.
1759
  August 1. Father killed at Battle of Minden.
1763
  February 10. Treaty of Paris: France, defeated in Seven Years' War, gives up all claims in North America.
1768
  January 12–March 2. The French government sends the Baron de Kalb to America to investigate the controversy between the colonies and Great Britain; he reports that the Americans are not ready to revolt.
  Moves to Paris; enters Collège du Plessis.
1770
  April 3. Mother dies.
  May. Inherits a large fortune from his grandfather.
1771
  April 9. Becomes a *sous-lieutenant* in the King's Musketeers.
1773
  February 15. Moves to the Hôtel de Noailles in Versailles, as a protégé of the Duc d'Ayen.
  April 7. Becomes a lieutenant in the Noailles Dragoons.
1774
  April 11. Marries Adrienne de Noailles.
  May 7. Death of Louis XV. Accession of Louis XVI.
  May 19. Becomes a captain in the Noailles Dragoons.
  Summer. On maneuvers with his regiment at Metz, under the command of the Comte de Broglie.
1775
  Becomes a Freemason.
  Summer. Stationed at Metz; at a dinner given by Broglie, hears the Duke of Gloucester speak of the American revolt.
  December 15. Daughter, Henriette, born.

1776
  April. French government decides to send secret aid to the Americans.
  June 11. Placed on reserve status.
  November. Broglie introduces Lafayette to the Baron de Kalb, who takes
    him to Silas Deane.
  December 7. Signs agreement to serve as a major general in the American
    army.
  December. A party of French officers, led by Kalb and the Vicomte de Mauroy, is
    prevented from sailing for America by the French authorities.
1777
  February. Buys *La Victoire,* in which he plans to carry a party of French
    officers to America.
  February 21–ca. March 9. Visits London.
  ca. March 13. Returns secretly to Paris.
  March 16–19. Travels to Bordeaux with Kalb.
  March 25–28. *La Victoire* sails from Bordeaux to Pasajes, Spain.
  March 31. Receives royal order to join the Duc d'Ayen at Marseilles.
  April 1–3. Travels from Pasajes to Bordeaux and reports to the royal com-
    mandant there.
  April 3–12. Sends letters to Paris requesting permission to go to America.
    Request denied. Pretends to leave for Marseilles, but waits outside Bor-
    deaux for reply to his final appeal.
  April 12–16. His courier and Mauroy arrive with news from Paris. Travels
    with Mauroy to Pasajes.
  April 20. Sails from Pasajes on *La Victoire* with fifteen other officers.
  June 13. Arrives at North Island, South Carolina.
  June 17. Arrives at Charleston, South Carolina.
  June 26. Sets out for Philadelphia.
  July 1. Daughter, Anastasie, born in Paris.
  July 17. At Petersburg, Virginia.
  July 23. At Annapolis, Maryland.
  July 27. Arrives at Philadelphia; reports to the president of Congress.
  July 31. Appointed major general, but without command. Meets Washing-
    ton; invited to join Washington's "family."
  August 1. Accompanies Washington on inspection of Delaware River for-
    tifications.
  August 8. Attends army review near Germantown, Pennsylvania.
  August 14. *La Victoire* sails from Charleston and founders on the bar.
  August 21. Attends his first council of general officers.
  August 24. Rides with Washington in parade through Philadelphia.
  August 25–September 11. Accompanies Washington in operations against
    British army invading from Chesapeake Bay.
  September 11. Wounded in the leg at the Battle of Brandywine.
  September 12. Transported to Philadelphia.
  September 18. Evacuated to Bristol, Pennsylvania, when Congress flees
    Philadelphia.
  September 19. Battle of Freeman's Farm.

September 21–October 18. At army hospital at Moravian settlement in Bethlehem, Pennsylvania.

September 27. Congress assembles at Lancaster, Pennsylvania. British occupy Philadelphia.

September 30. Congress moves to York, Pennsylvania.

October 4. Battle of Germantown.

October 7. Battle of Bemis Heights.

October 17. Burgoyne surrenders to Gates. Congress reorganizes the Board of War.

October 19–December 1. Attached to Washington's headquarters.

November 20–28. Detached with General Greene in New Jersey.

November 25. Commands at a skirmish at Gloucester, New Jersey.

November 27. Congress elects Gates president of the new Board of War.

December. Daughter, Henriette, dies in Paris.

December 1. Receives command of a division.

December 19. With the Continental army, establishes winter quarters at Valley Forge.

1778

January 23. Selected by Congress to lead an "irruption" into Canada.

January 28–February 5. Travels to York to discuss the campaign with Congress and the Board of War; returns to Valley Forge.

February 6. Franco-American treaties signed in Paris. (The news did not reach America until the end of April.)

February 7–17. Travels to Albany, New York.

February 19. Decides the Canadian expedition is not feasible. Assumes command at Albany.

March 1–11. Travels to Johnstown, New York, for an Indian treaty.

March 31. Leaves Albany to resume command of his division at Valley Forge.

May 18–22. Commands Continental army detachment at Barren Hill.

June 28. Battle of Monmouth Court House.

July 23–September 30. Serves with the Continental detachment in Rhode Island, in conjunction with d'Estaing's expeditionary force.

October 21. Given leave by Congress to return to France.

1779

January 11. Sails for France.

June. Appointed to the French army preparing to invade England.

November. The invasion is abandoned.

December 24. Son, George-Washington Lafayette, born.

1780

April 28. Arrives in Boston.

July–August. Takes command of the Light Division.

September 25–28. With Washington at West Point; Arnold's treason is discovered.

September 29. Appointed to a board of general officers to try Major André.

1781

February 22. Leads a detachment to Virginia to counter British forces under Arnold.

April 22–October 19. Commands Continental forces during the Virginia campaign against Cornwallis.

July 6. Battle of Green Spring against Cornwallis.

July 27. Cornwallis decides to occupy Yorktown; Lafayette besieges him.

September 2. De Grasse's fleet arrives at Yorktown; French marines placed under Lafayette's command.

September 14. Arrival of American and French forces under Washington and Rochambeau.

October 14. Capture of Redoubt No. 10 by troops under Lafayette's command.

October 19. Cornwallis surrenders.

December 23. Departs for France on board the *Alliance*.

1782

September 17. Daughter, Virginie, born.

October 24. Accepts position of quartermaster general of Franco-Spanish expeditionary force mobilizing at Cadiz.

1783

January 20. Preliminary peace, hostilities officially ended.

March. Becomes a *maréchal de camp* in the French army.

1784

August 4–December 21. American tour.

1786

Works for French trade concessions for the United States as a member of the "American Committee."

August. Buys plantation in Cayenne for experiment in slave emancipation.

1787

February 22–May 25. Attends Assembly of Notables.

May 24. Calls for toleration of the Protestants and reform of the criminal law.

1788

November 6–December 12. Attends Second Assembly of Notables; supports doubling of the Third Estate.

1789

March 26. Elected deputy to the Estates General from Auvergne.

June 27. Joins with the Third Estate, which had constituted itself as the National Assembly.

July 11. Presents draft for the Declaration of the Rights of Man and the Citizen.

July 13. Chosen vice-president of the National Assembly.

July 14. Fall of the Bastille.

July 15. Proclaimed commandant of the Paris National Guard.

October 5–6. Leads Paris National Guard to Versailles; brings the king to Paris.

1790

June 19. Supports decree abolishing titles of nobility.

July 14. Presides at Federation ceremony of the National Guard.

1791
  June 21. Flight of the king to Varennes.
  July 17. Demonstration at the Champ de Mars dispersed by the National
    Guard.
  October 8. Resigns as commandant of the Paris National Guard.
1792
  ca. January 1. Takes command of the Army of the Center at Metz.
  May–August. Commands the Army of the Left.
  August 10. Arrest of the king.
  August 19. Impeached by the Convention. Emigrates and is captured by
    the Austrians.
  September 18, 1792–September 19, 1797. Imprisoned at Wesel, Mag-
    deburg, Neisse, and Olmütz.
1795
  October 24. Joined by wife and daughters in prison at Olmütz.
1797
  September 19. Released from prison under the terms of the Treaty of
    Campo-Formio.
  November. Moves to Lemkhulen, Holstein.
1799
  ca. January. Moves to Vianen, Holland.
  November 9–10: 18 Brumaire. Establishment of the Consulate.
1800
  January. Establishes residence at La Grange.
1807
  December 24. Death of his wife, Adrienne.
1815
  Begins first of several terms in the Chamber of Deputies.
  June 18. Waterloo.
  June 22. Insists on Bonaparte's abdication.
1824
  August 16. Arrives in New York for American tour.
1825
  September 9. Sails for France.
1830
  July 28–30. Plays leading role in Revolution of 1830.
  August 16–December 26. Commandant of National Guard of the Realm.
1834
  May 20. Death in Paris.
  May 22. Buried next to his wife at the Picpus Cemetery in Paris.

GENEALOGICAL CHART

The immediate ancestors, close relatives, and children of Gilbert du Motier and Adrienne de Noailles, marquis and marquise de Lafayette

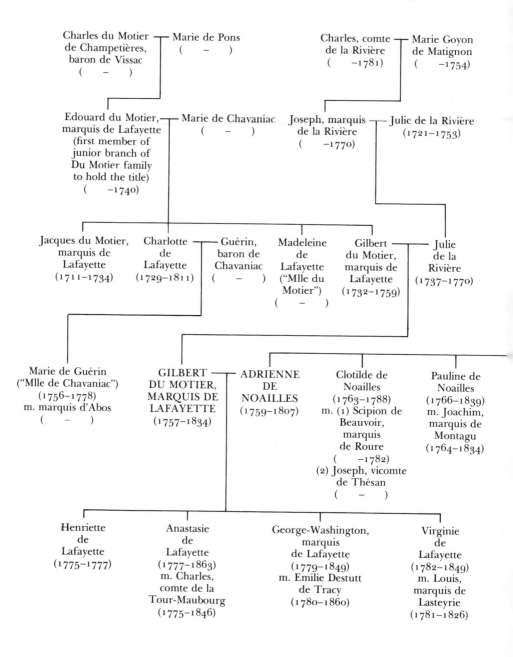

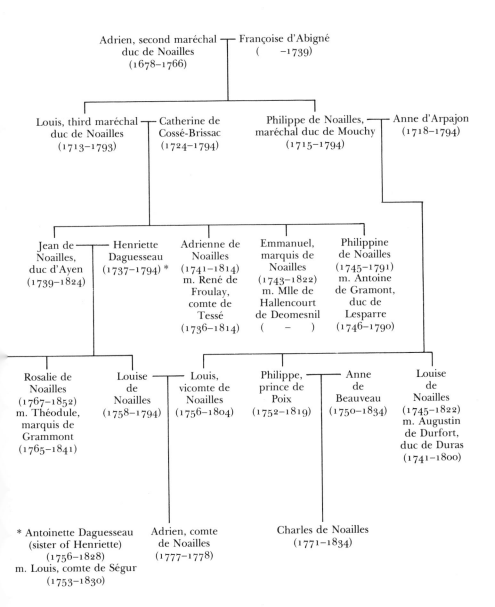

Adrien, second maréchal ┬ Françoise d'Abigné
duc de Noailles   (–1739)
(1678–1766)

Louis, third maréchal ┬ Catherine de   Philippe de Noailles, ┬ Anne d'Arpajon
duc de Noailles   Cossé-Brissac   maréchal duc de Mouchy   (1718–1794)
(1713–1793)   (1724–1794)   (1715–1794)

Jean de ┬ Henriette   Adrienne de   Emmanuel,   Philippine
Noailles, Daguesseau   Noailles   marquis de   de Noailles
duc d'Ayen (1737–1794) *   (1741–1814)   Noailles   (1745–1791)
(1739–1824)   m. René de   (1743–1822)   m. Antoine
                            Froulay,   m. Mlle de   de Gramont,
                            comte de   Hallencourt   duc de
                            Tessé   de Deomesnil   Lesparre
                            (1736–1814)   (–   )   (1746–1790)

Rosalie de   Louise ┬ Louis,   Philippe, ┬ Anne   Louise
Noailles   de   vicomte de   prince de   de   de
(1767–1852)   Noailles Noailles   Poix   Beauveau   Noailles
m. Théodule,   (1758–1794) (1756–1804)(1752–1819) (1750–1834)   (1745–1822)
marquis de   m. Augustin
Grammont   de Durfort,
(1765–1841)   duc de Duras
                                                                   (1741–1800)

* Antoinette Daguesseau   Adrien, comte   Charles de Noailles
(sister of Henriette)   de Noailles   (1771–1834)
(1756–1828)   (1777–1778)
m. Louis, comte de Ségur
(1753–1830)

Lafayette in the Age of
the American Revolution

PART I

FROM FRANCE TO
PHILADELPHIA

December 6, 1776–July 31, 1777

*. . . having to choose between the slavery that everyone believes
he has the right to impose upon me, and liberty, which called me
to glory, I departed.*

To Adrienne de Lafayette, April 19, 1777

The year that followed the Battle of Bunker Hill forced the American leadership to the conviction that there was little chance that independence would be won without foreign aid. Commercial treaties, alliances, war matériel, and loans were essential to American success. So was a judicious seeding of professional officers (especially engineers) who would provide models for the majority of American officers who had little or no experience in warfare, yet had to face the best professionals England could muster.

The French government was not averse to providing the aid the Americans needed, for an independent America would weaken Britain and help restore the balance of power with France's old enemy. When Silas Deane arrived in Paris as the agent of the Continental Congress late in the spring of 1776, he knew he was there with French encouragement; within a few weeks he was working closely with Beaumarchais on a plan to use French funds to ship supplies to the American forces. In addition, Deane contracted for the military engineers needed by the American army, and many additional officers were taken at their word when they presented their qualifications and were sent off to America with commissions by Deane. As Henry Laurens noted, just about the time Lafayette arrived in Philadelphia to a cool welcome, Deane could not say no "to any Frenchman who called himself a Count or Chevalier."

Among those Deane found irresistible were Kalb and Lafayette. Like the host of other officers who were willing to travel halfway around the world to fight on behalf of rebels against one of the greatest military powers of the age, Lafayette and Kalb could hope for mili-

tary advancement at home if they succeeded abroad. Yet the letters
and memoirs presented in this section suggest that there was a much
wider range and complexity of motives even among the small group
of voyagers on *La Victoire*. Some had little to lose and some incurred
great risk in the adventure; perhaps most of the volunteers shared at
least part of Lafayette's vision of an arcadian republic that would welcome chivalrous Frenchmen to their cause. It is one measure of the
difference between Lafayette and his companions that he seemed un-
dismayed by the rigors of the overland trip from Charleston and the
unhappy dénouement in Philadelphia; it was an accurate augury of
his future in America.

If I were to confuse obstinacy with firmness, as too often happens, I would blush to begin these memoirs that I have long refused to write, and to add further to the egotism of their content by my style, whereas it was necessary, at least, to cover myself with the cloak of the third person. But I shall not be even half-compliant to that sensitive and affected self-interest which would value the ephemeral honors of newspaper publication. It suffices for me to think that this account, intended for only a few friends, will never go further. My work even has two great advantages over many famous books: since it is not meant for the public, it does not need a preface, and the affectionate dedication does not require a letter.

It would be too poetical to place myself at once in another hemisphere, and too meticulous to dwell upon the particulars of my birth, which soon followed the death of my father at Minden; [1] of my education in Auvergne among loving and respected relatives; of my transfer, at the age of eleven, to a school in Paris,[2] where I soon lost my virtuous mother, and where the death of her father made me rich, though I had been born poor; [3] of some schoolboy successes, inspired by the love of glory and disturbed by that of liberty; of my entry into the Black Musketeers, which took me out of my class only on review days; [4] and finally of my marriage at the age of sixteen,[5] preceded by attendance at the Academy of Versailles.[6] I have still less to tell you of my entry into society, of the brief favor I enjoyed as a member of a youthful set, of some short tours of duty with the Noailles Regiment,[7] and of the unfavorable opinion that I incurred through my silence, because I did not heed and scarcely listened to things that did not appear to be worthy of discussion. That ill effect of disguised vanity, and of an inclination to be observant, was not moderated by the awkwardness of my manners, which, without being improper on great occasions, never succumbed to the graces of the court or to the charms of a supper in the capital.

⟨ I shall spare you also the confession of an unedifying youth, and even of the story of two romances dedicated to beauties who were then very celebrated, in which my head had a larger part than my heart. The first, scarcely begun, broke against the obstacles of jealousy with which I collided head-on. The other—in which I wanted at first to triumph less over the object herself than over a rival—I pursued,

Julie de La Rivière de Lafayette, Lafayette's mother

Gilbert du Motier, marquis de Lafayette, Lafayette's father

Lafayette at about the time of his marriage, at the age of sixteen

despite long interruptions, on every possible occasion. Our relationship went from esteem all the way to the contrary sentiment, and
was finally terminated by a catastrophe unconnected with me. It is more
pleasant for me to speak of the tender and stable affection that I
never cease to feel for the woman whom I had the good fortune to
marry.⟩ [8]

You ask me when I first longed for glory and liberty; I can recall no
time in my life when I did not love stories of glorious deeds, or have
dreams of traveling the world in search of fame. At the age of eight,
my heart pounded when I heard of a hyena that had done some
mischief, and caused still more alarm in our neighborhood, and the
hope of meeting it made my walks exciting. When I went to school, I
was never distracted from my studies, except by the desire to study
without constraint. I seldom deserved to be chastised, but, despite my

ordinary calm, it would have been dangerous to attempt it. I like to recall that in Rhetoric class, when I described the perfect horse, I sacrificed a chance of pleasing the teacher to the pleasure of depicting a horse that, on perceiving the whip, threw his rider. Republican anecdotes delighted me,[9] and when my wife's family obtained a place for me at court, I did not hesitate to be disagreeable to preserve my independence.[10] It was while I was in that frame of mind that I first learned of the troubles in America; they were not well known in Europe until 1776, and the memorable declaration of July fourth arrived there toward the end of the same year.[11]

After having crowned herself with laurels and enriched herself with conquests, after having mastered all the seas and insulted all nations, England had turned her pride against her own colonies. North America had long been offensive to her; she chose to add new vexations to the original shackles, and usurp the most sacred privileges. The Americans, attached to the mother country, limited themselves at first to complaints: they accused only the ministers, and the whole English nation rose up against the accusers; they were charged with insolence, and then rebellion, and were finally declared enemies. Thus did the obstinacy of the king, the rage of the ministers, and the arrogance of the English people force thirteen of their colonies to declare themselves independent. Never before had such a glorious cause attracted the attention of mankind; it was the final struggle of liberty, and its defeat would have left it neither asylum nor hope. Both the oppressors and the oppressed were to receive a lesson: either that great work would be accomplished, or the rights of humanity would be lost beneath its ruins. At the same time the destinies of France and her rival were both to be decided. England was to lose a great amount of commerce, of which she derived the sole advantage; a quarter of her subjects, continually increased by rapid multiplication and emigration from all parts of Europe; and finally more than half of the British territory—and the most beautiful portion, at that. But what if she had reunited herself with those thirteen colonies? That would have been the end of our Antilles and our possessions in Africa and Asia, of our maritime commerce, and consequently of our navy, and ultimately of our political existence.

When I first learned of that quarrel, my heart was enlisted, and I thought only of joining the colors. Some circumstances, which it is not necessary to relate, had taught me to expect from my family only obstacles to the attainment of my goal.[12] I therefore relied upon myself, and dared to take for a device on my coat-of-arms the words *Cur Non?*, which could serve me both as an encouragement and as a response.[13] Silas Deane was in Paris, but everyone was afraid to visit

him, and his voice was overpowered by the cries of Lord Stormont.[14]
Deane secretly sent to America some old weapons that were of little
use and some young officers who did little good, all of which was financed by M. de Beaumarchais.[15] When the English ambassador complained to our court, it denied having sent them, ordered the unload-
ing of the ships that had not yet sailed, and expelled the American
privateers from our ports. Wishing to address myself directly to
Mr. Deane, I became friendly with de Kalb, a German in our army,
who was applying for service with the "insurgents," as they were
called at the time, and who acted as my interpreter.[16] He was the one
whom M. de Choiseul had sent to visit the English colonies, and who,
on his return, had received some money but no audience—so little did
that minister think of the revolution for which some people later gave
him the credit.[17] When I presented myself to Mr. Deane I was just
nineteen years old, and I spoke more of my enthusiasm than of my
experience. I dwelt upon the minor sensation my departure would
raise, and he signed the agreement. The secrecy of those negotiations
and of my preparations was truly miraculous. Family, friends, ministers, French spies, English spies, all were blind to them. Among my
discreet confidants, I owe much to M. Duboismartin, secretary to the
Comte de Broglie, and to the Comte de Broglie himself, who, after
vain efforts to stop me, followed my activities with a paternal concern.

A ship was being prepared for America when very bad news arrived: New York, Long Island, White Plains, Fort Washington, and
the Jerseys had been the scene of successive destructions of the American forces by thirty-three thousand British or German troops. Only
three thousand men remained in arms, and General Howe was pursuing them. From that moment the insurgents' credit vanished; it became impossible to dispatch a ship. The envoys themselves thought it
their duty to admit their discouragement to me, and to dissuade me
from my project. I called upon Mr. Deane and thanked him for his
frankness. "Before this," I added, "you have only seen my enthusiasm; perhaps it will now become useful: I shall buy a ship to transport
your officers. Be confident. I want to share your fortune in this time
of danger." My idea was well received, but then it was necessary to
find the money to buy and arm a ship in secrecy. All that was soon accomplished with great dispatch.

We came, however, to the time for a trip to England, which had
been planned for a long while. I could not refuse to go without compromising my secret, whereas by accepting I concealed my preparations. This last measure was strongly supported by MM. Franklin and
Deane. The Doctor himself was then in France, and although I did
not go to his home for fear of being seen there, we corresponded

through Mr. Carmichael, an American who was less well known. Thus I arrived at London with the Prince de Poix, and saw Bancroft, the American,[18] and then His Britannic Majesty. At nineteen, one may take too much pleasure in mocking the tyrant whom he is about to fight, in dancing at the home of Lord Germain, minister for American affairs, and at the home of Lord Rawdon, who had just arrived from New York, and in meeting at the opera that Clinton whom I would meet again at Monmouth. But, while hiding my intentions, I displayed my sentiments. I often defended the Americans; I rejoiced at their success at Trenton, and my spirit of opposition earned me an invitation to breakfast with Lord Shelburne. I ⟨did not shut my ears to indiscretions, but⟩ declined offers to inspect the seaports and the vessels that were being sent out against the "rebels," and avoided everything [19] that I believed to be a breach of confidence. At the end of three weeks, when it became necessary for me to leave, I refused the invitation of my uncle the ambassador to go with him to court, and told him that I wanted to take a trip to Paris.[20] He proposed to say that I was ill until my return. I would not have proposed that stratagem myself, but I did not object to it.

After suffering cruelly on the channel crossing, during which I was comforted with assurances that it would soon be over, I arrived at M. de Kalb's house in Paris. I hid myself for three days at Chaillot, where I was visited by the Americans and a few friends, and left for Bordeaux, where several unexpected delays stopped me again. I took advantage of the delay to write to Paris, from which the news was not encouraging. But, since my messenger was followed by one from the government, not a moment was lost in setting sail, and the orders of my sovereign were able to overtake me only at Los Pasajes, a Spanish port at which we had to stop. The letters from my family were terrifying, and the *lettre de cachet* was peremptory: "You are forbidden to go to the American continent, under penalty of disobedience, and enjoined to go to Marseilles to await further orders." [21] The consequences of the anathema, the laws of the state, and the power and the wrath of the government were all well known. But the grief and the pregnancy of a cherished wife,[22] and the thoughts of his relatives and his friends, had a much greater effect upon M. de Lafayette. Now that his vessel could no longer be stopped, he returned to Bordeaux to justify his undertaking, and, in a declaration to M. de Fumel, took upon himself alone the consequences of his flight. Since the court did not deign to relax its position, he wrote to M. de Maurepas that such silence was tacit consent, and with that pleasantry he made his departure. After taking the route to Marseilles, he retraced his steps, and, disguised as a courier, he had almost escaped all dangers when a girl recognized him at Saint-Jean-de-Luz. But he signaled her to be silent, and she adroitly threw his pursuers off the track. Thus M. de Lafayette rejoined his ship, on April 26, 1777, and the same day, after six months of labor and impatience, he set sail for the American continent.[23]

As soon as his seasickness abated, M. de Lafayette began to study the language and the profession he had adopted. A sluggish ship, with two defective cannons and a few muskets, could not have escaped from the smallest privateer. In that situation, M. de Lafayette resolved to blow up his ship rather than surrender. The necessary measures were arranged with a brave Dutchman named Bedaulx, whose fate would surely be the gallows if they were taken.[24] The captain insisted upon putting in at the Antilles, but the *lettres de cachet* would have preceded them there, and, less from choice than from compulsion, they got him to follow a direct course.[25]

Forty leagues from the American coast they were met by a small ship. The captain turned pale, but the crew was attached to M. de Lafayette, and the army officers were numerous; they made a show of resistance. Fortunately, it was an American ship, which they attempted to accompany, but in vain. They were scarcely out of sight of the American ship when it met two English frigates; this was not the only time that the elements obstinately opposed M. de Lafayette in order to save him. After seven weeks of perils he arrived in Carolina, and anchored before Georgetown.[26] Ascending the river in a canoe, he finally stood upon American soil, and his first words there were an oath to conquer or to perish in that cause. Landing at midnight at the house of a Major Huger, he met there a person about to sail for France, who seemed to be waiting only for his letters. Many of the officers came ashore, others remained on board, and all hastened to reach Charleston.

That attractive city is worthy of its inhabitants, and everything there proclaimed comfort and refinement. Without knowing much about M. de Lafayette, Governor Rutledge and Generals Howe, Moultrie, and Gadsden hastened to welcome him. They showed him the new defensive works, and that battery which Moultrie defended so well, but where the British, it must be admitted, appear to have chosen the only plan of attack certain to fail. Many adventurers, the refuse of the Antilles, tried in vain to ally themselves with M. de Lafayette and to instill in him their prejudices. Having procured some horses, he left for Philadelphia with six officers. His ship had arrived, but it no longer had the same luck; when it departed again, it foundered on the bar off Charleston.[27]

To reach the Congress of the United States, M. de Lafayette traveled nearly nine hundred miles on horseback. He had to travel through the two Carolinas, Virginia, and the states of Maryland and Delaware before he reached the capital of Pennsylvania. As he traveled he studied the language and customs of the inhabitants, and saw new products and new methods of cultivation. Vast forests, immense rivers—nature adorns everything in that land with an air of youth and majesty. After a month of difficult, fatiguing travel, he came to Philadelphia, now so well known, whose future grandeur was determined when Penn laid the first stone of its foundation.[28]

After his able maneuvers at Trenton and Princeton, General Washington had remained in his camp at Middlebrook. Frustrated in their first hopes, the English combined their forces for a decisive campaign. Burgoyne was already advancing with ten thousand men, preceded by his savages and his proclamations. The famous Fort Ticonderoga was abandoned by Saint Clair; that made him very unpopular, but it saved the only unit about which the militia could rally. While the militia was being assembled, Congress recalled its generals, replaced them with Gates, and used all possible means to support him. At the same time a large British army of about eighteen thousand men had sailed from New York, and the two Howes united for a secret operation. Rhode Island was occupied by an enemy force, and General Clinton remained at New York to prepare an expedition. To parry so many blows, General Washington left Putnam on the North River, crossed the Delaware with eleven thousand men, and camped just outside Philadelphia.

That was the situation when M. de Lafayette arrived. Those circumstances, though crucial for the cause, were not favorable for foreigners. The Americans were disgusted by the conduct of several Frenchmen, and revolted by their pretensions. The impudence of the adventurers, the disgrace of those first chosen, the jealousies in the army, and national prejudices all served to confound zeal with self-interest and talent with charlatanry. Supported by Mr. Deane's promises, a large band besieged the Congress. Their chief was M. Du Coudray, a clever but imprudent man, a good officer but vain to the point of folly.[29] With M. de Lafayette, Mr. Deane sent another detachment, and every day so many foreigners arrived that the Congress no longer listened to any of them. The coldness of the first welcome accorded M. de Lafayette gave it the air of a dismissal. But, without being discouraged by the representatives who spoke with him, he entreated them to return to Congress and read aloud the following note: "After the sacrifices I have made, I have the right to exact two favors: one is to serve at my own expense, and the other is to begin to serve as a volunteer." [30] Such a novel tone caught their attention; they read the dispatches from the envoys, and, in a very flattering resolution, M. de Lafayette was appointed a major general. Among the officers he had brought to America, many were total strangers to him. He took an interest in all of them, however, and those whose services were not accepted received indemnities. A few months later, M. Du Coudray was drowned in the Schuylkill, and the loss of that troublemaker was perhaps a fortunate accident.

AM (NIC: Dean Collection), 54 pp., translation.

This is the first portion of Lafayette's earliest memoir, which covers the period 1757–1779. The Memoir will be presented serially in volumes 1 and 2, without further description, except for explication of specific textual problems. Annotation of the Memoir is limited to textual problems and the elucidation of issues and events that are not discussed in the other documents printed in this volume.

We have given the Memoir the title "Memoir of 1779" because we have determined from internal evidence that most of it was composed in that year. Lafayette did not give it its final form until much later. When he sent a copy of it to Jared Sparks in 1828, Lafayette noted that a rough draft of his memoirs for the years 1777 and 1778 had survived the French Revolution, but the first few pages were missing, and he had replaced them with the beginning of another journal. He added that the two drafts should have been integrated, but he preferred to copy them as they were written at the time (Autobiographical Notes I, fol. 1).

Lafayette's final draft of the Memoir actually consists of four distinct pieces. The first four pages, which Lafayette told Sparks he had detached from another journal, are written in the first person in Lafayette's nineteenth-century hand. Lafayette gave them the title, in pencil, "lettre à une amie." The remainder of this journal has not been found. The second piece is a short passage in the third person, written on a separate sheet in the hand of Virginie, Lafayette's daughter. The third is the original Memoir, also in the third person. It has been copied onto a series of small folded sheets, in Lafayette's hand of the period between 1782 and 1789. This section contains many ink and pencil amendations in Lafayette's nineteenth-century hand. Lafayette completed the Memoir with a two-page extract from a letter written during the period between the American and French revolutions. It is also in the first person (Autobiographical Notes I, fol. 27).

The Memoir was published, with further changes, three years after Lafayette's death, as "Mémoires de ma main jusqu'en l'année 1780," in Lafayette, *Mémoires*, 1:5–66. It could therefore be considered a literary work, which the author was free to amend for publication, but we have chosen to treat it as a historical document, and print it here without the amendations Lafayette made many years after the events described in it. Significant later changes are indicated in the notes, and passages omitted from Lafayette, *Mémoires*, are printed in angle brackets.

1. This is an error. As Lafayette noted in his other autobiographical notes, he was nearly two years old when his father died. Michel-Louis-Christophe-Roch-Gilbert du Motier, marquis de Lafayette, was born on August 13, 1732. He married Julie de La Rivière on May 22, 1754; their son, Marie-Joseph-Paul-Yves-Roch-Gilbert du Motier, was born at Chavaniac, in Auvergne, on September 6, 1757. When the elder Gilbert du Motier was killed at the Battle of Minden, on August 1, 1759, his son became the marquis de Lafayette.

2. From 1768 to 1772, Lafayette attended the Collège du Plessis, which was located next to the Sorbonne and operated under its direction. Its students were the sons of the greatest families in France, and they regularly took the highest honors in competitions among the schools of Paris. The Collège offered the standard curriculum of the time, which consisted mainly of the study of the Latin classics, but some of its teachers also put considerable emphasis on contemporary work in philosophy, theology, and physics,

and on the teaching of the French language (Martial Griveaud, "Essai historique sur le Collège du Plessis de l'Université de Paris [1318–1797]," *Positions des thèses de l'Ecole nationale des Chartes,* 73 [1922]:65–68; Henri Lantoine, *Histoire de l'enseignement secondaire en France au XVIIe et au début du XVIIIe siècle* [Paris, 1874], pp. 235–239).

3. Lafayette's mother died on April 3, 1770. When her father, the Marquis de La Rivière, died a few weeks later, Lafayette inherited his estates (mainly in Brittany and La Touraine), and his annual income increased from 25,000 livres to 120,000 livres. As he says, he was now rich.

4. Lafayette entered the Second Company of the King's Musketeers on April 9, 1771. His great-grandfather, the Comte de La Rivière, who took charge of his education in Paris, had commanded this company until his retirement in 1766.

5. On April 11, 1774, Lafayette married Adrienne de Noailles, who was only fourteen. She was the daughter of Jean de Noailles, duc d'Ayen, a member of one of the most powerful families in France, and Henriette Daguesseau, the granddaughter of the royal chancellor. Adrienne's dowry was set at 400,000 livres.

6. A riding academy attended by courtiers.

7. The Duc d'Ayen obtained a lieutenancy (April 7, 1773) and then a captaincy (May 19, 1775) for Lafayette in the Noailles Dragoons, the royal regiment in which the Noailles family held certain proprietary rights. It was agreed that Lafayette would not exercise his command until he was eighteen, but he went to Metz for his regiment's summer maneuvers in 1774 and 1775, and he took charge of his company in August 1775. When Minister of War Saint-Germain reformed the army, Lafayette was one of many officers placed in the reserve (June 11, 1776).

8. This paragraph was omitted from Lafayette, *Mémoires.* Neither of the ladies in question can be identified for certain, but Louis, comte de Ségur, describes in his *Mémoires* an incident with Lafayette during the winter of 1775. "In love with an amiable and beautiful lady, he mistakenly thought me his rival and, despite our friendship, spent nearly an entire night at my house in an access of jealousy, trying to persuade me to fight with him, swords drawn, for the heart of a beauty on which I had no claim" (Barrière, *Bibliothèque,* 9:72–73). During Lafayette's first trip to America, court gossip linked his name with that of Aglaé, comtesse d'Hunolstein (Louis Gottschalk, *Lady-in-Waiting* [Baltimore, 1939], pp. 12–15, 116).

9. This statement may also be read as a commentary upon Lafayette's education at the Collège du Plessis. His most challenging activity there was the mastery of Latin composition, but his models were works written under the Roman Republic, which contained many assertions of independence and examples of republican virtue.

10. The Noailles family had almost secured a post for Lafayette in the service of the Comte de Provence, the king's brother, but Lafayette managed to insult the comte, thus ending his chances for a career at court (Autobiographical Notes I, fol. 2).

11. The American revolt apparently first came to Lafayette's attention when the Duke of Gloucester, brother of King George III, visited Metz in 1775. The Comte de Broglie, commander of the army to which the Noailles Dragoons were attached, gave a dinner for the duke, and Lafayette was among the junior officers who attended. Broglie was already interested in the revolt, and Gloucester openly supported the American position. Lafayette related this story in 1828 (Sparks, *Writings of Washington,* 5:445). The French chargé d'affaires in London informed his government of the Declaration of Independence in mid-August 1776, but its signing was not generally known in France until Silas Deane received a copy in November.

12. The Duc d'Ayen had discussed the possibility of soliciting ministerial permission for his other son-in-law, the Vicomte de Noailles, to serve in the American army, but he flatly refused to make any such request for Lafayette (Gottschalk, *Lafayette Comes to America,* pp. 72–73).

13. *"Cur Non?"*—"Why Not?"—had also been the device of the Maréchal de Lafayette (ca. 1380–1462).

14. The French government did not officially recognize Deane, but his presence did not go unnoticed. On December 2, 1776, he wrote to John Jay: "Everybody here has taken it into their heads I am plenipotentiary. In consequence of which I have a levee

of officers and others every morning as numerous, if not as splendid, as a prime minister. Indeed I have had occasionally dukes, generals and marqueses and even bishops, and comtes and chevaliers without number, all of whom are jealous, being out of employ here, or having friends they wish to advance in the cause of liberty" (L. Bendikson, "Restoration of Secret Writing," *Franco-American Review*, 1 [1937]:248). Lord Stormont was the English ambassador.

15. Beaumarchais's firm, Roderigue Hortalez and Company, was financed by the French and Spanish governments, each of which made an initial contribution of one million livres. By October 1776 Beaumarchais reported he had used that capital to finance 5.6 million livres' worth of aid to the Americans (Samuel F. Bemis, *The Diplomacy of the American Revolution* [New York, 1935], p. 37 and note). Part of this aid did consist of obsolete weapons, but it also included 90 percent of the powder and ammunition available to the Continental army for the campaign of 1777, without which it could not have won at Saratoga the victory that made possible the French alliance (Orlando W. Stephenson, "The Supply of Gunpowder in 1776," *American Historical Review*, 30 [1925]:271–281). A number of the men Deane sent to America proved to be very effective officers in the Continental army.

16. See Kalb's description of his part in Lafayette's activities at this time, in Kalb to Saint-Paul, November 7, 1777.

17. Kalb was in America in 1768. Choiseul, the French minister of war, believed that the American colonies would eventually revolt against Britain, and that event would give France an opportunity to restore the balance of power. He refused to see Kalb because he felt Kalb had returned to France before his mission was completed. Choiseul promised to include Kalb's name in the next list of promotions to brigadier general, but he fell from power before he could fulfill that promise (Kapp, *Kalb*, pp. 52–73).

18. Bancroft wrote to Deane in the latter part of February 1777: "I am to meet yr. Friend the Marquis to morrow" (*Deane Papers*, 2:5). Bancroft was Deane's agent in London, and later became his secretary. He was also a British agent, but there is no evidence that he informed the British of Lafayette's plans, and it is quite possible that he did not know about the expedition.

19. The portion of the manuscript in the hand of Virginie de Lasteyrie begins here.

20. The Marquis de Noailles, Lafayette's wife's uncle, had recently been appointed ambassador to England.

21. Beginning with the words "to Marseilles," the manuscript is again in Lafayette's hand, and the narrative changes from the first to the third person. The letters from his family have not been found. Kalb wrote to his wife, on April 6, that Lafayette had received a letter from the Vicomte de Coigny just as the boat that was to carry them to their ship was leaving shore. The letter informed him that both his family and the king were very displeased at his actions. When the ship reached Pasajes, in Spain, Lafayette received a courier from the Comte de Fumel, commandant of the port of Bordeaux, transmitting the king's order for Lafayette to go to Marseilles and await the Duc d'Ayen and Mme de Tessé, whom he was to accompany on a tour of Italy (Kapp, *Kalb*, pp. 105–106). There is no evidence that the royal order, which also has not been found, was issued in the form of a *lettre de cachet* (Gottschalk, *Lafayette Comes to America*, pp. 101, 115, 145–146).

22. The Lafayettes already had one child, Henriette, born on December 15, 1775; Adrienne was now expecting a second.

23. The declaration to Fumel and the letter to Maurepas have not been found. Lafayette arrived at Pasajes on April 16 and that same day sent the ship's first officer to Bayonne to get one hundred muskets. It was also decided that the ship would be armed with six cannons (Segretain, ed., "Journal par Du Rousseau de Fayolle," p. 3). We have not been able to determine how many of these arms were obtained, or what became of them once Lafayette reached America. The ship finally set sail for America on the night of April 20–21.

24. Bedaulx, a Swiss by birth, had been a lieutenant in the British grenadiers and had also served in the Dutch army. He had sailed from Rotterdam in September 1776,

intending to offer his services to the American army, on a ship carrying powder and small arms to the insurgents. The ship was taken and Bedaulx was put in jail in England. He managed to get to France, and in December applied to Deane and Franklin for help in securing another passage to America. He was included in a group of officers led by Kalb and Mauroy, and when their departure was prevented he was included in Lafayette's group. Bedaulx describes his career in his petitions to Congress (February 2 and 4, 1778, DNA: RG 360, PCC 78, 2:375–382).

25. Lafayette gave Sparks a more detailed version of this incident in 1828:
The ship's papers were taken out for the French Islands in the West Indies, and the Captain sailed in that direction. While on the voyage Lafayette told him, that it was his intention to run directly for the coast of America. This was promptly declined by the Captain, on the ground that the papers protected the ship only to the French Islands; and should they be taken by the English in attempting to go into an American port, they would all inevitably be sent prisoners to Halifax, and detained in captivity no one could tell how long. This was a dilemma which Lafayette had not anticipated, and he finally told the Captain that the vessel was his property, that every person on board ran an equal risk, that he was determined at all hazards to sail by the shortest course to the American coast, and that, if he refused to put the vessel upon that track, he would deprive him of the command and give it to the next officer. The Captain acceded, but with a reluctance, which made Lafayette suspect there were other motives besides personal apprehension; and he found, on inquiry, that the Captain had goods in the ship to the amount of eight thousand dollars. When this was known, he offered a pledge of security, that in case they should be captured, and the cargo lost, he would pay this amount to the Captain, although the goods had been put on board without his authority. [Sparks, *Writings of Washington,* 5:449–450]

26. On June 13 the ship anchored at the mouth of Winyah Bay, before Georgetown, South Carolina.

27. The ship was loaded with rice for the French market and left Charleston on August 14 (*Gazette of the State of South Carolina,* September 15, 1777).

28. Lafayette left Charleston on June 26 and arrived in Philadelphia on July 27.

29. At the time of Lafayette's arrival in Philadelphia, Congress was trying to work out an agreement with Du Coudray and the officers who came with him from France, without offending American officers already in the service. According to a contract he had signed with Deane, Du Coudray was to be a major general, with command over the artillery and engineers, dating from August 1, 1776. This arrangement would have given him seniority over American major generals appointed after that date; Generals Sullivan and Greene and Brigadier General Knox, the American chief of artillery, threatened to resign if Du Coudray's agreement with Deane was honored.

30. The "note" has not been found. It is probably the letter summarized in Harrison to Washington, August 20, 1777. In offering his services as a volunteer, Lafayette had in mind the French practice by which a young noble was attached to a general officer, who taught him the art of war. A volunteer often performed the duties of an aide-de-camp and received the military courtesies of a staff officer, but had no official position. There were a number of volunteers who performed similar functions in the Continental army, but they usually became regular staff officers. A volunteer major general was an anomaly.

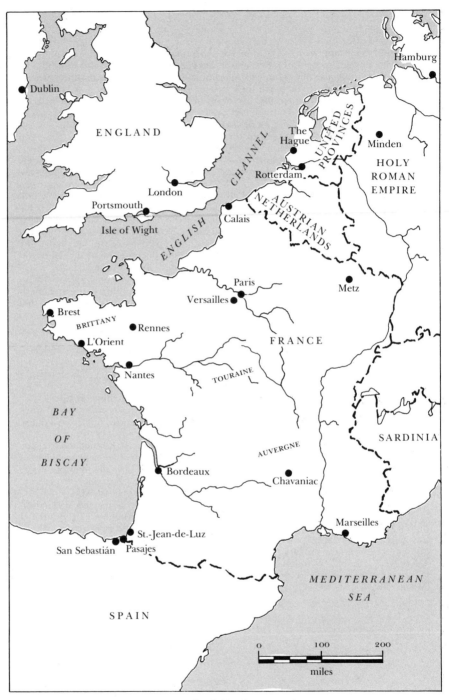

France and neighboring countries

Agreement with Silas Deane

Paris, December 7, 1776

The desire which Mr. the Marquis de la Fayette shews of serving among the Troops of the United States of North America, and the Interest which he takes in the Justice of their Cause making him wish to distinguish himself in this war and to render himself as useful as he possibly can; but not thinking that he can obtain leave of his Family [1] to pass the seas and serve in a foreign Country till he can go as a General Officer; I have thought I could not better serve my Country and those who have entrusted me than by granting to him in the name of the very honorable Congress the Rank of Major General which I beg the States to confirm to him, to ratify and deliver to him the Commission to hold and take Rank, to count from this Day, with the General Officers of the same degree. His high Birth, his Alliances, the great Dignities which his Family holds at this Court, his considerable Estates in this Realm, his personal merit, his Reputation, his Disinterestedness, and above all his Zeal for the Liberty of our Provinces, have only been able to engage me to promise him the Rank of Major General in the name of the United States. In witness of which I have signed the present 7th. of December 1776.[2]

SILAS DEANE
Agent for the United States of N. America

On the conditions here explained I offer myself, and promise to depart when and how Mr. Deane shall judge proper, to serve the United States with all possible Zeal, without any Pension or particular allowance, reserving to myself the Liberty of returning to Europe when my Family or my King shall recall me. Done at Paris this 7th. of December 1776.[3]

THE MARQS. DE LA FAYETTE

LbC (DNA: RG 360, PCC 103, p. 74). This translation was probably prepared for Congress soon after Lafayette presented his copy of the agreement (in French) to President Hancock, on July 27, 1777. That copy has not been found, but it was recorded in the congressional letter book (ibid., pp. 72–73). Deane's copy of the agreement, with Lafayette's signature, is in CtHi: Silas Deane Account Book. For a discussion of the agreement, see Shirley A. Bill and Louis Gottschalk, "Silas Deane's 'Worthless' Agreement with Lafayette," *Prologue: The Journal of the National Archives,* 4 (1972):219–223.

The agreement was prepared by Kalb. See Kalb to Saint-Paul, November 7, 1777.

1. His wife's family, the Noailles.

2. The agreement may be compared with those Deane made with other French officers at this time (*Deane Papers,* 1:359–360, 406–407). All the agreements state that

the appointments were subject to congressional approval, but Lafayette's appointment was the only one that Deane supported with a list of nonmilitary qualifications.

3. None of the other agreements cited above contain conditions about an officer's departure or return, and none of the other officers agreed to serve without pay.

A List of Officers of Infantry and Light Troops destined to serve in the Armies of the States General of North America Vizs.

Messrs.

le M. de la Fayette Major General from the 7th. of Decemr. 1776

le Baron de Kalb	Major General	7th. Novr.
Delesser	Colonel	1st. December
de Valfort	Colonel	1st. December
de Fayols	Lieutenant Colonel	20th. November
de Franval	Lieutenant Colonel	1st. December
de Boismartin	Major	7th. November
de Gimat	Major	1st. December
de Vrigny	Captain	1st. December
de Bedaulx [1] Capitaine	Captain	1st. December
de la Colombe	Lieutenant	1st. December
Candon	Lieutenant	7th. November

The mentioned Ranks and the Pay which the most honorable Congress shall affix to them to commence at the periods marked in the present List have been agreed to by us the undersigned. Silas Deane in Quality of Deputy of the American States General on the one part, the Marquis de la Fayette and the Baron de Kalb on the other part. Signed double at Paris this 7th. of December 1776.

DE KALB
THE MARQS. DE LA FAYETTE
SILAS DEANE

LbC (DNA: RG 360, PCC 103, pp. 71–72). This translation was probably prepared for Congress at the same time as that of Lafayette's agreement. The original has not been found, but the French text was recorded in the letter book (ibid., pp. 70–71).

Several men included in this list were part of an expedition headed by Kalb and the Vicomte de Mauroy which was scheduled to sail in mid-December but was stopped by the French authorities. See the list of officers dated December 1, 1776, ibid., pp. 65–67. All the men whose names appear on the list signed by Lafayette accompanied him to America; it may have been composed specifically for his expedition, in February or

March, and dated December 7, 1776, to make it conform with Lafayette's original agreement. Three other men—Dubuysson, Brice, and Mauroy—joined Lafayette's party after the list was composed.

1. In the LbC of the French text there is a bracket in the right margin, which probably indicated that Bedaulx was to receive the same rank, from the same date, as Vrigny. That interpretation is adopted by Peter Force, ed., *American Archives* (Washington, 1853), 5th ser., 3:1090.

To William Carmichael[T]

[Paris, February 1777]

I am very grateful, Sir, for the letter that you have been so good as to write to me.[1] I rely upon the good will that you have shown me for the success of our affair. I would go to see you tomorrow if I were not afraid of going too often to Mr. Deane's apartment, and of meeting people there. I would be delighted to receive you at my house, if you have the time.[2] I shall be there tomorrow at five o'clock in the afternoon. If you give me the pleasure of coming to see me, we shall talk about our affairs. I wish very much that you would be persuaded, Sir, of the tender attachment with which I beg you to believe me your very humble servant

THE MIS. DE LAFAYETTE

Silas Deane (left), the American agent in France whose freely dispensed commissions swamped Congress with foreign officers, and William Carmichael, his secretary, who assisted Lafayette and recommended him to his American friends

ALS (DNA: RG 233, HR 27A-G7.4, Papers of William Carmichael, tray 742, item 95), translation.
This letter was probably written at the beginning of February—after Lafayette visited Deane to announce that he was purchasing a ship to take French officers to America, and before the letter of February 11. Carmichael was Silas Deane's secretary.

1. Letter not found.

2. Deane's apartment at the Hôtel d'Hambourg on the Rue Jacob, the American headquarters in France, was watched by British and French agents, and Lafayette would have been much more conspicuous there than Carmichael would have been at the Hôtel de Noailles, on the Rue Saint-Honoré, where Lafayette resided with his wife's family.

To William Carmichael[T]

[Paris, February 11, 1777]
Tuesday, three o'clock

I do not leave for England until Sunday, Sir, so I shall have the time to see Mr. Franklin and Mr. Deane.[1] It is impossible for me to keep today's rendezvous because the queen is giving a ball which I am obliged to attend.[2] If I could see you tomorrow between six and seven o'clock, I would come and take you in my carriage, as I did the other day, and we could talk of our affairs. I announce to you with great pleasure, Sir, that I have just purchased my ship,[3] and that, in a month at the latest, I hope to be able to take to your country the zeal that animates me for their happiness, their glory, and their liberty. All your fellow citizens are dear to me, but I shall never find any of them to whom I can be more affectionately attached than to you.

THE MARQUIS DE LAFAYETTE

If you do not reply, that will be a sign that you will expect me tomorrow.

ALS (DNA: RG 233, HR 27A-G7.4, Papers of William Carmichael, tray 742, item 98), translation.
1. Lafayette did not meet Franklin until 1779.

2. Marie-Antoinette's Mardi Gras ball.

3. La Victoire, a ship of 220 tons with a crew of 30, had already served in the American trade. It was purchased at Bordeaux by François-Augustin Duboismartin, younger brother of the Comte de Broglie's secretary. In 1824 Duboismartin recalled that he had been sent to France by his regiment, on Santo Domingo, to purchase arms and clothing. When his business was completed, he told his brother he was looking for a ship to take him back to his post.

My brother advised me to wait and sail with Monsieur le Marquis de Lafayette, on the ship promised to Mr. Deane. I confess that I replied to my brother, rather heatedly, that when one was privileged to be a great lord, and very rich, like Monsieur de Lafayette, he did not wait for means that might never arrive, to launch an escapade; he procured them for himself, whenever he wished. My brother, much more calm than I, asked me: "Since you are so wise, what would you do in such a case?" I replied that I would procure and equip a ship, and sail in it with some officers of my choice. Then my brother asked me to write my ideas down, which I did. He took the paper upon which I had written and said: "I am going to find Monsieur le Marquis de Lafayette. I will tell him of your plan; go to your hotel and wait there for word from me on the subject." That evening I received a note from my brother, by which he informed me that he and Monsieur le Marquis de Lafayette would come to see me at eight P.M. They came and it was arranged between us that I would set off to execute my plan. I left the same night, and everything was arranged. [Exposé de François Aug. Du Bois Martin (MdHi: MS 307)]

Duboismartin neglected to mention his previous connections with Deane and the French officers he was sending to America. Duboismartin had handled some business at Bordeaux for Deane (see Deane to Saml. and J. H. Delap, Merchants, Bordeaux, November 13, 1776, in *Deane Papers*, 1:358), and Deane had agreed to send him to America as Kalb's aide-de-camp, with the rank of major (agreement with Kalb, November 22, 1776, and list of officers in the Kalb-Mauroy expedition, December 1, 1776, in ibid., 1:344, 405).

In 1824 Duboismartin told a reporter for the *Baltimore American* that the ship he purchased was named *La Bonne Mère* (Gilbert Chinard, *When Lafayette Came to America* [Easton, Pa., 1948], pp. 1–2). Lafayette later said he had changed its name to *La Victoire*, to make it an omen of success (Doniol, *Histoire*, 2:378 n.).

To Adrienne de Noailles de Lafayette[T]

[Calais] February 20, 1777

We have arrived at Calais without mishap, dear heart, ready to embark tomorrow, and see the famous city of London.[1] It will be painful for me to leave the shore; I leave behind all the people I love, I leave you, dear heart, and in truth without knowing why. But the die is cast, and I must go. We have proceeded at a very leisurely pace, we have broken down because it is my lot, and we arrived with the pleasant expectation of staying here five or six days. Tomorrow we shall be able to cross very quickly, and we shall have to endure the inconvenience of being sick for only four or five hours. Please tell my aunts[2] that you have heard from me, my dear. I shall write to you from London the moment I arrive, and I hope I shall soon receive a letter from you. I shall be very happy if you write to me punctually. Farewell, dear heart. Wherever I go, I shall always love you very tenderly. I wish you could know how sincere that assurance is, and how important your love is to my happiness.

AL (ALG, courtesy of the Comte de Chambrun), translation.

1. Lafayette was traveling with the Prince de Poix.
2. Madeleine de Lafayette, known as Mlle du Motier, and Charlotte Guérin, baronne de Chavaniac.

To Adrienne de Noailles de Lafayette[T]

[London] February 25 [1777]

We have arrived in London, dear heart, but not without difficulty. The time we spent at Calais was very boring, but we finally got here yesterday. I write to you from the home of the Marquis de Noailles, who received us very warmly. We have as yet seen only a few men this morning. We have just dined with our ambassador, and we are about to leave for the opera; then we are invited to a supper. At the ball tonight we shall see all the ladies. I still think Paris is preferable to London, even though we have been received very agreeably here. I am very impatient to see all the young women, and the famous Duchess of Devonshire. We make our entry into society this evening. I very much hope that the prince will conduct himself well. He claims that I am always afraid that he will say something stupid. Farewell, my dear,

Adrienne de Noailles de Lafayette, Lafayette's wife

I am so rushed that I have only time to tell you that I love you with all my heart.

AL (ALG, courtesy of the Comte de Chambrun), translation.

To Adrienne de Noailles de Lafayette[T]

[London, February] 28 [1777]

For once, dear heart, I am just like these gentlemen. London is a delightful city, I am overwhelmed with kindnesses, and I only have time for pleasure here. All the men are polite and obliging. To us, all the women are pretty, and good company. Amusements are more lively than in Paris. We dance all night, and, perhaps because my dancing is more on a par with everyone else's, I like the ball here, for there are some fine figures in my new country.[1] The Marquis de Noailles is charming, and very attentive to us. He is highly esteemed in London, and maintains his station very well. It is true that I am inclined to see everything in the best light. I am already almost as much a part of London society as I am of that of Paris. The post arrived today; I hoped to have news from you, and saw with chagrin that there wasn't any. I hope to have better luck with the next post. Farewell, dear heart, I have time to write only a few lines to you. I have a thousand things to do this evening, concluding with a ball, for we never retire here before five A.M.

AL (ALG, courtesy of the Comte de Chambrun), translation.
1. "Ma nouvelle patrie."

To Adrienne de Noailles de Lafayette[T]

[London, March 1777]

I was quite distressed, dear heart, not to receive any news from you for two posts. Fortunately, I know that you are not sick but only lazy, because we have had letters from the vicomtesse [1] and our other friends, who don't speak of you at all. The diversions of London maintain a rapid pace, and even I, who am not accustomed to a secluded life, am amazed at their liveliness. To leave the dinner table at seven-thirty and have supper between two and three A.M. at first

Jean-Paul-François de Noailles, duc d'Ayen, Lafayette's father-in-law

Henriette Daguesseau, duchesse d'Ayen, Lafayette's mother-in-law

struck me as a very bad practice. I am enjoying myself very much here. There are some truly charming women and some men who are very friendly and full of kindness for us. When you can draw the women from their precious gatherings, and the men from their clubs, to bring them into company [*one or two illegible words*], they are very agreeable. The period of your exile at Versailles approaches,[2] and I send you my regards on that. Tell M. le Duc d'Ayen that up to now I have not had a moment to myself, that I shall have the honor to write to him at the first opportunity, and to speak to him of M. de La Rochette. I find him so compatible that I am often perfectly happy to closet myself with him for a chat while M. de Poix goes to court the ladies. A thousand regards to Mme d'Ayen, a thousand compliments to my sisters;[3] don't forget to remember me either, dear heart, to my grandfather,[4] to my aunts, and to Mme d'Abos. I very much wish to learn that she has been presented at court. Farewell, my dearest, I must write on the run; my stay in London may be short and that makes my time more precious than if I were to spend four months here like my predecessors. If I needed new proof to convince myself how tenderly I love you, it would be the pain I have felt in not receiving any letters from you when I have had them from all of my friends. *Good day.*

AL (ALG, courtesy of the Comte de Chambrun), translation. The manuscript is faded in several places.
    1. Louise, vicomtesse de Noailles, Adrienne's older sister.
    2. Lafayette is probably referring to one of the Noailles family's regular periods of attendance at court.
    3. Adrienne's sisters.
    4. The Comte de La Rivière, Lafayette's great-grandfather.

To Adrienne de Noailles de Lafayette[T]

London, March 7 [1777]
    At last, dear heart, I have received news from you and with great pleasure.[1] I look forward to hearing more today; no matter how great the bustle of London, I am always thinking impatiently about post days, and I am elated when they arrive. We dance, we dine, we always stay up very late, and our activities have been related to scarcely anything but society. Today, however, I took a walk with M. de La Rochette (whom I can never leave) to the port of London and several notable places in this city. Tomorrow or the day after we are going to Portsmouth, armed with an ample supply of introductions, which will

enable us to see everything.[2] Therefore, I may not write you for one or two posts. They continue to overwhelm us with kindness in this country, and nowhere in the world could we be treated more pleasantly. M. de Poix is the great arbiter of fashion and creates hair styles for all these ladies,[3] but these ladies only. We are eagerly awaiting our friend Etienne, who is traveling slowly with the Duke of Dorset. However, we hope to have some news of him eventually. The English are convinced that there will be war, or rather they predict it. In truth, one need not be terribly shrewd to see that it will come, at least after a time. Here, however, I do not let on that I am convinced of it. Today I dine with a man whom I have met only when he was running about town with Mlle Grandi, and whom I was astonished to see again here in possession of a wife and a house, which is beautiful if not fine, whereas it is said that his wife is neither of those. All in all, I am annoyed to be obliged to go there and my ill humor about it is even greater as I am compelled to take leave of you. It is five-fifteen here, the time when people begin to ask if their carriage has arrived. I am going to hurry the prince, who is always on horseback and extremely busy buying horses.

Farewell, dear heart, a thousand regards to Mme d'Ayen, a thousand affectionate greetings to the vicomtesse, and to my sisters. I am always distressed when I leave you, even in writing, and it is my cruel star that keeps me moving constantly and which I must blame when I do not see you even a sixth part of the time that I would truly like to see you. But you know my heart, or at least its sincerity, and you will believe me, I trust, always, when I assure you that it loves you forever, with the strongest and most tender affection.

Kiss our dear Henriette twenty times for me.

Remember me to your father. Thus far, I have seen only feathers like those in Paris, and I am waiting to be able to give him an account of a more interesting stroll.

I hope to write you once more before my excursion.

AL (ALG, courtesy of the Comte de Chambrun), translation.

1. Letter not found.
2. Lafayette later remarked about his visit to London:

Although these two young Frenchmen [Lafayette and Poix] made friends with people of the opposition, they also made the acquaintance of several people who supported the ministry, especially at the home of the ambassador, their relative. The courtesies they received from the latter were perhaps due to a desire to demonstrate the good relations that existed between the two courts. But Lafayette, to the extent that his age and the amusements that were his sole interest gave him the opportunity, never hesitated to profess his support for the cause of the insurgents, and even his esteem for their agents in Paris. He saw the king only once and did not return to court. When Mr. Stanley, governor of the Isle of Wight, brought him and the Prince de Poix letters of introduction that would have permitted them to

visit the fleet at Portsmouth, where an expedition was being prepared for America, Lafayette believed that it would be an abuse of confidence, and did not take advantage of the opportunity. [Autobiographical Notes IV, p. 3]
Lafayette did not visit Portsmouth; he received word that his ship was ready, and hurried back to France. See following letter.

3. Lafayette's reference to Poix is explained by a contemporary newspaper item:
London. March 20. A gentleman just returned from Paris, desires to acquaint his fair countrywomen of the *Ton,* that her Majesty, hearing of the order of the Superintendent of the Opera-house for the ladies to abate their high head-dresses, thought it would have a better effect to set the example herself. She accordingly wears her hair *quite flat,* with a small wreath of artificial flowers in front;—which is now a fashion not only adopted by the whole Court, but advancing fast over all Paris. [*New-York Gazette and Weekly Mercury,* June 2, 1777, p. 2]
Lafayette's phrase is "coiffe toutes ces dames," which can also be translated figuratively as "infatuates all these ladies"—a nice double entendre.

To the Duc d'Ayen[T]

London, March 9, 1777

You will be astonished, my dear Papa, by what I am about to tell you; it has been more painful than I can say not to have consulted you. My respect, my affection, and my confidence in you must assure you of that. But I had given my word, and you would not have respected me if I had gone back on it, whereas the step that I am taking will, I hope, give you a favorable opinion, at least of my good intentions. I have found a unique opportunity to distinguish myself, and to learn my profession. I am a general officer in the army of the United States of America. My zeal for their cause and my sincerity have won their confidence. On my side, I have done everything I could for them, and their interests will always be more dear to me than my own. In short, my dear Papa, at this very moment I am in London, awaiting news from my friends. As soon as I receive it, I shall leave here and, without stopping in Paris, board a ship that I have equipped, and which belongs to me.[1] My traveling companions are M. le Baron de Kalb, an officer of the highest distinction, a brigadier general in the king's army,[2] and a major general in the service of the United States, like myself, and a few excellent officers who are willing to share my adventures. I am overjoyed at having found such a fine opportunity to do something and to improve myself. I know very well that I am making enormous sacrifices, and that it will be more painful for me than anyone to leave my family, my friends, and you, my dear Papa, because I love them more dearly than anyone has ever loved. But this voyage is not such a long one; people undertake longer ones every

Vous allez être ettonné, mon cher papa, de ce que je vais vous mander; il m'en a plus coûté que je ne puis vous exprimer pour ne pas vous consulter. mon respect, ma tendresse, ma confiance en vous doivent vous en assurer. mais ma parole y était engagée, et vous ne m'auriez pas estimé si j'y avois manqué; au lieu que la démarche que je fais, vous donnera, j'espère bonne opinion, au moins de ma bonne volonté. j'ai trouvé une occasion unique de me distinguer et d'apprendre mon métier. je suis officier général dans l'armée des états unis de l'amérique. mon zèle pour leur cause et ma franchise ont gagné leur confiance. de mon coté j'ai fait tout ce que j'ai pu pour eux, et leurs intérêts me seront toujours plus chers que les miens. enfin, mon cher papa, dans ce moment où je suis à londres attendant toujours des nouvelles de mes amis. dès que j'en aurai, je partirai d'ici et sans m'arrêter à paris j'irai m'embarquer sur un vaisseau que j'ai frêté, et qui m'appartient. mes compagnons de voyage sont mr le baron de kalb, officier de la plus grande distinction brigadier des armées du roi, et major général au service des états unis ainsi que moi, avec quelques officiers excellens qui veulent bien partager mes aventures. je suis au comble de ma joie d'avoir trouvé une si belle occasion de faire quelque chose et de m'instruire. je sais bien que je fais des sacrifices énormes, qu'il m'en coutera plus qu'à personne pour

quitter ma famille, mes amis, vous, mon cher papa, parceque je les aime plus tendrement
qu'on n'a jamais aimé. mais ce voyage n'est pas bien long, on en fait tous les jours de
plus considérables pour son seul plaisir, et d'ailleurs j'espere en revenir plus digne de tout
ce qui aura la bonté de me regretter. adieu, mon cher papa; j'espere vous revoir bientôt
conservez moi votre tendresse, j'ai bien envie de la meriter et je la merite deja par celle
que je sens pour vous, et le respect que conservera toute sa vie

votre tendre fils
lafayette

le 9 mars à londres 1777

j'arrive un instant à paris, mon cher papa, ne prenant que le temps de vous dire adieu
je voulais écrire a mon oncle et a ... de ... mais je suis si pressé que je vous prie
de vous charger de mes hommages

Lafayette's letter to the Duc d'Ayen, March 9, 1777 (*continued*)

day, solely for pleasure, and, moreover, I hope to return more worthy
of all who will have the goodness to miss me. Farewell, my dear Papa,
I hope to see you again soon. Keep your affection for me, for I want
very much to deserve it, and I already deserve it because of that which
I feel for you, and the respect that will endure for the rest of my life.
Your affectionate son

LAFAYETTE

[Paris, March 16, 1777]

I come to Paris for a moment, my dear Papa, but take only the time to
say good-bye to you.[3] I wanted to write to my uncle [4] and to Mme de
Lusignem, but I am in such a great hurry that I must ask you to
present my respects to them.

ALS (NIC: Dean Collection), translation.

1. Lafayette apparently received the news that his ship was ready from Kalb. See
Kalb to Saint-Paul, November 7, 1777. None of the letters Lafayette received in London have been found.

2. Kalb was the son of a German peasant, and not related to the Baron von Kalb
whose title he borrowed when he became a French officer. He did become a French
noble in 1769, when he acquired the fief of Milon la Chapelle. His highest rank in the
French army was lieutenant colonel, but he also held a commission of brigadier general
in the colonies, from the Ministry of the Marine.

3. When Lafayette reached Paris, on March 13 or 14, he found that the preparations
for his departure were not complete, and rather than return to the Hôtel de Noailles,
he took a room in the suburb of Chaillot. He apparently wrote the postscript just before
he set off for Bordeaux with Kalb, at noon on March 16.

4. The Marquis de Lusignem.

The Baron de Kalb to William Carmichael

[Paris,] March 14th. [1777]

Dear Sir

The Marquis does not dare to go out of his lodgings at Chaillot, he
is in great haste to be gone, and should be glad you would call on him
this Evening. He will tell you all his reasons not to tarry in Paris. I
believe he will propose to you, to detain here Mr. Price and his fellow
traveller,[1] till you have done all the Letters we are to be charged
with,[2] and that he and I could set out to morrow evening.[3] You will
do him a great pleasure to see him.

His Directon is à Chaillot, dans la maison de Mr. Marie, Jardinier
de l'Orangerie—à Côté des Cazernes suisses, vis à vis une porte

grillées. Demander un Monsieur qui y loge au premier.[4] (He must not be named.) I am yours,

DE KALB

ALS (DNA: RG 233, HR 27 A-G7.4, Papers of William Carmichael, tray 742, item 93).

1. Edmund Brice (not Price) was Lafayette's aide-de-camp, and his "fellow traveller" was probably one of the other men who were to sail on *La Victoire*. Brice was in Bourdeaux by March 21.

2. The letters included recommendations written for Kalb in December 1776, and new letters of recommendation for both Lafayette and Kalb to Deane's friends in Congress. See Deane to Hancock, March 16, and Deane to Kalb, March 18, 1777 (MH: Sparks MSS 52, 1:64). Sparks assigned the date of March 22 to the second letter, and it is printed in *Deane Papers*, 2:29–30, with that date.

3. Lafayette and Kalb left Paris on March 16 and arrived in Bordeaux during the night of March 19.

4. "At Chaillot, at the house of Mr. Marie, Gardener of the Orangerie—next door to the barracks of the Swiss troops, facing a barred gateway. Ask for a gentleman who is lodged on the first floor."

To Adrienne de Noailles de Lafayette[T]

[Paris, March 16, 1777]

I am too guilty to vindicate myself, but I have been too cruelly punished not to deserve a pardon. If I had expected to feel my sacrifices in such a frightful manner, I would not be at present the unhappiest of men. But I have given my word, and I would die rather than go back on it. M. le Duc d'Ayen will explain my foolish acts to you.[1] Do not be angry with me. Believe that I am sorely distressed. I had never realized how much I loved you—but I shall return soon, as soon as my obligations are fulfilled. Good-bye, good-bye, write to me often, every day. Embrace our dear Henriette. And, moreover, you are pregnant, all of which adds to my torment. If you knew how painful this is, you would surely be more sorry for me than you will ever be. To add to my misery, the people I love are going to believe that I am quite happy to leave. Besides, it is a voyage no longer than that of your father to Italy. I promise you it will be short. Farewell, I have saved this letter for last; I finish my good-byes with you. They are going to take me far away. It is terribly hard for me to tear myself away from here, and I do not have the courage to speak to you longer of a man who loves you with all his heart, and who cruelly reproaches himself for the time he will spend without seeing you.

L.

LbC (NIC: Dean Collection), in hand of Adrienne de Lafayette; translation. She entitled this letter book: "Letters that M. de Lafayette wrote to me during his voyages to America. First voyage, in 1777." She gave this letter the title: "First letter, at the moment of his first departure, of which I had known nothing." Lafayette later noted: "Several letters written from America had been copied by my wife for Dr. Du Breuil, who honored me with his friendship during his lifetime, and of whom I have always retained a deep and tender memory. That letter book was preserved; it would be appropriate to delete repetitions and insignificant details, but I retain nearly everything, because it pleases me, in putting this collection together, to recall the sentiments that moved me at various periods of my life" (Autobiographical Notes I, f. 35). This statement was included in a "Foreword by M. de Lafayette" in Lafayette, *Mémoires*, 1:vii–viii.

1. Lafayette probably wrote this letter at the same time as the postscript to his letter of March 9 to the Duc d'Ayen.

Silas Deane to [John Hancock]

[Paris, ca. March 16, 1777]

Sir,

The letters, to be delivered you by the Baron de Kalb, were wrote at the time fixed for his setting out in December last, which I hoped would have been the case, but many and unexpected accidents have prevented. At length, the Marquis de la Fayette, a young Nobleman of the first family and connexions at Court, viz. that of Noailles, has equipped a vessel, at his own expence, to transport him and the Baron, with other Officers, to America. As my letters were very particular at the time, and as we shall write express by Capt. Hammond in a few days, will not detain you more than to recommend this young Nobleman to your particular notice and attention. His family are of the first influence here, and have, for ages, been celebrated in the affairs of this Country, as well in peace as war. His fortune puts him above all pecuniary considerations, and he desires none, but wishes to rank with Gentlemen of the first character in the Army. The Baron du Kalb is an old experienced officer, having served during the last war as Adjutant General under Marshal De Broglio, who recommends him. His being a German, and speaking the English language, will undoubtedly be of great service, as well as his other qualifications, the whole of which he submits to the determination of the honorable Congress, to direct, as they shall judge proper.

Dr. Franklin is, at present, in the country, has a slight turn of the gout. I dined, however, with him yesterday in town, and have the pleasure to assure you etc.

I send you for your entertainment, by *Mr. Brice,* a young gentleman of Maryland, whom I think deserving your notice, as a worthy sensible young man, the London papers, in which you will perceive the character I have the honor of bearing in England, and that I have fled, &c. &c., which causes diversion here.

Mr. Carmichael is still with us, and has, on every occasion, shewn himself not only the true American, but has been of great real service to us; to me, I may say in particular, as a Secretary or Assistant. He is much esteemed in Paris, and should he return, as he proposes, soon to the Continent, my wishes are, that he may there find a sphere to act in, equal and agreeable to his capacity and disposition. At present, as no Secretary is sent out, he with Mr. Franklin,[1] supply the place, who is a young gentleman of great ingenuity, and gives the most favourable presages of future eminence. He has an animating example in his worthy Grandfather, who is universally esteemed and respected here, as well as in America, and, I may say, through the learned world.

My compliments to friends in general. My most profound respects to the honorable Congress, and, remembering your lady in the most affectionate manner, I have the honor to remain Your &c.

S.D.

L (MH: Sparks MSS 52, 1:52–53; by permission of Houghton Library, Harvard University); copy in secretary's hand, from Deane's letter book, with note in Sparks's hand: "The copy, from which this transcript was made, had neither date nor address, but was on a sheet with several others, dated as this is now dated." The other letters were dated March 22, and that was the date assigned by Sparks, but the letter must have been written by March 18, when Brice left for Bordeaux. It was probably written on March 16, at the same time that Deane wrote a letter to Robert Morris which included a request that he serve as Lafayette's banker: "This by the Marquis de La Fayette is to inform you, that this gentleman is of one of the most capital fortunes, and as he will incline to live up to his rank, as far as is possible in America at this time, he will have occasion to draw bills. I have, therefore, recommended him to your house for supplies, and to refund in bills—on which you may rely; he has at his own expense equipped the ship he goes out in" (MH: Sparks MSS 52, 1:60–61; by permission of Houghton Library, Harvard University).
1. William Temple Franklin, Benjamin Franklin's grandson.

William Carmichael to Richard Henry Lee

Paris March 17th. 1777

Sir

As your Brother Mr. Arthur Lee is not on the spot, I take the Liberty in consequence of his desire to inform you of his health, now at Burgos in Spain, at which place he remains at the desire of the Spanish Ministry, to negotiate on the behalf of the United States. From

Richard Henry Lee, member of Congress from Virginia, to whom Lafayette was recommended

what He writes me, I am in hopes he will at least get some money on
our acct. Your Brother the Alderman, as I am just informed by a
Gentleman from London is well. His prudence will I hope preserve
him from the malice of the Ministry armed now with pernicious powers by the Suspension of the Habeas Corpus act—Doctr. Bancroft, as
we just hear, having been confind. Your Eldest Son is at Nantes in the
Country House of a Mr. Schweighauser, a man of the first Character
in business there. Your second is left under my inspection at a military pension here, and improves fast in all his excercises. He will write
you fully by Captn. Hammond.[1] I take the liberty of introducing to
your Notice & protection the Marquis La Fayet & the Baron de Kalb.
The former of the first distinction for birth fortune & family connections here, the other of the highest repute in the Service & strongly by
the Marshal duc de Broglie & the Marshall de Maillebois. The
formers family are our strong support here. His Uncle is Embassador
at the Court of London & from his representations we hope to bring
on a war much sooner than otheways it would happen.[2] I hope He
will have every reason to think favorably of the Country & I do for
him to you what your Brothers absence hinders him from doing.
Should my name be mentioned in Congress in consequence of Letters
from hence, may I hope your kind attentions. I have the honor to be
with much respect sir your most Obedient humble Sert.

                                                     WM. CARMICHAEL

ALS (PPAmP).
  1. Richard Henry Lee was a member of the Continental Congress from Virginia. His
brother Arthur, who had spent many years in London, was sent to Paris to join the
American commission in October 1776. At the urging of his colleagues Deane and
Franklin, he went to seek assistance from the Spanish government in February 1777.
William Lee, a third brother, had been an alderman of London, but resigned at the
outbreak of war in America and received several American diplomatic appointments in
Europe. Neither Arthur nor William appears to have had any contact with Lafayette
before he went to America in 1777. A fourth brother, Francis Lightfoot, also represented Virginia in Congress. Richard Henry's sons were Thomas and Ludwell.
  2. Carmichael explained these remarks in a letter written to Charles Dumas, the
American agent at The Hague, on April 21, 1777.
      Knowing how much and how strongly the generality of our common people looked
   up to France, I encouraged a most promising young nobleman of high rank and
   fortune, married into the Noailles family, and nephew to the ambassador in England, to go out in a ship of his own to America with a few choice officers. I wrote
   and prepared all my acquaintance for his reception, insinuating that a man of his
   estate and rank would not leave France without knowing fully the disposition of its
   court; that their intentions certainly were war, &c. [Deane Papers, 2:49]
He put it a bit differently to General Cadwalader. In a letter dated October 8, 1777,
Carmichael said he was happy that Lafayette had joined the American army, "on acct.
of his Family connections & because his going out showd the English Nation on what
footing our affairs stood in France" (Henry Ammon, ed., "Letters of William Carmichael to John Cadwalader, Maryland Historical Magazine, 44 [1949]:16).
  On March 17, 1777, Carmichael also recommended Lafayette to Cadwalader (ibid.,

p. 6), and to Tench Tilghman, an aide-de-camp to Washington (New York *Sun,* June 1, 1902, p. 6).

Lafayette always denied that his uncle had any prior knowledge of his plans. As soon as Lafayette's departure was known, the ambassador protested his ignorance of the whole affair to his superiors, who replied that they did not hold him responsible for his nephew's folly (Noailles to Maurepas, April 8; Maurepas to Noailles, April 28; and Vergennes to Noailles, May 2, in Stevens, *Facsimiles,* nos. 1509, 1522, and 1525). The only members of Lafayette's family who then supported the American cause were the Vicomte de Noailles, Lafayette's brother-in-law, and the Comte de Ségur, his friend, who married Adrienne's aunt on April 30, 1777. Lafayette did not even tell them he was going to America until the morning he left for Bordeaux (Ségur, *Mémoires,* in Barrière, *Bibliothèque,* 19:73–74).

Act of Embarkation[T]

At Bordeaux, March 22, 1777

I attest that Sieur Gilbert du Moitie, Chevalier de Chavaillac,[1] age 20, tall, blond hair; Jean-Simon Camus of La Villedieu in Franche Comté, in the service of Monsieur le Chevalier, age 32, medium height, blond hair; Michel Moteau of Saclay, near Paris, age 27, medium height, blond hair, in the same service; François-Aman Rogé of Nantes, age 20, medium height, blond hair, in the service of Monsieur le Baron de Canne,[2] and Antoine Redon of Sarlat, age 22, medium height, chestnut hair, are Catholics of long standing who desire to embark on *La Victoire,* Captain Lebourcier, to go to Le Cap,[3] on business.

GILBERT DU MOTIER
J. S. CAMUS

DS (ADG), in clerk's hand; translation.

1. This is one of five acts of embarkation, dated variously March 21, 22, and 23, by passengers of *La Victoire,* in the Bordeaux Embarkation Register. There are many errors in these declarations. Some of them may be ascribed to the recording official, but Lafayette obviously intended to conceal his identity. His name was indeed Gilbert du Motier, chevalier de Chavaniac, but he normally signed himself "the Marquis de Lafayette." It was of course a common thing for eighteenth-century nobles to use one of their little-known titles when they were traveling incognito.

2. The Baron de Kalb.

3. On Santo Domingo, in the French Antilles.

To the Comte de Broglie[T]

Bordeaux, March 23, 1777

I have the honor to inform you, M. le Comte, that I leave for the country you know, and for that adventure which you counseled me not to risk. You will be astonished by my action, but it was impossible for me to do otherwise, and the proof of this truth is that I have not followed your advice. I have not even wished to discuss it with you again because, with the best will in the world, and despite myself, Fate has prevented me from following your counsel. You would have opposed my desires, and I already had enough obstacles to overcome. Now there is so much the less danger in taking you into my confidence, because this letter will leave for Paris at the same time I leave for Philadelphia, and then it will be useless to impress upon me the consequences attendant upon an action already taken, or, in common parlance, a folly already consummated. I dare hope that you will even help and encourage an enterprise that you are no longer able to prevent. For my part, I shall try to vindicate this thoughtlessness (I accept the term) as I acquire the knowledge and the means of distinguishing myself.

L (PRO: S.P. 78/302), copy in secretary's hand; translation.

The copy was made for Stormont, from a letter Broglie was circulating. Stormont enclosed the copy in his letter of April 9 to Weymouth, with the comment: "There is great Reason to believe that Count Broglie secretly encouraged this wild Enterprize of *La Fayette,* tho' He shews an ostensible Letter, that seems to prove the contrary. . . ." Many historians have questioned the authenticity of the letter, but its style and tone are unmistakably Lafayette's, and Lafayette's reasons for writing the letter are not difficult to understand. He later privately acknowledged his gratitude for Broglie's interest in his plans at this time (Lafayette to Duboismartin, October 23, 1777), but on March 23 he was waiting for his father-in-law's reaction to his departure (see following letter), and he obviously wrote to Broglie in an attempt to absolve him of responsibility for an act that might draw the wrath of the powerful Noailles family, and perhaps even that of the government. Kalb probably encouraged Lafayette to write the letter, and Lafayette may even have begun to compose it before he left Paris, because Deane had written to Kalb, on March 18: "You will remember the letters you mention from the Marquis, and favour me with one, if you have time" (MH: Sparks MSS 52, 1:64; by permission of Houghton Library, Harvard University).

The Baron de Kalb to Silas Deane

Bordeaux, March 25th., 1777, in the morning

I received by the Hands of Mr. Brice the honor of yours of the 18th. with several Letters for your Friends which we hope please God to deliver in a Short time.[1] Our Ship is already gone down the River, and this instant we will follow in a boat, as the weather Cleared up since yesterday, and the wind sitting fair we are in hopes of setting sail tomorrow. Every one of our Passengers are arrived; M. Le Chevr.

The Baron de Kalb, to whom Lafayette looked for guidance

Dubuisson too came here last night, so we are in all fifteen. I will follow your advice for my introduction to the Congress, as I should be glad to do on all occasions. I am sorry for our being very soon far asunder which will put it out of my reach and power to consult you about my further behaviour to render myself useful to the Country & People, & agreable to the Superiors, but I'll do my best. The Marquis I think has wrote to you to day or yesterday; his Letter must surprize you as much as his confidence, of having taken this step without advice from his Family, or consent from M. Le Duc d'Ayen his Father in Law, has surprized me when he first confessed it to me at his arrival here.[2] I hope it will involve neither you nor me in any difficulties about it, for we both were Confident that all was done in that matter by the advise & Consent of his nearest relations.[3] I can but repeat once more to you, my hearty wishes for your Welfare, Prosperity & Success in all your undertakings. Nobody Professes more esteem and respect for you than, Hond. Sir, Your most Obedient Humble Servant

DE KALB

My Sincere Wishes & Compliments to Mr. Carmichael. The Marquis as well as myself shall be glad to give your News to your Lady at her own Home.

L (DLC: Samuel Burch Papers), copy in secretary's hand.

1. The letters probably included Deane's recommendations to Morris and Hancock (see Kalb to Carmichael, March 14, 1777, note 2), and Carmichael's letters to Richard Henry Lee and Tench Tilghman (see Carmichael to Lee, March 17, 1777).

2. Letter not found.

3. See Kalb to Saint-Paul, November 7, 1777.

Silas Deane to Joseph-Matthias Gérard de Rayneval

[Paris,] 2 Apr. 1777

Sir

You have, enclosed, Two Original Letters from the Baron du Kalb,[1] which please to present, to his Excellency the *Comte De Vergennes*, and tell him I refer to my uniform Conduct to justify what I have had the honor of relating to You this Evening, as to the Facts. Mons. Comte de Broglio has received this Evening a Letter from Mons. *Le Marquiss de Fayette* which he will communicate.[2] I refer to that Nobleman, & am willing to rely on his relation of this Affair, for my Justification, more, for my Approbation, since to gain a most Gallant & Amiable Young Nobleman, to espouse Our Cause, and to give to the World a Specimen of his Native & hereditary bravery, surely cannot be deemed Criminal. I have nothing to add to what I have had the honor of relating to You personally on this Subject, except that I rely on the Comte de Broglio to explain, any and every part of my Conduct in this Affair; that my Colleagues have had no knowledge of it, as it was executed in November last, long before their Arrival, and that I shall do every thing in my power to Satisfy every one that my Conduct has been & shall be strictly honorable. I have the honor to be Your most Obed. & Very Hum. St.,

S. DEANE

The dispatches shall go by the first packet which will sail the 15th. inst. & I will send his Excellency a Copy of the Letters from me which shall accompany them.[3]

ALS (Stevens, *Facsimiles*, no. 673). Sent with a cover letter dated April 3 (ibid., no. 674).

1. One of the two letters must have been Kalb to Deane, March 25; the other has not been found.

2. Lafayette to Broglie, March 23.

3. The letters, dated April 5, to Washington and Hancock, warned them that Lafayette's departure, "being without the approbation or knowledge of the King, is disagreeable, and that his Majesty expects that you will not permit him to take any command under you; but that he should be directed immediately to return." They were enclosed in a letter of the same date in which Deane told Vergennes: "I have the honor of enclosing to your Excellency agreeably to my promise to Mr. Gerard, copies of my letters respecting M. La Fayette, which I hope will be agreeable. . . . P.S. If the enclosed letters to Genl. Washington and President Hancock are not quite agreeable to his Majesty's designs, I will alter them as I shall be directed" (*Deane Papers*, 2:38–40). Vergennes approved the drafts and returned them (Deane to Gérard, April 7 [MH: Sparks MSS 52, 1:77]). By the time Deane got them back, however, he had heard that Lafayette had decided to obey the royal order (Lafayette to Carmichael, April 3), and he informed Gérard that he would not be sending the letters about Lafayette to America (April 8, Stevens, *Facsimiles*, no. 680).

Lord Stormont to Lord Weymouth

Paris April 2d. 1777

My Lord

It is now very generally, and certainly known, that M. de la *Fayette* is gone to join the Rebel Army,[1] and has taken with Him twelve french officers, Nine of them, actually in this service: Three have sent their

Dismission. They embarked at Bordeaux on Board a french Vessel, which Mr. de la Fayette has freighted, and for which He gives fifty thousand Livres.[2] As soon as His Intentions were known here, a Courier was dispatched, with Orders to stop Him. His Brother in Law, the Vicomte de Noailles, likewise dispatched a Courier at the desire of his Family, and pressing him in their Name, to abandon this wild Enterprise, but both these Couriers arrived a few hours After he had sailed.[3] As Nothing further can be done in this Business now, I did not think it proper, to enter upon the Subject with M. de Vergennes. Another foreign Minister did speak to him of it as the news of the Day, and to that foreign Minister M. de Vergennes said, that for a Young Man of the first fashion, with every advantage of Fortune, and Situation, to engage in such an Adventure as this, was such unaccountable Folly, as there was no foreseeing, no guarding against. He then mentioned the Courier, that had been sent to stop M. de la Fayette, and added, that a *Batiment* was gone to endeavour to come up with Him, and bring him back.[4] It is very likely, continued M. de Vergennes, that the English will meet with him by the Way. If they do, they will pretend not to know him, and treat Him rather roughly, which will be treating him, as his folly deserves. This Folly however, *est montée dans la Tete de nos Jeunes Gens,*[5] to a degree that You cannot conceive. I have had numberless applications to me. My Answer to those who are absolutely free, is this, they may to be sure do as they please, but I tell them, that if they come to ask my advice, I give it strongly against their going, if they ask my Orders, *Je le defends.*[6] This My Lord is the Substance of what M. de Vergennes said, as repeated to me, by my Friend. It would I think, be no difficult Matter to collect M. de Vergennes real sentiments, and wishes, even from this Language, fair and guarded as He thinks it.

Mr. de la Fayettes Relations seem to be much displeased with his Conduct, most of them certainly were not privy to this Design. His Friends and the Public at Large appear to say, that to be sure this step is imprudent and Irregular, and in that Light liable to Censure, but that it shews a Spirit of Enterprize, and strong Enthusiasm in a good Cause. It is proper to inform your Lordship, that M. de la Fayette goes under a feigned Name. He calls himself *Gilbert Du Montier Natif de Chavaniaque.*[7] Monsr. de Lugny, Mr. Quade, an officer of some Reputation, and that Baron Kalb whom I have frequently mentioned to your Lordship are . . . three of the officers that are gone with Him.[8] I am with the greatest Truth and Respect, My Lord, Your Lordships most obedient humble servant

STORMONT

LS (Stevens, *Facsimiles*, no. 1504), in secretary's hand, endorsed, "Separate & Secret."
    This is one of more than thirty manuscripts in the *Facsimiles* which report information (often erroneous) about Lafayette's departure and the English reaction to it.
    1. Stormont had informed Weymouth on March 26 of Lafayette's intention to embark for America from one of the seaports, probably Bordeaux (Stevens, *Facsimiles*, no. 1497).
    2. The ship and its cargo cost 112,000 livres. Lafayette paid 40,000 livres in cash and promised to pay the rest in June.
    3. Kalb wrote to his wife on April 6 that Lafayette had received a letter at Bordeaux from the Vicomte de Coigny just as the boat that was to carry them to *La Victoire* was leaving shore. The letter informed him of the displeasure of his family and the king with his actions (Kapp, *Kalb*, pp. 105–106). At the insistence of the Duc d'Ayen, the king dispatched an order requiring Lafayette to go to Marseilles to await the arrival of d'Ayen and Mme de Tessé, and to accompany them on a trip to Italy. Lafayette received the king's order by a courier from the Comte de Fumel, commandant of the port of Bordeaux, at Pasajes, Spain, on March 31 (see Kalb to Saint-Paul, November 7, 1777). Neither Lafayette nor Kalb mentions a courier from the Vicomte de Noailles.
    4. As France was not yet prepared for war with England, the government had maintained a formal attitude of neutrality in the war between England and her colonies while giving secret aid to the insurgents. The clamor over the departure of a member of the royal court brought to light an expedition that the government could not publicly countenance, and Louis XVI signed an order to be sent to the French West Indies, forbidding all French officers to take service in America without his express permission. Any French officer, and in particular M. de Lafayette, who arrived there with the intention of going to America was to return immediately to France. Minister of War Montbarey sent the order to Sartine, minister of marine and the colonies, but Sartine favored French intervention on behalf of the colonies, and delayed issuing it. On April 2, 1777, he wrote to Montbarey that he had received only one copy of the order and that, to ensure its prompt and safe arrival in the colonies, it would be prudent for Montbarey to send him two copies of the order which could be sent by different ships. No duplicate order has been found (Doniol, *Histoire*, 2:395 and note).
    5. "Impassions our youth."
    6. "I forbid it."
    7. See Act of Embarkation, March 22, 1777.
    8. De Lugny and Quade were not among the officers who went to America with Lafayette. For Lugny, see Lafayette to Robert Morris, January 9, 1778, note 1. The ellipses appear in the manuscript.

To William Carmichael[T]

[Bordeaux, April 3, 1777]
    I have been detained by order of the king, my dear friend, and I am sending a messenger to obtain a cancellation of it. In the meantime I have put the ship and the other officers out of danger.[1] I am most unhappy that my good intentions toward you have met with such poor success. I am so hurried that I do not have the time to say any more to you. Please express my regrets to Mr. Deane. Good-bye. Force may prevent me from rendering you the services which I de-

sired, but, since it cannot act upon hearts, nothing will prevent me from being all my life your brother and your friend.

THE MQUIS. DE LAFAYETTE

ALS (DNA: RG 233, HR 27A-G7.4, Papers of William Carmichael, tray 742, item 97), translation.

1. At Kalb's suggestion, Lafayette had directed *La Victoire* to sail to Pasajes, Spain, where it could safely await the outcome of Lafayette's negotiations to get permission to go to America. Lafayette left Pasajes by land on April 1 and arrived on April 3 at Bordeaux, where he reported to the Comte de Fumel. From Bordeaux he sent a courier to Paris with letters requesting permission from Maurepas and d'Ayen (Doniol, *Histoire*, 3:209, and Kalb to Saint-Paul, November 7, 1777). Those letters have not been found.

Lord Stormont to Lord Weymouth

Paris April 9th. 1777

My Lord

I am now able to give your Lordship some further Particulars, relative to the *Brillante Folie de Monsieur de La Fayette,* as his friends, and the Public at large affect to call it. He is to have the Rank of Major General in the Rebel Army. This Project must have been long in Agitation, as there are Letters from St. Domingo, that mention his Intentions as known there. That they should not be known to any of his own Family, nor to any of the French Ministers, is very Extraordinary, and more than I can bring myself to believe, but I have good Reason to think, that M. de Maurepas was not in the secret, and that he is really displeased.[1] The french King has expressed his displeasure in the strongest Terms, and said it was highly blameable, in a Man of M. de la Fayettes Fashion, and Rank to go and assist *Rebels.*

The ship that M. de la Fayette has freighted, is called *la Victoire,* she has on board a great Quantity of cloth, and Ammunition, a large Part of which was purchased by M. de la Fayette, and is intended as a present to the Rebels.[2] This Expedition has already Cost him a good many thousand Pounds.

There are fourteen french officers gone with Him, I know for certain that one of them, who is to be *aide* de Camp to La Fayette and who is only a Lieutenant, tho' he has been eighteen years in the french Army, wrote to his Colonel the Day He embarked. In this Letter, some particulars of which are material, He says *Je vais m'embarquer moi Quatorzieme* not including La Fayette, I am the only one of the fourteen, who has not a *Congé* from Prince Montbarry. I beg that you would endeavour to obtain it for me. It is hard that I should be the only exception, and it is the more Extraordinary, as Count Broglie, whom I saw at Rouen, and who strongly advised the Step I have taken, promised to use his Interest with Prince Montbarrey. Upon the Receipt of this Letter, the Colonel tho' He had always given his Opinion strongly against the Lieutenants Resolution, went to M. Montbarrey, made the Application, and had a general Evasive Answer, *qu'il verroit ce qu'il y auroit a faire.*[3] Your Lordship may depend upon these particulars, as I have them from an intimate Friend of mine, who conversed with this Colonel, whom He would not Name, and heard Him read the Letter from the Lieutenant. There is great Reason to believe that Count Broglie secretly encouraged this wild Enterprize of *La Fayette*, tho' He shews an ostensible Letter, that seems to prove the contrary, LaFayette says in that Letter that He hopes Monsr. de Broglie will justify to the Public what He would not approve. I am with the greatest Truth, and Respect, My Lord, Your Lordships, most obedient, humble servant.

STORMONT

P.S. M. de la Fayette's Expedition has been a short one indeed: a Courier dispatched to St. Sebastian, where it was known, his Vessel was to put in, came up with Him there, and Signified to Him the french King's Order to return to France, which was so peremptory, that He could not but Obey. As the order was to M. de la Fayette only, the other officers will no doubt continue their Voyage.

S.

LS (Stevens, *Facsimiles*, no. 1510), in secretary's hand. Endorsement notes one enclosure, probably the copy of Lafayette to Broglie, March 23, found with this letter in the PRO.

1. It is difficult to believe that none of the French ministers had any knowledge of the preparations for the expedition, but there is no evidence that any of them knew Lafayette was planning to take part in it. The available evidence indicates that Lafayette's family first learned of his activities on March 16, when he sent the letter dated March 9 to the Duc d'Ayen. The French government first took notice of Lafayette's actions when d'Ayen asked Maurepas to have Lafayette stopped, and the British ambassador first notified his government of Lafayette's departure on March 26, after Louis XVI had issued an order for Lafayette's arrest.

2. Presumably Lafayette purchased a standard cargo for a ship sailing to the Antilles, which would have included dry goods. He expected to sell the cargo at a profit to pay the expenses of the voyage. He also obtained some muskets just before sailing from Spain on April 20, but these were intended primarily for the defense of the ship (Segretain, ed., "Journal par Du Rousseau de Fayolle," p. 3).

3. "He would see what might be done about it." The lieutenant was Louis Cloquet de Vrigny, who went to America as Lafayette's aide-de-camp. The king did grant him a leave and the commission of major in the colonies in 1777.

The Baron de Kalb to Silas Deane

On board the ship la Victoire
at the Passage in Spain, 17 April, 1777

Sir:

I had the honour of writing to you four days ago in a sad mood of mind, about all the difficulties which seemed to obstruct M. Le Marquis de la Fayette's generous designs; as I made you a partaker of bad news, I think it a piece of justice to impart to you a good one. The Marquis guessing, by all the letters he received, that the Ministers granted and issued orders to stop his sailing, out of mere compliance with the requests of M. Le Duc d'Ayens, and that in reality neither the King nor any body else could be angry with [him], for so noble an Enterprise, he took upon him to come here again and to pursue his measures. He arrived this morning nine of the clock to the great comfort of all his fellow Passengers.[1] M. de Mauroy arrived at the same time,[2] So we shall put out to sea again by the first wind, and strive to get to the Continent directly as much as possible. All these Gentlemen present you with their most sincere Compliments and good wishes.

I wrote to M. le Cte. de Broglie as well as to Madame de Kalb, if they had any letters to send to me before I could give them an account of myself after arrival at your army, to put them under cover, directed to Mr. Sam. Shoemaker at Philadelphia,[3] and desire you to get them over when opportunities will offer. I depend on this and all other occasions on your goodness and friendship, to which and Mr. Carmichael's I recommend myself particularly and am with all possible respect, Honoured Sir, Your most obedient humble servant

DE KALB

This letter will go by the to morrow's Post, but you shall hear from me the day of our putting under sail.

The marquis charges me peculiarly to acquaint you that his fear of involving you in some disagreeable Dilemma and of doing hurt to our friends interrest at the French court,[4] was what determined him most to comply with the king's orders and go back to Bordeaux; being willing to fall alone a sacrifice to resentment and make nobody share his misfortune, as long as he could believe these orders serious, and that it is only since he is sure of your and your cause's security he assumed anew his most darling Project.

L (*Magazine of American History,* 9 [1883]:384–385).

1. Kalb had written to his wife on April 15:

The marquis writes from Bordeaux, under date of the 12th inst. that he was on the point of leaving for Marseilles, where the royal order requires him to report himself to-day. He says that the court devotes great attention to this affair of his, but he still hopes to gain over the Duc d'Ayen, so as to be at liberty to rejoin me. He therefore requests me not to sail before receiving another letter from him from Toulon or some other point. . . . Lafayette's letter shows that the ship is still held in his name. He requests me to have an eye to his interests, and to see that his investment is realized as soon as possible. [Kapp, *Kalb,* p. 107]

2. Mauroy was the last officer to join the expedition before it embarked from Pasajes. He arrived in Bordeaux about April 12, carrying letters of introduction from Deane to Congress, and from Broglie to Washington, both dated April 8 (E. S. Kite, "Lafayette and his Companions on the 'Victoire,'" *Records of the American Catholic Historical Society,* 45 [1934]:159–160). As far as Lafayette was concerned, however, he was sent by Carmichael, Lafayette's special friend among the Americans (see Lafayette to Carmichael, April 19), and the information Mauroy brought with him helped Lafayette reach a decision. Kalb explained to his wife on April 19: "He made this decision according to assurances he received from all over Paris that the Duc d'Ayen alone solicited the order from the king, that everyone approved of his undertaking and blamed his father-in-law for wanting to stop him and that the ministers, when asked for their true disposition on this affair, responded that if the Duc d'Ayen had not complained they would have said nothing" (Doniol, *Histoire,* 3:211). This information about the disposition of the ministry undoubtedly came from Broglie, through Mauroy (see Memoir by the Vicomte de Mauroy, p. 53.

3. Kalb had been sent to America in 1768 by Choiseul, French minister of foreign affairs, to obtain information on the state of the American colonies' relationship to Great Britain. He spent a fortnight in Philadelphia and arranged for correspondents to keep him informed of developments in America. Samuel Shoemaker, one of the more influential men in Philadelphia before the Revolution, may have been one of these correspondents.

4. The friend whose interests at court might have been harmed was Broglie (see Doniol, *Histoire,* 1:636, and Lafayette to Broglie, March 23).

To Adrienne de Noailles de Lafayette[T]

On board *La Victoire,* April 19 [1777], at San Sebastián

Ah, dear heart, they thought that fear would have more effect upon me than love. They have misunderstood me, and since they tear me away from you, since they compel me not to see you for a year, and since they wish only to humble my pride, without affecting my love, at least that cruel absence will be employed in a manner that is worthy of me. The only notion that could detain me was the sweet consolation of embracing you, of being restored to you, and to all the people I love. Giving these reasons, I asked for a fortnight, only a fortnight to be with you, at St. Germain, or wherever they wished. My request was refused.[1] I refuse also, and, having to choose between the

An imaginative representation of Lafayette's departure on *La Victoire* from the port of Pasajes, Spain, on April 20, 1777

slavery that everyone believes he has the right to impose upon me, and liberty, which called me to glory, I departed.

My voyage will be no longer, perhaps shorter, and you will have news of me even more often. A thousand ships will bring it to you constantly. I shall not expose myself, I shall take care of myself, I shall remember that you love me, you can set your mind at ease. It is more as a philosopher than as a soldier that I shall visit all of that country. . . .[2]

I was received here with very flattering transports of joy, and I am liked here beyond all my expectations, but yet I am far from happy. My heart is broken. Tomorrow is the moment of cruel departure. I am writing to you on the day before to be more certain that my letter will be rational. If you do not send word to me that you still love me, that you forgive me, that you will take good care of your health, I shall be in despair. I swear to you by the most sacred honor, by my love for you, that my greatest regret in departing is to leave you, that my greatest anxiety is for you. Make me less unhappy by writing to me very soon. Farewell, I may return sooner than M. le Duc d'Ayen. Love me always, even at the moment when I deserve it only because of my anguish at leaving you, and because of my ardent affection.

Give our Henriette a hug for me. Take good care of our other child. I hope to be reunited soon with my whole family. Write to me at once, my address is Major General. . . .[3] You must go with Mme d'Ayen to Mr. Deane's house, to have your letter forwarded to me. He is a man of the greatest merit, the most honorable man in the world, and my friend. He will take care of your first letter. For the others, the Marquis de Coigny will give you the address.

Farewell. Once again, do not doubt the sentiment that I feel more than ever at this cruel moment. Nothing, not even adversity, seems to compare with the anguish of leaving you.

L.

LbC (NIC: Dean Collection), in Adrienne de Noailles de Lafayette's hand; translation. The letter is preceded by her note: "Second letter, written on the eve of his departure from San Sebastián, at a time when he was quite agitated and extremely irritated with what several people had written him, and with my father and Mme de Tessé. They took pleasure in contriving to do everything they thought appropriate to make him rebel against my family; my mother and I were the only ones spared. The projected trip to Italy is his reason for complaint."

1. Lafayette thought he might obtain d'Ayen's approval if he could go to Paris, but Commandant Fumel insisted that he obey the royal order and proceed to Marseilles.

2. A line and a half of elipses here in the LbC.

3. Ellipses here in the LbC.

To William Carmichael[T]

On board *La Victoire,* April 19 [1777]

Here, Sir, is the last letter you will receive from me in French, but I dare not write to you in your language yet, and I wish to make use of the one I know best, in order to make clear to you how happy I am to find myself here. The fear of doing some harm to my friends had forced me to make a cruel sacrifice; as soon as it disappeared, I did not lose a moment, and departed full of joy, hope, and zeal for our common cause. They told me that Milord Stormont had shown a bit of bad humor at my departure. On the whole, this affair has produced all the éclat I desired, and now that everyone's eyes are on us, I shall try to be worthy of that celebrity. I can assure you that I shall not be taken by the English, and I hope you will not be worried.

Edmund Brice, who went to Europe to study painting and returned to America as Lafayette's aide-de-camp

All the officers that I am taking with me have received me with an amity that augurs well for the future. Their number has been augmented by M. de Mauroy, whom you sent. Thank you very much for having given me Mr. Brice. I like him very much, and he is popular with everyone. We shall always be together, as you seem to have desired. I was also very pleased to make the acquaintance of M. Bedaulx. He has begged me to request that he always serve with me. I hope that you will be so good as to recommend us again in your letters. The only favor that I ask is that they give me every possible opportunity to make use of my fortune, my labors, and all the resources of my imagination, and to shed my blood for my brothers and my friends. The only recompense that I shall request, after success, is to obtain new means of being useful to them.

Do not worry about my family affairs, or even about that order I received. Once I have departed, everyone will agree with me; once I am victorious, everyone will applaud my enterprise. It is through your recommendations that I expect to obtain the means to have an effect that will be equally advantageous for all of us. I hope I shall become a good general as readily as I have become a good American, and I shall neglect nothing to merit your friendship and the public's esteem. I hope also that that may be a means of proving to you the tender and eternal attachment with which I have the honor to be, Sir, your most humble and obedient servant

THE MIS. DE LAFAYETTE

If by chance you ever have need of my friends, I have informed them that I shall recognize their affection for me only in proportion to the care they take to be useful to you.

ALS (DNA: RG 233, HR 27A-G7.4, Papers of William Carmichael, tray 742, item 99), translation.

Benjamin Franklin and Silas Deane to the Committee of Secret Correspondence[E]

Paris May 25 1777

. . . The Marquis de Fayette a young Nobleman of great Family Connections here, & great Wealth, is gone to America in a Ship of his own, accompanied by some Officers of Distinction, in order to serve in our Armies. He is exceedingly beloved, and every bodys good wishes attend him. We cannot but hope he may meet with such a Reception as will make the Country and his Expedition agreeable to him. Those who censure it as imprudent in him do never the less applaud his Spirit; and we are satisfy'd that the Civilities and Respect that may be shown him will be serviceable to our Affairs here, as pleasing, not only to his powerfull Relations & to the Court, but to the whole French Nation. He has left a beautifull young Wife big with Child: and for her sake particularly we hope that his Bravery and ardent Desire to distinguish himself will be a little restrain'd by the Generals prudence; so as not to permit his being hazarded much but on some important Occasion. We are very respectfully, Gentlemen, Your most obedient humble Servants

B. FRANKLIN
SILAS DEANE

LS (DNA: RG 360, PCC 85, p. 55), in secretary's hand, signed by Franklin and Deane; extract. Probably received by the committee on August 1 or 2, in a packet from the American commissioners (Burnett, *Letters,* 2:436).

The Committee of Secret Correspondence was established by Congress in November 1775, and eventually took charge of all American diplomatic activity. On April 17, 1777, its name was changed to the Committee for Foreign Affairs, but its representatives in France had not received word of that change when they wrote this letter.

Silas Deane to Robert Morris

Paris 26 May 1777

Dr. Sir

I cannot let the inclosed go without saying one Word on the Subject of Mons. Le Marquiss LaFayette, he is of the first Family & Fortune in this Kingdom [both by?] birth & Marriage. A generous reception of [him] will do Us infinite Service. He is above pecuniary Considerations; his Family have ever been distinguished in the first Military Line, in Europe, as the History of Europe witnesses. It has occasioned much Conversation here & tho' the Court pretends to know nothing of the Matter, his Conduct is highly extoll'd, by the first people in France. I am afraid his generous disposition may be Abused by Avanturiers of his Own Country, his Friends the *Marshall Duc De Noiailles,* the Duchess D'ayen his Wive's Mother & others of the Family have been with Me, & I assured them I would recommend him to the Care & oversight of one who would be as a Father to him on every Occasion and I could in such a Case think of no one in preference to You. He is expected to live in Character, & his Friends wish it, but they are apprehensive on the Score I hinted at; I have advised him to place the most implicit Confidence in You on every Occasion, & I am sure I could no way better employ the influence I have over him. All he seeks is Glory, and every one here, says, he has taken the most noble method to procure it. You may think it makes a great Noise in Europe, & at the same time see that well managed it will greatly help us. I refer to Our joint Letter in which You will see Dr. F.'s Opinion on the Subject.[1] I am with the greatest Esteem, Your Sincere Friend & Humle. Servt.

DEANE

ALS (DLC: Papers of Robert Morris). Manuscript torn where seal was broken.
1. See preceding letter.

Memoir by the Vicomte de Mauroy[ET]

I had been an infantry captain for fifteen years when in 1772 I obtained the brevet of lieutenant colonel. Several days later I was placed on active duty through a transfer to the post of lieutenant colonel of the Royal Grenadiers of the Franche-Comté, the regiment of which M. le Marquis de Mauroy was then colonel.

Monsieur le Comte de Saint-Germain reorganized the regiment, and the large number of officers put on reserve and left without employment did not allow him, or the ministers who succeeded him, to find a position for me.

It was in these circumstances that it was proposed I should go to America, and that Mr. Deane, sent to France by the thirteen united colonies, accepted us, the Marquis de Lafayette, the Baron de Kalb, and me, for service in the Continental army, with the rank of major general.[1]

I was in no position to be choosy, even though it was easy for me to foresee all the troubles that I would have to endure as a result. I thought I would at least get credit for my willingness to serve, and that the least favorable result I could expect would be to receive a position the moment I returned to France.

I received a brevet of brigadier general in the colonies, and orders assigning me to Santo Domingo. Then I allowed myself to entertain the most flattering hopes—the name of my master was enough to reassure me, and at the same time that everything told me the brevet was illusory, it was impossible for me to conceive that a name as respectable as *Louis* did not declare irrevocably the station of the one who has the honor to offer it as proof of his identity.

Be that as it may, I started out on April 10, 1777. I headed for Bordeaux, and six leagues from the city I was to join the Marquis de Lafayette.

According to public rumor, this nobleman, on his own account, and, it was said, by order of the minister, had decided to pretend that he had abandoned his project. He had taken the road to Italy, but he had stopped en route to wait for either new entreaties from his family or the considered opinion of the public. I arrived at the same time as his courier; we made a detour to avoid Bordeaux, and reached Pasajes, the first port in Spain, where we found *La Victoire*, a 250-ton ship. We sailed on April 20, without any means of defending ourselves if

The Vicomte de Mauroy, a major general without illusions and without employ

they wanted to intercept us, and without any other preliminary than our devotion to fortune.

My fellow passengers were in a laughable state of enthusiasm, and I certainly had no intention of trying to cure them of it, but the Marquis de Lafayette truly interested me. His youth, that ardent desire to distinguish himself, his name, his fortune, the pleasures that he had sacrificed to glory, his constancy in fighting against all obstacles, and the good luck he had met with in surmounting all of them made me very interested in his success. Whereas everyone around him took care to flatter his fondest hopes, I wanted by my objections to prepare him for the disappointments he would perhaps experience, and which would make too painful an impression upon him if he experienced them at the very moment when his imagination was the most inflamed on the subject of the Americans.

"Eh! What!" he said to me one day. "Don't you believe that the people are united by the love of virtue and liberty? Don't you believe that they are simple, good, hospitable people who prefer beneficence to all our vain pleasures, and death to slavery?"

If the savages of the new continent, I replied, had united to live together, if some man of genius, virtue, talent, and constancy, a new Timoleon, had given North America its laws, such a people could present to us the pleasant tableau you have just described, but it was people who were already civilized (and who had not been educated by such philosophers) who brought to a savage land the views and prejudices of their respective homelands.

Fanaticism, the insatiable desire to get rich, and misery—those are, unfortunately, the three sources from which flow that nearly uninterrupted stream of immigrants who, sword in hand, go to cut down, under an alien sky, forests more ancient than the world, watering a still virgin land with the blood of its savage inhabitants, and fertilizing with thousands of scattered cadavers the fields they conquered through crime. In this tableau, which is only too accurate, do you see any less horror than you see in the picture you are able to make of the continent we are leaving? I see you are about to raise the objection of the Quakers and the happiness that at least Pennsylvania must present to us, but besides the fact that such a point of view works to the disadvantage of the other colonies, it is a fact that these supposedly good people yield with regret to the projects of their neighbors, that they piously desire only peace and abundance, and that finally all powers are the same to them, because, under their truly monkish constitution, no power can bind them. That is the basis upon which I admit to you quite frankly that I expect to find in America only people like those of our own continent. I think that, because of

their prejudices, we French must be detested by them, when, as people who come to offer knowledge superior to theirs, we hurt their
pride in general and arouse their envy in particular. Don't worry,
though, it will be politic to welcome you. I do not know what resources M. de Kalb has, and since I have none I would be a total fool
if I did not at least reap from such a voyage the benefits that are
always within reach of those who retain their composure. . . .

AM (AN: AE III 219, fols. 1–2 vo.), extract, translation. Probably written for the
Comte de Broglie after Mauroy's return to France in 1779.
    1. Mauroy had signed an agreement with Deane on November 20, 1776 (*Deane
Papers*, 1:359–360). He and Kalb are listed as major generals on a list of officers dated
December 1 (ibid., pp. 405–406), but his name does not appear on the list of December
7, 1776, with those of Lafayette and Kalb.

To Adrienne de Noailles de Lafayette[T]

On board *La Victoire,* May 30 [1777]
    I am writing to you from very far away, dear heart, and to this cruel
separation is added the still more dreadful uncertainty of the time
when I shall hear from you. I hope, however, that it will be soon.
Among the many reasons that make me want to arrive at my destination, none make me more impatient than that. So many fears and so
many worries are added to the intense grief of leaving everything that
is most dear to me. How did you take my second departure?[1] Did you
love me less because of it? Have you forgiven me? Have you thought
that in any case I would have been separated from you, wandering in
Italy and leading a life without glory, amidst the people most hostile
to my projects and my way of thinking? All these reflections did not
prevent me from experiencing a terrible emotion during the awful
moments when we left the shore. Your grief, that of my friends,
⟨your pregnancy,⟩ Henriette—all came to my mind with a terrifying
vividness. It was then that I could find no more excuses for myself. If
you knew everything that I have suffered, dear heart, during the sad
days I passed in flight from everything that I love in the world! Must I
add to this the unhappiness of learning that you do not forgive me?
In truth, my dear, that would be too much to bear. But I am telling
you nothing about myself, about my health, and I know that such details interest you.
    Since my last letter I have been in the most tedious of regions; the
sea is so dismal, and I believe we sadden each other, she and I. I

should have landed by now, but the winds have cruelly opposed me, and I shall not see Charleston for eight or ten more days. That is where I expect to land, and it will be a great pleasure for me. Once I am there I shall have the hope, every day, of receiving news from France; I shall be informed of so many interesting things, both about what lies ahead, and above all about what I have left with so much regret! Provided that I learn that you are well, that you still love me, and that some of my friends do too, I shall be perfectly philosophical about any other news I receive, no matter what it is or where it comes from. But if my heart is wounded in a very tender spot, if you, dear heart, no longer love me as much, I would be unhappy indeed. But I do not need to fear that, do I, dear heart?

I was very ill during the first part of the voyage, but I could have given myself the consolation of the wicked, which is to suffer in a numerous company. I treated myself in my own way, and I recovered sooner than the others. Now I feel almost as if I were on land. Once I arrive, I am sure that I shall have acquired the hardiness that will assure me perfect health for a long time. Do not fancy, dear heart, that I shall run great risks in my service here. The post of general officer has always been regarded as a warrant for long life. I shall have functions different from those I would have performed in France, as a colonel, for example. In the former grade, one serves only in councils of war. Ask any of the French generals of which there are so many because, once they have reached that rank, they no longer run any risk, and consequently do not make room for others, as in the other ranks. To prove that I do not wish to deceive you, I shall admit that at present we are in some danger because we risk being attacked by English vessels, and my ship does not have the strength to defend itself. But once I land I shall be in perfect safety. You see that I tell you everything, dear heart, so have confidence in what I say, and do not be anxious without cause. I will not write a journal of my voyage for you; one day follows another here, and, what is worse, they are all alike. Always the sky, always the water, and again the next day the same thing. In truth, the people who write volumes about an ocean passage must be cruel babblers. For, like them, I have had contrary winds, I have made a very long voyage, I have endured storms, I have seen some ships, and they were much more interesting to me than to any other person. Well, I have not noticed anything that was worth the trouble of writing down, or which has not been described by everyone.

Now, dear heart, let us speak of more important things: let us speak of you, of dear Henriette, of her brother, or her sister. Henriette is so lovable that she gives me a liking for daughters. Whatever our new

child may be, I shall welcome it with great joy. Do not lose a moment
in hastening my happiness by informing me of its birth. I do not
know if it is because I am a father for the second time, but I feel more
like a father than ever. Mr. Deane and my friend Mr. Carmichael will
furnish you with the means; I am very sure that they will neglect
nothing to get the happy news to me as quickly as possible ⟨because
they are truly my friends⟩. Write, or even send a reliable man. It
would give me so much pleasure to question a man who had seen
you—Landrin, for example—in short, do as you think best. You do
not understand, dear heart, how ardent and tender my love is, if you
believe you may neglect anything that relates to you. You will receive
my news very late this time. But when I am established you will receive it often, and it will be much fresher. There is no great difference between sending letters from America and sending them
from Sicily.[2] I confess that I cannot stop thinking angrily of Sicily. I
believed that I was so close to seeing you again. But let us cut short
the discussion of Sicily. Good-bye, dear heart, I shall write to you
from Charleston; I shall write to you before I arrive there. Good
night for now.

June 7

I am still on this dreary plain, dear heart, and it is so dismal that
one cannot make any comparison with it. To console myself a little I
think of you, and of my friends. I think with pleasure of meeting you
again, my dear; what a delightful moment it will be when I arrive and
suddenly embrace you, when you do not expect me. Perhaps you will
be with our children. Even thinking of that happy moment gives me
the greatest pleasure. Do not fancy that it will be a long time. It will
surely seem long enough to me, but in fact it will not be as long as you
may imagine. Without being able to set the day, or even the month,
without seeing for myself the state of things, I can assure you that the
exile until the month of January prescribed by M. le Duc d'Ayen appeared to me so interminable that I am certainly not going to inflict a
truly long one upon myself. You must admit, my dear, that the employment and existence that I shall have are very different from those
to which I would have been restricted during that futile journey. As
the defender of that liberty which I idolize, freer than anyone else,
coming as a friend to offer my services to this most interesting republic, I bring there only my sincerity and my goodwill, and no personal
ambition or selfish interest. In striving for my own glory, I work for
their happiness. I trust that, for my sake, you will become a good
American. Besides, it is a sentiment made for virtuous hearts. The
welfare of America is intimately connected with the happiness of all

mankind; she will become the respectable and safe asylum of virtue, integrity, tolerance, equality, and a peaceful liberty.

We have from time to time some minor alerts, but, with a little skill and good luck, I am quite certain of getting through without trouble. I shall be all the more pleased at that because I am becoming more prudent every day. You know that the vicomte [3] is always repeating that "travel educates the young." If he only said it once every morning and once every evening, in truth that would not be too often, because I am coming to appreciate more and more the justice of the maxim. I do not know where that poor vicomte is, or the prince, or any of my friends, and this lack of news is a cruel thing. Every time that you chance to meet any of those I love, give them a thousand and ten thousand greetings for me. Embrace my dear sisters tenderly; tell them to remember me and love me. Present my sincere compliments to Mlle Marin. I recommend to you also, dear heart, the poor Abbé Fayon. As for M. le Maréchal de Noailles, tell him that I do not write to him for fear of boring him, and because I had nothing to tell him about except my arrival. I await his requests for some trees, or plants, or whatever he would like from me, and I truly hope that my exactitude will be proof of my affection for him. Also present my respects to Mme la Duchesse de la Trémoïlle, and tell her that I make the same offer to her as to M. le Maréchal de Noailles, either for herself or for her daughter-in-law,[4] who has a very beautiful garden. Also let my old friend Desplaces know that I am in good health. As for my aunts, Mme d'Ayen, and the vicomtesse, I am writing to them myself.[5]

That completes the list of my little commissions, dear heart; I have also written to Sicily.[6] Today we have seen several types of birds that indicate that we are not far from land. The expectation of arriving is very sweet because life in this region is so dull. Fortunately, my good health permits me to engage in some activity; I divide my time between military books and English books. I have made some progress in that language, which will soon be so necessary. Farewell, my dear, I cannot continue because night is falling, and I have forbidden all lights on my vessel for several days now. See how careful I am. Farewell, then, if my fingers are guided a bit by my heart, I do not need to see clearly to tell you that I love you, and that I shall love you all my life.

June 15, at Major Huger's house [7]

I have arrived, dear heart, in very good health, at the house of an American officer, and by the greatest luck in the world, a French vessel is just about to sail.[8] You can imagine how pleased I am at that. ⟨I have only the time to close this letter.⟩ This evening I go to Charleston; I shall write to you from there. I have no more interesting news. The campaign has begun, but there is no fighting, or at least very little. The manners of the people here are simple, honest, and in every way worthy of this land where everything proclaims the beautiful name of *liberty*. I had planned to write to Mme d'Ayen, but it is impossible. Farewell, farewell, dear heart. From Charleston I shall go by land to Philadelphia and the army. Is it not true, my dear, that you will love me always?

AL (NIC: Dean Collection), translation. The manuscript has been edited in pencil, in Lafayette's later hand. Significant passages omitted from Lafayette, *Mémoires,* are printed in angle brackets.

1. Lafayette's "second departure," from Pasajes on April 20, would have been a surprise to his family, who expected him to comply with the royal order.

2. The Duc d'Ayen's Italian tour included a trip to Sicily.

3. The Vicomte de Noailles.

4. The daughter-in-law was Marie-Maximilienne, princesse de Salm-Krybourg, duchesse de la Trémoïlle.

5. Letters not found.

6. To the Duc d'Ayen. Letter not found.

7. Benjamin Huger, a major in the South Carolina militia, was at that time in his summer home on North Island, South Carolina.

8. A ship was about to leave for France from South Inlet, the port near North Island (Kalb to Mme de Kalb, June 15, 1777 [Doniol, *Histoire,* 3:213]).

To Adrienne de Noailles de Lafayette[T]

Charleston, June 19 [1777]

If I had to hurry, dear heart, to finish my last letter, which I wrote five or six days ago,[1] I hope at least that the American captain (whom I believed to be French) will get it to you in the shortest possible time. That letter said that I have arrived safely in this country, after having been a bit seasick during the first few weeks; that I was then at the home of a very obliging officer, at whose house I had disembarked; that I had wished to go straight on; and that my voyage had lasted nearly two months. That letter spoke of everything that is closest to my heart: of my regret at having left you, of your pregnancy, and of our dear children. It also said that I am in splendid health. I give you this abstract from it, dear heart, because the English might enjoy seizing it en route. Yet I have enough faith in my star to hope that it will reach you. That star has already served me in a manner that astonished everyone here; have a little trust in it, my dear, and it will surely put you entirely at ease. I landed after sailing for several days along a coast that swarmed with enemy vessels. When I arrived here, everyone told me that my vessel had surely been taken, because two English frigates blockaded the port. I even sent orders, by land and sea, for the captain to put the men ashore and burn the ship, if there was still time. Well, by inconceivable good fortune, a squall had momentarily driven off the frigates, and my vessel arrived in broad daylight without encountering either friend or foe. At Charleston I found General Howe, a general officer on active duty; the president of the assembly is due to arrive from the country this evening,[2] and all the people with whom I have wished to become acquainted here have overwhelmed me with courtesies and attentions (and they are not the sort of courtesies one receives in Europe). I cannot help being pleased with the reception I have had here, even though I have not judged it proper to enter into any details about either my arrangements or my plans. I want to see the Congress first. I hope to leave in two days for Philadelphia,[3] an overland journey of more than two hundred and fifty leagues. We will separate into small parties; I have already purchased some horses and small carriages for transportation. There are some French and American vessels here, which will sail out together tomorrow morning, the instant the enemy frigates are out of sight. Moreover, they are numerous and armed, and they have promised me to defend themselves well against the small corsairs they will surely meet. I shall divide my letters among the various ships, in case something happens to one of them.

And now, dear heart, I shall tell you about the country and its inhabitants. They are as likable as my enthusiasm has led me to picture them. A simplicity of manners, a desire to please, a love of country and liberty, and an easy equality prevail everywhere here. The richest man and the poorest are on the same level, and although there are some immense fortunes in this country, I challenge anyone to discover the slightest difference in their manners toward each other. I began with country life, at the home of Major Huger; now I am in the city. Everything here rather resembles the English fashion, but there is more simplicity, equality, cordiality, and courtesy here than in England. Charleston is one of the most beautiful and well built of cities, and its inhabitants are among the most agreeable people I have ever seen. American women are very pretty, totally unaffected, and maintain a charming neatness. Cleanliness prevails everywhere here, and receives even more attention than in England. What charms me here is that all the citizens are brothers. In America there are no paupers, or even the sort of people we call peasants. Every individual has an adequate amount of property, ⟨a considerable number of Negroes,⟩ [4] and the same rights as the most powerful proprietor in the land. The inns are quite different from those of Europe. The innkeeper and his

A view of Charleston, South Carolina, from the south shore of Ashley River

wife sit at the table with you, and do the honors of a good meal. When you leave, you pay without haggling. When one does not wish to go to an inn, one finds houses in the countryside at which it suffices to be a good American to be received with the attention one would get from a friend in Europe.

For myself, I have received the most pleasant reception possible from everyone; for my companions, it suffices to have come here with me to be welcomed in the most gratifying manner ⟨and with the greatest eagerness imaginable⟩. I have just spent five hours at a grand dinner given in my honor by a resident of this city. Generals Howe and Moultrie and several officers from my group were there; we drank toasts and conversed in broken English—at present I am just beginning to speak a little of it. Tomorrow I shall take all those gentlemen with me when I call upon the president of the assembly, and I shall work on the arrangements for my departure. The day after that the generals who command here will take me on a tour of the city and all its environs, and then I shall leave to join the army. I must close and send this letter right away, because the vessel will go this evening to the entrance of the harbor, so that it can slip out tomorrow at five A.M. Since all the ships run some risk, I am dividing my letters among all of them. I have written to MM. de Coigny, de Poix, de Noailles, and de Ségur, and to Mme d'Ayen.[5] If any of their letters get lost on the way, give them the news about me.

Because of the pleasant existence I have in this country, dear heart, the openness that puts me as much at my ease with the inhabitants as if I had known them for twenty years, the affinity between their way of thinking and my own, and my love for glory and liberty, one would believe that I am very happy. But I miss you, dear heart, I miss my friends, and I cannot be happy when I am far away from you and from them. I often ask you, dear heart, if you still love me, but I ask myself the same question much more often, and my heart always answers yes. I trust it is not deceiving me. I await your letters with inexpressible impatience; I hope to find some of them at Philadelphia. My greatest fear is that the corsair that was to carry them to me will be captured on the way.

Although I fancy that I have greatly displeased the English by taking the liberty of departing, in spite of them, only to come face to face with them here, I swear, dear heart, that they will never have done with me if they capture that vessel, my fond hope, upon which I rely so much to bring me your letters. Write them to me often, please, and make them long. You cannot know how happy I shall be to receive them. Hug Henriette for me; may I say, dear heart: hug our children for me? Those poor children have a father who is something of a rover, but who is basically a good and honorable man, a good father who truly loves his family, and a good husband also, because he loves his wife with all his heart. Give my fond regards *to your lady friends* and to my friends (I would express them also to my lady friends, with the permission of the Comtesse Auguste and of Mme de Fronsac). By *my friends* you will understand that I mean that dear company the former Court Club, which through the passage of time has become the Society of the Wooden Sword; we other republicans feel it is much better as the latter.[6] This letter will be conveyed to you by a French captain, who I believe will deliver it in person.[7] But I must confide to you, dear heart, that I am preparing yet another transaction for tomorrow, which is to write to you by way of an American who is also departing, but later. Farewell then, dear heart, I finish for lack of paper, and lack of time, and if I do not repeat to you ten thousand times that I love you, it is not from lack of love but lack of modesty, because I have the confidence to hope I have convinced you of that. It is very late at night, it is frightfully hot, and I am being devoured by gnats, which cover one with large blisters, but even the best of countries have their discomforts, as you can see. Farewell, dear, farewell.

AL (NIC: Dean Collection), translation. The manuscript has been edited in pencil, in Lafayette's later hand. Significant passages omitted from Lafayette, *Mémoires,* are printed in angle brackets.

1. Letter of May 30–June 15.
2. John Rutledge, president of the South Carolina General Assembly.
3. Lafayette's party did not leave Charleston until June 26.
4. This phrase is crossed out in ink in the manuscript. It does appear in Adrienne's LbC (NIC: Dean Collection).
5. Letters not found.
6. Lafayette had been a member of the younger set at the French court, the self-styled Court Club, which centered around Marie-Antoinette and the Comte d'Artois. When court society began to frequent the new cafés on the right bank of the Seine, the group began to meet at the Café de l'Epée-de-Bois and to refer to themselves as the Société de l'Epée-de-Bois (the Society of the Wooden Sword). They occupied themselves with dancing, gaming, and horse racing, and tried to introduce a more chivalric mode of dress at court. They favored innovation and applauded republican scenes at the theater, daring new books, and philosophical discourses at the academies. The Comte de Ségur, a member of the group, says in his *Mémoires,* "Liberty, whatever its language, pleased us because of its courage, equality because of its convenience. It is pleasant to stoop as long as one believes he can get up again when he wants, and, without foresight, we enjoyed the advantages of the aristocracy and the charms of a plebian philosophy at the same time" (Barrière, *Bibliothèque,* 19:27).
7. Captain Foligné, commander of *Le Marquis de La Chalotais,* had escorted two American munitions ships from Nantes, and was in Charleston when Lafayette's ship arrived. His journal recounts his meeting with Lafayette:

As soon as M. de Foligné was informed of his arrival he repaired to the hotel where that gentleman was staying to pay his respects, offer him his services, and inform him of his approaching departure for France. Immediately after this first visit, he returned to his ship and gave the order to fire a fifteen-gun salute to this nobleman, to let him know the satisfaction the French felt at his fortunate arrival on the American continent after having run great risks. He received this homage with all possible gratefulness and attention. He asked M. de Foligné to take charge of his letters for France and to have the kindness, on his arrival in France, to go to Paris to give an account of his mission, and to see Madame la Marquise de Lafayette and assure her that he was in good health and was preparing to leave for Philadelphia. [Foligné Deschalonge, *Journal de navigation* (BN: Manuscrits français, nouvelles acquisitions, Collection Margry, fond 9416, fols. 75–76)]

To the Duc de Mouchy[T]

[Charleston, June 22, 1777]

Your indulgence for me, my dear uncle, makes me hope that you will share my happiness at my arrival in America. I was rather slow in coming to my second decision, but if I have done wrong I have yet to feel contrite, and shall add this mistake to the list of those sins that are so pleasurable to commit. Fortunately, I escaped the notice of the English frigates that wanted very much to meet me on this coast. It is impossible to be received with more enthusiasm, cordiality, or pleasantness than that with which I have been received by the American people and all the officials of this country. Monsieur Restarges, who will bring you this letter, can give you an account of that. He is charged with business in Paris, related to the interests of the new republic. He has lived in this country a long time, and can be considered a naturalized citizen. Can I count sufficiently on your goodwill, my dear uncle, to hope that your reception of an American at Bordeaux and the assistance you would be willing to offer him with regard to his affairs would begin to repay the kindness I have received from everyone in this country? I especially solicit your protection for our interests in everything that concerns your department. Farewell, my dear uncle, I do not wish to distract you from your affairs any longer. Maintain your indulgence for me, and I shall try to deserve it. The value I place on it equals the affection and respect with which I have the honor to be, etc.

LAFAYETTE

L (*Gazette de Leyde*, 67 [August 22, 1777], 4), translation.

This letter was printed in *L'Espion anglois* with a passage from a letter from Lafayette to "a friend": "I do not hear either king or ministers spoken of here; here only two sovereigns are cherished and idolized—Glory and Liberty" (M. Mairobert, *L'Espion anglois ou Correspondance secrète entre milord All'eye et milord All'ear*, 7 [London, 1783]:32n.). Several of Lafayette's letters were apparently in circulation, but publication of his letter to Mouchy was a different matter. In it he requests a royal governor to assist an American commercial agent, an act that would violate official French policy. The English ambassador reported that Mouchy was severely reprimanded for allowing the letter to be published (Stormont to Weymouth, July 30, 1777, summarized in Stevens, *Facsimiles*, no. 1600).

To Adrienne de Noailles de Lafayette[T]

Petersburg, July 17 [1777]

I am very happy, dear heart—if the word happiness is appropriate for me while I am far from all that I love. There is a ship here, ready to sail for France, and I may tell you, before I arrive at Philadelphia, that I love you, my dear, and that you may be perfectly at ease about my health. I have sustained the fatigue of the trip without noticing it. It was a very long and tedious journey by land, but it was even more so when I was on my sad vessel. I am now eight days from Philadelphia, and in the beautiful state of Virginia. All the hardships are past, and I greatly fear that those of the war will be very light, if it is true that General Howe has departed from New York, to go I know not where. But all the news is so uncertain that I shall keep an open mind until I arrive. From there, my dear, I shall write you a long letter. You should have received four from me, if they have not fallen into the hands of the English. I have not yet received your letters, dear heart, and my impatience to reach Philadelphia, in order to have them, is beyond comparison. You may imagine, my dear, the state of my mind, after such an immense period of time without receiving a single line from even one of my friends. In short, I hope that situation will end, because I cannot live in such a state of uncertainty. I have undertaken a task that is truly too much for me. I was not born for such suffering.

You will have learned of the beginning of my journey; you know that I departed most handsomely in a carriage; you will now learn that we are all on horseback after having broken the carriages, according to my laudable custom, and I expect to write to you in a few days that we arrived on foot. The journey is a bit fatiguing, but, though several of my companions have suffered a great deal from it, I myself have not felt it at all. Perhaps the captain who carries my letter will come to visit you; in that case, please receive him well.

I hardly dare think of the time of your confinement, dear heart, and yet I think of it every minute of the day.[1] I cannot dwell upon it without agitation and dread. In truth, my dear, I am very sorry to be so far from you. Even if you did not love me, you ought to pity me—but you do love me, and we shall always love each other, dear heart, and we shall always make each other happy. This little note is truly abridged in comparison with the volumes I have sent you, but you will receive another from me in a few days.

The farther I advance toward the north, the more I like both this country and its inhabitants. There are no courtesies or kind attentions that I do not receive, although many people hardly know who I am. But I shall write to you about all of that in more detail from Philadelphia; I have only the time here to entreat you, dear heart, not to forget an unhappy man who has paid most dearly for the offense he committed in leaving you, and who had never realized how much he loves you.

Give my respects to Mme d'Ayen, and my fondest regards to my sister. Let M. de Coigny and M. de Poix know that I am well, in case something happens to the letters I shall send by another means that I have heard about, and by which I shall write another line to you, but I am not so sure about it as about this one.[2]

AL (NIC: Dean Collection), translation.
1. On July 1, 1777, Adrienne de Lafayette gave birth to a daughter, Anastasie. Lafayette did not receive the news until December.
2. Letters to Coigny and Poix not found. The next surviving letter Lafayette wrote to his wife is that of July 23.

To Adrienne de Noailles de Lafayette[T]

[Annapolis,] July 23, 1777

Dear heart, I am always finding people who are just about to leave for France, but this time I have less than a quarter of an hour in which to write. The vessel is ready to sail, and I cannot inform you of anything except my safe arrival at Annapolis, forty leagues from Philadelphia. I cannot tell you what the town is like because the moment I dismounted from my horse I armed myself with a little quill dipped in invisible ink. You must have received five letters from me, unless King George has received some of them. The last was sent three days ago.[1] In it I informed you of my good health, which has not altered for a moment, and of my impatience to arrive at Philadelphia. I have received some bad news here. Ticonderoga, the strongest post in America, has been taken by the enemy. That is very unfortunate. We must try to make up for that. In retaliation, our troops have taken an English general officer near New York. I am every day more miserable for having left you, dear heart; I hope to receive your letters at Philadelphia, and that hope greatly increases my impatience to arrive there. Farewell, my dear, I am so hurried that I do not know what I am writing you, but I do know, dear heart, that I love you more tenderly than ever, that it took the pain of this separation to convince me how very dear you are to me, and that I would give half my blood to obtain the pleasure of embracing you just once, and of telling you just once how much I love you.

Give my respects to Mme d'Ayen, and a thousand compliments to the vicomtesse, my sisters, and all my friends; I have time to write only to you. Ah, my dear, if you knew how much I miss you, how much I suffer from being far from you, in truth you would find me somewhat worthy of your love. I have no space left for my Henriette—or may I say, for my children? Embrace them, dear heart, embrace them a hundred thousand times. I shall always share those embraces.

AL (NIC: Dean Collection), translation. The letter is addressed to "Mme la Mise. de Lafayette, from a loving son who embraces his mama with all his heart, in presenting to her his very respectful but even more affectionate regards." The address is in the same playful tone found in the letter and may have been written to mislead the British should the letter be intercepted.

1. Probably his letter to her of July 17.

Journal of a Campaign in America by Du Rousseau de Fayolle[ET]

The twelfth [of June] we sighted land at nine o'clock in the morning. We had hoped to enter a port that day, but our hope was vain. We tacked back and forth all day and all night, without getting anywhere.

The night of the thirteenth we had contrary winds. We stood out to sea, and during the day we came back to land and anchored near a small harbor called Georgetown.

M. le Marquis de Lafayette and M. de Kalb went ashore to gather intelligence. The ship lay at anchor and awaited the return of these gentlemen until noon the next day, the fourteenth. They told us that there was no other way to reach Charleston than to go on foot by terrible roads. Half of our party then decided to take their chances on land.

I was one of those who stayed on board. I could not have done better, since we arrived safely, but it was extremely risky as the English had been cruising attentively before the port of Charleston, which we entered on the eighteenth at ten o'clock in the morning. Our strategy was to run aground if we were pursued, but it would have been a nasty business. At last, after fifty-six days in the crossing, not counting our stay in Pasajes, we arrived safely at Charleston, a port in Carolina. We still have more than two hundred leagues to travel to reach Philadelphia, but we shall do it the only way we can—overland and at great cost, because everything is terribly expensive.[1]

The city of Charleston is quite pretty. The streets there are wide and well laid out and the houses well aligned, some of which are built of brick, others in wood, all of them roofed with wood. Entering Charleston harbor is very difficult because of a bar that has no water over it at low tide, and at high water, even with the highest tides, a vessel drawing more than seventeen feet of water cannot enter. Our ship, which draws only thirteen, struck three times; in fact, the tide was going out. At the end of this bar are two forts capable of firing broadsides at the river. Their batteries are very well constructed. The first is called Fort Moultrie, after the man who so valiantly defended it on the twenty-eighth of June in the year 1776, when the English tried to pass the bar on a high tide and enter the port of Charleston. Three frigates succeeded, but, not knowing the river, failed to get beyond the fort. They were battered by the fire from this fort, and the English have made no further attempts since that time.

Farther away is Fort Johnson, before which vessels must also pass to reach the city; there are two batteries, one on top of another, with about twenty guns in all. Work is going on at present to build batteries along the river to defend both the port and the entrance to the city, which has no fortification whatever on the landward side.

Our caravan, which left Charleston on June 26 for Philadelphia, was composed of six officers and four domestics or wagon drivers, which made ten persons in all.[2] We traveled in two wagons, each one harnessed to four horses. The wagon in which I was riding lost one of the shaft horses on the third or fourth day; it died on the road after an hour of colic. We were obliged to buy another one at a high price, but it was healthy.

We endured abominable heat in South Carolina, and to refresh ourselves at the end of each day we had to accept horrible lodgings and detestable water. Further, one of our band fell sick at Charlotte, the second town we came to.[3] It is one of the worst places imaginable. We found a doctor, however, who took great care of the sick man. He took him, as well as us, to his house, and I did not leave there until the sick officer was out of danger. In this same Charlotte we bought two more horses to add to the first four, who were overburdened, so that we could try to make up the time the illness had cost us.

The other wagon had continued on its way; it would be at least a fortnight ahead. As for me, I left on horseback, on July 19, to reach

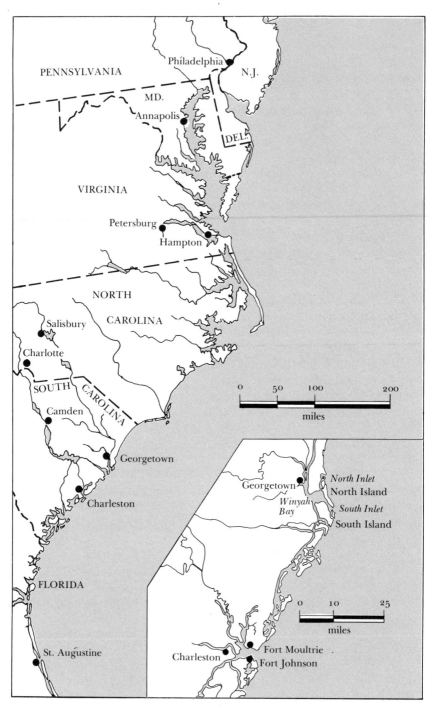

The journey from Charleston to Philadelphia

Philadelphia more quickly and obtain some financial assistance for the wagon that would arrive long after me. We had begun to be short of money because of the purchases and stops we had been forced to make.

One thing is certain—up to the present we have not been flattered with attentions. On the whole, people are not very obliging, and we have been able to find assistance only by paying for it. All the men are well built and lively, but the women are very sullen. I do not know whether the future will prove to be better for us, but things are not at all as they were described to us in France. The people are not united for the common cause, and I do not think that they will ever do anything spectacular. Vanity wounds them; they all want to be officers rather than soldiers, and are no better as one than as the other. One must wait until the end to be more certain of his judgment.

I expect to be in Philadelphia, if I have no accidents, between the eighth and the fifteenth of August. Our wagon had five good fresh horses when I left it, which makes me hope that it will arrive safely.

I arrived in Philadelphia on August 6, having endured extremely hot weather and travel on very poor roads. But on horseback one is spared much of it. My trip was safe and uneventful, even though I made it all alone and crossed six hundred miles of country, the greater part of which is completely forested. However, the differences between colonies are very great, and Virginia, which is two hundred leagues wide and almost three hundred leagues long, is the one that furnishes the most and is the wealthiest and best cultivated on this continent. Maryland is also beautiful, but I saw only thirty or forty miles of it. Pennsylvania is the oldest and therefore most cultivated, but I do not believe it is richer than Virginia.[4]

Philadelphia, the capital of Pennsylvania, is a beautiful and large city, but dreary because of the width of the streets and the low height of the houses. The latter are well built, however, of brick and roofed with wood. It seems to be wealthy, but the war has made great changes there.

Our reception by the Congress in that city was not what we expected; on the contrary, it could not have been more uncivil. It even made us suspect that they were very surprised to see us. Moreover, we wanted, most of us, to return to France. M. le Marquis de Lafayette, who had particular cause to complain, after the generous and honorable things he had done on their behalf, finally obtained the rank of major general from them. That produced the desired effect, and he became their zealous partisan as before, despite the poor arrangement of everything that affects the improvements he would like to make in both civil and military affairs. It is impossible to find anything with a more disorderly appearance than everything that relates to the war here. Their army is miserable in every respect, and even more so in the composition of its officers, of which one cannot even give an idea. No form of discipline exists, but what is even worse about them is their ignorance and false vanity, which do not allow them to resist the forces of the English general if he wants to make an attempt to conquer their country, which would be very easy. It is even incredible that he should have lacked the means to succeed before now. No doubt he has political reasons for that.

What is certain is that I have no desire whatever to fight for their liberty, considering that the only thing to be gained here by honorable men is dishonor or death. One can count on nothing when one takes a forward position. This spirit of liberty, which inspires their actions now, produces a wholly different effect on them, and, far from trying to promote the good intentions one might have, they say that they do not want to go on at all and that they would prefer to turn back, which they do at once. Moreover, if it is most decidedly raining, they will not march at all. The description of their absurdities would be endless.

I left Philadelphia the fourteenth of September 1777 to go to Boston, but I did not leave until I had received a leave from Congress and a letter of exchange for Paris to pay for my return to France.[5]

M (Poitiers, Archives de la Société des Antiquaires de l'Ouest: Mélanges Bonsergent, carton 2, pièce 4), probably in Du Rousseau de Fayolle's hand; extract, translation. Two manuscript pages are now missing from the journal. The first portion of our extract is therefore taken from Segretain, ed., "Journal par Du Rousseau de Fayolle" (pp. 5–7), which was printed before the manuscript pages were lost.

Du Rousseau de Fayolle was one of Broglie's protégés. His journal begins with *La Victoire*'s departure from Bordeaux on March 26, 1777, and ends on May 5, 1780. He was with Lafayette for only short periods during the span of the journal, but he gives details and commentary on these experiences not found elsewhere.

1. End of portion taken from the printed "Journal."

2. The officers were Mauroy, Du Rousseau de Fayolle, Capitaine, Franval, Dubois-martin, and Candon.

3. The sick officer was Capitaine, who remained for several months at an inn in Salisbury, North Carolina (see Lafayette to Laurens, November 18, 1777, and Laurens to Lafayette, January 25, 1778).

4. The Pennsylvania colony was not established until 1680, whereas Virginia was first permanently settled in 1607 and Maryland in 1634.

5. On September 14, 1777, Congress resolved to pay the expenses of Du Rousseau de Fayolle and the other French officers who had not received commissions and wanted to return home (*JCC*, 8:743–744). Du Rousseau de Fayolle then went to Boston, where he remained for ten months, waiting either for a call from Congress to serve or for a ship going to France. He did see service as a volunteer in July and August 1778, when he served as an aide-de-camp to Lafayette in Rhode Island.

Memoir by the Chevalier Dubuysson [T]

I shall say nothing of our passage. A thousand small adventures, long to relate and important to us at the time, would have little interest now for my readers. It should suffice to say that the vessel purchased by the Marquis de Lafayette left Bordeaux on March 26 and arrived at Charleston on June 20.[1] The causes of such a long passage were our forced stay on the Spanish coast, waiting for the Marquis de Lafayette and M. de Mauroy, some long periods of calm, and winds that were often against us. Poor management of our provisions, which were distributed in profusion at the beginning, forced us to be very frugal during the last days of our voyage.

We planned to go straight to the port of Charleston, but ocean currents and the fear of falling into the hands of the English made us land twenty-five leagues farther north. After some information had been obtained, the Marquis de Lafayette, the Baron de Kalb, six officers, and two servants went ashore there.[2] The others remained on the ship, which did not arrive at Charleston until four days later. We went there by land and on foot, because we had been able to find only three horses. Some of us were wearing riding boots, but we were not able to walk in them, and we were forced to take them off and finish the trip barefoot, which was an uncomfortable means of travel on burning sand and in the woods. For the next two weeks my legs were swollen to the size of my thighs. We had chosen to carry arms rather than clothing, to defend ourselves against marauding Negroes, and thus we arrived at Charleston, after three days of walking, looking very much like beggars and brigands. We were received accordingly. We were pointed at in scorn by the local populace when we said we were French officers, motivated solely by the desire to attain glory and defend their liberty, and we were treated as adventurers, even by the French, who are very numerous in Charleston. Most of these Frenchmen are officers who are deeply in debt, and some of them have been discharged from their units. Many of them come from the French colonies, whose governors get rid of as many of the bad ones who arrive from France as they can, by giving them letters of recommendation to the Anglo-American generals. The first ones were very well received, but their conduct showed them for what they were. The Americans no longer have any faith in letters of recommendation, and they pay very little attention to the people who bear them. On the whole, the

The Chevalier Dubuysson, who became Kalb's aide-de-camp

French are very poorly repaid here for their sacrifices on behalf of an ungrateful and undeserving people.

The day after our arrival the Marquis de Lafayette's vessel entered the port in triumph, and caused a complete reversal of opinion about us. We now received the warmest welcome possible, and the French officers, who had been the first to jeer at us, came in crowds to fawn upon the Marquis de Lafayette and try to join his party.

The people of Charleston, like all the people of this part of the continent, detest the French and heap abuse on them. That was not the case in the better circles, however, where we were warmly welcomed and entertained everywhere. We spent eight days in festivity and celebration. We had one of the most magnificent parties in a fort six miles from the city, where the Marquis received honors suitable to a marshal of France, or the protector of liberty.

This fort is interesting because of its construction (I shall bring back a plan of it), because of the eighty artillery pieces taken from the French on the vessel *Foudroyant,* [3] because of its vigorous defense last year, but most of all because of its interior and exterior walls, constructed of palmetto logs laid one upon the other and strongly fastened together. This tree is so spongy that cannon balls are stopped, and enter the wood without exploding. The hole closes by itself, with the result that the English made the fort stronger by bombarding it, because it is now studded with cannon balls.

We had planned to leave on June 25, but an entirely unforeseen obstacle arose. The Marquis had a rich cargo on board his ship, all of which he had advertised for sale, and he had expected to make a three or four hundred percent profit on it. With such a large sum he hoped to be able to take care of all of us, and we expected to live comfortably in this country for two or three years. Thus we were astounded when the captain of the ship brought the Marquis a note for 40,000 livres in favor of the company that had supplied the ship and signed by Lafayette. The note stated that the vessel and its entire cargo should return to France to be sold, and that from the proceeds the company would deduct the 40,000 livres due it, and thirty-five percent in addition—twenty-five percent for insurance and ten percent for commission. At Bordeaux the Marquis had signed without examination every paper placed before him by the man who offered to aid him in his pursuit of glory. At Charleston he suffered cruelly because of these advantages that had been taken of his obliging nature, and we were lucky to borrow 36,000 livres, at very high interest. [4] With that sum we puchased equipment and prepared to leave for Philadelphia.

We divided ourselves into three parties. In the first, six men purchased two wagons for 7000 livres.[5] That initial expense was greater than ours, but their trip was nevertheless much less expensive than ours, because they were fortunate enough to be able to carry all their baggage with them, without being robbed as we were. A second party of three, who did not fear being taken by the English, went by sea.[6] In the third group, Lafayette, the Baron de Kalb, and those of us who had landed with him hired four wagons for 5700 livres to carry us and our baggage. The Marquis's aide-de-camp took it upon himself to serve as our guide, even though he had no knowledge of that part of the country.[7]

Our party left Charleston in the following order. Our procession was led by one of the Marquis's servants, dressed as a hussar. The Marquis's carriage was a sort of uncovered settee, supported by four springs, with a forecarriage. Beside his carriage he had a servant on horseback, to perform the functions of a squire. The Baron de Kalb was in the same carriage. The two colonels, Lafayette's advisers, followed in a second two-wheeled carriage.[8] The third carriage was for the aides-de-camp, and the fourth was for our baggage. The column ended with a Negro on horseback.

I shall omit the details of our adventures en route, as I have those of the voyage, even though they included several remarkable things and some rather interesting and curious events. I shall wait to relate them in person.

By the fourth day some of our carriages were in splinters. Several of our horses, nearly all of which were old and weak, either died or went lame, and we had to buy others along the way. These expenditures consumed all our funds. We were forced to leave part of our baggage behind, and part of it was stolen. We traveled a great part of the way on foot, often sleeping in the woods, starving, prostrated by the heat, and some of us suffered from fever and dysentery.[9] At last, after thirty-two days of travel, we arrived in Philadelphia in a much more pitiful condition than that in which we entered Charleston. I think it is safe to say that no campaign in Europe could be more difficult than this journey. The hardships there are never continuous, and they are even made bearable by many pleasures, whereas on this journey our misery increased each day, and our only solace was the hope of arriving at last in Philadelphia. The pleasant expectation of the reception we would receive there sustained us, and I can truly say that we would have undertaken the hardest labors with the same zeal and composure that I exhibited once I had made up my mind to complete the journey. We were all animated by the same spirit. Lafayette's enthusiasm would have sustained anyone who had less than he.

We arrived on the morning of July 27. After cleaning ourselves up a bit, we went to see the president of the Congress, to whom we handed our letters of recommendation and credit, and our agreements. He sent us to a member of Congress named Morris, who asked us to meet him the next day at the door of the Congress. In the meantime, our papers were read and examined. We were punctual the next day, but we had to wait a very long time. At last Mr. Morris appeared with another member of Congress and said: "This gentleman speaks French very well. He is in charge of all dealings with people of your nation. Thus it is with him that you will deal in the future." [10] He went back inside, and the other gentleman received us in the street, where he left us, after calling us adventurers—in very good French, He finished his harangue by saying, "Gentlemen, have you seen Mr. Deane's commission? We empowered him to send us four French engineers. Instead he sent us M. Du Coudray with some men who claimed to be engineers, but were not, and some artillerymen who have never served. We asked Mr. Franklin to send us four engineers, and they have arrived. French officers are very forward to come and serve us without being asked. Last year we did lack officers, but this year we have plenty, and all of them are experienced." [11]

Such was our first reception by Congress. We did not know what to think. It is impossible to be more astounded than we were. MM. de Lafayette, de Kalb, and de Mauroy, accompanied by ten officers with recommendations like ours, and at least tolerated if not openly acknowledged by the French government—could we have expected such a reception? Baron de Kalb, among others, was known in this country, and even by the Congress.[12]

We decided to wait and seek the reason for this affront before we complained about it. We rightly attributed it to the bad conduct of the Frenchmen who preceded us. We learned, in fact, of the misconduct of several, and of the discredit that their conduct had brought upon the letters of recommendation that they brought from our colonies. There were several other reasons: the incompetence of M. de Fermoy at Fort Ticonderoga (this M. de Fermoy is French and holds the rank of brigadier general); the contempt felt for M. de Borre, also French, by all the officers of his brigade; the excessive and sometimes rash and indiscreet zeal of a Marquis de La Rouerie, who raised a regiment here at his own expense. Everything serves to make the French detested here, for those who have conducted themselves very well contribute to this end as much as those about whom I have just spoken.

A N.W. VIEW OF THE STATE HOUSE IN PHILADELPHIA taken 1778

M. de Conway, brigadier general, is detested by the officers of his brigade and envied by all the generals, including Washington, because he makes his brigade work and personally drills and instructs it, instead of leaving it idle in camp.

But I believe M. Du Coudray has done us the most damage, because he has disgusted the whole Congress. He arrived here with the airs of a lord, and let on that he was one, as well as a brigadier general in France, adviser to the royal ministers, and friend of all the princes and dukes, from whom he carried some letters.[13] He presented to Congress an agreement signed by Mr. Deane, by which he was to have the rank of major general and to be commander in chief of the artillery, the engineers, and all the forts, including those not yet built, with the power to create positions, appoint and dismiss men from them, etc., with accountability only to the general and the Congress, with a salary of 36,000 livres, and a promise of 300,000 more after the war. He even had the impudence to say and write to Congress that all the aid sent from France was the result of his ardent and pressing solicitations.

Congress did not dare either to grant his enormous demands or to refuse them outright, but when the four engineers sent by Mr. Franklin arrived, M. Du Coudray was confronted with them at a session of Congress. He was unmasked, and it was proven that he had deceived the Congress about everything, even his status, because he was the chief of an artillery brigade, and not a brigadier general, and the son of a wine merchant of Rennes.[14] Du Coudray has presented a memorial in which he reviles all the Frenchmen, even the Marquis de Lafayette, to whom he wrote a very rude letter.[15]

When we had obtained this explanation of the reasons for the Congress' conduct toward us, we sent it a memorial in which we asked to be either given commissions or repaid for our expenses and sent back home. Lafayette, the Baron, and M. de Mauroy let it be known that they were not the sort of people to be treated like the adventurers who had presented themselves as officers and gentlemen. Congress sent them Mr. Lovell, the same who had received us so badly. He was accompanied by another congressman who was more polite and adroit, and they made some sort of apology to Lafayette. The second representative, of whom I have just spoken, apparently had instructions to sound out Lafayette. He spoke to him in private, promised him wonders, and learned from him everything he wanted to know.[16] In a second interview with Lafayette, he got him to agree to accept from Congress the rank of major general, but only from that day, without regard to the earlier agreement, without pay or command, and made him promise that he would never make any claim to the command of a division.[17] Two hours after he had made that promise, they sent him his sash, with a letter from Congress that said that "in consideration of his name, his great connections, and the sacrifices he had made through his love for liberty, Congress was pleased to make him a major general, from this day, with the understanding that he would have no claim to a command, a salary, a pension, or any of the perquisites of that rank." [18] He was taken at once to General Washington, who paid him a thousand compliments, and persuaded him to establish his quarters in his household and dine at his table for the whole campaign. In short, he was so dazzled that he forgot us for a moment. But I must do him justice, he has too good a heart to allow his forgetfulness to last very long. He did his utmost to obtain positions for us, but in vain, as he has no influence. Yet if he had stuck to it the Baron de Kalb would have been a major general, and all of us would have received positions. They gave the marquis the rank of major general out of regard for his name, and not for himself, because that rank will be without functions. By the same considerations, we would all have obtained positions, according to the agreement, if only he had insisted upon making common cause with us. He was very sorry to have accepted the sash. He wished to send it back, but they persuaded him to keep it, with more promises, and sent him a carriage and four horses to stop his complaints. Lafayette was taken at once to camp. As for us, we were left at Philadelphia, and the Congress sent us 18,000 livres' worth of American paper money to pay our debts, without making any other reply to us.

When it appeared to be decided that we would all return to France, with the exception of the marquis and his aide-de-camp, I drew up an individual memorial for the general, and another for Congress. In the memorials I said that since I had come with Lafayette, was his relative, had served in the same regiment, and was recommended by the same people, in order to justify my return I would have to say in France that Lafayette does not even have enough influence here to obtain a position for the only officer in whom he has a personal interest. I sent these memorials to Lafayette at camp, for him to sign.[19] He came to see me at Philadelphia the next day. He promised me that I would be made a major of a cavalry regiment if I wished to wait and stay with him. That was all I asked, and I gladly consented to remain. He thanked me for not abandoning him, and promised that he would set to work for me. After some time had passed and nothing happened, I spoke of my hopes to a member of Congress with whom I lodge. He confessed to me that the marquis was mistaken if he believed he could obtain a position for me, because it had been decided that no Frenchmen were wanted. Further, General Washington, far from giving a division to Lafayette, as he had told me, had complained about him to the president of Congress, saying that he was tormented by the latter's requests for a division, and did not know how to get rid of him.[20] The Congress was very displeased, because the marquis had promised in writing that he would never ask for a division.

When I saw that I had no more hope of obtaining a position, I sadly decided to return with my comrades and the Baron de Kalb as soon as we had obtained the last things we requested for our return. But first I wished at least to see the army, and I asked Congress for permission to serve as a volunteer, receiving nothing but rations to live on until the time of our departure. That favor was refused, on the grounds that if I happened to perform some action that deserved reward, I would again ask for a position, which they did not wish to give to any Frenchman.[21]

In undertaking such a long voyage, I was not moved solely by ambition. I was very disappointed to have come so near to the theatre of war without being able to take part in it, and without gaining any of the knowledge I had come to seek. I decided to go to camp in spite of the refusal we had received. I put a shirt in my sack, took a musket and a bayonet, and offered my services to M. de Conway, the brigadier general who is said to have the best instructed and disciplined brigade. He received me very warmly. He gave me a mattress in his tent and permitted me to serve as a volunteer in his brigade. I served in that capacity for some time, and I obtained some idea of the American army and its troops. The maneuver that it executes the best, or rather the only one it executes, is to deliver a very accurate volley from behind some bushes (that is to say, the heather, which attains a height of five feet, is extremely common, and grows around the edges of cleared land). A regiment places itself behind some of these bushes and waits, well hidden, for the enemy. They stick their muskets through the bushes, take careful aim, fire, and fall back, leaping over several bushes with all possible agility. They go a quarter of a league, to wait for the enemy behind some more bushes. If the enemy appears, they repeat the same maneuver several times. Since I found nothing in this type of service that was instructive enough to make it worthwhile for me to continue to do it as a simple volunteer, and since my comrades were all at Philadelphia, from which it was necessary to depart immediately, I went back there to join them.

The American forces consist of 25,000 men who are supposedly regular troops and 50,000 militiamen.[22] The units of the first type are badly clothed and undermanned, and half the officers are always absent, on the pretext of recruiting. The militia units are much finer and very complete. The main cause of the difference between these two types of unit is that the Congress gives a bounty of only 200 [livres] to each man who enlists for the duration of the war in the regular army, while the militiamen serve only four months, after which they are replaced by others.[23] Further, everyone is called to serve, and rich men fulfill their obligation by paying as much as eleven hundred [livres] to those who take their place. Congress and Washington say to one, "You will be a soldier," and to the other, "I appoint you lieutenant, captain, colonel, drummer, or general." They say to the first, "You defend the common liberty, and for that you will serve in the army, where you will be in charge of the storehouses." To the others they say, "You will achieve the same glory by following the army as a commissary agent, baker, butcher, etc." They have cried to everyone, "Liberty!" Everyone has responded to that call, and they have believed themselves in earnest, and a nation of heroes, so long as they saw no danger. But then the cowards, and they are the majority, said: "We agree that we must defend our liberty, and that of our compatriots, but since the army needs carpenters and commissaries, we would rather be the general's carpenters than have the rank of lieutenant, for the latter dies of hunger while the former lives well, yet both serve the same cause. We would rather be commissary agents than captains, because both work for the same cause, but the former get rich without ever having to be afraid, and the latter often know great fear without getting rich." What reliance can be placed upon troops who think that way? [24]

It would be superfluous to enter into the details of the causes of this war. Everyone in Europe knows what they are. But what they may not know is that it would end today if England agreed to the annulment of the debt of thirty millions that America owes her, and for which the notice of default was the raising of the standard of revolt. It is said quite openly that peace depends only upon that condition, and a promise of support in a similar default with the European powers.

Peace is desired by many people. The Quakers, who are in the majority in this province, are nearly all royalists, and hasten the arrival of Howe at Philadelphia as much as they can. They have been driven to that by the vexations that Congress has made them suffer, while excluding them from all government offices under the pretext that they refuse to fight. They secretly furnish provisions to the enemy army.[25] The inhabitants of this country, having few pleasures, are very attached to the few luxuries that they are able to enjoy, with the result that the privation of tea, Madeira wine, some spices, etc., is much more painful to them than it would be to a European, and makes them long for peace. Many people who have relatives and friends in the English army also desire it. This war must then be regarded as a civil war, rather than as the revolt of a people who seek to shake off the yoke of its sovereign. And from that one may safely predict that it will not be a long war.

Today, the fifteenth of August, we have finally obtained a positive response from Congress. It has decided to send all of us back, except for Lafayette, and to pay for our passage.[26] We have submitted our final requests, which consist of the following: first, that all our expenses be paid; second, passports from the English general, or permission to go over to the English army, and from there to England and on to France; third, a certificate attesting that Mr. Deane, the congressional envoy in France, has the power neither to send over French officers nor to make agreements with them. Congress agreed to all of them, with the exception of permission to pass over to the English army. Thus we are all thinking of our departure, which we would take immediately if our baggage were not scattered in several places. I greatly fear that we shall be obliged to return to Charleston to pick up part of our baggage, or else abandon it. In any event, we hope to be in France before the end of January.

Extract from the letter that accompanied this memoir:

September 12 [1777]

Our situation remains unchanged, and we are leaving without having been able to obtain positions or to persuade the Marquis de Lafayette to return with us. He was wounded on August 11 by a ball that struck him in the leg, but he has totally recovered from it, and he comported himself with great valor in that battle.[27]

Things have taken a very bad turn in America. You may report that the following information is very accurate. On July 10, General Howe landed 18 leagues from Philadelphia with 12,000 men, 500 horses, and 50 pieces of artillery. Washington stationed his army of nearly 25,000 men 8 leagues from the English, and 10 from Philadelphia. He fortified an unassailable position, and let Howe make his landing.[28] Rather than attack Washington's army, Howe hoped to take Philadelphia within two weeks' time. As soon as his troops were rested, Howe made an all-night march and took a position on Washington's right, at the same distance from Philadelphia. This movement forced Washington to give up his position, and there was a rather brisk skirmish.[29] On August 11[30] at nine A.M. the English made a feint with their right, while covering their front with considerable artillery fire. When Washington maneuvered to meet the feint, the English left attacked very rapidly and in good order, and threw back every American unit they met. Only the divisions of Milord

Stirling and M. de Conway held out for any length of time. The Marquis de Lafayette joined the latter, where there were some Frenchmen. He dismounted and did his utmost to make the men charge with fixed bayonets. The Frenchmen personally attached their bayonets for them, and Lafayette pushed them in the back to make them charge. But the Americans are not suited for this type of combat, and never wanted to take it up. It was there that Lafayette was wounded. Soon that brigade fled like the rest of the army, which rallied four leagues away.

Yesterday, September 11, it was said that Washington's army wanted to have its revenge, but it is predicted that it will be beaten again, and it appears that Howe will be master of Philadelphia within six days. Our departure has been delayed while we wait for our baggage to arrive. If we had had it with us, we would have left long ago. For the last two months Baron de Kalb and I have had only two shirts and a single ragged coat, but we are in good health, and in spite of my troubles I am very happy to have made this trip. My constant misfortune has taught me to suffer patiently and find moments of pleasure in the midst of troubles and misfortune. I sent copies of the enclosed memoir to M. le Comte de Broglie and to my uncle two weeks ago, but the letters we write to Europe are delivered only with great difficulty, and it is possible that they have not been received.[31] In that case, please have copies sent to them.

M (Stevens, *Facsimiles*, no. 754), copy in two hands; translation. The memoir is followed by a contemporary extract of a letter from Dubuysson to an unknown recipient, dated September 12 [1777] (ibid.), which continues the narration of the memoir. The two pieces were copied as one manuscript and are therefore printed together here. The copyist's note precedes the memoir: "Copy of a memoir by one of the French officers who went to America with the Marquis de Lafayette, which was sent from Philadelphia about the twelfth of September [1777], and arrived in France at the beginning of December."

1. *La Victoire* arrived in Charleston on June 18.

2. The six officers with Kalb and Lafayette were Dubuysson, Lesser, Valfort, Brice, Gimat, and Bedaulx. These officers traveled overland together to Charleston, and all but one of them—Bedaulx—journeyed together from Charleston to Philadelphia.

3. In reporting the British fleet's unsuccessful attack on Fort Sullivan of June 28, 1776, the French chargé d'affaires in London remarked, "The peculiar thing about all this is that the batteries that worked so well were composed of 40 guns from the *Foudroyant,* the beautiful ship which we lost so unfortunately during the last war [the Seven Years' War]" (Garnier to Vergennes, August 23, 1776, in *Naval Documents of the American Revolution,* ed. William James Morgan [Washington: Naval History Division, Department of the Navy, 1972], 6:569–570).

4. Pierre de Basmarein had made the arrangements by which his firm, Reculès de Basmarein, Raimbaux & Cie., sold Lafayette the ship and cargo for 112,000 livres, of which Lafayette paid 40,000 before leaving France. The remaining 72,000 livres was to have been paid in June (Kalb to Mme de Kalb, April 1, 1777, in Vicomte de Colleville, *Les missions secrètes du Général-Major Baron de Kalb et son rôle dans la Guerre de l'Indépendance Américaine* [Paris, 1885], p. 132). Because Lafayette was a minor, Basmarein's

agent in Charleston insisted on having a release from the shipping company before Lafayette could take the proceeds from the sale of the cargo, which Basmarein intended him to have. Lafayette's business agent in Paris wrote Mlle du Motier that he had heard from the shipping firm and had written to Lafayette: "I also inform him that I have been notified by the shipping firm at Bordeaux that they received word from the continent that the ship and cargo were insured there. Monsieur de Lafayette has received or should have received the proceeds from the sale of the cargo he carried from France and the insurance money from the ship and the cargo he was sending back when the ship sank—all of which should have given him a considerable sum. Such being the case, I immediately requested him to be so good as to send me as much money as possible to assist me in continuing to discharge his debts" (Jean Gerard to Mlle du Motier, December 27, 1777, in Louis Gottschalk and Janet L. MacDonald, "Letters on the Management of an Estate during the Old Regime," *Journal of Modern History*, 8 [1936]:80). Gerard also mentioned various bills of exchange Lafayette had drawn on him, including one from Charleston for 27,428 livres, 10 sous (ibid., pp. 80–81). See Kalb to Saint-Paul, November 7, 1777, for additional information about Lafayette's finances at this time.

Lafayette did not hold Basmarein responsible for the misunderstanding. In 1798, when he wrote a letter of recommendation for Basmarein's son, who planned to go to America, he praised the efforts of Basmarein, Raimbaux & Cie. to aid the American cause: "I have been the better enabled to know their sentiments and to witness their exertions as they did furnish me with the means for the first time to go over to America and that in the particular circumstances attending that expedition the part they acted by me has been very liberal and friendly" (Robert Castex, "L'Armateur de Lafayette," *Revue des questions historiques*, 102 [1925]:127).

5. The party whose trip to Philadelphia is described in Du Rousseau's Journal. Mauroy was the leader of this party, but he left it at Camden, South Carolina, and made his own way north with a servant (Mauroy, Mémoire [AN: AE III 219, fols. 2–4]).

6. Probably Bedaulx, La Colombe, and Vrigny.

7. The guide was Brice, an American.

8. Lesser and Valfort.

9. Kalb wrote his wife from Annapolis that Gimat had become ill and stayed behind at Petersburg, Virginia; Dubuysson had the fever and planned to rest a few days at Annapolis (Kalb to Mme de Kalb, July 23, 1777, in Doniol, *Histoire*, 3:214).

10. Lafayette and Kalb presented their letters to John Hancock, who referred them to Robert Morris, a member of the Committee for Foreign Affairs and Deane's main correspondent in Congress. Morris turned them over to James Lovell, a chairman of the Committee on Foreign Applications and a member of the Committee for Foreign Affairs.

11. Mauroy later recalled: "Lovell, a former schoolmaster in Boston, who was in charge of Frenchmen, assured M. le Marquis de Lafayette that His Royal Highness the Prince de Condé would solicit in vain a division of the American army, and that such a thing would be a direct affront to their constitution" (Mauroy, Mémoire [AN: AE III 219, fol. 4 vo.]).

12. Dubuysson is probably referring to Kalb's visit to America in 1768. In addition, Deane had sent a copy of his agreement with Kalb to the Secret Committee of Congress on December 6, 1776 (*Deane Papers*, 1:343–345, 404–405), and on March 19, 1777, Congress had instructed the committee to "write a respectful letter to the General de Kalb, thank him for his obliging offer, and decline accepting it at present" (*JCC*, 7:185). By then Kalb was in Bordeaux, waiting for *La Victoire* to take him to America.

13. Du Coudray's claims to connections at the French court were justified. As an artillery expert, he had taught the martial arts and given lessons on artillery to the royal princes, and was a technical adviser to several successive ministers of war. His brother, Alexandre, was legal counsel to Marie-Antoinette.

14. The brigade Du Coudray commanded in the French Royal Artillery was the equivalent of an infantry battalion, and as *chef de brigade* he ranked with the majors of the other services. His family was from Reims.

15. The memorial and Du Coudray's letter to Lafayette have not been found.

16. Mauroy later recalled:

> The next day they came to present some propositions, and even some flattering compliments, to the Marquis de Lafayette. As the Marquis did not wish to accept unless all our claims were granted, I took the liberty of explaining that our cause was not his, and since all obstacles had been removed for him, I urged him to worry only about his own success. We do not enjoy in France, I said, an importance so great that our fate would cause a sensation there; your story is entirely different. I follow its plot with the greatest interest, and, provided you succeed, I resign myself willingly to all the troubles that I have yet to endure here. My career is too far advanced for me to hope for great military rank, but you begin yours under the best possible auspices, and I have an opinion of you that redoubles my wishes for your success and which you will undoubtedly justify. [Mauroy, Mémoire (AN: AE III 219, fols. 4–5)]

17. The second representative, William Duer, assured Congress that Lafayette did not want to have a command, but would serve as a "volunteer." Congress, on the basis of this assurance, granted Lafayette a commission of major general. Although Congress' resolution (July 31) did not specify that Lafayette's commission was without command, it was generally understood in Philadelphia that he would not be given a division. Benjamin Marshall wrote to his father on August 3, 1777: "The Congress have made him a Major Generall tho' not to have any Brigade neither will he receive any pay or pension but bear the whole Expences himself, only to have Liberty to be with Gen. Washington in every Engagement, a noble Instance of Honour . . ." ("Correspondence of the Children of Christopher Marshall," *Pennsylvania Magazine*, 17 [1893]:340). Washington was also informed that Lafayette would be a volunteer (Washington to Harrison, August 19, and Harrison to Washington, August 20, 1777).

18. Letter not found.

19. Memorials not found.

20. No such letter from Washington to Hancock has been found, but see Washington to Harrison, August 19.

21. No written communications between Dubuysson and Congress have been found.

22. These estimates are clearly wrong. There are no official figures on the size of the Continental army at this time, but Lafayette later estimated the number of troops under Washington's command at the Battle of Brandywine (September 11) to have been 13,000 regulars and 3,000 Pennsylvania militia (Memoir of 1779, pp. 92, 94).

23. In September 1777 the congressional bounty for men enlisting for the duration of the war was $20, 100 acres of land, and a $20 suit of clothes, or that amount in cash if the recruit had purchased his own clothing. Bounties for enlistment in state militia regiments were often higher, and served to discourage re-enlistment in the Continental regiments.

24. The portion of the manuscript that follows is copied in a different hand.

25. The Quakers were not a majority in Pennsylvania at the time of the Revolution. Some of them did sell provisions to the British army, but they were not the only Americans who did so. Dubuysson's statement reflects opinions held by many American patriots and accepted by the foreign officers in the Continental army.

26. On September 14, 1777, Congress resolved to pay the French officers' expenses and their return passage, but only Candon and Valfort went back to France that year. Duboismartin returned to Santo Domingo, Franval settled in the United States, and Du Rousseau, Lesser, and Mauroy remained there for many months. The other officers eventually received commissions from Congress. On September 15 Kalb became a major general, Dubuysson received a brevet of lieutenant colonel as his aide-de-camp, and Bedaulx was offered a captaincy. Four other Frenchmen eventually received commissions as Lafayette's aides-de-camp: Brice as a major, Gimat and Vrigny as lieutenant colonels, and La Colombe as a captain. Capitaine became a captain of engineers.

27. Lafayette was wounded at the Battle of Brandywine on September 11. The copyist has erred in copying the dates here and in the next paragraph.

28. Washington learned that Howe's fleet was in the Chesapeake, and the Continen-

tal army moved to the Wilmington area on August 25. Howe landed his army near Head of Elk the same evening.

29. The skirmish is probably that of Cooch's Bridge (Iron Hill) on September 3. Maxwell's Light Infantry had been sent there to harass Howe's advance from Head of Elk. Washington did not move from Wilmington to Chadd's Ford until September 9.

30. September 11.

31. No other copies of the memoir have been found. Dubuysson's uncle may have been Pierre-Ulric Dubuisson, writer, dramatist, and active participant in the French Revolution. One of his books, *Abrégé de la Révolution de l'Amérique angloise* (Paris, 1778), is a history of the American Revolution from 1774 to January 1778.

Request for Verification of Appointments for Valfort and Lesser[T]

[Philadelphia, ca. July 29, 1777]

The Sieurs Delessers and Valfort, colonels in the French army, request that the persons who have been charged with giving them a hearing grant them justice by employing them as brigadier generals in the army of the United States of America.

Mr. Deane, envoy from these states in France, at first listed these two officers only as colonels on the list addressed to Congress, claiming that he was afraid of multiplying too greatly the number of general officers in America. Since these arrangements were made at the moment of their departure, the Sieurs Delessers and Valfort did not think it necessary to insist, because they were assured that the professional soldiers of their government who had thus far offered their services to the United States had obtained a rank higher than the one that they had held in France.

THE BAR. DE KALB
THE MARQUIS DE LAFAYETTE

DS (DNA: RG 360, PCC 156, p. 340), in Valfort's hand, signed by Kalb and Lafayette; translation.

Lesser was refused a commission and eventually returned to France. Valfort was a less experienced officer, but if illness had not obliged him to return to France he would probably have become a brigadier general. Lesser wrote to Lafayette in March 1778 that Valfort had been offered the rank of brigadier in the American service, but had not wanted to accept it (Lasseray, *Français*, 2:415). There is no record of such a commission in the congressional journals.

Resolution of Congress

July 31, 1777

Whereas the Marquis de la Fayette, out of his great zeal to the cause of liberty in which the United States are engaged, has left his family & connexions & at his own expence come over to offer his service to the United States without pension or particular allowance, and is anxious to risque his life in our cause:

Resolved That his service be accepted and that in consideration of his zeal, illustrious family and connexions, he have the rank and commission of major general in the army of the United States.

D (DNA: RG 360, PCC 1 [Rough Journals], 10:16–17).

Congress' special consideration for Lafayette's "zeal, illustrious family and connexions" indicates their intention that the commission be an honorary one, and distinguishes the resolution from others granting commissions. Congress' resolution on Kalb's commission, September 15, reads simply, *"Resolved,* that another major general be appointed in the army of the United States; the ballots being taken, the Baron de Kalb was elected" (*JCC,* 8:746).

Henry Laurens discussed the commission in a letter to John Gervais on August 8, 1777:

A Commission of Major General is granted to the Marquis de la Fayette the young Nobleman who lately came from Charles Town. He required no pension no Special Command; the honour of fighting near General Washington & having rank in the Army was all he coveted except opportunities to shew his Zeal for the glorious cause of American Freedom either in the Field, or at Court when it Shall be judged he can be more Servicable at Versailles. This illustrious Stranger whose address & manner bespeak his birth will have a Short Campaign & then probably return to France & Secure to us the powerful Interest of his high & extensive connections. [ScHi: Henry Laurens Papers]

PART II

FROM BRANDYWINE
TO GLOUCESTER

August 13–December 1, 1777

Consider, if you please, that Europe and particularly France is looking upon me—that I want to do some thing by myself, and justify that love of glory which I left be known to the world in making those sacrifices which have appeared so surprising, some say so foolish.

To George Washington, October 14, 1777

In July 1777 the British commanders in North America began major operations designed to crush the American rebellion. John Burgoyne advanced from Canada toward the Hudson River, and Sir Henry Clinton later moved north from New York City to meet him. Sir William Howe sailed from New York, landed his troops at the head of Chesapeake Bay, and marched toward Philadelphia, the largest city in America and the seat of the Continental Congress.

Part of the Continental army was sent to the northern department under the command of Philip Schuyler, who was soon replaced by Horatio Gates. Gates defeated Burgoyne at Freeman's Farm (September 19) and again at Bemis Heights (October 7), and the British army surrendered on October 17. Most of the Continental forces remained under the command of Washington, who hoped to stop Howe, but when they met the British at Brandywine Creek on September 11, the Americans were outflanked and defeated. Washington lost only part of his forces, but he was not able to prevent Howe from occupying Philadelphia on September 19. Congress fled to Lancaster and then moved on to York, Pennsylvania.

Washington's army inflicted heavy losses on a large British detachment at Germantown (October 4) and American morale greatly improved, but the British were able to consolidate their hold on Philadelphia by clearing the Delaware River of American fortifications and obstructions. The last Continental unit in that area, commanded by

Nathanael Greene, rejoined the main army on November 30. By that time Washington was beginning to look for winter quarters.

During these four months, Lafayette established his position in the Continental army. He began as a volunteer aide-de-camp to Washington, with the rank of major general, and quickly established a close relationship with the commander in chief. Lafayette distinguished himself at Brandywine, where he was wounded in the leg. He recuperated at the Moravian hospital in Bethlehem, and during this time he became acquainted with Henry Laurens of South Carolina, who soon succeeded John Hancock as president of Congress. Lafayette returned to staff duty in October and then joined Greene's expedition to New Jersey. Greene was unable to save the Delaware River forts, but Lafayette led a successful militia attack against part of the British force commanded by Cornwallis. With this further proof of Lafayette's courage and ability, Congress accepted Washington's proposal that he be given command of a division of the Continental army (December 1).

The two Howes had appeared off the Delaware capes, and General Washington came to Philadelphia. There M. de Lafayette saw that great man for the first time. Although he was surrounded by officers and citizens, the majesty of his figure and his height were unmistakable. His affable and noble welcome to M. de Lafayette was no less distinguished, and M. de Lafayette accompanied him on his inspections. The general invited him to establish himself in his household, and from that moment he looked upon it as his own; it was with such simplicity that two friends were united whose attachment and confidence were cemented by the greatest of all causes.[1]

A few miles from Philadelphia, the army waited until the enemy's movements were determined. The general reviewed his army, and M. de Lafayette arrived there the same day.[2] About eleven thousand men, poorly armed and even more poorly clothed, offered a singular spectacle. In that motley and often naked array, the best garments were *hunting shirts,* large jackets of gray linen commonly worn in Carolina. As for tactics, it suffices to say that, for a regiment formed in battle order to advance on its right, instead of a simple turn to the right, the left had to begin an eternal countermarch. They were always formed in two ranks, with the small men in the front; no other distinction as to height was ever observed. Despite these disadvantages, they were fine soldiers, led by zealous officers. Virtue took the place of science, and each day added to their experience and their discipline. Lord Stirling, who was more courageous than judicious; a general ⟨Stephen⟩ who was always drunk,[3] and Greene, whose talents were, as yet, known only to his friends, commanded as major generals. General Knox, who had transformed himself from bookseller to artillery expert, was there also. He trained the other officers, and created an artillery unit. "We should be embarrassed," said General Washington, "to show ourselves to an officer who has just left the French army." "I am here to learn, and not to teach," replied M. de Lafayette, and that tone produced a good effect, because it was unusual for a European.

After threatening the Delaware, the English fleet disappeared again, and for several days it was the object of many pleasantries.[4] Its arrival in the Chesapeake ended the joking, and, in order to be closer to the British disembarkation, the patriot army passed through Philadelphia. With their heads adorned with green branches, and marching to the sound of drums and fifes, these soldiers, despite their nakedness, presented a pleasing spectacle to the eyes of all the citizens. The general shone at their head, and M. de Lafayette was at his side.[5]

The army stationed itself on the heights of Wilmington, and the enemy disembarked on the Elk River, at the head of Chesapeake Bay. The same day that the enemy landed, General Washington imprudently exposed himself to danger. After a long reconnaissance, he was overtaken by a storm, on a very dark night. He took shelter in a farmhouse, very close to the enemy, and, because of his unwillingness to change his mind, he remained there with General Greene and M. de Lafayette.[6] But when he departed at dawn, he admitted that a single traitor could have betrayed him.[7] Several days later, Sullivan's division joined the army, increasing it to thirteen thousand men.[8] Major General Sullivan ⟨was very vain, but did not lack talent. He⟩ had made a good beginning, but had not succeeded in a surprise attack on Staten Island.

If the English committed grave errors in planning a campaign that was too extensive, it must also be admitted that the American defense was not irreproachable. Burgoyne, with his many cannons and fine carriages, blindly and doggedly marched along a single road through a forest from which he could not extricate himself. Certain of not being outflanked, the Americans disputed every step he took. This kind of warfare attracted militiamen, and Gates received reinforcements every day. Each tree concealed a skilled marksman, and the English found that their own tactics, and even the talents of their leaders, were useless. The army left in New York could, it is true, scorn Putnam's forces, but it was too weak to go to Burgoyne's aid, and consequently it depended upon his success instead of assuring it.

During all this time Howe thought only of Philadelphia, and, at the expense of the northern operation, he headed for it by a lengthy roundabout route. Yet, on the other hand, why were the English permitted to land without hindrance? Why was an opportunity allowed to pass when the Elk River divided their army? Why was there so much wavering and inconsequential activity in the south? It was because the Americans had previously had skirmishes but no true battles, and because, instead of harassing an army and disputing defiles, they now had to protect an unfortified capital and maneuver in the open against an enemy that could destroy them if it outflanked them. If General Washington had followed the advice of the people, he would have imprisoned his army—and the American destiny—in Philadelphia. But, to avoid that folly, it was necessary to give the nation a

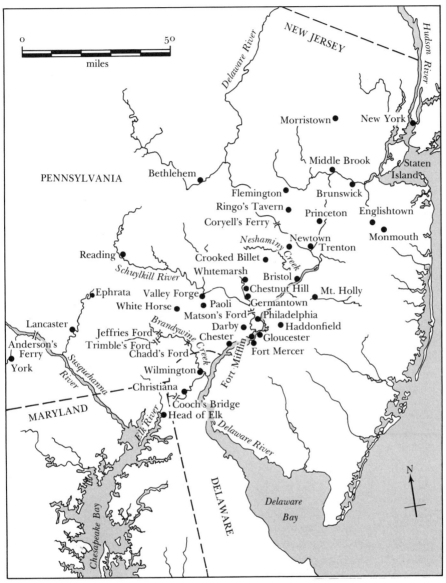

Eastern Pennsylvania and New Jersey

battle. Europe also expected it, and even though he had been made dictator for six months, the general thought it necessary to submit everything to the orders of Congress and the deliberations of his own councils of war.[9]

After advancing as far as Wilmington, the general detached a thousand men under Maxwell, the senior ⟨but also the most inept⟩ brigadier general in the army. At the first advance of the English, he was beaten by their advance guard near Christiana Bridge, and during that time the American army established a poor position at Newtown. We dug some earthworks and awaited the enemy there for two days. Then, just as they were marching toward our right, a nocturnal council of war decided to move the army to the ⟨heights of⟩ Brandywine. The Brandywine covered our front, and Chadd's Ford, which was near our center, was defended by artillery. It was in this poorly reconnoitered position that, in obedience to a letter from Congress, we awaited the battle.[10]

On the evening of September tenth, Howe advanced in two columns. By a skillful maneuver, the left column (about 8000 men, counting grenadiers and guards, under Lord Cornwallis) marched toward the fords of Birmingham, three miles to our right.[11] The other column continued its march, and about nine o'clock in the morning it appeared on the other side of the stream. The edge of the woods was so near the riverbank that it was impossible to judge the size of the enemy force, and time was lost in mutual cannonading. General Washington walked the length of his two lines, and was received with acclamations that should have promised victory. We had some information about Cornwallis's movements, but it was confused and contradictory. The similarity of the names of two parallel roads caused the best officers to be mistaken in their reports. The only musket shots that had been fired came from Maxwell's brigade; it killed several of the enemy, but had already been driven back over a ford on our left. Three thousand militiamen who had been added to the army stood in reserve even farther away, but they took no part in the action. Such was our situation when the first clear information arrived about Lord Cornwallis's march toward the scarcely known fords of Birmingham. Three divisions, containing nearly 5000 men, were detached under Generals Sullivan, Stirling, and Stephen. M. de Lafayette, as a volunteer, had always accompanied the general, but since the left was quiet and the major thrust would come on the right, he obtained permission to join Sullivan. At his arrival, which the troops appeared to appreciate, he found that the enemy had crossed the ford, and Sullivan's corps had scarcely had time to form one line in front of a thinly wooded forest. A few moments later Milord Cornwallis's men suddenly emerged from the woods in very good order. Advancing across the plain, his first line opened a very brisk fire with cannon and muskets. The American fire was murderous, but both their right and left wings collapsed. The generals and many officers joined the central division, where M. de Lafayette was with Stirling, and where 800 men were brilliantly commanded by M. de Conway, an Irishman who had served in the French army. By separating that division from its two wings and advancing across an open plain, where they lost many men, the enemy was able to concentrate its fire on the center. The confusion became extreme, and it was while M. de Lafayette was rallying the troops that a ball passed through his leg. At that moment the remaining forces gave way, and M. de Lafayette was fortunate to be able to mount a horse, thanks to Gimat, his aide-de-camp. General Washington arrived from a distance with fresh troops, and M. de Lafayette was about to join him when loss of blood forced him to stop and bandage his wound. He was again very nearly taken, and retreating soldiers, cannons, and wagons flowed pell-mell along the road to Chester. The general took advantage of the remaining daylight to delay the enemy's advance. Several regiments had done well, but the rout was complete. During that time, the enemy forced its way across Chadd's Ford and took the American cannon, and the whole American army retreated along the road to Chester. In the midst of that horrible confusion, in the gloom of night, it was impossible to recover. But at Chester, twelve miles from the field of battle, there was a bridge that had to be crossed, and M. de Lafayette applied himself to stopping the retreating troops there. He had re-established a degree of order when the generals and the commander in chief arrived, and M. de Lafayette finally had time to have his wound dressed.[12]

Thus, twenty-six miles from Philadelphia, the city's fate was decided. Every cannon shot was heard there, and the two parties, separated in two groups in all the squares and public places, awaited the result in silence. Finally the last messenger arrived, and the friends of liberty were dismayed. The Americans had lost between 1000 and 1200 men. There were approximately 15,000 in Howe's army. Their losses were so considerable that their surgeons and those of the local area were not sufficient, and they asked us to provide some for the prisoners. If the enemy had marched to Derby, the American army would have been cut off and destroyed; the English lost a precious night, and it was perhaps their greatest error in a war in which they committed many.

M. de Lafayette was transported to Philadelphia by water, where he was overwhelmed by citizens who were interested in him because of his youth and situation. The same evening, the Congress decided to depart, and a multitude of inhabitants left their homes. Entire families abandoned everything and, no longer sure of anything, sought refuge in the mountains. A boat carried M. de Lafayette to Bristol; he there encountered the fugitive Congress, which assembled again only on the other side of the Susquehanna. He himself was conducted to Bethlehem, a Moravian settlement, where the mild religion of that brotherly people and the community of goods, education, and interests among that large and simple family made a striking contrast to scenes of carnage and the convulsions of civil war.[13]

After the rout at Brandywine, the two armies maneuvered along the Schuylkill. General Washington always remained above the enemy, out of their reach, and they never got another chance to cut him off. Wayne, an American brigadier general, was detached to observe the British, but he was surprised in the night by General Grey, near the White Horse, and lost a large part of his unit.[14] Finally Howe crossed the Schuylkill at Swede's Ford, and Lord Cornwallis entered Philadelphia.

Despite the independence of the new states, everything now bore the characteristics of a civil war. The names *Whig* and *Tory* distinguished the republicans and the royalists; the British army was still called the *regular troops,* and when one spoke of the *king,* it was understood that he meant the British sovereign. The violence of party spirit divided provinces, cities, and families; one saw brothers, officers in the opposing armies, meet by chance in their father's house and seize their arms to fight each other. In their arrogant rage, the British committed horrible acts of license and cruelty, and dragged in their train those hired Germans, who knew only how to kill, pillage, and burn houses. In the same army there were American regiments that trampled their brothers under their feet, and enslaved their devastated country. Every township contained a still greater number of people whose sole object was to hinder the friends of liberty, and warn those of despotism. To these inveterate Tories must be added those who opposed the war through fear, private interest, or religious principles. If the Presbyterians, the descendants of Cromwell and Fairfax, hated royalty, the Anglicans, who had sprung from it, were more divided. The Quakers ⟨plebian Jesuits⟩ hated the carnage, but served as guides to the royal troops. Insurrections were not uncommon. Near the enemy posts, farmers often shot each other, and thieves were even encouraged. *Rebel* [15] leaders ran great risks when they traveled about the country. They would announce that they were going to stay in one house, and then move into another, where they would barricade themselves and sleep with their weapons at their sides.

In the midst of these troubles, M. de Lafayette was no longer considered a foreigner, and no other adoption was ever so complete as his. While in the councils of war he trembled to think that the voice of a twenty-year-old might decide the fate of two worlds, he was also initiated into those deliberations in which, by reassuring the Whigs, intimidating the Tories, supporting a sound currency, and redoubling their firmness in a time of adversity, the leaders of the revolution guided it through so many obstacles.

M. de Lafayette was confined to his bed for six weeks, where he suffered from his wound and even more from inaction. The good Moravian brothers loved him, and lamented his warlike folly; while listening to their sermons he dreamed of setting both Europe and Asia ablaze. Since he could no longer do anything but write, he wrote to the commander of Martinique [16] and proposed an attack upon the English islands under American colors. He wrote to M. de Maurepas and offered to lead some Americans to the Isle de France,[17] where he would have coordinated attacks by private individuals on the English trading posts. From what has been learned since, the India project would have succeeded, but it was rejected at Versailles, and M. de Lafayette's letters still went unanswered. Bouillé was more energetic and endorsed the whole plan, but he could not act without permission, and these delays led up to the epoch of the war that M. de Lafayette hoped to bring on.

During his stay at Bethlehem the British entrenched themselves at Philadelphia. The two rivers that encircle the town were joined by a chain of wooden palisades and good redoubts, which were partially flooded. A portion of their army was camped at Germantown, five miles in advance of their lines. General Washington attacked it on October fourth, and even though his left column, retarded by an absurd precedence dispute between divisions, strayed in a thick fog, and even though the advance guard, under Conway, attacked from the front a position that should have been attacked from the flank, the enemy was nonetheless surprised and beaten, and the general, with his victorious wing, crossed the whole extent of the British camp. All went well, but then a false movement of the left column, and worse, an attack on a stone house that should have been outflanked, gave the enemy the time to rally. Howe considered a retreat, but Cornwallis arrived with reinforcements. The Americans passed back through the British camp, and the action ended with their general defeat. The losses were heavy on both sides. General Agnew, an Englishman, and General Nash, an American, were both killed. The American forces included some dragoons under Pulaski, the only member of the Polish Confederation who had refused to accept a pardon. He was an in-

trepid and virtuous chevalier, who was both devout and licentious,
and a better captain than a general. He insisted upon being a Pole
wherever he went, and M. de Lafayette, after having helped him obtain a command, often labored to reconcile him with the Americans.

Without waiting for his wound to close, M. de Lafayette returned to
headquarters, twenty-five miles from Philadelphia.[18] The enemy had
fallen back upon its own lines and attacked Fort Mifflin, which was on
an island, and Fort Red Bank,[19] on the left bank of the Delaware. At
that point in the river, chevaux-de-frise, protected by the forts and
some galleys, delayed the British fleet that was bringing supplies and
troops from the Chesapeake.[20] Among the skirmishes that occurred
between small detachments, the most remarkable was the ambush of a
militia unit at Crooked Billet, where the British burned a barn where
the wounded were being held.[21] Such was the situation in the south
when the news of Burgoyne's surrender arrived.

When that general left Canada, he had hoped to have a division on
his right, but St. Leger failed to take Fort Schuyler, and Burgoyne
himself appears to have lost much time in his advance toward Albany.
Gates added many militiamen to his Continentals. Every citizen was
armed and a member of the militia, and all of them assembled when
the alarm was sounded, or when they received marching orders from
the government. But if that crusade was only voluntary, their discipline and the length of their stay in camp was even more so. The
Continentals, on the contrary, served the thirteen states, each of
which furnished some regiments. Such soldiers served for the duration of the war, or for three years, a dangerous alternative, but one
that was required by republican jealousy. These regular troops were
subject to military regulations and maintained proper discipline. The
officers from each state vied with each other for promotion.

Gates had established an entrenched position on the road to Albany, in the midst of the woods, and with the North River on his
right. The enemy invasion threatened New England, and its brave
militiamen swelled Gates's force to 16,000.[22] The militia had already
proven itself at Bennington, where Stark had surrounded and destroyed one of Burgoyne's detachments. The enemy advanced to
within three miles of Gates's position, and since they could not go
around it without abandoning their wagons and cannons, they tried
twice to storm it. But as soon as they began to move, Arnold's division
fell upon them, and in those woods full of sharpshooters they could
not reach the entrenchments. In the second engagement Arnold's leg
was shattered, and Lincoln, the other major general, was also
wounded. It is true that 4000 men had embarked at New York and

ascended the Hudson, and while Vaughan needlessly burned Esopus, Clinton had taken all the forts that defended the river. They were hardly bothered by old Putnam, the man who, when the troubles first began, had left his plow and given the army more zeal than talent. But the British diversion was too weak, and a note that a captured spy swallowed, but which a dose of emetic forced him to surrender, showed that Clinton was aware of his weakness. Burgoyne, abandoned by his Indian allies, grieving the loss of his best soldiers, and of Fraser, his best general, was reduced to 5,000 men who lacked provisions. He tried to retreat, but too late, and his communications were cut off. At Saratoga, a few miles behind his camp, he signed the famous surrender. A brillant gilded troop came out with Burgoyne, and met Gates and his officers, all clothed in gray. After a frugal repast the two generals watched the defeated army file out, and, as a member of Parliament asserted, "five thousand men crossed rebel territory to take up their winter quarters near Boston." Clinton then returned to New York and the militiamen returned to their homes. Gates's chief merit was in his choice of a position. Burgoyne's misfortune lay in the nature of the countryside, which was impassable and practically uninhabited. Gates's enemies criticized the terms of the surrender, but M. de Lafayette eagerly celebrated his glory. He did blame Gates, however, for having rendered himself independent of his general, and for then retaining the troops that he should have sent to him. To get them back, it was necessary to send out Hamilton, Washington's personal aide-de-camp, an intelligent and talented young man whose sound advice carried great weight.[23]

The forts on the Delaware still held out, and the one at Red Bank, with a garrison of 400 men, was assaulted with cold steel by 1600 Hessians. The area of the fort had been reduced, on the advice of Mauduit, a young Frenchman, and the two sides fought between the old trench and the new one. The enemy was repulsed, with a loss of 700 men, including Count Donop, their commander, whose last words were: "I die the victim of my own ambition and the avarice of my sovereign." [24] The fort was commanded by Greene, an old and respected colonel, who three years later was massacred by the British, to whom he had surrendered. A faithful Negro covered his body with his own and died heroically. Fort Mifflin, attacked by land and by water, defended itself no less valiantly. The *Augusta,* an English ship of the line, had been blown up, and a frigate had also perished there, and Colonel Smith did not even think of surrender. But the island was outflanked through an unknown passage; the fort was assaulted from the rear and had to be evacuated. When Lord Cornwallis and 5000 men invaded the Jerseys, it was also necessary to abandon Red Bank, which was blown up. General Greene crossed the river at Trenton and opposed Cornwallis' detachment with a force of equal size.[25]

Although M. de Lafayette's wound was still open and he could not wear a boot on that foot, he accompanied Greene as far as Mount Holly, where he detached himself to reconnoiter, and found the enemy on November 25 at Gloucester, opposite Philadelphia. They were transferring the provisions they had foraged across the river, and to make certain of their activities M. de Lafayette went out on Sandy Point. That imprudence would have cost him dearly if those who had the chance to kill him had not depended too much upon the dragoons, who should have taken him prisoner. After having somewhat calmed his guides, at about four o'clock he found himself two miles from the British camp, facing a unit of 400 Hessians with cannon. He had with him only 350 men, most of whom were militiamen, but he attacked suddenly, and the enemy gave way.[26] Lord Cornwallis came up with his grenadiers, but, believing he was engaging Greene's entire force in those woods, he let himself be pushed back to the outskirts of Gloucester, with a loss of about sixty men. Greene arrived during the night but did not choose to attack, and Lord Cornwallis crossed the river. The American detachment rejoined the army camped at Whitemarsh, twelve miles from Philadelphia. For a month it had occupied some excellent heights; the general's accurate eye had discerned the spot for the camp on the other side of an almost impenetrable wood.

The little success at Gloucester pleased the army, and especially the militia. It was resolved by Congress that it would be extremely agreeable to them to see the Marquis de Lafayette at the head of a division. Thus he ceased to be a volunteer, and replaced Stephen ⟨the old drunkard⟩ as commander of the Virginians.

AM (NIC: Dean Collection), translation. Significant passages of the Memoir not printed in Lafayette, *Mémoires,* are printed here in angle brackets. Annotation of the Memoir is limited to textual problems and the elucidation of issues and events that are not discussed in other documents printed in this volume. See p. 12 for a description of the manuscript and a discussion of editorial procedures for the Memoir.

1. The meeting occurred on July 31, 1777. In 1828 Lafayette recalled more details for Jared Sparks:

The first introduction was at a dinner party, where several members of Congress were present. When they were about to separate, Washington took Lafayette aside, spoke to him very kindly, complimented him upon the noble spirit he had shown and the sacrifices he had made in favor of the American cause, and then told him, that he should be pleased if he would make the quarters of the Commander-in-chief his home, establish himself there whenever he thought proper, and consider himself at all times as one of his family; adding, in a tone of pleasantry, that he could not promise him the luxuries of a court, or even the conveniences, which his former habits might have rendered essential to his comfort, but, since he had become an American soldier, he would doubtless contrive to accommodate himself to the character he had assumed, and submit with a good grace to the customs, manners, and privations of a republican army. [Sparks, *Writings of Washington*, 5:454]

Thus Lafayette finally received a place in the Continental army—as a volunteer, attached to the commander in chief.

2. The review took place near Germantown, on August 8.

3. "Un Gal. Stevens toujours ivre" changed in pencil, in Lafayette's later hand, to "un Gal. souvent ivre." Lafayette, *Mémoires*, 1:21, reads: "un autre général souvent ivre." In November 1777 a court-martial convicted Major General Adam Stephen of "unofficerlike behavior" and "drunkenness," and Washington approved the court's recommendation of dismissal from the service (General Orders, November 20, 1777, in Fitzpatrick, *Writings of Washington*, 10:88–89).

4. The destination of the British fleet was discussed in a council of general officers on August 21. Lafayette signed the minutes: "The Mquis. de Lafayette, M. G.," as the most junior major general present (DNA: RG 360, PCC 169, 3:413–415).

5. The parade took place on Sunday, August 24. The term "naked," often applied to the Continental troops by contemporaries, may sometimes be taken in its literal sense, but in this case it refers to the fact that most of the troops wore whatever clothes they had, rather than proper uniforms.

6. Added here, in pencil, "et leurs aides-de-camp" (and their aides-de-camp).

7. The date was August 26. Both Greene and Lafayette berated their chief for his lack of caution.

8. The figure of 11,000 men, given by the standard authorities, is taken from an unsupported statement in George W. Greene, *Life of Nathanael Greene* (New York, 1867–1871), 1:443.

9. Congress did not give Washington that title. The powers it granted him, on December 27, 1776, were limited to those necessary to recruit, equip, and provision his army for a period of six months, and Congress reserved the right to terminate those powers before the six months expired (*JCC*, 6:1045–1047). Washington's special powers ended on April 27, 1777, and he was not granted new ones until September 17, a week after the Battle of Brandywine (Freeman, *Washington*, 4:629 and note).

10. Congress naturally expected Washington to halt Howe's invasion, but there is no evidence that it issued any specific military instructions to him at this time, or that he received any written message that could be construed as an order to stand and fight.

11. Birmingham was the site of the most important fighting, later that day (September 11), but it was nearly two miles to the rear of the original position of the American right wing. The British column crossed the branches of the Brandywine at Trimble's and Jeffries' Fords. Lafayette's confusion here, and about the two parallel roads below, points up the basic reason for the American defeat at Brandywine: Washington and his staff failed to secure adequate information about the terrain they had chosen to defend. See Freeman, *Washington*, 4:471–489.

12. Lafayette described the battle in his letter of December 16, 1777, to the Duc d'Ayen. In 1828 he provided some additional details for Sparks:

Firing was heard at a distance up the river, & Lafayette, with the permission of Washington, advanced to the scene of action. He found Lord Stirling who was just bringing his division into action, which was then beginning to grow warm. He was on horseback at first, but as the men began to retreat he dismounted, entered the ranks, & endeavored to rally them. While in this act he was wounded by a musket ball in the leg. He remained in the ranks, however, for some time, till the troops were so hard pressed by the enemy as to be compelled to retreat precipitately. The blood began to run from his boot, & he mounted his horse. He met Dr. Cochran in the rear, who put a light bandage on his leg in a great hurry, as the enemy was close upon them. Lafayette rode immediately to Chester. [Autobiographical Notes V, pp. 173–174]

Lafayette's actions at Brandywine are also described in Dubuysson's Memoir, pp. 83–84. Mauroy's Mémoire mentions Lafayette's wound, and notes that Lafayette confided to Mauroy his astonishment at the ease with which the American forces had been routed (AN: AE III 219, fol. 5 vo.).

Washington's report to the president of Congress (September 11; Fitzpatrick, *Writings of Washington*, 9:207–208), which mentioned Lafayette's wound, was published by order of Congress and reprinted in Europe (e.g., *Gazette de Leyde* [in French translation], vol. 90 [November 11, 1777], and *The Remembrancer, or Impartial Repository of Public Events for the Year 1777* [London, 1778], pp. 432–433). *The Annual Register . . . for the Year 1777* also described the battle and included some general observations:

> The present unhappy contest was so interesting to foreigners, and rendered America so conspicuous a theatre of action, that it drew bold and enterprizing spirits, from different parts of Europe, either merely in search of glory and rank, or to acquire military experience and improvement. Among the numerous instances of this nature which might be given, a few are necessary, and will be sufficient. The Marquis de la Fayette, a young French nobleman, of the first rank, and of large fortune, was so carried away by this enthusiasm, as to purchase and freight a ship with military stores (in which he embarked with several of his friends) for the service of the Americans; he bore a command, and was wounded in this action. [(London, 1778), 1:130]

The *Register*'s "Chronicle" section also mentioned Lafayette's departure from France, under the date of April 4 (ibid., 2:176).

13. Congress received word of the approach of the British army on September 18, and the evacuation of Philadelphia took place during that night. From Bristol, Lafayette was taken to the army hospital in Bethlehem by Henry Laurens (Laurens to Robert Howe, October 20, 1777, in Burnett, *Letters of Congress*, 2:525). The diary of the Moravian congregation noted:

> September 21 (Sunday).—Our friend and protector Henry Laurens, of South Carolina, with many other notables arrived. . . . Among others arrived . . . the young Marquis de La Fayette, with a suite of French officers. . . .

> October 18.—The French Marquis de La Fayette left us to-day for the army, in company with Gen. Woodford. We found him a very intelligent and pleasant young man. He occupied much of his time in reading, and, among other matter read an English translation of the History of the Greenland Mission. With the accounts given by the missionaries he expressed himself highly pleased, pronouncing some of their descriptions *pompeux*, and their narrative of facts simple and truthful. Before bidding us adieu, he requested to be shown through the Sisters' House, a request which we were pleased to grant, and his admiration of the institution was unbounded. [John W. Jordan, "Bethlehem during the Revolution," *Pennsylvania Magazine*, 12 (1888):406; 13 (1889):75–76]

14. On September 21, 1777, Wayne lost nearly 400 of his 1500 men in the "Paoli Massacre." Wayne had recently moved his forces from a position near the White Horse Tavern to one nearer the Paoli Tavern.

15. Changed in pencil to: "Republicains."

16. The Marquis de Bouillé.

17. Mauritius, in the Indian Ocean.

18. Lafayette arrived at Washington's headquarters, in Worcester Township, Pennsylvania, on October 19.

19. Fort Mercer, at Red Bank, New Jersey.

20. Chevaux-de-frise were portable obstacles constructed of heavy timber frames studded with iron-tipped spikes. Lafayette refers to the ones adapted for use in the Delaware River, where they were placed on the bottom to rip the hulls of ships that passed over them.

21. The engagement at Crooked Billet occurred on May 1, 1778.

22. Gates's returns for October 16, the day Burgoyne surrendered, listed 16,056 officers and men fit for duty (Charles H. Lesser, ed., *The Sinews of Independence: Monthly Strength Reports of the Continental Army* [Chicago: University of Chicago Press, 1976], pp. 50–51), but for the battles of Freeman's Farm (September 19) and Bemis Heights (October 4) he had no more than 7000 men against Burgoyne's 6000.

23. From the inception of the Continental army, the commander of the northern army had been independent of Washington, and the commander in chief specifically accepted that situation when Gates was appointed to that command in August 1777 (Rossie, *Politics of Command*, pp. 37, 95, 164). Gates appears to have complied with Washington's request for all the troops the northern army could spare before Hamilton arrived (ibid., pp. 184–186, and Knollenberg, *Washington and the Revolution*, pp. 30–36). Lafayette's comments reflect the common opinion at Washington's headquarters in the fall of 1777.

24. Lafayette told Sparks that Du Plessis and Colonel Greene heard Donop say those words (Notes for Sparks, November 22, 1828, NcFayM).

25. Cornwallis led approximately 3000 men to New Jersey on November 18, but the total British force under his command numbered nearly 8000. General Greene led about 2000 men to New Jersey, but by November 26 he also commanded a force of nearly 8000 (Samuel S. Smith, *Fight for the Delaware* [Monmouth Beach, N.J.: Philip Freneau Press, 1970], pp. 38–41, 50).

26. At the time of the skirmish, Lafayette reported that the numbers were 350 Hessians and 300 Americans; General Greene reported 300 enemy and 400 Americans (Lafayette to Washington, and Washington to Congress, November 26, 1777).

To John Hancock

[Philadelplia,] the 13 august 1777

Sir

I beg that you will receive yourself and present to Congress my thanks for the Commission of Major General in the Army of the United States of America which I have been honor'd with in their name.[1] The feelings of my heart, long before it became my duty, engaged me in the love of the American cause. I not only consider'd it as the cause of Honor, Virtue, and universal Happinness, but felt myself empressed with the warmest affection for a Nation who exhibited by their resistence so fine an exemple of Justice and Courage to the Universe.

I schall neglect nothing on my part to justify the confidence which the Congress of the United States has been pleased to repose in me. As my highest ambition has ever been to do every thing only for the best of the cause in which I am engaged, I wish to serve near the person of General Washington till such time as he may think proper to entrust me with a division of the Army.[2]

It is now as an american that I'l mention every day to Congress the officers who came over with me, whose interests are for me as my own, and the consideration which they deserve by their merits, their ranks, their states and reputation in France &c. I am Sir with the sentiments which every good american owe to you Your most obedient servant

THE MQUIS. DE LAFAYETTE

ALS (DNA: RG 360, PCC 156, pp. 1–4). Addressed to Mr. Hancock, president of Congress.

This is the earliest extant Lafayette letter in English. He probably had help in composing most of his early letters in English. The letter was read in Congress and referred to the Board of War (August 13, *JCC*, 8:634).

1. Lafayette immediately accepted the congressional resolution of July 31, and during the next few weeks he appeared at official functions wearing the sash of a Continental major general, but he did not accept the commission in writing for two full weeks, apparently because of his misgivings about accepting an appointment when his companions had been rejected. See Dubuysson, Memoir, p. 80.

2. This is the earliest extant indication that Lafayette had a conception of his agreement with Congress which differed from the one held by Congress and the other French officers. They understood that he had promised "he would never make any claim to the command of a division . . ." (Dubuysson, Memoir, pp. 79–80).

George Washington to Benjamin Harrison

Neshamony Bridge August 19. 1777

Dear Sir

If I did not misunderstand what you, or some other Member of Congress said to me respecting the appointment of the Marquis de Le Fiatte, he has misceived the design of his appointment, or Congress did not understand the extent of his views, for certain it is, If I understand *him*, that he does not conceive his Commission is merely honorary; but given with a view to command a division of this Army. True, he has said that he is young, & inexperienced, but at the same time has always accompanied it with a hint, that so soon as *I* shall think *him* fit for the Command of a division, he shall be ready to enter upon the duties of it; & in the mean time, has offer'd his service for a smaller Command, to which I may add, that he has actually applied to me (by direction he says from Mr. Hancock) for Commissions for his Two Aid de Camps.[1]

What the designs of Congress respecting this Gentn. were—& what line of Conduct I am to pursue, to comply with their design, & his expectations, I know no more than the Child unborn, & beg to be instructed. If Congress meant that this Rank should be unaccompanied by Command I wish it had been sufficiently explain'd to him. If on the other hand it was intended to vest him with all the powers of a Major Genl., why have I been led into a contrary belief, & left in the dark with respect to my own conduct towards him? This difficulty with the numberless applications for Imployment by Foreigners, under their respective appointments, adds no small embarrassment to a command which, without it, is abundantly perplexed by the dif-

ferent tempers I have to do with, & different modes which the respective states have pursued to nominate & ar[range] their officers,
the combination of all which, is but a too just representation of a great
Chaos from whence we are endeavouring (how successfully time can
only tell) to draw some regularity & order.

George Washington, 1777

I was going to address Congress for Instructions in the case of the
Marquis de Le Fyatte, but upon second thoughts concluded to ask
some direction of my conduct in this matter through a Member; and
therefore have imposed this task upon you. Let me beseech you then
my good Sir to give me the sentiments of Congress on this matter,
that I may endeavour, as far as it is in my power, to comply with
them. With respect to Commissions for his Aid de Camps, I told him
that I should write to Mr. Hancock about them and wish to be instructed. The Marquis is now in Philadelphia but expected up this day
or tomorrow. With sincere regard, I am, Dr. Sir, Your most affecte.

G. WASHINGTON

L (DLC: George Washington Papers, Series 4), copy in the hand of Richard Meade,
Washington's aide-de-camp.
    1. Gimat and Brice.

Benjamin Harrison to George Washington

Philad. Augst. 20 1777

Dear General,
    I remember well a Conversation's passing betwixt you and I on the
subject of the Marquis de la Fyattes Commission, & that I told you it

was merely Honorary. In this light I look'd on it, and so did every other member of Congress. He had made an agreement with Mr. Deane, but this he gave up by Letter to Congress, not wishing as he said to embarrass their affairs.[1] Mr. Duer who presented this Letter assur'd us he did not wish or desire Command, but gave us to understand his chief motive for going into our Service was to be near you, to see Service, and to give him an Eclat at home, where he expected he would soon return. These you may depend on it were the Reasons that induced Congress to Comply with his request, and that he could not have obtain'd the Commisn. on any other terms; the other Day he surprised every body by a letter of his, requesting Commissions for his officers, and Insinuating at the same time that he should expect a Command as soon as you should think him fit for one.[2] Depend on it Congress never meant that he should have one, nor will not countenance him in his applications. I had it not in my power yesterday to get their opinions on the subject, but will do it soon.

"Where can Howe be gone," we begin to be under great Apprehensions for South Carolina, and think he must have been heard off if he had taken any other course. Can not a blow be given Burgoyne in his absence? If something can not be done in that quarter soon, N. York will certainly be lost, our eastern Friends have certainly behaved most shamefully. Where the Devil is Gates, why dos he loiter so on the Road, the weather has been hot it is true, and so is the Service he is going to. I am my Dear Sir, Your affect. Hble. Servt.

BENJ. HARRISON

ALS (DLC: George Washington Papers, Series 4).
1. Letter not found. It is probably the "note" mentioned in Lafayette's Memoir of 1779, p. 11, and summarized in Dubuysson's Memoir, pp. 79–80.
2. Probably Lafayette to Hancock, August 13.

To James Lovell

                                                    head quarter 21 august 1777
Sir

The bearer of my letter is the Count de Pulaski who will be in your departement as a stranger officer asking the live [leave] of fighting for our liberty. Though I did not know him, as I recieved a particular account about him, I think proper to acquaint you with it.[1] He was one of the first member of the confederation of Polland, the most dinstinguished officer, and the most dangerous ennemy of the tyrants of his

country. He deserved a great reputation by his bravery and intelligence in the war, and his noble and fiery conduct after the de-
struction of the unhappy Polland.

I reccommend to you, Sir, the businesses of all the gentelemen coming over with me, and I hope that you'l receive the assurances of attachement which I am with Sir your most obedient servant

THE MQUIS. DE LAFAYETTE G. M.

ALS (DNA: RG 360, PCC 41, 8:27).

1. Pulaski had come to America by way of Paris, where he met Madame de Lafayette,
and he brought a letter from her to her husband. See Adrienne de Lafayette to Casimir
Pulaski, May 27, 1777 (CtY: Benjamin Franklin Collection), and Lafayette to Adrienne
de Lafayette, October 1. He probably also carried Deane's letter of May 29 to Tench
Tilghman, which recommended Lafayette and Kalb. See Massachusetts Historical
Society, *Proceedings*, 18 (1880–1881): 287, and Carmichael's letter of May 29, 1777, in
"Letters of William Carmichael to John Cadwalader," ed. Henry Ammon, *Maryland His-
torical Magazine*, 44 (1949):7.

On August 24 Pulaski wrote to Congress:

I desire to obtain a Single Company of voluntiers of Cavalry with a title which will
authorize me to command an entire Division when I shall merit it.

My first military years were passed in very rough tryals. I may be permitted to
aspire to an Employ in which I should be Subject only to the orders of the Commander in Chief of the Army. If that cannot be yet joined to the Marquis de
Fayette. I would take pleasure in sharing his laboures and executing the orders of
the Commander in Chief as Subaltern of the marquis. . . . [DNA: RG 360, PCC
41, 8:21, 25]

Pulaski's letter was referred to a committee that included Lovell. It decided "that a
Compliance with those Expectations would be . . . highly impolitic" (August 25, *JCC*,
8:673 and note). Washington also supported Pulaski's petition, however, and on September 15 Congress resolved to appoint a commander of the light dragoons, with the
rank of brigadier general, and selected Pulaski for the post (Washington to Congress,
August 21 and 28, 1777, in Fitzpatrick, *Writings of Washington*, 9:112, 143–144, and
JCC, 8:745).

The American Commissioners to [George Washington]

[Passy, ca. August–September 1777]

Sir

The Marquis de la Fayette, a young Nobleman of great Expectations & exceedingly belov'd here, is by this time probably with you. By
some Misapprehension in his Contract with the Merchants of Bordeaux he was prevented from using the Produce of the Cargo he
carried over, & so was left without a Supply of Money. His Friends
here have sent him over about 500 £ Sterling; and have propos'd
sending him more. But on Reflection, knowing the extream Generosity of his Disposition, & fearing that some of his necessitous & artful

Countrymen may impose on his Goodness, they wish to put his
Money into the Hands of some discreet Friend, who may supply him
from time to time, and by that means knowing his Expences may take
Occasion to advise him if necessary, with a friendly Affection, and
Secure him from too much Imposition. They accordingly have desired us to name such a Person to them. We have not been able to
think of one so capable, & so suitable from the Influence of Situation
to perform that kind Office, as General Washington, under whose
Eye the Gentleman will probably be. We beg therefore in his Behalf,
what his Friends out of Respect would not take the Liberty of asking,
that your Excellency would be pleased to furnish him with what
Money he may want in Moderation, and take his Drafts payable to us
for the Sums paid him, which we shall receive here and apply to the
publick Service. We also join with his Family in their earnest Request
that you would favour him with your Counsels, which you may be assured will be an Act of Benevolence gratefully remembered & acknowledged, by a Number of very worthy Persons here who interest
themselves extreamly in the Welfare of that amiable young Nobleman. With the greatest Respect we have the honour to be, Sir, Your
Excellency's m. o. h. S.

L (DLC: Franklin Papers, Series 2, Vol. 10), draft in Franklin's hand. This letter was
written after news of Lafayette's problems with the sale of the cargo reached France,
probably in early August 1777, and before news of the loss of *La Victoire* arrived there,
probably in late September 1777. See Dubuysson, Memoir, p. 75. The George Washington Papers (DLC) contain no record of the receipt of this letter, and it is probable that it never arrived, since many of the commissioners' letters to America were intercepted or destroyed in the fall of 1777. The commissioners were Franklin, Deane,
and Arthur Lee.

To Adrienne de Noailles de Lafayette[T]

Philadelphia, September 12 [1777]
I send you a few lines, dear heart, by some French officers, my
friends, who came here with me but have not obtained positions and
are returning to France. I shall begin by telling you that I am well,
because I must end by telling you that we fought in earnest yesterday,
and we were not the victors. Our Americans, after holding firm for a
considerable time, were finally routed. While I was trying to rally
them, the English honored me with a musket shot, which wounded
me slightly in the leg. But the wound is nothing, dear heart; the ball
hit neither bone nor nerve, and all I have to do for it to heal is to lie

27
1777

Lettre septième. ce 12 7bre a philadelphie.

cette lettre fut ecrite le lendemain de la bataille de Brandywine, ou il fut blessé, il est difficile de deviner par la maniere dont il s'exprime, les details de la conduite en cette journée, la premiere qu'il fut témoin d'une bataille rangée

je vous ecris deux mots, mon cher coeur, par des officiers françois de mes amis, qui étoient venus avec moy, et que n'ayant pas été placés, s'en retournent en france. je commence par vous dire que je me porte bien, parceque je veux finir par vous dire que nous nous sommes battus hier tout de bon, et nous n'avons pas été les plus forts. nos americains apres avoir tenu ferme pendant assés longtems, ont fini par etre mis en deroute, en tachant de les rallier, messieurs les anglois m'ont gratifié d'un coup de fusil qui m'a un peu blessé a la jambe, mais ce n'est rien, mon cher coeur, la balle n'a touché, ni os, ni nerf, et j'en suis quitte pour etre couché sur le dos, pour quelques tems, ce qui me met de fort mauvaise humeur. j'espere que vous ne serés pas inquiette, cela au contraire une raison de l'etre moins, parceque me voila hors de combat pour quelque tems, étant dans l'intention de me bien menager, soyez en bien persuadée, mon cher coeur, cette affaire aura je crois, de bien facheuses suites pour l'amerique, il faudra tacher de reparer si nous pouvons. vous devés avoir reçu bien des lettres de moy, a moins que les anglois n'en veulent a mes epitres autant qu'à mes jambes. je n'ai encore reçu qu'une fois de vous, et je soupire apres des nouvelles. adieu, on me defend d'ecrire plus longtems, depuis plusieurs jours, je n'ai pas eu celui de dormir, la derniere nuit a été employée

First page of Adrienne de Noailles de Lafayette's letter-book copy of Lafayette's letter to her dated September 12, 1777. Her note translates: "This letter was written the day after the Battle of Brandywine, where he was wounded. It is difficult to tell from the manner in which he expresses himself the details of his conduct on that day, the first time he witnessed a pitched battle."

on my back for a while—which puts me in very bad humor. I hope, dear heart, that you will not worry; on the contrary, you should be even less worried than before, because I shall now be out of action for some time. I intend to take good care of myself; you may be sure of that, dear heart. This battle will, I fear, have unpleasant consequences for America; we must try to repair the damage, if we can. You must have received many letters from me, unless the English are as hostile to my letters as to my legs. I have received only one from you so far, and I long for news.[1] Farewell. They won't let me write longer than this. For several days I have not had time to sleep. Last night was spent in our retreat and in my journey here, where I am very well cared for. Let all my friends know that I am in good health; give a thousand tender respects to Mme d'Ayen, and a thousand compliments to my vicomtesse and my sisters. These officers will leave soon; they will see you—how fortunate they are! Good night, dear heart, I love you more than ever.

AL (NIC: Dean Collection), translation.

Adrienne de Lafayette noted in her letter book (NIC: Dean Collection): "This letter was addressed to my mother, in a double envelope, so that she could explain everything to me before I read it." There may have been a separate letter to Madame d'Ayen, but none has been found.

1. The letter (not found) that Pulaski brought to Lafayette.

To Henry Laurens

Bethleem 25 September 1777

Dear Sir

Troublesome it will be to you for ever to have been so Kind with me, because it seems me Now that I became in right by my first obligations, of disturbing you for my businesses. Therefore I take the liberty of reposing myself upon your friendship about one very great interest of my heart. I Know that a large packet is arrived for my from France. It was told so some days ago to an officer in Philadelphia, who finding an occasion for Bristol proposed to send those letters to me; but it was answered at the post office that they were already sent. I heared too that a paket was arrived for Congress in which some thing perhaps is included for me. I fancy that my dispatches must be in Mr. Moriss's hands, and I adress myself to you because I do not know in what place he lives.[1]

Henry Laurens of South Carolina, elected president of Congress on November 1, 1777, began a close friendship with Lafayette on the journey to Bethlehem.

Major Gimat who comes to day from Camp told to me that Mr. John Laurent was in very good health. You know certainly the niews from the army better than I do, and that the ennemy crossed the Sculchill.

The bearer of my letter is a genteleman who came with me upon my assurance that he would be employed. He is of a very good birth, and a sensible young man. He wants only a commission of lieutenant, and General Canaouay is desirous of having him in his brigade. As Congress did not comprehend him in sending back the others I hope that he will be received in our service. Will you be so good to speack about it when you'l find some occasions?[2]

My leg is about in the same state and without your kindness would be in a very bad one. For my heart he is full of all the sentiments of gratidude and affection which I have the honor to be with Dear Sir Your most obedient servant

The Mquis. de Lafayette

ALS (ScHi: Henry Laurens Papers).

1. Robert Morris was one of Silas Deane's main correspondents, and Deane had asked him to serve as Lafayette's American banker (Deane to Morris, May 26).

2. The bearer of the letter was La Colombe. He had a strong claim to Lafayette's support, because their families were closely connected in Auvergne, and he was the only officer in Lafayette's party who was not put there by either Broglie or the American commissioners. La Colombe was not included in the list of officers whom Congress sent back to France (JCC, 8:721–722 [September 9]). The next day it voted to give him nine months' pay as a lieutenant (the rank Silas Deane had promised him), but gave him no specific assignment (JCC, 8:728).

To Henry Laurens

[Bethlehem,] the 27 September 1777

Dear Sir

The bearer of my letter is Mr. Dorset french officer who (thro' I did not Know him in France) desired me to add some words to his request, and to give him a letter for a member of Congress.[1] I beg your Pardon for choosing you amonghst the others, but I see that my first obligations will be followed by great many others. What engaged me to grant to this gentleman the favor of being addressed to you, is the zeal which he came over with in order to be employed in our service. But that seems to me very difficult, though it could be advantageous to get officers who have made the war. I would have wrot rather to Mr. Lovell if I did Know where he lives now.

I congratulate you, Sir, and myself with you for the good niews which we heared About the colonel's of the queen's light dragoons rgt. army. *His royal* Master will not be very much satisfied with the conduct of that noble instrument of his justice, and I hope that we schall make too a proclamation one day or another before the walls of Quebec.[2] I am Sir with the warmest affection Your most obedient Servant

THE MQUIS. DE LAFAYETTE

I hope that you will be so good as to remember the Mr. de Valfort's businesses;[3] I expect yet the young genteleman whom I desire some employement for, and I wishoud that he could arrive with my letters from France and the declaration of war between France an England.

ALS (ScHi: Henry Laurens Papers).
1. See Recommendation for François Dorset, September 27.
2. General Burgoyne, who held the colonelcy of the Queen's Light Dragoons, had been defeated at Freeman's Farm on September 19. For his proclamation, see Laurens to Lafayette, October 23.
3. At this time Lafayette still hoped that Valfort would be commissioned a brigadier general, as Deane had promised.

Recommendation for François Dorset

Bethleem the 27 September 1777

As Mr. Dorcet who came over at his own expense with the warmest zeal for serving in our cause, desires me to add some thing to his request, I can inform the honorable Congress that the corps where he told me that he made the war in, was one of the best of our army and full of excellent officers. I assured too Mr. Dorcet that even out of the reccommandations of *Doctor Franklin,* and the Count de *Clermont Tonnerre,* he was to put the greatest confidence in the justice of the honorable Congress if it was by circumstances impossible to grant to him the employement which he desires so warmly.[1]

THE MQUIS. DE LAFAYETTE

ALS (DNA: RG 360, PCC 41, 2:419), on back of Dorset's petition to Congress (ibid., p. 418).
1. Du Coudray's death had left Dorset without a position. In November 1777, at the very time that men more closely associated with Lafayette were receiving commissions, Congress sent Dorset back to France. Henry Laurens had supported Dorset's petition, and finally sent him to Charleston, South Carolina, to seek "employment in his profession" (Laurens to Gervais, November 18, 1777 [ScHi: Henry Laurens Papers]).

To Adrienne de Noailles de Lafayette[T]

Bethlehem, October 1, 1777

I wrote to you, dear heart, on the twelfth of September; the twelfth is the day after the eleventh. About that particular eleventh, I have a tale to tell you. To put the best face on it, I could tell you that mature reflection had induced me to remain in my bed for several weeks, sheltered from all danger. But I must admit that I was invited to stay there because of a very slight wound in the leg. I do not know how I received it; in truth, I did not expose myself to enemy fire. It was my first battle, so you see how rare battles are. It is the last of this campaign, or at least the last big battle, it appears. If any other action occurs here, you see that I could not be present. Consequently, my dear heart, I take pleasure in reassuring you that you have no need to worry. While I tell you not to worry about me, I tell myself that you love me, and this little conversation with my heart pleases it very much, for it has never loved you more tenderly.

The day after that battle, my first thought was to write to you. I told you then that the wound was nothing, and I was right. The only thing I fear is that you have not received that letter, for if, when General Howe gives his master the king some slightly inflated details about his exploits in America, he reports me wounded, he could just as well report me killed. That would cost him nothing. I hope that my friends, and you especially, my dear heart, will never believe the reports of those people who last year even dared to print a story that General Washington and all his general officers were in a boat that capsized and all of them were drowned.

But we were speaking of my wound; the ball passed through the flesh and touched neither bone nor nerve. The surgeons are astonished by the rate at which it heals; they are in ecstasy every time they dress it, and maintain that it is the most beautiful thing in the world. I myself find it very foul, very tedious, and rather painful; there is no accounting for tastes. But, finally, if a man wished to be wounded just for his own amusement, he should come and see my wound and have one just like it. There, dear heart, you have the story of what I pompously call my wound, to give myself airs and to make myself interesting.

Now, since you are the wife of an American general officer, I must give you some instructions. People will say to you: "They have been beaten." You will reply: "That is true, but between two armies *of equal size,* in open country, old soldiers have the advantage over new ones; besides, the Americans had the satisfaction of killing many more of the enemy than they lost." [1] After that they will add: "That is all very well, but Philadelphia, the capital of America and the bulwark of liberty, is taken." You must politely reply: "You are simpletons. Philadelphia is a dismal city, open on all sides. Its harbor was already blocked, and I do not know why the residence of Congress there made the place famous. ⟨It is full of a wretched sort of people, the ridiculous Quakers, who are fit only to gather in a hall with large hats on their heads whatever the weather. They wait there in silence for the Holy Spirit until one of them, wearied from not seeing it appear, gets up and utters a great deal of tearful nonsense. There you have the people of Philadelphia, who, moreover, never fight.⟩ There you have that famous city which, by the way, we will make the British surrender to us sooner or later." If they continue to press you with questions, you will send them about their business with language that the Vicomte de Noailles will teach you; I do not wish to lose so much time talking politics in my letter to you.

I have saved this letter until the last moment in the hope that I would be hearing from you. Then I would be able to answer yours while I give you the latest reports on my condition. But I am told that if I do not send this immediately with a captain who is going to the Congress, seventy-five miles away, [2] he will be on his way and I shall have lost the chance to write you. That is why my scribble is even less readable than usual. Besides, if I wrote you anything but a scrawl, I would have to ask your pardon for presenting you with such a novelty. Just think, dear heart, that I have heard from you only once, by way of Count Pulaski. That is a stroke of bad luck and it makes me miserable. Judge for yourself how horrible it is to be so far away from all that I love and in a desperate state of suspense. It is unbearable. Yet I feel that I have no right to complain; why did I madly insist upon coming here? Too sensitive, dearest, to perform such deeds, I have been thoroughly punished. You would pity me if you knew all that I suffer, especially at this time when any news from you would be so welcome. I cannot think about a letter from you without trembling. I am told that mail has arrived from France. I have dispatched expresses to every crossroad, and I have sent an officer to Congress.[3] I await his return daily, and you can imagine with what impatience. My surgeon is anxious for his arrival too, because my restlessness makes by blood race and he is trying to keep me quiet. Good heavens, dear heart, if only I receive good news about you and all those I love, if those delightful letters arrive today, how happy I shall be! And how excited I shall be as I open them!

Do not be concerned, dear heart, about the care of my wound. All the physicians in America are paying close attention to me. I have a friend who has spoken to them in such a way that I can be assured of the best care. That friend is General Washington. This estimable man, whom I at first admired for his talents and qualities and whom I have come to venerate as I know him better, has become my intimate friend. His affectionate interest in me soon won my heart. I am a member of his household and we live together like two brothers in mutual intimacy and confidence. This close friendship makes me as happy as I could possibly be in this country. When he sent his chief surgeon to care for me,[4] he told him to care for me as though I were his son, for he loved me in the same way. Having learned that I wished to rejoin the army quickly, he wrote me a very fond letter, urging me to take care of my health first.[5] I give you all these details, my dear heart, so that you may rest assured that I am receiving the best of care. Among the French officers, all of whom have shown interest in my welfare, I have M. de Gimat as an aide-de-camp. Both before and since the battle he has followed me like a shadow and has shown every proof of devotion to me. So, dearest, you may be at ease on this matter now and in the future.

All the foreigners who are with the army (for I speak not only of those who have not received commissions and who, upon their return to France, will give unjust accounts of America, since offended and vengeful men are not reliable), all the other foreigners who have been commissioned here are discontented. They complain; they detest others and are detested. They do not understand why I am the only foreigner in America who is loved, and I cannot understand why they are so hated. As for my part in the typical disputes and discussions found in all armies, especially when officers of several nations are together, I am always even-tempered and easygoing and am happy to be liked by everyone, foreigner or American. I like them all. I hope to merit their esteem, and we are satisfied with each other.

I am at this moment in the solitude of Bethlehem, of which Abbé Raynal has spoken so much.[6] This establishment is truly touching and very interesting. The people here lead a gentle and peaceful life; we shall talk about that when I return. I expect to bore those I love, you most of all, when I give an account of my travels; you know what a prattler I am.

You must become my voice, dear heart, in all that you say for me to Henriette, my poor little Henriette; hug her a thousand times, speak to her of me, but do not say all the bad things about me that I deserve. My punishment will be not to have her recognize me upon my arrival; that will be the penance Henriette will impose upon me. Has

The Moravian settlement of Bethlehem, Pennsylvania, where Lafayette recuperated from his wound

she a sister or a brother? It does not matter to me, as long as I have the pleasure of being a father a second time, and I hear about it soon. If I have a son I shall tell him to examine his own heart with care. If he is at all tenderhearted, and if he has a wife whom he loves as I love you, I shall advise him not to be carried away by enthusiasms that will take him away from the object of his affection, for that affection will then be the source of a thousand torments.

⟨Am I able to tell you, dear heart, that I am leaving for France on a particular day? I can at least assure you that I shall leave here as soon as possible. I shall be here only as long as I believe I am being kept here by the requirements of my honor. I wish so much to see you again that I believe, God forgive me, that if I could I would be in Paris tomorrow, and then return to America if I thought myself obliged to do so. But no, I shall go soon, I hope—if *soon* is a word by which my impatience may be eased when I count the time in months—and it will be for good.⟩

I am writing by another occasion to various other people, but I am writing to you as well. I think that this letter will arrive soonest. If by chance this ship gets there and the other letters are lost, I have sent the vicomte the list of letters I have written him.[7] I forgot my aunts; give them news of me as soon as this reaches you. I have not made any copies for you because I have written you at every opportunity. Give news of me also to M. Margelay, Abbé Fayon, and Desplaces. A thousand tender regards to my sisters; I allow them to despise me as an infamous deserter, but they must love me nonetheless. My respects to Mme la Comtesse Auguste and Mme Fronsac. If the letter to my grandfather has not yet arrived, give him my respects. Farewell, farewell, my dear heart, love me always; I love you so tenderly.

Give my compliments to Dr. Franklin and to Mr. Deane. I want to write them but do not have the time.

AL (NIC: Dean Collection), translation. The manuscript has been edited in pencil, in Lafayette's later hand. Significant passages omitted from Lafayette, *Mémoires*, are printed in angle brackets.

1. British losses were 90 killed, 448 wounded, and 6 missing, compared with American losses of approximately 200 killed, 500 wounded, and 400 captured (Peckham, *Battle Casualties*, p. 40).

2. It was approximately seventy-five miles from Bethlehem to Lancaster, Pennsylvania, where Congress assembled after it left Philadelphia. Lafayette apparently did not know that it had moved to York, twenty-five miles farther west, on September 30.

3. La Colombe.

4. Dr. Cochran.

5. Letter not found.

6. Abbé Raynal's *Histoire philosophique et politique des établissements et du commerce des Européens dans les deux Indes* (many eds., 1770– ?) was the only work Raynal had then published about America. None of the editions describes Bethlehem, but every one of them contains a section on the Dumplers of "Euphrate," Pennsylvania (e.g., vol. 7 of the

edition published in The Hague, 1773–1774, pp. 18–22). That sect, also known as the German Baptist Brethren, or the Dunkers, was established at Ephrata. It was entirely separate from the Moravian Brethren of Bethlehem, but the two communities were similar enough to be confused by a foreigner. It is also possible that Lafayette had actually heard Raynal discuss the Bethlehem community.

7. Not found.

To Robert Morris[E]

Bethlehem, Oct. 6, 1777

As I did not know the place where you were in, I sent to Mr. Laurent my letters for France, which, I pray, have been sent to you.[1] I dispatched them immediately because a Captain coming from Niew Yorck told me that he was ready to sail by order of Congress and very certain of arriving safe. I fear that the English amplification and British generals's laying [lying] temper could have put my family and acquaintances in a great pain about my wound, and I would let know to them how trifling it was.

I am in the most cruel inatitude [incertitude] about the late operation of our army, it is not for Want of accounts, but on the contrary I got too many and not one like the other, however I know very certainly that we have had a great advantage in the beginning, but nothing more.[2] I expect further intelligences at every hour with the Warmest impatience, and I directed [*ellipses in printed text*] my aid to camp [3] to go to the army and be acquainted in the head quarter itself. It is indeed very unhappy to lay down in a bed in such circumstances. . . .

L extract (Henkels, *Confidential Correspondence of Robert Morris,* pp. 124–125).
1. See Laurens to Lafayette, October 12.
2. The Battle of Germantown, October 4.
3. Brice or Gimat.

From Henry Laurens

York 12th. Octobr. 1777

Sir

I have had the honour of receiving your favours under the 27th. Septembr. & 3d. Currt.[1] The Gentleman [2] whom you directed to call on me received my advice to apply to the Committee of Foreign Affairs to which I added an assurance of doing him all the service in my power if his application should come before Congress, Since which I have learned nothing more of the Subject nor seen him.

If you committed any charge to me respecting Mr. de Valforts my memory has been so treacherous as to lose it, for which I beg pardon, & request a repetition when I have your Commands, in writing my Eyes will assist & my inclination will be prompt upon every occasion to demonstrate my respect & attachment.[3]

I could find upon enquiry no good or certain conveyance for your packet from any of the neighbouring ports, how can there be one when all are hemmed in by the Enemy's Ships of War? Having therefore a faithful Messenger going to Charles Town I have sent it directly to Mr. President Rutledge endorsing your request in a particular manner of his attention to send it forward & referred to the directions which you had superscribed. It will probably be delivered into his hands on the 25th. Inst. & I am morally certain he will find a good conveyance before this Month expires.[4] I shall be happy if this measure meets your approbation.

No Letters that I can learn of are arrived for you from France but I here Inclose one which was delivered to me by Monsr. Dubuysson.[5]

The Aspect of our Northern affaire is a little Clouded. Genl. Putnam writes on the 5th Inst. that 2000 of the Enemy conducted from New York in Transports & Convoyed by Men of War had landed within five miles of Peek's Kill that he had not 1000 Continental Troops with him & few militia—of these he had made the best disposition, that Governor Clinton had arrived at Fort Montgomry whose presence he hoped would animate & bring in the Militia, but that in his present weak state although he would exert every nerve in the defense of the important posts committed to his charge, he could not warrant & did not hold himself answerable. He is a brave Officer in the field, cautious & timid only upon paper therefore I am not diffident of his success. Before this day I should suppose somewhat decisive has been done in the special department under Genl. Gates.[6]

The Action of the 4th at German Town is a subject for a condolance & congratulation. Tis very evident we run away from complete victory which had [invited?] us to proceed & embrace her. It cannot be doubted but Your Excellency is acquainted with particulars therefore I will only add that the several & distinct Accounts of four Genl. Officers of the Enemy Viz: Agnew, Sr. W. Erskines, Kniphausen & Grant having fallen are attended by such circumstantial proofs as put them little below the line of certainty.[7] I have the honour to be with the most respectful esteem &tc.

LbC (ScHi: Henry Laurens Papers).
1. Letter of October 3 not found.
2. Dorset.
3. See Lafayette to Laurens, September 27.
4. The packet probably contained the letters to France mentioned in Lafayette's letter of October 1 to his wife.
5. Letter not identified.
6. The American forces won the Battle of Bemis Heights on October 7, but Congress did not receive the news until October 18.
7. Of the four generals listed, only Agnew was killed at Germantown.

To Horatio Gates

Bethlehem 14 october 1777

Dear general

I Can't let go your express without doing myself the pleasure of congratulating you About your happy and glorious succès.[1] The fine opportunity of your victory, and the circumstances (the taking Fort Montgommery) which it meet with, is to add some thing yet and to your glory and to the gratefulness of every one who loves the cause we fight for. I find myself very happy to have had the pleasure of your acquaintance before your going to take the command of the northen army. I am very desirous, sir, to convince you how I wish to cultivate your friendschip. It is with such sentiments and those of the most perfect esteem that I have the honor to be dear Sir Your most obedient servant

THE MQUIS. DE LAFAYETTE

I do not wraït from our camp because I am detained yet in this place for some days by my vound of Brandywine. Mr. Hugley who is here desires me to present you his compliments.

ALS (NHi: Gates Papers, Box 8).
1. Gates's victory at Freeman's Farm, September 19.

To George Washington

[Bethlehem,] the 14 october 1777

My dear general

I do not do myself the honor of wraïting to you as many times as I would chuse, because I fear to disturbe your important occupations—

but I indulge now that pleasure to me on the occasion of the two nominations of Congress. General Connay is a so brave, intelligent, and active officer that he schall, I am sure, justify more and more the esteem of the army and Your approbation.[1] For the Baron de Kalb who is unknown to your excellency I ca'nt tell any particularity of his arrangements since his niew convention with Congress, because I am not well acquainted with them.[2] He was employed with succès in the last war in the part of ammunition and fourages. I wrote to Cannay to congratulate him and I believe indeed that he will acquitt himself ⟨with his functions⟩ as well as possible.[3] For the Baron de Kalb I do not know where he is.[4] I do'nt take the liberty of asking the sentiments of your excellency about those promotions because I do not think that Congress could be able of doing such a things in the army without your petition and approbation.[5]

I can'r express to you, dear General, with what pleasure I heard General Gates's advantages upon the queen's light dragoons's colonel—without speaking of my very sincere love for our cause, without speaking of Congress ⟨which (betwen us) I am not so fond of as I was in France⟩, every thing important to your own succès, agreement, and glory procures me the greatest happinness.

Give me leave, dear general, to speack to you about my own business with all the confidence of a son, of a friend, as you favoured me with those two so precious titles. My respect, my affection for you, answer to my own heart that I deserve them on that side as well as possible. Since our last great conversation I would not tell any thing to your excellency, for my taking a division of the army—you were in too important occupations to be disturbed—for the Congress he was in a great hurry, and in such a time I take my only right of fighting; I forget the others. Now that the horable. Congress is settled quiete, and making promotions, that some changements are ready to happen in the divisions, and that I endeavoured myself the 11 september to be acquainted with a part of the army and Known by them, advise me, dear general, for what I am to do. It is not in my character to examine if they have had, if they can have never some obligations to me, I am not usued to tell what I am, I wo'nt make no more any petition to Congress because I can now refuse, but not ask from them, therefore, dear general, I'l conduct myself by your advices. Consider, if you please, that Europe and particularly France is looking upon me—that I want to do some thing by myself, and justify that love of glory which I left be known to the world in making those sacrifices which have appeared so surprising, some say so foolish. Do not you think that this want is right? In the begining I refused a division because I was diffident of my being able to conduct it without Knowing the character of the men who would be under me. Now that I am better acquainted no difficulty comes from me. Therefore I am ready to do all what your excellency will think proper. You know I hope, with what pleasure and satisfaction I live in your family. Be certain that I schall be very happy if you judge that I can stay in America without any particular employement when strangers come to take divisions of the army,[6] and when myself by the only right of my birth should get in my country without any difficulty a body of troops as numerous as is here a division.[7] We have there different ways of advancement as the different ranks of men. I know it is not right—but I would deserve the reprochs of my friends and family if I would leave the advantages of mine to stay in a country where I could not find the occasions of distinguishing myself. I do not tell all that to my general, but to my father and friend. For Congress I'l tell never nothing to them because tho' I like very much some as Mr. Lee, Mr. Lawrence &c. some others did not behave with me with that frankness which is the proof of an honest mind. All what I have the honor to wraït to your excellency in this letter is, if you please, under the most intimate secret, and confidence. I schall conduct myself entirely by your advices, and if You say that some thing is proper I'l do it directly—I desire only to know your opinion.

Among the officers who came on board of my ship, this whom Congress did pay the less regard to, is the very same whom I reccommended as the most able and respectable man and my best friend—he was coming only for me.[8] If I was to be at the head of a division and your excellency would be master of it, (as I am told that Stephens gives his dismission) [9] I can not help to tell you that a division of Virginians as they are, principally with General Woodfort would be the most agreable for me.

I hope that I'l be in camp in three or four days where I'l be able to speack to your exellency about all my businesses. I beg your Pardon for being so tedious—it is for You a very disagreable and troublesome proof of my confidence—but that confidence is equal to the affection and respect which I have the honor to be with Your Exellency's the most obedient servant

THE MQUIS. DE LAFAYETTE

ALS (NNPM). The manuscript has been edited, in ink, in Lafayette's later hand. The text of significant deletions has been restored in angle brackets.

1. Thomas, Comte de Conway, an Irishman who had attained the rank of colonel in the French army, was recruited by Deane. When Du Coudray delayed his departure from France, Conway took charge of the officers and military supplies Du Coudray had collected and brought them to America on *L'Amphitrite*. Washington recommended Conway to Congress, which made him a brigadier general (Washington to Congress, May 9, 1777, in Fitzpatrick, *Writings of Washington*, 8:30–31; May, 13, 1777, in *JCC*, 8:349). He commanded a brigade at Brandywine and Germantown, and made a very favorable impression upon his superior, General Sullivan.

2. On September 15 Congress created an additional major-generalcy and elected Kalb to it (*JCC*, 8:746). When Conway heard that Kalb had become a major general, he protested to Congress that Kalb was his inferior in the French army, and demanded the same rank for himself (Conway to Congress, September 25, 1777 [DNA: RG 360, PCC 159, p. 453]). Kalb refuted Conway's assertion in a letter to Richard Henry Lee (September 28, 1777 [NHi: Vail Collection, 1:136]), and, far from promoting Conway, Congress rejected a motion to have Washington investigate "the priority of rank between the Baron de Kalb and General Conway in France . . ." (October 3, 1777, in *JCC*, 9:762). Conway wrote to Congress again on October 19 to express his surprise at hearing that some members had been offended by "the boldness and freedom" of his letters. The letter was referred to the Board of War, and no further action was taken on Conway's request until November (DNA: RG 360, PCC 159, pp. 457–460).

3. Letter not found.

4. Kalb told Henry Laurens he had avoided the towns where Congress met, because he did not want to be accused of "having Sollicted the influence of friends to be employed" (Kalb to Laurens, October 5, 1777 [ScHi: Henry Laurens Papers]). He passed a few weeks in the vicinity of Lancaster and York, and finally accepted the commission in mid-October. See Kalb to Saint-Paul, November 7.

5. Washington wrote to Richard Henry Lee about the rumor that Conway had been promoted. If it were true, he said, it was "as unfortunate a measure as ever was adopted. I may add (and I think with truth) that it will give a fatal blow to the existence of the Army." Washington asserted that Conway's "importance to this Army exists more in his imagination than in Reality." His importunities and self-advertisement had made him unpopular, and were he promoted over the other brigadiers, all of whom were his seniors, they would resign. "To Sum up the whole, I have been a Slave to the service: I have undergone more than most Men are aware of, to harmonize so many discordant parts; but it will be impossible for me to be of any further service, if such insuperable difficulties are thrown in my way" (October 17, 1777, in Fitzpatrick, *Writings of Washington*, 9:387–389). Lee replied: "No such appointment has been made, nor do I believe it will, whilst it is likely to have the evil consequences you suggest" (Lee to Washington, October 29, 1777, in ibid., p. 389n).

6. At this point, only Kalb fitted that description.

7. Lafayette might eventually have been able to purchase the command of a French regiment, and the Noailles might have been able to obtain an even larger command for him, but when he left France he was only a reserve captain.

8. La Colombe; see Lafayette to Laurens, September 25.

9. Adam Stephen was not dismissed until November; see p. 101, note 3.

To Henry Laurens

Bethlehem for the last time the Saturday [October 18, 1777]
Dear Sir

At lenght I go to camp, and I see the end of my so tedious confinement. My wound (thro' the skin is not yet quite over) seems to me in so fine a way of recovery that I judje myself able to play my part in our first engagement.[1] Receive, Sir, as a good american, my very sincere compliments about the heroïc bravery, and most finest action in Germain town which illustrated one of your countrymen, who by the same time is so happy as to be a son of yours.[2]

The bearer of my letter is a french officer of reputation and merit

who came here on board of an american privateer, and could not
since three months get from Congress a *yes* or *not* about the proposition of serving in our army at his own expense. He is going back to
home. I beg your pardon for giving you such accounts, but I think
that it is better to let you know (betwen us) those little things.

I heared with pleasure the promotions of Congress, and I hope that
they will be confirmed; Cannway deserves such a distinction for his
fighting so well this Campaign, his coming here without particular arrangements, and his leaving a corps where he was actively employed
and considered in as a man of great talents. If we do'nt give in our
army particular rewards to merit and good behaviour as in all well
disciplined ones, all is lost. I speack not only for the first rancks but
for those of soldiership as non commissioned officers &c. in going up
to the first commissions.

Do'nt forget Sir to mention to Congress that an immense quantity
of clothes, are arrived from France I do'nt know where since last winter, and that our poor soldiers the respectable instruments of our
glory and liberty are indecently nacked for the next one. I could answer in the name of the nation which furnished them, that their destination is for General's Washington army which they ca'nt be taken à
way from, without robbery.[3]

According to my most dearest friend Mr. de Valfort colonel in the
french service, man as distinguished by his merit and reputation in
war, as by his exquisite virtüe, I'l tell you, Sir, that Congress ca'nt do
myself a greater pleasure than in engaging him to stay here as brigadier general. I Know that he wo'nt accept it, perhaps (betwen us) the
first reception disgusted him a little. I hope however that a very polite
letter could make him receive the favor of Congress. I do'nt ask a
brigade but only the rank to be in my family when I'l get a division of
the army. He is sick at ten miles from Yorck-town. I hope, Sir, that a
second pacquet of letters is arrived for me because they have been
seen by several officers, and some from the same pacquet belonging
to them taken by themselves in the post office in Lancaster. I'l be
much obliged to you to send them to the head quarters by a express
for the first one as Mr. Bedaux dutch officer, and Mr. Buchanan
american, will sawar [swear] that the post master told them in Philadelphia, that *he had sent a large pacquet for me.* I wishoud that you
would be so good as to let the matter be cleared up by way of tryal if
necessary, because I fear that some unknown spy should have done a
little present of it to his excellency General Howe. Therefore I'l have
perhaps some knowledge of them in the english papers of the next
months, and my only consolation would be to let the bearer be
hang'd.

I beg your pardon Sir for a letter which I coul'd not ride [read] myself through. I could wraït it for your unhappiness but I am in the hurry of my so pleasant departure. Will you present my compliments to M. Lee and other members of Congress of my acquaintance. Farewell, dear Sir, I am with the most tender affection for ever Yours

THE MQUIS. DE LAFAYETTE

ALS (ScHi: Henry Laurens Papers).

1. Lafayette wrote to Robert Morris on October 20: "I have had yesterday the pleasure of arriving at camp, and, through not quite recovered, I am able to ride a little without inconvaient" (Henkels, *Confidential Correspondence of Robert Morris,* p. 125).

2. John Laurens had been wounded at Germantown, on October 4.

3. Lafayette refers to the shipments sent to America by Caron de Beaumarchais's firm of Roderigue Hortalez and Company, which was secretly financed by the French and Spanish governments.

From Henry Laurens

York. 23d. Octobr. 1777.

Sir—

It is with the utmost degree of pleasure I congratulate with you on your recovery & return to the Army, where I hope every circumstance will conspire to make you happy that you may have opportunities of gratifying your thirst for glory & I pray God to protect & preserve your valuable Life.

Permit me the honour Sir, to congratulate with you on the amazing Success of the American Arms in the Northern department. I scorn to triumph over even an ungenerous Enemy, but from my own feelings I am persuaded if I had been capable of publishing such a Braggadocio proclamation as we saw in the month of July & of following it with such daring menaces & unmanly acts of murder upon Women & Children as we have been witnesses of, I should have surrendered my self to a pistol Ball in preference to becoming the prisoner of those people whom I had reviled by the Epithet of Rebels & every ignominious term.[1] From the advantages of a River an opposite Shore & a numerous powerful fleet I can scarcely hope & yet I cannot repress the wish, that your Army may have the honour of adding a Knight of the Bath to the list of English Captives.[2]

Your polite notice of Mr. Jno. Laurens lays a further obligation on me, it afforded me pleasure to learn he had done his duty & I flatter my self he will persevere. If Genl. Sir William Howe will faithfully transmit accounts of all preceeding actions & consequences, in the present Campaign he will afford his Master new matter for a speech to Parliament.

I have not seen the french Gentleman who did me the honour to bring your Letter, but will enquire of your black Servant [3] where he may be found & you may depend upon me Sir to attempt, at least, to Serve him, nor shall the Subject concerning Mr. De Valfort depart from my mind. I will this very morning inform myself of the opinions of the War Office respecting that Gentleman. Mr. de Valfort is here, he called upon me the day before yesterday in order to get me to interpose in a dispute Subsisting between himself & a Waggoner relative to the Freight of Baron de Kalb's Baggage, I censured the delinquent Carrier in Severe terms & recommended Mr. de Valfort to apply to two Gentlemen to arbitrate in the Case & I am told they have done him justice by mulcting the Waggoner very considerably. I do not think the Justice complete—it was easy to demonstrate the Baron's damages to have exceeded the Amount of the whole intended Freight.[4] If Baron d'Kalb is not in the Army I know not where to address him, therefore think it best to return your Letter under this Cover.[5]

Congress are apprized of large quantities of Clothing arrived from France & Spain but unfortunately at the distant ports of Boston, Charles Town & New Orleans, distant as these are I have strongly urged the necessity of bringing the Clothing even in Waggons, the expense is not to be set in competition with the Lives of our poor Soldiers, and if we consider, not too deeply, we might add our own Lives also, but I am afraid no measures for effecting this great purpose are yet in motion—I do not count the lost days to be in October but in January when the Cold will be intense. I will without fear of offence move again in this matter before the present day passes.

I have enquired very minutely of Mr. Morris relative to Packets for you from France. He declares he never Saw nor heard of one, will it be difficult Sir to confront the Post Master by Mr. Bedaux & Mr. Buchannan? A Letter to the Post Master might bring about an explanation. If he is in this Town you will soon hear further on the Subject, I will take the Liberty to question him very closely.

I have seen a Letter containing London Intelligence pretty late in July. The Privateers in Capt. Weeks's Squadron of three not very capital Ships out of France had made immense prizes in the Irish Channel & Spread such terror the Linnen Ships expected from Dublin &tc. were detained in port & the great annual Fair at Chester intirely empty & disappointed, a circumstance which never before happened from its commencement. Capt. Weeks with 3 little Barques has effected more than has ever been done by the United powers of France

& Spain. I construe this event in a manner differing from the opinions of Wiser politicians, the people in general in Ireland are our friends & will use Stratagem to frighten the Ministry. Weeks however & his Subcommanders were ordered by the French Ministry to be taken into Custody immediately upon their return & were actually in confinement at the Same time their Ships were with great celerity fitting out for another Cruize.[6]

"The Merchants had made two Representations to Lord North, in one was stated the Loss of Great Britain at Sea Three Million Six hundred thousand pounds Sterling—in the other a much deeper Loss by the Balance of Trade with America thrown into the Lap of a Rival power. The Loan for five Million had been soon filled by Subscription but payments were exceedingly tardy. Stocks had in earnest begun to fall & foreigners had also in earnest taken the alarm."

Nothing that has happened in America Since July can administer that distracted Country, consolation. If these things are not new I have been impertinent, I beg you will be so good as to ascribe the trouble to that sincere respect & regard with which I profess my self, &c.

LbC (ScHi: Henry Laurens Papers).

1. General Burgoyne's proclamation, issued on June 23, 1777, appealed to American loyalty to the king, and threatened to unleash thousands of Indians against those who rejected his appeal. At the same time, Burgoyne ordered his Indian allies to refrain from all violence, except against armed rebels. The patriots were outraged at the proclamation, and it was soon widely satirized.

2. General William Howe had become a Knight of the Bath in 1775.

3. Edmund Brice had purchased a slave for Lafayette on August 4, for the sum of 180 pounds (MdHi: Brice-Jennings Papers, MS. 1997).

4. Valfort, Kalb, Lesser, and Dubuysson had hired William McCafferty, of Charlotte, North Carolina, to transport their baggage from Charleston to Philadelphia for the sum of 900 pounds in South Carolina currency. McCafferty set out with the wagoners who had been hired to carry the rest of the baggage for Lafayette's party to Philadelphia, but he went only as far as Charlotte. Kalb appealed to Laurens for help in a letter of August 28, 1777 (ScHi: Henry Laurens Papers).

5. Letter not found.

6. Laurens refers to a raid led by Captain Lambert Wickes, of the Continental navy, in June 1777.

To Monsieur Duboismartin[T]

Camp at White Marsh, October 23, 1777

Here, sir, is a sad but sure occasion to write to you, and I shall not let it escape. M. de Valfort is leaving me, or, rather, he cannot stay here because the frightful state of his health obliges him to return to

France just when I need him most and have assurances of obtaining what he asks. He knows all about my affairs, and I have communicated all my ideas to him. Thus he will be able to give you all the news about me which the friendship I know you hold for me will surely require of him. I wish, however, to tell you myself how closely I am attached to you. This sentiment, sir, which I shall cling to all my life, depends neither upon the trouble I have given you nor upon the proofs of concern I have received from you, nor even upon all my obligations to you, to be truly frank and sincere.

I have written to Monsieur le Comte de Broglie since I was wounded and once by ship before leaving Charleston. I write to him now by a mail boat sent by Congress, and I am trying to have M. de Valfort sent on the same ship.[1] If by chance that is not possible, I enclose here the letter I am sending to M. de Maurepas—that is, a copy made by M. de Gimat, in whom I rightly have complete confidence.[2] You will find in the letter some ideas that are quite extraordinary, completely mad, and perhaps very ridiculous, but, tortured by the longing to accomplish something to satisfy my vanity and the needs of my fatherland in this country, I could not resist submitting my plan to your judgment, and that of M. le Comte de Broglie. If you do not find it unreasonable, would you be good enough to forward my epistle to the current first minister, whatever nature and origins he may have, for who knows what may have become of M. de Maurepas?[3] I shall not dwell upon the reasons that make me fond of my project; your extensive knowledge of the Indies will make my rationale appear pitiful enough. Simply reflect, if you will, that the odds would need to be only one in four, for me to undertake it, and that, until now, the risks I have taken have not had unfavorable results. Bear in mind that the enterprise of M. d'Estaing had some success.[4] Besides, an equivocal consent from the minister will shelter me from most dangers. I shall say no more, sir. Judge me, indulge me, and serve me in my enterprise, if it is feasible; at least forward the letter by M. de Valfort, if it is forwardable. I do not think it necessary for him to act as though he knows its contents, and as for M. le Comte de Broglie, he can judge whether it is worthwhile for him to be involved in it, or whether he should be unaware of it also. I depend so much upon his goodwill—my confidence is so complete—that I dare not doubt that he will interest himself on my behalf in this affair as in the other one.[5]

Would you believe that I add to the present ridiculous effort that of writing seriously to M. de Bouillé to convince him to close his eyes to an expedition that would be based upon his island? It would not take even two months of this winter. One would have to furnish some ships with congressional commissions, take some men from the estates of my cousin the governor, and fall on some small English islands where the Negroes would cover the cost of the enterprise.[6] But that, like Asia, is another one of my castles in the air. It is for Asia, if I go there, that your counsels would be of value to me!

You will have seen your brother; I am sorrier for myself than for him that he did not stay here with me.[7] I shall not go into the details of this subject, which I have already repeated to you, as well as to M. le Comte de Broglie. I shall be content with repeating to you that several members of Congress had made many misjudgments. Du Coudray made them lose their heads, but there are some men of virtue and merit in Congress. As for the rest, among all the accusations and injustices, I hope that we always except General Washington, my friend, my intimate friend, and since I like to choose my friends, I dare say that to give him that title is to praise him.

If all the divisions of our army were commanded by French general officers (and I have the honor to know many of them), I would not be so impertinent as to take one of them, but since the disproportion is not the same, and, besides, having a mind to make something of myself and occupy my time, I shall not hesitate to ask General Washington to give me one. The opportunities for doing something outstanding (assuming I would know how to profit from them) are rare for a foreigner. This situation always causes jealousy or stifles the good that one can do in any country in the world; at least, that is what the French who are employed here are saying, and they are shrieking like devils. As for me, I have nothing to complain about. I cannot join the lament. I can even boast that I get along perfectly with everyone, and the general's friendship gives me every possible pleasure. So long as this is the case it would be graceless for me to be offended.

I also wish to caution you about the error of thinking we are three times stronger than the enemy, an error that always diminishes the honor of success and augments the unpleasantness of defeat. I shall amuse myself by making war all winter. It is impossible to leave America when things are going so well, and at such a decisive moment. If my project gets me recalled, I shall lose no time. In any case, please let me know what you think about my return, about the good or bad effects it would have, etc. Since circumstances are infinitely variable, I seek counsel that will guide me in a wide range of possibilities. By all appearances, however, I shall be here for the next campaign if I do not receive any other news. The outbreak of war would impel me to leave immediately, even if I had to swim back. Alas! sir, if there is to be an invasion of England, for God's sake do not forget me!

If all this has not annoyed or wearied you too much, M. de Valfort will tell you the rest. You can understand, by the close attachment and friendship that unite the two of us, how much I desire that M. le Comte de Broglie will become interested in his welfare. Farewell, sir, I send you my heartfelt embraces.

LAFAYETTE

Please give my compliments to your brother and our fellow voyagers. My letter is surely not full of common sense, but a campaign is being planned behind me, which makes it difficult to think because the disputants are contending so noisily.

ALS (AN: AE II 1018), translation.

Duboismartin was the Comte de Broglie's secretary and Lieutenant François Duboismartin's elder brother.

1. None of these letters have been found. The ship was the *Randolph;* see Lafayette to Lee, October 28.

2. Copy not found.

3. As a royal minister and personal adviser to Louis XVI, Maurepas performed the functions of a first minister, but that office had been abolished half a century earlier. In 1774, when Maurepas came to power at the age of seventy-three, many people thought he was senile and did not expect him to last very long.

4. D'Estaing had led an expedition against the English settlements on the Persian Gulf in 1769.

5. See Lafayette to Broglie, March 23, 1777.

6. Bouillé was Lafayette's cousin. In February 1777 he had been appointed governor of Martinique and Saint Lucia, with authority to take command of all the French Windward Islands whenever necessary. His main task was to maintain French neutrality in the principal entrepôts for European trade with the Americans, while preparing for war with England. See René de Bouillé, *Essai sur la vie du marquis de Bouillé* (Paris, 1853), pp. 46–53; Lafayette, Memoir of 1779, p. 97; Lafayette to Laurens, December 14. 1777; Bouillé to Lafayette, March 8, 1778 (DNA: RG 360, PCC 156, pp. 21–23).

7. François Duboismartin had declined to serve as Kalb's aide-de-camp and returned to his unit on Santo Domingo. Lafayette apparently believed he had returned to France.

To [*the Comte de Maurepas*]^T

At Whitemarsh camp in Pennsylvania
October 24, 1777

Sir,

You were imposed upon, despite my wishes to the contrary, by the part you were obliged to take in my first schemes; [1] you are going to be bothered again, in spite of yourself, by the consideration that I dare to ask for my new ones. They may seem as little worthy as the others of occupying your valuable time, but now, as before, my goodwill (though it may be misdirected) will serve as my excuse. My age could perhaps be a justification as well. All that I ask now is that it not prevent you from considering whatever may be reasonable in my ideas.

I do not venture to examine the nature of the assistance received by the noble cause that we are defending here, but my patriotism makes me reflect with pleasure on the number of aspects from which England's domestic troubles may be advantageous to my country. There is one especially that, in every case, and *whatever happens,* would seem to me to offer so much utility that it would be pursued by stronger means, and I feel that I would already solve one problem by proposing myself for its execution. I speak of an expedition, more or less extensive, against the East Indies.

Without giving myself the airs of a prophet in current affairs, but genuinely persuaded that to inflict harm on England is to serve (do I dare say revenge?) my country, I believe this idea is designed to put to use the particular resources of every individual who has the honor to be French. I came here without permission; I serve without any approbation but that of silence; I could allow myself yet another little voyage without authorization. If success is doubtful, I have the advantage of endangering only myself, and what prevents me then from being daring? However little I should succeed, the flames of the smallest English settlement, though they might consume part of my fortune, would satisfy my heart by increasing my expectations of a more propitious occasion.

Guided by the feeble knowledge that my ignorance has permitted me to obtain, here, sir, is how I would attempt that enterprise. An American commission to make my operation legal, plus the slight help necessary to sustain it—which would be furnished in the French Antilles, through the speculation of a few merchants, or the goodwill of a few traveling companions—such are the slight resources that would lead me quietly to the Isle de France. There I believe I would find both privateers to assist me and men to follow me—at least enough to ambush ships returning from China as a source of additional means, perhaps enough to descend upon one or two of their settlements and destroy them before they can be relieved. With forces such as I dare not expect, especially with abilities that I am still very far from having acquired, could we not draw some advantage from the jealousy of quarreling nabobs, the hatred of the Mahrattas, the venality of the sepoys, and the indolence of the English? Could we not usefully employ the crowd of Frenchmen scattered along that coast? As for myself, the fear of compromising my country would in every case keep me from glorifying myself with that name, much as the nobility in certain provinces sometimes lay aside their marks of honor only to reassume them at a later date.

Although I am not at all blind to my imprudence, I would have risked this voyage alone if the fear of harming the interests I wish to serve, out of an incomplete knowledge of them, or of prejudicing some better planned expedition, had not held me back. For I am vain enough to believe that a project roughly similar to this one could someday be carried out on a grander scale by more capable hands. At least it could be executed in a manner that would seem to me almost certain to succeed if I could expect from the government, not an order, not assistance, yet not a simple indifference, but something for which no language provides me with a sufficiently nuanced expression. In such a case, an order from the king, deigning to *recall me for a while to my family and friends* without *forbidding me to return, would signal me* to arm myself with American Continental commissions. At the same time, some instructions and some preparations in France would precede this pretended return, and would send me straight to the East Indies. *Then that same discretion which* at another time might have been harmful, becoming a sacred duty, would serve to hide my true destination, and especially the extent to which it was officially approved.

Such are the ideas, sir, which, though I am fully aware of my incompetence and the shortcomings of my youth, I nevertheless presume to submit to your judgment, and (should they please you) to the various modifications you will think necessary. I am certain, at least, that they are not ridiculous, because they spring from too respectable a motive, the love of my country. I ask only the honor of serving my country under another flag, and I love to see her interests united to those of the republicans for whom I fight, even though I wish I might soon be permitted to serve actively under the French colors. Then I would rather be a grenadier in the king's army than hold the highest rank in a foreign army.

I reproach myself too much, sir, for having heedlessly offered you Asian projects to trace for you even more clumsy descriptions of America, embellished with unsolicited reflections that are of no interest to you. Moreover, the zeal that led me here, and above all the friendship that unites me to the commander in chief, would cause me to be suspected of a partiality from which nevertheless I believe myself free. I shall only reserve for myself the honor of speaking to you on my return, on behalf of the officers of merit who came to this continent out of love of their profession. Everyone who is French, sir, has the right to have confidence in you. It is by this right that I ask your indulgence. I have a second claim to it in the respect with which I have the honor to be, sir, your very humble and obedient servant.

LAFAYETTE

This letter will reach you, sir, by a means that is perhaps too reliable, if the letter troubles you. I confide it to Monsieur de Valfort, captain in the Regiment of Aunis with the brevet of colonel in our colonies, whose talents, reputation, and virtue make him valuable to this country, and who would be retained here by the wish of General Washington if his health had not absolutely obliged him to return to France. I shall await here your orders (which do not reach American ports without difficulty) or I shall go seek them, depending on the circumstances, not having received any that could direct me since my arrival.

ALS (Stevens, *Facsimiles*, no. 756), translation.
In 1829 Lafayette sent Sparks a copy of this letter with the notation that it had been addressed to Vergennes (MH: Sparks MSS 85, pp. 1–5), and it was printed in Lafayette, *Mémoires*, 1:108, with that label, but Lafayette's contemporary references to the letter (in letters to Duboismartin, October 23, and Laurens, December 14, and in Memoir of 1779, p. 97) indicate that it was written to Maurepas. Vergennes probably did see the letter, which was deposited in the Archives of the Foreign Ministry.
1. The Duc d'Ayen had secured the royal order forbidding Lafayette to go to America from Maurepas, and Lafayette had appealed to the minister to have it withdrawn.

To Richard Henry Lee

Head Quarters, the 28th. October, 1777

Dear Sir—

Receive my very sincere thanks for the advice you favoured me with.[1] I am yet more sensible of such a service, when I consider my friends must be in the same want of news, as I am myself, without being happier perhaps in their expectations; however, I'll write by every good opportunity—some letters will escape, and let them know that I am alive. I am not in any doubt, that the English will kill me in Europe, when they expect to take me in America, according to their New York papers.[2] I take therefore the liberty, of enclosing you a letter for a friend of mine, where I give to him some accounts in general; none of my acquaintances shall receive a word from me, without political and American reflections.[3] I know well the . . . genius of our enemies, that I'll endeavour all my powers, to let the truth . . . in Europe, of their ridiculous relations. For a long time, nobody would think himself a true friend of mine, without being what they call, a *good insurgent*. I dare hope, that I can raise in my own country, as strong a party as can be there, of the most agreeable and polite. Though I wrote several letters upon the same principles, I send you but one; the others will be carried by Mr. de Valfort, actually at, or very near York, whom I will introduce to my friends in France. I beg from you . . . the occasion of this gentleman the greatest pleasure and most interesting service; he is my intimate friend, and I wish warmly to obtain the following favour. He came over on board of my vessel by a sincere attachment for me, and with the hope of being always in my family; if he could stay, I would now trouble Congress, in order to get employment for him, but the deplorable state of his health obliges him to return home. He has not a moment to lose—his life depends on his safe and speedy arrival in France. I understand that Congress would engage the captain of their packet, to take him on board, alone, or if possible, with one of his friends; it is much better, than exposing him to the dangers of a merchant vessel. Will you be so good, sir, to inquire yourself, where my friend can be; Mr. Lawrens, who will receive a letter from his son,[4] is able, I believe, to give you that intelligence; then you'll engage Mr. de Valfort, to take that opportunity, and the captain, to embark him in his vessel, at whatever price he will choose.[5] Perhaps 'tis not . . . to our business, that my letters could arrive soon. I know by my experience, that a great authenticity is desired in the American views; however, I give you one, which in all cases, will acquaint my societies in Paris, of John Burgoyne being prisoner of war. Farewell, sir, I will not detain your despatches, therefore it shall not give me the pleasure of presenting you in long terms, with the assurances of my affection and esteem, with which I am, yours,

THE MARQUIS DE LAFAYETTE

[October 30, 1777]

I add here, sir, the letters of several gentlemen, and one from myself to the French ambassador, which you can read, and seal after if you please.[6] A meeting of general officers yesterday, prevented me of sending my despatches.[7] I enclose too, a letter from his excellency, General Washington, for you. Sir, be pleased to let Mr. Carrol get the other one.[8]

L (Richard Henry Lee, ed., *Memoir of the Life of Richard Henry Lee and His Correspondence* [Philadelphia, 1825], 2:103–104). The printed text contains apparent inaccuracies of transcription and unexplained ellipses.
    1. No letter from Lee has been found.
    2. The only references to Lafayette that we have been able to find in the New York

newspapers of the period are the following: On June 30, 1777, the *New-York Gazette and Weekly Mercury* reported that Lafayette had been arrested in France (p. 1). On September 22 it carried two pieces about the Battle of Brandywine which mentioned Lafayette: Washington's report of September 11 to Congress, which said that Lafayette had been wounded, and a British report that "two Generals were wounded, one a Frenchman, thought to be mortally . . ." (p. 3).

3. Perhaps the letter of October 23 to Duboismartin, or a copy of it.

4. Letter not found.

5. Lee was a member of the Marine Committee, which had ordered Captain Nicholas Biddle to take his frigate, the *Randolph*, from Charleston to France (Marine Committee to Biddle, October 24, in *Out-Letters of the Continental Marine Committee and Board of Admiralty, 1776–1780*, ed. Charles O. Paullin [New York, 1914], 1:161–162).

6. Lafayette apparently enclosed a letter (not found) to the Marquis de Noailles, and some letters by other French officers for Lee to forward to Valfort.

7. The minutes of the council of war, October 29, are in Ford, "Defences of Philadelphia," 20:223–227.

8. Letters from Washington to Lee and Charles Carroll not found.

To Adrienne de Noailles de Lafayette[T]

At camp near Whitemarsh
October 29 [1777]

I am sending you a completely open letter, my dear heart, in the person of M. de Valfort. He is my friend, and I beg you to treat him as such. He will give you a lengthy account of me. For myself, I want to tell you how much I love you. I enjoy that feeling too much to deny myself the pleasure of repeating it to you, a thousand times if I could ⟨but the unhappy fate that binds me here prevents that most cruelly⟩. I have no other resources, dear heart, than writing, and writing again, without the hope that my letters can ever reach you, trying to console myself with the pleasure of conversing with you about my sorrow, my extreme anguish at not receiving a line from France.[1] It is impossible to express to you how much my heart is troubled, and often tortured, by this silence. I would not want to describe that torment for fear of spoiling the sweetest moments of my ⟨sad⟩ exile, those when I can speak to you of my affection. ⟨What a way to express it to you! When will I be able to ask her pardon, to swear to her, in person, to love her always?⟩ Do you, at least, pity me, understand how much I suffer, how I have been punished ⟨for an ill-considered course that I ventured to take, not knowing the constraints of my heart? It cannot bear such a separation from all that it loves.⟩ If I could at least know what you are doing, where you are, I would know it much later, but at least I would not be separated from you as if I were dead. I await your letters with an eagerness from which nothing can distract me. I am

promised that they will arrive soon, but can I rely upon it? Don't neglect any opportunity to write me, my dearest, if my happiness still
matters to you. Repeat to me that you love me. The less I merit your
affection, the more your assurances of it are a necessary consolation
for me.

You must have received enough news of my trifling wound so that
repetitions would be useless. In any case, if you have believed that it
was anything serious, M. de Valfort can undeceive you. In a very
short time I shall not even be lame. ⟨From now on, I shall not need to
show or expose myself, and I assure you I shall be careful. Moreover,
the war is presently being carried on by small detachments that will
not involve me. The friend I send to you is fondly attached to me, but
he is obliged to leave me, and the separation is painful for both of us.
A heart broken by great shocks is thereby made more sensitive to
slight sorrows. The loss of a man in whom I have confidence brings
cruelly to mind the awful losses I have suffered of all that is dear to
me. I have made a great blunder, dear heart, and the pleasure with
which I serve here is a very meager consolation for such great unhappiness. Be very gracious to M. de Valfort, I have assured him you
would receive him well. I look forward eagerly to seeing him in
France, because he joins a wide knowledge to the best heart and the
highest virtue.⟩

⟨There has been some difficulty with my finances; M. de Valfort
will explain it to you.[2] I think there is a remedy, however. I spend as
little as I can, and yet I spend a good deal; the abominable expense of
even the smallest articles and the depreciation of paper currency are
the causes. The largest expenditure here, after my journey from
Charleston, was for the six weeks I stayed at Bethlehem recovering
from my wound, and you can guess that I had no frivolous expenses
there. In general, it cannot be said that love of pleasure holds me in
this country, where people either think only of politics or occupy
themselves only with the horrors of a kind of civil war. The problem
of money is very much on my mind, and I assure you I seek only what
is absolutely necessary. It piques me that it has cost me so much to
make myself unhappy. As my ship was insured, I hope that everything is not lost, the letter of insurance having been sent off before
the ship went down. At least it is said that this is the merchants' rule.⟩

Isn't it awful, dear heart, to think that it is by the public, by the English papers, by newspapers coming from the enemy that I hear news
of you? In a rather useless article about my arrival here, they end by
speaking of you, of your pregnancy, of your confinement, of that object of my fears, my hopes, my trembling, and my joy.[3] What happiness it would be for me were I to learn that I am a father a second

time, that you are well, that my two children and their mother are preparing to make me happy for the rest of my life. This country is a charming place for paternal, maternal, or filial love—where it is pushed to the extreme of passion, to truly touching solicitude. The news of your delivery will be received joyfully here, especially by the army, and above all by him who commands it. ⟨Even though he is my good friend I am impatient to bid him good-bye. How quickly I would be willing to risk being taken, and satisfying our friends the English! But I cannot know yet the exact day I shall have the happiness of embracing you, although I can promise you to depart as soon as I believe I can honorably leave the army in which I serve.⟩

⟨This army still has several things to do. If we were as strong in proportion as Gates was to General John Burgoyne, we could play the same trick on Mr. Howe, then quickly take New York, and in a fortnight I would set sail. Not that I expect to see the end of this war in America—God forbid! As soon as I can honestly desert, I am all yours, dear heart, and (if things develop as I would like them to) you will see me arrive sooner than one might think. If anyone thinks my stay here is not long enough, I shall send him off to try a short voyage of a year or eighteen months, far from all that he loves, to see how he likes it. Neither fair nor foul times will decide my return. I shall not leave the war for a ball; it is not for such pleasures that I would abandon an army fighting both for liberty and against the English. But I shall return to see you and to see my friends. I shall return because I no longer have the patience to stay. Any month would be a good one in which to leave, but the earliest one will always suit me best.⟩

I shall find my poor little Henriette a very amiable child when I return. I hope she will give me a lecture ⟨on my silly military adventure⟩, and speak to me with all the candor of friendship. For my daughter will always be, I hope, my best friend. I want to be a father only for love, and paternal love goes marvelously with friendship. Give her a hug, my dear—should I say, give them a hug?—for me. But I don't want to dwell on how much I suffer from this uncertainty; I know that you share the sorrows of my heart, and I don't want to afflict you. Last time I wrote to Mme d'Ayen.[4] Since I received my wound, I have written to everybody. But perhaps these letters have been lost; it is not my fault.[5] I can do a bit of harm to these letter-stealing villains when they are on land, but on the open sea I have only the consolation of the weak, which is to curse very heartily those upon whom one can no longer take revenge. A thousand tender respects to your mother, a thousand regards to my sisters. Remember me to Monsieur le Maréchal de Noailles, to your paternal and maternal relatives. I received four foolish lines from the Maréchal de

Mouchy which do not say a word about you.[6] I swore at him in every language. Farewell, my dear, farewell. Question my good and honest friend M. de Valfort. I am running out of paper; it is terrible to be reduced to writing when one loves as much as I love you, dear heart, and shall love you until my dying breath.

I have not neglected any opportunity, even the most indirect, to write to you. Do as much for me, dear heart, if you love me. I would be very ungrateful and very insensitive if I were to doubt that you do.

AL (NIC: Dean Collection), translation. The manuscript has been edited in pencil, in Lafayette's later hand. Significant passages omitted from Lafayette, *Mémoires,* are printed in angle brackets.

1. Pulaski had brought Lafayette one letter (not found) from his wife, in August.

2. Caused by the dispute over the sale of *La Victoire*'s cargo in Charleston and the loss of the ship itself on the Charleston bar. See Dubuysson, Memoir, p. 75.

3. The English newspaper account has not been found.

4. The letter (not found) in which he enclosed his letter of September 12 to his wife.

5. Only the letters of October 23 to Duboismartin and of October 24 to Maurepas have been found.

6. Letter not found.

To John Sullivan

[Whitemarsh, November 1, 1777]

Dear Sir

I would have been glad you had lett me known the form of the certifitate you are wanting; such a want seems to me so extraordinary after having seen you in the field, that I did not know how to express my being so sensible of your bravery as by telling you what every soldier who was with us that day, must be acquainted with.[1] I did not answer directly to your request, because I was engaged in business with Genl. Washington. I will always do myself the greatest pleasure to pay a due justice to your merit, and desire your being no less convinced of my affection. I am Yours

THE MARQUIS LA FAYETTE

L (NhHi), copy in secretary's hand.

1. On September 9 Congress had ordered an inquiry into the failure of Sullivan's attack on Staten Island (*JCC,* 8:727 n.). Some Congressmen also believed Sullivan was responsible for the defeat at Brandywine, and Sullivan collected testimonials from a number of officers about his performance in both of those actions (*Sullivan Papers,* 1:552–565, and Rossie, *Politics of Command,* pp. 181–183). The court of inquiry cleared Sullivan; Congress accepted its report on October 20, but did not send that information to Washington's headquarters until November 4 (*JCC,* 9:822–823 and note). For Lafayette's later assessment of Sullivan, see Memoir of 1779. p. 92.

Certificate for John Sullivan

at camp near White Marsh the 1st november [1777]
Tho' very far from thinking that Major General Sullivan could ever
want such a certificate, however it is with the greatest pleasure that
(according to his own desire) I repeat here how sensible I have been
of his bravery at the affair of Brandiwine the 11 7bre. I can assure
him that such courage as he shewed that day will alwais deserve the
praises of every one.

THE MQUIS. DE LAFAYETTE
Mjor. Gral. in the Army
of the Unit. St. of America

ADS (NhHi).

George Washington to the President of Congress[E]

Head Qrs., near White Marsh, November 1, 1777
Sir:
. . . I would take the liberty to mention, that I feel myself in a delicate situation with respect to the Marquis Le Fayette. He is extremely
solicitous of having a Command equal to his Rank, & professes very
different Ideas as to the purposes of his appointment, from those
Congress mentioned to me. He certainly did not understand them. I
do not know in what light they will view the matter, but it appears to
me, from a consideration of his illustrious and important connections—the attachment which he has manifested to our cause, and the
consequences, which his return in disgust might produce, that it will
be adviseable to gratify him in his wishes—and the more so, as several
Gentlemen from France, who came over under some assurances, have
gone back disappointed in their expectations. His conduct with respect to them stands in a favorable point of view, having interested
himself to remove their uneasiness and urged the impropriety of their
making any unfavorable representations upon their arrival at home,
and in all his letters has placed our affairs in the best situation he
could. Besides, he is sensible—discreet in his manners—has made
great proficiency in our Language, and from the disposition he dis-

covered at the Battle of Brandy Wine, possesses a large share of bravery and Military ardor.

There is a French Gentn. here, Monsieur Vrigney, in whose favor the Marquis seems much interested. He assures me he is an Officer of great merit, and from that motive & a regard to the service wishes to see him promoted. The Rank he holds in France and his present expectation are contained in the inclosed Copy of a paper, given me by the Marquis.[1] Monsr. Vrigney also has Honble. certificates of his services nearly corresponding with the Marquis's account of them. If Congress are pleased to honor him with a commission in the Army of the States, I must try to imploy him. . . .

LS (DNA: RG 360, PCC 152, 5:165–166), in the hand of William Grayson, Washington's aide-de-camp.

1. See Lafayette's recommendation, which follows.

Recommendation for Cloquet de Vrigny

[Camp near White Marsh, ca. November 1, 1777]

Mr. de Vrigny who has now the commission of Major in the french service begun by being in the rgt. *of family* de Noaïlles, Cavalry,[1] from the year 1754 till 1758. He made in that intervall two campaigns of war near the person of my uncle the Marechal Duc de Mouchy then lieutenant general who gave him an honourable certificate of good conduct and behaviour.

He was received after it in the corps of *horse rangers* under the famous partisan Ficher as lieutenant;[2] which corps was granted (Ficher being dead) to the Mquis. de Conflans officer of the greatest reputation in our service. That general who is a friend of mine gave me the best accounts of Mr. de Vrigny who is yet Captain in the same rgt. called now *houzards de Conflans* with commission of Major as I mentionned above.[3]

As I think that the military knowledge and experience of this genteleman, principally in the kind of war used till this moment by our light dragoons, could be useful to our excellency's Gral. Washington army, I wishoud that he could be employed in it with the rank of lieutenant colonel.

AD (PEL: Hubbard Collection).

This recommendation was given to Washington, who sent a copy of it (written by John Laurens, in better English) with his letter of November 1 to the president of

Congress. An extract of Washington's letter and the copy of Lafayette's recommendation are in DNA: RG 360, PCC 82, 1:39–41.

1. The Noailles Dragoons, Lafayette's regiment.

2. Fischer's Chasseurs had been organized as a special unit for gathering intelligence (see E. de Ribancourt, *Vie militaire et exploits de J. C. Fischer* [Paris, 1939]).

3. Deane had promised Vrigny the rank of captain as commander of his own "Free Company," and on August 11 Vrigny had petitioned Congress for permission to raise such a company from men he had met in Charleston (DNA: RG 360, PCC 41, 10:313–316). Washington was trying to strengthen his light cavalry, and had already supported Pulaski's similar petition. See Lafayette to Lovell, August 21, note 1. The letters recommending Vrigny were referred to the Committee on Foreign Applications.

To Adrienne de Noailles de Lafayette[T]

Whitemarsh camp, November 6, 1777

You may receive this letter, my dear heart, in five or six years, for I am writing you by an indirect route, which I don't know much about. Just look at the journey my letter is going to make: an army officer will carry it to Fort Pitt, 300 miles through the hinterlands of the continent; it will then be shipped down the great Ohio River, through countryside inhabited only by savages; once it arrives at New Orleans, a small ship will transport it to the Spanish islands; then a vessel of that nation will take it (God knows when) when it returns to Europe. But it will still be very far from you, and it is only after having been fouled by the dirty hands of all the Spanish postmasters that it will be permitted to cross the Pyrenees; it may be opened and resealed five or six times before reaching your hands. Then it will be a proof that I do not neglect even the most distant opportunity to give my dearest my news and to repeat to her how much I love her. Yet it is scarcely for my own gratification that I have the fresh pleasure of reciting this to you; when this letter arrives I hope to have the satisfaction of throwing it in the fire myself, since I shall be there and my presence will make this scrap of paper entirely useless. The idea is very dear to my heart; I surrender to it with ecstasy; oh, how delightful it is to foresee the moments when we shall be together, but how cruel it is as well, my dearest, to think that my affection can as yet only feed on illusions, and that the reality of my happiness is two thousand leagues from me, across immense seas infested by those knavish English vessels. Those vile ships make me very unhappy; a single letter from you, only one, my dearest, has yet come to hand.[1] The others are mislaid, taken to the bottom of the sea, by every appearance. I can only blame the enemy for this terrible privation, for you, surely, would not neglect to write me by every port, by every packet from Dr. Franklin and Mr.

Deane. Yet some ships have arrived; I've dispatched messengers to every corner of the continent, and all my hopes have been frustrated. Apparently you are not well informed. I beg you, my love, inquire with great care about the means of sending me a few letters. It is so painful to be deprived of them; I am so unhappy to be separated from all that I love! Though I am guilty of creating my own unhappiness, you would pity me greatly if you knew all that my heart suffers ⟨from being so far from you and from all that can possibly be dear to me⟩.

What is the use of sending you news in a letter destined to travel for years, which will perhaps reach you in pieces, and which will describe antiquity itself? All my other dispatches have informed you of the remaining events of the campaign. The Battle of Brandywine, where I cleverly left a little bit of my leg; the occupation of Philadelphia, which is so far from having the ill consequences of which they are persuaded in Europe; an unsuccessful attack on the camp at Germantown, in which I didn't participate because I had very recently been wounded; the surrender of General Burgoyne with five thousand men, that same Burgoyne who tried all spring to swallow us, and who in autumn found himself made prisoner of war by our northern army; finally our present position facing the enemy four leagues away, and General Howe established at Philadelphia, making every effort to capture certain forts that do not yield, and having already lost both a large and a small vessel. There, my dearest, you are as fully informed as if you were commander in chief of one of the two armies. I shall only add here that that wound of September 11, of which I have already spoken to you a thousand times, is almost completely healed, although I still limp a bit; but in a few days it will no longer be noticeable, or at least not very much. But all these details, my dearest, will have certainly been related to you in full by my friend Monsieur de Valfort, to whom I gave a letter for you, and in whose report you can have the most complete confidence.[2] I have just learned that he did not leave on a packet, as I had thought, but on board a good thirty-five-gun frigate. Thus there would be some harm if he were taken. From him, and the letter I entrusted to him five or six days ago, you will learn all that your love for me could make you wish to know. I wish very much that you might also know the exact day of my return, for I am very impatient to establish it myself, and to be able to tell you with a joyful heart which day I leave to join you, to recover the happiness ⟨that I so foolishly lost⟩.

A little gentleman volunteer, in a white jacket with lemon-yellow cuffs, of German nationality, who has come here to offer services that will be rejected, and murders the French language, told me that he had set out in August. He spoke to me of politics and ministers, he overturned Europe in general and every court in particular, but he knew not a word of what was dearest to my heart. I approached him from every side, I named fifty names, but he always said, "Me not know those lords there." ⟨Finally I asked him if he had read the gazettes, and if there was any news of society; he said yes, that everyone was well, and that there was nothing new. Thus his interrogation ended, and I was none the wiser. How cruel it is to be reduced to that!⟩

I sent you, by way of Monsieur de Valfort, a full accounting of my finances ⟨by which you will see how reasonable I have become, but if I repeated them here my duplicate explanation would cause you a double and very unnecessary ennui⟩. The loss of my ship has been very painful to me, because that ship would have settled my affairs like a charm. But it is no more, and I would really reproach myself for having sent it off if I had not been forced to settle my affairs because of my minority. Everything here is unbelievably expensive, but we have the consolation of the wicked in reflecting that the shortages are even worse in Philadelphia. In war, one consoles oneself by thinking of worse things one could suffer, and by making things four times worse for the enemy. Besides, food is abundant here, and I learn with pleasure that it is no longer the same for the English.

Don't think of being worried about me at present. The season for great actions is past; at present there will be at most some trifling skirmishes that do not concern me. Thus I am as secure in camp as in the center of Paris; ⟨the only difference is that I am not so happy here. Still,⟩ if all the pleasure possible in serving here, if the favor of the army and all its men, if a tender union, sustained by a reciprocal confidence, with the most respectable and admirable of men, General Washington, if the affection of all the Americans by whom I could desire to be loved, if all this sufficed for my happiness I would have nothing to wish for, but oh, how far my heart is from being at peace! You would indeed be touched, my dearest, if you knew what it feels and how it loves you.

We are now in a season that makes me hope for a few letters. What shall I learn from them? What should I fear, what should I hope for? Oh, my dearest, how cruel it is to suffer from this frightful uncertainty about an event so important to my happiness. Do I have two children? Has a second object of my affection joined my dear Henriette? Hug my dear little daughter a thousand times for me, *hug them both* very tenderly, my dearest; I hope they will one day know how much I love them.

A thousand regards to Mme d'Ayen, a thousand endearments to

the vicomtesse and my sisters, and a million of them as well to all my friends. Take charge of presenting my respects to everyone. Goodbye, my love, take care of your health, send me very detailed news, believe that I love you more than ever, that I look upon you as the first object of my tenderness and the most certain assurance of my happiness. The feelings engraved upon a heart that is wholly at your service will be preserved there until the end. Will you love me always, my dearest? I dare to hope so, and that we shall make each other happy by a love that is as tender as it is eternal. Farewell, farewell, how sweet it would be to embrace you now, to tell you myself, my love, that I love you more than I have ever loved before, and that it shall last all my life.

AL (NIC: Dean Collection), translation. The manuscript has been edited in pencil, in Lafayette's later hand. Significant passages omitted from Lafayette, *Mémoires,* are printed in angle brackets.

1. The letter (not found) brought to Lafayette by Pulaski in August.

2. The letter of October 29.

The Baron de Kalb to Pierre de Saint-Paul[ET]

With the army of the United States
of America, November 7, 1777

If I have not had the honor of writing to you for a long time, sir, it is not because I have forgotten, or can ever forget, the marks of good will and friendship with which you have always honored me, [1] and thus I earnestly request their continuation for me and my family, especially since they will be prevented from seeing me again for some time by my acceptance of a commission as major general in the Continental army. My silence has been due only to the long time it has taken the Congress to decide whether or not to employ the French officers who arrived with me, or at the same time as I did. When it finally decided to reject all those who do not speak the language of the country, I was uncertain whether I (practically the only one of my party) should accept or reject the rank offered to me by unanimous vote of Congress.[2] On the one hand, I was afraid of being reproached in France for not having shared the lot of those who returned home, and, on the other, of being accused of inconsistency for having made a long and difficult journey without having attained the object for which it was undertaken, when I could even serve with distinction because of the solicitations that were made for me. Thus I have made an agreement with the Congress, in writing, that I shall serve with the reservation that I may quit its service if my decision is disapproved in France, by either the ministers or my friends, or similarly if, because of some unpleasantness or other trouble, I should believe I had reason to return to France.[3] These conditions having been accepted,[4] and having been assured command of a division, I went to the army to see whether General Washington, or any of the American general officers whose interests might be adversely affected by my arrival, had any objection to make. I stayed there for three weeks, and, with the chief's assurance that my service could only be agreeable to the army, I collected my equipment, and I have just now rejoined the army in camp at Whitemarsh, thirteen miles from Philadelphia.

The Congress believed that my refusal of a commission at first derived from discontent with the preference shown to M. le Marquis de Lafayette, to whom they had given the rank of major general, without pay or command. They offered to antedate my commission relative to his, but I refused that provision and chose the same date (both are from July 31), so that it will be in my power to let him outrank me, since he was at the Battle of Brandywine, near Wilmington, at a time when they had not yet formally engaged me to stay here.[5] The friendship with which he has honored me since I made his acquaintance, and that which I have vowed to him because of his personal qualities, oblige me to have that deference for him. No one is more deserving than he of the consideration he enjoys here. He is a prodigy for his age; he is the model of valor, intelligence, judgment, good conduct, generosity, and zeal for the cause of liberty for this continent. His wound is healing very well. He has just rejoined the army, so as not to miss any chances for glory and danger. I have heard that his family was convinced that I had a part in his decision to come to America. I must vindicate myself from that imputation, if it really has been made, and I would be very glad to do it through you, if you have occasion to speak of it, or if the question is ever raised with the ministers or with you, sir. Therefore I would like to explain to you everything I know for certain about the matter.

M. le Vicomte de Noailles and M. le Marquis de Lafayette came to see me at the beginning of November 1776 (I had not had the honor of knowing them previously) to tell me that M. le Duc d'Ayen had agreed that both of them could offer their services to the Americans, through Mr. Deane, if they were made general officers. They also congratulated me about what they had heard of my arrangement with the American agent, and said they would take great pleasure in serving in the same army with me. They concluded by asking me to present them to Mr. Deane someday, and I promised to do so at their convenience. A few days later M. le Vicomte de Noailles wrote to tell me that he had given up the idea of going to America. M. le Marquis de Lafayette, on the contrary, came back several times, and I presented him to Mr. Deane and served as the interpreter for his proposal, always adding that M. le Duc d'Ayen desired and consented to it. We saw each other every day. He came to my home openly and without the least secrecy, and without suspicion I also went to see him at home, at the Hôtel de Noailles, where he had me admitted without difficulty, even when Mme de Lafayette was with him. Therefore I never had any reason to imagine that all his proceedings were made without the knowledge of his family. At the end of the same month of November he signed his agreement with Mr. Deane (it is true that I composed and wrote it down, at their request).[6] I left Paris on December 8 to embark at Le Havre. I said good-bye to M. de Lafayette, and he said, "Until we meet in America." When the ship was prevented from sailing, I returned to Paris, and for a time the voyage was out of the question. In February 1777 Mr. Deane again took up his plan of sending me off, and M. le Marquis de Lafayette, wishing to be included in the party and being too impatient to endure a long delay, proposed to equip a vessel at his own expense, which he did without my having the slightest part in the matter (because I also counted entirely upon the vessel that Mr. Deane wished to equip for me). He furnished [*illegible word*] which he filled with silver, and had it sent to Bordeaux.[7] He himself left for London with M. le Prince de Poix, to remain there until word arrived that his ship was ready to sail. I wrote to him about it in care of M. le Marquis de Noailles, ambassador to England, in accordance with the letters I had received from Bordeaux. On March 13 or 14 he returned to Paris, or rather to Chaillot (on the pretext of avoiding a scene of tenderness and distress with Mme de Lafayette), and we left together from my home (to which he came the same day, his carriage having been sent there two days before) on March 16, at noon.

I was utterly astounded when, upon our arrival at Bordeaux, he confessed to me that his departure, as well as his plan to serve in America, was unknown to his whole family, and that he was going to send a messenger to Paris to discover the effect produced by the letters he left to tell them about it. His messenger returned on the morning of the twenty-fifth with terrifying letters from his friends, about the anger of the king, and above all that of M. le Duc d'Ayen. My advice was to abandon his plan, return immediately to Paris, and leave his ship in the care of his outfitters. But all I could get him to do was put into another port, where he could receive confirmation of the royal orders that his friends had said were being issued. The port of

San Sebastián, in Spain, was convenient for that, and there he received a courier from M. le Comte de Fumel, commanding at Bordeaux, on account of which I persuaded him to yield to the orders of
His Majesty and the wishes of his family. He departed then, on the
express condition that I [would] not set sail again until I had heard
from him, because he was going to make every possible effort to obtain permission to depart. I could not refuse such a reasonable
request, especially since the vessel belonged to him. . . .[8] that they
tacitly approved of his enterprise, and we sailed forthwith, on April
20.

As for his financial affairs and expenses, I have involved myself in
them only to advise economy, and if at Charleston I endorsed letters
of exchange for 28,000 livres drawn on his agent at Paris, it was only
because otherwise he would not have been able to obtain any money,
owing to his age. M. Raimbaux's correspondent was not willing to advance it to him against the value of the cargo of his vessel before he
had a release from the shipping company in Bordeaux, in confor-
mance with an agreement between M. le Marquis and the latter. He
received all of it and disposed of it as he saw fit. Even though he was
rich, I wanted him to exercise more control over his generosity and
liberality. I have not failed to speak of this to him often. The few
purchases that he asked me to make for him, the cost of our trip from
Paris to Bordeaux, and of that from Charleston to Philadelphia,
together with the sums I have given him or paid for him on several
occasions, were computed and paid in a final account executed in
duplicate between us on September 1 last. He then owed me 388
livres, 18 sols in cash, for which he gave me a draft, payable upon
demand, against his business agent, and 30 piastres or dollars in
paper money, which he paid me. These details make my letter longer
than I would have wished, and I fear that they may bore you, but I
wanted you to know what my conduct was in this matter.

I shall not speak to you of the discontent that M. le Vicomte de
Mauroy, M. de Lesser of the Aunis Regiment, M. le Chevalier de
Fayolle of the Brie Regiment, and the others who are returning to
France may perhaps appear to feel because I have agreed to serve,
while no service has been offered to them, and they appear not to
have even cared about it.[9] Nevertheless, they cannot say that I have
not worked very hard to help them obtain reimbursement for their
expenses and the means for their return. Since some of them undoubtedly imagine that I have neglected their interests and thought
only of myself, and they may perhaps make some sort of complaint
against me to M. le Comte de Broglie, I have asked M. de Valfort of
the Aunis Regiment to tell everything he knows about that, and he

knows better than anyone what has occurred and what I have done. He is a man of honor and good sense who will gladly do me justice in that regard. I shall say no more about it, except that I have nothing with which to reproach myself.

I shall finish my letter by giving you some news about our war, including both successes and failures. . . .

L (*American Historical Review*, 15 [1910]:562–567), extract, translation. The letter was among the papers of the *Venus* prize, which were deposited in the Public Record Office, London, but the letter can no longer be found among the prize papers there.

1. Saint-Paul, as first secretary of the bureau of appointments, decorations, and pensions at the Ministry of War, had handled Kalb's requests for a regular military position after he returned from America in 1769.

2. September 15, 1777 (*JCC*, 8:746). No figures for the vote were recorded.

3. Kalb stated his terms in a letter of September 18 to Richard Henry Lee (Joseph R. Rosengarten, *The German Soldier in the Wars of the United States*, 2nd. ed. [Philadelphia, 1890], pp. 107–109). They included provisions for Dubuysson as Kalb's aide-de-camp and a request that Kalb's commission bear the same date as Lafayette's.

4. Congress accepted all of his terms except those relating to pensions for Kalb's family and to Dubuysson, which it rejected on the grounds that such provisions had not been made for other foreign officers (October 4 [*JCC*, 9:769]).

5. Congress apparently made the offer because Kalb had written to the president of Congress on August 1:

> What is deemed Genérosity in the Marquis de la Fayette would be downright madness in me, who am not one of the first rate fortunes, if I was in his circumstances I should perhaps have acted like him. I am heartily glad you granted his wishes, he is a worthy young man, and no one will outdo him for Enthusiasme in your cause of Liberty and independance. My Vows will be allways, that his Successes as a general officer may answer his zeal and your Expectations. But I must confess to you, Sir, that this distinction between him and me is painfull and very displeasing to me. We came on the Same Errant, with the Same promesses, and as military men, and for military purposes, I flatter myself, that preference, if there was to be any, was due to me; 34 years of constant attendance on Military Service, and my Station and rank in that way, may well be laid in the Scale with his disinterrestedness, and be at least of the Same Weight and value. Said distinction is very unaccountable in an infant State of a Commonwealth, but this is none of my Business, I want only to know whether Congress will agree me as a Major General and with the Seniority I have a right to expect, (for I cannot stay here in a lesser Capacity) it would look very odd, and I think very diverting to the French Ministry and to all old military men to see me under the Command of the Marquis de la Fayette. [DNA: RG 360, PCC 164, p. 308]

On September 15, Congress voted to date Kalb's commission from July 30, 1777, but that resolve was later crossed out of the record (*JCC*, 8:747).

6. The agreement with Deane, which is dated December 7, 1776.

7. The missing word is probably *bourse*, purse, or *caisse*, chest.

8. Ellipses in printed text. Kalb probably said much the same thing that he had said in his letter of April 17 to Deane: "The Marquis guessing, by all the letters he received, that the Ministers granted and issued orders to stop his sailing, out of mere compliance with the requests of M. Le Duc d'Ayens, and that in reality neither the King nor any body else could be angry with [him], for so noble an Enterprize, he took upon him to come here again and to pursue his measures."

9. Kalb dealt with this matter in a letter of November 2, 1777, to Broglie (Stevens, *Facsimiles*, no. 757). When Mauroy heard of Kalb's appointment, he accused Kalb and Congress of deliberately tricking him out of pressing his own claim to a major gen-

eralcy, but he specifically disclaimed such feelings about the other member of his party who had attained that rank: "All the World will know that the Marquis de Fayette whom no Body can reproach (unless with being a frenchman, and the sacrifices he has made to your interest), was retained in your service from political reasons only . . ." (Mauroy to Congress, November 1777 [DNA: RG 360, PCC 78, 15:279–282).

From Horatio Gates

                                                          Albany, November 12th. 1777

Dear General

In the Letter you have honoured me with, from Bethlehem, dated the 14th. Ult. you have expressed for the noble Cause you most disinterestedly engaged in, an attachment, which proves that the Wound you have received in its Defence, is truly honourable. Now, dear General, you may have some Idea of the Pleasure I felt, when I was informed your Cure was so far advanced as to promise you the Opportunity of soon testifying again, in the Field, the Sincerity of that Zeal.

I always Shall, as a principled Soldier, endeavour to Preserve your Esteem, and can but gratefully remember the valuable Offer you have tendered me of your Friendship. The Intercourse which I earnestly wish it may produce, not being likely to suffer the least Interruption from Wars, similar to those, by which the Individuals of different States are but too often divided, your kind Offer gives me the most agreeable Sensations.

It naturally leads me to observe the happy Situation of the present King of France, ever since he ascended the Throne. The deepest, as well as the Soundest Policy pointed out to him, to his Friends, and his Enemies, the prodigious Increase of Wealth, and relative Power, which, to his Kingdom, must be the Fruits of his Uprightness and Moderation, without enlarging his Territories by burthensome, envied, and precarious Acquisitions.

As soon as the British Parliament dismembered these vast Countries from their Empire, by absurdly declaring us to be no more under their Protection, all Europe saw, with impotent Jealousy, that France could, whenever she should think fit, reduce the most powerful, and the most dangerous of her Rivals to the Class of Secondary Powers. The unsullied Reputation of her young King, inspiring the United States with Confidence in him, his natural Enemies who now are ours, cannot succeed in thwarting his success, by raising in us that Spirit of Distrust, which cannot fail to attend our Negotiations with every Prince of ruined, or even an equivocal Character. May he wisely per-

Horatio Gates, president of the Board of War, whose reputation as the victor at Saratoga was sullied by the rumors of the Conway Cabal

sue his truest Interest! May an indissoluble Alliance between him and the American Commonwealth, be grounded on the Certainty of reciprocal Advantages, and Safety! And, may it be soon manifested to the World!

I have the Honour to be, with the purest Esteem, Dear General Your most obedient and most humble Servant

H. G.

L (NHi: Gates Papers, Box 19), in secretary's hand.

To Henry Laurens

Head quarters 18 november 1777

Dear Sir

It is now to the President of Congress as well as to a friend of mine that I have two rights of being troublesome for my own, and sometimes for strangers businesses. My sentiments upon your election are as follows—it will engage you in infinite, difficult, tedious, occupations, on the other side I think that Congress pay'd to you a düe and convenient mark of his Consideration, I think too that the advantage of justice, equity, public interest is much concerned in such a choice— therefore if compliments are to be done 'tis not to the niew president.[1]

As being honour'd with the name of french, I consider it my duty, to reccommend you every honest contryman of mine, when desired. Mr. de la Balme the late inspector of our cavalry told me that he intends to apply to Congress for a certain sum of monney which is ackowledged belonging to him, but is to be pay'd in paper currency, when expensed in hard monney. I assured him that he would find in you and Congress all the justice he could wish, and in same time it was impossible (too in such a case it must be useless) to refuse mentionning his name to you.[2]

I told very long ago to Mr. Lovell, that a french officer belonging to me, and (according to the american expression) to my family, was left in Salsbury North Carolina, and detained there by Sikness. I desired Mr. Lovell to send him (on my account if he judged it to be better) every supplie of monney he could want. I desired him to facilitate by the same occasion the carrying some baggage left in the same place. I have been answered very politely that every proper measures were taken and for the trunks and for the officer whom I prevented being

inclosed in the general late arrangement for sending back all the Gentelemen of the french army arrived with me. As I have seen just now a
letter from the same Mr. Capitaine dated Salsbury the 28 october
Where he seems very much concerned to be left by me since five
months in a inn at a very great expense and therefore engaged in
many debts, without receiving any order, and any direction, I incline
to believe that some thing was misunderstood in it.[3]

You know, Sir, that Mr. de Conway is going home—as that gentleman is well acquainted with our wants of every kind I mean cloathes
&c. I mean principally cartrige boxes that so very interessant part of
military drest, which seems here more done to receive than to prevent
raining in, if in short his care could be of some use to us, I think that I
schould know it before his departure from Reading. Mr. Connway
will do great many things for Congress itself, but however as we'l
meet again together in France I would do some for me.[4] I have seen
with great pleasure the Baron de Kalb in the army, and am fully convinced of his being useful to our cause.

You heard as soon almost as myself of all the interesting niews on
the Delaware. The gallant defense of our forts deserves praises—
praise and her daughter emulation are the necessary attendants of an
army. I am told that Major Fleury and Captain du Plessis have done
theyr duty. It is a pleasant enjoyement for my mind, when some frenchmen behave *à la francoise*, and I can assure you that everyone who in
the defense of our noble cause will show himself worthy of his
country shall be mentionned in the most high terms to the king,
ministry, and my friends of France when I'l be back in my natal air.

If I had not in execration that kind of men who are alwaïs complaining what was neglected, without thinking of what is now to be
done, I schould express you my being surprised, that when so many
ingeniers or self thinking ingeniers were disputing theyr ranks in
Philadelphia, none of them has been employed with succes to fortify
again that so important passage in the river.[5] I fancy that Colonel Por-
tal is now brigadier general, and for my being very sensible of his
merit, moderation, and honest mind, I'l be very glad to see him enabled to be more useful yet than he could have been before.

I hear from every where strong rumours of war betwen France and
England. How many reasons I have to wish it of all my heart, it would
be too long to explain—but my known in the whole world love of your
cause, my warm patriotism, my Sentiments *very warm too* against the
english pride, all can answer for my good warlike intentions. What
disappoints me to the last degree is the unhappy ignorance where I
live in of all my friends, connexions in France, of all what can be
dearest to my heart, when I am sure that some of 'em don't miss a

single day without wraïting some lines to me. As soon as I'l receive
some important intelligence, it shall be laid immediately before Congress. How I am sincerely and warmly concerned in the cause of liberty, how I'l employ every exertion in my power to serve your interests, it will be known as far as your confidence will intrust me with the
occasions of showing the feeble dispositions or talents which nature or
art gave me in a way where I dare say that I have some hopes to succeed.

Thoug I am near a very hot fire, however as my eyes fall in this
moment upon three poor quite nacked fellows, it congeels my blood
and obliges me to tell you again how happy I would be if our army
was drest in a confortable manner. That army is not a very strong
one—great many losses, and fiew recruits—indeed, Sir, I wish heartly
that some changements in raising militia could help our inlisting continental soldiers—if the sixht part of that american militia was under
our command and discipline. . . .[6]

Mr. de la Balme is the bearer of my letter—his little fortune does
not en[able him] to make sacrifices. I beg your pardon for so long a
letter and I am, with the most tender affection and highest esteem
Dear Sir Your most obedient servant

THE MIS. DE LAFAYETTE

I received a letter from Mr. de Valfort to let me know all his obligations towards you. Tho' you do'nt permit me any thanks of all your
kindness, I ca'nt help joining my aknowledgment to this of the poor
colonel; I would be on the french shore to see the majestous and fine
Randolph arriving in the harbour, and followed I hope by good many
glorious prizes.[7]

ALS (ScHi: Henry Laurens Papers).
1. Laurens had been elected on November 1 (*JCC*, 9:854).
2. Augustin Mottin de La Balme had resigned his position as inspector of the Cavalry rather than serve under the orders of Pulaski (La Balme to Congress, October 3
[DNA: RG 360, PCC 41, p. 142]). Congress had already accepted La Balme's resignation and agreed to pay his expenses in a combination of American and French money
when Lafayette wrote to Laurens (*JCC*, 9:797, 864, 878; and La Balme to Congress,
November 5 [DNA: RG 360, PCC 78, 7:143]). The settlement apparently satisfied La
Balme, because his next letter to Congress dealt only with his proposal for an expedition to Canada (December 5 [ibid., p. 145]).
3. Capitaine's letter not found. See Laurens to Lafayette, January 25, 1778.
4. On November 14 Conway had returned his commission to Congress with the explanation that he could not serve as a subordinate to either Kalb or the Chevalier de
Preudhomme de Borre, because both were his inferiors in the French army (Conway to
Charles Carroll or the secretary of Congress [DNA: RG 360, PCC 159, pp. 461–468]).
His letter was read in Congress on November 24 and referred to the Board of War
(*JCC*, 9:958). There is nothing in Conway's letter to Congress about aiding the American cause in France; Lafayette apparently refers to the proposed attack on the British
colonies in the Indian Ocean, which he had discussed with Conway.

5. Lafayette refers to the dispute between Du Coudray and the four French engineers (described by Dubuysson, Memoir, pp. 77, 79) and the passage in the Delaware River which the fall of Fort Mifflin (November 15) had opened to the British.

6. Lafayette's ellipses.

7. Valfort had sailed from Charleston on the *Randolph,* which reached L'Orient in December (Stormont to Weymouth, December 25, 1777, in Stevens, *Facsimiles,* no. 1799).

To Henry Laurens

the 20 november [1777] head quarters

Dear Sir

His excellency wrote to Congress some days ago in order to reccommend Mr. de Vrigny, actually Major in the french service, who desires to be employed in this with the rank of Lieutenant colonel. After General Washington's speacking for him, any thing from me can be but very weak and even very useless. However I think it my duty, as well as becoming to desire of seeing him employed to let you know, Sir, how interesting it seems to me to have that officer in our cavalry—a good officer of horse is not a short matter to be formed—Mr. de Vrigny enjoyed a fine militar reputation in a corps much reputed itself in our army last war. His kind of duty had a great likeness with this of our light dragoons, and Gral. Pulaski well convinced how such a man could be useful and to himself and to the advantage of the service expressed me the greatest desire of his being employed and in expecting an answer from Congress took him at his quarters.[1]

I gave you by my last the trouble of sending some supplies to that poor fellow who expects from me since five months.[2] As Congress has been kind enough as to except him from the general arrangement I am not in any doubt about his getting a commission in my family.

I am just now going from this place with a detachement under Mjor. Gral. Greene.[3] I hope my wound w'ont be much hurted. I shall never reproach myself loosing any occasion of doing some thing, as far as it can be for my present situation, or to speak better the inaction I am in. With the greatest affection and esteem I am till the last moment of my life Dear Sir Your most obedient servant

THE MIS. DE LAFAYETTE

ALS (ScHi: Henry Laurens Papers).

1. See Washington to Congress and Lafayette's recommendation for Vrigny, November 1. Vrigny did not get a commission at this time.

2. Capitaine (see Laurens to Lafayette, January 25, 1778).

3. Greene had been ordered to cross the Delaware at Bristol to deal with Cornwallis if he attempted to sweep through New Jersey.

To George Washington

Dear General

I went down to this place since the day before yesterday in order to be acquainted of all the roads and ground arround the ennemy. I heard at my arrival that theyr main body was betwen Great and Little Timber Creek since the same evening. Yesterday morning in recconnoitring about I have been told that they were very busy in crossing the Delaware. I saw them myself in theyr boats and sent that intelligence to General Greene as soon as possible as every other thing I heard of—but I want to acquaint your excellency of a little event of last evening which tho' not very considerable in itself will certainly please you on the account of the bravery and alacrity a small party of ours showed in that occasion. After having spent the most part of the day to make myself vell acquainted with the certainty of theyr motions I came pretty late into the Glocester road betwen the two creeks. I had ten light horse with Mr. Lindsey, almost hundred an fifty riflemen under Colonel Buttler, and two piquets of the militia commanded by the Colonel Hite and Ellis. My whole body was not three hundred. The Colonel Armand, Colonel Laumoy, the Chevaliers du Plessis and Gimat were the frenchmen who went with me. A scout of my men with whom was Mr. du Plessis to see how near were the first piquets from Glocester found at two miles and a half of it a strong post of three hundred and fifty hessians with field pieces (what number I did know by the unanimous deposition of theyr prisoners) and engaged immediately—as my little recconnoitring party was all in fine spirits I supported them—we pushed the hessians more than an half mile from the place were was theyr main body, and we made them run very fast. British reinforcements came twice to them but very far from recovering theyr ground they went alwaïs back. The darkness of the night prevented us then to push that advantage, and after standing upon the ground we had got I ordered them to return very slow to Haddonfield—the ennemy knowing perhaps by our drums that we were not so near came again to fire at us—but the brave Major Moriss with a part of his riflemen sent them back and pushed them very fast. I understand that they have had betwen twenty five and thirty wounded, at least that number killed amonghs whom I am certain is an officer some say more, and the prisoners told me that the[y] have lost the commandant of that body. We got yet this day fourteen prisoners. I send you the most moderate account I had from themselves. We left one single man killed a lieutenant of militia and only five of ours were wounded. Colonel Armand's, Chevalier du Plessis's and Major Brice's horses have been wounded. Such is the account of our little entertainement, which is indeed much too long for the matter, but I take the greatest pleasure to let you know that the conduct of our soldiers is above all praises. I never saw men so merry, so spirited, so desirous to go on to the ennemy what ever forces they could have as that little party was in this little fight. I found the riflemen above even theyr reputation and the militia above all expectations I could have. I returned to them my very sincere thanks this morning. I wish *that this little succès of ours* may please you—tho' a very trifling one I find him [it] very interesting on account of the behaviour of our soldiers.

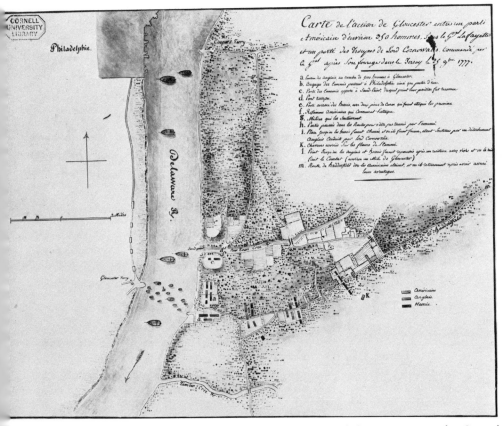

Map of the engagement at Gloucester between an American party of about 350 men under General Lafayette and a party of Lord Cornwallis's troops foraging in New Jersey, November 25, 1777"

Some time after I came back Gral. Varnum arrived here. General Greene is too in this place since this morning. He engaged me to give you myself the account of that little advantage of that small part of the troops under his command. I have nothing more to say to your excellency about our businesses on this side because he is wraïting himself.[1] I should have been very glad if the circumstances had permitted me to be useful to him upon a greater scale. As he is obliged to march slow in order to attend his troops, and as I am here only a volonteer, I'l have the honor to waït on your excellency as soon as possible, and I'l set out to day. It will be a great pleasure for me to find myself again with you. With the most tender affection and highest respect I have the honor to be, dear general, Your excellency's the most obedient humble servant

⟨THE MIS. DE⟩ LAFAYETTE

I must tell too that the riflemen had been the whole day running before my horse without eating or taking any rest.

I have just now a certain assurance that two british officers besides those I spocke you of have died this morning of theyr wounds in an house. This and some other circumstances let me believe that theyr loss may be greater than I told to your excellency.[2]

ALS (PEL: Hubbard Collection). The manuscript has been edited, in ink, in Lafayette's later hand. The text of significant deletions has been restored in angle brackets.

1. See Washington to the president of Congress, November 26, which includes an excerpt from Greene's letter.

2. On November 27 John Laurens wrote to his father that Lafayette's men "kill'd 20, wounded about as many and took 14 prisoners . . . having lost only two men kill'd and three or four wounded" (*Correspondence of John Laurens*, p. 87). In a letter of November 29 he told his father: "It appears that two British captains were kill'd and two wounded in the Marquis de la Fayette's combat" (ibid., p. 89).

George Washington to the President of Congress[E]

Head Quarters Nov. 26th. 1777

. . . I must take the liberty to request the decision of Congress . . . respecting the Marquis de la Fayette. He is more & more solicitous to be in actual service, & is pressing in his applications for a Command. I ventured before to submit my Sentiments upon the measure, and I still fear a refusal will not only induce him to return in disgust but may involve some unfavorable consequences.[1] There are now some vacant Divisions in the Army, to one of which he may be appointed, if it should be the pleasure of Congress. I am convinced he possesses a large share of that Military ardor which generally characterizes the Nobility of his Country. He went to Jersey with Genl. Greene, and I find he has not been inactive there. This you will perceive by the following Extract from a letter just received from Genl. Greene. "The Marquis with about 400 Militia & the Rifle Corps, attacked the Enemies Picket last Evening—killed about 20—wounded many more & took about 20 Prisoners. The Marquis is charmed with the spirited behavior of the Militia and Rifle Corps. They drove the Enemy about half a mile and kept the ground untill dark. The Enemys Picket consisted of about 300 and were reinforced during the skirmish. The Marquis is determined to be in the way of danger." [2]

LS (DNA: RG 360, PCC 152, 5:224–225), in Robert Harrison's hand, extract. Read in Congress on December 1.
1. Washington to Congress, November 1.
2. Extract from Greene to Washington, November 26, in George W. Greene, *Life of Major-General Nathanael Greene* (New York, 1871), 1:527–528. Washington's last two sentences and the excerpt from Greene's letter were published by order of Congress (e.g., *The Independent Chronicle and Universal Advertiser* [Boston], January 1, 1778). Another account of the engagement appeared in the *New-Jersey Gazette* [Burlington], December 5, 1777, p. 3.

To Richard Butler

                                         Head Quarters the 29 November 1777
Dear Sir
    It is with the greatest pleasure that I follow his excellency's order, in acquainting you that he desires his thanks should be made to the Officers and soldiers of the brave detachment of riflemen under your's and Major Moriss' command. The general is very sensible of the alacrity and gallant conduct they showed the 25th. instant in having attacked and repulsed with a great loss an enemy much superior in number and force. I congratulate you and them, Sir, for having so well deserved his approbation. With the greatest affection and esteem I have the honor to be, dear Sir your most obedient servt.
                                         THE MARQUIS DE LAFAYETTE (MG)

My compliments if you please to Colonel Morgan and Major Moriss.

L (*Pennsylvania Magazine,* 14 [1890]:83).

To Henry Laurens

White Marsh the 29 november 1777

Dear Sir

How I am obliged to you for the charming parcell of letters I received yesterday.[1] All the feeling of Your heart will certainly convince you if you remember in this moment every thing, every body, love or friendship has ever given your soul an attachement for. I found there that my friends of all age and sex were in very good health the 14 july. I found that they keep the remembrance I can wish, of that man who is called in France the american entousiast. I found also that I was lately father of a female child—but nothing about war, and indeed the date is too old for any good niews of that kind.[2] I received your's some days ago with the greatest pleasure, and all your intelligences seem to me so strong that I have no more any doubt or at least very light ones about France being ready to over power proud England under the superiority of her arms.[3] I'l be much obliged to you if you are so good as to let me know every niews you'l hear from my country.

The bearer of my letter is Mr. de Fleury who was in Fort Miflin, and as he is reccommanded by his excellency I have nothing more to say but that I am very sensible of his good conduct.[4]

I'l be much obliged to you if you let me know when I can wrait to France. I chuse rather to put my letters in pacquets going from Congress by *paquet boats* than to send them on board of merchant schips even of armed ones—those pacquet boats arrive always very fast and very safe. As I fancy that some of them will go of very soon I wish to know when I must send my pacquets. Amongs the other letters I'l inclose one for the first minister where I shall acquaint him that General Bourgoïgne is going over to England.[5] If war was not declared that advice would be perhaps an inducement to begin real hostilities. I wishoud you would be so good as to tell me what you think about Bourgoïgne's embarkation and where vessels of transport and provisions will come from.

His excellency has been pleased to let you know a very small engagement on the other side of Delaware. Tho' it is very trifling in itself, tho' no kind of merit at all can be on the account of the general officer who was by chance with them, however I have had the greatest pleasure to see by my own eyes with what bravery and alacrity a little

recconnoitring party of less than three hundred men the half militia
has repulsed very far with a great loss a body of 350 hessians with
field pieces, nowisttanding two british reinforcements and strong ones
(for two english captains have been killed there). General Greene who
arrives just now acquaints me that besides those above mentionned
captains and the killed hessian officer, two captains of the same nation
have been wounded—therefore I hope theyr loss greater than I
thaught. I was there nothing almost but a witeness, but I was a very
pleased one in seeing the behaviour of our men.

Mr. de Fleury receives just now the commission of lieutenant colonel, I think he wo'nt go to day to Congress, and I send this letter by
one other occasion—with the most tender sentiments of an eternal affection I have the honor to be Dear Sir Your most obedient servant

THE MQUIS. DE LAFAYETTE

All the letters I receive from frenchmen are full of theyr gratefulness
for your own particular kindness towards them. Will you be so good
as to accept my thanks for them and for myself, and to join here my
sincere ones on account of the appointement of Mr. de la Colombe? [6]
My compliments, if you please to Mr. Richard Henry Lee, Mr. Moriss
and the other gentelemen of my acquaintance.

ALS (ScHi: Henry Laurens Papers).
1. Laurens's letter book (ibid.) contains a note saying that he had written to Lafayette
on November 21, and again on November 22, when he forwarded letters from France.
None of the letters, from Laurens or from France, have been found. The packet from
France probably included the letter from the Maréchal de Noailles mentioned in Lafayette to the Duc d'Ayen, December 16. It probably also contained letters from the
Maréchal de Mouchy (July 6), from Leonard Lafitte (July 3), and two letters from the
Prince de Poix (one of which was dated July 14). Duplicates of these four letters,
together with two more from Lafitte to Lafayette (July 30 and August 3), and one from
Lafitte to Randall and Sons of Philadelphia (August 8, asking them to serve as Lafayette's bankers), were sent on a ship that was taken by the British, and they were read
by King George himself. The letters were deposited in the Home Office Admiralty
Series at the Public Record Office; that series has been reclassified, and the letters can
no longer be found. They are summarized in DLC: Benjamin F. Stevens, Catalogue
Index of Manuscripts in the Archives of England, France, Holland and Spain Relating
to America, 1763 to 1783, Chronological Index, vols. 46–47.
2. Anastasie, Lafayette's second child, was born on July 1.
3. Probably Laurens to Lafayette, November 21, not found.
4. Fleury had been promoted on November 26.
5. Lafayette to Maurepas, not found.
6. Lafayette had renewed his solicitations in La Colombe's behalf in a letter of October 27 to Laurens (ScHi: Henry Laurens Papers). On November 15 Congress adopted
the recommendation of the Committee on Foreign Applications, that "the Chevalier de
la Colombe . . . may be usefully employed in the quality of captain in the family of the
Marquis during his service in the American service" (JCC 9:930–931).

To [Denis Du Bouchet][T]

> In camp at Whitemarsh
> December 1 [1777]

I am very sorry, sir, that your health obliges you to leave us; it is always very pleasant to find oneself in a foreign country with compatriots who conduct themselves there as you do. You may rely upon it that I add a very personal interest to this general sentiment; I have learned with great pleasure how well you were liked and esteemed in the army in which you served, and I assure you that I would have been delighted to wage a campaign in it with you.[1] I cannot take advantage of your gracious offer to carry my letters to France; we shall, unfortunately, have an earlier occasion with M. de Conway, whom, I fear, we are about to lose for good. I expect to hear from him any day now. I recall with great pleasure, sir, having been at school with your brother, and I pray you will give him my warmest regards when you see him. I truly hope you will not be taken at sea, but in case of mishap you must remember that you have many friends in General Washington's army who are very much disposed to serve you. I hope you will have no doubts about the sincere attachment with which I have the honor to be, sir, your very humble and obedient servant

> THE MQUIS. DE LAFAYETTE

Please give my affectionate regards to General Gates. Also tell Generals Arnold and Lincoln how eager I am to make their acquaintance.

ALS (PEL: American Friends of Lafayette Collection), translation.
1. Du Bouchet was Conway's brother-in-law. Gates had used his authority as commander in chief of the northern army to promote Du Bouchet to major in recognition of his distinguished service and his notable bravery at Saratoga (Gates's certificate, December 8, 1777, in Lasseray, *Français*, 1:264). Congress approved the promotion on January 1, at the same time that it accepted Du Bouchet's resignation for reasons of health and agreed to pay his passage to France (*JCC*, 10:8–9).

Memorandum on Winter Quarters

> [Whitemarsh, December 1, 1777]

Your excellency ordered me to give my opinion about these three places for winter quarters 1° the chain from about the Schulchill till

Betheleem—2° this from Reading to Lancaster 3° building hutts about and quartering in Willmington.[1]

I must confess My being prevented of fixing my Sentiments in a decicise manner by my want of knowledge about very interesting points amongs them as

1° How far we should distress and perhaps disaffect those persons who schould be turned out from the diferents places they are in.

2° How far we may expect to collect and keep with the army all the officers who perhaps will think themselves intitled to go home, to occupate themselves with theyr businesses or pleasures if we are not in a kind of warlike quarters, and then we will loose the same advantage of theyr being instructed and disciplined we schould endeavour to gain in going into peaceful places.

3° What effect can it make upon the people our leaving the country entirely oppened to the excursions, cruelties and also to the seductions of the ennemy, when we schall give them all the opportunities they can wish to draw all the provisions from every where and in the same time to inlist provincial soldiers.

4° If our giving a greater idea of the army in covering the country and laying near the ennemy will more facilitate our making recruits than if we were in good confortables towns and not in a place and in a manner, which will seem to the eyes of people a kind of winter campaigne.

5° Till what point those different measures will please or distress the officers and (what is generally in the militar world the less attended to, and deserves the greater attention) our private soldiers.

6° Till what point we may depend upon our intelligences and light troops to avoid equally and being surprised and tiring the troops by false alarms.

7° If we can hope that the soldiers will now receive cloathes &c. in order to be fit for some winter marches and operations, if in case where they schould be defeated we may hope to meet them again.

Such are the points of knowledge which I am deprived of by my being stranger in this country, and my being stranger in the army, if I can speak so, for I have no officers no soldiers under my particular direction whom I could consult and know theyr temper, theyr inclinations, and all what it is possible to expect from them.

However I'l tell to your excellency my very imperfect sentiments about the matter

1st. The first proposition seems to me the less eligible, and my reason for it is the scarcity of villages and principally the report of the commissaires and other gentelemen who know the country.

2° The second seems to me the most prudent. There we schall be quiete, there we can discipline and instruct our troops, we can be able to begin a early campaign, and we shall not fear to be carried into a winter campaign if it pleases General Howe. Therefore in consulting only prudence, and as far as my little knowledge can go, I am at less certain that I'l have nothing to reproach to me in giving my choice to this second proposition.

However (and in making excuses to your excellency for such an indecision and refering myself to your knowledge about the suppositions I will make) if it was not distressing neither for officers neither for soldiers, if going to Lancaster &c. will disaffect and make a bad impression as far as to prevent our recruiting, if we can keep better our officers when we schall be in a kind of encampement near the ennemy, if principally you think that we schould be fit for some winter march's we should be able to support some disadventages then I am fully and with a great chearfulness of opinion that we must go to Willmington. My reasons would be then

1° This position enable us to do in the course of the winter what we shall think proper to annoy, to deprive of rcsources of every kind, to attack if possible the ennemy.

2° This position has something shining and military like which will make the best effect and upon the continent and even in Europe.

3° The doctors, and american ones who know the manners and phisik constitution of our soldiers say that nothing is so confortable as well made hutts.[2]

Prudence orders me to choose Lancaster but if the inconveniences I fear (without being able to know them) if those inconveniences I explain to your excellency are not as strong as they can be, if principally our present civil situation ask from us some thing shining and perhaps bold then I give all my wishes and all my choice to Willmington.

THE MQUIS. DE LAFAYETTE, M.G.

AMS (DLC: George Washington Papers, Series 4). Received by Washington on December 1.

A council of general officers was held on November 30 to discuss three alternate locations for winter quarters. No decision was reached, and Washington asked each of the officers to submit a written opinion. Their replies are in Ford, "Defences of Philadelphia," 20:228–247, 391–403.

1. The first proposal was to find a site in Tredyffrin township of Chester County, in the "Great Valley." Valley Forge is in that township. The second proposal was to quarter the troops in Reading, Lancaster, and the towns between them. The third site was Wilmington, Delaware.

2. General Sullivan questioned the advisability of quartering the troops in huts: "One great objection to Hutts is that they are exceedingly unhealthy and are at Best but a miserable Shelter from the Inclemency of the weather. The mortality among the Hessians at Brunswick Last Spring as well as common observation will justify this assertion" (Ford, "Defences of Philadelphia," 20:229).

The President of Congress to George Washington[E]

York 1st. Decemr. 77

Sir

. . . I am also ordered to Signify to Your Excellency it is highly agreeable to Congress that the Marquis de Lafayette be appointed to the Command of a division in the American Army. Your Excellency will find a minute from the Journal of Congress on these points here inclosed.[1] I hasten this forward in order to transmit at the Same time the following intelligence deliverd to me by the Board of War. This I am persuaded will afford your Excellency a particular degree of pleasure & the account may have some good influence in the approaching conference between Your Excellency & the Committee deputed by Congress.[2]

LbC (DNA: RG 360, PCC 13, 1:52), extract.

1. Henry Laurens had written to his son John on November 30: "Several Members of Congress who have called here this Morning to read Gen. Washington's Letter of the 26th. have expressed their wishes that the Marquis may be appointed to the Command of a division, therefore I have no doubt when the Letter is Read and the subject considered to morrow in Congress, I shall be charged with a Resolve equal to the Marquis's wishes . . ." (Burnett, *Letters of Congress*, 2:577 and note). On December 1, Congress "Resolved, That Genl. Washington be informed, it is highly agreeable to Congress that the Marquis de la Fayette be appointed to the command of a division in the continental army" (*JCC*, 9:982–983). Washington announced the appointment in the General Orders for December 4: "Major General, The Marquis La Fayette is to take the command of the division lately commanded by General Stephen" (Fitzpatrick, *Writings of Washington*, 10:138).

2. Congress had resolved on November 28 to send a committee of three "to repair to the army, and, in a private confidential consultation with General Washington, to consider of the best and most practicable means for carrying on a winter's campaign with vigour and success, an object which Congress have much at heart, and on such consultation, with the concurrence of General Washington, to direct every measure which circumstances may require for promoting public service" (*JCC*, 9:972). Robert Morris, Elbridge Gerry, and Joseph Jones were chosen for the committee.

PART III

VALLEY FORGE

December 3, 1777–January 22, 1778

> It would be a too great pity that slavery, dishonor, ruin, and un-
> happiness of a whole world schould issue from trifling differents
> betwixt some fiew men.
>
> To George Washington, December 30, 1777

In December 1777 and January 1778 the remnants of the Continental army settled in their winter quarters at Valley Forge while the
Continental Congress adjusted to its new quarters across the Susquehanna in the small town of York, some sixty miles to the west.

The loss of Philadelphia and the lack of a striking success at Germantown, contrasted with the victory at Saratoga, naturally led many
in Congress to compare the generalship of Washington and Gates, to
Washington's disadvantage. The Congress continued to send committees of conference and members of the reconstituted Board of War to
Valley Forge with the intention of rectifying discipline, proposing new
means of obtaining supplies, and suggesting new military actions
aimed at retaking Philadelphia. The commissary and quartermaster
departments had been ineffectual for months and were to remain that
way for some time; in addition, the army was destitute of both the
training and the numbers necessary for any action beyond a desperate
defense if it was attacked by Howe's forces.

Notwithstanding a universal disdain for "party" and "faction," there
was partisanship in both the army and the Congress. The best example of it in this period was the ill-conceived, inchoate wish or design to replace Washington as commander in chief which historians
have called the "Conway Cabal." The cabal is misnamed, for Conway
was guilty chiefly of making critical remarks in letters that came to
Washington's attention, and Conway's sentiments were echoed by
some members of Congress, who re-created the Board of War with
Gates as president. Washington was prevented from making a public
defense of his position because that would have revealed the weakness
of his forces to both the British and the American public, but he did
respond firmly and powerfully, in letters to Conway, Gates, and the

Congress, to the gossip that made up much of the cabal. For the rest, his own ardent partisans (Lafayette is typical) made sure that he had their vocal support; any plan to replace Washington was snuffed out before it really got started. At the same time, the unity and morale of his officers who remained at Valley Forge was strengthened by their successful resistance to the cabal, as well as by their common sufferings and the good cheer with which they endured that terrible winter together.

The letters in Part III cover the first weeks after Lafayette received his long-coveted command. They illustrate both his constant concern for his troops' welfare and his new-found caution about risking his soldiers in rash enterprises. In addition to expressing these basic concerns, Lafayette continued to importune all and sundry to provide positions for his compatriots, and he became deeply involved with both the president of the Continental Congress and his own commander in chief in the debate over Washington's position vis-à-vis Gates and Conway.

When the brigadier generals protested to Congress the elevation of Conway to major general in December, it is remarkable that they specifically exempted Lafayette from their strictures about the appointment of general officers without regard for seniority. Despite his lack of experience and his close relationship with Washington, Lafayette never seemed to be the object of jealousy among his fellow officers. Perhaps his letter to the Duc d'Ayen on December 16, with its frank avowals of his loyalties, his motives, and his actions, gives us the clearest view of the man after his first six months in America, and explains in part why his fellow officers considered Lafayette a friend as well as an asset to the American cause.

Memoir of *1779* (continued)^T

Since it took Cornwallis only a few hours to join forces with Howe, and it required several marches for Greene to join Washington, one wonders why General Howe gave him the time to get there, and did not move his army to Chestnut Hill, three miles from Whitemarsh, until December fifth.[1] After testing the right wing, which overawed him, Howe threatened the extreme left, and that wing, following his movement, spread itself out along the brow of the hill. Several shots were exchanged between the British soldiers and the Riflemen—skillful marksmen from the untamed frontier. Since he could not attack that position, or easily outflank it, Howe returned to Philadelphia on the fourth day.[2] Despite the reinforcements from the north, the Americans were reduced to nine thousand, and the lateness of the season accelerated the depletion of their forces. The protection of the country had cost the army dearly. On December 15 the army finally marched toward Swede's Ford, where by chance Lord Cornwallis was foraging on the other bank of the river. M. de Lafayette, the major general of the day, was reconnoitering a position when his escort and the enemy opened fire on each other.[3] The uncertainty was mutual, and Lord Cornwallis and General Washington both halted their march. The British withdrew during the night, and the American army crossed the Schuylkill and entrenched itself in a camp at Valley Forge, twenty-two miles from Philadelphia.[4] By skillfully arranging the trunks of small trees, they built a town of wood there in a few days,[5] and the whole army settled into its melancholy winter quarters. A small unit, under Brigadier Smallwood, was detached to Wilmington, where it fortified itself.

Despite the victory in the north, the American situation was never more critical. Its paper money, which had no solid foundation and was not supplemented by any specie, was counterfeited by the enemy and discredited by their partisans. The Americans were afraid to establish taxes and had still less power to collect them. Since the people had revolted against English taxes, they were astonished to have to pay even more now, and the government lacked the power to force them to pay. On the other hand, New York and Philadelphia overflowed with gold and merchandise, and the threat of a death penalty could not stop such easy trading. By refusing to pay taxes, depreciating the paper money, and feeding the enemy, one could easily make a fortune. Misery and privations fell only upon good citizens. Each English proclamation was sustained by the seductions, wealth, and plotting of the Tories.

While a large garrison lived sumptuously in New York, a few hundred men, poorly dressed and poorly nourished, camped along the Hudson.[6] Newly recruited in Europe and abundantly furnished with everything, the army of Philadelphia numbered 18,000 men; that of Valley Forge was successively reduced to 5000, and a two-day march along the fine Lancaster road, where the line of storehouses was located, would have placed the British behind our right flank, rendered our position untenable, and left us with no way out. The unfortunate American soldiers lacked everything—coats, hats, shirts, and shoes. Their feet and legs turned black with frostbite, and often had to be amputated. For lack of money, they had neither food nor means of transportation. The colonels were always reduced to two rations, and sometimes to one. The army lacked provisions for entire days, and the patient virtue of the officers and men was a continuous miracle, constantly renewed.

But the sight of their misery halted enlistments. It became almost impossible to recruit, and it was easy to desert into the countryside. The sacred fire of liberty still burned, and the majority of citizens abhorred British tyranny, but the victory in the north and the tranquillity in the south had put two-thirds of the country to sleep. The rest of it was harassed by two armies, and the greatest difficulty in this revolution was always that, in order to hide weaknesses from the enemy, it was necessary to hide them from the people. If the latter had been awakened to the truth of the situation, the former would have learned it also and would have struck a mortal blow before a slow-moving democracy could provide the remedy. Because of this, the strength of the American army was always kept a deep secret, even from Congress, and the generals themselves were often deceived. General Washington's confidence in other people always had limits, but for M. de Lafayette it had no bounds, because it came from the heart. As the situation grew more critical, discipline became more essential. In the course of his nocturnal rounds in the deep snow, M. de Lafayette had some negligent officers broken to the ranks. In his dress, his food, and his habits he adopted American customs, but he was even more simple, frugal, and austere than anyone else. He had been raised in a genteel fashion, but now he suddenly changed his whole way of living, and his temperament became adapted to privation and fatigue. ⟨In all matters⟩ he had maintained his right to communicate freely with Congress. He sometimes imitated the prudence of the general, however, and stated his opinion to a few members of that body, or to a state assembly, so that it could be adopted by them and thus submitted to the Congress.

In addition to the difficulties already described, which lasted throughout the war, the winter at Valley Forge brings to mind other troubles that are even more distressing. At York, beyond the Susquehanna, the Congress was divided into two factions that, despite their designations as *the east* and *the south*, actually divided the representatives of states in both parts of the country. The representatives substituted their private intrigues for the wishes of their fellow citizens. Many impartial men had withdrawn, and some states had no representatives there, or only one. The factional spirit was so great that the effects of it were still felt in Congress three years later. An important issue reawakened their patriotism, however; when Burgoyne declared that the terms of his surrender had been broken, they were wise enough to prevent the departure of his troops, since everything—for instance, the small quantity of provisions for the transports—clumsily betrayed his true intention.[7] But the worst result of these divisions in Congress would have been the loss of the only man capable of conducting the revolution.

⟨Intoxicated by his victory,⟩ Gates was at York, and ⟨the old general⟩ made a great impression on the Congress because of his manner, his promises, and his European expertise. Among the representatives who supported him one may distinguish the Lees, who were Virginians and enemies of Washington, and the two Adamses ⟨who were rigid republicans, but more capable of destroying than preserving the republic⟩. Mifflin, the quartermaster general, aided him with his talents and his brilliant eloquence. They needed an *enfant perdu*, and they selected Conway, who fancied himself a party leader. Some political and military groups praised Gates only as a pretext for speaking of themselves. The people become attached to victorious generals, and the commander in chief had not been fortunate. His character inspired respect and even love, but Greene, Hamilton, and Knox, his best friends, were slandered. The Tories fomented all these dissensions. The creation of a presidency of the Board of War for Gates restricted the powers of the general. This was not the only humiliation Washington endured. A congressional committee came to camp and dared to propose an attack upon Philadelphia. It is singular that the shrewdest people did not believe that Gates was the true object of the intrigue. He was a good officer, ⟨but he had neither the talent, the intelligence, nor the willpower necessary for supreme command. He would have been crushed by the burden,⟩ [8] and he would have given way to the famous General Lee, who was then a prisoner of the British, and whose first action would have been to sell out his friends and the whole American cause.

M. de Lafayette was attached to the general, and still more so to the cause, and he did not waver. Despite the flatteries of the other party, he remained faithful to the one whose ruin was predicted. He saw his friend every day and wrote to him often to discuss either reforms of the army or his personal situation. The general, having brought his wife to camp, displayed in society the noble calm of a strong and virtuous spirit. "I did not seek this position," he said to M. de Lafayette; "if I displease the people, I will go, but until then I will resist all intrigue."

AM (NIC: Dean Collection), translation. Significant passages of the Memoir not printed in Lafayette, *Mémoires,* are printed here in angle brackets. Annotation of the Memoir is limited to textual problems and the elucidation of issues and events that are not discussed in other documents printed in this volume. See p. 12 for a description of the manuscript and a discussion of editorial procedures for the Memoir.

1. Cornwallis's forces returned to Philadelphia from New Jersey on November 26. On the same day, Greene received Washington's letter of November 25, ordering him to return with his detachment to Whitemarsh (Fitzpatrick, *Writings of Washington,* 10:104–105). Greene's detachment was back in camp by November 30.

2. On December 5 there was light skirmishing between British advance parties and a small detachment of Pennsylvania militia. Finding the American camp defended by abatis and covered by large fieldpieces, Howe tried to outflank the American left during the night of December 6–7. Around noon on the seventh, the British assaulted the American right and managed to force the Americans to retreat behind their abatis. On the American left, Morgan's Riflemen and the Maryland militia skirmished with British advance parties, but the Americans refused to be drawn out of their positions. Howe returned to Philadelphia on December 8 (Fitzpatrick, *Writings of Washington,* 10:143–144).

3. The encounter between Cornwallis's foraging party and the Pennsylvania militia took place at the Gulph, near Matson's Ford on the Schuylkill River, just southeast of Swede's Ford, on December 11.

4. The American army remained encamped near Gulph Mills until December 19, when it marched to Valley Forge.

5. The huts were not completed until mid-January.

6. General Israel Putnam, in command of the Hudson Highlands, had only a small number of militiamen with him because he had sent his Continental troops to New Jersey in November to reinforce the main army.

7. Sir William Howe, who was to have provided transports to return the troops to England, had secretly planned to take the British infantry and artillerymen to New York and return only the foreign troops to England (Howe to Burgoyne, November 16, 1777, in "The Convention Troops and the Perfidy of Sir William Howe," ed. Jane Clark, *American Historical Review,* 37 [1931–1932]: 722–723).

8. Changed in pencil in Lafayette's later hand to "but he did not have the ability to succeed" (our translation).

Memorandum on a Winter Campaign

[Whitemarsh, December 3, 1777]

The project of calling a large body of militia for such a day in order to attack the ennemy in Philadelphia, seems to me attended with so many difficulties, inconveniences and bad chances, that if it is not looked upon as a necessary and almost desesperate enterprise, tho' it is a very shining and highly pleasing idea, however I can not think it is a prudent and reasonable one. The reasons for my rejecting it are as follows.

1st. I do not believe that any body could advise your excellency to attack only the redoubts in front, whatever could be our force; such an attack would be attended with a greater loss but not a greater succès than if we had only continental troops.

2° We must therefore expect the moment where the ice upon the Schullchill will oppen to us all the left side of the ennemy's lines and encampements. But or the climate makes a great difference betwen this country and the european ones, or one single fine day may frustrate all our hopes and preparations in pulling à way all the ice. Then we schould expect one other moment before dismissing the troops, and in my actual supposition they are to be kept a very schort time.

3° In Europe ice is brocken every night when it can facilitate the projects of the ennemy; if All is not cleaned, at least a ditch can be formed in the river. I know that we schould annoy theyr workmen, I know that such an operation would be very hard an troublesome for them. But in the first case I'l answer that every where military works are performed with the same inconveniences, in the second the people of Philadelphia can be employed there. When I say that we could trouble theyr operation, I suppose that our winter quarters are not in the back country.

4° We ca'nt expect any secrecy in our collecting those forces, we ca'nt deceive the ennemy for theyr destination. Therefore (unless we could have a respectable body in the Jersay) he can go of before fighting and then we Must not entertain the hope of oppressing and destroying all that army, but only of recovering Philadelphia.

5° Supposing that we could go upon the ice we have one only way of attaking. For if we put the militia in first line, they will fall back upon the continental troops, and we can not depend enough upon our men to believe that we could maintain order and resolution amongs them. If the militia is in rear, and the regulars were repulsed certainly they will not advance where continentals troops do'nt succeed. If amongs us, I do'nt believe it would do better. Therefore our only way should be to make false attacks of militia and true ones of continental troops, to have a curtain—what we call in french un rideau—of troops in the whole lenght of the Schulchill and on this side, of the redoubts, in order to cover the heads of our columns, and our points of attack, and to put the disorder amongs the ennemy by an easy fire. I wishoud too a body could be in the Jersay *in case it would be possible for the ennemy to retreat by the Delaware.* And does your excellency think that such a quantity of troops could be raised?

6° When I consider all the difficulties of turning out some militia in interesting occasions I c'ant flatterer myself that all that people could be sent to your army for such a day, without the utmost difficulties. Each state will have an excuse for not sending as many men as they'l be desired. The cold, the rivers, the want of cloathes of every thing will seem sufficient reasons, if not to stay at home at least to arrive after the time of the rendez vous. Every one will trust upon the another and if we do not succeed all will be against us.

7° Have we in the continent all the cloathes, arms, ammunition &&c. which would be necessary for so many soldiers? [1] Would it be possible to find subsistances enough in cattle, forage &c.? All things which I ca'nt know, but however I think worthy of being mentionned and that principally because the want of exactitude, the necessity of giving to them a light idea of what they are to do will engage us to keep them longer than we think.

8. I know that all those inconveniences can not be together; because if we keep them some time, then we schall find an opportunity of going over the Schulchill in case that we can prevent theyr braking the ice; on the other hand if we have them only for few days, difficulties of subsistence will be much lesser; and if it is impossible for the ennemy to pass the Delaware, certainly a body in Jersay is quite useless. I can add that in case we could not go over the ice, it is possible to throw bridges upon the river. But, Sir, I have mentionned all the difficulties which strike me, because my opinion is not to begin such an enterprize unless we shall be certain of succeeding. A great schame for our arms, a great michief for our cause would attend our being repulsed when we schould attack a part of the british forces with all the united forces of America. Europe has a great idea of our being able to raise when we please an immense army of militia, and it is looked upon as our last but certain ressource. If we fall this phantom will fall also and you know that the american interest has alwaïs been since the begining of this war to let the world believe that we are stronger than we can ever expect to be. If we destroy the english

army, *our generous effort* will be admired every where, if we are repulsed it will be called *a rash and laughable expedition.* Therefore we
must not let a shining appearance and the pleasing charms of a bold
fine enterprise deceive us upon the inconveniences and dangers of a
Gigantesque and in the same time decisive expedition.

However perhaps the interest of America, the wish of all the States,
the instructions of Congress, the necessity of finishing soon the war,
all those circonstances which are unknown to me, make it necessary
for your excellency to hazard some thing in this occasion. Perhaps the
difficulties in the phisick and moral ressources of this country are not
so great as I am affraïd to find them. Perhaps it is possible to raise,
to arm, to cloath, to subsist, to keep together and give some instructions
to that so considerable army which according to my opinion is necessary; perhaps the weather is not so changeable in this country as it is
in Europe, or some other means than going upon the ice could seem
eligible to Your excellency. But if the difficulties which I fear are
indeed true (what you can judje, and I can not know myself) then I
am not for that expedition in considering it as only a militar one.

If however I was deceived, or if politic circumstances schould make
it necessary to try such an enterprize, the following precautions seem
me to be taken

1° I do not ascertain the number of militia to be raised because it
must be as large as we can arm, cloath and subsist.

2° All possible exertions are to be taken for having them at the appointed time which time must be now as soon as it is possible.

3° Some instructions should take place before the operation, only
for some days, because if they were marched to the ennemy without
the less idea of marching together such a disorder would prevent the
succès of the less difficult enterprize.

4° The continental troops schould be sent in theyr winter quarters
as soon as possible, to take a good rest, to recomfort themselves, to be
reinforced by theyr men now scattered every where,[2] by some recruits, and the whole to be managed and exerced by theyr genl.
officers under that point of vüe, and principally cloathes should be
delivered to them, and theyr arms put in a good order. (It seems to
me that this prospect could engage us to be nearer from the ennemy
than Lancaster is.)

5° The soldiers and pricipally the officers of our army schould not
be permitted to go home till it would be over.[3]

6° Proper means for recruiting the army schould be taken as soon
as possible. One of the best according to my opinion would be (after
having suppressed the substitutes)[4] to annex a part of the militia of
each state to theyr continental divisions in order to serve there for

twelve months. I think that such a regulation is eligible in all cases. For a strong continental army well managed and disciplined, and ready to begin an early campaign and to make use of all the unforeseen and soudain occasions, would do much greater service than all the militia in the world, and then militia should be made use of only in a less great number or in particular circomstances.

THE MQUIS. DE LAFAYETTE M.G.

AMS (DLC: George Washington Papers, Series 4). This memorandum is in response to Washington's circular letter to the general officers on December 3: "Sir: I wish to recall your attention to the important matter recommended to your consideration sometime ago; namely, the advisability of a Winters Campaign, and practicability of an attempt upon Philadelphia with the aid of a considerable body of Militia, to be assembled at an appointed time and place, particular reasons urge me to request your Sentiments on this matter by the Morning, and I shall expect to receive them accordingly [in writing] by that time" (Fitzpatrick, *Writings of Washington*, 10:135).

A council of general officers met on November 24 to consider the advisability of a winter campaign, and a majority of the officers were against it. But Congress was anxious for the army to carry on a vigorous campaign against the British in Philadelphia, and a congressional committee was then at camp to consult with Washington about the best method of carrying it out. Washington again solicited the officers' opinions on a winter campaign, and this time they were unanimously against it (ibid., pp. 103n and 144n).

1. Sullivan pointed out that one-third of the army was already confined to their tents and huts for lack of shoes, stockings, and other clothing, and Varnum complained that the commissary department was scarcely able to provide the army's daily provisions (Ford, "Defences of Philadelphia," 20:521, 548).

2. As the weather became severe and clothing and provisions scarce, more men "deserted to their own homes." Sullivan asserted that there were upwards of a hundred such deserters from the Delaware regiment and an equal proportion from many of the other regiments. These men would have to be brought back to the army before the beginning of a spring campaign (ibid., pp. 523–524).

3. Sullivan maintained that a winter campaign would only increase the great dissatisfaction among the officers and added, "I am fully convinced and fear the Event will prove that more than half your officers will leave you in a month, unless some Remedy is found out to quiet their minds & relieve their Distresses" (ibid., pp. 521–522). The congressional committee at camp noted that dissatisfaction among the officers was one of the major reasons for abandoning the idea of a winter campaign (Fitzpatrick, *Writings of Washington*, 10:144n).

4. For the substitute system, see Lafayette to Clinton, March 16, 1778, note 13.

From Henry Laurens

York 6th. Decemr. 1777

Sir—

I have in view the Several Letters which you have honoured me with under the 18th. 28th. & 29th. of the Month past.[1]

Permit me Sir in the most respectful & Cordial terms to congratulate with you on your Successful enterprize in New Jersey—the agreeable accounts which you have received from home & more particularly on the birth of a daughter—events which conspire to transfuse mutual joy to your Noble Family & to your numerous friends on each Side of the Atlantic.

I have not been so attentive to all your Commands as I ought & as I wished to have been, but believe me Sir, the delinquency has been absolutely unavoidable. The business of Congress has lain heavy upon me for fourteen days past. Their Session each day very long & intervals too Short for dispatching the necessary Resolves & Recommendations to the States, to Officers &c. without intrenching deeply on the Night & constantly rising before day light Some times one or two, Some times four hours—this is almost as hard work as one Night a Bed in a Camp. Indeed these Candle light hours contain the only moments, I can pass at the writing Table with any degree of tranquility, while day light continues & almost all the Evening, I am exposed to incessant attacks, too many of them very trifling, but 'tis necessary to hear all before judgement can be formed & it often happens, the most impertinent plunder the most of ones time. Besides we are not in the most convenient Situation in This Town. Where one cannot exercise a right to arrange family economy, circumstances will occur to interrupt & impede the progress of business. I am lodged where everybody Strives to make me happy, but it would be too unreasonable to expect from them to vary all their movements according to the pressure of my Duty, & impossible to accomodate them to the very irregular periods of our adjournments. I have taken the liberty of obtruding this prolix detail in order to account for my tardiness & in Some measure to plead my excuse, especially for my neglect of your intimation relative to Monsr. Capitaine, which has been with me nine days, yet I have not at all interfered in the business—the Subject important as it is, had wholly escaped my memory. Let me incur your Censure Sir, in preference to the reproaches of my own mind, or an attempt to insult you, which would follow a fallacious apology. But Sir, before you will have an opportunity of Superceding the power you have vested with me, I shall have Set myself so heartily to the discharge of that trust as will render it unnecessary for you to employ another Attorney & I am not without hope of regaining your confidence. Be assured Sir I will not lose Sight of the Subject until I have done everything that shall be practicable for accomplishing your desires.

Monsr. Craignée, Monsr. d'Balm & Some other french Gentlem. are retained at the public expence while measures for gratifying their wishes consistent with the Service of these States are under consideration.[2] These Gentlemen have many good friends here & Some, more able to Serve them, than I am, but my best endeavours shall never be wanting to forward their attempts in measures calculated for promoting our great Cause.

General Conway has devoted much of his time in York to our Marine Committee by planning & recommending in particular explanations, a scheme which is very inviting & which, when we are able, will undoubtedly be carried into execution.[3] To part abruptly with that Gentleman would be a circumstance extremely mortifying to a few persons here who hold themselves to be of the best friends to the United States. Had he served any particular State in the Union with the Same Zeal & good effect which have been conspicuous & universally acknowledged in his Military efforts in the Service of the Thirteen—a deputation would have waited on him long before this hour, either with honorable propositions for retaining, or Commands to take leave of him, in terms suitable to his merits. We have Something in view which we hope will hold the General longer in America—when the business is matured you shall be duly informed—whether our wishes succeed or not.

Monsr. Duplaisis was not overlooked in the act of promotion to Monsr. Fleury. I hope this has been sufficiently explained by that Gentleman's particular friends.[4]

Every account which we have lately received except those from Sir William Howe's printers in Philadelphia indicate the near approach of a Rupture between France & England. The general Embargo throughout the French West India Islands is undoubtedly a Strong prognostic & this fact is asserted by very good authority from St. Domingo.[5]

Your condescension Sir to take notice of the naked condition of our Soldiery is a mark of paternal regard for those your adopted Sons. When I reflect seriously upon this branch of our distress—I see clearly black faults in Individuals & shameful neglect at fountain head. My resentment is excited against Men, who, however they are Safely hedged in by partial favor deserve to be charged. The retrospect is extremely painful. The consequence of Some Men's Self Interestedness & the gross partiality & inattention of those whose duty it was to Superintend & to correct betimes, has already appeared in the loss of Some lives, cruel Sicknesses, boundless desertion & what is to follow, God only knows.

I presume the conference now on the Tapis or possibly just finished between His Excellency the General & the Committee from Congress will determine the question relative to Winter Quarters. We are morally certain of Sending you a pretty large Supply of Blankets & Cloths before Christmas. I hope these will reach the Army time enough to give new cause for thanksgiving on the 18th.[6]

The Committee for foreign Correspondence will dispatch to Boston, to morrow or next day, Letters for France to go by the hands of the Honble. John Adams Esquire appointed one of our Commissioners at the Court of Versailles. A Vessel will be purposely equipped for his accomodation & Safe passage. I am sure that Gentleman will be happy in being the bearer of your Commands or in disposing of them in the best manner, if he Should decline this duty to which he is elected by Congress & I believe you will find Safe & expeditious conveyances from Camp to Boston.[7]

In time of War with France there will be no tolerable assurance of reaching our friends on t'other Side the Water oftner than one out of Six Letters. I always practiced in former Wars Sending at least a Sixth Copy of every Letter of any importance & found great advantages result from my care, while my Neighbors, less attentive often Suffered Losses.

I cannot inform you Sir any particulars concerning the intended embarkation of Lt. Genl. Burgoyne's conquered Troops. I have dispatched to Boston Several Official Letters on that Subject to which I every day expect answers. In the meantime 'tis probable, necessity will oblige Sir William Howe to Support the remains of them where they are, during the present Winter. I have the honour to be, with the highest Respect & Esteem &c.

LbC (ScHi: Henry Laurens Papers).

1. The letter of the "28th." was dated November 20 and was received by Laurens on November 28.

2. "Craignée" is Crozat de Crénis. Congress paid his expenses on February 8, 1778, but did not give him the lieutenant colonel's commission he sought until November 7, 1778. Congress paid La Balme's expenses on February 13, 1778, and informed him that his services were no longer required (JCC, 10:138, 157; 12:1109).

3. A letter from the Committee for Foreign Affairs to the commissioners in Paris, December 2, 1777, suggested an expedition that may have been the same one Conway discussed with the Marine Committee (Wharton, *Diplomatic Correspondence*, 2:440–441). The plan was essentially the same one Lafayette outlined in his letter to Maurepas, October 24, 1777.

4. On November 26, 1777, Congress appointed Fleury lieutenant colonel and proposed but postponed a resolution to commend and promote Du Plessis (JCC, 9:967).

5. William Bingham had written Congress on October 13 from Martinique that the French governor Bouillé had received orders from his government to put a general embargo on all ships destined for Europe to prevent their falling into the hands of the English (DNA: RG 360, PCC 90, 1:5–12).

6. Congress had declared December 18 a day of prayer and thanksgiving in gratitude for the American victory at Saratoga (JCC, 9:854–855).

7. See Lafayette to Adams, January 9, 1778.

From Charlotte Bentinck

Hamburg 8th. December 1777

Sir

I hesitated a long time before I yielded to the extreme desire of taking a step, in appearance rather singular—to address to you who are in the remote region of America, a Letter signed with a name which will not even be known by you—but recollect Sir that Sentiment and Glory alone induced you to quit the most brilliant situation in Europe; and condemn if you dare, a person who without having it in her power to do as great actions as you, is however determined by the same principles on this occasion. The late Duke of Tremorille my Grand Uncle, was the happy spouse of Mary Magdelane de La Fayette: this seems to give me a kind of title to address you.[1] I have lived beyond half a Century, without ever imagining that to belong by chance to the greatest princes, could for a moment flatter the vanity of a reasonable being—but to have the honor of the least proximity to such a man as you are, appears to me, I confess a glorious advantage, and whence it is impossible for me not to derive a delicious vanity.

Besides you defend a cause Sir, which is that of Humanity. It does not become a female to decide the rights of Sovereigns and Nations— we have often been accused of too great a fondness for heroes; I detest Conquerors. I abhor Tyrants, I would sacrifice the few remaining years of my life for the illustrious Washington. Ancient and modern history have made me acquainted with a number of brave Warriors; but he is the only one I have ever known, that answers the idea which I have of a truly great man who unites to genuine heroism, humanity, equity, disinterestedness; who hating war, carries it on from duty and necessity; in a word a man, whose character I should have thought the brilliant fiction of a poetical imagination; and which I must have seen in order to believe its possibility and existence. To snatch oneself at an age like yours from the bosom of felicity to go and attach oneself to such a guide, is perhaps to equal him. The Excess of Veneration, of Esteem which I cannot refuse to Virtue, forces my hand to pay him this feeble homage. We live at a time when men are scarcely sensible of great actions. I date myself from an age, in which they made more lively impressions.

America has however in our pretend Republic of Hamburg,[2] where I reside, many zealous partisans. I have a small number of friends, people of worth, sensible minds, who resort to my house, as to the Temple of a more than Demi God; of the Hero of Liberty and Humanity—the great Washington—to bring their Vows, their fears, their admiration, their hopes to the Altar of honor and Sentiment which I have consecrated to him.[3] You share in all these tributes of the heart. It is impossible that great minds such as yours can feel an indifference to them. But what cruel Uneasinesses, this noble and interesting cause makes us experience. We pass weeks, and months in suspense—at every instant some threatening news overpowers us—and even our consolations are uncertain. If you are touched with the Justice which I do you, if you deign to confess the honour which I have in belonging to you—if the purity of motives which animate me appear to merit some consideration—be so generous as to make acceptable to your illustrious General, the Tribute which sensible and worthy hearts Address him from the midst of another world—and which perhaps he will not judge unworthy of him. His happy fellow Citizens scarcely make more tender vows for him than we do. May it please heaven to listen to them. May a Nation still exist on earth, possessed of Liberty, happiness and Virtue.

The second Request which I take the liberty of making you, seems still more indiscreet—but the feelings with which I am animated get the better of me. I cannot resist continual anxiety for yourself, your Chief, and 13 United States, exposed to the Malice of British Brokers, & to the repetitions of Gazeteers of every country—we are in too much perturbation here. Have the charity for people who are attached to you, to acknowledge by a line the receipt of this letter—which I entreat Mr. Franklin to convey to you and the answer to which may come the same way—and be so good as to order your Secretary to add a few lines, to inform me that *you* and the *General* are in *good health*—that all is not going to ruin, and that we need not despair.[4] It is not Curiosity, it is Sentiment, Zeal, the purest affection which animate us—we do not desire to be informed so much as to be tranquilized. Be as careful of yourself Sir as your Courage and the noble Task which you have undertaken will allow. Remember that an amiable Wife, an illustrious family, a whole Nation expects it of you. There is perhaps only one Marquis de la Fayette, only a single Nobleman of his age and birth capable of doing what he has done. Does not that alone render him more pretious.

Pardon me I entreat you. My abuse of your leisure, my justification must be in your heart, or my cause is lost without resource. I have the honor to be with the most distinguished esteem Sir Your &c.

CHARLOTTE SOPHIE COUNTESS DOWAGER OF BENTINCK
born COUNTESS OF ALDENBERG [5]

L (DLC: George Washington Papers, Series 4), copied, and probably translated, by John Laurens.

1. Jacques-Roch Motier de La Fayette, Lafayette's uncle, had inherited the La Fayette lands from Marie-Madeleine Motier de La Fayette, a distant cousin in the elder line of the family. Her husband was Charles-Louis Bretagne de La Trémoïlle, prince de Tarente, duc de Thouars.

2. Hamburg was a free city of the Holy Roman Empire, but it was dominated for the first half of the eighteenth century by the king of Denmark. It was only in 1768 that it obtained representation in the Imperial Diet.

3. In 1738 Charlotte Bentinck began her travels to the European courts, where she met such people as Frederick the Great, Voltaire, Maria-Theresa, and Count Wilhelm von Schaumburg-Lippe. She maintained an extensive correspondence with her illustrious contemporaries, and when she settled in Hamburg, in 1767, her house became a meeting place for statesmen, artists, and men of letters.

4. Lafayette's reply has not been found.

5. An error for Uldenburg.

To Horatio Gates

At the Gulph the 14 december 1777

Dear Sir

I have received with the greatest satisfaction the favor of yours.[1] The idea of obtaining your friendship is highly pleasant to me—be certain, sir, that you can depend upon my attachement for ever. The only love of glorious and great actions, schould have inspired me with such sentiments—but the Knowledge I got of your character adds infinetely to the pleasure which my heart feels in receiving the assurances of your future affection towards a young soldier who desire it very heartely.

The bearer of this letter has the advantage of having been the witness of your succès. I would reccommend him to you, if I was Not convinced that you know how that gentleman deserves the regard of Congress—be so good as to be his advocate there. I do'nt see any thing unjust in his desire to be appointed colonel, any impossibility in this of being at the head of a corps, of canadians if he could inlist them, and to be annexed to some division in the army. Such an officer will Certainly be of a great use to the cause principally if he is vith men whom he can understand and where he will make himself understood.[2] With the greatest esteem and affection I have the honor to be dear sir Your most obedient servant

THE MQUIS. DE LAFAYETTE

ALS (NHi: Gates Papers, Box 8).

1. Gates to Lafayette, November 12.

2. Lafayette had also recommended the bearer, the Chevalier de Failly, to Henry Laurens (Lafayette to Laurens, December 3, 1777 [ScHi: Henry Laurens Papers]).

To Henry Laurens

At the Gulph the 14 december 1777

Dear Sir

I advise you to take care for yourself in making the least excuse to me, because thousand and thousand will fall immediately upon you, with all the rapidity of a torrent, and then my heart will indulge itself the repeated and tedious assurances of my gratefulness, which you deserved by this apology of your last letter.[1] But, Sir, friendship do not admitt such compliments, and, therefore I wish heartely they should be removed from us. I am very well convinced of that immense quantity of businesses which employ all the moments of your life. Give me leave to tell you that you would be quite in rung [wrong?], if Your time was spent in serious occupations as far as to hurt your health and constitution. Then the trifling advantage of some hours would certainly prevent you from being useful to your country for months or years on account of sickness and disconveniences attending too hard and tiring occupations. However, tho' troublesome I might be, my confidence is such that I'l apply always to you in the least circumstances, and the president of Congress as well as my friend will receive all my adresses in every occasion. I beg only leave of making two rules betwen us—the first, that when I schall ask some thing to you improper, unjust, or not becoming with the regulations or interests of your country, the president of Congress will never Know any thing of the matter neither take any notice of it. My second rule is that you schall never think yourself obliged to any answer, to any execution of my desires &c. &c. till the moment where your businesses will have you in full liberty of doing it. Such is the plan which must be fixed upon among us.

The bearer of the present the Chevalier de Faïlly ran à way from you some days ago without any leave, without thinking of his rendésvous, on account of the approach and fihgting-like maneuvre of General Howe. I assured him that you would excuse such an impolite desertion. He feels the greatest gratefulness for your kind reception. These are the sentiments of all the french gentelemen who have had some occasions of Knowing You. I can tell you without compliment that never man Acquired the love and confidence of a stranger nation, so far as you are beloved and trust upon by all my country men I know here. I wish the same way schould have been taken every where and every body would have been satisfied with much lesser expense of Congress, and greater advantages on both side.

I received a letter from the Viscount de Montroy who has the same rank in France as the Baron de Kalb, and made the same convention with Mr. Silas Deane. He seems to me very affronted to have been left when the Baron de Kalb was admitted in our service. This genteleman my countryman is one of the most reccommendable in this part of the world for his wit, genius, and civil reputation—however Mr. Lovell told to a french officer that he had wrote A very improper letter to Congress. I hope that you will be so good as to let me know the truth of it.[2]

I am very sensible of the mark of confidence I received from Congress in being appointed to a division of the army. I wish to deserve it by my own and my division's conduct principally when happy occasions may present themselves to us. My tenderest and warmest attachement for our respectable and great general has made myself very desirous to be at the head of his country men. It is with a great pleasure that I heard a plenty of cloathes and blankets would arrive soon in camp. Give me leave to make to you the following reflexion—do'nt you think that as the Northen provinces [3] have been well provided since the beggining of the war (and indeed I saw yet yesterday large parcels of goods distributed among them) some more attention schould be payed to our poor nacked virginians who have alwaïs fought without any ressource, alwaïs in the oppened field, and under General Washington? I wishoud that a great plenty of coats could arrive together in camp, and not parcel by parcel, in order to distribute them at once and make some uniformity in the several regiments which is a thing much more important than it seems to be. When a small quantity is brought here we are obliged to attend first those unhappy wretches whom theyr nackedness prevents entirely from making any duty, and who expect the moment of perishing by sickness or changing theyr deplorable situation by desertion. Of those quite nacked fellows incapable of service for want of cloathes, shoes &c. I have many in my division, and I can't express to you how it makes myself uneasy.

I have been acquainted with a very great pleasure of the measures which Congress will take for the sake of this army—first in giving to our officers that consideration, and idea of themselves which is absolutely necessary.[4] Military Life is full of labours, dangers, inconveniences of every kind. In the middle of theyr distresses, and sufferings we want to entertain merry, willing, and alwaïs ready spirit—but how can you expect that they will go through the hardships of war with that so desirable alacrity, if honor, if even a Kind of pride does not sustain them? Honor will raise from praises düe to bravery and good conduct. Do'nt tell never *he has done his duty,* the men must receive thanks for doing merely that very same duty as well as they ought to be punished when they neglect it. The other point schall be carried on in making the commissions honorable and desirable for every gentleman of whatever fortune he can be. I'l let you know as my friend that I intend for this purpose to pay to the lieutenants of my division the same politeness and regard which is payed here to Generals officers and sometimes refused to a colonel. One other thing very agreable to me is to hear that the divisions and regiments will be completed this winter by taking them out of militia. It is the only way of getting an army; it is, I dare say, the only way of opposing ourselves to whatever ennemy England can send to us. The same men who are now scatered in the country, plundering the inhabitants, and bold every where but before the ennemy, will make Good, fine, disciplined Soldiers, under the niew stricts rules which, I hope, will be established upon a general plan and calculated upon the best military principles.[5]

I received several letters from General Connway by which I foresee he will stay in this country.[6] According to that highly pleasant project he spoke you of, I believe that you mean some ideas about the East Indias. As Mr. de Cannway has been in Garrison in the *Isle de France* I desired from him several times some particularities about the matter. That project wants a man at the head of it who by his weight in France could undertake things which would loose a Gentleman less firm in that country by his connexions and all our others french prejugces. Influence about court is not only necessary, he must have some fortune to risk expensive enterprizes. These considerations engaged me to believe that I could be of some use to America if in the same time that I am fighting here I would induce the french ministry in supporting enterprizes which schall certainly finish by a war betwen France and England. I have therefore the pleasure to inform you that by Mr. de Valfort I wrote a long letter to the Count de Maurepas, whom I desire to consider himself and propose to the King in my name the following project [7]—intrusted with commissions of Congress, with very smallest succours (because I represent that in this circomstances America ca'nt make great efforts) I offer myself to engage a part of my fortune in collecting some vessels arms &c. I ask only from the King to order the governors of the french american islands, and principally this of the Isle de France in the Est Indies, not to put any obstacle to my operations, and even to favour them. Then I answer to them that some english establishements (perhaps all) will be destroïed without any expense neither from France neither from America. This project want's to be explained in very long terms what

I'l do at our first enterwiew. To be short on the matter I'l tell only to you—first that I employed all the Knowledge of this court I can have to make the King and his minister in love with this project—the second that I engaged no body there but myself, that I have promised nothing in the world to them, because I think a plan betwen both nations must be calculated for theyr common advantage in it—the third that I selected from all that romanesque of this project, all what it has reasonable and praticable in itself—the fourth that I am certain that in our first conversation you'l find that what I have done and mean to do answers every purpose for the interests of America.

I have wrote by the same occasion to the governor of Martinico,[8] a gentleman whom I can depend upon, and I am certain he will do every thing in his power for me. I propose to him the following enterprize—I could make a voyage in these islands for two months in all—and from there I'l take proper measures to fall in the english possessions, destroy the habitations, take à way the negros &c. &c.—which operations tho' done in my name, upon my credit, and under American colours, would certainly be the cause of a great dispute betwen France and England, as well as of some advantage for America. I expect answers about those two points, and if they are agreed I schall lay down my projects before Congress and submit them to theyr jugement and instructions. I ask from you, Sir, a great secrecy, you can only let them be Known to few members of Congress you can depend upon as upon yourself. But if some others schould be acquainted of it, I foresee indiscretions and bad consequences. In case the above projects schould take place, and the operations of war schould want my presence here, than I'l direct officers and gentlemen I can depend upon to act under my name, my expenses and my instructions.

You will be perhaps surprised that I did not speack to any body in America about those ideas and untertakings of mine—but, Sir, it would not answer any purpose but to let me have some assurances that America is satisfied with my conduct—And tho' agreable and highly pleasant it could be to me to think that this country believes myself of some use to it, however I want more to serve America and the cause of liberty and mankind than to be thanked for those services. I wishoud therefore to conceal my measures till the moment when favorables answers should make myself able to proceed directly to the execution, and in case of refusals no body schould have Known any thing of it. But as I see Congress ready to engage itself in some undertakings of that Kind I thaught it my duty to let you Know what I have already done. By the first opportunity you'l furnish me with I'l explain myself upon a greater scale.

If I had had the pleasure to be better acquainted with Mr. Jonh Adams or he had applied to me, I would have given to him every instruction in my power for his succès in that country. It seems to me by your letter that some time will be spent in the preparations of his vessel. Be so good, Sir, as to let me Know how long you think that time will be, because I'l have my letters ready and I wish to send them as late as possible. I am sorry I have not seen that genteleman. He will have thousand questions made to him about me. Thousand particularities will be inquired in on the same subject. I do not Know how he will answer—for there he will hear more from me perhaps in two hours, than he ever heard since my arrival. For avoiding to him the trouble of answering to thousand about a point he do'nt Know much of, make to him a little lesson he will repeat the first day, and after it he must shut the shop, and all those importune questions about a man unknown to him must be over.

I do'nt deserve indeed, sir, any compliment for our little victory of the Jersays. That advantage had (I must confess) some thing very clever but it is much more owned to the bravery of my little party than to any disposition or operation on my part. I was there nothing more than a witness.

I am indeed very importune to waït so long a letter. You'l find me very troublesome, and I make haste to put an end to it by the short assurance of the eternal friendship I am with—Dear Sir Your most obedient servant

THE MQUIS. DE LAFAYETTE

The Chevalier de Faïlly if he obtains the levée of a canadian corps Desires very much he could be annexed to my division, and indeed that idea is very pleasing to me.

As the french war is not confirmed I begin to conceive some very bad doubts, on this matter. I wish with a great ardour to get clear of them.

ALS (ScHi: Henry Laurens Papers).

1. Laurens to Lafayette, December 6.

2. A bitter letter from Mauroy, complaining of the treatment he had received from Congress, was read in Congress on December 8 (Mauroy to Congress, November 1777 [DNA: RG 360, PCC 78, 15:279–283]). Lovell wrote to Samuel Adams on the same day: "Among friends, we have received a most impudent letter from Mauroy. Tis impossible to take any notice of it to him without putting him in Jail" (Burnett, *Letters of Congress*, 2:583).

3. The regiments of the northern states. The Continental regiments were clothed by the states that levied them.

4. The congressional committee at camp had been sent there to confer with Washington about a winter campaign, but concluded that such a campaign would be impossible, in part because of the officers' discontent with conditions in the army. On De-

cember 10 the committee sent Washington the recommendations it intended to present to Congress for improving those conditions, including the establishment of a regular line of promotion (Fitzpatrick, *Writings of Washington,* 10:144n).

5. Congress had given the Board of War the task of establishing the exercises and maneuvers for drill in the army, but nothing was done until the spring of 1778, when Steuben began to drill the troops and prepare a manual of arms.

6. Letters not found.

7. Lafayette to Maurepas, October 24.

8. This letter, to Bouillé, has not been found. See Lafayette to Duboismartin, October 23.

To the Duc d'Ayen[T]

> In camp at Gulph in Pennsylvania
> December 16, 1777

This letter, if it ever arrives, will at least find you in France;[1] some risks are avoided because of that. However, I should not flatter myself too much, for I never write a word to Europe without pitying in advance the fate that awaits it. I have certainly written more for Lord Howe than for any of my friends. This is the winter season, and the English ships will fortunately be obliged to leave off their accursed cruising. Then I shall get some mail, and I shall be able to count upon some of mine getting there. That will please me and will keep me from burdening you with a repetition of matters I want you to know about, but which I do not want to make you recall each time.

I am impatient for news about your trip and am relying principally upon the kindness of Mme de Lafayette for some details; she certainly knows how eager I am to have them. M. le Maréchal de Noailles tells me that the letters he receives from Italy assure him that all the travelers are in good health and their expedition is going very well. He also told me about the accouchement of Mme de Lafayette.[2] He did not speak of it as the happiest event in the world, but my anxiety was too great to bother about distinctions of sex. The fact that he was good enough to write and give me all the news gave me a hundred times more pleasure than he could imagine in telling me that I only had a daughter. So the Rue St. Honoré is discredited forever, whereas the other Hôtel de Noailles has gained fresh luster through the birth of Adrien.[3] It is truly shameful to have committed this wrong in a family where I have received so many kindnesses.

At this moment you must be freezing on the highroads of France; those of Pennsylvania have also become very cold, and I try vainly to persuade myself that the difference in latitude should provide us a pleasant winter compared to Paris. I am told it will become even more severe. We are fated to spend the winter in huts twenty miles from Philadelphia, as much to protect the countryside as to take advantage of circumstances that may arise. At the same time, while we hold our troops together, we are able to give them the training they need. Perhaps it would have been much better to go quietly into real winter quarters, but political considerations have obliged General Washington to choose a middle ground.

I wish I were capable of giving you a satisfactory account of military events in this country. Aside from my inadequacy, you know I could not put in a letter, liable to interception by an English ship, information that could explain many things if I had the pleasure of talking about them with you. I am going to try to relate to you once more, however, the interesting aspects of this campaign; my gazette, to which I shall not add any comments, and which is all the better for that reason, will always be preferable to the European ones, because the man who sees with his own eyes, however imperfectly, is always more reliable than the one who has seen nothing at all. As for the gazettes with which the English flood us, their only purpose is to amuse the sedan-carriers over their mugs of porter, and even then they would have to drink quite a bit to be able to swallow all the lies.

It appears to me that the plan of the English ministry was to cut America along a line extending from Chesapeake Bay to Ticonderoga. General Howe was ordered to Philadelphia by way of the Elk River, Burgoyne was to descend upon Albany, and Clinton was to travel up from New York by way of the North River. The three generals would by this means join hands. They would have received, or pretended to receive, the submission of the provinces they claimed to have conquered, and we would have been left with the hinterlands for our winter quarters and the four southern states for our sole resource. Perhaps an attack upon Charleston was also projected. Thus was America nearly conquered in the king of England's council. Happily, Providence has permitted some alterations in the execution of this fine plan, in order to test, for some time yet, British constancy.

When I reached the army in August, I was quite surprised not to find the enemy. After some uneventful maneuvers into Jersey, General Howe embarked at New York. We were camped near Philadelphia and were waiting for their landing on the Chester side of the river when we learned that they were at the mouth of the Elk River. General Washington marched to meet them and, after taking several positions, decided to wait for them on some excellent heights at Brandywine Creek. The British came to attack us on September 11. While they diverted us with a cannonade and many movements before our front, they filed off the largest part of their army, with the elite of their forces and all their grenadiers, commanded by General Howe himself and Lord Cornwallis, to cross a ford four miles to our right. As soon as General Washington knew of this maneuver, he detached his entire right wing to meet them. The first reports of the British movement were then contradicted by some wretched intelligence that appeared accurate, and the detachment was so long delayed that when it arrived on the field the enemy had already crossed the ford. Then it had to engage on open ground against superior numbers; after sustaining a brisk exchange of fire and killing many of the enemy, both American wings gave way. Some were rallied and brought back; that is when I was wounded. Finally, to cut short the account, everything went wrong ⟨on all sides⟩; General Washington had been beaten for the same reason that he had not been able to win the first general battle of this war.[4]

The army reassembled at Chester. Having been removed a good distance from it, I was not able to follow its movements. General Howe took advantage of the disorder that a frightful downpour caused in our army to cross the Schuylkill. He marched to take Philadelphia, and took a position between the city and Germantown. General Washington attacked him on October 4. One could say that our general beat theirs, for our troops surprised the British and even pursued them for a long time, but British experience eventually gave them the victory over our untried officers and soldiers. Some time before this an American brigadier, with a detachment on the other side of the river, had been attacked at night in his camp and lost ⟨quite⟩ a few men.[5] There you have all the events of interest until the time I returned to camp after six weeks in bed, waiting for my wound to close.

During that same time we received some good news about General Burgoyne. When I first joined the army, while General Howe was still at sea, I heard that the Americans had hastily evacuated Ticonderoga, leaving behind a large quantity of cannon and all kinds of munitions ⟨without taking the time to destroy them⟩. This ⟨unexpected⟩ success inflated the pride of General Burgoyne ⟨and he then began to think seriously of accomplishing his mission⟩. He issued a pompous and ridiculous proclamation for which he has since paid dearly. His first step was to send a detachment, which was repulsed. Undiscouraged, he pushed on ⟨heedlessly⟩ through immense forests, in a country that had but a single road. General Gates commanded 15,000 or 16,000 soldiers, who harassed the enemy by firing at them from the cover of trees. Victor or vanquished, Burgoyne became weaker as each mile cost him many men. Finally, surrounded on all sides, dying of hunger,

he was obliged to sign a convention by virtue of which he was conducted by the New England militia to the very "province" of Massachusetts in which, he had boasted in London, he would take up his
winter quarters. With the remnants of his 5000 men, he will be taken
from there to England at the expense of his master, the king. Ticonderoga has since been evacuated by the British.

General Clinton had ⟨by his own choice⟩ delayed his departure
from New York. After having taken and destroyed Fort Montgomery
on the North River, he tried to reach Gates's rear; but, having heard
of the convention, he returned by the same road on which he had
come. If Clinton had acted more quickly, Gates would have had a
more difficult time.

When, after six weeks, the condition of my wound enabled me to
rejoin the army, I found it fifteen miles from Philadelphia. Reinforcements had arrived from the north. General Howe, in Philadelphia,
was much inconvenienced by two forts, one on the Jersey shore and
the other on the little Mud Island you will find on your map just
below the Schuylkill. These two forts were protected by chevaux-de-
frise in the Delaware River, and had held out for a long time against
British land and sea forces. Two young Frenchmen serving as engineers there acquired much honor: Monsieur de Fleury of the
Rouergue Regiment, and Mauduit Du Plessis, who commanded the
artillery, of which he is an officer in France. The Hessians, commanded by Count von Donop, attacked the fort where Mauduit was,
and were repulsed with heavy losses. Count von Donop was taken,
mortally wounded. The forts were evacuated after a vigorous defense.
Lord Cornwallis then went over to Jersey with 5000 men; an equal
number of our troops were there under one of our major generals.[6]
Being still only a volunteer, I went along with him, and, when I found
myself by chance with a detachment close to the enemy, the fine conduct of my troops justified an imprudent attack. Everyone told us that
his lordship had been wounded there.[7] He crossed the river again,
and we did the same. A few days later the whole army mustered at
Whitemarsh, thirteen miles from Philadelphia. General Howe's troops
moved to attack us, but after four days of hesitation, during which
they surveyed our position from all sides, they concluded that a night
withdrawal was more prudent. We then pursued our plan of crossing
to this side of the Schuylkill, but we were delayed on the other bank,
where we encountered part of the enemy army (though the action was
limited to a few cannon shots). They left the way open the next day,
and we shall all be in our huts for the whole winter.

Here the American army will attempt to clothe itself, because it is
practically naked, to improve itself, because it is in great need of train-

ing, and to rebuild itself, because it is very deficient in numbers—but the states will take care of that by sending us more men. My division will, I hope, be one of the strongest, and I shall do all I can to see to it that it is the best in every respect.

The present situation of the enemy is not at all disagreeable. Burgoyne's army is fed at the expense of the republic, and the few men they are able to send back (for many will be lost en route) will be at once replaced by other troops. Clinton is quite at ease in New York with a large garrison; in Philadelphia, General Howe is paying court to the belles ⟨of whom he is a great connoisseur⟩. The liberties the British take in stealing and pillaging from friend and foe alike puts them completely at ease. At this moment their ships can come up to the city, but not without danger. Not counting the sixty-four-gun ship and the frigate that were burned in front of the forts, and all those ships I trust the ice will deliver to us, several are lost each day through the hazards of passage up the river.

The loss of Philadelphia is very far from having the importance given it in Europe. ⟨This city, the least disposed of all to the cause of liberty, does not merit the title "capital of America," with which it is honored in France. It is a dreary place, populated chiefly by tiresome Quakers, whose virtue is less acknowledged here than it is in Abbé Raynal's book.[8] All the respectable people have withdrawn to the Lancaster area.⟩

If the difference of circumstances, of terrain, and of proportion between the two armies were not so manifest, General Gates's success would be quite surprising, compared with recent events here, especially in view of the notable superiority of General Washington over General Gates. Our general is a man truly made for this revolution, which could not succeed without him. I am closer to him than anyone else, and I find him worthy of his country's veneration. His warm friendship and his complete confidence in me regarding all military and political matters, great and small, put me in a position to know all that he has to do, to reconcile, and to overcome. I admire him more each day for the beauty of his character and his spirit. Certain foreigners, piqued because they did not receive commissions (although such things were not within his authority),[9] others whose ambitious projects he did not wish to serve, and still other jealous intriguers would like ⟨perhaps⟩ to tarnish his reputation, but his name will be revered down through the centuries by all those who love liberty and humanity. While I am duty bound to honor my friend, I believe the role that he plays gives me the right to make known how much I admire and respect him. There are many important matters I cannot

put on paper. We can speak of them someday. On these I ask that you
suspend judgment; they will redouble your esteem for him.[10]

America waits with impatience for us to declare for her. I hope
France will one day decide to humble ⟨insolent⟩ [11] England. This consideration, and the measures America appears willing to pursue, give
me great hope for the glorious establishment of her independence.
⟨Freed from my first enthusiasms⟩ I no longer see us [12] as strong as I
believed to be the case ⟨when I was in Europe⟩, but we are able to
fight and we shall do so, I hope, with some success. With the help of
France we shall win, at some expense, the cause that I cherish because
it is just, because it honors humanity, because it concerns my country,
⟨because it will hurt England⟩ and because my friends [13] and I are
deeply committed to it.

The next campaign will be interesting; we are told that the English
are sending us some Hanoverians. Much worse, some time earlier
they threatened us with Russians. A small threat from France would
lessen the number of these reinforcements. The more I see of the English, the more I understand that one must speak out to them.

After I have wearied you with public affairs, I must also bore you
with my private ones. No one could spend each day more agreeably in
a foreign country than I do here. I have only praise for what I see,
and every day I am more satisfied with the conduct of Congress toward me. Though my military duties have permitted me to know only
a few of its members, they have overwhelmed me with civilities and
kindnesses. The new president, Mr. Laurens, one of the most respected men in America, is a special friend of mine. As for the army,
I have had the happiness of gaining the friendship of everyone ⟨and I
flatter myself that it is impossible to desire to be better off than I am
here⟩. No occasion is lost to give me proofs of it. You know my intention was to command a division, yet I went the whole summer without
such a command. All that time I spent in General Washington's
household, just as though I were in the home of a friend of twenty
years. After my return from Jersey, he asked me to choose from several brigades the division that would suit me best. I have taken one
composed entirely of Virginians. It is undermanned at the present,
even in proportion to the weakness of the whole army; it is almost entirely naked, but I have been led to believe that I shall get some cloth
with which I shall make some clothing, and some recruits of whom I
must then make soldiers at about the same time. Unhappily, one task
is more difficult than the other, even for persons who are more adept
than I am. If I haven't already practiced my profession enough to be
proficient at it, this work will be very useful for my development. A

major general replaces a French lieutenant general and a *maréchal de camp* in their most interesting activities; thus I would be able to make good use of my talents and my experience, if Providence and my baptismal certificate have given me reason to boast of either one. I read, I study, I examine, I listen, I think, and out of all of that I try to form an opinion into which I cram as much common sense as possible. I shall not talk very much for fear of saying something stupid; for I am not disposed to abuse the confidence that the Americans have deigned to show me. Such is the plan of conduct that I have followed and shall continue to follow. But when I have ideas that I think might be valuable, with a little alteration, I do not hesitate to bring them to a noble arbiter, who has given me reason to believe that he is pleased with them. On the other hand, when my heart tells me that a favorable opportunity has presented itself, I am inclined to run the necessary risk. But I do not think that a thirst for glory permits us to hazard the well-being of an army, or even a part of it, which is neither ready nor designed for an offensive. If I dared risk a maxim without uttering an absurdity, I would say that, given the forces we have, we must rely upon a purely defensive plan except for those times when we are forced into an action; for I think I have observed that British troops are more surprised by a brisk attack than by a firm defense.

⟨As for my return to France, it seems to me that it was your opinion, as well as that of all those persons who have my welfare in mind, that I should remain here for more than one campaign. That opinion will bind me; besides, as the present campaign is not ended and we are only partly situated in what cannot really be called winter quarters, I believe in conscience, as well as in deference to the advice I most respect, that I am obliged to remain here for some time yet.⟩

This letter will be brought to you by the famous Adams, whose name is surely known to you. Since I have never permitted myself to leave the army, I have not been able to meet him. He wished that I should introduce him in France, and particularly to you. May I hope that you will be good enough to see him, and even to give him some understanding of how things stand at present? I imagine that you would not have cause to regret talking with a man whose merits are so well known. His ardent wish is to obtain the esteem of our nation; one of his friends told me that himself.

AL (NIC: Dean Collection), translation. The manuscript has been edited in Lafayette's later hand. Significant passages omitted from Lafayette, *Mémoires,* are printed in angle brackets.

A nineteenth-century copy of the letter is preceded by Lafayette's note: "The Duc d'Ayen, my father-in-law, was not among the least severe critics of my departure, but he restored me to his affection with all the kindness and sincerity which characterize him. His friendly congratulations touched me deeply, and this sentiment moves me again today to repeat here some details contained in two letters which were addressed to him" (Autobiographical Notes I, fol. 46).

1. D'Ayen left Rome and his traveling companions on October 22 to return to France (Comte de Tessé, Journal de mon voyage en Italie en 1777 [NIC: Dean Collection]).

2. Probably one of the letters mentioned in Lafayette to Laurens, November 29.

3. Lafayette and his wife lived in the Noailles house on the Rue St. Honoré. Adrienne de Lafayette's sister Louise and her husband, the Vicomte de Noailles, had just had a son. The vicomte belonged to the Mouchy branch of the family. It was their home that Lafayette referred to as "the other Hôtel de Noailles."

4. Howe's plan at Brandywine was similar to that at the Battle of Long Island (August 27, 1776): part of his force created a diversion while his main army turned the exposed American flank.

5. General Wayne lost about 150 men in an engagement near Paoli Tavern on the night of September 21, 1777.

6. General Greene. He and Cornwallis eventually had approximately 8000 troops each. See p. 103, note 25.

7. A rumor that Cornwallis had been killed at Gloucester persisted into 1778. John Thaxter wrote John Adams from York on January 10:

> Lord Cornwallis, it is said, was kill'd in an Action lately, in which the Marquiss de Fayette was engaged. The Report seems tolerably well founded. Dr. Rush says the following facts are well attested, viz., That an Officer was seen carried off the field, to a certain House—that about a fortnight after, a very elegant Coffin was carried to that House—that a most pompous funeral was made—and that the Officers of the Army wear black Crape on their Arms. The Doctor, however, is not positive. There is an Account also that his Lordship's baggage is on board the Vessel bound to England, but no Certainty of *his* being on board; it is said he is not. [L. H. Butterfield, ed., *Adams Family Correspondence* (Cambridge: Harvard University Press, 1963), 2:383]

8. Abbé Raynal discusses the Quakers in glowing terms in *Histoire philosophique et politique des établissemens et du commerce des Européens dans les deux Indes* (The Hague, 1773–1774), 7:1–39.

9. Congress officially conferred commissions, but Washington's recommendations as commander in chief carried great weight with its members. Congress had followed Washington's recommendations in appointing Conway a brigadier general and in giving Lafayette command of a division.

10. Lafayette is probably referring to the Conway Cabal. See Lafayette to Washington, December 30.

11. Changed in Lafayette's later hand to "the proud."

12. "Us" here refers to Americans. At the beginning of this paragraph "us" refers to the French.

13. Changed in Lafayette's later hand to "American friends."

To [Henry Laurens]

At the Gulph's camp the 18 december 1777

Dear Sir

Is it not very importune to send you not only the very tedious letters I trouble You with, but even those which are directed to several gentlemen some of 'em you never saw in your life. But, Sir, friendship and confidence are to live in the same family to which is added in-

dulgence, and this I hope I schall alwaïs find in you. Letters are generally so neglected, so badly directed, and forwarded, that I took
upon myself to desire you to have them sent or by occasions or by the
post office at York town when you will have time or you will think of
it. I believe that I schall be obliged too to beg your care for my french
dispatches when You'l tell to me in what time they may be directed to
Mr. Adams. The occasions for Boston seem to me very uncommon in
camp.

I have been glad to see that a medall was presented to General
Gates in order to perpetue the memory and have a Kind of triumphi-
cal mark of his succès.[1] Such a reward is the most noble and flattering
for the man who received it, and in the room of General Gates it
would seem to me the most agreable one. It is about as when the
republic of Genoes [Genoa] erected a statue to the Duke de Richelieu for a much less important service.

Let me speack not to the president of Congress but to my friend
about a matter which concerns me very much. Monsieur le Chevalier
de Gimat my first aid de camp is a man of birth, education, and
merit. He came over vith the desire of being in my family and never
asked neither desired any monney since the begining of this expedition. He is now captain of infanterye in the french service not captain
by *commission or retreat* [2] but captain in a rgt. where he has done two
campaigns of war. Do'nt you think that if that gentleman schould ask
here the commission of lieutenant colonel following the army he
would not obtain it? Tho his being in my family prevents his advancement—what is your opinion about the matter? Must I apply to the
president of Congress? All what I wraït here is entirely unknown to
Mr. de Gimat who never spoke to me a word of it.

I received letters from France but indifferent ones. The last one is
from a valet de chambre of mine [3] who speaks much about the good
health of my family but nothing about war—however you think that
such a man can not be as well acquainted with the projects of the
Governement as one of my friends could be. He promises me several
letters by the same occasion which I did not receive—perhaps they
will come. The letter of that valet de chambre is dated the 7 september. A french officer has got one from the 1st. october by which he is
acquainted that the old Count de St. Germain had given since fiew
days his resignation. Mr. de Montbarrey who was under him and
succeeds now to the ministry has not strengths enough to stay a long
time against powerfull efforts. Then no other minister (I believe so)
can't be done but a particular acquaintance of mine [4]—if I am not
mistaken who ever it will be of those two or three concurrents I can
answer he will be fond of war. I dare not hope that the Duke de

Choiseuïl would be immediately elected—the queen is for him but the King has strong prejugces against him—however after having settled there some of his friends he will perhaps come himself in spite of every body. I tell you in confidence all what I know about the matter. If you have received intelligences or niews papers from France be so good as to let me have them. We are setting out to morrow if the weather is tolerable for our hutting ground.[5] It is a very soldier-like habitation, therefore I am very fond of it for my own satisfaction and pleasure.

With the highest esteem and tenderest affection I have the honor to be Dear Sir Your most obedient servant

THE MQUIS. DE LAFAYETTE

ALS (NjMoW: Manuscript Collection).
1. On November 4 Congress resolved to present Gates with a gold medal commemorating the victory at Saratoga (*JCC*, 9:866–867).
2. By "commission" Lafayette probably meant a commission by brevet, which promotes an officer to a higher rank without an increase in pay and with a limited exercise of the higher rank. By "retreat" he meant on reserve status.
3. Desplaces. Letter not found.
4. Lafayette may be referring to the Comte de Broglie.
5. Valley Forge.

From Henry Laurens

York 20th. Decemr. 1777

Sir—

From the morning of the 9th. Inst. to this minute I have been close prisoner to the Gout, much the greatest part of the intermediate time, in very great pain & at this Instant unable to put a foot to the floor, Sitting in Bed & writing in the most awkward positions from Morning to Night for these reasons forgive me, Noble Marquis, for barely acknowledging the Receipt of your favor of the 14th. Inst. Be assured Sir, I will pay that regard which is due to your Commands as soon as it shall please the superintendent of Gouts to discharge me from the present Billet.

I have the honour of inclosing you a small packet which I hope is from France because it came to my hands with other Letters from thence, via Boston.

If Sir, you incline to write by Mr. Adams be assured your own Commands will be a sufficient introduction, he well knows your Style & title & I am sure he reveres your Character & Merits. The addition of a Line recommending him to the countenance of your Noble friends in France will not only lay him under great obligations, but be a means of enabling him to be more serviceable in his ambassadorial capacity & consequently be serving the general cause of these States. I have the honour to be Noble Sir—Your obliged & most obedient humb. Sert.

LbC (ScHi: Henry Laurens Papers).

To Adrienne de Noailles de Lafayette[T]

In camp near Valley Forge, December 22 [1777]

I have been taken by surprise, dear heart; I had reserved your letter for last, expecting to have plenty of time to write it, but the person who is to take my letter to Mr. Adams has just informed me that he must leave immediately. I had already prepared a long letter to M. le Duc d'Ayen, one to the prince, and another to my grandfather.[1] Now I have time only to say hello to you. A longer letter that I shall send to you by another means will perhaps arrive even sooner.

I have received the news of your happy delivery, and it fills me with the purest and keenest joy. I was never so happy in my life as at the moment the news arrived. I have not received any letters from you on the subject, but I have been informed that some have arrived in five or six American ports. You can appreciate how impatient I am to receive them. I have written to you since I heard of your delivery, and you should have received that letter.[2] This one will be taken to you by the famous Mr. Adams, whom I beg you to favor with every possible courtesy. Since I have been with the army all the time, I have not had the opportunity to get to know him very well, but I know that his intelligence is equal to his attainments, and he is very unpretentious. I hope that the courtesies he receives from you and my friends, and the acquaintances you procure for him, will be partial repayment for all those I have received here.

M. le Duc d'Ayen, and especially the prince, will tell you at greater length the details of what has happened to me. Dear heart, I shall content myself with repeating to you here, with a pleasure that is always new, that I love you with an inexpressible tenderness, that I love you more than ever, and that I hope we shall be happy all our lives in our mutual love. I embrace our two dear daughters thousands of times. Tell them that their papa loves them madly, as he does their charming mother. You must believe that I shall not lose a moment in rejoining you as soon as I can. Farewell, farewell, I embrace you ten million times.

A thousand fond regards to Mme la Duchesse d'Ayen, to M. le Maréchal de Noailles, etc. Farewell, farewell, love me always.

I hope that Mr. Adams will tell you a great deal about my close and charming friend, the great and honorable General Washington.

L.

LbC (NIC: Dean Collection), in Adrienne de Lafayette's hand; translation.
1. Letter to d'Ayen, December 16. The other letters have not been found.
2. Letter not found.

Memorandum on Dress and Appearance

At Camp the 28 December 1777

Some of the general officers gave yesterday theyr opinion to your excellency for the form of our niew cloathes. I beg leave to explain here my ideas about this point.[1] In considering our scarcity I try to make them as confortable as possible.

1st. The hat must be round and turn'd up in one side, the bream of about three inches—such an hat would be very good against the sun and the rain. We have not new hats enough to turn them up in any other uniform manner, and those little hats would look very cleverly. It will be perhaps possible to adorn them with a little feather.

2d. The stock must be black made with hair, leather, or some slight black stoff with a leather in the inside to keep it firm around the neck.

3d. Each soldier must have three and never less than two good shirts. Otherwise it is impossible to have him clean. If we can't get shirts we must [im]press them in the several states.

4th. Theyr hair must be cut very short no lower than the beginning of the stock and wash'd every day.

5th. The blanckets must have one or two buttons to surround the breast and be a kind of great coat.

6th. The coat must be only a waïst coat (at the french military fashion) with large lapels, which are turn'd back in a fair weather, and buttonn'd upon the breast against the cold, rain &c., a standind collar of one inch and a half, the sleeves [2] of three inches and half. I wish'd if possible that the ground would be uniforme, the lappels to distinguish the states, and the collar and sleeves to distinguish the regiments. Those waist coats are to have lanings of the same color as the lappels if possible. Some gentlemen in the army have the dimensions of those waist coats.

7. They men should have a little jacquet without belt neither pocquet and a pair of over alls under which they could have stockings and breaches if they can get some, [otherwise] they'l do without. The jacquet and over all to be of woollen—this is for the winter. In summer time they will have linen over alls and jacquets under the waïst coat without breaches neither stockings, even when they could get them. The little jacquet in the over alls with two buttons to keep it.

8. The schoes to be made with a great care and pretty easy. The skins of all the beefs killed in the army or in publick departements schould be employed to it. If we could have little half boots not heavy but as a kind of little half gaitter it would do much better. This to be alwaïs without stockings, and the inside of the schoe greased every day—those half gaitters would save the bucles for the shoes.

9. The men should comb theyr hair every day after washing it, cut theyr beard twice a week and alwaïs when they are upon parade for guards, and take baths when they will have opportunity to it.

10. The men should pass every day (principally those who are upon duty) a review of cleaneness to know if they are not dirty and drest in an unbecoming manner. The commanding officer of each compagny schould muster twice a week the cloathes of theyr men, and theyr bags to know both if they have the due cloathes, soap, grease &c. and if they have nothing more. In the first case that the loss should be repaired at theyr expense and themselves punished, in the second it must be confiscated for the publick.

11. The non commissioned officers are to be distinguished, therefore I give to the sergeants two pieces of stoff of a different color arround theyr arms close by the sleeves and one to the corporals.

12. I wish'd too that the officers and each rank among them could be distinguished by theyr epaulets, or any other manner, and the general officers to take care that all the officers should preserve such distinctions. It would prevent the several mistakes which happen every day in the army, and oblige the soldiers to pay due respects to theyr officers. They should be ordered to put theyr hands to theyr hats (without pulling them of) when they cross an officer, to present theyr arms, when upon centry, to the general officers and field officers of theyr own rgt. and officers of the day, and to shoulder theyr arms for the others.

13. As I include the cartrige boxes among the cloaths I wish that some proper means should be taken for getting better ones.[3]

14. The field officer commanding a regiment is to review his regi-

ment every week, look very attentively the arms, cloathes, bags &c. &c., know the employement of every piece which is not to be found, inquire if it has been repaired at the expense of the soldier, and punish every officer or soldier who is guilty of neglect in that point. The same thing to be done by the brigadier twice in a month, and by the commandant of a division when he pleases to arrive in a moment where he will be unexpected.

15. The review of cleaness to be alwais attended by the commissioned officer every day.

16. Such are the ideas which I submit to your excellency. I know that the circumstances should admit some variations. But in taking à way the ornaments of my scheeme, I think that it offers the most confortable and easy manner of cloathing our troops.

THE MQUIS. DE LAFAYETTE M.G.

If we could get materials enough it would be possible to have a large belt out of the jacquet and independant of it, which could be tide upon the belly. The bags must be strong and [held] by the two shoulders in crossing upon the breast.

AMS (ScHi: Henry Laurens Papers). Written for Washington; enclosed in Lafayette to Laurens, January 2.

1. There are memoranda from two other general officers at this time in the George Washington Papers (DLC: Series 4) which suggest improvements in the army, but there are no others that specifically discuss dress and appearance.

2. Cuffs.

3. Most of the cartridge boxes were made of leather with a wooden insert to hold the cartridges. Many lacked leather flaps on either the outside or the inside to keep the ammunition dry in the rain, and the powder was often ruined in a storm.

To [Robert Morris]

Camp the 30 december 1777

Dear Sir

I Come again to trouble you about my busineses—but I want some dollars from you which I desire you would send me by Some opportunity.[1] We schall make the the same conditions or any other as you will be pleased. I expect gooddill of currency paper from Charlestown [2] and if you choose I could let you have it with any interest you'l think proper. In all I desire you to be alwaïs master of the conditions betwen us. I took already the liberty of taking from Count de Pulaski two hundred dollars which he was to send to you. Mr. Robert Buchanan will ask to you thirty seven pounds 10d. or perhaps more which I beg you would give to him or any body from him. For the remains out of those two employements I hope you will be so good as to send it to me by some occasion. I beg you thousand pardons for being so troublesome, but my confidence issues from your kindness for me since the first moment of my arrival in this country.

I gave in landing at Charlestown every guinea I had for currency paper. I thought that I could never leave soon enough that [h]eavy gold for continental monney, and as some body proposed me some trifling advantage I made to him the most severe reproaches. However I wish'd now to have about fifty guineas if it was possible, and to give for it what interest or bills of exange you would think proper.

We have no news in camp since the ennemy went again into Phila-delphia. It is very desagreable to be obliged by common sense and every rule of war to aknowledge that we can not attack those redoubts in our present circumstances without the total ruin of the american army. Attacking must not be our present scheme. Let us have men to fight—this is the first thing. Let us make soldiers of those men as far as a so little time will permit. Those things will not be done before the spring, and if they are done in a right manner then we must exert ourselves in the field. The building of our hutts is advancing —there I hope our men will be very confortable. I have been very glad to hear that Virginia took the resolution of filling up all his reg-ular rgts., for my division is very far from being strong in conse-quence of the most part being to be dismissed soon. However before my coming there great many of 'em have been reinlisted for the war on the condition of going on furloughs immediately. With the most affectionnate Sentiments I have the honor to be dear Sir Your most obedient servant

THE MQUIS. DE LAFAYETTE

Will you be so good as to send this letter to Colonel Armand.[3]

ALS (PHC: Charles Roberts Autograph Letters Collection).
1. Robert Morris was acting as Lafayette's banker at this time, lending him money whenever he needed it. Henkels, *Confidential Correspondence of Robert Morris*, p. 125, lists a receipt signed by Lafayette for money received from Morris (amount not specified), December 30, 1777.
2. Lafayette still had not received money from the sale of the cargo he had brought from France. It was being held by Basmarein's agent in Charleston and was to be sent to Lafayette as soon as the agent received a release from Basmarein's firm in France (Kalb to Saint-Paul, November 7).
3. Letter not found.

Robert Morris, member of the Continental Congress's Committee for Foreign Affairs and Lafayette's banker

To George Washington

My dear General

I went yesterday morning to Head Quarters with an intention of Speaking to Your Excellency But you were too Buzy and I Shall lay down in this letter What I Wished to Say.

I don't Need telling you How I am Sorry for all what Happens Since some time. It is a necessary dependence of my most tender and Respectful friendship for you, Which affection is as true and Candid as the other Sentiments of my Heart and Much Stronger than a So new acquaintance Seems to admit. But an other Reason to Be concerned in the present circumstances is my ardent, and perhaps enthusiastic Wishes for the Happiness and Liberty of this Country. I See plainly that America Can defend Herself if proper measures are taken and now I Begin to fear that She could Be lost By Herself and Her own Sons.

When I was in Europe I thought that Here almost every man was a lover of liberty and would Rather die free than live slave. You Can Conceive my astonishment when I saw that Toryism was as oppenly professed as Wighism itself. However at that time I Believed that all good Americans were United together, that the Confidence of Congress in you was Unbounded. Then I Entertained the Certitude that America Would Be independant in case she would not loose You. Take a way for an instant that modest diffidence of yourself (which, pardon my freedom, my dear general, is Sometimes too Great, and I wish you could know as well as myself, what difference there is Betwen you and any other man Upon the continent), You Shall See very plainly that if you were lost for America, there is nobody who could keep the army and the Revolution for six months. There are oppen dissentions in Congress, parties who Hate one another as much as the Common Ennemy, stupid men who without knowing a single word about war undertake to judge you, to make Ridiculous Comparisons; they are infatuated with Gates without thinking of the different Circumstances, and Believe that attaking is the only thing necessary to Conquer. Those ideas are Entertained in their minds By some Jealous men and perhaps secret friends to the British Government who want to push you in a moment of ill Humour to some Rash enterprise upon the lines or against a much stronger army. I should not take the liberty of mentionning these particularities to you if I did not Receive a letter about this matter from a Young Good natured Gentleman at York whom Connway Has Ruined By His Cunning Bad advice But Who Entertains the Greatest Respect for You.[1]

I have been surprised at first [2] to see the niew establishement of this board of war, to see the difference betwen northen and southern departement, to see resolved from Congress about military operations—but the promotion of Canway is beyhond all my expectations.[3] I should be glad to see niew major generals after me, because as I know that you take some interest to my happiness and reputation, it is perhaps an occasion for your excellency to give me more agreable commands in some interesting instances. On the other hand Gal. Connway says he is entirely a man to be disposed of by me, he calls himself my soldier, and the reason of such behaviour for me is that he wishs to be well spoken of at the french court, and his protector the Mquis. de Castries is an intimate acquaintance of mine—but Since the letter of Lord Stirligg I inquired in his caracter.[4] I found that he was an ambitious and dangerous man. He has done all [in h]is power by cunning maneuvres to take off my confidence and affection for you. His desire was to engage me to leave this country.[5] Now I see all the general officers of the army ⟨revolted⟩ against Congress.[6] Such disputes if known by the ennemy, can be attended with horrid consequences. I am very sorry when ever I perceive troubles raised amongs the defensers of the same cause, but my concern is much greater when I find officers coming from France, officers of some character in my country to whom any fault of that kind may be imputed. The reason of my fondness for Connway was is being by all means a very brave and very good officer. However that part of maneuvres &c. which seems so extraordinary to Congress is not so very difficult for any man of common sense who applies himself to it. I must pay to Gal. Portaïl and some french officers who came to speack to me the justice to say that I found them as I could wish upon this occasion—for it has made a great noise amongs many in the army. I wish indeed those matters could be soon pacified. I wish your excellency could let them know how necessary you are to them and engage them in the same time to keep peace and simulate love among themselves till the moment when those little disputes schall not be attended with such inconveniences. It would be a too great pity that slavery, dishonor, ruin, and unhappiness of a whole world schould issue from trifling differents betwixt some fiew men.

You will find Perhaps this letter very useless and even very importune—but I was desirous of having a pretty long conversation with your excellency upon the present circumstances to explain you what I think of this matter. As the proper opportunity for it is not to be found, I took the liberty of laying down some of my ideas in this letter, because it is interesting for my satisfaction to be convinced that you, my dear general, who have been indulgent enough as to permit me to look on you as upon a friend, could know the confession of my sentiment in a matter which I consider as a very important one. I have the warmest Love for my country and for every good frenchmen. Theyr succès feels my heart with joy. But, sir, besides Connway is an Irishman, I want country men who deserve in every point to do honor to theyr country. That gentleman had engaged me by entertaining my head with ideas of glory and shining projects, and I must confess for my shame that it is a too certain way of deceiving me.

I wish'd to join to the fiew theories about war I can have, and the fiew dispositions nature gave perhaps to me, the experience of thirty campaigns, in hope that I schould be able to be more useful in the present circumstance. My desire of deserving your satisfaction is stronger than ever, and every where you'l employ me you can be certain of my trying every exertion in my power to succeed. I am now fixed to your fate and I shall follow it and sustain it as well by my sword as by all means in my power. ⟨I beg you will keep the letter secret.⟩ You will pardon my importunity in favor of the sentiment which dictate it. Youth and frienship make perhaps myself too warm, but I feel the greatest concern of all what happens since some time. With the most tenderest and profond respect I have the honor to be, dear general, Your most obedient humble Servant

⟨The Mquis. de⟩ Lafayette

ALS (PEL: Hubbard Collection). The manuscript has been edited in ink, in Lafayette's later hand. The first page is marked "copy" and the first two pages have been recopied in Lafayette's later hand. The text of significant deletions has been restored in angle brackets.

1. Possibly Thomas Mullens, Conway's aide-de-camp.
2. End of recopied pages.
3. On December 13 Congress created two inspectors general to be responsible for troop instruction and discipline. Congress unanimously elected Conway to one of the positions and promoted him to major general. The other position was left vacant (*JCC*, 9:1023–1026). Conway arrived at Valley Forge to take up his new position about December 29.
4. In his letter of November 3 to Washington, Stirling enclosed an extract he said was taken from an October letter from Conway to Gates. Colonel James Wilkinson (just arrived from Saratoga with news of the victory) had transmitted the extract to Stirling's aide, Major William McWilliams. It read: "Heaven has been determined to save your Country; or a weak General and bad Counsellors would have ruined it." Stirling commented: "Such wicked duplicity of Conduct I shall always think it my duty to detect" (DLC: George Washington Papers, Series 4). Washington showed Stirling's letter only to members of his military family and to Lafayette, since Conway had already spoken to him about it (Washington to Gates, January 4, 1778, in Fitzpatrick, *Writings of Washington*, 10:264). Despite Washington's discretion in showing the letter to only a few people, by the beginning of January 1778 the letter and Conway were the subjects of camp gossip. Conway was represented as one of the leaders of a cabal, formed by Washington's

detractors in the army and Congress, to replace Washington with Gates as commander in chief. The cabal had no basis in fact, but Conway was discredited because of it and could not assume his position as inspector general (Knollenberg, *Washington and the Revolution;* and Rossie, *Politics of Command,* pp. 188–202). An additional result was a sort of cabal formed in Washington's favor, such that a former friend of Conway's in Congress told him that "any Body that Displeas'd or did not admire the Commander in chief ought not to be kept in the army" (Conway to Gates, June 7, 1778 [NHi: Gates Papers, Box 9]).

5. A reference to the plan Lafayette discussed with Conway for an expedition against the East Indies, which required that someone go to France to make preparations.

6. On January 2 a protest by the general officers was submitted to Washington through Sullivan. It complained of Conway's promotion over other brigadiers who were his seniors and of Congress' promotion of Wilkinson (given a brevet of brigadier general for bringing the news of Saratoga to Congress). The officers requested that Congress "settle a regular Line of Promotion, not to be departed from, but in Cases of extraordinary Merit, or upon great political Principles. Under this Exception, we are happy to mention the Marquis Le Fayette, whose Sacrifices to our Cause, and personal Merit highly deserve the Honor bestowed upon him" (*Sullivan Papers,* 1:606–608; 2:1).

From George Washington

Head Quarters Decr. 31st. 1777

My Dear Marquis,

Your favour of Yesterday conveyed to me fresh proof of that friendship and attachment which I have happily experienced since the first of our acquaintance, and for which I entertain sentiments of the purest affection. It will ever constitute part of my happiness to know that I stand well in your opinion, because I am satisfied that you can have no views to answer by throwing out false colours, and that you possess a Mind too exalted to condescend to dirty arts and low intrigues to acquire a reputation. Happy, thrice happy, would it have been for this Army and the cause we are embarked in, if the same generous spirit had pervaded all the Actors in it. But one Gentleman, whose name you have mentioned, had, I am confident, far different views.[1] His ambition and great desire of being puffed off as one of the first Officers of the Age, could only be equalled by the means which he used to obtain them; but finding that I was determined not to go beyond the line of my duty to indulge him in the first, nor, to exceed the strictest rules of propriety, to gratify him in the second, he became my inveterate Enemy;[2] and has, I am persuaded, practised every art to do me an injury, even at the expense of reprobating a measure, which did not succeed, that he himself advised to.[3] How far he may have accomplished his ends, I know not, and, but for considerations of a public nature, I care not. For it is well known, that neither ambitious, nor lucrative motives led me to accept my present appointments; in the discharge of which, I have endeavoured to observe one steady and uniform conduct, which I shall invariably pursue, while I have the honour to command, regardless of the Tongue of slander or the powers of detraction.

The fatal tendency of disunion is so obvious that I have, in earnest terms, exhorted such officers as have expressed their dissatisfaction at General Conway's promotion, to be cool and dispassionate in their decision upon the matter, and I have hopes that they will not suffer any hasty determination to injure the service. At the same time, it must be acknowledged that Officers' feelings upon these occasions are not to be restrained, although You may controul their actions.[4]

The other observations contained in your Letter, have too much truth in them, and it is much to be lamented that things are not now as they formerly were; but we must not, in so great a contest, expect to meet with nothing but Sunshine. I have no doubt but that every thing happens so for the best; that we shall triumph over all our misfortunes, and shall, in the end, be ultimately happy; when, my Dear Marquis, if you will give me your Company in Virginia, we will laugh at our past difficulties and the folly of others; where I will endeavour, by every civility in my power, to shew you how much and how sincerely, I am, Your Affectionate and obedient servant,

G. WASHINGTON

LbC (DLC: George Washington Papers, Series 3H).

1. Conway.

2. Conway complained to Gates on January 4, 1778 about his reception at camp: "I have been cooly received at my arrival here. I ask'd Leave of the commander in chief to Beginn without Delay the instruction of the troops, as the Different returns necessary for the reviews were not yet ready. He answer'd that when the Regulations for the purpose would be [made] by the Board of War he would give the necessary orders to have them carried into execution. He added some remarks upon my appointment which Does not seem to please him" (NHi: Gates Papers, Box 9). As the Board of War moved slowly, it would be some time before Conway could exercise his duties. Washington maintained that Conway was "received and treated with proper respect to his Official character, and that he has no cause to justify the assertion, that he could not expect any support for fulfilling the duties of his Appointment" (Washington to the president of Congress, January 2, 1778, in Fitzpatrick, *Writings of Washington,* 10:249).

3. A reference to the alleged cabal to remove Washington as commander in chief. See preceding letter.

4. Sullivan informed Washington on December 30 of the general officers' intention to protest Conway's promotion and requested him to "Defer announcing in orders any promotions among the General officers which have Lately taken place in Congress" (*Sullivan Papers,* 1:605–606). Washington tacitly endorsed the protest by delaying the announcement of Conway's promotion and appointment as inspector general.

To George Washington

Walley Forge Decr. 31, 1777

Dear General

I Schould have much more reproached myself the liberty I took of wraïting to your excellency, if I had believed it could engage you in the trouble of answering to that letter—but, now, as you have wrote it, I must tell you that I received this favor with the greatest satisfaction and pleasure.[1] Every assurance and proof of your affection fills my heart with joy because that sentiment of yours is extremely dear and precious to me. A tender and respectful attachement for you, and an invariable frankness will be discovered in my mind the more as you will know me better—but after those merits I must tell you that very few are to be found. I never wish'd so heartely to be intrusted by nature with an immensity of talents, than on this occasion ⟨where my frienship⟩ could be then of some use to your glory and happiness as well as to mine own.

⟨[What?] man do not join the pure ambition of glory with the other ambitions of advancement rank and fortune. As an ardent lover of laurels I can not bear the idea that so noble a sentiment should be mixed with Any low one.⟩ In your preaching moderation to the brigadiers upon such an occasion, I am not surprised to find your virtous character. As I hope my warm interest is known to your excellency, I dare entertain the idea that you will be so indulgent as to let me know every thing concerning you when ever you will not be under the law of secrecy or particular circumstances. With the most tender and affectionate friendship with the most profond respect I have the honor to be, Dear General, Your most humble and obedient servant

⟨THE MQUIS. DE⟩ LAFAYETTE

ALS (PEL: Hubbard Collection). The manuscript has been edited in pencil and in ink, in Lafayette's later hand. The text of significant deletions has been restored in angle brackets.

1. See two preceding letters.

To Henry Laurens

in Camp the 2nd. day of the year [1778]

I am undone, my dear Sir, our cloathes, the fair object of my Most charming hopes, they are, I am told, detained in York town and confined in a dark jail. Consider, if you please, that they are innocent strangers, travelling tho' this state, and very desirous of meeting the virginian regiments they belong to. If they are detained only for exerting the most respectable rights of hospitality receive here my thanks in the name of Virginia. But if it is possible, I do not want they should be entertained longer, and I wish very heartely they schould appear soon upon the nacked backs of our honest virginians soldiers for whom they have been destinated, pay'd and sent to the army by the way of York town where they have been so kindly received as I was told yesterday night.

It has been objected to me by an officer of an other state, that Virginia was indebted for cloathes with the other provinces, and that Congress would avoid troubling her for the pay'ment of them. But, Sir, rags had been given to us, and rags are upon our backs since the begining, which we schall deliver very heartely when asked for. It is just in case our Virginia schould be indebted that she would press in his own bosom the düe quantity of scattered and non uniforme cloathes she has received, (if however the other provinces have furnished a greater proportion, in distinguishing provincial and continental cloathes) but in the same time it would be unfair to deprive us of those uniforms which are our property, and schall be I hope our safety, happiness, and pride in the next campaign.

I Am told that my division will be about five thousand strong—reduce it to four and five hundred for *reasons obvious*.[1] I was in hopes that those men would be drest in a convenient uniform and confortable manner, and now I begin to give up those flattering ideas. If I could receive at once cloathes for the whole, then I should not trouble any body about the matter till the end of this war, if this war is to be carried on in a vigorous manner, which do not so much depend on the warlike resolveds than the civil exertions of Congress. I send you (*for you*) the manner in which I desire my men could be drest, not however as a scheme-maker, but because that plan seems agree with the wiews of his excellency.

We are at the begining of the year. I desire you could have hundred happy ones before you—to see your good intentions accomplished, to see peace, union, and love and glory attend all the right enterprizes of this for ever free continent, to see all my american friends beloved and respected in it, to see you, Sir, who is among the most intimate and dearest I ever had any where, alwaïs happy and satisfied as well in your family as in public businesses, because you schall never have any satisfaction but in the good and the right, are the most ardent wishes of Dear Sir Your most obedient servant

THE MQUIS. DE LAFAYETTE

I desire you would be so good as to speack about those cloathes to the Virginian gentlemen in Congress.

ALS (ScHi: Henry Laurens Papers); erroneously dated 1777. Encloses Lafayette's Memorandum on Dress and Appearance of December 28.
  1. Lafayette means 4500. On January 1, 1778, his division had 3086 men ("Arrangement of the Army for the Campaign of 1778 & present state of the Battalions," in Fitzpatrick, *Writings of Washington,* 10:opposite p. 246).

To Patrick Henry

Camp near the Valley Forge the 3d January [1778]

Sir

Give me leave to make you my thanks for the civilities which I received from you in one of your letters to his excellency Gal. Washington.[1] I am very happy to find this occasion of telling you how I am desirous of being acquainted with you, and how much I wish'd to deserve your esteem. I am highly sensible of all the advantages I obtained in being intrusted with the command of a virginian division, and I dare entertain the idea that such a favor will intitle me to some connexions with that state. I hope that Virginia will be satisfied with the conduct of those of her brave sons I'l have the honor to fight with. Glory and prosperity are done to attend your country, and she will receive a niew splendor by that hero who is born in her bosom for the happiness of America and the admiration of the world.

I have heard with the greatest pleasure that Virginia had taken the most fine and useful resolution of compleating her regiments in the army immediately, in order to have them ready for the next so interesting and perhaps decisive campaign.[2] I wish such a step could be followed by all the states, and then we could depend upon a very respectable army. Our cloathes are, I am told, arrived in York town, and I desire very heartely to see them in camp. As officers will be useful for bringing here the men who are to be sent, I desired (according to our general's orders) those who are gone home to Mention theyr arrival to Your excellency and take your directions to know if they can be of some use when they'l come again to the army at the end of theyr furloughs.

Receive, Sir, my sincere thanks for the trouble you have taken in sending me some letters from France. Is it not very uncivil to be importune upon the same matter? But I have heard from a gentleman in Hampton who is reccommanded to me and is just now arrived with a parcel of letters. His vessel has been sunk by some eglish frigate, three men only have escaped, he did not save any thing but a trunk and a bag which, he says, have been broked and plundered à schore. He seems in a great distress. I take the liberty of giving to him some hopes by the inclosed letter that you will be so good as to order some notice to be taken of him.[3] I desire him also to direct his dispatches to your excellency in case you would Give yourself the trouble of sending them to General Washington as you have done for the others. I beg you, Sir, to receive my thousand very sincere and humble excuses for making myself so free in the first letter I have the honor to adress you. This liberty will increase yet my obligations, and I wish'd to be able to convince you of all the gratefulness I entertain for your kindness towards me.

With the greatest desire of your acquaintance and ambition of your esteem with the most sincere respect I have the honor to be Your excellency's the most obedient servant

THE MQUIS. DE LAFAYETTE

In case that gentleman would be in any want of monney I dare hope you would be [so kind] as to order some to be Given to him for me.

ALS (ViHi); erroneously dated 1777. Patrick Henry was serving as governor of Virginia.

1. Henry wrote Washington on December 6: "I take the Liberty to send under cover to your Excellency two Letters from France to the Marquis dela Fayette. One of them is from his Lady I believe. I beg to be presented to him in the most acceptable manner. I greatly revere his person & amiable Character" (DLC: George Washington Papers, Series 4).

2. On December 4 the Virginia House of Delegates resolved to complete their Continental regiments, and to replace the Ninth Virginia Regiment, captured at Germantown, with the First Virginia State Regiment (*Journal of the House of Delegates of the Commonwealth of Virginia*, October 20, 1777–January 24, 1778 [Williamsburg, 1778], pp. 57–58).

3. Moré de Pontgibaud related the story of his eventful arrival in America in his memoirs and recalled his meeting with Lafayette at Valley Forge (incorrectly placing the event in November): "I presented myself to him, and told him frankly my whole story. He listened to my history with attention and kindness, and at my request enrolled me as a volunteer. He also wrote to France and before long received a reply confirming the truth of my statements; he then appointed me one of his *aides-de-camp*, with the rank of Major, and from that moment never ceased to load me with benefits and marks of confidence" (Chevalier de Pontgibaud [Charles-Albert de Moré], *A French Volunteer of the War of Independence*, trans. and ed. Robert B. Douglas [1897; reprint ed., Port Washington, N.Y.: Kennikat Press, 1968], pp. 41–42).

To Henry Laurens

[Valley Forge, ca. January 5, 1778]

Dear Sir

My attachement for your cause, for yourself, for General Washington engages me to express freely the sentiments of my heart. You will find perhaps my confidence very importune upon a so delicate point—but it is in the same time a so important one that I want to know if my fears are groundless or if I must give up the flattering hopes which upon this occasion every lover of liberty and mankind had a true right to entertain. I am fully convinced that if any dissenssion take place in the Congress, in the army, or betwen the militar and the civil power of this niew feeble country, America is lost for ever. What must I think when I hear from every where the party of such a one, this of one other, the northen, the southern interest and all those distinctions betwen members of a body which can not have any strenght but by the most strictest union.[1] Remember, my dear Sir, what Lord North promised to your most cruel and tyrannic ennemys, when he foresaw in one of his speeches that dissensions should take place one day or another amongh the several States, the several members of Congress, and facilitate in the succès and vengeance of a master who is now as thirsty of your blood as he was before of your liberties and properties. In all the niews papers, in all the conversations, in all the speculations of ministers and powerfull men I have alwaïs heard those two ideas united together. "Some members of Congress" (as we are told) "do not agree amongs themselves, therefore America is lost and submitted." Heaven has removed till this time from our ennemies the perfect knowledge of great many particularities which strike my eyes, which I see with the greatest concern, but they will know it soon. You are surrounded by secret ennemys, you have thousand amongs you, some perhaps in Congress itself. If Howe should know in this moment our present circomstances, I dare not say what my mind foresees.

It is perfectly Clear to every body that Congress is divided in three parts. The first and I wish it can be the more numerous, those virtous citizens, who desire truly happiness succes and freedom to the whole continent, without any base self-interest, without particular ambition, without hainouseness for any part of that world which they try to make happy. The second part is what is called the southern party, or Gates's faction, or Miflin's forces, and every other denomination ac-

Thomas Mifflin, quartermaster general until his appointment to the Board of War in November 1777, a reputed enemy of Washington

cording to the power of the gentlemen who are concerned in it.[2] The third part is the northen faction. Those two last were since a long time silentely working one against another, but now ready to breake up in open dissenssions. Let us consider what has been done since some days.

General Gates's succès have turned all the heads and raised his party to the highest degree. Some have been audacious, ungrateful, and foolish enough as to hope it would reflect on General Washington's reputation and honor—men indeed to be pitied as well as despised. They erect themselves absolute judges without having the less idea not only of military knowledge, but even of common sense. Genl. Gates (and I did not believe that any comparison could be ever made betwen both) General Gates, I say, was in the middle of the woods, expecting an ennemy who could arrive to him by one single road—no danger of being turned by the right or the left—no march to be made without his knowledge—a great superiority of number. It was almost impossible to him not to conquer.[3] Which marches, which movements, what has he done in all to compare him to that hero who at the head of sixteen hundred peasants pursued last winter a strong disciplined army through an open and vast country—to that great general who is born for the salvation of his country and the admiration of the universe? Yes, Sir, that very same campaign of last winter would do one of the finest part of the life of Cesar, Condé, Turenne, and those men whose any soldier can not pronounce the name without an entousiastik adoration. In the last summer obliged to give battles in a plain (in that moment where the troops are all, and the general almost nothing in comparaison of his influence in the course of the campaign), he has been defeated by a superior number, by the discipline, by the moral and phisick necessity he was under to loss the first general engagements in open field. The great Condé would have been defeated in such circomstances. And yet, if in German Town his order of battle (one of the finest I ever Saw) had been followed by some general officer whom I will not name, perhaps he would have been successfull.[4] There are men who are surprised that he do'nt attack the redoubts because Gal. Gates has been into some trifling lines. Believe me, Sir, I am candid and frank, I dare say that I am not quite stranger in the military way, if we go there in our present circomstances we are ruined for ever. Consult if you will General Portaïl one of the best and most honest officers upon this continent, he will tell you that taking Philadelphia is as impossible as to storm the moon. I told to General Washington and I repeat to you, if we attack now those redoubts I make very willingly the bargain of coming back with one single arm and the half part of the army, and certainly it would be a very advantageous one. But, Sir, all those men who talk of storming the lines of beating Gl. Howe are or stranger to our circonstances, or desirous to engage Gal. Washington in a step where he could fall. Believe that upon my word.

However if you should loose that same man, what would become of the American liberty? Who could take his place? Certainly some body should raise from the earth—for now I do not [know] any body, neither in the south, neither in the north, neither Gates, neither Mifflin, neither Greene (you see that I put them all without distinction) who could keep an american army for six months. General Washington is my friend my tenderest friend it is true, but I assure you that I have not the least partiality in what I wrote to you. For Gal. Gates, I consider him, I have a great regard for him, I think he deserves the praises as well as the gratefulness of every one in his country, but I do not bear any comparaison vith our general.

Give me leave to tell you how I am surprised of the little regard pay'd to Gal. Washington in this last instance. Since some time a board of war has been established and taken in a certain faction to restrain his authority.[5] A distinction has been made betwen his army and this of General Gates—the northen departement the commander in chief of the northen troops and so on. Gates himself did never give to him any account of his operations and succès. Resolveds of Congress (and which resolveds good God!) are sent every day to stop his operations and push him in very bad ones.[6] And now a major general, inspector general, a kind of superintendant of all the army with about the same rights as Du Coudray could ever desire in the artillerie is sent to him without his participation.[7] He is not acquainted of a word of it till Gnal. Connway appears himself. Indeed he does not deserve that neglect, I say more that kind of insult. If you could know in what circumstances it happens—what letter had been wrote [8] by the same gentleman—but if General Washington has been moderate enough as to keep the silence about this matter I schall imitate him.

I want however to let you know which effects that promotion has made in the army. Every brigadier thinks himself affronted to the last degree. All will give theyr dismission. What circumstances if the ennemy had some knowledge of it. Try, my dear Sir, to establish some peace in all that confusion, the sooner will be the best, if it would go a degree further great inconveniences should arise.[9] Congress is not to make use of his authority in this instance. Such a step in this moment would be too dangerous.[10] Believe me, Sir, believe my interest for the cause, for yourself, for Gal. Washington, this is one of the most important crisis America has ever been in.

General Connway is a good an brave officer (and without minding his moral qualities) as he is an excellent major of infanterie, he could be useful for the instruction of our troops. Do not believe however that the departement of maneuvres, administration of rgts. &c. &c. is a very difficult thing, every man who is not stupid and has been six month in a french garrison must be pretty far advanced in that so easy knowledge, but certainly no body can deny that kind of merit to Mr. de Connway to a very high degree.

I am sorry that Congress is so far advanced. It will be desagreable to be obliged to go back. It will be very dangerous to proceed. I admire in this occasion the perfect silence and moderation of our commander in chief.

I know very well your sentiments upon those matters—however I desire to have a line from you upon these subjects. I promise you the same secrecy and care of burning your letters which I beg for the present. Explain me, Sir, by what chance so little regard is pay'd to General Washington. I am very certain you do not approuve such a neglect. I am not in any doubt about your sentiments for that ungratefulness which some reward that respectable man with. I beg your pardon in being so free, but as I am a friend of Peace those dissentions revolt me so much that I could not help myself of mentionning it to you.

I have been very sorry to hear how you was under the tyranic domination of a troublesome goute. Slavery in general and so bad one as this should never attend you. Farewel my dear Sir and worthy friend, I am with the most tender affection, the most warmest wishes for the liberty, happiness of your country, for the union of her sons, the succès of our cause, and your own satisfaction, Your most obedient servant

THE MQUIS. DE LAFAYETTE

ALS (ScHi: Henry Laurens Papers), undated but endorsed by Laurens, "Recd. 5 January 1778."

1. See Laurens to Lafayette, January 12, for Laurens's comments on factionalism in Congress.

2. It was rumored at Washington's headquarters early in 1778 that General Thomas Mifflin was the pivotal figure in the cabal to replace Washington with Gates, and that Conway was his right-hand man. In describing "Gates's faction" as "Miflin's forces," Lafayette reflects the uncertainty of Washington and the officers around him about the extent of Gates's involvement in the cabal. Washington, Tench Tilghman, and John Cadwalader thought Gates merely the instrument of Mifflin, while Greene suspected that Gates was a conscious party to the cabal (Kenneth Rossman, *Thomas Mifflin and the Politics of the American Revolution* [Chapel Hill: University of North Carolina Press, 1952], pp. 125–134).

3. A line following this, "It would have been impossible to every one who schould have been in his room," was excised at the time of writing and "almost" was added above the line in this sentence.

4. General Stephen was dismissed from the service on November 20, partly as a

result of his "unofficerlike behavior" at Germantown (Fitzpatrick, *Writings of Washington*, 10: 89).

5. A reference to the "new" Board of War, created by Congress in the fall of 1777 to replace the existing board with one composed of experienced military men who were not members of Congress. Congress selected only men who had worked closely with Washington: Thomas Mifflin, quartermaster general; Timothy Pickering, adjutant general; Horatio Gates, a former adjutant general; Joseph Trumbull, former commissary general; and Robert Harrison, Washington's secretary, who did not accept. Lafayette here expresses the feeling, common among Washington's officers, that because Mifflin and Gates were on the board, it would be used against Washington; but at the time Lafayette wrote this, the new members had not yet arrived in York for their first meeting.

6. Only a few such resolves arrived at camp in December, but Washington's responses show how difficult it would have been for him to carry out Congress' wishes. A resolve of November 28 recommended a winter campaign (*JCC*, 9:972), which proved infeasible. On December 10 Congress directed Washington to obtain supplies from the Philadelphia area, where they were plentiful (ibid., pp. 1013–1015). Washington replied on December 15: "Congress seem to have taken for granted a Fact, that is not really so. All the Forage for the Army has been constantly drawn from Bucks and Philadelphia Counties and those parts most contiguous to the City, insomuch that it was nearly exhausted and intirely so in the Country below our Camp. From these too, were obtained all the Supplies of flour that circumstances would admit of" (Fitzpatrick, *Writings of Washington*, 10:159). In response to a resolve of December 19, asking Washington what was to be done to protect Pennsylvania east of the Schuylkill and the state of New Jersey (*JCC*, 9:1036), he wrote: "It would give me infinite pleasure to afford protection to every individual and to every Spot of Ground in the whole of the United States. Nothing is more my wish. But this is not possible with our present force" (December 22, 1777, in Fitzpatrick, *Writings of Washington*, 10:186).

7. Conway, as inspector general, did not have the command powers Du Coudray was to have had as commander in chief of the artillery, the engineers, and the forts, nor did he have Du Coudray's power to create positions and appoint and dismiss men from them. Conway said of his new position, "If the commander in chief would explain or even read to the brigadiers the Resolve of Congress [concerning my] appointment they would find that I have not the power of appointing as much as a corporal" (Conway to Gates, January 4, 1778 [NHi: Gates Papers, Box 9]). Washington and his general officers thought it advisable to have an inspector general who would establish a uniform set of regulations and maneuvers, but the consensus was that any such regulations should be previously "settled or agreed to by the Commander in chief or a board of officers appointed by him for that purpose" ("Circular to the General Officers," October 26, 1777, in Fitzpatrick, *Writings of Washington*, 9:441–442).

8. "Against him" deleted here at the time of writing. Conway's letter is discussed in Lafayette to Washington, December 30, note 4.

9. Conway had hoped to serve the cause as inspector general and, much disappointed, wrote to Gates about the dissensions at camp:

> Two other objections are that I have been intriguing at Congress with General Mifflinn and you in order to remove General Washington, and that I gave myself the Merit of the Germantown affair. Such Low calumnies I Did not think worth my answering. . . . You see, Dr. General, that I am here in a Disagreeable situation. I am stopp'd in [my] functions, can not be usefull and Do not chuse to struggle with cabales. I wish I could be sent some where else, or [order'd] to France where I am persuaded I can be of some service to the main cause which will always be Dear to me in spite of the many Difficultys and the temporary Disgusts I meet with. [Conway to Gates, January 4, 1778 (NHi: Gates Papers, Box 9)]

10. The following sentence was deleted here, probably at the time of writing: "I am afraid when I talk upon our present state."

To George Washington

[Valley Forge,] the 5 January 1778

Dear General

As your excellency's opinion seems to agree with my ideas for taking in our service those Non commissioned officers who came with Mr. Du Coudray, I schall take the liberty of telling you what I know about the matter. How useful they would be in this army is a thing obvious for every body. Those men join to a pretty great theory the greatest practice of theyr art. ⟨Security and exactitude attend alwaïs theyr firing,⟩ and not only they would be useful by themselves, but they could form our gunners, and sergeants of artillery. In the same time theyr pretentions schould not be so extensive, tho' theyr service could be greater than if you were to take officers of theyr corps. However pretty great advantages schould be proposed to them, because they enjoy in theyr own country both a good state and a flattering consideration. They have been, I believe, disatisfied with Congress when sent back. If your excellency would speack to the committee who is to come here, if General Knox was to receive orders of making to them good propositions when it would be only for a campaign, if Mr. Du Plessis (I suppose his business will be soon done) was to engage them, and promise them in my name that I schould take care of 'em, perhaps they could be induced to stay with us, and it would be a good acquisition ⟨—it is useless to have so many field pieces if they are not so used as they ought to be⟩.

I did not hear any thing about Mr. Connway's businesses since three days, but that he has proposed to Congress an expedition against St. Augustin, with troops raised in Europe. As soon as my cloathes will be here I schall make out a waïst coat and every other part of the drest, to show it to your excellency.

⟨They are drest so badly all add to that.⟩ I think your excellency will be obliged to make a general order, about every thing which is to be done since the moment where a guard arrive upon the parade till this where they go off from duty. ⟨What if the officers do not know what they are to do, and the Service is done in many different ways— attending punctually the parade with men as clean as they can be, filing off in a good order before the general officer, relieving the other guards in a proper manner, sending an orderly man from the picquet [1] to know where they are, the picquets laying arround one or at most two fires without pulling down theyr cloathes, neither allowing

any fire to theyr centrys, recconnoïtring those who come in camp principally when numerous by a corporal and four men, and for the
centry challenging in the night, and in day time schouldering theyr
arms for any officer or troop who pass by, and presenting them to
general officers, are things which I take the liberty of mentionning to
your excellency, because I have seen myself several faults of all those
points, and it has been answered to me by officers and soldiers that
they did not know what they were to do.⟩

Give me leave to mention to you a thing which I have thaught of
and could be perhaps attended with advantages. There are in
⟨your⟩ [2] army some scattered frenchmen who tho' they fight very
well in the moment of an action are however troublesome to theyr
officers and undisciplined beyhond all expressions. They excuse themselves desobediency to the orders, by telling that they do'nt understand what is told to them. They will never be kept by theyr officers
and perhaps they will spoil the others—but if they were collected in a
body, and under some officer Who could speack with them they
would be quiete and disciplined and I thing some advantage schould
arise from that arrangement. When the fight is over theyr officers do
not know what to do with them. I wishoud to give them to that little
french officer who was in the northen army and whom I can answer
for, as an honest man and a good officer.[3] They schould have whatever denomination you would think proper, corps, regiment, compagny, but conneked to a division or rather to Morgan's corps and not
independant, for a military independance should ruin the civil one.
As that officer is neither an imprudent neither a young man I could
answer for the discipline and good order of that corps *if not independant.* I would take care myself of theyr conduct. My reason in speacking so is that I do not like to see any michief done in this country by
frenchmen, and I am sure if that measure is not taken that I schall
have alwaïs the disagreement to hear from every where many instances of undiscipline and libertinage by those scattered men. I do
not inclose the canadians compagnies of Colonel Hazen in my project.
I am alwaïs affraïd that our reinforcements will not arrive soon
enough. Collecting, inoculating marching them, and the whole attended with many deliberations of Congress of the several states, &c.
&c. will all that be done for begining an early campaign? For not only
our interest but even the want of provisions will chace us very early
from this place. ⟨I had entertained the idea that this country was
more plentifull than it is.⟩

Do'nt you think, Sir, that if we have a very large army as I hope we
schall, and I think we must absolutely, that a quarter master general
with the rank of General officer with a considerable departement as in

Last page of Lafayette's letter to Washington, January 5, 1778, in which he gives his "young and inexperienced ideas" on military affairs. The passages Lafayette deleted from the letter in 1828 are restored in the printed text.

the european armys schould not be very useful? ⟨I pray it schould be a man who would have been in Europe in the staff of big armies.⟩

Is it not very importune and even very impertinent to lay before you my young and unexperienced ideas ⟨about what is to be done⟩? But if they are unjudicious and unacceptable, I hope at least that you will not miss the sentiment which dictate them. I am very far from thinking myself able to give any advice in this army, but I dare hope that my warmest wishes for the good and right could inspire me some times with some tolerable ideas, and as I have no pretentions in it I'l see myself deceived by false ones without being surprised at all.

I am just now coming from the parade, where a french officer who has been those past days in Lancaster, told me that there are to be heard the most extraordinary, and indecent things about the present businesses. They speack of Conway as a man sent by heaven for the liberty and happiness of America. He told so to them and they are fools enough as to believe it. He has desired Congress to send him as an ambassador to France or as commander in chief in Georgia in case he could not stay in this army to superintend it.

I am very glad to hear that Colonel Pickering is in the board of war because he is an honest man, I wish he could have strengths enough as to oppose ⟨himself⟩ to the factions.

With the varmest affection and greatest respect I have the honor to be dear general Your excellency's the most obedient servant

⟨THE MQUIS. DE⟩ LAFAYETTE

⟨I have not been to head quarters by fear of troubling you, and I schall have the honor of wraïting to morrow your excellency.⟩

ALS (PEL: Hubbard Collection). The manuscript has been edited in ink, in Lafayette's later hand. The text of significant deletions has been restored in angle brackets.
1. An outlying guard post.
2. Changed later to "the."
3. Failly.

To Adrienne de Noailles de Lafayette[T]

In camp near Valley Forge, January 6, [1778]
What a date, my dearest, and what a country to be writing from in the month of January! My destiny is strange indeed. In a camp, in the middle of the woods, fifteen hundred leagues from you, I am confined by the winter ⟨when I should have been with you two months

ago—when, my dear, all my desires and even good sense obliged me to depart. But a delicate sentiment that is stronger than reason, and which you understand better than I can express to you, has always detained me here from day to day. We other Frenchmen have always made it a point of honor not to depart before the conclusion of a campaign. This one has not ended, and I have found myself imperceptibly carried along until the present moment, when I am astonished and almost alarmed to find myself in the wilds of America). Not very long ago we were separated from the enemy by only a little river; now we are seven leagues from them, and here the American army will pass the winter in little huts that are no more pleasant than a dungeon. I do not know whether it will suit General Howe to come and visit our new town; if he does we shall try to give him a proper welcome.

The bearer of this letter will describe the pleasant abode I prefer to the happiness of being with you, with all my friends, in the midst of all possible pleasures.[1] Honestly, dear heart, do you think that it would not require very strong reasons to induce me to make this sacrifice? Everything tells me to depart, but honor has told me to remain; and truly, when you know in detail the circumstances in which I find myself, the situation of the army, of my friend who commands it, and of the whole American cause, you will pardon me, dear heart, you will even excuse me, and I almost dare to say you will approve. If only I could have the pleasure of telling you all my reasons in person, of embracing you and asking you for forgiveness, which I would then be sure to obtain. But do not condemn me without a hearing; besides the reason that I have already given you, I have another that I would not relate to everyone because it would appear that I am ridiculously conceited. My presence is more necessary to the American cause at this moment than you could imagine. So many foreigners who have not received commissions, or who then have not been allowed to fulfill their personal ambitions, have made powerful cabals. They have tried all sorts of tricks to disgust me with both this revolution and the one who leads it; they have spread the rumor as widely as possible that I have left the continent. On the other side the English have said it openly, and their hatred for me seems to grow stronger every day that I stay here. I cannot in good conscience prove all of those people to be right. If I depart, many Frenchmen who are useful here will follow my example. General Washington will be truly unhappy if I speak to him of leaving. His confidence in me is greater than my age allows me to admit. In his position, he is surrounded by flatterers and secret enemies. He finds in me a trustworthy friend to whom he can open his heart, and who always tells him the truth. Not a day passes that he does not have long conversations with me or write me long letters, and he likes to consult me about the most important matters. At this very moment there is a particular matter in which my presence is of some use to him; this is not the moment to speak of leaving.

At present I am also engaged in an important correspondence with the president of the Congress, who, after the general, is my best friend in this country. ⟨I have a great desire to see this revolution succeed.⟩ The humiliation of ⟨insolent⟩ England, the advantage to my country, the welfare of humanity, for which it is important that there be in the world a people who are entirely free, and the sacrifices that I and my friends have already made for this cause—all oblige me not to abandon it at a time when my absence could do some harm.

Moreover, after a small victory in the Jerseys, the general, with the unanimous approval of Congress, persuaded me to take command of a division of the army, to train it as I see fit, insofar as my meager talents will permit. I could not respond to these marks of confidence by asking what he would like me to do for him in Europe. These are, dear heart, some of the reasons that I confide to you in secret; I shall tell you in person many others that I cannot risk putting in a letter. ⟨You must not think that my stay here entails the necessity of waging the next campaign. A thousand circumstances may provide me with the occasion to leave soon, and be assured, my dear, that I shall decamp as soon as I can decently get away. You must be aware that it is not for my pleasure that I remain buried in this wretched place, while every possible happiness awaits me in Paris, in the midst of all my friends, and in the arms of a charming wife whom I love more than ever. If you could see for a moment what is in my heart, I would have no need of excuses; and if my feelings affect you ever so little, I dare say that you will be content with the sentiments that I express.⟩

This letter will be given to you by a respectable French gentleman who has traveled a hundred miles to pick up my messages for France. ⟨I am very grateful for that. Receive him well, dear heart; soon after his arrival he will depart for this country. Take advantage of that to write to me, and even though your letter may well arrive long after I have left, write anyway, in case I may be so unfortunate as to be here still, to soften a bit the boredom and sorrow of my exile.⟩ I sent you a letter a few days ago by way of the famous Mr. Adams,[2] ⟨whom I recommended to you. I hope you will give him a cordial reception;⟩ he will help you get letters to me. You should have received by now the letter I sent to you as soon as I heard of your delivery. How happy that event has made me, dear heart! I like to mention it to you in all my letters because I enjoy thinking about it constantly. What a pleasure it will be to embrace my two poor daughters, and have them ask their mother to forgive me. You must not believe that I am so insensitive, dear heart, and at the same time so ridiculous, that the sex of our new child has diminished in the slightest my joy at her birth. We have not become so decrepit that we shall need a miracle to have another child. That one absolutely has to be a boy. For the rest, if one must worry about the family name, I declare that I have decided to live long enough to bear it myself for many years, before I am obliged to bequeath it to another being. I received the news from M. le Maréchal de Noailles. I am very impatient to receive it from you.

The other day I received a letter from Desplaces that mentioned an earlier one, but the capriciousness of winds and fleets, not to mention encounters with the English, often disturbs the order of my correspondence.[3] For several days I have been concerned about the Vicomte de Coigny, whom I have heard was getting worse, but that letter from Desplaces, which did not mention him, and which told me that everyone was well, has reassured me. I have also received some others that do not mention his health. When you write to me, dear heart, please send me plenty of news about all the people I love, and even about society. It is very strange that I have not yet heard about Mme de Fronsac's confinement. Present a thousand fond and respectful compliments to her and to Comtesse Auguste for me. If those ladies do not understand the reasons that force me, despite myself, to remain here ⟨from day to day⟩, they must think me a very ridiculous person, especially since they are able to see my dear heart, that charming wife from whom I separate myself. But that same idea must impress them with a sense that ⟨if I remain, if I sacrifice pleasure to boredom, happiness to sorrow, life in the most amiable company to the dreary life of a savage, if, in short, dear heart, I am far from you instead of being near⟩ it is because I have overwhelming reasons for making that decision. ⟨I think no one will go so far as to imagine that it is to amuse myself that I bury myself in this wilderness.⟩ Several general officers have brought their wives to camp, and I am very envious, not of their wives ⟨who are rather dull⟩, but of the pleasure they have in being able to see them. General Washington has also just decided to send for his wife, a modest and respectable person who loves her husband madly. The English gentlemen ⟨have decided, I believe, to make use of the wives of others, for want of their own. They⟩ have received, in addition, a reinforcement of three hundred girls from New York, and we have taken from them another ship filled with chaste officers' wives who were going to join their husbands. They were very much afraid that they would be kept ⟨for the winter⟩ for ⟨the use of⟩ the American armies.

You will learn from the bearer of this letter that my health is very

good, my wound has healed, and the change of climate has not affected me at all. ⟨Le Blanc and Baptiste are not so fortunate: the latter nearly died, and I would have been very upset about that, for he is
a good fellow.⟩ [4] Don't you think, my dear heart, that after my return
we shall be mature enough to establish ourselves in our own house,
where we shall be happy together, receive our friends, establish an
easy freedom, and read the foreign newspapers without having the
curiosity of going to see for ourselves what is happening? I love to
build castles of happiness and pleasure in France. You are always a
part of them, dear heart, and once we are reunited nothing will separate us again and prevent us from enjoying together both the
sweetness of loving each other and the most delightful and tranquil
felicity. Farewell, my heart, I truly wish that that arrangement could
begin today. Would it suit you, my dear heart? Present my fondest
regards to Mme d'Ayen, embrace the vicomtesse and my sisters a
thousand times. ⟨Present my compliments also to Abbé Fayon and
Mlle Marin. A thousand regards to my grandfather; I wrote to him
the other day, and I shall write to him again if I have time.⟩ Farewell,
farewell, my very dear heart, love me always, and never forget for a
moment the unhappy exile who thinks always of you with a new tenderness.

AL (NIC: Dean Collection), translation. Erroneously dated 1777. The manuscript has
been edited in pencil, in Lafayette's later hand. Significant passages omitted from Lafayette, *Mémoires,* are printed here in angle brackets.
   1. The bearer of the letter has not been identified.
   2. Letter of December 22.
   3. Mentioned in Lafayette to Laurens, December 18.
   4. These were Lafayette's two servants who accompanied him to America.

To John Adams

[Head Quarters, 9th. Jany. 1778]

Sir

   As General Knox will have the pleasure to see you before your
going to France, I took the liberty of entrusting him with the inclosed
letters for you, which you will find very importune, but I hope you
will excuse on account of my being very desirous to let hear my
friends from me by every opportunity. Such a distance, so many ennemies, are betwen me and every relation every acquaintance of mine,
that I wo'nt reproach myself any neglect in my entertaining with 'em
the best correspondance I can. However, to avoid troubling you with

two large a parcel of letters, I'l send my dispatches by two ways as one other occasion is offered to me in this very moment. I must beg your pardons, Sir, for making myself free enough as to reccommend you to some friends of mine in France—but as I don't believe you have many acquaintances in that country, I thaught it would not be des-agreable to you, if I would desire Mde. de Lafayette, and the Prince de Poix to whom I wraït, to introduce you to some of my other friends.[1] Before indulging myself that liberty, I asked the Gal. Knox's opinion who told me that he did not find any miss in it tho' I had not the honor of your particular acquaintance.

I told to Gal. Knox some particular advices which I could believe to be not desagreable to you. I hope you will hear good news from here, and send very good ones from there, such is the desire of a friend to your country and the noble cause we are fighting for; I wish you a pleasant and safe voyage, and with the highest esteem and greatest af-fection for a man to whom the hearts of every lover of liberty will be indebted for ever, I have the honor to be Sir Your most obedient ser-vant

THE MIS. DE LAFAYETTE

ALS (MHi: Adams Papers); dated in an unknown hand.
1. See Lafayette to his wife, December 22. Letter to the Prince de Poix not found.

To Henry Laurens

[Valley Forge, ca. January 9, 1778]

Dear Sir

Alwaïs new letters from me; but the matter I will mention is too in-teresting, and I am too sensible of the confidence I am intrusted with in this occasion to differ a single instant more.

A french gentleman mestre de camp in second (as we call it) in the Regiment of Chartres dragoons whose name is much known to me tho' I never saw himself, Mr. de *La Tour du Pin-de-Montauban* is pos-sessed with the desire of taking his part in our noble cause. His prop-ositions are as moderate as disinterested—and tho' I do not know him he honoured me with his confidence, and desired me to lay his inten-tions before Congress. He is so polite as to wish to make the next cam-paign with me, and I schall aknowledge his politness and good opin-ion by the strictest attendance to his businesses. I am alwaïs happy to see my countrymen worthy of the name of french they are honoured with, and I am no less satisfied to see them coming here without any interested neither too ambitious intentions.

That gentleman proposes to come over with ten good experienced officers, and one among them has made the last war in America. Twenty four soldiers who will be the non commissioned officers of his corps—this corps to be raised among the british or hessians deserters, among the american themselves, till the number of two hundred men. In case it would be impossible to raise them in the continent he schould endeavour to obtain leave for recruiting in or about France. He will bring with him arms, cloathes, shoes &c. &c. for his troop and this at his expense. He does not ask any appointements to Congress for himself but only for his officers and soldiers and I am to know at what rate they will be pay'd, which commissions they will get. There will be also three field pieces with a quantity of powder, and two sergeants of artillery with four soldiers to serve them. He intends to join to the whole a surgeon a taylor, a shoe maker &c. In all America will have a corps of two hundred men with proper officers non commissioned officers and every thing to enable that corps to be useful and well attended to. Such are the propositions which he made to me, and I do not see any thing there but very moderate and advantageous to the cause. Be so good, Sir, as to answer as soon as possible upon that article, because I'l give My letter to Gal. Knox for Boston,[1] and I schall inclose to that officer the exact words of your letter, and whatever Congress will approve or resolve upon the matter. With the most tenderest affection I have the honor to be Dear Sir Your most obedient servant

THE MQUIS. DE LAFAYETTE

D'ont forget our good cloathes for the sake of our naked shoulders.

ALS (ScHi: Henry Laurens Papers), endorsed by Laurens, "no date Recd. 12 Jany. 1778."
   1. Knox was to deliver letters to Adams to carry to France.

To Robert Morris

9 January, at head quarters, [1778]

Dear Sir,

I am sorry not to be able to give you the intelligence you want about the gentleman who came privately to this Country. His name is entirely unknown to me, and I did not hear of such a name from any French officer in the army. I dare [say] that if he was arrivd I would have got some intelligence of his being among us or by himself because great many Gentlemen whom I was not acquainted with wrote me when they heard that I was here, or by some of the officers of my nation who are in or about this army. I know very well the Duke de *Luines* [maréchal] de camp, General of all the dragoons; but I am certain he did not mind to come hear and he has but a girl. I do not know any brother or cousin of his, and his name will finish with him. If somebody of his relations had been to this Country certainly the Duke de Luines schould have wrote me. Even the ortograph is not the same thing, and that name is the only one I know of which can answer to what Doctor Franklin wraits about him; however I'l ask to every french gentleman I shall meet if they know the name of *Luigné* and I'l send you every intelligence I can about this matter.[1]

I took the liberty of asking you a sum of money some days ago—but I do not want so much presently,[2] and if you are so good as to send me only two hundred dollars out of what I have begged from you to pay to the bearer of my first letter (thirty seven pounds I believe) I shall be under great obligation to you. I hope too that you will be indulgent enough as to pardon me the liberty which I take of troubling you so about my business.

If General Howe gives to us a good chance of beating him certainly we must not lose it, but if he stays at home, if in all it would be imprudent to meet him, with his actual forces against ours, then, my dear Sir, we must be quiete and try to have an army before having any fight. I am sorry my contience obliges me to have an opinion which is so much against my inclination—but what I look upon as to be the advantage of our cause shall always go before any interested ideas for my own reputation and pleasure. As I came here to fight, fighting is the most pleasant occupation I can wish, and I shall be the happiest of men when I shall believe it can be attended with any advantage for America, but sir we have at our head a great judge, a man whom America and principally the army is to have a confidence as extended as the love he derives from them, and when he will think proper to fight, then I shall believe alwais that we have good reason for it.

Be so good, sir, as to send the enclosed letter to Colonel Armand. I shall be alwais sorry to see him far from us, and I should be very happy if we had again the pleasure of saluting him in camp.[3] With the greatest regard and affection I have the honor to be, dear Sir, your most obedient servant,

THE MRQUIS. DE LAFAYETTE

L (*Collections of the New-York Historical Society*, 11 [1878]:410–412). Erroneously dated 1777.

1. Franklin's letter has not been found; a letter from Silas Deane to Morris also inquired about a "Marquis de Luigné" who had left France, without letters of credit or introduction, to join the American army (Frederick R. Kirkland, ed., *Letters on the American Revolution in the Library at "Karolfred"* [Philadelphia: privately printed, 1941], 1:50). The final entry in the Comte de Luigné's file at the Ministry of War shows that the twenty-five-year-old captain in the Royal Lorraine Cavalry resigned his commission suddenly on August 27, 1777, "because his affairs made it impossible to rejoin his regiment" (Vincennes, Service historique de l'Armée: dossier "Luigné"). No record has been found showing that a Luigné served in America during the revolution.

2. In his letter of December 30, Lafayette had asked Morris to send him fifty guineas in addition to the dollars he requested.

3. Letter not found. Armand was in York, trying to organize his legion before the opening of the spring campaign.

From Henry Laurens

[York,] 12th. Jany. 1778

Sir—

I am grieved by reflecting upon the length of time I have been indebted for the several Letters which you have lately honoured me with under the 14th. & 18th. of the past, 2d. & 5th. of the present Month, & more because it is not in my power even now to return such answers as these demand & as I wish to give. That condescension however which is apparent in your kind & indulgent expressions on this head, afford me encouragement & forbid a laboured apology either for past or present unavoidable remissness. I say present, because I confess I am urged to this address by the inclosed Letter which I received from France last Night & which I am anxious to forward without delay, perhaps if this circumstance had not happened I might from a desire of answering all your favours have deferred some days longer. Now I shall confine my self to that of the 5th.—I say I shall, in obedience to an hundred other calls which say I must.

Very early after my arrival at the State House Philadelphia I discovered the spirit of party triumphant. I lamented the prospect exhibited to my view & predicted certain evil consequences which have naturally followed. I was a stranger, a by stander, I was careful to take no decided part except that of speaking & voting according to the dictates of conscience.

I will not boast of having been instrumental in promoting beneficial measures which from all appearance would otherwise have failed, nor of defeating attempts which if they had succeeded would greatly have injured our Cause. You would smile Sir to hear me say that America is a little indebted to me for her successes against the threatning flood of the invincible Burgoyne. If I were to attempt to prove this, it would be with no other view but this of showing my steady opposition to party. You will conclude therefore that upon questions I have not been found always on one side.

I mean only to say, Yes Sir, I have long known there were divisions among those, whose duty required from them as honest Men, Strict Union. I have observed fuel to be so carefully supplied as never to fail of keeping up a spark of discord. Hence I have often been induced to believe there were Agents from our Enemies if not within Doors, yet too closely connected with some who sat there.

You will however be pleased to observe Sir, or I should rather say, you very well know Sir, there is no subject more abstruse than this of party. It is said to be the sinews of Liberty. I have neither Leisure nor abilities for going deeply into the enquiry, nor is it necessary. I will only say that party animosity between the Eastern states & the Inhabitants of New York is almost inexistent with the *Inhabitants.*

These are the grand divisions. Each has its atmosphere, they are sometimes very troublesome in their disputes which are carried to such extremes as seem to threaten a dissolution of all friendship, nevertheless, danger from a common Enemy will reduce them to good order & as it were by a Charm, instantly establish a coalition. I have said so much on this subject in order to remove in some degree the strong apprehensions which you seem to be under from reports of prevailing parties in Congress. They make the Road rough but not impassable. So much upon party in general concerning the particular influences which you speak of, I must acknowledge your conjectures are not illfounded. But I think the friends of our brave & virtuous General, may rest assured that he is out of the reach of his Enemies, if he has an Enemy, a fact which I am in doubt of. I believe I hear most that is said & know the outlines of almost all that has been attempted, but the whole amounts to little more than tittle tattle, which would be too much honoured by repeating it.

All Men acknowledge General Washington's virtue, his personal Bravery, nor do I ever hear his Military abilities questioned but comparatively, with the fortunate event which you allude to, why cannot Genl. Washington grasp Genl. Howe abounding with every advantage of situation & every necessary article for defence or attack—as Genl. Gates conquered Genl. Burgoyne, under disadvantage of situation & reduced to the last extremity? Answers are easily given to such silly remarks, when one is disposed to reply.

In a word Sir, be not alarmed I think it is not in the power of any junto to lessen our friend without his own consent, I trust his good sense & his knowledge of the World will guard against so fatal an error. If you desire it Sir Mr. John Laurens will communicate what I have written in confidence to him.[1] I say in confidence, not because I am afraid of having my sentiments known, I speak them honestly & unreservedly upon every proper occasion but I very much dislike correspondencies which may be misconstrued & charged with design to foment dissentions. It is my constant endeavor to reconcile & make peace.

I am not insensible that Genl. Washington has been in several Instances extremely Ill used by the neglect of those who ought to be his grand support & to prevent every cause of complaint on his part, but if I were with him half an hour & could persuade my self he wanted information, it would be very easy to convince him there has not any thing been *designedly* done or omitted to affront him. I speak of so large a majority as 9 in 10.

The General very well knows what we are, & will continue to make suitable allowances for all defects seeming or real. We are in a State of Infancy, yet thank God, we are not quite so foolish nor so wicked as our Parent. Men whisper & very harmless things too of Genl. Washington. Loud bellowing scandal appears in every News paper upon the name of his Antagonist Sir William—but I will dwell no longer upon these matters. A large Committee appointed by Congress of four of its own members & three from the New Board of War will shortly be in Camp in order to concert measures with the Commander in Chief for the reformation of the Army.[2] God grant every good purpose may be answered by their consultations. To these Gentlemen Sir you are particularly referred for an answer to your last favor without date relative to Monsr. du Pin de Montauban, & also for the desired promotion of Monsr. Gemaut.[3] The powers of this deputation are very ample I will not say unlimited.

The Clothing which you had been informed of, Colo. Lee assures me is little more than a collection of old wearing apparel of all shapes & sizes & that the whole is appropreated.

You will learn by the dispatches now sent to Genl. Washington, that Mr. Burgoyne is destined to pass the present Winter in Massachusets Bay & the reasons which urged Congress to a determination which must undergo the Criticism of all the Politicians in the Civilized World. I shall be happy to have the approbation of those in our own Country. If I had not honestly thought the measure justifiable as well as necessary I would not have been a strenuous advocate in favor of it. I think he will appear to have been the dupe of his own policy. The intimation which he gave to Gen. Gates who was at Albany of a breach of Public faith was artfully enough insinuated, calculated for a particular purpose but not intended for the view of Congress. If in this we have acted wisely—it will be set to our Credit in opposition to some of our supposed errors.[4] I have the honour to be Noble Sir &c. &c.

LbC (ScHi: Henry Laurens Papers).
    1. Laurens's long letter of January 8–10 to his son John assures him that Washington is much respected and cannot be replaced without his own consent. It is less moderate, however, on the spirit of party in Congress and those who foment it, including "Characters of whom your friend [Washington] entertains the most favorable sentiments" (Burnett, *Letters of Congress*, 3:21).
    2. Congress resolved to send a "Committee of Conference" to camp, specifically to attempt to reduce the number of regiments (many of them understrength), reform abuses in the different departments, and generally "to adopt such other measures as they shall judge necessary for introducing oeconomy and promoting discipline and good morals in the army" (*JCC*, 10:40). The four committee members from Congress were to be Richard Dana, Joseph Reed, Nathaniel Folsom, and John Harvie. The Board of War was to be represented by Gates, Mifflin, and Pickering (Proceedings of January 10 and 12, 1778, in *JCC*, 10:39–41). See also Laurens to Lafayette, January 22.
    3. La Tour du Pin de Montauban is discussed in Lafayette to Laurens, January 9, and Gimat in Lafayette to Laurens, December 14.
    4. On January 8 Congress considered the implications of Burgoyne's accusation that the Americans had failed to comply with the terms of the surrender at Saratoga. Burgoyne did not seem to believe himself and his army bound by the terms of the surrender, and Congress determined it could no longer have faith in his "personal honor." It therefore resolved "That the embarkation of Lieutenant General Burgoyne, and the troops under his command, be suspended till a distinct and explicit ratification of the convention of Saratoga shall be properly notified by the court of Great Britain to Congress" (*JCC*, 10:29–35).

To George Washington

[Valley Forge, ca. January 13, 1778]
Dear General
    I Schall make use in this particular instance of the liberty you gave me of telling freely every idea of mine which could strike me as not being useless to a better order of things.
    There were two gentlemen, same rank, same duty to perform, and same neglect of it who have been arrested the same day by me. As I went in the night arround the piquets I found them in fault, and I gave an account of it the next day to your excellency. You answered that I was much in wrong not to have had them relieved and arrested immediately. I objected that it was then very late for such a changement, and that I did not know which was the rule in this army, but that the gentlemen should be arrested in that very moment. The last answer of your excellency has been, "They are to have a court martial,

and you must give notice of it to the adjutant general." Therefore Major Nevill made two letters in order to arrest them, one *for having been surprised in his post* and the other, for the same cause and *allowing his centrys to have fires which he could see in standing before the picquet.* I give you my word of honor that there was not any exageration.

Now I see in the orders the less guilty punished in a manner, much too severe indeed, and dismissed from the service (it is among all the delicate minds deprived of his honor) when he was only to be severely reprimanded, and kept for some time under arrest—but it can be attributed to a very severe discipline.

What must I think of the same court when they unanimously acquit (it is to say that my accusation is not trüe) the officer who joins to the same fault, entirely the same, this of allowing his centrys to have fire in his own sight. For in every service *being surprised* or being found in the middle of his picquet without any challenging or stopping centry, as Mjor. Nevil riding before me found him, is entirely the same thing—and Mjor. Nevil riding before me when I was busy to make a centry pull off his fire, can swear that such was the case with that officer.[1] He can do more than swearing, for he can give his word of honor—and I think that idea *honor* is the same in every country but the *prejugées* are not the same thing—for giving publickly the Best of such a dispute (for here it becomes a trial for both parties) to an officer of the last military stage against one of the first, schould be looked on as an affront to the rank, and acquitting a man whom one other man accuses, looked upon as an affront to the person. It is the same in Poland for Count de Pulaski was much affronted of the decision of a court martial entirely acquitting Colonel Molens.[2] However as I know the english costoms I am nothing else but surprised to see such a partiality in a court martial.

Your excellency will certainly approuve my not arresting any officer for being brought before a court martial, for any neglect of duty, but when they will be robbers, or cowards, or when they will assassinate, in all when the[y] will deserve being cashiered or put to death.

Give me leave, to tell your excellency how I am adverse to court martials. I know it is the english costom, and I believe it is a very bad one. It comes from theyr love of lawers, Speakers, and of that black apparate of sentences, and judgements. But such is not the american temper, and I think this new army must pick up the good institutions, and leave the bad ones where ever they may be. In France an officer is arrested by his superior, who gives notice of it to the commanding officer and then he is punished enough in being deprived of going out of his room in time of peace, of doing his duty in time of war. No body knows of it but his comrades. When the fault is greater he is confined in a common room for prisonner officers and this is much more shamefull. Notice of it is immediately given to the general officer who commands there. That goes too to the King's minister who is to be reimplaced here by the commander in chief. In time of war it goes to the general in chief.

Soldiers are punished the same or next day by order of proper officers, and the right of punishing is proportionate to theyr ranks.

But when Both officers and soldiers have done something which deserves a more severe punishement, when theyr honor, or theyr life, or theyr liberty for more than a very short time is concerned, then a court martial meets, and the sentence is known. How will you let an unhappy soldier be confined several weeks, with men who are to be hanged, with spies, with the most horrid sort of people, and in the same time be lost for the duty, when they deserve only some lashes— then almost no proportion in the punishements?

How is it possible to carry a gentleman before a parcel of dreadful judges at the same place where an officer of the same rank has been just now cashiered, for a trifling neglect of his duty, for, I suppose, speaking to his next neighbour in a maneuvre, for going into a house to speack to a pretty girl, when the army is on his march and thousand other things? How is it possible to bring to the certainty of being cashiered, or dishonored, a young lad, who has made a Considerable fault because he had a light head, a too great vivacity, when that young man would be perhaps in some years the best officer of the army, if he had been friendly reprimanded and arrested for some time, without any dishonor?

The law is alwaïs severe, and bring with it an eternal shamefull mark. When the judges are partial as in this occasion, it is much worse, because they have the same inconveniences as law itself.

In court martials men are judged by theyr inferiors. How [*page torn; several words missing*] to discipline I do'nt want to say. The publication exposes men to [be] despised by the least soldier. When men have been before a court martial they schould be or acquitted or dismissed. What do you think can be produced by the half comdemnation of a Gal. officer? What necessity for all the soldiers, all the officers, to know that *General Maxwell has been prevented from doing is duty by his being drunk?* [3] Where is the man who will not laugh at him if he is told by him *you are a drunkard* and is it right to ridicule a man respectable by his rank, because he drank two or three gills-of-rum?

There are my reasons against court martials, when there is not some considerable fault to punish. According to my affair I am sorry in seeing the less guilty being the *only one punished.* However, I shall send to court martials but for such a crimes, that there will be for the judges no way of indulgence and partiality. With the most tender respect I am Your excellency's the most obedient servant

THE MQUIS. DE LAFAYETTE

ALS (PEL: Hubbard Collection).
1. The results of the courts-martial of these two officers were published in General Orders on January 13:

At the same Court held 6th. instant Captain Flagg charged with "neglect of duty 1st. in suffering the Marquis de la Fayette, when Major Genl. of the day to come in the night to the center of his Picquet, without being stopped or challenged; 2nd. for permitting his sentries to have fires in his sight" was tried and acquitted by the unanimous opinion of the court. The Commander in Chief approves the sentence.

At the same Court held 7th. instant Captn. Laird, charged with "Neglect of duty, in suffering the Major General of the day to surprize him at his picquet in the night," was tried and found guilty and sentenced to be dismissed from the service. [Fitzpatrick, *Writings of Washington,* 10:298]

2. Colonel Stephen Moylan, one of Pulaski's regimental commanders, was "charged with 'Disobedience of the orders of Genl. Pulaski, a cowardly and ungentlemanlike action in striking Mr. Zielinski, a Gentleman, and officer in the polish service when disarmed; and putting him under guard; and giving irritating language to Genl. Pulaski.' The Court were of opinion that Col. Moylan was not guilty, and therefore acquitted him of the charges exhibited against him" (General Orders, October 31, 1777, in Fitzpatrick, *Writings of Washington,* 9:472).

3. A court of inquiry had investigated a complaint that General William Maxwell was prevented from doing his duty by being drunk while he commanded the light troops. They found it groundless, but admitted that his spirits had been elevated on several occasions by spirituous liquor and submitted to Washington's judgment whether he ought to be court-martialed. Washington ordered the trial (General Orders, October 26, 1777, in ibid., p. 438), and Maxwell was fully acquitted (General Orders, November 4, in ibid., 10:3–4).

To Henry Laurens

Camp the fifteenth janry. 1778

Dear Sir

It is with the greatest pleasure that I see the Chevalier de Mauduit du Plessis, Going to Congress with a reccommandation suitable to his merit. That gentleman is distinguished by all what can make a man vorthy of an universal esteem and affection. His military learning, and strict attendance to his duty, his knowledge of the world through which he has amasingly travelled for his age, his unbounded and alwaïs ready courage, the goodness of his heart, modesty of his temper, and elevation of his mind, intitle him to be called on every point *A fine young man.* So I love to see french-men. Such is, give me leave to say, the trüe french character. There is no stranger in America who has showed a more disinterested love for the cause, and given more repeated and essential services. I am not in any doubt of his having the same commission and the same date to it as Colonel Fleury, according to the general's desire, this of the army, and I may add my very earnest one.[1] He was with me in the Jersays (where I have been lately confirmed by a deserter that our parcel of three hundred men had the honor of fighting with his Lordship's own person at the head of the two hessian and british detachements) and as I had desired him to take a small little party to come near the ennemy, he attaked them with his usual boldness.[2] The chevalier's conduct in that occasion is really to be mentionned in the list of his other military actions.

Do not loose any time, my dear Sir, to send down that ever expected committee, which stops the course of every thing till they will have settled many important matters. I expect my much beloved virginian cloathes with the greatest impatience, and they will be a very delightfull sight for me. Did you hear if our recruiting and drafting departement was carried on with a great vigour? Let us try to be able to keep the field before the ennemy will think of leaving the philadelphian girls, or be cured of the cruel cupid's wounds. God bless you, my dear Sir, and our noble cause, with such blessings, and good cloathes, good discipline, good bayonnets, we schall disappoint all the barbarous projects of tyranny. With the greatest affection, and highest regard I have the honor to be Dear Sir Your most obedient servant

THE MQUIS. DE LAFAYETTE

You remember that the chevalier was one of the two glorious, heroïc young men who attaked the stone house in Germain Town.

ALS (ScHi: Henry Laurens Papers).
1. Washington's letter of January 13, recommending Fleury, was read in Congress on January 19, and Fleury was appointed lieutenant colonel, his commission to be dated from November 26, 1777 (*JCC*, 10:64).
2. The skirmish with Cornwallis's forces at Gloucester, New Jersey, on November 25, 1777.

To Henry Laurens

Camp the 15 january 1778

Dear Sir

The bearer of this letter is a french officer who came over with a warm desire of being received in the american army.[1] He brought with him many reccommandations for me, and a firm confidence that I schould obtain some emploïement for him from Congress. I wish'd that idea could be a little lessened in the minds of my countrymen, who send me gentlemen with that very sentence; *I hope you will not refuse to have a commission from the United States for M. such a one.* However I wrote to my friends not to presume in that bold manner *of my powerfull protection.* Otherwise they could have the desagreement of seeing the bearer of theyr letters going back with a negative answer not from me but from Congress. However I wish'd it could not be the case for this gentleman. I am told that he is of a very good family, a sensible, brave, honest young man and vorthy of every regard. My desire would be to see him obtain a commission which I leave to your own choice (he was lieutenant in France, and, has been three years before volonteer in one other regiment which rank of volonteer is highly considered by every rank of frenchmen).[2] I could annex him *without any command* to some rgt in my division. He has with him a letter from Doctor Franklin to Mr. Peters which I beg you would read because I do'nt know the contains of it.[3] It would be desagreable if that poor young man was refused after coming with a plain confidence in my reccommandation and this letter of the doctor. He is himself a very good gentilhomme of a province in which lies a small part of my estates. I do'nt believe he is by any means a rich man. Great many of our french gentils hommes have nothing but theyr swords, but the know how to make a noble use of it according to the virtuous and glorious example of theyr ancestors. With the greatest affection I have the honor to be Dear Sir Your most obedient servant

THE MQUIS. DE LAFAYETTE

I desired Mr. le chevalier de Mauduit du Plessis to take along that gentleman with him, and tell you what he has seen of his reccommandations.

ALS (ScHi: Henry Laurens Papers).
1. Louis Gaetan de Sigounié.
2. On the "volonteer" in the eighteenth-century French army, see p. 15, note 30.
3. Letter not found.

To George Washington

[Valley Forge,] the twenty [January 1778], a half past one
Dear General

I have received just now a letter from Gal. Connway who is gone on to York town, and Mullens his aid de camp who is not a wit, lets me know that his going there is in consequence of two repeated letters from Gal. Gates and Miflin. That same man thinks that there are some projects to send Connway to Canada.[1] They will laugh in France when they'l hear that he is choosen upon such a commission out of the same army where I am, principally as he is an irishman, and when the project schould be to show to the frenchmen of that country a man of theyr nation, who by his rank in France could inspire them with some confidence—but I mention that only as a remark ⟨of theyr folly, Sir⟩. I do not entertain myself any idea of leaving your army neither my virginian division, but I would not loose a moment to wraït your excellency of that journey towards Congress which means perhaps some much worse scheme against yourself or your army.

Our making fashines goes very slow.[2] We are obliged to take alwaïs the same men. We want axes and when I ask some, five or six are sent for the whole wing. No spirits to be issued to the men. There have been too complaints for provisions principally in General Waine's division; I am about to inquire if they are right, and in that case who is guilty for those fatigue partys being not supplied. However we'l do as fast as circumstances may permit. With the most tenderest affection and highest respect ⟨I have the honor to be⟩ Your excellency's the most obedient servant

⟨THE MQUIS. DE⟩ LAFAYETTE

⟨I am told that Mullens is to be lieutenant colonel, if it is so, as that the same commission was done for Mssrs. de Fleury and du Plessis who are on every respect so much out of the line of Mullens who being by his birth of the lowest rank, and not so long ago a private soldier, I hope that those gentlemen are to be at least brigadier generals.⟩

ALS (PEL: Hubbard Collection). The manuscript has been edited in ink, in Lafayette's later hand. The text of significant deletions has been restored in angle brackets. Lafayette apparently edited the manuscript after he had it copied for Sparks in 1828 or 1829, because the postscript, all but obliterated in the ALS, is legible in the Sparks copy, where it is deleted with a wavy line (Autobiographical Notes I, fol. 189 vo., 190).

1. Letters from Gates and Mifflin to Conway, and from Conway to Lafayette, not found. See Gates to Lafayette, January 24, and Lafayette to Laurens, January 26, in which the incursion into Canada is discussed.

2. Fascines: tightly tied bundles of brush, used to strengthen earthworks or for building temporary fortifications.

To [Adam Hubley]

[Valley Forge,] the twenty jan'y 1778

Sir

Your letter of yesterday came this morning into my hands, and I do not loose any Moment to answer to its several articles.[1] You have seen, since it was wrote, a gentleman I had sent to you with some directions about making picquets.[2] I desire you would carry that work with all possible expedition, because as soon as it will be done I'l go with the engeneers for tracing out the fortifications of the right wing. You have received the number and the dimensions of those picquets; therefore as soon as it will be almost done be so good as to give me notice of it, and I schall go upon the ground with the engeneers. Such a trifle will be the affair of few moments.

When I'l have the pleasure to see you, before your going to the fashines, I'l try to get some more axes from the quarter master general. We'l speack too for some better place tho' I do not know any very convenient to the purpose. I think it would be possible to get small hatchets in the several brigades of the right wing, I beg you would take some informations of it as you will work before the front of each brigade—however I schall ask some to the quarter master general.

I hope you will have to day the men from General Poor's brigade. At the end of our work if some thing remains to do, that brigade could reimplace the day where they have not been emploïed.

According to provisions, there is not the smallest doubt that men must not be sent to work before eating any thing, or taking along provisions with them. I even thaught yesterday that, mentionning it was useless. When you'l let me know that the picquets are far advanced to be done, (and certainly it wo'nt be long) then I schall come immediately, and we'l regulate together this matter.

I am, Sir, infinetely obliged to you for all the trouble you take in this occasion and I have the honor to be very sincerely Your most obedient servant

THE MQUIS. DE LAFAYETTE

ALS (PHC: Charles Roberts Autograph Letters Collection).
The General Orders of January 15, 1778, put Lafayette in charge of construction of the defenses for the army's right wing:
The works marked out by the Engineers for the defence of the camp are to be executed with all possible dispatch, and the commander in chief requests the favor of

General Greene, Lord Stirling and the Marquis de la Fayette (General Sullivan being upon other duty) to consult with Genl. Portail on the proper means and number of men necessary to execute the works in the different Wings and Second line and give orders accordingly, and that each of them appoint proper officers to Superintend and push forward the defences. [Fitzpatrick, *Writings of Washington,* 10:306]

1. Letter not found.
2. Pointed stakes used in military stockading.

From Henry Laurens

[York,] 22d. Jany. 1778

Sir—

The 19th. Inst. I was honoured by the Receipt of your favor of the 16th. by the hands of a French Gentleman whose name you have omitted & I have not seen him since he brought me the Letter.[1] Be assured Sir, it will afford me the highest satisfaction to serve you effectually in all your Commands—& yet I almost despair of succeeding in the present trifle, for it seems by Mr. Duplessis' report the Gentleman would be content with a Lieutenancy but you Sir, are now a better judge of the State of our Army than I am. I learn however from all quarters, there are very many supernumerary subalterns, a certain number of these I apprehend will be reduced. There could never be a more improper juncture for applying for new Commissions—in this view I feel myself unhappy because I cannot do all that I wish. Nevertheless my endeavors shall not be wanting to give a lift to this Young Soldier, I have just sent to seek him in order to offer at least, my countenance, & in a word Sir, I will make him a witness of my gratitude to Marquis dela Fayette for his friendship to my Country.

The Committee appointed to confer with His Excellency the Commander in Chief in Camp, are now stripped of all their intended Military Coadjutors & will consist of Members of Congress—perhaps I ought to except Colonel Reed who is at the same time a Member of Congress & a Military Man. Genl. Gates, Genl. Mifflin & Colonel Pickering are called to attend the duties of their appointment at the Board of War.[2] An application to that Committee will be as likely a measure for obtaining employment for the Young Gentleman as any I can think of, but it is much against him that he speaks not a word of English.

P.M. Just returned from Congress, where a Report was made from the Board of War marking out a separate Command for Major Genl. Marquis dela Fayette.[3] This will undergo debate this Evening & probably you will very soon receive minute information from the Board of War or from the President of Congress. If the plan is Resolved upon the Young Gentleman in view will be provided for. I continue in the most sincere Esteem & Respt.

LbC (ScHi: Henry Laurens Papers).

Laurens wrote Lafayette a short note on January 22 which may have been enclosed in this letter: "Sir—Here Inclosed I have the honour of transmitting an Act of Congress of this date for payment of your Aids de Camp in the usual mode of the Army" (DNA: RG 360, PCC 13, 1:23). The resolve directs Lafayette's aides to be paid "as the aids of other major generals are paid" (*JCC*, 10:84). Lafayette served without pay. ·

1. Lafayette to Laurens, January 15, carried by Sigounié.

2. On January 20 Gates offered "strong reasons" why he should not go to camp with the congressional members of the Committee of Conference. One of those reasons may have been talk of the Conway Cabal current at camp. Congress excused Gates, Mifflin, and Pickering from attendance on the committee to allow them to begin the business of the Board of War, and added Charles Carroll and Gouverneur Morris to the committee (*JCC*, 10:66–67).

3. Congress resolved on January 22 to authorize an "irruption" into Canada. The vote on general officers to lead the expedition was taken the next day, and Lafayette, Conway, and Stark were elected (ibid., pp. 84–85, 87).

PART IV

THE CANADIAN
EXPEDITION

January 24–March 30, 1778

. . . if I meet with some good luck, I can hope to have the pleasure of wraïting you from *Camp before Quebec* . . .
To Henry Laurens, January 27, 1778

Canada, the "fourteenth colony," loomed large in the imaginations
of the political and military leaders of the American Revolution. From
late June 1775, when Congress suggested the first ill-fated invasion of
Canada, to the peace in 1783, an invasion of Canada was continually
considered. Invitations to revolt were couched in terms of a common
cause that the Canadians should feel with the United States against
British despotism; political feelers or rationales usually preceded the
expeditionary forces. If not the fourteenth state, Canada might be the
first colony to profit from the influence of the American Revolution;
if neither, Canada would be a valuable trump in peace negotiations,
and possession of her would deprive the British of their main base of
operations in America.

Armies in Canada and in the northern military department (upstate
New York and part of present-day Vermont) operated independently
of the main army under Washington; it was Congress that formulated
their operations. Congress gathered, received, and reviewed the intelligence from Canada, and planned or approved Canadian expeditions. Though it was customary to consult the commander in chief
before initiating such military operations, it was not extraordinary for
Congress to inform Washington of its plans for Lafayette to command
an incursion into Canada only by sending him Lafayette's letter of appointment.

Congress learned very slowly and only by repeated example that
Canadian invasions were not feasible, given problems of climate, supplies, and provisions and a hesitation on the part of the Canadians to
embrace their "liberation." The invasion of 1775–1776 was a fiasco, yet
in the autumn of 1777 both Schuyler and Gates were drafting pro-

posals for another invasion attempt. From these proposals evolved the expedition that Lafayette expected to lead in the winter of 1777–1778, and when the expedition proved abortive, new means of penetrating Canada were immediately sought. Lafayette, greatly discouraged by the inadequate preparations for his first expedition, later proposed grand invasions of Canada by combined French and American land and naval forces in 1778, 1779, and 1780, and also in 1782 and 1783, when he expected Spanish assistance. These proposals received an attentive hearing in Congress and in the French ministries.

Thus it is not surprising that in the winter of 1777–1778, when the weakened and impoverished main army was immobilized in winter quarters at Valley Forge, Congress, searching for some decisive action following Gates's success over Burgoyne in the north, settled upon an invasion of Canada, though it should have known what the results would be.

Albany, at the time of the Revolution, was a city of fewer than 4,000 people; the population of upstate New York, exclusive of the Indians, was under 65,000. Lafayette assumed command of this near-wilderness area after he had abandoned his plans to invade Canada. As commanding officer at Albany, he worked in close conjunction with the civil authorities to obtain necessary provisions and supplies, and to provide for the common defense. Besides attending to the countless details of military administration, Lafayette cooperated with the local committees in maintaining internal security, forwarded to the state government representations on behalf of prisoners and Loyalists, and assisted the Indian commissioners in their dealings with the Six Nations. The correspondence in Part IV illustrates more than the follies of Canadian expeditions; it shows as well the confusion and disruption that war entails on the local level.

On January twenty-second Congress resolved to invade Canada, and M. de Lafayette was chosen to lead the expedition with Generals Conway and Stark. Hoping to seduce and govern so young a commander, the Board of War, without consulting General Washington, ordered M. de Lafayette to go to Albany to await its instructions. But with the approval of the congressional committee at Washington's camp, Lafayette hastened to York, where he declared that he required detailed orders, a statement of the means to be employed, the assurance that he was not deceiving the Canadians, more general officers, and commissions for several Frenchmen. He added that he was well aware of the duties and advantages provided by a name such as his, and thus his first condition for accepting the position was not to be independent of General Washington, as Gates had been. He defied Gates's party at the general's own quarters, and embarrassed them by making them drink to the health of their commander in chief.[1] Under the able presidency of Laurens, Congress granted everything he required. The instructions from the Board of War promised that there would be 2500 men assembled at Albany, a large body of militiamen at Coos, two millions in paper money,[2] some silver money, and the means for crossing the ice of Lake Champlain. After having burned the British flotilla, he was to fall upon Montreal and act there as the situation required.

Recrossing the Susquehanna, which was not without danger since the river was full of enormous ice floes, M. de Lafayette set out for Albany. Despite the hazards of ice and snow, he made the 400-mile trip very quickly.[3] As he traveled on horseback he observed the simple customs of the inhabitants, especially their patriarchal society and republican spirit. The women are devoted to their families and delight in making a comfortable home for them. One speaks of love to the girls, and their flirtatiousness is as amiable as it is modest. In the marriages of convenience that are made in Paris, a wife's fidelity is often repugnant to nature, reason, and even the principles of justice. In America one marries one's sweetheart; to break that valid agreement would be like having two lovers at the same time, because the two parties understand why and in what manner they are bound to each other. The men work at their business affairs in the midst of their families and assemble to discuss those of the government. While they drink they talk politics, and patriotism warms them more than the strongest liquor. Children cry at the very word "Tory" and old men pray to heaven that they may be permitted to see the end of this war. During his repeated and rapid journeys, M. de Lafayette mingled with all classes of citizens and was not useless to the great cause, to the interests of the French, and to the party of General Washington.

When M. de Lafayette arrived at Albany, he was very disappointed. Instead of 2500 men, there were not even 1200, and Stark's militiamen had not even been notified. The supply of all the items necessary for that frigid expedition—clothing, provisions, stores, sleds, and snowshoes—was entirely insufficient. If the preparations had been better, and the general appointed earlier, success would probably have been possible. Some Canadians were already restless, and they had begun to take a great interest in M. de Lafayette. But it would have required two months to gather the necessary supplies and men, and by the middle of March the lake begins to thaw. At the age of twenty, M. de Lafayette had become the general of a small army and had been placed in charge of an important and unique operation, authorized by Congress, and encouraged by the expectations of America, which would soon be those of Europe as well. Thus he had many good reasons for taking great risks. On the other hand, his resources were slender, and time was too short. The enemy was in a good position, and Lieutenant General Carleton was preparing another Saratoga for M. de Lafayette. Forced to make an immediate decision, he wrote a restrained letter to Congress, and with a sigh abandoned the Canadian expedition.[4] At the same time, Congress had become a bit less confident and sent him inconclusive advice, which, arriving too late, served only to compromise the general and exonerate the government. But M. de Lafayette's prudence was later applauded by Congress and the people, and he commanded in the northern department until the beginning of the next campaign. He found there the intrepid Arnold, who was still detained by his wound, and who since . . .[5] He also became well acquainted with Schuyler, Gates's predecessor. Disgraced like St. Clair, Schuyler still served the cause and was very useful because of his superior intellect, his presence in that part of the country, and the confidence that the state of New York, of which he is a citizen, had in him.[6]

Even though Canada did not launch another invasion, all the Indians were bribed, and, under the protection of British parties, the Hurons and the Iroquois devastated the frontier. A few baubles or a barrel of rum put war clubs in their hands, and, falling upon villages, they burned houses, destroyed crops, and massacred everyone, without regard to age or sex. On their return they received a bounty for every bloody scalp. A young American girl whose fiancé, a British officer, was waiting to marry her, was killed by the Indians he had sent to escort her.[7] Two Americans were eaten by the Senecas, and Colonel Butler [8] was one of their guests. "It is thus," the Indians were told as they drank at their council fires, "that you must drink the blood of the rebels."

Because M. de Lafayette could not guard such a vast territory, he had quarters prepared everywhere, as if troops were about to arrive in every district. That stratagem stopped the Indians, who rarely attack when they expect much resistance. But he kept together the Albany garrison, obtained part of the pay that was due them, provisioned the forts that had been hitherto neglected, and forestalled a plot the details of which have never been precisely known.

He found George Clinton, the governor of the state of New York, resolute, enlightened, and cooperative. A little later, Schuyler and Duane, commissioners for Indian affairs, scheduled a general assembly at Johnstown on the Mohawk River. Recalling the Indians' former attachment to the French, M. de Lafayette went there by sled to show himself to these nations that the English had tried to raise against him. Five hundred men, women, and children, gaudily painted and bedecked with feathers, their ears pierced, their noses ornamented with jewels, and their nearly naked bodies marked with various designs, attended these councils. As the old men smoked, they discoursed very well on politics. The balance of power would be their goal, if their drunkenness with rum, like drunkenness with ambition in Europe, did not often divert them from it. They adopted M. de Lafayette and gave him the name Kayewla, which had formerly been borne by one of their warriors and by which he is known to all the Indians. Next to the English presents, a few louis d'or in the guise of medals and some cloth from the state of New York were not very impressive. A treaty was made and a few of the Indians observed it; the troubles were at least suspended.[9] The Oneidas and the Tuscaroras, our only true friends, asked for a fort, and M. de Lafayette left with them M. de Gouvion, a French officer who had a rare combination of intelligence, talent, and virtue. Whenever the army needed Indians, or there was any business to be conducted with those tribes, they always had recourse to the influence of M. de Lafayette, whose necklaces and words the Indians respected.

Upon his return, M. de Lafayette found that a new oath had been established. Every civil and military officer was required to take it, following the practices of his religion. "An acknowledgement of the independence, liberty, and sovereignty of the United States, an eternal

renunciation of George III, his successors and heirs, and every king
of England, a promise to defend the said states against the said
George III." This oath was sworn before M. de Lafayette throughout
the northern department.[10]

AM (NIC: Dean Collection), translation. Significant passages of the Memoir not
printed in Lafayette, *Mémoires*, are printed here in angle brackets. Annotation of the
Memoir is limited to textual problems and the elucidation of issues and events that are
not discussed in other documents printed in this volume. See p. 12 for a description
of the manuscript and a discussion of editorial procedures for the Memoir.

1. Lafayette described the incident to Sparks in 1829. Upon receiving notice of his
appointment, Lafayette declared to the Committee of Conference that he would never
accept any command that was independent of Washington. Lafayette

> set out for Congress, and arrived at the quarters of General Gates, who was dining
> with several of Washington's opponents. A toast was drunk to the United States
> and to Congress, and people began to rise from the table. "You have forgotten to
> drink to the health of General Washington," Lafayette said to them. When the
> toast had been drunk, Lafayette very openly declared his sentiments to Gates, con-
> cerning the command which had been given him. He told him that if his military
> duties should require him to correspond directly with the Board of War, he would
> only send them copies of letters addressed the same day to General Washington,
> whom he always regarded as his commander in chief. [Autobiographical Notes I,
> fol. 116]

In another memoir Lafayette commented that the party drank his toast, "but not with
much exhuberance of feeling. Lafayette's purpose was answered, however, which was
to let them see at the outset the tone and tendency of his sentiments" (Autobiographical
Notes V, p. 180). Lafayette's memoirs appear to be the only source for the incident,
which has been embellished in the historical literature. See Knollenberg, *Washington and
the Revolution*, pp. 203–206.

2. Lafayette probably means $200,000.

3. The distance between York and Albany was closer to 300 miles.

4. Lafayette to Congress, February 20, 1778.

5. Lafayette's ellipses. From February 1779 to January 1780 Benedict Arnold was
fighting court-martial charges of peculation, which arose from his command of Philadelphia during the last half of 1778. Lafayette could still call Arnold "intrepid" in 1779;
in 1781, when he commanded against Arnold in Virginia, Lafayette claimed that "a
Correspondance with Arnold is so very Repugnant to My feelings that I Can Never
Conquer them so far as to Answer His Letters" (Lafayette to Nathanael Greene, May
18, 1781 [MiU]).

6. Both Schuyler and St. Clair had been relieved of their commands in the northern
department and faced an investigation of their conduct with respect to the evacuation
of Ticonderoga and Mount Independence in July 1777.

7. Jane McCrea.

8. Changed to "a colonel of the British army" in Lafayette, *Mémoires*.

9. James Duane's account of the treaty at Johnstown, March 7–9, 1778, indicated
that over 700 Indians attended the council. The speech from Congress contrasted "the
glorious and upright conduct of these States towards the Six Nations, with their own
Ingratitude, Cruelty and Treachery," and "peremptorily commanded" satisfaction. In
response, an Onondaga chief blamed "the Headstrong Warriors who no longer would
listen to advice, laid a proper stress on the example of our own internal divisions and
Oppositions and printed in Strong Terms the influence of the Bribery and artifices
employed by Butler and the other creatures of the Crown." The Oneidas and Tuscaroras were excepted from the censures and commended for their faithfulness; they
warned the commissioners that the Onondagas, Senecas, and Cayugas were likely to
renew hostilities in the spring (Duane to Clinton, March 13, 1778, in *Magazine of American History*, 13 [1885]:177–180). The speech prepared by Congress is in *JCC*, 9:994–

998 (December 3, 1777); the sachems' speeches of March 7 and 9 are in NN: Schuyler Papers, Box 14; and a speech by the Oneidas and Tuscaroras [April 1778] is in NHi: Misc. MSS Willett (copied on the back of Jeremiah Van Rensselaer to Marinus Willett, April 1, 1778). See also Barbara Graymont, *The Iroquois in the American Revolution* (Syracuse, N.Y.: Syracuse University Press, 1972), pp. 162–164.

10. Lafayette commented to Sparks in 1829: "It is rather remarkable that the American commander destined to receive this oath throughout such a vast part of the former colonies was a twenty-year-old Frenchman" (Autobiographical Notes I, fol. 18).

From Horatio Gates

War Office Jany. 24th. 1778

Sir,

Congress having thought proper and in compliance with the wishes of this Board, from a Conviction of your Ardent Desire to signalize yourself in the Service of these States, to appoint you to the Command of an Expedition meditated against Montreal it is the Wish of the Board that you would immediately repair to Albany, taking with you Lt. Colo. de Fleury, and such other gallant French officers as you think will be serviceable in an Enterprise in that Quarter.

It being of Importance that you should lose no Time in repairing to the Northward, the Board have thought proper to give you immediate Notice of your Appointment and will transmit to you by Genl. Conway particular Instructions, which will explain to you the Principles on which this Expedition is formed, and the Opinion of the Board with respect to the best mode of Executing it.[1]

The Board flatter themselves that the Officers appointed by Congress to cooperate with you in this matter will be acceptable, the one being a Expd. Officer with whom you are personally acquainted, and who wishes to serve under you, and the other an officer, who has the Confidence of the Troops who will be employed with you, from the Victory gaind at Bennington.[2]

Should you arrive at Albany before Genl. Conway, Colo. Hazen who is engaged as D. Q. MG [3] on this Expedition, will communicate to you the orders he has received from this Board and follow your further Directions.

As Mr. Duane who is now at Albany, has been appointed by Congress to confer with Genl. Stark on an Expedition against St. Johns,[4] You will be pleased to confer with him on this Subject; whenever you shall think it requisite for the good of the Service.

The Board doubt not, but that Gentleman, and every other Person of Influence, whom you and he may deem prudent to consult on the

Execution of this Enterprise will afford you every assistance in their Power, which may contribute to the Success of the Plan, and to your own personal Honor.

The Board deem it needless to recommend to you as much Secrecy in this matter as the nature of the thing will possibly admit of, as your own Prudence will suggest to you that much of the Success of such attempts depends upon the Caution of those concern'd.

I have the Honor to be, Dear Marquis, Your Most Affecte. Hum. Serv.

HORATIO GATES
P. of the B. of War

ALS (NHi: Gates Papers, Box 19), draft.

The letter had been enclosed with other Board of War materials to Washington, who replied to the board on January 27: "As I neither know the extent of the Objects in view, nor the means to be employed to effect them, It is not in my power to pass any judgment upon the subject. I can only sincerely wish, that success may attend it, both as it may be advancive of the public good and on account of the personal Honor of the Marquis de la Fayette, for whom I have a very particular esteem and regard. Your Letter was delivered him in a little time after it came to my hands, and he proposes to set out for York Town to morrow" (Fitzpatrick, *Writings of Washington*, 10:356).

1. Conway did not deliver the instructions; Lafayette went to York and received them there. See Instructions, January 31.

2. Conway and Stark.

3. Deputy quartermaster general.

4. Duane described the plan to Clinton on March 13:

The Plan of Congress, when I was last upon the Floor was by a sudden Irruption with 3 or 400 Volunteers, to attempt to burn the Enemy's shipping at St. John's and to offer a very considerable Bounty in case of success. The command to be given to General Starke who was supposed to be very popular in New Hampshire the western frontiers of the Massachusetts & the Grants and in every other respect qualified for the undertaking. The adventurous spirit of the Inhabitants in those parts, the danger to which they must be exposed while the British vessels command the Lakes and the prospect of a Great Reward if they should succeed in the attempt, were thought sufficient considerations to justify the proposition. To me it was given in charge by Congress, to confer with General Starke & deliver him his instructions and explain their views. This occasioned my repairing to Albany as soon as I could give him notice to meet me. At first he seemed sanguine that the scheme would be acceptable and vigourously supported by those over whom he had an immediate influence; but on examination it was found that a Reward which depended only on a prosperous Issue was too slender a Motive for the undertaking. A proposal was therefore made to Congress to allow the Volunteers pay at all events, & the Bounty in case of success. But on General Gates' arrival at Congress the Plan was enlarged into its present Form, and the Command conferred on the Marquiss. [*Magazine of American History,* 13 (1885):178]

James Duane, member of Congress, who served as a semiofficial adviser to Lafayette during his command at Albany

From Henry Laurens

[York,] 24th. Jany. 1778

Sir—

I had the honour of writing to you by Monsr. Duplessis who left York yesterday.[1] I find the Board of War have transmitted you the Intelligence of your appointment by Congress to a Command—to which I shall add no opinions of my own. If you accept it, Monsr. Sigongné will probably be provided for & therefore I have said nothing to restrain his desire of returning to Camp.[2] I had conferred respecting him with Mr. Lovel, who promised me his aid in procuring a Lieutenancy for this young Gentleman, but some difficulties were started from a consideration of the arrangements intended & expected at Camp which I alluded to in my Last. To keep this Gentleman wasting his time & money in this extravagant Market would be cruel. He will learn at Camp your determination & at the same time will have an opportunity of being presented to a Committee of Conference, therefore Sir, I have rather encouraged his inclinations to do the same. I am writing with a frozen hand & the Gentleman waiting at my Elbow your kindness will overlook imperfections of the present address & believe me to be with the warmest respect & cet.

LbC (ScHi: Henry Laurens Papers).
1. Laurens to Lafayette, January 22.
2. Sigounié did join Lafayette on the Canadian expedition.

From Henry Laurens

[York,] 25th. Jany. 1778

Sir—

I had the honor of writing to you yesterday by the hand of Monsr. Sigougné as I omitted to inform you that by a Vote of Congress, Genl. Conway is appointed second & Genl. Stark third in Command for the intended Northern expedition.

On the 6th. Decemb. I made to you Noble Marquis very sincere promises of attention to your affairs at Salisbury,[1] the day or the second day after that event, I was arrested by the Gout & confined to Bed, the consequence of which has been a total neglect of all my own private businesses & a mortifying delay in the execution of the above mentioned engagement. I have been able in the mean time barely to discharge the duties of my public character. Indeed I had spoken to Mr. Lovel again & relied upon him. Yesterday that Gentleman called on me & delivered a memorandum of Monsr. Capitaine's Name & Rank & informed me he had done nothing. I will therefore instantly set about the business & send this very day to Salisbury & will pursue such measures as I hope will prove effectual for the purposes intended.

Inclosed you will find a Letter which you sent some time ago for Mr. Pliarne, it has lain on my Table because I had expected him again in this Town & knew not precisely how to direct to him—but having learned of his death I judge it proper to return the Letter to you. I have the honour to be & cet.

LbC (ScHi: Henry Laurens Papers).
1. Capitaine was still stranded in Salisbury, North Carolina. See Lafayette to Laurens, November 18.

To Henry Laurens

[Valley Forge, January 26, 1778]

Dear Sir

I have received two letters from you by Lt. Colonel du Plessis, and one by the young Gentleman whom I had directed to you some days ago [1]—in those favors you mention to me a particular point upon which Mr. du Plessis gave me in your name a more extended explanation.[2] I wish'd, my dear Sir, to be able to express you in better and stronger terms how flattered and honour'd I find myself by that precious mark of confidence from the Congress of the United States. I am young, I am therefore unexperienced, but every mean in my power, every knowledge in the military way I can have got since the first days of my life, every thing nature could have granted to me, all my exertions, and the last drop of my blood, schall be employed in showing my acknowledgement for such a favor and how I wish to deserve it. I schould never think of asking any command, but I believe it is of my duty as well as of my gratefulness and my own satisfaction not to decline a so honorable mark of confidence. If by every exertion in my power, if principally by the advices of my officers and spirited bravery of my troops, I am happy enough as to meet with some good luck, then, sir, my greatest satisfaction schall be to serve the noble cause of liberty, and in the same time not to be useless to the succès and future glory of our respectable friend—for I dare hope, that Congress will permit me to look upon myself only as a detachement of General Washington's army, and an officer under his immediate command.[3] There is, Sir, a very particular instance about my going to engage the english to leave the country called some time ago the *niew France*. It is that one of my ancestors, marshal of France under the french king Charles Seventh, the *Marshal de Lafayette* at the head of the army, and an immense number of volonteers, was happy enough as to drove the english from *old France* which they had invaded, after having defeated them in a large battle and killed the Duke de Clarence the English king's brother with his own hand.[4]

You will be surprised to hear that I have not received any intelligence about that Appointement from any member of Congress or of the board of war but from the President of Congress.[5] Perhaps a man [6] who is not unknown to you has contrived some base scheme to stop the expedition of it. I am told by the Baron de Kalb who has received a letter from a gentleman in York town, that the same man is appointed to be under me in the command I am intrusted with. The baron is very angry against him on account of his publishing every where that almost all the french officers are disatisfied with the american service and Gal. Washington, and that he himself *Baron de Kalb* without speaking a word of it is put by Gal. Connway at the head of the list. I desire you would receive soon this letter to know which is my way of thinking about those matters.

Amongs All the men who could be sent under me Mr. Connway is the most disagreable to me and the most prejudiciable to the cause. I Confess you that love and friendship have alwaïs been my düties. This last sentiment I feel to the most perfect degree for General Washington. How can I support the society of a man who has spocken of my friend in the most insolent and abusive terms, who has done, and does every day all his power to ruin him, who tries to spend the fire in every part of the army and the country? On the other hand I am very certain that every one who can find one single reason of refusing düe respect and love to Gal. Washington will find thousand ones of hating me to death. Such sentiments would be attended with horrid circumstances and I do assure you that if any officer schould do in my army what he has done in this, he would be confined immediately, and cashiered by a court martial. I know that Connway will sacrify honor, truth, and every thing respectable to his own ambition and desire of making a fortune. What engages me to despise him more is that he is with me as submist, as complaisant, and low than he is insolent with those he do'nt fear.

I want, Sir, to have with me men who hearty for the cause, respected by theyr virtue, candid in theyr advices, ponctual in the execution of our projects, quiete by theyr temper and moderate in theyr discourses, as well as theyr actions, could engage the confidence of the people, give good exemples to the officers, help the young commander in chief both by wise and sincere advices and by trüe exertions for the common cause, who in case I was killed could take immediately my place, till farther orders, and be depended upon by Congress in all cases, even when stranger inductions and hopes of fortune at home could engage them to make a bad use of the confidence of Congress and this of the Canadians.

You have among you a man of real virtüe, a man who loves truly his country the brave and prudent MgDougall. This is a man entirely convenient to me—the coldeness of his age will calm the ardor of my twenty years.[7] I came with the Baron de Kalb in this country, he is wise, he is a good officer, he is not over-powered by the clamours of an unbounded ambition. I am sure both will be glad to come with me. One reason more to desire Gal. MgDougall is that being amongs Canadians I schall be obliged to *francise* myself, and speak much about *the french blood* to gain theyr hearts. I wish'd to have with me a man of a great judgement, and ardent lover of his country to prevent the ideas of diffidence which are unhappily so frequent among a free people.

I fancy that great many french officers, and even french soldiers scaterred in the army will be given to me to establish the confidence of our fourteenth state. I hope that some other means of succeeding *in supplies artillery &c.* will be granted to your much too young deputie in Canada. I expect with a great impatience the appointment and other orders in order to know what I am to do. I schall not loose a minute to execute every thing I'l be directed to. I do not believe that any large number of troops could be taken out from our present army without great inconvenience. If some are selected Colonel Smith's and Jackson's niew regiments from New England, who do'nt belong to any body and above all Colonel Hazen with his canadians compagnys are I believe to fill up the list.

Lt. Colonel du Plessis is I believe the best man to command the artillery in the world. Tho' he is young he is a gentleman of superior habilities, high virtue, and most respectable and noble sentiments. I schall be highly pleased if he is given to me in that appointement and that will be a way of taking along with me the french *officiers de fortune* as it is the intention of Congress. You can speak freely about my business to Col. du Plessis.

As soon as I will receive the appointement of Congress, I schall direct to you a letter of thanks which you'l be pleased to read in the house. I'l beg you to keep secrete the injurious personnalities which are in the present, but if there are some things you think proper to communicate I give you my full liberty for it, and I am certain you will attend my interests as a true friend.[8]

With the sentiments of a warmer lover of your country than I have ever been, with the greatest gratefulness of the confidence of Congress, and the most tender affection for his respectable president, I have the honor to be dear Sir Your most obedient servant

THE MIS. DE LAFAYETTE

When I had just finished Mr. Moriss [9] came into head quarters and as I did Know that he was a friend of ours I have communicated to him almost all my letter. He will wrait to You.[10] I have been very happy to hear that he was of the same opinion as myself for Gnl. MgDouggal.

ALS (ScHi: Henry Laurens Papers). Endorsed: "Marquis de la Fayette supposed to have been written 26th. Recd. 27 Jany. 1778."
1. The two letters of January 22 and the letter of January 24, 1778, carried by Sigounié.
2. Lafayette's appointment to command the Canadian expedition.
3. Commanders of previous expeditions to Canada had been independent of Washington (see Memoir of 1779, p. 99; and p. 103, note 23).
4. In one of his memoirs, Lafayette correctly stated that he was distantly related to the Maréchal de Lafayette, but not descended from him (Autobiographical Notes III, p. 1). The maréchal commanded at the battle of Beaugé, where Thomas, Duke of Clarence, was slain, in 1421. The English were not expelled from France until 1483.
5. Lafayette did not receive Gates's letter of January 24 until January 27.
6. Conway.
7. McDougall was forty-six years old; Conway was forty-five.
8. Laurens wrote to a friend on January 30: "We have now in motion an Irruption into Canada under the Command of Marquis de Lafayette, provided he will condescend to accept of Mr. Conway for his second. If I may judge from his Letters to me in which he speaks of this Officer with the utmost abhorrence, he will not. What Congress may then determine is uncertain" (Laurens to Isaac Motte, January 26–30, 1778, in Burnett, *Letters of Congress*, 3:53).
9. Gouverneur Morris, a member of the Committee of Conference appointed by Congress.
10. See following letter.

Gouverneur Morris to the President of Congress

Camp 26th. Jany. [1778]
Sir

I have taken occasion to speak to the Marquis de la Fayette upon the appointment you know of. The Sentiments of his Heart which are

Drawn from the life by Du Simitier in Philadelphia. _Engraved by B. L. Prevost at Paris._

N.º 7

Gouverneur Morris, a firm supporter of Washington and a member of the Committee of Conference that counseled against a Canadian expedition

fully expressed in a Letter to you [1] do him so much Honor that any Expressions of mine would be impertinent. I am deeply surprized at the mature Judgment & solid Understanding of this *young* Man for such he certainly is.[2] The Impropriety of having the first and second in Command from a foreign Country is strongly stated by him, and his apprehensions that it would be disagreable to the Subjects of America are certainly not ill founded, for great Liberality in vulgar Minds is not common even in America. It deserves the Consideration of Congress whether in Case an Accident should happen to the Commander in Chief it would be prudent to trust a Person [3] whose object it is to push his Fortunes in France with an opportunity to imbue the Minds of the Canadians with a Love of the Grand Monarque who may as probably like Canada as any of his Predecessors. This Consideration has not the *less* Weight from being mentioned by the Marquis. His having pitched upon McDougall who you may remember I wished to have with him may have prepossessed me in Favor of what some Gentlemen may call his Prejudices and this Prepossession is as you may well suppose not weakened by his Declaration that he would willingly act under him as second in Command if deemed necessary for the Service. I write standing in the midst of Company. You will therefore be so kind as to excuse the Stile of this Letter which upon Perusal I find to be very defective. I have the Honor to be with very great Respect Sir your most obedient & very humble Servant

GOUVR. MORRIS

ALS (DNA: RG 360, PCC 78, pp. 295–298).
1. See preceding letter.
2. Lafayette was then twenty; Gouverneur Morris was twenty-five.
3. Conway.

To Henry Laurens

the 27 [January 1778, Valley Forge]

Dear Sir

You will have certainly received a long letter from me by Lt. Colonel Du Plessis,[1] before this falls into your hands—but as I send a servant of mine to York for several businesss belonging to his province, I wo'nt let pass this occasion of presenting you a niew assurance of my attachement. I schall mention in the same time two or three points relative to my glorious and flattering appointement.

I have received a letter signed Connway where he informs me

under the most strictest secrecy of what he can no more conceal from me.[2] He presents me that commission under the two points of wiew he knows to be the most agreable to me, the utility of this country of the american liberty, and my own glory. He assures me how happy he finds himself to serve under my orders. He swears that he feels a much greater pleasure to be under me than if he was commander in chief, too happy, says-he, if he can by every exertion in his power contribute in some thing to my reputation, and he begs, he expects with a great respect an answer. However, I have thaught that even the most strict duty of politeness could indulge me to wait one or two days before answering to that honest gentleman.

We have, Sir, in the army a man who would be of a great use to me—more useful even to the northen than the southern part of your army. This is Gal. Portaïl—you will be surprised at my begging the chief of the ingeneers, to be merely in a detachement of General Washington's grand army—but I pray you'd reflect that (without mentionning any fort) if I meet with some good luck, I can hope to have the pleasure of wraïting you from *Camp before Quebec* and then it will be the true business of the chief of Your ingeneers to take the only one fortified town to be taken, or at least the strongest one of America. (I do'nt include St. Augustine because Gnl. Connway will take it with fifteen hundred men coming from Mr. de Borre's country.)[3] Gal. Portaïl would be intrusted too with the care of marking out, fortifeïng if necessary and distributing our camps. So I would divide the place of quarter master general and leave the other employements to a country man officer, an active friend of ours, pointed out near or upon the spot, and very well acquainted with Canada.

I must confess to you that I am wraïting this after the most warm desire of Mr. du Portaïl, declared to me in the most expressive terms. He would take along with him the youngest of his ingeneers and leave Colonels La Radiere and Laumoy, and the new Major Villefranche with some other strangers to do the duty in General Washington's army. I dare hope that such a plan would agree without difficulty with his excellency.

If I had that gentleman and the most respectable MgDouggall, I schould be very happy. I want, my dear Sir, to have men whom I can extract from, as much prudence and as many years (without any sensible injury to theyr persons) as I believe there is necessary to fill up in my age, which years I think must have a general to be in his point of perfection—and it is my opinion that even when a man is born with those so superior and uncommon talents for the great art of war, the best age for his generalship, after a continued study and experience is betwen forty and fifty.

Can I dare hope, my good friend, that Congress will add yet to his confidence and my gratefulness in granting me as much power as to reform abuses, punishing, or rewarding upon the spot, in all to establish that strict discipline which will give to the Canadians a great idea of our justice, our strengths, and our soldiership? I fancy and I wish very heartely that I schall be directed to settle my plan and my businesses with the committee of Congress actually in camp—for the board of war, you know, is not in the interest of the friends of Gal. Washington. I fancy too that I schall after waït on Congress and its president to take farther instructions.

There is a point upon which I did not hear any thing this of monney. Do'nt you think that gold is absolutely necessary? I'l tell you what I can make upon that matter and I hope you know too well my heart and my love for Your cause for injuring me with any thanks. I have about seven thousand guineas of actual revenüe, I have an hôtel in Paris, I have in plate, diamonds, &c. too about the double of that summ I can dispose of or make a borrowing upon. If Congress wants a warrant for borrow immediately that monney from some stranger I schall give my name to it—but in case it was useless, then, Sir, I beg you would find for myself about five or six thousand guineas to borrow, which I am certain it will be necessary for me to spend from my own pocquet in liberalitys, pious charitys to clergymen &c. &c. &c. &c. and it is only with the power of spending from my own that sum that I wish'd to undertake the expedition—if you could not find that I schould be obliged to borrow those five thousand guineas at some foolish and ruinous interest.[4]

the same day at 2 o'clock

When I was wraïting this your letter and this of Mr. Duer fell into my hands,[5] and I see with the greatest concern that the two greatest ennemys and most insolent calumniators of my friends are directed to follow me, Cannway as second commandant, and Duer as volonteer. The first you know my way of thinking for—the second has the reputation in the country to be a tory, and you'l know by several instances that he is a rascall.[6] I tell you, Sir, freely not as to the president of Congress but to my friend that if it is not altered at least for the first I am obliged to decline the appointement. If they go there I am sure they will prevent my succeeding. If my endeavourings to do well are attended with such impassables obstacles, my hating cabals and cabaleurs will send me back to France. Mr. de Gimat is going to York. I tell to him not to mention that I have received those two last letters even this of Connway—that Connway is so much despised by every honest frenchman, that no body will serve under him—and those who do not know him yet, will be lighted on his conduct as well as I have been myself. What Mr. de Gimat will tell you, you can put the same confidence in as if it was myself.

LE MIS. DE LAFAYETTE

ALS (ScHi: Henry Laurens Papers).

1. Lafayette to Laurens, January 26.

2. Letter not found.

3. Conway had earlier proposed an expedition against St. Augustine, Florida, a fortress considered difficult to capture. Preudhomme de Borre had resigned from the Continental army to avoid a court of inquiry into his competence; Lafayette's sarcastic comment about capturing St. Augustine with only 1500 men of Borre's stamp would not have been lost upon Laurens.

4. A guinea was twenty-one shillings; it was worth a little more than $5 at the beginning of the American Revolution. On February 19, Duane wrote to Clinton about Lafayette and an incident "which shews the Liberality of his disposition": "He determin'd on his entering Canada to supply his army thro his own private Bills on France, to the Amount of 5 or 6000 Guineas, and to present that sum to Congress, as a Proof of his Love to America & the Rights of human Nature!" (NHi: Duane Papers).

5. Laurens to Lafayette, January 25; Duer's letter not found.

6. William Duer wrote to Francis Lightfoot Lee on February 14 that he was awaiting a letter from York,

> the Substance of which, is (I am told) a very Extraordinary Conversation betwixt the Marquis de la Fayette, and Genl. Conway, of which I had the Honor of being the Topic. In the Course of a Discussion betwixt these Officers of the Expedition against Canada, the Marquis Exprest his Astonishment, that *I* should be trusted to go on it, as he had been inform'd that my political Character was that of *a Tory. Risum teneatis, Amici?* . . . I think it is no difficult Matter to guess at the Quarter, whence this Insinuation comes, or the Purpose for which it is design'd. I am happy, however, to learn it in Time, for, however I despise the Insination it will furnish me with this Useful Lesson not to risque my own Reputation, and Ease of Mind by troubling the Young *Telemachus* with the Presence of a Person, whom he cannot consider as a *Mentor.* Before I was informd of this Matter my Imagination suggested to me that the Pleasure, which the Marquis Exprest of my going with him as a Volunteer appeard more the Result of French *Politesse* than of Inclination; yet, as I was of Opinion my Presence might be useful to the Public, I was willing to sacrifice my own feelings to a more important Consideration. To persist in this Resolution at present would be a Breach of Self Duty, as I must in such Case sacrifice my own Ease, and (possibly) my Reputation, without the Hope of possesing with the Marquis that Influence, which might be necessary for Effecting Purposes beneficial to the public Weal. I have thought it my Duty to communicate this Matter to you in order that you may mention it to the Board of War and to Congress, who probably depend on my going into Canada, and may thereby be prevented from taking such Measures with respect to that Expedition, as Policy may suggest. I think a Committee of Congress ought without Delay to be sent into Canada should our Troops oblige the Enemy to retire to Quebec; and though, I owe too much to my own Feelings to Volunteer it, where I am look'd upon in a Suspicious Point of View, I will, if Congress think proper, act as one of such a Committee. . . . [Louis Gottschalk and Josephine Fennell, eds., "Duer and the 'Conway Cabal,'" *American Historical Review,* 52 (1946):90]

From Henry Laurens

York 28th. Jany. 1778

Sir—

Very late last Night (& it is now not day light), I had the honour of receiving your favour by the hands of Colonel Duplessis.[1] I perused it very carefully & will pay the most honorable regard to the Contents. Forgive me Dear Marquis, for expressing some regret that you disclosed any part of them to a Gentleman who though very sensible appears to me, & has given some proof, to be often guardless & incautious.[2] You command me to keep parts of your Letter in confidence, be assured Sir, the whole will be held in that Esteem. If I can produce or procure any good from the knowledge which you are pleased to communicate, it shall be effected without disclosing the source.

I know from the Gentleman himself that Genl. Conway is desirous of accompanying your Excellency upon the intended expedition & I am equally sure a rejection on your part will be received as a great disappointment. I took the liberty of intimating that it would be decent if not necessary to consult Your Excellency upon the Question of who should be your second—but the thing had been not only preconcerted but apparently predetermined. Indeed by some contrivance I was deprived of the honour, & the means of doing my Duty, of informing you Officially of the appointments.

As I do most sedulously avoid even the appearance of being a party Man, Your Excellency will the more readily excuse me for speaking only in general terms. I think I can discern on which side Virtue & honour predominate as well as that where Craft & design are lurking under specious guise, when perhaps the party themselves are blinded by prejudice & not sensible of their own errors, & as I judge charitably I would endeavour to act circumspectly even with such Characters, who divested of the Spirit of party may be valuable Men in community.

I have taken such measures as I think cannot fail to bring Monsr. Capitaine & the Baggage forward. Major Polke who left the Army last Week has engaged not only to deliver my Letter but to exert his utmost endeavors that my direction & requests shall be duly executed.[3] I have the honour to be with the most sincere attacht.

LbC (ScHi: Henry Laurens Papers).
1. Lafayette to Laurens, January 26.
2. Gouverneur Morris.

3. Laurens directed his acquaintances in Salisbury to settle Capitaine's accounts and arrange for his journey to York, drawing upon Laurens for any expenses (Laurens to Matthew Locke, to Matthew Troy, to Michel Capitaine, to William Polk, all January 25, 1778 [ScHi: Henry Laurens Papers]).

To Robert Morris

[Lancaster?] The 29 january 1778

Dear Sir

According to your directions I have applied to Colonel Lutterloh for getting some monney, but was answered by that gentleman that all the monney he had belonging to you was disposed of. I'l beg you to let me have by the bearer two thousand pounds because I want immediately ressources for the northen expedition, if this is acceptable on every respect. I hope you will pardon my being troublesome to you, and beg you would be convinced of the most sincere attachement I have the honor to be with dear Sir Your most obedient servant

THE MIS. DE LAFAYETTE

ALS (DLC: Robert Morris Papers). Endorsed: "Camp, 29 Jan. 1778. Marquis de lay Fayette for £2000 credit & his receipt for it." The letter was probably written while Lafayette was on his way to York from Valley Forge.

Instructions for the Marquis de Lafayette Major Genl. in the Army of the United States of America, and Commanding an Expedition to Canada

[York, January 31, 1778]

The Troops selected for the above Service, consist of the following Corps. Vizt.:

Brigr. General Nixons Brigade
Col. Van Schaicks Regiment
Col. Warners _____
Col. James Livingstons _____
Col. Hazens _____
Col. Bedels _____
and Capt. Whitcombs Rangers.

These Corps will at a low estimate make two thousand five hundred Combatants, and all except Bedels Regiment will rendezvous at Benington. That will march from Co'os where it is raised, to the mouth of Onion River; the place appointed for the general Rendezvous.

As most of the Troops ordered for this Service, have been upon Duty in Canada, there will be no want of any other Guides than such as may be chosen from among them. Genl. Stark, Col. Warner and Col. Bedel, with the Assistant Deputy Quarter Master General Colonel Hazen, know every Road, Pass and Post in the Country.

You have only to consult with them as you advance, and if absolutely necessary upon your Retreat.

Colonel Greaton, the Commanding Officer at Albany, has Directions in concert with the Quarter Master Genl., the Commissary General, and the Commander of the Artillery at Albany, to provide Ammunition, Provisions, Stores, and as many Carriages as may be requisite for the intended Service.[1] Col. Hazen is sent forward to expedite the execution of these orders.[2] You need therefore be under no concern for Supplies.

As Success will depend principally upon the vigour, and alertness with which the Enterprise is conducted, the Board recommend it to you to lose no time. The rapidity of your motions and the consternation of the enemy will do the business.

The Season of the Year being severe though healthy, the Commissary of Cloathing at Albany [3] is ordered to furnish all the Woolens, and every Comfort his Stores can afford. You will constantly be in the Woods at Night, where the Troops are so well acquainted with the mode of covering themselves, that you would find Tents unnecessary and cumbersome. The Proper officers are now providing Forage at the general and particular Places of rendezvous.

Upon your gaining possession of St. Johns or Montreal, you will publish a Declaration of your Intentions, to the Canadians; and invite them to join the Army of the United States.

Colonel Hazens Regiment of four Battalions, is to be first completed to the Establishment, and the Officers and Soldiers who inlist, are to be allowed the Bounty and Reward offer'd them by Congress in their Resolutions of _____ 1776.[4] Unless you shall be of opinion, after considering the political Complexion of the Inhabitants, that it is not a proper Crisis, for inviting the Canadians to take an open Part with these States—in which case you will publish a Manifesto, requiring a strict neutrality on the part of the Canadians, and suggesting such other Considerations, as you shall deem adapted to the Situation of Affairs.

If upon your entering Canada, you find a general disinclination of the Natives, to join the American Standard, You will destroy all the works and Vessels at St. Johns, Chamblee and the Isle aux Noix, and

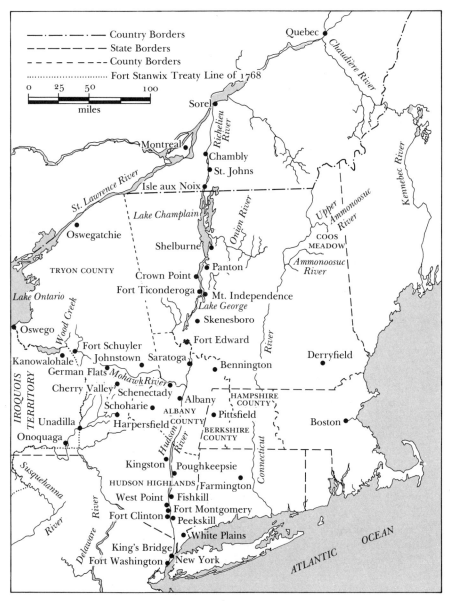

New York and the Northern Department

retire by the best route to the Settlements, then to Saratoga, and our present advanced Posts, on the Wood Creek and Hudsons River.

If on the contrary the Canadians are ardently desirous of assisting to establish the Freedom and Independence of America, you will inform them, that when they embark in the common cause, they must determine to receive the Resolves of Congress and the Currency of America, with that Reverence and Alacrity, which have ever been manifested in the Acts and Dealings of the Subjects of the United States.

They are then to be requested to send Delegates, to represent their State in the Congress of the United States, and to conform in all Political Respects to the Union and Confederation established in them.

In taking possession of Montreal, which is a principal Object of this expedition, you will take into your possession, for the use of the Publick, all the Arms, Ammunition and Warlike Stores, together with all the Linnens, Woolens and Indian Goods that may be found in or near the City of Montreal making such allowance for the private Property so secured, as you shall think most consistent with Justice and sound Policy and the Merits of the respective individuals. In transacting this business, you will take effectual care to prevent every Species of Plunder, and embezzlement, as these may tend to raise Suspicions in the minds of the Canadians that may be both dishonorable and prejudicial to the Interest of the United States.

[This Board would suggest to you the propriety of calling upon the Governor, Senate, & Assembly of the State of New York, now sitting at Poughkepsie, on your way to Albany, & taking their Advice upon all such matters as may contribute to the Glory, & Success of your Expedition.]

General Washington has ordered Col. Hazens Regiment to march from its present Station to Albany; this Corps will therefore if possible be added to your Strength.[5]

The Board confiding in your discretion and the advantages which you will derive, from the advice of all the principal officers who will accompany you on the expedition, deem it not only unnecessary but even impracticable to enter into a minute detail of the Conduct proper to be observed by you, in conducting it.

They content themselves with suggesting, that the Design of this Expedition may not be misunderstood, that its Grand Object is to destroy, or possess the Enemys Vessels and Stores of every kind upon Lake Champlain and in the City of Montreal; and all Clothing and Stores of every kind, in the possession of private Persons, which may be necessary for the Service of the States, or Serviceable to the Enemy. The Consequences which may arise from Success, are to be viewed in a secondary Point of Light, and therefore the holding the Country or prevailing upon the Inhabitants to confederate with the States, is not to be undertaken but with the greatest Prudence, and with a Prospect of durable Success. By order of the Board.

H. GATES

President

D (DLC: George Washington Papers, Series 4), copy in John Laurens's hand, probably made from the instructions Lafayette received from Gates in York.

On February 16, Congress asked the Board of War for a copy of these instructions (*JCC*, 10:172). The last paragraph of the version that the board presented to Congress (DNA: RG 360, PCC 156, pp. 55–64) was composed from memory; it does not differ significantly from the DLC copy. A paragraph was also added instructing Lafayette to consult with the governor and the assembly of New York; that paragraph has been inserted in the transcription in square brackets.

1. Udny Hay, Jacob Cuyler, and Ebenezer Stevens. See Gates to John Greaton, January 24 (NHi: Gates Papers, Box 19).

2. Gates to Moses Hazen, January 24 (ibid.).

3. George Measam.

4. The resolutions of September 16 and October 8, 1776, authorized a bounty of $20, a grant of land, and a suit of clothing each year for anyone who enlisted in the Continental army for the duration of the war (*JCC*, 5:762–763, 855).

5. This paragraph does not appear in the DNA copy.

To [the President of Congress]

York town this 31 january 1778

Dear Sir

I beg you would receive yourself and present to the honorable Congress my Warmest thanks for the mark of confidence they have honoured me with in appointing me to the command of a northen army. I schall be very happy if circumstances, I mean such ways of succeeding as will be granted to my desires on every point, enable me to accept a favor which I have received with the most sincere gratefulness. As soon as I received notice of the propositions which were made to me by the board of War, I desired the opinion of the gentlemen from Congress who were in camp,[1] and seeing them convinced as well as myself that *I schould come* here before going to Albany, I got this leave from his excellency Gal. Washington, and I repaired to this place in order to know in which light I could consider the expedition Proposed to me *against Montreal.*

I have been surprised to receive the niews of my appointement, and the instructions of my commission by any other hand than this of my general. It engaged me to make this very stranger to my mind and very strange in itself reflexion, that I was not perhaps looked on as a detachement of his excellency's army under his immediate command. However I hope that idea was groundless, and I find even it was a ridiculous one. I look upon it as a much higher honor and a much pleasanter satisfaction for me, to be considered only as an officer of his under his immediate orders, than if I was in any other light. It is not for satisfieing my own pride that I speack so, but for the advantage of the thing in itself, and for compliying to the sentiments which I know to be in the hearts of all the *frenchmen* who are to come along with me.

It is, Sir, an highly pleasant idea for me, to think of a large parcell of my countrymen, driving theyr natural and tyrannical ennemy out of the lands they had taken from 'em, and enjoying all the advantages of liberty by theyr strict union with thirteen other states. How happy I would be had I the satisfaction of being an instrument of such a revolution, my love for the freedom of mankind in general, and in this particular instance, my consanguinity with the Canadians and the name of french man I am honoured with, will be sufficient proofs. If I had believed that I am not sent for doing good and right to the Canadians, then I schould not have hezitaded an instant to decline this Commission—but as I am fully convinced that I would promote theyr happiness as well as the advantage of the United States, I schall undertake it with the greatest chearfulness, if those means are taken which I'l think proper to succeed. It is far from the temper of my mind, to accept the governement of any business which I could not carry to my own honor, and the utility of the people who have put theyr confidence in me.

Gal. Gates has been pleased to communicate to me one part of the project. Other instructions will come soon in my hands—but I was anxious to make as soon as possible my thanks to the honorable Congress, and in the same time to let them know which were some of my sentiments about this matter. I went for that purpose as soon as I received the letter of the hble. board of war.

I schall make use with the greatest pleasure of the liberty which has been granted to me of taking along with us some of the french men who are here, and to choose those I am more acquainted with. I dare answer that the Unit. States will be satisfied with theyr services, and the canadians pleased with theyr manners and good exemples. I inclose here the list which I have been permitted to make out.[2] We know all that the name of french men imposes to us great duty to deserve it, but no exertions will be forgotten on our part to show ourselves worthy of the country we have had the advantage to be born in.

I entertain the hope that such a collection of frenchmen, among whom some are not unknown to the english nation, going for helping canadians against the common ennemy, will spend troublesome reflexions in the hearts of many in theyr ministry, and be of some weight for declaring war to France. This I desire heartely because I am fully convinced that it is the advantage of my country to take now a more active part in the present contest.

The honorable Congress will give me leave to mention them, as a thing of the highest moment that for my operations, principally for my councils, and for giving to me theyr advices I have not a sufficient number of general officers with those whom I find the Congress and board of war have been pleased to appoint to me. The only troops who will be at or about Albany are more numerous than any division is now in the army and if we have some succès I understand it will increase every day amasingly. But it is the least matter, and we must not so much consider the number of men as the importance of our business. There will be great many instances where I'l want the advice and exertions of more than two Gal. officers. I think it is as much of my duty as of my delicacy to confess all what I schould need, before the same men who appointed me, and wish the succès of the enterprize. I had desired Gal. MgDouggall, not that I am very intimately acquainted with him, but by the knowledge I have of his rigid and imperturbable virtüe. The state of his health would not permit his going now in a so cold country—but there is the Baron de Kalb who has seen more wars than any officer in the continent, who came over with me, who if I was to point out any of the general officers who are to be in that expedition, had an indubitable right to my mentionning his name. He desires to come with me, he will be much more useful to America if he is employed there. I take the liberty of reccommanding that article in the most strongest terms, not at all because there where are more than two brigadiers, it seems it schould be two major generals, but because I think very firmly that for the good of the service, and the succès of the enterprize it is of the highest importance and of an absolute necessity.

You will find me, Sir, very difficult, and rather too cautious—but it comes chiefly from by being strongly convinced how far indebted I am to the Congress of the United States for the confidence they honor me with. I want to deserve it, and when matters will be settled, then no exertion schall be forgotten on my part for showing myself worthy of such a commission. My first step towards Albany will be decisive for my fate—therefore I must avoid any inconsidered one. If before venturing myself to it I would not insist upon the means of succès I look upon as necessary, then myself and the french officers whose attachement has connexed theyr going there with my having that command, we schould take the place of men who could perhaps give a greater weight to that expedition in Europe, gain better the hearts of the Canadians, and engage them with lesser difficulty to raise up against the common ennemy.

When I will get the detaïl of my instructions, the returns of my ressources of every kind, and as many intelligences as I can get from the board of war, then the board will give me leave to consider deeply which objections I can make (for the advantage for the expedition) to what schould be granted to me. Knowing the just time at which things will be ready is by circumstances of the highest importance. The quantity and quality of cloathings, of arms which will be delivered to our soldiers, those which are destinated for as many Indians as will be in our party, and as many canadians as will serve under the american colours, our magasines, stores of every kind, our provisions, waggons, horses &&c. are things of which a single one may throw down all the enterprize. But as it is not prohibited to look in a fair prospect as far as it can go, if circumstances would permit to us a longer stay, if a siege of a greater importance was thaught proper and ordered by Congress then other steps schould be taken and foreseen. There is one other thing of the greatest importance to provide for—it is to prevent the ennemy coming up in our rear or obliging us by the least motion to make a precipitate retreat. By my being sent there on a political as well as a military wiew I am intitled to beg to Congress instructions from themselves for what I am to do in that first way, and to give me officers to whom I can have the greatest confidence on every respect. What I promise must be relligiously kept, and my honor as well as my love for the french blood obliges me to take care not to make the least misunderstanding. As many things as can be foreseen I want to have them cleared. For the others I fancy some liberty will be granted to me, and then I'l judge according to my conscience and the advice of every honest man and warm friend to the american cause I may consult. I fancy that I will get the answers Congress will be pleased to make to the several articles of this letter about in the same time that my most interesting business with the board will be done. Then, Sir, if I can hope to satisfy the wiews of Congress and the feelings of my own heart, I'l repair immediately to camp, and after taking leave and the last orders of my general, I'l go as fast as possible with the officers who are to follow me, to the place where I hope to show by my conduct my gratefulness and my warm attachement for the United States of America.

With the highest regard I have the honor to be Sir Your most obedient servant

THE MIS. DE LAFAYETTE

ALS (DNA: RG 360, PCC 156, pp. 5–8).

With the start of the Canadian expedition, Lafayette began to separate his private from his official correspondence with Henry Laurens, president of Congress. Lafayette's public and private letters were usually written concurrently. We have indicated the distinction in the titles: public letters are entitled "To the President of Congress," and private ones "To Henry Laurens."

1. On February 11, after Lafayette had left for Albany, the Committee of Conference wrote to Congress—with apologies for its "Presumption"—to voice its "deep Concern" that the Canadian expedition proposed by the Board of War would "involve the most serious Consequences." If the expedition failed

> it would produce Desertion among the Troops . . . Disgrace to our Arms, and all its Consequences upon our Money, upon our People, upon our Friends in Europe, and upon the Enemies we have in our own Bowels. . . . And on what do we build our Hopes of Victory? Have not Montgomery and Burgoyne demonstrated the Imprudence of distant Expeditions across an inhospitable Wilderness where there is but one Road by which to advance or retire? Is not the very Season against us? Our Troops are unprovided against its Rigors, and when it abates which will probably happen by the Time they have crossed the Lake, then they will be deprived of the Means of accomplishing a Retreat. To these Considerations let us add that those Troops cannot be fed. . . . The Army in Canada tho crowned with Laurels must . . . undoubtedly starve. [DNA: RG 360, PCC 78, 7:167–170]

The letter was read in Congress on February 16, and "referred to the Board of War, who are directed to report specially thereon, and to lay before Congress a copy of the orders given to the officer commanding the irruption." On February 24, Congress ordered Lafayette to "regulate his conduct according to the probability of success" (*JCC*, 10:172, 193).

2. List not found; see Resolution of Congress, February 2, 1778.

To Henry Laurens

[York, January 31, 1778]

Dear Sir

If my business are done very early be so good as to give me notice of it to prepare myself to my departure.[1]

To the reason that I do'nt seem to like the expedition you can answer that I like it very well and my propositions to you about monney are a good mark of it.

For the Baron de Kalb they must reflect that as the baron will go of[f] with me he will not be more useful to Gal. Washington in France than in Canade and by the same occasion they will loose Gal. Portaïl and all the engeneers, Gal. Pulaski, Armand, Duplessis &c. &c. &c.

If my going there is not agreed upon immediately I'l resign this evening and the other french generals and officers will send theyr resignation in two days.

You can say too that I must set out immediately for France by the occasion of the man I had sent for bringing to me that fregate of 24 guns.

If I go there I'l wrait to France a letter to my friends, one to the french ambassador, one to the members of the opposition in the two houses which I'l show you.

If no french officers as it will be go to Canada, then no canadians will join under that irish man [2]—principally when they will see us going of[f] and publishing the reasons which distify [dissatisfy] Gal. Washington, myself and all the french officers, to whom Congress has been so ungrateful.

At half past nine

I am Coming from that board.[3] I spoke to them with a great frankness and finished by telling that if they do'nt give me MgDougall or Kalb, and the french officers appointed according to my ideas I decline the appointement and will go to France with most all the french officers in the army. I am sorry my dear Sir, to think that two or three rascals oblige me to make out such a conditions and take such steps. Mr. Lee was I believe for me, Duer quite against, the secretary charmed vith that dispute, and the old fellow scretching his wigg.[4] I think they'l beg Congress to meet to morrow tho' it is Sunday. There my proposition and my leave in case of refusal will be layd down in the worse light possible. I told them that such I wish would be my instruction from Congress: "When you'l repair to camp you'l send in our name an order to General MgDouggall to follow you, and you'l proceed towards Albany, but if his health do'nt admitt then you'l leave to Gal. Washington a letter which upon MgDouggall's answer he will deliver to the Baron de Kalb to order him to go up." Then I am certain to have one or another, and more certain yet to have the baron tho' I would like better the other.

If you are not so good as to make out before Congress will meet a little cabale in my favour, then I'l be lost and as I ca'nt go back obliged to keep my word in going home. At least I could give directly my commission and be yet three or four weeks with his excellency as a volonteer.

Good Night, my dear Sir, I am going to bed. Be so good as to wrait to me or send for Mr. de Gimat when you will be up.

L. F.

ALS (ScHi: Henry Laurens Papers).

1. Lafayette refers here to the proposals contained in his letter to Congress, January 31.

2. Conway.

3. The Board of War.

4. Francis Lightfoot Lee; Richard Peters and Gates.

Resolution of Congress

February 2, 1778

Resolved that General Washington be informed that in compliance with the request of the Marquis de la Fayette Congress are willing that Major Genl. McDougal should proceed on the intended incursion into Canada, if his state of health will admit of it; but if not that the Baron de Kalb be directed to follow the Marquis on the said expedition in case Genl. Washington shall judge it proper. That it is not however the intention of Congress that the Marquis should be detained till Genl. McDougall's intention can be known, as the success of the expedition depends upon its being executed without loss of time.

That in compliance with the request of the Marquis de la Fayette, commissions be granted to the following french gentlemen who have produced to the Board of War credentials of their rank and military merit in the French service and are moreover recommended by the Marquis to be employed under him agreeable to their respective ranks in the intended incursion into Canada, the said officers to be appointed to the command only of such Canadians as may be embodied in Canada viz.

Mons. Jimat, at present aid de camp to the Marquis
     de la Fayette to be appointed .... lieutenant Colonel.
Mons. de Vrigny to be appointed .... lieut. colonel
Chevr. de Pont Gibaut .... Major
Mons. de Sigonie .... Captain
Monsr. de Lomagne .... Captain
Baron du Frey .... Captain

D (DNA: RG 360, PCC 1, 13:106).

To Adrienne de Noailles de Lafayette[T]

February 3, [1778,] at York

I shall never reproach myself, dear heart, with having let an opportunity to write you go by, and I find one through M. Du Bouchet, who has the good fortune to be leaving for France. ⟨How I envy him, dear heart! I often hate myself and go into a rage against my foolish judgment, which has launched me into a situation from which I can no longer withdraw. They have just made me commanding general of an army in the north, destined for an expedition into Canada. However flattering this appointment may be, and however gratifying it would be to succeed, considering the immense difficulties, I assure you, dear heart, that I would much prefer to leave for France. What those in the army call *homesickness* begins to take hold of me and I am experiencing its painful symptoms. The same things that would have turned my head at my arrival no longer give me any pleasure. The love of my calling and an inclination to be something in the military line (I am not speaking of rank), together with my friendship for General Washington and an estimable president now at the head of Congress, plus the advances I have already made for this American cause—these are the reasons that send me so far in the winter, and impel me now to accept a command that I would gladly exchange for that of a small vessel going to France. I am sad, dear heart; and I am unhappy. While I must present a smiling face to the people to whom I cannot reveal my feelings and attend to the ten thousand things with which I am occupied, my heart grieves in secret, and I am all alone to complain to myself.⟩

⟨This letter will be delivered to you by the brother-in-law of one of the general officers who will serve under me.[1] He is a young man who is as estimable for his noble sentiments and his conduct as he is for his bravery and his merit. He served in the north under General Gates, which gives him stature, and everyone has spoken well of him to me. Receive him well, dear heart, show an interest in him and speak earnestly of him to M. de Causan, his colonel, when you meet him at Mme de Fresnet's.⟩

⟨Although it is for me, dear heart, one of the greatest pleasures I can enjoy here to write you, my heart aches in telling you that it is another than myself who is destined to give you my news. If I am melancholy in this country, there is no way to share my feelings with all the strangers who surround me, and I cannot help being tedious on the rare occasions I find to open my heart. I would much prefer that you could believe me entirely happy and content, because that would prevent your suffering my pain; but, dear heart, I would be lying to you if I told you that my soul is satisfied far from you and from all that I love. The first moment of enthusiasm can prevent backward glances for a little while, but then, my dear, I discover that as long as one has a sensitive spirit, he soon repents of an ill-considered course.⟩

You will already have received several letters in which I speak of the birth of our new child and of the joy this delightful event has given me. If I thought that you suspected this satisfaction suffered some diminution because our Anastasie is only a daughter, in truth, my dearest, I would be so angry with you that for a few minutes I would love you only a little. Ah, dear heart, what a delicious pleasure to embrace you all! What consolation to be able to lament with my other friends the one I have lost.[2]

I shall not give you a lengthy account of the mark of confidence with which America has honored me. It will be sufficient for you to know that Canada is oppressed by the English ⟨and ⟨between us⟩ it has had no reason to be satisfied with the Americans⟩. All that immense country is in the possession of the enemy; they have a fleet, troops, and forts there. For myself, I am going with the title of commanding general of the northern army, and at the head of about [three?] thousand men, to see if some harm can be done to the English in those regions. The idea of liberating all of New France and freeing it from a heavy yoke is too splendid to stop there. Then my army would be greatly enlarged, and it would be augmented by Frenchmen. ⟨A great many French officers are accompanying me there, and I feel very glorious at their head.⟩ I am undertaking a terrifying task, especially with so few resources. As to my personal resources, they are practically nonexistent for such a position; and at twenty, one is not prepared to be at the head of an army, responsible for all the numberless details that devolve upon a general, and having under my direct orders a great expanse of country.

The number of troops I shall have under me, which would be negligible in Europe, is considerable in America. What gives me the greatest pleasure in all this is that in some way or other ⟨this campaign will be shorter than if I had stayed in General Washington's army, and⟩ I shall be in a position to join you sooner. ⟨I long for that happy moment.⟩ How delightful it would be to take care of my business with the English up there quickly ⟨and decamp immediately for my fine homeland⟩. I am leaving immediately for Albany, and from there for another place about a hundred and fifty leagues from here; from there I shall set to work. This month is not pleasant for traveling; I shall make part of the journey in sleighs. Once arrived up there I shall travel only on the ice.

I am not writing to any of my friends by this occasion. I have a great number of concerns, and there is an infinity of political and military matters to be settled, so many things to put in order, so many new obstacles to overcome, that in truth I would need forty years of experience and superior talents to avoid coming out of it disagreeably. At least I shall do my best, and should I succeed only in occupying their attention in the north while doing them no other harm, that is always of great service, and my little army will not be useless. Do me the favor of telling the prince ⟨, the vicomte, and all my friends my news. Assure the prince⟩ that his puny captain, commanding general though he is, knows little more about warfare than he did at the *polygone*,[3] and, unless chance or a good angel provides the inspiration, he hardly knows how to account for the confidence that is placed in him. A thousand fond regards to Mme d'Ayen; a thousand assurances of my tender affection to the vicomtesse and to all my sisters. Remember me to your friends and to your father, Mme de Tessé, M. le Maréchal de Noailles, etc. Farewell, farewell, dear heart, embrace our dear children. I embrace their charming mother a million times; when shall I find myself again in her arms?

AL (NIC: Dean Collection), translation. The manuscript has been edited in pencil, in Lafayette's later hand. Significant passages omitted from Lafayette, *Mémoires*, are printed in angle brackets.

1. Du Bouchet was Conway's brother-in-law.
2. Adrienne noted in her letter book (NIC: Dean Collection) that the friend Lafayette had lost was the Vicomte de Coigny.
3. The Prince de Poix was colonel of the regiment in which Lafayette had been captain. A *polygone* was a field used for military maneuvers.

To Henry Laurens

Anderson Ferry [1] at three o'clock in a great hurry
[February 3, 1778]
Dear Sir

I have the pleasure to inform you that I have over taken Colonel Troop, tho' he was to make his incursion into Albany with all the possible rapidity.[2] As a large river was before him, no boat to cross and his escaping by any way entirely impossible, he surendered himself to me, and the condition of our treaty as been that we schould meet again at Lancaster where he will take a letter for the inspector gal. of the army without inspection, and second commander of the incursion without any particular command.[3] However the military postillon [4] was very anxious to be at Lancaster before me, which I thought it was kind to indulge him. I found at the same river one other rapid incursor from the board going to Reading—and I'l go myself with all the imaginable rapidity to head quarters and from thence to Albany.

There is a letter which I desire you would send to Mr. de Valfort and from hence to France *but in proper hands because I speack of Gal. Washingtons business.*[5] I schould be very happy if that old friend of mine would come again with me.

Do'nt forget to put in the fire the little note I had given yesterday for rememberance in Congress. I forgot to ask you if I was to wraït again to them for granting my desires but however I believe it is useless.

This letter will be delivered by Mr. de la Nieuville coming from the french islands and reccommanded to me. If some other officers were sent to me or employed in the grand army be so good as not forget him. He is a quite young man and I do'nt know better his pretensions than his merit but I wish to show some regard for the reccommandation. We shall mention him again in our letters. The other is a captain in the same regiment entirely unknown to me, but both are frenchmen and I ca'nt refuse a letter for the president of Congress.

After reflexion if Valfort is not at Charlestwon and you do'nt find a quite sure occasion, let the letter be thrown in the fire.

I desire Du Plessis schould be send to his business without delay. I beg your pardon my dear Sir of the impropriety of this letter, but I have only a minute, and I must make an incursion into the boat with all possible rapidity. With the most tender affection and highest regard I have the honor to be Yours

THE MIS. DE LAFAYETTE

My most respectfull compliments to the ladies, I never drank a so good thé than this morning. Indeed my dear Sir you must have a great indulgence for me if you pardon *mon griffonage*.[6]

ALS (ScHi: Henry Laurens Papers).

1. Anderson's Ferry crossed the Susquehanna at the site of present-day Marietta, Pennsylvania.

2. Robert Troup, Gates's aide-de-camp, carried his own instructions from Gates:
    You will proceed, without delay, to Albany with the Packet committed to your Charge; which you are to deliver to Major General the Marquis De Fayette, provided he arrives in Albany, Time enough to be at the Rendezvous appointed for the Troops who are ordered to Canada, and which, it is designed the Marquis shall command. If you find upon your Arrival in Albany, that General Fayette is not likely to arrive in Time, as the Orders already given, & the Season of the Year will not admit of the least Delay in the marching of the Troops; you will in that Case deliver the Packet, entrusted to your particular Care, to Major General Conway, who is instantly to take the Command of the Expedition, and act accordingly. [Gates to Troup, February 2 (NHi: Gates Papers, Box 19)]

3. Conway.

4. By referring to Troup as a *postillon*, Lafayette describes him as a messenger boy.

5. The preceding letter.

6. "My scrawl."

From John Adams

Braintree Feb. 3. 1778

Sir

I had Yesterday the Honour of receiving, from the Hand of my worthy Friend General Knox, your kind Letter to me, together with five others, which, with Submission to the Fortune of War, shall be conveyed and delivered as you desire.[1] I am happy in this opportunity to convey Intelligence from you to your Friends, and think myself greatly honoured and obliged by your Politeness and attention to me—a Favour which makes me Regret the more my Misfortune in not having had the Honour heretofore of a more particular Acquaintance, with a Nobleman, who has endeared his Name and Character to every honest American, and every sensible Friend of Mankind by his Efforts in favour of the Rights of both, as unexampled as they were generous. I thank you, Sir for the kind advice, communicated by General Knox, to which I shall carefully and constantly attend—shall at all Times be happy to hear of your Welfare, and to have an opportunity of rendering you any Service in my Power. I have the Honour to be with the greatest Respect and Esteem, Sir your most obedient and most obliged humble Sert.

LbC (MHi: Adams Papers).
1. Lafayette to Adams, January 9.

From John Stark

Derryfield 3d. feby. 1778

Sir

Being Informed by the Honble. General Gates that you are appointed to Command an expedition against the British troops in Canada, & that I am to go on the same expedition, should be glad to know as soon as possible what Number of troops you expect I shall Bring with me, what States I shall Raise them in, the place of rendevouz & when to Be rendevouzed, & I shall leave no method untried to Answer your expectations. I am dear General your most obedt. Humble servant.

JOHN S. STARK

L (DNA: RG 360, PCC 166, pp. 57–58), copy in Gimat's hand, enclosed in Lafayette to Congress, February 20.

Stark's letter was the first Lafayette received in Albany (Lafayette to Washington, February 19). Gates had written to Stark on January 24 to inform him that: "Congress having thought proper to direct an irruption to be immediately made into Canada, and their design being in part communicated to you by Hon. James Duane, Esq., I am directed . . . to acquaint you that, for wise and prudential reasons, they have appointed Lafayette, first in command, and . . . Conway, second in command who will act in concert with you in promoting the interest and political views of the United States in Canada." Gates added that he expected Stark to "cordially coöperate with them in every measure and move to the public service," and requested his "hearty agreement with, and officer-like assistance to the gentlemen above mentioned," but he did not inform Stark of his intended role in the expedition (Caleb Stark, ed., *Memoir and Official Correspondence of Gen. John Stark* [1860; reprint ed., Boston: Gregg Press, 1972], p. 142).

To Henry Laurens

[Lancaster, February 4, 1778]

Dear Sir

There is Lieutenant Colonel Fleury who not only out of my esteem and affection for him but even by a particular reccommandation of the board of war is destinated to follow me to Canada. I schould have desired of Congress every thing or employement which I could have believed more convenient to his wishes, had I not expected to see him before—you know he was upon my list. He desires to be at the head of an independent troop with the rank of Colonel. I do'nt know which will be the intentions of Congress but every thing which can please Mr. de Fleury not only as a frenchman but as a good officer, and *as being Mr. de Fleury* will be very agreable to me.

I travel very slow, and I am angry against the roads, against my horse, against every thing which stops me. However I am not so quite exesperated against a swet parcel of letters coming thro' the hands of Mr. de Francis, which I have received very kindly. My family was then very well.[1]

I was thinking of the title of that man going to Canada. I am affraïd some body will call him commander in chief in order to excuse himself—but I desire it would be called only General and commander of the northen army. I do'nt say I will so much, but I say positively I will no more, neither any expression which could hurt the commander in chief's rights.[2]

I have showed to Colonel Fleury the first lines of my letter, in order to let him know my giving willingly the reccommandation he asks for you. You know that gentleman's merit and that Duplessis and himself were made lieutenant colonels as reward of fine actions. With the most tenderest affection and highest regard I am Dear Sir Your most obedient servant

THE MIS. DE LAFAYETTE

ALS (ScHi: Henry Laurens Papers). Endorsed: "Recd. 6th. Feby. 1778."
1. Letters not found.
2. Lafayette here expresses his concern that only Washington bear the title "commander in chief."

From Henry Laurens

[York,] 5th. Febry. 1778

Sir—

Virtue & fortitude will subdue "Troops," countermine Cunning Inspectors & bring Presidents embarrassed & entangled between native honour & party plots to subscribe very unprecedented engagements.[1]

The Convention of Susquehana, affords me Dear General, the highest satisfaction although I am under some apprehension for the article to be complied with at Lancaster.[2] Be that as it may—you will be at the heels of the contrasting party, my fears are therefore confined to the little mischief which an almost exhausted Treasury may suffer by a demand for an unnecessary & expensive Courier. The Eye of my mind is always fixed on that poor battered Treasury badly filled from a want of judgement & scandalously plundered by the effects of folly & dishonesty.

Proper care shall be taken of Monsr. Valfort's Letter & the disposal duly notified.

There will be an excellent opportunity for writing to France about 10 days hence from Baltimore.

The little Note was destroyed the Morning it was delivered to me. Unless the New Monsr. Lanuville will follow Your Excellency's fortunes as a Volonteer I have no prospect in his favour.

Congress have Resolved to detain the Artillerists &c. at Boston on certain terms which Col. Duplessis is possessed of, advancement of Rank & the pay of the Army. If they have not Stratagems in their heads, considering what they have already received, they will accept. If they have, they will be left to prosecute them.[3] I have the honour to be with every Sentiment of respect & attachment &c.

LbC (ScHi: Henry Laurens Papers).

1. "Troops," "Inspectors," and "Presidents" are Troup, Conway, and Gates.

2. A reference to Troup's "surrender" to Lafayette at Anderson's Ferry and their agreement to meet at Lancaster. See Lafayette to Laurens, February 3.

3. The artillerymen who had come to America with Du Coudray were waiting in Boston for Congress to decide their fate: they would either receive positions in the Continental army or be reimbursed for their time and given their passage home. Lafayette had been an advocate of their cause before the Board of War during his stay in York (Lafayette to the Board of War [DNA: RG 360, PCC 156, pp. 25–26]). They were offered positions in the Continental army on February 4 (*JCC*, 10:118–119).

To Alexander McDougall

[Valley Forge]
Camp the 5 february 1778

Dear Sir

My happiness and the succès of an interesting enterprize depend on your present health, for I hope if you are well that you would not disappoint my most ardent wishes. Congress desiring an incursion to be made into Canada has appointed me to the command of that body of troops. Gal. Connway and Gal. Stark were appointed to go with me—but I have expressed my earnest desire of going with you, and Congress has at lenght granted this point. The object is to go upon the ice to get St. Johns and Montreal, and try the affection of the people. The little army will begin his march by the twentieth or twenty second of the present month from above Albany at Oignon River. The ice obliges us not to loose any time. As that country is unknown to me, I am obliged to rely entirely and put a full confidence in what I am told by the board of war which is very sanguine upon the matter. I have not, Sir, the pleasure of being since long acquainted with you, but your reputation on every respect and what I know and I have seen or heard myself from you, makes me look upon your presence as very necessary to the succès, if there succès are to be met with. I set out to morrow for Albany. Try, my dear Sir, to consult your forces, and I schall be very happy if they enable You to be at time for our expedition. Be so good as to send your answer to his excellency, because in case of a refusal the Baron de Kalb will join me immediately. Gals. Connway and Stark are already at the rendés vous. With the greatest desire of deserving your esteem and frienship I have the honor to be Dear Sir Your most obedient servant

THE MIS. DE LAFAYETTE

ALS (NHi: McDougall Papers).

Robert Troup to Horatio Gates[E]

Bethlehem [February 6, 1778]
1 oClock AM Friday morning

I came here this moment, & am now setting off for Nazareth, where I expect to see General Conway. As the time for the. Rendez-vous of the Troops is near at Hand I shall Hurry him to Albany. There is now a Prospect of good sleighing, & I believe I shall arrive there on Tuesday next.

I left the Marquis at Lancaster. He seems to be strongly tinctured with the Fabian Principles of Head-Quarters.[1] I asked him "how long he intended to stay at Camp." His Answer was "four or five Days."

My opinion is, that he will be too tardy to reap the Benefits Congress promised themselves from the Expedition. I shall therefore endeavour to forward it not only by delivering my Packet to Gen. Conway, but by every other Means in my Power. . . .

ALS (NHi: Gates Papers, Box 10), extract.
1. Troup found Conway at Nazareth later the same day and wrote to Gates again: "Gen. Conway believes that the Cabal at Head Quarters want the Marquis to take Kalb in order to prevent his doing any Thing that may contribute to his own Honor, in the interest of the States" (NHi: Gates Papers, Box 10).

To Henry Laurens

[Valley Forge]
the Seventh [February 1778] à five in the morning

Dear Sir

I am not yet out of camp tho' I did not loose a minute, but the roads and my business detained me longer than I thaught—however I'l push now very quick and you will hear very soon from me. The bearers of those letters are two gentlemen whose the first is I believe intended by his excellency to be an ingeneer, the second wants too some employement. They were, say they, strongly reccommanded to me by one other schip who was taken. If you see only one of those officers it will be a mark that the first schall be reccommanded by his excellency himself. There will be an officer *de line* already emploïed in our army to whom I'l beg you to say that I have mentionned him for going in the northen army. I can not be so hot for men unknown to me, but as french men I'l reccommand allwaïs them and make the best wishes for theyr succès. I am glad they could know that I have mentionned them. Do'nt forget if you please the little Martinican who brought letters for me.

You have seen Mr. de Fleury. I fancy *entre nous* that he will not be satisfied in so high pretensions. He is very unhappy that Mr. Duer is no more in Congress because he is his intimate friend and confident—that will perhaps surprise you.[1] Mr. de Fleury is *entre nous* a fine officer but rather too ambitious. When I say such things I beg you to burn the letters.

I inclose here two lines for Gal. Gates.[2] You will hear from me by the first opportunity. Be so good as to pay my excuses to the gentlemen of my acquaintance in Congress whom time prevented me from paying a visit to. I have only this of presenting you the assurance of my warmest friendship I highest regard, I have the honor to be with Dear Sir Your most obedient servant

THE MIS. DE LAFAYETTE

Mr. John Laurens is in a very good health. Present if you please my respectfull compliments to your fine land lady and the most charming Miss Ketty.[3]

ALS (ScHi: Henry Laurens Papers).
1. Duer was still a member of Congress but was absent from York.
2. See following letter.
3. Catherine Alexander, daughter of General William Alexander, Lord Stirling.

To Horatio Gates

[Valley Forge]
Camp the 7 february 1778

Dear Sir,

I'l trouble you with these fiew lines to let you know that my journey has been stopped till this time by the badness of the roads and necessary business in camp—but I am going off immediately, and no time schall be lost to be at the appointed rendes vous. You will hear soon from me, and I will be very happy of this occasion of entertaining a correspondance with you. I schould be in a terrible concern about my means of succeeding and the immensity of things which I must be provided for, had I not the greatest confidence in your frienship and your good care of my reputation as well as the public interest. This project is yours, Sir, therefore you must make it succeed. If I had not depended so much on you I would not have undertaken the operation. I am fully convinced that the warmest acknowledgement will be joined to the warm affection and high regard I have the honor to be with, Dear Sir, Your most obedient servant

THE MIS. DE LAFAYETTE

ALS (NHi: Gates Papers, Box 9).

From Henry Laurens

[York,] 7th. Febry. 1778

Sir—

I had the honour this Morning of receiving your Commands by the hands of Lt. Colo. Fleury.[1]

This Gentleman notwithstanding the aid of some able advocates in Congress has failed in his pursuit of a Colonel's Commission. You will wonder less, when you learn that the preceeding day I had strove very arduously as second to a warm recommendation from a favorite General, Gates, on behalf of Monsr. Failly, for the same Rank, without effect. The arguments adduced by Gentlemen who have opposed these measures, are strong & obvious. "We are reforming & reducing the Number of Officers in our Army, let us wait the event, & see how our own Native Officers are to be disposed of"—& besides, there is a plan in embrio for abolishing the Class of Colonel in our Army, while the Enemy have none of that Rank in the Field.[2]

Some difficulty attended obtaining leave for Monsr. Fleury to follow Your Excellency, Congress were at first of opinion he might be more usefully employed against the shipping in Delaware & formed a Resolve very flattering & tempting to induce him—but his perseverence in petitioning to be sent to Canada, prevailed.

Monsr. Fleury strongly hopes Your Excellency will encourage him to raise & give him the Command of a distinct Corps of Canadians. I am persuaded you will adopt all such measures as shall promise advantage to the Service & there is no ground to doubt of your doing every reasonable & proper thing for the gratification & honour of [a] Gentleman of whom Your Excellency speaks & writes so favorably.

The kings' speech of the 20th. Novemr. which I presume you have seen at Camp, according to my reading & interpretation, is intended as harbinger to propositions. The tone will be raverbrated by Lord North's puppets, & the scene will open.[3]

It is remarkable that on the 20th. Novemr. the Capture of Philadelphia had not been announced in England—& not less *remarkable,* that except the Speech there is not a Single insertion of European intelligence in the Philadelphia Gazette 31st. Jany.

I congratulate with your Excellency on the pleasing accounts received from the spot from whence you are now wandering. If fretting, or wishing, would rand the Roads I would enter heartily upon so cheap a mode of scavaging [4]—such as they are, may God conduct you, Noble Marquis, happily successfully, through them, that when, *You shall think it proper,* you may return & fill those tender breasts with joy which till that time will be the subjects of anxiety.[5] I have the honour to be with great regard &cet.

LbC (ScHi: Henry Laurens Papers).
1. Lafayette to Laurens, February 4.
2. Congress wished to abolish the rank of colonel in order to simplify the exchange of prisoners; the exchange was rank for rank and the British did not have that rank among their field officers.
3. As reported in the *Pennsylvania Gazette,* February 7, George III's speech ended: "I shall consider the greatest happiness of my life, and the greatest glory of my reign, the restoration of peace, order and confidence of my American Colonies." Laurens's interpretation was accurate; the North ministry named the members of the Carlisle Peace Commission in the middle of February.
4. "Rand" means to repair; "scavaging" is cleaning or clearing.
5. A reference to the ladies in York.

To Henry Laurens

Flemmingtown 9 february 1778

Dear Sir

I think indeed that I go back as much as I go on, and I am asham'd to see me so far from the famous place where I am expected. How the second in command must be frightened and unhappy at my being detained so long You can easely conceive by this gentleman's character—I had forgotten mentionning you from camp that he never sent a copy of his letter to Gal. Washington.[1]

My road has been rectified by Lord Stirling and rewiewed by every one who has some topographical, jerjayan,[2] Knowledge. Mr. William Duer was not at the appointed rendés vous near Coriel's Ferry, and I must confess I never entertained great hopes of finding him there.[3] I dare say he is by this time hurriying every thing for the alert and expeditious incursion, and calculating very kindly every accident which can broke the neck of a gentleman from head quarters to Albany.

For Mr. Troop he must fly over like a bird for no body has seen him along that very road where he was to get every thing ready for me. However he took my letter for Gal. Connway where I direct him to go on in case I schould not be in Albany by the 25th.[4]

The "most charming Miss Ketty," Catherine Alexander (left), daughter of Lord Stirling, and William Duer, whom Lafayette considered a "rascall" and a "tory." They married in July 1779.

I have received your last favour by Mr. du Plessis.[5] It would be, my dear Sir, a fine work of Yours if it was possible to open the eyes, schut the ears, and direct again the conscience of a certain honest old man.[6]

[I aver?], Sir, the charming Miss Ketty has told what You flattered me with, but if sche had taken any Notice of what my eyes could have signified, she would have read there the greatest admiration for all her accomplished person. With the greatest affection and highest regard I have the honor to be, Dear Sir Your most obedient servant

THE MIS. DE LAFAYETTE

ALS [photostat] (DLC: Papers of Lafayette). The present location of the manuscript is unknown.
1. Conway had not sent his letter of appointment to Washington.
2. Jerseyan.

3. Duer had already decided not to join the expedition (see Lafayette to Laurens, January 27, note 6).

4. Letter not found.

5. Laurens to Lafayette, February 5.

6. Gates.

To George Washington

At Flemming town
the Nineth february [1778]

Dear General

I can not let go back my guide without taking this opportunity of wraïting to your excellency tho' I have not yet Public business to speak of. I go on very slowly sometimes pierced by rain, sometimes covered with snow, and not thinking many handsome thoughts about the projected *incursion* into Canada. If Succèss were to be had it would surprise me in a more agreable manner, by that very reason that I do'nt expect very shining ones. Lake Champlain is very cold for producing the least bit of laurels, and if I am neither drawned neither starv'd I'l be as proud as if I had gained two battles.[1]

Mr. Düer had given to me a rendés vous at a tavern, but no body was to be found there. I went by Coriel-Ferry in compliance to the directions of Lord Stirling, and the advices of Mr. Tilmangh and Gibs.[2] I fancy Mr. Düer will be with Mr. Cannway sooner than he had told me. They'l perhaps conquer Canada before my arrival, and I expect to meet them at the governor's house in Quebec.

⟨I have been told by the people in going along that on the other side of the Delaware, there was a great plenty of scheep which the ennemy could take of very easely and which ought to be secured. That I ca'nt give any particular intelligence about but I thought it proper to mention that report to your excellency. I have heard too that the ennemy keeps a great correspondance with the Jersays by Coopers Ferry.⟩

Could I believe one single instant that this *pompous command of a northen army* will let your excellency forget a little an absent friend, then I would send the project to the place it comes from. But I dare hope that you will remember me sometimes. I wish you very heartely the greatest public or private happiness and succès. It is a very melancholy idea for me that I ca'nt follow your fortune as near your person as I could wish—but my heart will take very sincerely his part of every thing which can happen to you, and I am already thinking of the agreable moment were I'l come down to assure myself Your excellency of the most tender affection and highest respect I have the honor to be with dear General Your most obedient servant

THE MIS. DE LAFAYETTE

Will you give me leave to inclose here my most affectionate respects to your lady and my best compliments to your excellency's family.

ALS (PEL: Hubbard Collection). The manuscript has been edited in ink, in Lafayette's later hand. The text of significant deletions has been restored in angle brackets.

1. Lafayette had originally written "as proud as any president"—reference to Gates—but crossed out "any president."

2. Tench Tilghman and Caleb Gibbs, officers on Washington's staff.

To Moses Hazen

Albany Feby. 18. 1778

Sir

As I have been much disappointed at my arrival in this place, when I seen such a diffirance between what was promised me by the Board of War and what I have found since yesterday Evening (for I have not lost a minute in making myself acquainted with everything I could learn here concerning the Expedition).[1] I intend to make a particular Inquiry in every department which can interfere in this matter. I know you have shewed the greatest activity and imployed great Exertions in all the parts concerning you as being Depty. Quarter Mastr. Genl. of the Troops intended for this Expedition. Therefore I request you to let me know by writing what you have provided in your department, where those things have been got, where they are to be found, how many Slay's &c. &c. you have now in your Disposition. I want particularly to know how much Forrage you have in this moment, how much you are certain to get yet at such a Time, & from where, which are the means of having ready and forwarded to me sixty days Provisions and all the necessary Baggage, Artillery, Amunition for an army of three Thousand men. As you have been directed too to inquire in our present Sittuation for Cloaths and all the Comforts the present season makes necessary, I'l beg you to let me know what you have been acquainted of. You have wrote to several officers and several States. What are their answers? In a word Sir, I desire you to let me know in the greatest detail what Intelligence you have got, which Steps you have taken and what I can depend upon in every thing belonging to your department and the Instructions you have received from the Board of War. I am fully convinc'd you have done every thing in your power, and I make you my very sincear thanks for all the Activity and Zeal you have shewn in this occation, but I want as well for your Intrest as my own to know very minutely how all your Exertions have succeeded.[2] With the greatest regard I have the Honor to be Sir Yr. most Obet. Servt.

                                              THE MIS. DE LAFAYETTE

L (DNA: RG 360, PCC 166, pp. 59–61), copy in Presley Neville's hand, enclosed in Hazen to Gates, February 20, 1778 (ibid., pp. 117–120).

1. Lafayette had arrived in Albany on February 17.

2. On February 20, Hazen told Gates: "I am convinced there has been Great Pains taken by some Ill minded people to fix the failour of this expidition on the Quarter Master Generals Department, holding up as I concive the Difficulty, or rather as they term it the impossibility of my being able to provide Carriages and Forrage Necessary for the expidition" (DNA: RG 360, PCC 166, p. 117). See also Troup's comments to Gates in Lafayette to Laurens, February 19, note. John Laurens had written to his father on January 28 that Hazen, "who is appointed Q. master for this expedition, is said to be a man skilfull in enriching himself at the public expense" (*Correspondence of John Laurens*, p. 113).

From Moses Hazen

                                              Albany 18th. February 1778

Sir

In obedieance to your commands I have the Honr. and Particular Satisfaction to acquaint you, that from the Precautions which I have taken as well to execute as to expedite the buisness of the Quarter Master Generals Department on the intended expedition to Canada, I am not under the least apprehensions of any Defect or delay in the buisness which I have undertaken, as I am invested with authority from the State of the Massachusetts Bay to impress any no. of Carrages in the Counties of Hampshire and Barkshere which may be wanted for this public Service, as also an ordinance from the State of New York impowering me to impress five hundred Carrages and Drivers, and to retain them in the Service for 24 Days, and from the State of Vermount I shall be able to Collect a number of Carrages.[1] As to the Article of Forrage I have provided a Magazene at Pitsfield, at Bennington and on Otter Creek. I have ordered Magazenes to be

Laid in, the Perticular Quantities I cannot yet assartain. Col. Hay will also be able to furnish me with Twenty Tons purchased by him at Panton on Lake Champlain. Mr. Jacob Cuyler Commissary of Purchases has this Day furnished me with a Return of Provisions intended for this Expedition amongst which are 174 head of Fat Cattle, which he will order to Pitsfield and Bennington.[2] Them I propose to yoak in Sleighs, Load them with Salt Provisions and Drive them on with the Troops. They may be killed and Issued to the Troops at your pleasure, which will greatly Diminish the number of Sleighs that would otherwise be wanted, and of course a Saving to the Public. But Suppose I had not a Bushell of Grain or a pound of Hay Provided and that the Army was to be Fed intirely with Salt Provisions to be Transported in Carrages. Yet, as 7 or 800 Sleighs 10 or Twelve days only will be Sufficent to move at once all the Provisions, Artillery, warlike Stores, Hospital Stores and Baggage of the Army to St. Johns or Montreal, and that these Sleighs may take with them Twelve days Forrage each, that from the Authority given before mentioned, It is next to impossable that I should fail in the Number of Sleighs, and the Article of Forrage cannot effect the Expedition. 500 Snowshoes are at Bennington, 500 falling Axes I brought from Boston, which togeather with an additional Number and other implements provided at this place will be Sufficient for the Expedition; I therefore humly conceive the only Difficulties which will attend your proceeding on the Expedition is the want of the Number of men intended for this Service, and the Necessarys of Cloathing for them. To the one and the other I have paid Dilligent attention, and have in some measure been successfull. A Copy of the Return of Cloathing you have inclosed as also my Letter to the Committe at Bennington, there answere and my Letter to Colol. Easton, who has since told me that in consiquence thereof he Hopes to be able to collect 400 men. I also wrote to General Baley & Colol. Bedle at Coohaas, in the same pressing terms. To the latter I have sent Five thousand Dollars, to forward this Service. Their answere I have not yet receiv'd.[3] It is likewise necessary to acquaint you Sir that at my request the Council and Assembly of the Massachusetts Bay Authorised Genl. Heath to Commission a Subaltrn and impowered him to raise Twelve men at the Head of Kennebec River who are to march to the inhabetants on the Shaudier near Quebec and there give out as a Secret in Confidence that they were sent forward to mark a Road for three thousand men who were soon to follow them.[4] This Diversion as they will in all probability be in time may have a very good effect. I have the Honr. to be Sir your most obedt. and most Devoted Humbl. Servant

MOSES HAZEN

L (DNA: RG 360, PCC 166, pp. 67–70), copy in Neville's hand; with multiple enclosures (see note 3). This letter was in turn enclosed in Hazen to Gates, February 20 (ibid., pp. 117–120).

1. Massachusetts, *Journal of the Honorable House of Representatives* ([Boston, 1778]), pp. 172–173 (February 2–3, 1778); *Votes and Proceedings of the Senate of the State of New-York* (Fishkill, 1777 [–1779]), pp. 51–53 (February 9–10, 1778); *Journal of the Assembly of the State of New York* (Poughkeepsie, 1778), pp. 47–49 (February 10, 1778); Vermont Council to Udny Hay, February 9 (*Chittenden Papers*, pp. 224–225).

2. Cuyler's Return of Provisions, February 18 (DNA: RG 360, PCC 166, pp. 101–102).

3. Enclosures: Return of clothing (not found); Hazen to the Vermont Council of Safety (also called the Bennington Committee), [February 9, 1778] (not found); Vermont Council to Hazen, February 9 (*Chittenden Papers*, p. 225), announcing, in response to Hazen's letter of February 9, its decision to raise a corps of 300 men (see also ibid., pp. 224–236 passim, for the Council's orders to levy troops); Hazen to James Easton and to Jacob Bayley (not found); Hazen to Timothy Bedel, January 29, 1778 (*New Hampshire State Papers*, 17:212–213). Bedel reported to Hazen on February 7 that although he had been pessimistic about the success of the proposed expedition, he was encouraged to learn that Lafayette had the command, and he expected to march within eight days, assuming that he could procure necessary provisions and supplies (DNA: RG 360, PCC 166, pp. 63–64; probably enclosed). Bayley to Hazen not found.

4. See William Heath to Henry Laurens, February 7, 1778 (Massachusetts Historical Society, *Collections*, 7th series, 4 [1904]:212–213).

From Alexander McDougall

Morris-Town 18 February 1778

Sir,

I was not honored with your favor of the 5th. Current untill Yesterday. The excursion into Canada, is of great moment, & the obliging manner, in which you are pleased to express my Importance, to that Service demands my Sincere Acknowledgements. But it gave me great concern, that a Letter of such Importance, shou'd have been detained so long, and I am very sorry, that it's out of my Power, to gratify your Wishes; which are expressed in such pressing & Polite Terms. Altho' my health is restored, yet such is the State of my Strength, that I cannot flatter myself, my going with you into Canada, wou'd advance the Service, for Strength is necessary in a Soldier, to endure the fatigue of the excursion mentioned; and I have not yet ventured on Horseback. Agreeable to your desire, Immediately on receipt of yours, I informed His Excellency, of my inability to go on that Service. The Officers of my Acquaintance, who wou'd be of any particular Assistance to you, are too far from you, to be collected in time, to Answer your Purpose.

The Service you are going upon, is very Critical; Remember the fate of General Burgoyne: take Care, that your Retreat be Secure, and some provisions deposited at proper Stations, on the Rout, on which its probable you may return, otherwise your Troops will be in danger of perishing. If you Return, on the Ice by Onion River it is of importance Boats shou'd be built, without Loss of time, sufficient to Secure the Retreat of your Corps, over the Lake; if we have not that Number in our possession. What we have, shou'd be ascertain'd, & Congress wrote to, for means to provide the defficiency. It is of importance to you, to know, that there is a Season, in which you cannot pass Lake Champlain in Boats, or on the Ice. This is occasioned, by the Latter's not being Strong enough to bare travelling on it, and yet so Strong, as to impede the Navigation. General Schuyler will be able to inform you, when this State of the Ice may be expected and many other matters, relative to that Country which may be of use to you.

The "brave and prudent" Alexander McDougall, whom Lafayette wished to have with him on the Canadian expedition

Great attention shou'd be paid to the Quality &. temper of your Troops; on this depends the Success of almost every enterprize. Convince the New England Troops, that you will take all the Care of them in your Power, and exercise steady Discipline on them. And I can assure you, from experience, they will Render you every Respect you cou'd wish, and endure fatigue with a patience equal to any Men. But too severe discipline breaks their Spirits. This is the Line of Conduct I wou'd observe to the Continental Troops. As to the Militia under General Starks, as he is best acquainted with their Temper, I wou'd therefore leave the Management of them to him in matters of discipline. I have taken the liberty to Suggest these hints to you, at the instance of our mutual Friend General Green, who Signified to me it was your desire.[1]

As I am totally ignorant of the information, on which the Board of War have been encouraged, to Sett this Expedition on foot, & of the Country, it Puts it out of my power, to give my Sentiments on this

Subject, so fully as I cou'd wish.[2] I have inclosed a Small Map of Lake Champlain, it may be of some Use & Amusement to you.[3] If any of your Family can Copy it, you will oblige me, in preserving the Original. I Sincerely wish you Success and beleive me to be with great truth & regard. Your most obedient and Most humble Servant.

ALEX. McDOUGALL

LS (NHi: McDougall Papers).

1. Nathanael Greene wrote to McDougall on February 5:
   The Marquis de la Fyette is appointed to command an expedition against St. Johns & Montreall. . . . *Major* General Conway was appointed the second in command, but the Marquis at his special request has obtain'd leave for you to accompany him provided your health permits. If not the Baron de Calb is to go. I wish the plan appear'd to me ellegible and you in a condition to undertake the execution with the Marquis; he is a very cleaver honest fellow. He wishes you to go exceedingly for many reasons. . . . If you are not able to undertake the expedition—the Marquis desires you to give him such advice and information as you may think necessary to direct his conduct. If you have any acquaintances that may be useful to him he begs you'l favor him with some Letters. [NHi: McDougall Papers]

2. McDougall did voice his sentiments in a letter to Nathanael Greene, February 28:
   I am of opinion with you, that the Force going into Canada is much too great for a coup de main on the shipping, and I cannot conceive on what principles or information the Congress or Board of War have carried their views any farther, while we are unable by our Supineness to expel the Enemy out of our states. This I confess appears to me a new Maxim of carrying on a war. . . . If the Juncto expect by this expedetion, to raise a Pillar for their ambitious Fabric, I fear they will be dis-appointed. I wish therefore, for the sake of the Marquis, and the other Honest fellows who are to accompany him there the object of the expedition had not been so extensive. [Ibid.]

3. Map not found.

To the Albany Committee

Albany Feby. 19th. 1778

Gentlemen

Relying on your Zeal for the publick Good and your vigorous exertions on all former Occasions I have made free to address myself to you on the present Emergency. The Honble. the Congress and the Board of War thinking it absolutely necessary that an Incursion should be made into Canada this Season have honoured me with the Command. I arrived in Albany two Nights ago & very contrary to the Intelligence I received from the Board of War find that matters here are by no Means prepared for the Expedition. There are a Number of Men wanting and a great Quantity of Cloathing to render the Soldiers equal to their duty in that Country at this Season. Besides these there are a Number of other Matters very necessary for carrying on the Expedition such as Forrage, Slays &c. &c. Now Gentlemen I request the Favour of you to let me know if those wants can be supplied, by what means, from where, and how soon. I wish you to be very particular as I mean to transmit a Copy of your Answer to Congress. I hope the Nature of the case will excuse my giving you the Trouble. I have the Honor to be with sincere Respect Gentlemen Yr. most Obedient Servant.

THE MARQUIS DE LAFAYETTE

L (DNA: RG 360, PCC 166, pp. 105–106), copy in Neville's hand, enclosed in Lafayette to [Congress], February 20.

The Albany Committee of Correspondence, authorized under the state constitution of 1777, exercised all the functions of civil government in Albany County, and, in conjunction with the smaller district committees, was responsible for the maintenance of internal order and the detection and regulation or prosecution of the disaffected. The committees were expected to assist the military in procuring supplies and provisions.

To Thomas Conway

Albany the 19th. February 1778

Sir,

As I am writing to Congress, and the Board of War about the intended Expedition into Canada, I desire to have, by Writing, your Opinion upon the Matter. You arrived here before me, and therefore had some Time more to make yourself acquainted with the different Circumstances. You have wrote before I was at Albany to Genls. Schuyler, Lincoln, & Arnold.[1] You had conferred with several other Gentlemen, and the greatest Part of the Intelligence I have got, I got them by you. On the other Hand, You have shewed the warmest Desire of succeeding. You have inquired into every Point belonging to the Matter with the greatest Activity and in the same Time you told me that there was Nothing to do, you assured me how happy you would be, could I carry this Expedition to some honorable End, for you & myself. All these Circumstances, besides your military Knowlege, & Experience enable you to advise me better than any Body, & to find, if possible, some Means or another to carry a point which the Board of War, & several Members are so sanguine upon, & which I want to succed in, by every Exertions, when I can find any Probability not to ruin, or dishonor the Troops under my Command. I am, Sir, Your most obedient Servant

THE MIS. DE LAFAYETTE

L (NHi: Gates Papers, Box 9), copy in Troup's hand.

1. Letters not found. Conway had arrived in Albany on February 14. On February 16 he wrote to most of the general officers around Albany concerning the advisability of proceeding with the planned expedition. Lafayette enclosed the replies to Conway's letter in the packet he sent to Congress on February 20.

To Henry Laurens

Albany the 19th. February 1778

Dear Sir

I intend to wraït to you as the president of Congress but now I will explain my heart to my friend, and let him know which hell of blunders, madness, and deception I am involved in.

It is impossible that things could have been turned up in a so little time, and I do not believe that an expedition which would have had some degree of probability could be immediately cut of[f] on every point. Therefore I am inclined to believe that people as been rather fool than wicked in this particular circumstance.

You will find by my letter to Congress how much I had been deceived, and neither words of honor, neither wraïting assurances, my travel to York my conversations &c. have been able to prevent what I was much affraïd of, it is my being sent with a great noise a schining apparate.[1] For what? For nothing at all. You will condemn, I am sure, Gal. Stark's conduct,[2] but you will be more surprised that Gal. Gates seems not so well acquainted with the northen departement as myself who am here since two days. The immense number of debts, the want of cloathing, want of men, want of every thing indeed to be wanted had not only [3] been taken notice of by the future commander in chief of the american forces.[4]

I have found a spirit of disatisfaction every where, every eye seems to say to me, where are you going to bring those unhappy wertches, let it be a natural or an infused disinclination, it is sufficient to ruin the expedition.

I was expected in this town the 25—however I arrived the 17th. Connway has been here only three days before me. He was already very well with the three gal. officers then in Albany—but I ca'nt conceive how he could have altered the matter at such a point in such a time, principally when *Hazen* who has reasons to be, and indeed is very sanguine upon the expedition, was to over look him—and that Hazen himself aknowledges the expedition to be impossible by want of men and cloathes.[5] There is in that ridiculous and schoking affair a piece of folly or a piece of villainy behond all expressions.

General Arnold tho' he was sick and not able to do any thing had taken some notice of my coming to command here. I have wrote to him to day in order to ask his intentions about our present situation, and his commands as being by the date of his commission above me.[6] He his an inveterate ennemy to Gal. Gates and calls him *the greatest paltroon in the world* and many other genteel qualifications of that kind.

What is your opinion, Sir, about my present situation? Do you think it is a very pleasant one? How schall I do to get of[f] from a precipice where I embarked myself out of my love for your country, my desire of distinguishing myself in doing good to America, and that so false opinion that there was in all the board of war some feeble light of virtue or common sense? My situation is such that I am reduced to wish to have never put the foot in America or thaught of an american war. All the continent knows where I am, what I am sent for, I have wrote it through the whole France and Europe (as I had been expressely desired).[7] The world has theyr eyes fixed upon me, and me, myself, I'l be obliged to end an operation which may be looked on as untertaken, in the same ridiculous way as I do'nt know which man by the name of a general has carried on one in the easted. Men will have right to laugh at me, and I'l be almost ashamed to appear before some, because Mr. such a one is a fool, Mr. such a one is a rascal. No, Sir, this expedition will certainly reflect a little upon my reputation, at least for having been too confident in men who did not deserve it, but it will reflect much more upon the authors of such blunders. I'l publish the whole history, I'l publish my instructions *with notes* through the world, and I'l loose rather the honor of twenty Gatess and twenty boards of war, than to let my own reputation be hurted in the least thing.

I was very glad and quiete with my division, but now, sir, as by the impulsion of many in and about Congress I have vrote to my friends that I had the command of an army, an army must be given to me at the head of which I could do some thing to throw a schade upon this very desagreable part of my military life—unless leave schould be granted to me to go and laugh in France of the niew military american ministry of war. However if you can give me a good reason for coming back to my first military post with any decency I have no objection to it. But if you think that the noise my letters and these of all the other french officers will have done in Europe, that the expectations of everyone in America, the expectations of the british army must not end in this schort and laughable Manner then, Sir, you can enable me to show that I can be at the head of an army and that I can conquer when an army is to be found.

I can not give up all ideas of penetrating into Canada, but I give up this of Going there this winter upon the ice. I will take farther informations, I'l try farther exertions. I Confess that I am exesperated to the utmost degree, and was I certain to carry the least point, whatever might happen, I schould go on—but, sir, you'l see such a difference betwen what was promised to me and what I have found, that indeed nothing appears to be done. You know that the whole expedition has been put on foot in order to satisfy one single Man's ambition.[8] The behaviour and *underhands* of this man here I cannot conceive, neither understand yet; but he is well with every body and the most inveterate ennemys of General Gates. I must not forget mentionning to you that Arnold has desired me to take the command here.[9]

There is a project which could make honor to myself good to the country, and mind a little the business—it is if I was directed to go with a part of the northen forces which I could then command to defend the North River or attak Niew York. That attak if it is a possible one would make a good diversion for Gal. Washington. Is it true that Gates is Yet commander in chief in the northen departement?

One of my aids de camp will call on you two days after you'l have received this letter, be so good as to waït by him to me very *fully and very plainly* which effect my melancholy niews have done upon Congress, what they have determined upon about me. As I do not believe they have in theyr power or theyr will to mind my ridiculous travel by some glorious and figting chief command, I fancy *entre nous* that I'l be then induced to repair home—for you know, my dear sir, every body will laugh at my expedition. With the greatest regard and most tenderest friendship I have the honor to be my dear sir Your most obedient servant

THE MIS. DE LAFAYETTE

I am told Gal. Putnam is not to stay in the post he holds now.[10] I beg you would engage Congress to read over all the papers I send to them.

ALS (ScHi: Henry Laurens Papers).

On February 19 Troup wrote two letters to Gates from Albany. To Gates, president of the Board of War, he reported the unanimous opinion at Albany that the Canadian expedition was impossible (NHi: Gates Papers, Box 9); to Gates, his general, he wrote:
> Inter Nos: The trouble General A[rnol]d has given himself to prejudice people against the Expedition to Canada, is one grand Reason why it failed. The Malice of this Man is so bitter and his spirit so vindictive that he scruples not to say, it was formed by you & Col. Hazen—'two ignorant, & designing men.'

All who possess the least share of understanding treat these ungenerous Insinuations with the Contempt they deserve. But there are some on whom they make the deepest Impression. . . .

In the above Class, I may justly rank the Marquis, who affects to be highly displeased with the assurances you gave him, at York-Town. He cannot conceive, how you came to be so little acquainted, with the situation of Affairs, in this Department. I have therefore had several skirmishes with him, in one of which, I gave him a Wound, that he does not relish as well as the tear in his Leg.

As a Change of Measures has produced a Change in his Circumstances, it might be proper to ask 'what you intend to do with him?' A Regard to his Reputation, without considering the public Weal, prompts me to wish he would join his Division in the Southern Army. There, the Blunders of his Youth, & Inexperience, will pass as Manoeuvres in the Sublime Part of War. [NHi: Gates Papers, Box 9]

1. Lafayette to [Congress], February 20. *Apparat* is the French term for ostentation or parade.

2. See Lafayette to [Congress], February 20, and Stark to Lafayette, February 3.

3. "Not even."

4. Gates—another reference to the Conway Cabal.

5. Hazen called the lack of clothing and men "difficulties" in his letter to Lafayette of February 18. By February 19, however, he may have concurred in the general sentiment that the expedition was impossible. In a letter of February 20 to Gates, Hazen's main concern was to vindicate his own exertions on behalf of the expedition (DNA: RG 360, PCC 166, pp. 117–120).

6. Letter not found.

7. See Lafayette to Adrienne de Noailles de Lafayette, February 3. Although Gates had advised Lafayette on January 24 to proceed with as much secrecy as possible, Lafayette told Washington on February 19 that members of Congress had instructed him to announce abroad his command of the expedition. Duane repeated Lafayette's claim in a letter to Clinton, March 13: "He has, it must be confessed, some Reason to be vexed and disgusted, advised, as he was, to announce to his Court the confidence reposed in him by being elevated to the command of such an expedition . . ." (*Magazine of American History*, 13 [1885]:177). See also Lafayette to Laurens and to Congress, January 31. European newspapers carried garbled reports of Canadian insurrections and invasions in May and June 1778 (e.g., *Gazette de Leyde*, 38, supplement [May 8, 1778]:1; 48, supplement [June 16, 1778]:3).

8. Conway.

9. There were three officers senior to Lafayette in Albany when he arrived: Schuyler was under investigation, and had been relieved of his command on August 4, 1777; Arnold and Lincoln were recuperating from wounds, and thus were not fit for active duty. Because Lafayette had been appointed commander of the irruption into Canada, when the expedition was abandoned he was uncertain of the extent of his authority at Albany. With Arnold's blessing and by default, Lafayette was commanding officer at Albany, but he was astonished to learn that Gates still held the chief command in the northern department.

10. Putnam was the commander of the Hudson Highlands. On November 28, 1777, Congress called for an investigation of the conduct of the commanding officers in the loss of Forts Montgomery and Clinton (*JCC*, 9:975–976). On March 16, 1778, Washington ordered Putnam to report to the court of inquiry at Fishkill. McDougall, in addition to presiding over the inquiry, was to assume the command of the Highlands. The court exonerated Putnam, but he was not given any important post thereafter (Fitzpatrick, *Writings of Washington*, 11:94–95; *JCC*, 11:803–804).

To George Washington

Albany the 19th. february 1778

Dear General

Why am I so far from you, and what business had that board of war to hurry me through the ice and snow without knowing what I schould do, neither what they were doing themselves? You have thaught perhaps that theyr project could be attended with some difficulty, that some means had been neglected, that I could not obtain all the succès and the immensity of laurels which they had promised to me—but I defy your excellency to conceive any idea of what I have seen since I left the place where I was quiete and near my friend, to run myself through all the blunders of madness or treachery (God knows what). Let me begin the journal of my fine and glorious campaign.

According to Lord Sterling's advices I went by Coriels Ferry to Ringo's tavern were ⟨the worthy⟩ Mr. Düer had given me a ⟨certain⟩ rendes vous—but there no Düer to be found, and they did never hear from him. From thence I procedeed by the state of Niewyork and had the pleasure of seeing the friends of America as warm in theyr love for the commander in chief as his best friend could wish. I spoke to Governor Clinton and was much satisfied with that gentleman. At lenght I got Albany the 17th. tho' I was not expected before the 25th. Gal. Connway had been here only three days before me and I must Confess I found him very active, and looking as if he had good intentions—but we know goodile upon that subject. His first word has been to tell that the expedition is quite impossible.[1] I was at first very diffident of this report, but have found that he was in right. Such is at least the idea I can form of this ill concerted operation since these two days.

Gal. Schuïller, Gal. Lincoln, Gal. Arnold had writen before my arrival to Gal. Connway in the most expressive terms that in our present circumstances there was no possibility to begin [now?] an enterprize into Canada. Hay dep. quartermaster gal., Cuyler dep. commissary Gal., Meassin dep. clothier Gal. in what they call the Northen departement are entirely of the same opinion. Colonel Hazen who has been ⟨with great impropriety⟩ appointed to a place which interferes in the province of the three others above mentionned,[2] was the most desirous of going there. The reasons of such an ardor I think I may attribute to other motives than a mere love of the american cause.

However (tho' he says he is himself ready in every thing concerning his duty what I ca'nt be certain of) the same Hazen confesss we are not strong enough to think of the expedition in this moment—for the troops they are disgusted, and (if you except some Hazen's Canadians) affraïd to the utmost degree to begin a winter incursion in a so cold country. I have consulted every body, and every body answers me that I schould be mad to untertake this operation.[3]

I have been ⟨schamefully⟩ deceived by the board of war. They have by the strongest expressions promised to me, and three thousand, and (what is more to be depended upon) they have assured to me by wraïting *two thousand and five hundred combattans at a low estimate*. Now, sir, I do not believe I can find *in all* twelve hundred fit for duty, and most part of those very men would be naked even for a summer campaign. I was to find Gal. Stark with a large body, and indeed Gal. Gates had told to me *Gal. Stark will have burnt the fleet before your arrival*. Well, the first letter I receive in Albany is from Gal. Stark who wishes to know *what number of men, from where, for which time, for which rendes vous I desire him to raise*.[4] Colonel Bedels who was to raise too would have done something *had he received monney*.[5] One asks what encouragement his people will have, the other has no cloathes, not one of 'em has received a dollar of what was düe to them. I have applied to every body, I have begged at every door I could since two days and I see that I could do something was the expedition to be begun in five weeks—but you know we have not an hour to looze, and indeed it is now rather too late, had we every thing in readiness.

There is a spirit of disatisfaction prevaling among the soldiers and even the officers which is düe to theyr not being pay'd since an immense time. This departement is much indebted, and as near as I can ascertain for a so little time, I have already discovered near eight hundred thousand dollars due to the continental troops, some militia, the quarter masters's departement &c. &c. &c. It was with four hundred thousand dollars whose only the half part is arrived to day that I was to untertake the operation, and satisfy the men under my commands.[6] I send to Congress the account of those debts.

Some cloathes by Colonel Hazen's activity are arrived from Boston, but not enough by far, and the greatest part of it is not cut of[f].

We have had an intelligence from a deserter who makes the ennemy stronger that I thaught. There is no such thing *as straw on board of the vessels to burn them*. I have sent to Congress a full account of the matter.[7] I hope it will oppen ⟨a little⟩ theyr eyes. What they will resolve upon I do not know, but I think I must waït here for theyr answer. I have inclosed to the president the copys of the most important letters I had received.

It would be tedious for your excellency, was I to undertake the minutest detaïl of every thing. It will be sufficient to say that the want of men, cloathes, monney, and the want of time deprives me of all hopes about this expedition. If it may begin again in the month of june by the easted, I can't venture to assure—but for the present moment such is the idea I conceive of the famous incursion as far as I may be informed in a schort time.

You excellency may judge that I am very distressed by that disapointement. My being appointed to the command of the expedition is known through the continent, it will be soon known in Europe as I have been desired by members of Congress to write to my friends my being at the head of an army. The people will be in great expectations, and what schall I answer?

I am affraïd it will reflect on my reputation and I schall be laughed at. My fears upon that subject are so strong that I would choose to come again only a volonteer unless Congress offers me means of mending this ogly business by some glorious operation—but I am very far from giving to 'em the least notice upon that matter. Gal. Arnold seems very fond of an diversion against Niew York and he is too sick to take the field before four or five months. I schould be happy if some thing was proposed to me ⟨about⟩ in that way, but I will never ask or even seem desirous of any thing directly from Congress. For you, dear General, I know very well that you will do every thing to procure me the only thing I am ambitious of. Glory.

I think your excellency will approuve of my staying here till farther orders and of my taking the liberty of sending my dispatches to Congress by a very quick occasion without going through the hands of my general—but I was desirous to aquaint them soon of my desagreable and ridiculous situation. With the greatest affection and respect I have the honor to be Your most obedient servant

THE MIS. DE LAFAYETTE

Will you be so good as to present my respects to your lady?

ALS (PEL: Hubbard Collection). The manuscript has been edited in ink, in Lafayette's later hand. The text of significant deletions has been restored in angle brackets.
1. Conway reported to Gates on February 19:

I arriv'd here the 14th. inst. and I immediately ordered the Commanders of the several Regiments to give me exact returns of what men they had fitt for marching. I Deliver'd these returns to Marquis De La Fayette who arriv'd here the 17th. The number of men is infinitely short of what was expected by the Board of War. The Men were Destitute of every article necessary for a long and severe march. Coll. Hazen who has been extremely active and Diligent in his Department procur'd some cloathing from Boston but not half sufficient. There is a general claim and

Dissatisfaction here for want of money. The Men have not been [paid] these five months pass'd. . . .

The intelligence from Canada is not encouraging. . . . Indeed I found here a general aversion to the expedition. . . . I have this Day reviewed the troops of this place and promis'd that Congress had order'd them their pay and that they would soon receive it. This seemingly appeas'd them. I am going tomorrow on the same errand to Schenectady and Johnstown. [DNA: RG 360, PCC 166, pp. 111–114]

2. Hazen had been appointed deputy quartermaster general for the Canadian expedition. To prepare the expedition, he had to compete for resources that were also needed by the supply officers for the northern department.

3. Hazen wrote to Gates on February 20: "I am now greatly hurt at the thoughts of the Canada expidition being laid aside. I am also Sorry for the Marquis, his Disapointment is great and mortifying, he was very anxious to push forward and at the same time prudently cautious of acting contrary to the intentions of Congress and your Honble. Board. He has been very assiduous in obtaining information of every possible means of carrying on this expidition, and he has, as was natural to suppose, consulted with the Principle Officers in this place, on the facillity of the enterprize, and I have reason to believe their opinion has Dissuaded him from proceeding further in it." Of his own regiment, Hazen said: "They are so warm for the expidition that they would consent to go almost naked into Canada. I wish I could see as much forwardness in the other Troops" (DNA: RG 360, PCC 166, pp. 117, 119).

4. Troup commented to Gates on February 19 that Stark's letter "shews me the Folly of looking to him for the least Assistance. The whole Tenor of it wears the appearance of Disgust, & it is altogether silent about the Men he was ordered to recruit for an Enterprise against the Fleet" (NHi: Gates Papers, Box 9). Troup's assessment is unfair, considering that Stark had only just received Gates's letter of January 24 (see Stark to Lafayette, February 3, note).

5. Bedel summarized the situation in a letter to Gates on March 14:

Agreeable to your orders I raised my Regt.—but it was not in my power to supply them with every necessary for the Expedition. . . . I also recd. a Letter from Brigr. Starks informing he had the Commd. of the Expedition, and also informed me there was every necessary supply ordered to be forwarded immediately to Co'os. Immediately after the Rect. of his Letter I recd. orders from Colo. Hazen to march that the Marquiss de la Fayette had the Command. I immediately mustered my Men found the Regt. Compleat and some over. The day we were to march I recd. orders from Genl. Conway to remain at Co'os untill further orders and in a day or two after recd. orders from the Marquiss to repair to Albany, and I find the Expedition entirely stopt. . . . For all which I have never recd. one Shilling Public Money only what I borrowed in a Private way. [New Hampshire State Papers, 17:218–219]

6. Lafayette probably refers to the money that was appropriated by Congress on January 3 and February 2, 1778, for the northern department. Two warrants, each for $200,000, were issued in favor of the Board of War, to be transmitted to the deputy paymaster general for the northern department (JCC, 10:15–16, 110). The first of these appropriations reached Albany on February 19 (Conway to Gates, February 19, 1778 [NHi: Gates Papers, Box 9]). For Lafayette's belief that the money was intended for the expedition, see Lafayette to Clinton, February 23, and Lafayette to Gates, February 23 and March 11.

7. In his letter to Congress of February 20, Lafayette enclosed a copy of the deposition, which gave the strength of British forces and artillery stationed along the route to Montreal, and reported that the British fleet was under the cover of Fort St. Johns (DNA: RG 360, PCC 166, pp. 75–76).

From the Albany Committee

Albany. Committee Chamber
19th. Feby. 1778

Hond. Sir

We were favoured with your Letter of this date and in Answer to the several Matters therein stated beg leave to observe that the Troops are by no means cloathed equal to the Inclemency of the weather they are to undergo in the intended expedition against Canada, nor is it in our Power to furnish them with any, being entirely cut off from any Sea Port Town, and all the necessaries the Inhabitants of this unfortunate County and State may stand in need off they must receive from the Eastern States.

As to the Number of Men wanting necessary to carry on the Expedition we are no Judges of, nor does the raising of them come under the Jurisdiction of this Committee.

The Forrage has ever been supplied by a Commissary employed for that express purpose. This Gentleman as he has made it his constant Business will be better enabled to inform you whether the Forrage necessary for such an Expedition can be procured. We can only in general observe that there is not the Forrage in this part of the State as usual, owing to the depradations of the Enemy, the Quantity consumed by our Army, and the loss of that Article by means of the Cultivatures being called out to defend their Country at the Season when the same was fit and ought to have been gathered.

Colo. Hazen Deputy Quartr. Mastr. Genl. a few days ago laid before this Committee certain Resolutions of the Senate and Assembly of this State empowering him to empress for the public Service five hundred Sleighs from several of the Counties of this State and also circular Letters to the Committees whence the Sleighs were to be taken from.[1] We then informed Colo. Hazen that we would render him all the Aid in our power in procuring those from this County since which we have heard nothing on this Subject, we are however of Opinion that the Sleighs from this County can be procured, but it will be attended with more than usual Trouble & Time owing to the Averseness of the People's undergoing such a tedious and hazardous a Journey.

Upon the whole Sir we beg leave with Submission to observe that after the Sleighs, Forrage and other Necessaries to carry on the Expedition are procured there will be such a Relapse of Time before these Articles are brought to the proper places of Rendezvous that it may probably be the means of delaying the Transportation of the necessary supplies for the Garrisons and removing and securing the Contil. stores.

You may however rest assured Sir that we shall be ever ready to render you all the Assistance in our Power to carry the Orders of Congress into Execution. We are Hond. Sir with great Respect, Yr. most Obedient & very humbl. Servt. By Order

JOHN BARCLAY, Chairman

L (DNA: RG 360, PCC 166, pp. 107–109), copy in Neville's hand, enclosed in Lafayette to [Congress], February 20.
    1. For the resolutions, see Hazen to Lafayette, February 18, note 1.

To [the President of Congress]

[Albany, February 20, 1778]

Dear Sir

I have had the honor to receive your favor of the Nineth instant concerning the oath desired from every one who holds commission from Congress, and I'l take the greatest pleasure in receiving it from the army in and about this place in obedience to your directions.[1]

The sending of my distpatches has been stopped by the following reason. Tho' Gal. Connway is as averse to the expedition as any man can be in our present circumstances, I was desirous to have by wraïting the same opinion which he has given to every body *that the expedition was quite impossible by want of proper measures taken at time* &c. &c. That gentleman is gone on from this town to see some troops and forgot giving that letter to me, I have sent after him, but as I did not receive it Yet, and his opinion has been expressed by him in the strongest terms, I wo'nt detain the dispatches longer. With the highest regard I have the honor to be dear Sir Your most obedient servant

THE MIS. DE LAFAYETTE

ALS (DNA: RG 360, PCC 166, pp. 83–84).
    1. By the resolutions of Congress of February 3 (*JCC*, 10:114–118; enclosed in the president of Congress to Lafayette, February 9 [DNA: RG 360, PCC 13, 1:179]), all military and civil officers were required, by oath or affirmation, to renounce allegiance to the British king and to pledge support of the United States. Anyone who handled public funds or stores was required to take an additional oath or affirmation of integrity, vowing to be accountable for any money or items entrusted to his charge.

To [*the President of Congress*]

Albany the twentyth February 1778

Dear Sir

If I have ever been intitled to ask any favor from the Congress of the United States, I beg in this occasion your and theyr particular attention for what I am to tell them by this letter. The love of this country, the desire of complying with the ardent wishes and sanguine hopes of Congress (so has been the matter represented to me) and the most solemn promises which have been made to me that I schould find here a large field of glory, have engaged me in the present enterprize.

I hope you will have my instructions represented to you, and I think you will not find my confidence in what they contain greater than this which becomes an honest man—let us not mention the promises which have been told, but only those which have been wrote to me.

I was to find at *a low estimate* two thousand five hundred combattans only with the troops mentionned in the instruction—but a much larger body was foretold.

Gal. Stark would have been ready with his men, and indeed the board of war thaught the fleet could be burnt before my arrival.

I need not to be under any concern about provisions, fourage, slays, of any kind &c. The ennemy's forces were very feeble, the vessels, ready to be burnt with the straw which the ennemy had taken care of providing for that purpose, and there I knew the politness of Sir Guy Carleton.[1]

Four hundred thousand dollars were deemed very sufficient to obviate to every thing.

I need no more be under any concern about cloathes, the cloathier general beeing directed to furnish every thing his stores can afford.

The matter was so easy that the rapitity of my motions and the consternation of the ennemy would do the business.

I arrived, Sir, the 17th. tho' I was expected the twenty fifth, and Gal. Connway was here only three days before me. His first word has been to tell me that the expedition was quite impossible.

Inclosed I have the honor to send you several papers interesting to give some intelligence about this matter, among which are

A letter from Gal. Stark, who having heard of some expedition for this winter desires me to let him know where he is to raise troops &c.

A return of our present strength as near as we can ascertain where are inclosed the boys and old men unfitt for the present expedition.

The deposition of a deserter taken under oath by which you will see the matters very different from what had been told to me.

A letter from the Committee of Albany to whom I have applied for assuring myself not to forget any thing.

A letter from the Governor Clinton to Gal. Connway.

Other letters to Gal Connway concerning this expedition.

An account as good as I could get it in a so little time of what is düe in this departement without mentionning what I could not get notice of.[2]

You will see very plainly that if proper orders, proper monney had been sent some time ago we could have been able to carry the expedition, but the time is now too schort.

There is nothing, or almost nothing at all in the cloathier general's stores; Colonel Hazen has brought some cloathes from Boston. They are much insufficient, and indeed those had not been foreseen in my instructions.

Colonel Hazen is convinced that every thing in his departement will be ready in a little time, but is the only one of this opinion. That gentleman has showed the greatest activity and zeal, as exertions from him have been untried, and he thinks however that by want of men and cloathes the expedition is not possible in this time.

I have found a great disatisfaction among the troops owing to the want of cloathes and monney which could be attended with dangerous circumstances. That same want of monney has thrown many departements in confusion and stopped theyr operations.

It is the full opinion of Gal. Schuyller, Gal. Arnold, Gal. Lincoln, Gal. Connway, Mr. Duane (for I never saw Mr. Düer), Colonel Hazen, Colonel Hay dep. quarter master, Mr. Cuyler dep. commissary, Meassin cloathier gal., it is this of every one in the army I have spoken to (each of those gentlemen in theyr departement) that the enterprise falls, and can not be carried on by want of proper measures taken at time.

If we had three or four weeks before us it would do very well, but I am told that the ice is bad by the twentyth of March, and be pleased to consider how far it is from here to St. Johns.[3]

It will be a reflexion upon us, upon myself that such an expedition can not be carried on but an inconsidered step could bring an eternal dishonor upon the army and the general who commands it. I may add that I have been directed to attak so many forces with so many men, and I find a great misrepresantation of facts in those accounts.

If, as soon as the intended expedition began to run in the streets of

York, General Washington had been desired of giving me the order to repair to Congress, we schould have had some time before hand.

I think the honor of the american arms requires those preparations of a northen army would be directed against some other point, unless an expedition in the same country would be thought possible in the summer by the easted—and indeed two projects could be carried on one after an other—but I am not to day so fond of schemes as to propose any to Congress.

Tho' I see so many difficulties to carry the expedition *against of for* Montreal as it was intended by the honorable board of war, I'l do however as if I was in hopes to raise them till the last extremity—if any idea, any niew other way of getting in two or three days men and cloathes strikes me I schall be very happy. The troops are mustering to day and to morrow, and I'l get exact returns.

As I am the officer commanding in this departement (for Gal. Ar-

Philip Schuyler, major general and commissioner for Indian affairs, who requested Lafayette's presence at the Johnstown council

nold wrote me to take the command without difficulty) I think it is my duty to provide as soon as possible the important Fort Schuyller.[4] I schall go there myself—Gal. Schuyller thot I would be useful to the cause in showing myself and my french officers in the meeting he intends to have with the Indians.[5]

I have received the first two hundred thousand dollars yesterday.[6] I have thaught it of an absolute necessity to employ about 100,000 in paying the troops till november last, 50000 to the quarter master who had particular orders from Gal. Gates to get things absolutely necessary for the next campaign, 10000 to the hospital, and the rest in the chest—I have taken the advice of Mr. Duane member of Congress.

Why has been so much noise made about this expedition? Why have I been so desired to wraït to my friends, and let know to the whole Europe that I was at the head of an american army directed to do great things? It is no more time to recall my letters. I do not make any complaints, I'l make in my country a candid account of my disappointement. What my perhaps too quick and too warm heart must feel after being so much deceived, every sensible man must have some idea of. What can be done for me in this occasion I leave to the own feeling of the honorable Congress. It is in expecting theyr niew instructions for what I am to do and to be, that I have the honor to be, Sir, Your most obedient servant

THE MIS. DE LAFAYETTE

ALS (DNA: RG 360, PCC 166, pp. 97–98). Enclosures:
Stark to Lafayette, February 3.
Deposition of a Deserter, ca. February 1778 (DNA: RG 360, PCC 166, pp. 75–76).
Arnold to Conway, February 16 (ibid., pp. 70–72): "As this Expedition appear impracticable perhaps it may not be amiss to sugest to Congress the propriety of turning their Arms against New York as soon as the season will admit, by which time three or four thousand Continental Troops might be collected, and Militia to make an Army of Ten thousand Men, . . . and if the Affair is conducted with prudence, & Spirit I have no doubt of it succeeding, which in my opinion would be of more Consequence than the reduction of Montreal and St. Johns."
Lincoln to Conway, February 16 (ibid., pp. 81–82): ". . . the sooner all ideas of executing that Plan are quitted, the more it will be for the interest of the United States."
George Clinton to Conway, February 17 (ibid., pp. 87–89): "I am sorry to learn that the means for carrying on the Expedition falls so much short of your Expectations, tho indeed ever since I heard of the Expedition I feared this would be the case as I had frequently heard the Troops to the northward were for a long time unpaid and naked for the want of cloathing which had induced the Officers to suffer many of them to go home on Furlow."
Schuyler to Conway, February 17 (ibid., pp. 93–95): "I say, in this Situation of Affairs, I conceive the Intentions of Congress are frustrated, for I believe, no person whatever will venture to affirm that with so small a Body of Troops and in such a Condition it would be prudent to make the Attempt."
Lafayette to the Albany Committee, February 19.
Albany Committee to Lafayette, February 19.
Return of Troops under Lafayette's Command, February 20.
Account of Debts (see note 2).

Kosciuszko carried the packet sent to York from Albany on February 20 (Schuyler to Gouverneur Morris, February 20, [1778], Vt-SS: Stevens Papers). Along with Lafayette's letter to Congress and its enclosures, the packet contained several dispatches from the northern department to the Board of War. The address leaf of John Pierce's letter to the Board of War, February 20, appears to have been the cover sheet for the whole packet (DNA: RG 360, PCC 166, pp. 115–116, address leaf p. 100). Lafayette's letter to Congress was not removed before the packet was delivered to the board on February 24 or 25. There was no address on the letter, and it was opened and read by the board and then sent to Laurens "for the information of Congress" (see Laurens to Lafayette, March 4). This "piracy" occasioned much discussion in Lafayette's subsequent correspondence with Laurens and Gates.

1. On December 29, 1777, Bedel had informed Schuyler: "The Batteaus are hawled up at Saint John's & the shippg lie there, they have carted about 400 load of straw tied up in Bundles and put on board which they say is to set the shipping on fire upon the approach of the Rebels" (NHi: Gates Papers, Box 8).

2. No formal account of debts in the northern department has been found. Lafayette may be referring to Pierce's letter to the Board of War, February 20: "Words cannot express the distress we are in for want of Money. . . . The Regular Troops have five Months Pay due the 1 Feby. & some of them more, which will amount, together with the Departments for which warrants are drawn, to more than 450,000 Dollars—after which the Pay of the Militia, the Rations & Staff of the Army must make a large sum and probably will arise to 250,000 more. There is then this Month's Pay left unprovided for as also many other matters which must enevitably arise" (DNA: RG 360, PCC 166, p. 115).

3. The distance between Albany and St. Johns is approximately 190 miles.

4. Arnold's letter has not been found. For the command situation in Albany, see Lafayette to Laurens, February 19, note 9. Fort Schuyler (Fort Stanwix) marked the border between Iroquois territory and the state of New York, as established by the Treaty of Fort Stanwix in 1768, and blocked the main access to the Mohawk Valley from Canada.

5. For the Johnstown Treaty, see Memoir of 1779 (p. 247 and p. 248, note 9).

6. See Lafayette to Washington, February 19, note 6.

Observations on the Return of Troops

[Albany, February 20, 1778]

General Nixon's Brigade has been mustered yesterday, & several of the men mentioned in the present Return fit for duty, are by youth, or old age, some being twelve, & some sixty years old, unable to perform a Long & quick march.

N.B. Colonel Hazen's Regiment, will take almost all the cloathing, being already in hands of the clothier general.

The other Regimens are wanting of every thing & can not possibly be suplyed of cloth, the clothier general having not one single more, than the necessarys to Colonel Hazen, & yet scarcely.

N.B. There has been made a mistake. Colonel Hazen will not take all the cloathing tho' he wants a great part of it, but I'l take care they

General Return of the troops under the Command of marquis de la fayette major general.

20 February 1778. Albany.

fit for duty. — articles wanting — cloth &c.

Brigades & Regiments	colonels	L. colonels	majors	captains	lieutenans	ensignes	adjutant	q. master	2. master	surgeons	mates	serjeans & corporals	drum & fife	privates	TOTAL	coats	vetcoats	breeches	shirts	hoses	shoes	caps	leggins	unkwn shoe	socks	blanket	snow shoes	mittins
nixons brigd. 9. Regimens	1	2	2	9	22	19	2	2		2	1	51	29	475	611	205	290	167	262	205	255	244	929	626	565	505	609	
Van Schaicks 1. R	1	1	1	4	11	4	1	2	1	1	1	39	8	218	291	64	207	64	579	913	208	48	.	016	205	254	307	
Warner's 1. R	.	.	.	1	.	.	all unknown								50	unknown												
livingstone's 1. R	.	.	.	.	.	.									100	100	100	100	100	100	200	100	100	.	100	100	100	
hagens 1. R	.	.	2	7	19	.	.	1	.	.	.	93	16	267	345	"	"	"	"	compleated in cloth	"	"	"	"	"	"	"	
Selets 1. R	.	.	.	.	all	.	unknown	.	.	.	.	absolutely unknown			unknown													
Whetcomb. Rangers	.	.	.	.	all	.	unknown	.	.	.	.	.	.	.	40				unknown									
TOTAL	2	9	4	21	52	17	9	4	1	9	2	125	53	960	1437	569	924	667	716	721	692	429	941	953	657	906		

Lafayette enclosed this return in his packet to Congress, February 20, 1778

schould be distributed in [a sure?] equitable proportion—but we are very far from having all the necessary parts of cloathing.

N.B. Warner has about hundred men fit for duty, but out of the present return we must not forget that we'l find a large number of boys and old men.

D (DNA: RG 360, PCC 166, p. 80). The return (see facing page), and the observations written on the verso, are in Fleury's hand, except for the last two paragraphs of the observations, which are in Lafayette's hand. Enclosed in Lafayette to [Congress], February 20.

Hazen wrote to Gates from Albany on February 20: "My Regiment arrived here in time. It is three Hundred sixty six present effective good men, Officers included. . . . I obtain'd in Boston suitable Cloth for 800 pair of Legings, am sorry to informe you that General Arnold will not suffer a pair of them to be delivered to my Regiment, or evan all such other Necessaries of Cloathing as is immediately wanted" (DNA: RG 360, PCC 166, p. 119).

To Horatio Gates

[Albany] the twentyhe February 1778

Dear Sir

I dare say you will be much surprised of the most disagreable disapointement I meet with. I have been conducted here by my Confidence in your word and assurances—how far I have been deceived you will know by my letter to the hon. Congress to which letter I take the liberty of refering you. I am sorry that a so displeasant affair came through your hands, but I am not in any doubt that you were fully convinced of every thing you induced me to built my hopes upon. However I'l try again if I can find some means of giving any probability to the project. If ever any other one strikes you, you will find me alwaïs willing for the cause of your country. My conduct, I dare hope, will meet with your approbation. In expecting further instructions for what I am to do, I have the honor to be Sir Your most obedient servant

THE MIS. DE LAFAYETTE

ALS (NHi: Gates Papers, Box 9).

From Thomas Conway

Schenectedy February 20th. 1778

Sir,

I was honored with your Letter of the 19th. Instant, by which you desire my Opinion upon the intended Expedition. At my Arrival here I procured, as soon as it was possible, the Returns of the different Troops in this Department. Finding that these Returns fell much short of the Expectation of Congress, and that they were mostly naked, I did not think myself justifiable in proceeding to Onion River with less than half the Forces intended by Congress, and that half destitute of necessary Cloths. I consulted upon this Important Matter with Generals Schuyler, Arnold, & Lincoln. You are furnished with their Answers.[1] They were unanimous in their Opinions. I was still in Hopes that the Clothing procured from Boston, by Col. Hazen, might remove the greatest Difficulty.

But finding that this Clothing is not sufficient, my Opinion is that in sticking to the Letter of the Instructions, by which you are directed to carry on the Expedition, with twenty five hundred Men, at the lowest Estimate, you are not to proceed with half that number, because that if the Intention of Congress had been such, it would have been certainly mentioned in your Instructions. The Board of War cannot judge of the situation of the Troops, in this Department, otherwise than by the Returns, But as it appears that since these Returns have been sent, the commanding Officers suffered many of their Men, for Want of Clothing & Pay to go Home upon Furlough, as it is mentioned by Governor Clinton,[2] it is no Wonder that the Number of effective Men should fall so short of the Estimations of the Board of War.[3]

However, Sir, if you think proper to proceed I am ready to march, & will cheerfully obey your Order. I am, with Respect, Sir, Your most humble and obedient servant

Thos. Conway M.G.

L (NHi: Gates Papers, Box 9), copy in Troup's hand. Troup told Gates on February 24 (ibid.) that he had mistakenly dated the copy February 20, but the letter had actually been written on the nineteenth.

Lafayette had not yet received Conway's letter when he sent his packet to Congress (Lafayette to [Congress, February 20]). Troup sent this copy to Gates on February 23, and implied that because Conway had exculpated the Board of War from any censure for the Canadian expedition, Lafayette had purposely concealed his letter (NHi: Gates Papers, Box 9). His assertion seems improbable, since on February 23 Lafayette sent

Gates a copy of a letter from Conway (presumably this letter), which he asked him to present to Congress. The only copy of Conway's letter that has been found, however, is the one Troup sent to Gates.

1. Enclosed in Lafayette to [Congress], February 20.

2. Clinton to Conway, February 17, enclosed in Lafayette to [Congress], February 20.

3. Conway repeated his assertion in a letter to Gates, February 19: "Whatever might be suggested I Do not think that the Board of War can be Blam'd, for the Board being three hundred miles from this place could not judge of the situation of things otherwise than by returns, if those returns are not exact the fault Does not Lie with the Board of War" (DNA: RG 360, PCC 166, p. 113).

To George Clinton

Albany the 23d. february 1778

Sir,

I Can not venture to say you will be surprised, but I am certain you will be sorry of the disappointement I meet with in an affair where the advantage of the american cause was so much concerned. However, Sir, I think (even in making proper deductions) I was in right to expect, if some thing less than I was promised by word and wraïting at least some thing more than I found in arriving at this place. The letter of the same Gal. Stark whom *I was to find at the head of a large body and indeed who would have begun the business,* acquaints me that he wants to know where to raise his men &c. The quantity of cloathes is insufficient—the number of Continental soldiers smaller than what I had been told. The expedition displeases every body, and there is in the army a general spirit of disatisfaction owing to the want of pay (for this departement is much indebted). In all, Sir, I think I schould have been very imprudent, had I not sent a full account of the matter to Congress and expected theyr farther directions. Your excellency, I hope, will not disapprouve my Conduct.

If I had been acquainted sooner of the intentions of Congress, if proper orders had been given, proper monney sent, proper measures taken at time, we schould have been able to do great and useful things—for my greatest concern is to See that every necessary things are not far out of our hands and we want only time to collect them. Time will prevent us from doing some thing, unless the intelligences or means of succeeding were stolen out of my sight by a mutual agrement of so many men, that I ca'nt entertain such a suspicion.

I am sorry it has pleased Congress and the board of war to make such a noise about this operation—however you'l Confess with me that a less dishonor will fall upon the american arms by giving up the

idea of marching the troops that way, than if we were to begin and
meet with some unlucky adventure. I wish'd some other plan would
be fallen upon immediately. There is a fine one. . . .[1] How far it is
practicable I can not ascertain. I am told also that we can get in the
heart of Canada in the summer. I dare hope you'l be so kind as to
favor me with your opinion about those matters.

There is now a thing of the highest moment to provide for—the
provision of Fort Schuyler. That fort I understand to be the key of all
the wested. I intend to go there myself, and I will not forget any
precaution on that subject. I have had the pleasure to pay a little part
of the debts of the departement, and nothing now is düe to the soldiers till the month of november last. I thaught it of my duty as the eldest officer here (after Gal. Arnold desired me to take the Command)
to clear the debts in the best possible way as far as the monney I can
get may afford. I did receive yet but 200,000 dollars (and they were
indeed for the expedition tho' it has been wrote also that they were
for the departement) [2] and the debts I could get notice of amount betwen seven and eight hundred thousand dollars.

Colonel Hazen who got from this state an order for slays and slay
men is very anxious how they will be pay'd and dismissed. He thinks
that detaining or not paying them will be attended with the most terrible consequences. However it seems to me the old debts of the same
kind ought to be pay'd first, and they can be very necessary in every
case, principally if we could find some ways of doing any michief to
the fleet by surprise (what I must Confess seems a very difficult matter). Therefore, Sir, to satisfy every body I directed the dep. quarter
master g. of this departement not to detain any one but those who
would willingly stay, and give some trifling monney in expecting *better
somes*. If, Sir, you think this niew debt is to be attended to before the
others, as we have no public monney, can I hope you would be so
good as to order them to be pay'd on my private account and credit—
which engagement I will satisfy to in as little time as it is necessary to
receive the sum from Mr. Robert Moriss? I expect with great impatience the directions of Congress, the board of war, and Gal. Gates
who holds yet the title and authority of commander in chief of the
northen departement.

The young british officer I had the honor of introducing to your
excellency [3] di'nt go very far. He met upon the road a french officer
who found him drunk, making great noise in a tavern, and swearing
much against the very *same rebels and french* who had assisted him.
Things went so far that the young english man has been arrested and
the monney with the letters I had given to him were delivered back to
me. However the age of the gentleman and his being an ennemy in

our hands engage me to indulge his going to Boston, can I hope if you approuve my conduct that you'l be so good as to let the inclosed letter be silled and forwarded to Fishkill? I dare hope too that if he was in any want of monney your excellency will let him have some, only to get to Boston.[4]

You will find me very free, Sir, to trouble you about my private as well as my public business. Tho' I have not the honor of a long acquaintance with you, I begin already to use of the friendship you have been so kind as to promise me. I'l be very happy, sir, if I can Convince you how much I wish to deserve it, with such sentiments and those of the highest regard I have the honor to be Your excellency's the most obedient humble servant

THE MIS. DE LAFAYETTE

As we have no printing schop in or about this town, can I hope you will be so good as to order blank certificates to be Printed in Pookepsie or Fishkill for the two oaths requested by order of Congress? [5]

ALS (PPRF). Clinton was governor of New York.

1. Lafayette's ellipses. The plan Lafayette contemplated was an attack on New York (see the following two letters, and Lafayette's letters to Laurens and Washington, February 19.

2. See Lafayette to Gates, February 23, note 5.

3. Lafayette had visited Clinton at Poughkeepsie on his way to Albany.

4. John Laurens wrote to his father on February 9, 1778 about

> a handsome young lad, who call'd himself Cope, and said he was an ensign in the 55th. British. He said that in an affair of honor, he had killed his man, and fearing the consequences, threw himself into our protection. . . . A collection of clothes and money was made for him; the Marquis took him with him, and is to furnish him with letters for his friends in France. We have since discovered that he is an impostor. . . . It is probable that he is some young officer who has been obliged to fly in consequence of some disgraceful action, or perhaps a series of follies. I just had time to send the Marquis a message by Duplessis to put him on his guard. [*Correspondence of John Laurens,* pp. 123–124]

See also Lafayette to Washington, February 23, and Clinton to Lafayette, February 26. Lafayette's letter for Cope has not been found.

On May 24, 1778, Lafayette wrote to General William Heath: "I understand that one little Coope whom I confess I had patronized is yet in Boston; I have receiv'd letters from the english army where his history is related to me in terms very unfavorable to his character. The first word of the letter is that he never fought a dwell but deserted for an affair of money" (MHi: Heath Collection).

5. For the two oaths, see Lafayette to [the president of Congress, February 20, 1778], note 1.

To Horatio Gates

Albany the 23d. february 1778

Dear Sir

When this letter will fall into your hands you'l have received one other which will have disapointed you as much as I have been distressed in arriving here. I confess I was perhaps too sanguine in my hopes, or too quick in my feelings when I saw them deceived—but consider, Sir, the charming prospect I had before my eyes, and you will conceive how concerned I must be in this occasion. What hurts me more is to think that we want only time, and was I in the month of january I would be certain of carrying the business. I dare say you will be yourself very surprised to see things so different from what they had been represented to you and you had represented to me. Be certain, sir, I was never so unhappy as in this circumstance, tho' the general opinion of every rank and condition in the civil as well as the military line assures me that I could not do any thing in our present situation.

However I can not give up all ideas of doing some thing in that quarter. I hear every scheme on this subject and find very little probabilities of succès. No body thinks the grand expedition could be carried, but some speak of burning the fleet by surprise with a detachement. Gal. Connway is much against it, and I confess it seems to me he is in right—tho' doing or trying nothing in this moment is exesperating to the last degree.

I expect farther directions from you with the greatest impatience—my present situation is rather disagreable by my not knowing well what I am here and what I am to do—however as being the eldest officer I'l do for the best till I hear from you.

Gal. Connway came this morning from rewiewing Lewingston's and Wanschais rgts.[1] I think it is my duty to take a great care Fort Schuyller schould be provided for six months, I'l Go to that fort, and I'l have the honor to wraït you how I have found it. My intention if I have time is to examine myself and look very attentively those fields of glory which you have covered with laurels, in expecting some possible occasions could be given to me of acquïring some honor on my account.[2]

I hope you will approuve the disposition of the monney. Colonel Hay is gone on this morning to Boston—I thaught he was very necessary here, but as he had orders from you to buy those things, I would not take upon myself to send any other in his room.[3] Every body is after me for monney—be so good as to let me know how I must do. I have given leave to every one in public departements if they could borrow on my private credit for paying the debts, to do it without difficulty.[4]

It seems to me that the people is rather found of an expedition against New York. I am told that in the month of june there is a very easy way into the heart of Canada. In every thing you believe I'l be useful to the american cause, till the moment perhaps not very far where my business will oblige me to leave this continent, be certain, sir that I schall be always ready—and I dare say where I am obliged to stop nobody will go on. With a great impatience to hear from you, a great confidence in Your friendship, and the highest regard I have the honor to be dear Sir Your most obedient servant

THE MIS. DE LAFAYETTE

Inclosed I have the honor to send to you two copys which I beg you would present to Congress. Colonel Faïlly and Monsieur de Luce came here, and told me that they have been promised I schould give them the commissions of Colonel and Major.[5] If it is so I want only blank commissions.

I was a little distressed to know how to employ the monney which I thaught was for *the expedition* till I saw in one of your letters to Cl. Hay that it was coming for the departement.[6]

ALS (NHi: Gates Papers, Box 9), enclosing copies of letters from John Fellows (not found) and Conway (probably his letter of February 20). See Lafayette to Laurens, February 23.

1. Livingston's and Van Schaick's regiments.

2. Lafayette probably visited the Saratoga area from March 26 to March 28 (Schuyler to Duane, April 1, 1778 [NHi: Duane Papers]).

3. Hay wrote to Gates on February 20: "As the money is now received I shall probably sett out in a very little time for Boston, to procure the most necessary articles wanted for opening the Campaign. Notwithstanding the great plenty of many of those articles there, I am inform'd the price is beyond measure extravagant . . ." (DNA: RG 360, PCC 166, pp. 91–92).

4. Lafayette may have spent nearly $50,000 of his own money while commanding in Albany. Upon his return to Valley Forge in April he wrote to Laurens:

I had the intention of sending to you the receipts of the monney I have pay'd on public account which is pretty high. That is chiefly for officers who wanted a part of theyr pay to join theyr regiments, who were sent on command and had not a farthing. . . . But very unhappily I cannot find those papers. . . . In expecting they would be found I intend to pay what I owe. What is düe to me will be pay'd when it will please to God as I am much more concerned for the former part. I expect to hear to day or to morrow from Mr. de Francy who in a very obliging manner has desired me to take monney from him upon whatever terms I'll choose to direct. As soon as it will come to hand I schall settle my debts to the public. I was a little schort of monney as that fine journey has cost of extro'rdinary to me, in advancing money to officers, in paying some public accounts, in giving to the indians,

&c &c about twelve thousand dollars more than I schould have expended—*that only between us.* ["Letters from Lafayette to Henry Laurens," *South Carolina Historical and Genealogical Magazine,* 8 (1907): 62–63 (April 14, 1778)]

See Lafayette to Laurens, January 27 and February 23, and to Robert Morris, January 29, for the amounts Lafayette borrowed for the expedition. Lafayette submitted some of the receipts for his public expenditures to Laurens on April 26 ("Letters from Lafayette," 8:124).

5. Gates had recommended to Congress that Failly and Luce be given these commissions, but his request was refused (Gates to Congress, [February 1778?] [ScHi: Henry Laurens Papers, no. 16]; February 5, 1778, *JCC,* 10:123). Gates may have "promised" them commissions from Lafayette (as commander of the expedition) after Congress denied them.

6. Gates's letter to Udny Hay has not been found. On January 24, Gates wrote to John Greaton that $200,000 was being sent to Albany to "pay off Debts, & enable the Officers in the Public Departments to Comply with every Demand that can at present be made upon them" (NHi: Gates Papers, Box 19). This sum was probably the January appropriation for the northern department (see Lafayette to Washington, February 19, note 6).

To Henry Laurens

                                                    Albany the 23d. February 1778
Dear Sir

I am so busy the whole day and so troubled for trifles that I am obliged to spend the nights in wraïting, and it is at three à clock in the morning that I come to recall the canadian commander in chief to your memory. You will have received, my dear sir, a sorry letter of mine where I let you know all the disapointements I met with.[1] You can not conceive at which point I am distressed and unhappy by that affair—it is the most disagreable I have found, and I dare say, I'l find in my life. More I consider the matter, more I see that it was impossible to go on. Let it be a deception, a treachery, what you please, it was impossible for one single man to run through that dark cloud I run alwaïs surrounded with—I want rather to omitt an occasion of distinguishing myself than If I was to loose an army trusted to my care and bring an eternal dishonor upon the american arms.

Certainly there is some ⟨villainy⟩ in that affair—I am almost sure it is—but however we had no means of proceeding. I hope you will be so good as to let me know every thing which has been told about me even by the public. I send this night to Gal. Gates the copy of two letters from Gal. Connway and Gal. Fellow which I desire him to present to Congress. I hope you will take care he do'nt forget them.

⟨I am in Suspicion of a great scheme which I will advise you of. You do not know perhaps that Gal. Gates holds yet the title and authority of commander in chief in the northen departement. [He wants?] to see me go out and put Gal. Connway immediately under him. Connway is more polite with me than with most, he seems [occupied?] with every thing, and very gay and certain of himself. He begs to [see every paquet?] [*one illegible line*]. [His hope is?] I believe that after this disappointement [I wo'nt hesitate?] to go home, and then he'l be master of the field.)

I confess, sir, that after such a noise made on account of my commanding an army, I expect and wish much to be put in a separate command to do some thing. I am told an attak upon Niew York is not looked on as impossible, and the people is very willing to go on that expedition. The command of the North River can be interesting, this of the northen departement could be added. In all, my dear sir, I speak here as a friend because this letter is a private one, I want much to be enabled to mind my reputation and the honor of the army under my command, on account of theyr not going to Canada—but take care of Connway. If however things do'nt go in a decent way I'l have alwaïs the pleasure to see you and embrace you *at the french fashion* before my leaving this country.

I am busy in paying debts. Every departement cryes after me for monney. I have given leave to them to borrow on my private credit, and satisfy the people as fast as they can—for the public credit is very low. I try to do here for the best, but am however very distressed by my not knowing the bounds of my power in this departement—they do'nt know any thing but a commander in chief.

Here are more than twenty french officers all very willing to stay or go of[f] with me. I do'nt know what I can do for them. Mr. de Faïlly and Mr. de Luce have told to me that they had been promised I schould give them Colonel's and Major's commissions—but I have no blank ones. I have sent to Pookepsie to print certificates of the oath of alleagance.

You have acquainted me, sir, that monney was very easely to be found at four for one in giving bills for France. Be so good if it is possible as to direct your young man to borrow five or six tousand dollars at that rate.[2] I beg you thousand pardons for such a commission, but frienschip excedes all.

If there are some niews, some niews papers &c. &c. be so kind as to forward them to me. I beg you above all to be very very particular about every thing which has been said publikly or privately of the canadian expedition and the commander in chief. Do'nt be affraïd to forward any disagreable compliment. With the warmest attachement and highest regard I have the honor to be dear Sir Your most obedient servant

THE MIS. DE LAFAYETTE

The gentleman who was to carry this letter has forgotten it. I give to one of General Connway's acquaintances,[3] be so good sir as to answer me soon because I do'nt know how to do in the present circumstance.

ALS (ScHi: Henry Laurens Papers); inscribed by Lafayette: "private affairs." Portions of the text are nearly obliterated in the same ink as that in which the manuscript is written. The cancellations were probably made by Laurens as a discretionary measure. The text of these deletions has been restored within angle brackets.

1. See Lafayette to Laurens, February 19, and to Congress, February 20.

2. See also Laurens to Lafayette, March 6.

3. Captain Kennedy; Dr. Browne carried Lafayette's other letters of February 23 (Troup to Gates, February 24, 1778, NHi: Gates Papers, Box 9).

To Robert Morris

Albany the twenty 3d. february [1778]

Dear Sir

Inclosed I have the honor to send you the bills of exchange.[1] I beg your pardon to have been so long, but could not have a moment to me, and I must confess I had forgotten the sending of them from head quarters. You can send them or not as you please, but I beg leave to object that it would be much more convenient to me was you so kind as to keep them at what interest you'l be pleased to judge. Every body proposes me to find monney at four and five for one, but I like much better drawing it from you, and I wish'd you would enable me to do alwaïs so by making an arrangement for the paying of it which would agree with me much better.

You have been certainly acquainted of the disapointement I met with when after being sent with such a noise and apparate I find nothing ready for the intended expedition. We want only time, but on account of the ice, time will prevent us from doing anything. How sorry I am of that very disagreable event you may be able to judge by the fiew knowledge you may have of the temper of my mind.

AL (DLC: Papers of Lafayette). The manuscript has been mutilated and the last quarter of the sheet is missing.

1. These bills of exchange were probably for the money that Lafayette had requested from Morris in his letter of January 29.

To George Washington

[Albany,] The 23d. february 1778

Dear General

I meet with an occasion of wraïting to your excellency which I wo'nt miss by any means, even schould I be affraïd of becoming tedious and troublesome. But if they have sent me far from you for I do'nt know what purpose, at least I must make some little use of my pen to prevent all communication be cut of[f] betwen your excellency and me. I have writen lately to you my distressing, ridiculous, foolish, and indeed nameless situation. I am sent with a great noise at the head of an army for doing great things, the whole continent, France and Europe herself by in by, and what is the worse, the british army are in expectations.[1] How far they will be deceived, how far we schall be ridiculized, you may judge very well by the candid account you have got of the state of our affairs.

There are things, I dare say, in which I am deceived—Colonel ⟨Troop⟩ is not here for nothing [2]—one other gentleman [3] became very popular before I went in this place. Arnold himself is very found of him. Every part I mean to look at, I am sure a cloud is drawn before my eyes. However there are points I can not be deceived upon. The want of monney, the disatisfaction among the soldiers, the disinclination of every one (except the canadians who mean to stay at home) for this expedition, are conspicuous and as clear as possible. However I am sure I will become very ridiculous and laughed at. My *expedition* will be as famous as the *secret expedition* against Rhode Island.[4] I confess, my dear general, that I find myself of very quick feelings whenever my reputation and glory are concerned in anything. It is very hard indeed that such a part of my happiness without which I ca'nt live, would depend upon the schemes ⟨of some fools⟩ which I never knew of but when there was no more time of putting them in execution. I assure you, my most dear and respected friend, that I am more unhappy than I ever was.

My desire of doing some thing was such that I have thaught of doing it by surprise with a detachement—but it seems to me rash and quite impossible. I schould be very happy if you was here to give me some advices—but I have not any body to consult with. They have sent to me more than twenty french officers. I do'nt know what to do with them. I beg you would give me the line of conduct you advise me to follow on every point. I am at a loss how to act, and indeed I do'nt know what I am here myself.

However as being the eldest officer (after Gal. Arnold has desired me to take the command) I think it is my duty to mind the business of this part of America as well as I can. Gal. Gates holds yet the title and power of commander in chief of the northen departement—but as 200,000 dollars are arrived I have taken upon myself to pay the most necessary part of the debts we are involved in. I am about sending provisions to Fort Schuïller. I'l go to see the fort. I try to get some cloathes for the troops, to buy some articles for the next campaign. I have directed some monney to be borrowed upon my credit to satisfy the troops who are much discontented. In all I endeavour to do for the best tho' I have no particular authority or instruction and I'l come as near as I can of Gal. Gates's intentions—but I want much to get an answer to my letters.

I fancy (betwen us) that the actual scheme is to have me out of this part of the continent, and Gal. Connway in chief under the immediate direction of General Gates. How they will bring it up I do not know—but be certain some thing of that kind will appear. You are nearer than myself, and every honest man in Congress is your friend, therefore you may foresee and prevent if possible the evil hundred times better than I can. I would only give that idea to your excellency.

After having wrote in Europe (by the desire of the members of Congress) so many fine things about my commanding an army, I'l be ashamed if nothing can be done by me in that way. I am told Gal. Putnam is recalled,[5] and Goodell is expected on that part—but your excellency knows better than I do what could be convenient; therefore I do'nt want to mind those things myself.

⟨The young british officer I came with do not seem a very good subject. After he left me, he was met by Mr. Du Plessis in a tavern where he got drunk and made such a noise, and told so many indecent things, that Du Plessis arrested him till he could hear from me. I have writen to him that he could go to Boston. That little fellow is the greatest lyar I ever saw.[6]

I have heard of a robbery from my late landlord which if it is true deserves he schould be hanged.⟩

Will you be so good as to present my respects to your lady? With the most tenderest affection and highest respect I have the honor to be Your excellency's the most obedient servant

⟨The Mis. de⟩ Lafayette

ALS (PEL: Hubbard Collection). The manuscript has been edited in ink, in Lafayette's later hand. The text of significant deletions has been restored in angle brackets.

1. Sir Guy Carleton, the British commander in Canada, appears to have been informed of Gates's preparations for an invasion of Canada in the winter of 1777–1778. In January 1778, Carleton billeted his troops along the Richelieu River and placed the militia on alert (Sanguinet, "Temoin oculaire de l'invasion du Canada par les Bastonnois," in *Invasion du Canada*, ed. H.-A.-J.-B. Verreau [Montreal, 1873], p. 151). William Howe wrote to George Germain on March 24, 1778: "I have the honour to inform your Lordship that the enemy's intended invasion of Canada by way of the Lakes, as mentioned in my last dispatches, has failed from disappointments in collecting the troops and stores proposed for that enterprise" (*Clinton Papers*, 3:306).

2. Troup, Gates's aide-de-camp, was charged with the instructions for the commander of the Canadian expedition (see Lafayette to Laurens, February 3, note 2). He reported some of his intended functions on the Canadian expedition: "You may rest assured that I shall endeavour to promote Friendship, & good Understanding between the several officers who are to be employed on this Expedition. Upon my Arrival in Albany I shall speak to the QMaster & Commissary, & spur them on in the Execution of their Duty" (Troup to Gates [February 6, 1778], NHi: Gates Papers, Box 10). Troup does not appear to have had any official position on the expedition.

3. Conway.

4. The amphibious attack planned against the British on Rhode Island in October 1777, under Joseph Spencer's command. The attack had to be abandoned at the last moment because of bungling, bad weather, and British intelligence of the projected expedition.

5. Though an inquiry into his conduct had been ordered, Putnam had not yet been relieved of his command. See Lafayette to Laurens, February 19, note 10.

6. For the British officer, Cope, see the following letter and Lafayette to Clinton, February 23.

From George Clinton

Poughkeepsie 26th. Feby. 1778

Sir

I am favoured with your Letter of the 23d. Instant. It gives me real Concern to learn that the Preparations made for the Expedition which you was to have commanded fall so far short of what you had Reason to expect as to prevent your attempting it with a Prospect of Success. Tho I cant say I am in the least surprized at it as from the Accounts I have had from that Quarter in the course of the Winter it is what I expected. I had Reason to believe that there were large Arrears of Pay due to the Soldiery, that they were badly cloathed & the Business of the Department much deranged so that to have made proper & Timely Provision for such an Enterprize it woud have been necessary to set about it much earlier than the Date of your Appointment. I fully agree with you Sir that to make the Attempt without a very fair Prospect of Success woud be wrong & woud most probably prove very Injurious to the American Cause.

Fort Schuyler is Sir as you observe a Post of great Importance and therefore too much Attention cant be paid to its Security tho In my

Oppinion it does not afford full Security to the Western Frontiers. I
have lately received repeated Accounts from Schoharry, Harpersfield
& Cherry Valley of the Hostile Dispositions of the Indians residing at
& near Aaghquagee & Unadilla who joined by a Number of disa-
fected Scotch Inhabitants Have People in that Quarter apprehensive
of immediate Danger from those Indians, and Refugees are already
moving in which if not prevented by removing their Apprehension of
Danger will be attended with unhappy Consequences. I submit therefore to you Sir whether it woud not be prudent to order thither two
or three Companies of the Troops now at Schenectady until relieved
by such Guards as the States may be able to furnish the Inhabitants
there.

It is certainly Right that the Eldest public Debts of the same Nature
shoud be first paid & I woud hope that the People seeing the Justice
& propriety of the Measure, it will not be attended with the bad Effects apprehended by Colo. Hazen. I have sealed and forwarded your
Letters to Fishkill & directed my Friend there to furnish the Young,
may I not venture to say Foolish, British Officer with Cash to carry
him to Boston. Believe me Sir I shall always be happy in being Honored with your Commands & that I am with the most perfect Esteem
& Respect, Your most Obed. Servt.

AL (DLC: George and James Clinton Papers), draft.

To George Clinton

Albany 27 fevrier 1778

Sir

As we are in this place very far from head quarters, expresses are
excessigly dear for the public, and I understand you have occasions
for sending letters almost every day, can I hope your excellency will
forward this to General Washington? I beg your pardon for the trouble I take the liberty to give you, but if your excellency do'nt find I
make myself too free and rather troublesome, I'l send to Pookepsie
such letters as I wish to be delivered by a safe and short way. General
Washington is the only commander in chief I know of in America by
that very reason that I have very seldom seen two heads upon the
same body, and I must refer immediately to my general every step I
am obliged to take by my being so far from the main army.

I have not yet received the answers of Congress. That they had been deceived, and schall be strangely disappointed, I am much confident of. What they will do and direct I do not know at all. In waïting for theyr decision I try to make myself as useful as my being the eldest officer here arround can enable me to. I pay debts as fast as monney comes viz.—very slow. I am going to the convention of the indians because Gal. Schuyller has told me that a parcel of french men would be of some use to the cause. From thence I'l go to Fort Schuyller, and be back for receiving the answers of Congress. I hope too, Sir that I'l hear from your excellency. The defense of North River is a point of the greatest importance. I have desired the Baron de Kalb who will command here in that little absence of five days to give every assistance in his power for every thing which will be asked from him on that account. With the highest regard and respect I have the honor to be Sir Your most obedient Servant

THE MIS. DE LAFAYETTE

ALS (PHi: Gratz Collection), transmitting Lafayette to Washington, February 27.

To George Washington

Albany the 27 february 1778

Dear General

I hope your excellency will have received two letters from me, one by Major Brice, and the other by a doctor who was going to head quarters.[1] You will have seen very sorry accounts of our disappointement. That such an expedition they were so sanguine upon has not been prepared before hand, that or themselves or at least myself has been deceived so much, are things very surprising for every one who will inquire into the matter. However those very blunders will make the expedition, the troops intended for it, and myself ridiculous to the world, unless some means are given to me to mind our business and prevent people from laughing at us. I assure you, my dear general, that I find myself much concerned and unhappy in this affair.

You could perhaps think that the means of succès have been afterwards stolen out from me for particular reasons you know of—but I do'nt believe they had time to do it, and had been the expedition conducted for all points in theyr own way, we schould have been prevented from proceeding by want of men, cloathes, pay, forrage, and by the general disinclination for the enterprize.

I expect with the greatest impatience letters from your excellency and Congress, I hope you will excuse the impropriety of my sending immediately my dispatches from here, about that very business of the expedition, but you will easely conceive my reasons for acting so. Now tho' I do not know yet what I am neither what I schall be, my being considered (by Gal. Arnold's desire) as the commander officer here gives me the right to do what I think best for the good of the service. I schould [be] very happy had I by a greater proximity, the opportunity of asking oftener your excellency's orders and advices.

My first care has been to pay the most necessary debts out of the 200,000 dollars which came in my hands. I have thought very necessary to send six month's provisions to Fort Schuyller. I have hurried the sending for the canon at Tyconderoga which will be mended if possible as fast as we'l be able to work. Most part of 'em are desired for the defense of North River. I will give every assistance in my power for that so important defense, and indeed I am affraïd it w'ont be finish'd in time. I wish'd that point was not so far of[f] to be able of giving an account of it to your excellency. Our cloathier's stores are very poor. They keep immense quantities of 'em in and about Boston. It is very wrong.[2]

I have found the departement of artillery stores in a very good order but much weakened by the last envoy you certainly know of.[3] The hospitals are amizingly well. The soldiers in this town have a pretty good appearance. As I have been desired by Gal. Schuyller to meet along with him the indians at a grand treaty, I'l go to morrow by Sconnectedy to Johns'town, and if possible to Fort Schuyller, then I'l be able to give your excellency an account of the troops in those quarters.

I have received some applications for arms, but I w'ont dispose of any before knowing very certainly your intentions. The Baron de Kalb is arrived, and choses to stay in this town during my little travel. Albany is full of french officers who came to join me and I do not know how I will have them employed schould I stay in some particular command. I hope to receive in a fiew days orders from your excellency, and when I'll be back I'l be able to send you a more particular account of every thing.

General Gates, they say, is yet *commander in chief of the northen departement* but accounts will come by the nighest way from me to you, till the moment he will signify his holding the northen command, and then I schall see what to answer.

I understood that John Adams spoke very disrespectfully of your excellency in Boston.[4] I do not know if it is true, but in that case I schould [be] very sorry to have given to him letters for France. Give me leave to say my opinion, my dear general; those ennemy's of yours are so low, so far under your feet, that it is not of your dignity to take much notice of 'em. I do'nt speack however of the honorable the Continental Congress—for if I was General Washington I schould wraït very plain to them. With the greatest respect and most tender affection I have the honor to be Your excellency's the most obedient servant

THE MIS. DE LAFAYETTE

ALS (PEL: Hubbard Collection). This is one of the few Hubbard Collection letters that has not been edited.

1. Lafayette's letter of February 19 was carried by Brice; Dr. Browne carried the letter of February 23.

2. The Continental army depended upon foreign sources for its clothing supplies. With New York occupied by the British, most cargoes were carried to New England ports, where they accumulated, in part because of the difficulty of overland transport (Erna Risch, *Quartermaster Support of the Army: A History of the Corps 1775–1939* [Washington, D.C., 1962], p. 30). On February 4, Knox wrote to Washington from Boston that "Goods of every kind are here in great plenty, but very high priced" (DLC: George Washington Papers, Series 4).

3. Probably a reference to the artillery pieces that were sent to Farmington, Connecticut, early in 1778, by Gates's order (see Washington to the Board of War, February 21, in Fitzpatrick, *Writings of Washington,* 10:486–487).

4. The incident to which Lafayette refers has not been identified. John Adams related in his *Autobiography* (written in 1806):

> The News of my Appointment [as commissioner to France] was whispered about, and General Knox came up to dine with me, at Braintree. The design of his Visit was As I soon perceived to sound me in relation to General Washington. He asked me what my Opinion of him was. I answered with the Utmost Frankness, that I thought him a perfectly honest Man, with an amiable and excellent heart, and the most important Character at that time among Us, for he was the Center of our Union. He asked the question, he said, because, as I was going to Europe it was of importance that the Generals Character should be supported in other Countries. [L. H. Butterfield, ed., *Diary and Autobiography of John Adams* (Cambridge: Belknap Press of Harvard University Press, 1961), 4:5]

To George Clinton

Stonectady, the 3d. March, 1778

Sir:

Your favor of the twenty-sixth last came into my hands and I found myself very happy to be confirmed in the idea I had entertained of your opinion about the Canadian expedition. My being a stranger in this country (tho' I don't believe I'd be ever taken for a tory), my age which tho' very pleasant for myself can however be a half-argument for the half-critics, and my perhaps too quick feeling for my glory, have engaged me to consider very deeply what could be said by the fools, as well as by the wits, by the wise as by the mad people upon this ridiculous enterprise. I think that by the tenor of my instructions, and the date of my being instructed, if there is any blame it must go down towards York. For my part I have acted as my honor, and the military principles of the whole military world have urged me to do, and I feel the greatest pleasure to meet with an approbation I have so high regard for, as this of your excellency.

Agreeable to your letter, sir, two companys of Wanschoy's regiment will be sent to Schoary, and I directed the q. m. and com't, to have ready lodgings and provisions; as there are no barracks the men must be billited as thick as possible and much upon theyr guard—but before any disposition of this kind I want to be better acquainted with the situation of the place. I have been detained in this town since yesterday for a business of the greatest importance.

I schould not think of my travel, sir, as of an useless one, was I happy enough to discover a secret train which would throw this state and perhaps the whole continent in ruin and confusion. Such I begin to believe, could be the case. I mean to give only to your excellency an idea of this affair, in hopes that I'l be able to send you before long a better account.

I fancy that there is some conspiracy under hand for to strike in the same moment this state from every where, and be master of it at the oppening of the river before we could think of a defence—Indians, torys and regulars to come from Fort Schuyller and Schoary—Clinton to come up—and traitors to take arms and burn towns, rebels in the very moment when we should be quiet and happy. I'l explain your excellency some of the reasons my suspicions are built upon.

Four days ago the committe of Albany sent me an annonymous letter, where the writer confesses he was one of the men enlisted to burn the town and vessels of Albany—that many citizens were to be assassinated by theyr own negroes—that the British used to go disguised and enlist people for the conspiracy—that they were expecting the opening of the river, &c. &c.; several men were mentioned, one Duncan, one Cuyler, Holland, Thusman, and three or four more.[1] I had a conversation with the committee, and agreable to theyr desire partys and orders were sent, so that the next morning at six o'clock every one I was to apprehend was taken up with theyr papers—but nothing interesting to be found and the committee desired me to dismiss 'em.

Two days ago one of Gen'l Conaway's aid de camps who don't know any thing of the matter, reported to the General that he was sitting and drinking with two British officers who after some bottles were empty, told that *the next spring America would be theyrs.*

Yesterday I got [to] this Place to go to John's town and Lt. Colonel Wanday told me he had confined a soldier of his, formerly a Britsh deserter, *who had proposed to one Mr. Mackeon lately captain in the regiment to speak with Major Castleton.*[2] I have spent with Gen'l Connrway the half part of the last night in examining the man. No exertions have been forgotten to obtain some words of truth—what we have extorted from him is such.

That Major Castleton his excellency's own nephew has been disguised in Sarectady, inlisting tories, making provisions and every preparation necessary for the fatal day—that the plan was to take away the tories from this part of the state, and take advantage of the first panic to burn, destroy and murder every thing before them—that the lands of the murdered rebels should be granted to the tories—that great many were in the plot—that the principal place of the rendezvous are Schoary and Alibery [Albany?], in order to get from thence to Oswego and Oswegaschy, where they would meet with the regular forces and indians. The whole was to march towards Fort Schuyller and the Germaine Flats. The intention is to permit the indians to scalp, &c. &c.,—such is about the deposition of the man, which I hope to be much amplyfied when I shall send him to be hang'd.

Partys have been sent to the houses where I understand are some provisions and munitions. I have sent too after Major Castleton, but am much afraid that the develish nephew will be too cunning for us. I'd give every thing in the world to catch that fellow.

As soon as I get some more intelligence about the British plot I'l let you know every thing, and will be then able to send a full account of the matter to General Washington and from thence to Congress—but your excellency could now mention to them what you will think proper.

I am here commanding officer pro tempore—but if you could give me leave to tell my sentiment upon the matter I'd say that we have very few troops collected upon this continent. We here indeed think more of peace than of war and however the spring is coming very fast. Don't you believe, sir, that orders should be given now to the militia of this part, and proper dispositions made, to have a kin[d] of army collected and partys to be had under hand, at the first notice—for some secret stroke must be expected from the enemy?[3] I'd be very glad to receive your excellency'[s] directions and advices upon this matter as soon as possible.

The defence of the North River, principally towards General Putnam's army, is the most agreeable command in America for an officer *who wants to do.* For my part I think it is a much more agreeable one by the pleasure to be near your excellency and the allowance of keeping a good understanding, in procuring the good of the land as far as it is in our power. But I have made myself a point never to seem more inclined towards a military employment than another, principally in any other country than this where I have the honor to be born. Congress has been so good as to promise me they should furnish me with the occasions of distinguishing myself. I expect the answer without telling what I'd do in each case.

Whenever I have the advantage to command in this part of America no exertion will be forgotten on my part to deserve the approbation of the Governor and state of New York. I have had always a particular inclination for this part of the continent, and I schould be very happy to schow it by my zeal in putting things in good order and discovering an important conspiracy, 'till I'l be able to act in the fighting way.

After we'l have got some intelligence I intend to proceed with Gen'l Connway to the treaty where I am told my presence will be of some use. I imagine you will hear soon from me—and in expecting your answer I have the honor to be with the most perfect esteem and highest regard, Your excellency's The most obedient servant,

THE M'QS. DE LAFAYETTE

Can I hope your excellency will be so good as to present my respects to his family? We are in a distressing want of news and newspapers which I hope you will pity as far as to let us have some.

L (NN: Bancroft Collection), clipping from unidentified newspaper.
1. Anonymous letter to Colonel Beeckman [February 27, 1778] (*Clinton Papers,* 2:851).
2. Christopher Carleton, nephew of Guy Carleton, the commander of the British forces in Canada. See Lafayette to Peter Gansevoort, March 5.
3. General orders were issued at Albany on March 24, 1778, instructing the commanding officer of every regiment to "order all Soldiers on Furlow immediately to join their respective Regiments . . ." (PHi: Orderly Book 632).

To the Chairman of the Albany Committee

Schonectady 3rd. March 1778
Sir,

By new intelligence I got in this place I find our Suspicions very far from being groundless. A Soldier who I think is a Spy has been taken up and examined by me Yesterday. It has been impossible to obtain a true Confession from that Man, but I can however assure you that there is a Conspiracy and an important one. Major Carleton, [the]

General's own Nephew, was some days ago disguised in this Town and making preperations. Two parties are gone on after him but I question much if they will be successful. I have been detained in this place for that business, and intend to go to night as far as Johnstown. Two Companies of Van Schaick's Regt. will go to Schohary, where a number of true Rebels, Vizt. Rebels to the authority of the United States had designed to fix one of their Rendezvous. I hope I'll be back soon at Albany, where I'll have the Honor to confer with the Committee. My intention was only, Sir, in giving an account of what I had discovered, to put the Honourable Committee upon their Guard more than ever. Perhaps some of you Gentlemen will be able to get intelligence which united with mine can bring us to a Certainty.

With the greatest desire to deserve the approbation of the Committee and the highest regard I have the honor to be Sir Your most Obt. Serv.

THE M's. DE LAFAYETTE

L (*Clinton Papers*, 2:852–853), enclosed in Albany Committee to Clinton, March 5, 1778 (ibid., pp. 848–851).

Although the committee originally believed that the report of a conspiracy "was a fiction calculated to alarm and not inform," they reported to Clinton that the intelligence Lafayette sent them "caused us to alter our opinion and give Credit to our first information" (ibid.).

From Henry Laurens

[York,] the 4th. March 1778

Sir

I am much honoured by the receipt of your Excellency's Letter of the 19th. Febry. which was delivered to me by Colo. Kosciuszko in person, but not early enough by 24 hours to prevent my troubling Baron de Kalb to say, "I had nothing to offer the Marquis de Lafayette on the 25th. except respectful Compliments & good wishes." [1] This would not have been true, had your Excellency's favor been delivered to me, soon after the delivery of a Letter dated the 20th. Febry. & signed by your Excellency which was sent to me by the Board of War uncovered for the information of Congress.[2]

I had read this last mentioned Letter to Mr. Lovel before the meeting of Congress & remarked to him that from the Stile & tenor, it must have been intended for the president of Congress. This sentiment which scarcely required further aid, was confirmed beyond all doubt, by the preface of your Excellency's private letter, "I intend to write to you as president of Congress"—but unluckily this was not presented to me till the afternoon of the 26th. It was then the Colo., introduced by Genl. Gates, did me the honour to call at my little apartment. I can account in no way for the miscarriage of the Letter intended for Congress, but by concluding an error in the Superscriptory, & the omission within, of the customary direction—for it cannot be believed the Board of War would otherwise have made so unbecoming an appropriation; & their hurry of business apologizes for the want of that nice attention which was necessary to discover from the contents of the Letter that it was manifestly designed for Congress. From this mistake, if it be really one, it follows that I have no Commands on me from Congress directed to your Excellency, who will hear from the Board with whom your Excellency apparently corresponded.

Nevertheless, as it is neither out of the Line of the president's Duty, [nor] inconsistent with his Right as a Delegate, I shall do myself the honour of conveying a Copy of the Act of Congress of the 2d. Inst. passed upon Resolving to suspend the intended Irruption; meaning from thence to prove that Congress maintain an high opinion of your Excellency as a Soldier & a Gentleman & you may depend upon it Sir, the approbation contained in that Act, is genuine, not merely complimentary.[3] Admitting the phraseology to be not quite unexceptionable, I should be criminally silent were I not to declare, the intentions of Congress respecting your Excellency's honour & merits, are altogether one. I will in this case presume to answer for each Individual Member. I love to walk in the Light & to dwell on these bright scenes. Your Excellency, I flatter myself, will indulge my silence on some particulars alluded to in your Excellency's Letter of the 19th.[4] I might be led to disclose Sentiments which might seem unfavorable to a Gentleman, whom I esteem a man of good & upright intentions, whose mistakes are more the effect of credulity than of turpitude of mind or principles. Those who mislead him will be dragged forth at length to public view—methinks they are in such hands at present as will not spare them; you Sir, who are a Bystander are best qualified to judge, & most likely to judge impartially.

My wish is, that we may detect & punish all peculators, projecting, insidious mischievous Knaves, & that no Name under Heaven may screen the villain. But I would deal gently with those whose errors are of the head, whose general tone speaks the public good. And at all hazards & expences I will to the utmost of my abilities support & defend the disinterested patriot—at the same time most sedulously avoiding every whisper which may tend to fan the flame of party.

Hence your Excellency will perceive my motives for touching certain Subjects with caution. When I am clear, no Man will speak with more chearful boldness—but by casting at an object in a mist, I may wound an Innocent, or a friend.

If ever Man Stood on a firm Base, you do My Dear General, you are possessed of what Bacon calls the "vantage ground of Truth"— from whence you may look down upon the Crooked vales & paths below.[5]

My hopes are sanguine that from the American patriotism of Marquis de Lafayette & from his native virtue a power will be raised which will effectually repress the Monster, party, now ravaging the fairest Characters in this Country. God forbid Sir, you should entertain a thought of leaving our United States at this juncture.

"My opinion Dear General of *your situation*" is, that you are at Albany & often in very good Company, & very far from the inglorious precipice which you seem to suggest. The notoriety of your whole conduct & the Resolves of Congress shield you against every possible unfavorable insinuation. Your Excellency will find, that Body, Congress, however it may, by artful men, be sometimes a little Bamboozled, consist of honest well disposed minds, and if Wisdom is justified of her Children, I appeal to their Acts in general. Fall the blame of the late abortion where it ought, or where it may, or by good maneuvring on one side & tameness & acquiescence on the other, let a thick veil be drawn over it; not the smallest spark or speck of Censure can possibly light on Marquis de Lafayette; that General has performed every thing which had been prescribed to him. He has overshot the expectation of some who presumed to believe & assert, that he would be deficient in "activity," & the intended expedition "some days advanced before his appearance at Albany." [6] In a word, 'tis but just that I should repeat, your Excellency is spoken of by Members in Congress with Respect & Admiration. The Air around the Marquis is serene & his own Breast tranquil; a Blunder, not his own, has afforded an opportunity for a display of Wisdom which has gained him the confidence of the people. Hence my Dear Sir, you will perceive that you may with very great propriety & decency return to your late Military Post.

I shall add to the Act of Congress above mentioned one of the 24th. Ulto. which by three last words added at my particular request, injoins you to report the reasons of your Conduct "to Congress." Your Excellency may possibly think this anticipated by the Letter of the 20th. Febry.—& if the Board of War shall have transmitted Copies of these Resolves the present Inclosed will appear to be superfluous.[7] I have however confined my self within the sphere of my Duty, relying upon your Excellency's indulgence to excuse me for making an adress which is altogether private, the Vehicle for public Acts.

I know not what to say relative to Genl. Putnam's Command, it appears to me that Gentlemen wish him away, & at the same time are loth to offend the good old man. If it be from his unfitness their wishes arise, the sacrifice is very impolitic & unwarrantable.

I remarked in a late Act by Genl. Gates he retained the stile of Commander of the Troops in the Northern department. I know of no Resolve by which he has been divested of that Command & I have heard it said lately that there would be a necessity for his taking the Field again in the Spring.

Your Excellency having now a proper opening to correspond with Congress may, if you shall judge it proper to suggest a plan for employment of such troops as are at present under your Command & such as may be collected. I feel the utmost confidence that Congress will pay becoming attention to everything your Excellency shall be pleased to offer. I have the honour to be with the highest Esteem and Respect.

P.S. I should not like our correspondence to be talked of by every one who calls himself or who may seem to be friend—I am afraid of nothing but lies & misrepresentation.

A note in the Margin of your Letter [8] "I beg you will engage Congress to read over all the papers I send to them," is a clear proof the Letter of 20th. Febry. was intended for Congress altho' it might have been by mistake directed to the Board of War. I had not perceived this Note till the present Moment.

LbC (ScHi: Henry Laurens Papers).

1. Laurens to Kalb, February 25, 1778 (ScHi: Henry Laurens Papers).

2. See Lafayette to [Congress], February 20, note. Lafayette's letter was read in Congress on February 26 (*JCC*, 10:197).

3. Congress resolved on March 2 "that the Board of War instruct the Marquis de la Fayette to suspend for the present the intended irruption, and at the same time, inform him that Congress entertain a high sense of his prudence, activity and zeal, and that they are fully persuaded nothing has, or would have been wanting on his part, or on the part of the officers who accompanied him, to give the expedition the utmost possible effect" (*JCC*, 10:217).

4. Probably Lafayette's comments on Gates.

5. Francis Bacon, "Of Truth," *Essays* (1625).

6. See, e.g., Troup's comments to Gates, [February 6, 1778].

7. On February 24, before Lafayette's letter of February 20 had been received, Congress ordered the Board of War to instruct Lafayette to "regulate his conduct according to the probability of success" (see Lafayette to Congress, March 11). Lafayette received copies of this resolve both from Laurens and from the Board of War. The copy sent by Gates only instructed him to report to the board (Lafayette to Congress,

March 12). The journals of Congress direct Lafayette both to the board and to Congress. In the rough journals the connecting "and to" has been crossed out, but it appears in the transcript journals (DNA: RG 360, PCC 1, 14:29; PCC 2, 7:2031).

8. Lafayette to Laurens, February 19.

To Peter Gansevoort

Johns Town the 5th. march 1778

Sir

As the taking of Colonel Carleton [1] is of the greatest importance, I wish you would try every exertion in your power to have him aprehended. I have desired Colonel Lewingston who knows him to let you have any intelligence he can give, and join to them those I have got by one other spy about the drest and figure of Carleton.[2] You may send as many partys as you please and every where you'l think proper, and do every convenient thing for discovering him. I dare say he knows that we are after him and has nothing in wiew but to escape, which I beg you to prevent by all means. You may promise in my name *fifty guineas hard monney* [3] besides every monney &c. they can find about Carleton, to any party of soldiers or Indians who will bring him alive. As every one knows now what we send for there is no inconvenience to scater in the country which reward is promised in order to stimulate the Indians. I have the honour to be, Sir, Your most obedient servant

THE MIS. DE LAFAYETTE

ALS (NN: Gansevoort-Lansing Collection), enclosed in James Livingston to Gansevoort, March 6, 1778 (extract in William W. Campbell, *Annals of Tryon County . . .* [New York 1831], p. 159).

Gansevoort was the commanding officer at Fort Schuyler.

1. Christopher Carleton was a major at this date. This is the only instance where Lafayette calls him colonel.

2. A contemporary wrote: "Carleton, of the 31st. English Regiment, first *aide-de-camp* to his uncle, the general and governor, has lived several years . . . among the savages. His whole body has endured their savage tests of bravery and is adorned with wild figures which he permitted to be cut or burned in." He "has painted his face, wears a ring in his nose, and dresses like a savage" (Ray W. Pettengill, trans., *Letters from America 1776–1779, Being Letters of Brunswick, Hessian, and Waldeck Officers with the British Armies During the Revolution* [Boston and New York: Houghton Mifflin, 1924], pp. 55, 38).

3. By the standard established in June 1775, 50 guineas would be $262.50. Because Continental currency had depreciated, a reward offered in specie was worth considerably more.

From Henry Laurens

York Town 6th. March 1778

I feel myself very happy Dear General upon reflecting that the Letter which I had the honour of writing yesterday [1] has nearly anticipated the necessary answers to Your Excellency's favor of the 23d. Febry. which I am honoured with this afternoon. Had not Major Brice been detained by the Board of War my said Letter would have been one day's Journey advanced.

Were I to attempt an intimation of the public opinion of Your Excellency, the whole would end in repetition of what is contained in my last. I may nevertheless add by way of anecdote the remark of a sensible candid Man, when he had heard your Letter of the 20th. Febry. read. "I," said he, "was averse to this Irruption into Canada not because I thought badly of the scheme but because I feared the Marquis being a Young Man full of Fire would have impetuously rushed our soldiers into too much danger. But his present conduct convinces me he is wise & discreet as well as brave, I now esteem him a worthy valuable Officer." Once more, be assured you have gained great reputation in this Country & that there is not the smallest ground for your apprehensions of the contrary.

I know not how to account for the Ideas of those who planned & announced the intended Expedition, it is probable if they are ever called upon they will be at as great a loss in that respect as I am. A subject this, which I wish not to dwell upon. With regard to you Sir, it is clearly evident, that the part which Your Excellency has acted will be known throughout America & spoken of with applause. I dare not predict the sentiments of Congress respecting a seperate Command, however, I am persuaded every Individual holds you equal to the trust. If you are pleased to propose an eligible plan I may say with confidence it will receive a respectful consideration & 'tis my private sentiment there will be little hesitation upon availing the public of your Excellency's offers of service.

I submit to you Sir, in such Case, the propriety of corresponding directly with Genl. Washington & procuring his opinion to be transmitted to Congress & also with Genl. Gates as an Officer & a patriot not as part of the Board of War.

I am sensible of the distress the Northern department has been in, from want of Money. Of late there have been large remittances & such further sum will immediately follow as the Treasury Board assure me will afford complete relief.[2] If we all followed your Excellency's example & attended business at all hours until it was finished our affairs would be in much better plight than they are.

I don't know who promised Monsr. Failly a Colonel's Commission; I know Congress refused him one, altho' he applied under the strongest recommendation from Genl. Gates.[3] I cannot, even with Mr. Brice's aid, decypher the name coupled with that of Monsr. "Failly." [4]

If it shall be determined that your Excellency shall remain in the Northern department it will become necessary in a proper part of some one of your Letters to Congress to require Blank Commissions.

When a proper opening invites, I shall with great pleasure intimate your Excellency's attention to the Interests of these States demonstrated in pledging your own in support of the public Credit, which I am persuaded will be gratefully received & acknowledged.

I have ordered 6000 Dollars of my own funds to be packeted & delivered to Major Brice for which I have taken his Rect. to deliver the same to your Excellency.[5]

I shall put that Gentleman in the way to inquire the course of Exchange in Lancaster. If he finds it at 400 percent or upwards, Bills for about the value of One Hundred Louis d'or each set may be transmitted & made payble to me. I will endorse them to the purchasers. There ought to be at least five Bills to a set.

Major Brice will inform your Excellency how closely I am confined to this Table at all intervals from personal attendance in Congress & plead an excuse for all my errors & omissions.

I am just closing dispatches for Lieut. Genl. Burgoyne who having found a pen capable of writing Congress properly has obtained leave to embark himself & family for Great Britain.[6] I will in a few days transmit to your Excellency the particulars of this negotiation. At present I am obliged to conclude—which permit me to do by repeating that I am with the most sincere & respectful regard & attachment Sir Your Exely's obliged & obt. Servt.

P. S.
I have this moment a hint given me that the Board of War mean to recommend the recall of your Excellency & Genl. de Kalb to join Genl. Washington & that Genl. Conway will remain where he is. Do not Dear Marquis suffer this to discompose you. I shall expect—I was going to say—that Congress will well weigh this point—but that Inst. Genl. Gates came in, I put the question to him, he says it is intended

to make it agreeable to your Excellency because there is no Command yonder worthy of you.

LbC (ScHi: Henry Laurens Papers).
1. The letter was dated March 4.
2. A total of $450,000 had been appropriated for the northern department in January and February 1778. See Lafayette to Washington, February 19, note 6, and resolution of Congress, February 16, 1778, in *JCC*, 10:174. On March 2 Congress allocated an additional $500,000 for the department (*JCC*, 10:217).
3. See Lafayette to Gates, February 23, note 4.
4. The name is Luce.
5. Receipt for $6,000, signed by Edmund Brice, March 5, 1778 (DLC: Henry and John Laurens Papers).
6. President of Congress to Burgoyne, March 6 (DNA: RG 360, PCC 13, 1:208).

From Henry Laurens

[York,] 7th. March 1778

Sir—

Major Brice left me yesterday & carried with him Six Thousand Dollars on Account of your Excellency & two Letters which in obedience to your Excellency's command I had the honour of writing under the 4th. & 6th. Inst.

I spoke again this morning to Genl. Gates on the subject of recalling your Excellency to Genl. Washington's Army & although we differed in opinion I really believe he means well. However when the recommendation came before Congress, I could not, consistently with honour & Love to my Country, forbear intreating Congress to hear my sentiments. I marked out the good your Excellency was performing in the Northern department & the effect which an Order of recall *from the Board of War,* might have. The House agreed to postpone the Consideration of that Report & nothing will be done until we hear from your Excellency.

When your Excellency writes to Congress you will certainly take no notice of the above. You may ask us how you are to be disposed of & so forth, in which your Excellency needs no hint or information from me. Permit me to intreat you Sir, if you speak of or refer to the Letter of the 20th. Febry.—avoid disclosing that kind of resentment which may bring on disagreeable altercation. I dread the consequences of keeping up the flame of party by disputes among ourselves & so far as I feel myself affected or affronted I am willing to make a sacrifice to peace by passing quietly over the bagatelle. If there was any design in the forestalling that Letter, Major Brice has said enough, to inflict ample punishment upon the offender. The dread of being detected & brought to light will be no small degree of punishment.

The stream of Tallow Candle which just now fell on the paper will shew your Excellency that I am writing when many other people are fast a sleep or otherwise amusing themselves in Bed & upon my honour I have not time to Copy again. I know your Excellency's goodness will accept of a sincere inclination to wait on you, in atonement for these imperfections.

Your Excellency desired to have News Papers. I may have some to send by the next Messenger some five or six days hence, at present I am without any. I do not account the inclosed York Print to be a News paper.

By this conveyance I transmit to Govr. Clinton an Act of Congress for the Commanding Officer in the Northern department—relative to obstructing the passes in Hudson's River & I know not to whom it will be delivered, the direction is general & 'tis late Saturday Night when no explanation from Congress can be had.[1] Adieu Dear General permit me the honour again of subscribing—Yours &c.

The Gentleman [2] who was to have met or gone Volunteer, with your Excellency I am informed is yet within 40 miles of York & I am afraid his spirit is transfused by every opportunity & that it is always more or less at work here.

LbC (ScHi: Henry Laurens Papers).

1. President of Congress to the commanding officer of the army in the northern department, March 7 (DNA: RG 360, PCC 13, 1: 213). Lafayette was the recipient of the letter (see Lafayette to Congress, March 20).

2. Duer.

From George Clinton

Poughkeepsie 8th. March 1778

Sir,

On the 3d. Inst. I did myself the Honor of acknowledging the Receipt of your Letter of the 27th. Ultimo, inclosing one to his Excellency Genl. Washington which I have forwarded to Head Quarters by a safe Hand.[1] Rest assured, Sir, it will always afford me Pleasure to serve you, tho' it may not be amiss to inform you, that Expresses from hence to Head Quarters are not so frequent as you are lead to believe,

George Clinton, governor of the State of New York, who had greater concern for the defense of settlers than for the proposed invasion of Canada

so that, to prevent Delay you will please to mention when your Letters are of such a Nature as that you would wish them to be forwarded by Express, & it shall be done.

I am also favoured with your Letter of the 3d. Instant. It can't be of much Importance to know what the Fools & the Mad say concerning the Northern Expedition; I have the Pleasure to assure you, Sir, that the Sober & Wise, with whom I have had an Opportunity of conversing on the Subject, fully approuve your Conduct on the Occasion, tho' I cant with equal Justice add, that those who planned the Enterprize without providing properly for its Execution pass without a Share of Censure.[2]

I flatter myself the two Companies of Vanschaik's Regiment, will be of real Service at Schohary, & if the Idea of the Northern Expedition is entirely given up by Congress and the Disposition of the Indians shoud be in the least Doubtful, a few more Troops in that Quarter may be necessary for the Protection of the Frontiers.

I have the utmost Reason to believe that there [are] a number of Persons imployed recruiting for the Enemy's Service in the Neighbourhood of Albany, & that they have been but too successfull in that Business. Some Important Information, which I received on this Subject, I transmitted three Days ago, with the Names of a Number of the Persons concerned, to the Mayor of the City of Albany, and desired him to apply to the Commanding Officer for Aid to apprehend them.[3] Perhaps this may produce a further Discovery of the Conspiracy you mention, & enable you by a sudden Stroke to crush it in an early Stage. It is with Pain I confess that too little Pains have been taken to recruit our Army.

At first setting out the Hopes of Reconciliation injured us greatly; it induced many to consider the War to be a mere Temporary Business & since, we have not been as Industrious as we might & ought to have been. This State has been the Scene of War almost from the Beginning, & considering the many Disadvantages it labours under on that account, & for Internal Enemies much more coud not have been reasonably expected from it.

The Defence of the River is an Object of the last Importance to America. Little is yet done for its Security tho I have used every Exertion in my Power to effect it. We are now busied in arranging the Militia of this State & I have called on Massachusetts & Connecticut to furnish 2000 of theirs to assist in the Defence of the River & Country.[4] I am much of the Oppinion that there is not a Command in which a Gentleman may have a better Opportunity of distinguishing himself than that which Genl. Putnam now holds & shoud it be your

Lott to succeed him the Change will afford real, Pleasure to your Most Obed't Serv.

I am sorry I am not able to send you a word of News. I have not a single Paper at present worth reading. The first I get you shall have.

L (*Clinton Papers,* 3:3–5).

1. Clinton to Lafayette, March 3, 1778, not found.

2. E.g., Duane wrote to Clinton on February 19, concerning Lafayette: "His zeal for this Country, for which he has given marks even of Enthusiasm, & his ardent Desire for glory, lead him to wish the Expedition practicable; but he is too considerate to pursue it rashly, or without probable grounds for a successful Issue" (NHi: Duane Papers). Clinton wrote to Gouverneur Morris on March 4: "I trust you had no great Hand in planning the intended Northern Expedition. As Matters now stand, it will at least have answered some good Purpose. Old Debts will be paid, the Troops Cloathed a Department most horridly deranged, reduced to a Degree of order" (*Clinton Papers,* 2:838). On March 5 Clinton wrote to Hamilton: "I need not ask you who contrived & planned the Northern Expedition, I have seen the Marquis's Instructions. They are a Curiosity indeed. They suppose the Enemy are to be pannic Struck & fly on the Approach of our Army" (ibid., p. 865).

3. See Clinton to Abraham Yates, March 4, 1778 (ibid., pp. 839–840).

4. See Clinton to the governors of Massachusetts and Connecticut, March 6, 1778 (ibid., pp. 872–873). Clinton requested 2300 men from these states.

From George Washington

Head Quarters March 10th. 1778

My Dear Marquis,

I have had the pleasure of receiving your two favors of the 19th. and 23d. February, and hasten to dispel those fears respecting your Reputation, which are excited only by an uncommon degree of Sensibility. You seem to apprehend that censure proportioned to the disappointed expectations of the World, will fall on you in consequence of the failure of the Canadian Expedition. But in the first place, it will be no disadvantage to you to have it known in Europe, that you had received so manifest a proof of the good opinion and confidence of Congress as an important detached Command—and I am persuaded that everyone will applaud your prudence in renouncing a Project, in pursuing which you would vainly have attempted Physical Impossibilities. Indeed unless you can be chargeable with the invariable effects of natural causes, and be arraigned for not suspending the course of the Seasons, to accommodate your march over the Lake— the most prone to slander can have nothing to found blame upon. However sensibly your ardour for Glory may make you feel this disappointment, you may be assured that your Character stands as fair as ever it did, and that no new Enterprise is necessary to wipe off this imaginary stain. The expedition which you hint at I think unadvisable in our present circumstances [1]—anything in the way of a formal Attack, which would necessarily be announced to the Enemy by preparatory measures, would not be likely to succeed. If a stroke is meditated in that quarter it must be effected by troops stationed at a proper distance for availing themselves of the first favorable opportunity offered by the Enemy, and Success would principally depend upon the suddenness of the Attempt. This therefore must rather be the effect of time & chance than premeditation.

You undoubtedly have determined judiciously in waiting the farther orders of Congress. Whether they allow me the pleasure of seeing you shortly or destine you to a longer absence, you may assure yourself of the sincere good wishes of Dr. Sir &c.

P.S. Your directing payment of such debts as appear to be most pressing is certainly right as there is not money enough to answer every demand,[2] and I wish your supplies of Clothing had been better. Your ordering a large Supply of provisions into Fort Schuyler was a very judicious measure and I thank you for it.

G. W.

LS (DLC: George Washington Papers, Series 4), draft in John Laurens's hand, with signed postscript in Washington's hand.

1. An attack on New York (Lafayette to Washington, February 19).

2. There is one canceled line at this point in the draft: "but as a friend my dear Marquis I would . . ." Washington apparently intended to offer Lafayette some advice but decided against it.

To Horatio Gates

Albany the 11th. March 1778

Dear Sir

Your favor of the 25th. came into my hands yesterday, and I found that you began then to fear some difficulties in the intended expedition.[1] I have been very glad to see that the opinion of Congress agrees with what I have been obliged to fix upon without expecting theyr directions, for you know they could not arrive in time. I expect with the greatest impatience letters from Congress and the board of war where I'l be acquainted of what I am to do. I hope the good intentions of honorable board in my favor could be employed in a better occasion.

Indeed, Sir, there has been good deal of deception and neglect in that affair.

I wraït to the president of Congress where I accuse the reception of theyr resolve and your letter.[2] I give them also an account of a discovery which they will communicate to you, and you'l see that this part of the world is not to be neglected. Your reflexions about the magazines are very just, but let them be europeans or americans they schould not at any rate be so empty, principally this of monney. We want monney, sir, and monney will be spoken of by me till I will be enabled to pay our poor soldiers. Not only justice and humanity but even prudence obliges us to satisfy them soon. All the monney goes by other ways. I have seen a letter to Colel. Hay where you tell him that the very same 400,000 dollars you told me were for me, are destinated to him.[3] Colonel Hazen has the leave of taking what he wanted for the expedition. There are more warrants than monney and agreable to your orders the[y] refuse what I think absolutely necessary for our troops. Give me leave to advise you, sir, that tho' commander in chief in the northen departement, as your head quarters are pretty far from the main army it schould be better to alter that plan till you will leave the cabinet for the field; indeed in this moment some speedily measure schould be taken for satisfying men who have contributed to your glory and want to collect niew laurels when some notice will be taken of 'em on account of theyr former victorys. With the highest regard I have the honor to be Sir Your most obedient servant

THE MIS. DE LAFAYETTE

The Major Carleton whose it is spoken of is General Carleton's own nephew.[4]

ALS (NHi: Gates Papers, Box 9), enclosed in Lafayette to Gates, March 12.
1. Letter not found.
2. "Accuse the reception": acknowledge receipt. See following letter.
3. Letter not found.
4. See following letter.

To the President of Congress

Albany the 11th. March 1778

Dear Sir

I have just received a resolve of Congress dated the 24th. February where it is reccommanded to me not to untertake the expedition of

Canada if I do'nt find a probability of succès without running any apparent hazard, also a letter from the board of war dated the 25th. where some ideas are given of every thing being not in a so good order as they had believed, but that to gain some thing, some thing must be risqued.[1] Those ideas of the hble. board of war could have been streghtened by my letters which I understand were arrived the day before this was wrote. However the letter of the board as well as the directions of Congress could not have any influence in the present affair, for they arrived about the time that the lakes begin to be impassable, or at least very few days before. The hble. Congress must have got now a report of the reasons of my conduct in stopping the intended incursion. A single one of 'em was sufficient to give up all ideas of making the enterprize. I can assure you that never any disapointement afflicted me so much as this I met with in the present occasion.

I am coming this morning from the Indian treaty where I am told our presence, as frenchmen, was not quite useless to the negotiation. I wish it may have been so.

I have wrote four days ago to Governor Clinton about an affair of some importance,[2] and had deffered my giving notice of it to Congress in hopes that I'd be able to get a greater light about it, and indeed to aprehend the leader of the plot—but such are the only things I have discovered which I think of my duty to mention here to give a niew instance of the humane projects of our ennemys.

Before I went to John's Town an anomius letter was brought to me where I found intelligence of a plot carried on to burn the city of Albany, the stores, magazines, batteaux as soon as the rivers would oppen—that troops were inlisted for the purpose, that many officers and gentlemen were to be assassinated by theyr own Nigroes &c. &c. &c. Some persons were designed who at the request of the committee were taken up at the same hour tho' very distant one from another, but it was impossible to get any intelligence from 'em neither any proof against them. The next day I was acquainted in Scnectady that a soldier had been put in goal for some plot of desertion. Gal. Connway and myself spent a part of the night in examining him. The next day I ordered a court martial, and inclosed you'l find here what intelligence I have been able to collect.[3] Some other reasons as conversations heard betwen british officers &c. engage me to believe that there is some thing of that kind under hand which being half discovered is also half prevented provided we can have men to fight and every thing necessary for them. I have sent partys every where, I have promised fifty guineas to any one who could aprehend Carleton, but I did not find again either magazine or the major himself. If he is taken what I do'nt despair of, I'l Get from him before he'l be hang'd every possible intelligence which I'l forward immediately.

I am very sorry, Sir, to inform you that the troops are much dissatisfied by want of pay. For instance (and it woud be too long to name them all) Clel. Lewingston's rgt. at John's Town complains very much and do'nt choose to receive any part of theyr pay till they will have the whole. The colonel di'nt believe prudent to sent too compagnies of 'em to a particular post till they would be pay'd. I sent therefore to Albany, but the dep. paymaster refused to comply to the order, and represented to me himself that he was not to obey to me, because Gal. Gates has forbidded him to give any monney but upon his own warrants, as holding yet the immediate command of the troops in this departement, and those warrants have been given to any other but the troops.[4] Therefore I find myself unable to satisfy them, and obliged to pay them from my pocquet as far as I'l have monney. Without monney and without cloathes we ca'nt have soldiers.

With the greatest impatience I expect the directions of Congress for what I am to do and to be. I am obliged tho' with reluctance to advertize you, Sir, that there are about this place a schamefull niews running in many mouths which I am as far to believe as I have an high respect for the honor, virtüe, and give me leave to say, the good sense of those of the Congress of the United States who are now in York. They speack of a kind of accommodation under the name of truce where the independency and rights of America as a free country are not acknowledged.[5] I wish'd to know what punishment inflige to those bad wishers to the country who spread such rumours. With the highest regard I have the honor to be, dear Sir, Your most obedient servant

THE MIS. DE LAFAYETTE

ALS (ScHi: Henry Laurens Papers), enclosed in Lafayette to Congress, March 12.

1. For the circumstances behind this resolution, see Lafayette to Congress, January 31, note 1.

2. Lafayette's letter to Clinton was dated March 3.

3. Enclosure not found; for the deposition, see Lafayette to Clinton, March 3.

4. Pierce was the acting deputy paymaster general for the northern department of this time. On February 15, 1777, Schuyler had written to Congress: "It is certainly imprudent for any but the Commander in Chief of the Department to draw upon the Military Chest. I shall therefore . . . direct the pay master to pay no warrants but those signed by the Commander in Chief, or the Commander in Chief of the Department. The Commissioners will probably advise Congress of the Necessity of such an order" (DNA: RG 360, PCC 153, 3:89).

5. For similar reports, see Troup to Gates, March 9, 1778 (NHi: Gates Papers, Box 9), and Kalb to Henry Laurens, March 10, 1778 (ScHi: Henry Laurens Papers, no. 16).

To Horatio Gates

Albany the 12th. march 1778

Dear Sir

My letter No. 1st. inclosed in this was not yet sent à way when I received the dispatches from Congress and your several favors.[1] I am very happy to find that I met with theyr approbation, and indeed as you say very well, sir, the *fault is not mine* if the expedition has been thrown down. The note about provisions will be to morrow in general orders. I expect the arrangement about the general officers of this part of the continent, and I have the honor to wraït to Congress on this subject—for, sir, by one *other copy* of theyr resolves I am directed to give them an account of my conduct.[2] Colonel Lewis, sir, who was here just now assures me that a million of dollars are very far from paying the debts of this departement. Let me intreat General Gates commander in chïef of the northen army, to represent to General Gates president of the board of war that his poor soldiers are an object of pity for every humane man, and that theyr not being pay'd can be attended with bad circumstances. Very sincerely I have the honor to be Sir Your most obedient servant

THE MIS. DE LAFAYETTE

I am told, sir, that a letter from me to the president of Congress has been oppened in your office. It can have only been done by some servant, and I think the fellow schould be punished.[3] As you have told to Mr. de Faïlly and Mr. de Luce that I'd give them commissions of Colonel and major be so good as to send me some blank ones.

ALS (NHi: Gates Papers, Box 9), enclosing Lafayette to Gates, March 11.
1. Gates's letters not found.
2. See Laurens to Lafayette, March 4, and Lafayette to Congress, March 12.
3. Lafayette believed that Richard Peters, secretary of the Board of War, had opened the letter (Lafayette to Laurens, March 20).

To the President of Congress

[Albany] the 12 march 1778

Dear Sir

My letter was not yet sent à way when the dispatches of Congress and the board of war came by Mjor. Brice into my hands which I am going to answer and I will inclose the former letter in the same pacquet. There were in that former letter some reflexions of mine about certain rumours concerning an accomodation betwen England and what they call theyr colonies, which I am very happy to find groundeless.

I declare now, Sir, that I have the honor to wraït to the president and Congress of the United States. This precaution you will find not quite useless if you rembember that my letter favoured by Clel. Kosiasko has been oppened before arriving in the hands of the president.[1] Such mistakes schould not happen too often an this for reasons obvious.

I hope the gentlemen who have so kindly taken care of my letter have not forgot any thing in all the copys inclosed in it. I schould be particularly sorry had they lost an account of those of the debts in this departement (amounting to about eight hundred thousand dollars) which I could have known in a so little time.[2] To avoid any mistakes of this kind I take the liberty of sending the whole packet to Congress, and I hope, Sir, you'll be so good to send those who are directed to the board of war after having read them.[3]

Tho' I was confident I had acted according to my conscience and the common Sense, I must however confess the approbation of Congress afforded me the greatest pleasure. Things are some times so badly represented at four hundred miles. From the motives who brought me to this country, from those who have detained me till this moment, you may easely conceive, Sir, how happy I am to meet with the satisfaction of the representatives of a people whose interests have alwaïs been so dear to me.

I have the pleasure to inform you that I got intelligences of two mortars, many balls and small arms burried by Gal. Burgoïgne in his retreat from Sarathoga.[4] I'll send there to morrow morning to know the truth of that report, and try to get out that very small little supply for our stores.

In one of the resolves of Congress who have been sent to me by Gal. Gates it is said that I'l *give accounts of my conduct to the board of war,* in this you are so good as to send me I am directed to give that account to *Congress* and the board.[5] It is to comply to this last that I have the honor to wraït the present letter.

The board of war speacks alwaïs to me of those 400,000 thousand dollars, but besides the[y] can not pay 800,000,[6] the board knows very well that this monney will not be sufficient to pay the warrants already given.

Gal. Gates tells me that a niew arrangement will be made for the general officers in this part of the continent. That sentence I do'nt well understand, but was interpreted to me in this way—*the Marquis and General Kalb will leave to Gal. Connway the chief command of the troops.* If it is so (unless such a disposition has been made out of a particular consideration for General Washington's reccommandation) I'l beg leave to object that in my country we hold a particular military command as an honorable mark of confidence—that if I am recalled to leave this command in the hands of a gentleman who comes from Europe as well as myself, who is not above me neither by his birth neither by his relations or influence in the world, who has not had any more particular occasion of distinguishing himself than I have had, who has not the advantages I can glory myself in, of being born a french man, I will look upon myself as not only ill used but very near being affronted—and such will be the sentiment of all those of my nation and Europe whose opinion is dear to me.

I am very far from making complaints—but as I hope Congress returns me some of the warm attachement I have schowed for theyr country, they will permit and approuve my going to France immediately. I am sorry that this going à way will take of[f] from the army many french officers more useful than myself—but I schould be very ungrateful for General de Kalb, Gal. Portaïl and the engeneers, the Mis. de La Rouerie and almost all the french officers now in the continental army, was I to refuse theyr instances for following me in my going over to France. Those who are at Albany have renewed them to me when they heard of General Connway commanding here and my being recalled.

Do'nt believe, Sir, that I speack here out of any particular ambition of supreme command. I was very well, I was very happy and quiete near the most respectable friend and the best general I can meet with. But I have been sent to command in chief in a particular place, the expedition is stopped, and immediately after a chief command is given to one of my officers when I am directed to repair to the main army. How do you think such a treatement will look? How can I agree to it? I am wraïting here upon an uncertainty, for the intelligence of Gal. Connway commanding this army is not yet given to me *in form.* But, Sir, if the niews is true I desire my intentions schould be known soon, if not, I have no objection to the Congress knowing what I think my reputation would have obliged me to do in such a case. My heart schall alwaïs be oppened, my frankness is as well known in courts as any where else, and I do'nt fear to tell freely my sentiments upon every happened or to happen occasion. Congress can read in my mind, and they will find the warmest attachement for theyr cause joined to the love of my own glory.

I am sure that I'l never meet with desagreaments of this kind from the court of France *not even in favor of Monsieur de Connway,* but even then the case would be different. Love and duty bound me to the service of my country and there I'l serve as chearfully grenadier as general. In America, Sir, I am only bounded by a friendship independent of any duty as soon as I am out of the service.

Was I to give out schemes, I would desire ardently to be directed to find if there is some propability of succès in an enterprize against Niew York; was I to desire some particular post, and was I certain of what every body tells me about Gal. Putnam leaving the service, I schould say that Fishkill is a very agreable command, when it would bc only for being *a portée* [7] of receiving General Washington's orders and instructions more frequently than in this place. Was I to give an advice, I schould say that any military post who is not under General Washington's immediate command is a very improper one.

In expecting your answer with a very great impatience because time is schort, and the campaign ready to be oppened, I have the honor to be with the greatest respect Sir Your most obedient servant

THE MIS. DE LAFAYETTE

ALS (ScHi: Henry Laurens Papers), enclosing Lafayette to Congress, March 11.
1. See Lafayette to [Congress], February 20, note, and Laurens to Lafayette, March 4.
2. See Lafayette to [Congress], February 20, note 2.
3. Lafayette to Gates, March 11 and 12.
4. On January 8, 1778, Hugh Hughes had informed Gates that a British deserter "said he knew where a Number of Howitzers, Cannon, small Arms &c. were sunk in the Fish Creek, previous to the Convention." In a postscript to the letter, January 13, Hughes reported that the information had been sent to General Lincoln at Albany (NHi: Gates Papers, Box 9).
5. See Laurens to Lafayette, March 4.
6. The $400,000 that Lafayette expected to receive for the expedition had been allocated for the northern department in January and February; $800,000 was his estimate of the northern department's indebtedness.
7. Within reach.

To Henry Laurens

Albany the 12th. march 1778

Dear Sir

I beg you would oppen my public letters and then you will see that I need only to send you some fiew private lines on the subject. Recalling me, and leaving Gal. Connway in a separate command is a thing which neither me neither any friend of mine will ever suffer, and I beg you would read my letters to Congress with those I direct to General Gates.

I see nothing in the conduct of Gal. Connway and the board of war but deception and treachery. The conduct of the board schall be brought to the light and I'l take care of the insolent fellow who oppened my letter to you.[1]

Was I to make an agreable plan I would command at Fishkill, be directed to try if an enterprize against Niew York is possible (what I am sincerely confident can be done) an[d] then if they leave Connway at Albany at least he must be under my immediate command.

But if it is not so I will call immediately to see you and General Washington and set out for our country with Kalb, Portail &c. &c. &c. I beg, my dear sir, you would hurry the decision of Congress because in every case preparations are to be made for putting my army upon a good footing or arming my vessel. The bearer of this letter is Colonel Armand who desires for three American officers some thing which seems to me very just and I beg you to help him.[2] I have very unhappily lost the resolve by which Mr. du Plessis has been made lieutenant colonel with some lines from you. Be so good as to send me by the Colonel Armand an extract from the minutes and do'nt forget your note.[3]

I think of a scheme which would suit every body very well, if General Putnam was more satisfied of being at Albany and General Connway under him, I could be stationned at Fishkill answering not to General Putnam but to General Washington, and we schould after see which other gal. officers would be given to me. In case you think that project can do, be so good as to propose it to Congress in my name. Governor Clinton has wrote to me how glad he schould be was I to command where was Gal. Putnam.[4] I confess you *entre nous* that this post of Fishkill would make me very happy and I am sure we could do something.

I hope my dear sir that those noises of truce and peace are groundless, but if they were not so . . . Ah my good friend, schall I see the name of Laurens at the end of such a convention when this of Henkock was at the end of the declaration of independency?

Those who hate frenchmen have a fine occasion to see them all go off, but those who love them as my good friend the president of Congress will be I dare say a little sorry if my reputation forbids me to fight for the cause of this country which has alwaïs been so dear to me.

Do you think, my dear friend, that they will grant me this separate command at Fishkill? If it is so I'l be very happy. I beg your pardon to wraït you that *galimathias* [5] but I am in a great hurry to send of[f] the colonel who is so good as to carry my dispatches. With the warmest affection I have the honor to be dear Sir your most obedient servant

THE MIS. DE LAFAYETTE

ALS (ScHi: Henry Laurens Papers); inscribed by Lafayette: "private letter."

1. Lafayette believed that Richard Peters had opened his letter to Congress of February 20.

2. Colonel Armand desired captain's commissions for Charles Markle and George Schaffner, and probably a lieutenant's commission for John Sharp. These three men had accompanied Armand to Albany and became officers in the partisan corps that Armand was recruiting. See Armand to Washington, ca. March 22, 1778, November 1778, and June 3, 1782, in *Collections of the New-York Historical Society*, 11 (1878): 290–291, 303–305, 336–337.

3. January 19, 1778, *JCC*, 10:64. Laurens's note not found.

4. Clinton to Lafayette, March 8.

5. Gibberish.

To the Baron von Steuben[T]

Albany, March 12, 1778

Sir,

I am pleased to acknowledge the letters you did me the honor to write.[1] They arrived at nearly the same time, and I have postponed my reply to the first so as to be able to give you some detailed information on the expedition with which I have the honor to be charged. My ardent desire to merit the esteem of a man such as you and my keen appreciation for the obliging letters I have received from you make me very eager to know your opinion on this matter. I am a very young soldier, sir, and consequently more subject than anyone to error, yet I dare say that necessity has dictated my conduct, for the simple reason that I had no other choice. I find but a third of the troops that were promised me, and I find them ripe with discontent because their pay has been dreadfully neglected. With no money, clothing, carriages, provisions, or stores ready, time was our ruling factor, and since it would have taken us beyond the season when the lake is passable to procure even half of what was needed, I preferred to stop right away rather than expose the American troops to certain shame in a poorly planned enterprise. The particulars of what has just happened to me would seem extraordinary in Europe, but in a young country one must have patience and yield to circumstances. Congress has replied to me that it approved the line of conduct that I was obliged to follow.

I don't know yet, sir, in which part of this continent I am destined to serve. I would think myself very fortunate to have the occasion of making your acquaintance, of cultivating it, and of meriting your friendship and esteem. Even though I risk losing much of the inflated opinion that my friends wished to give you of me, I assure you that my fears on that account will easily be overcome by the pleasure of seeing you, and the benefit I hope to draw from your counsels, if I can persuade you to grant them to me.

Allow me, sir, to congratulate you on being so near General Washington.[2] This great man has no enemies but those of his own country, and yet every noble and sensitive soul must love the excellent qualities of his heart. I think I know him as well as anyone, and that is precisely the idea I have of him. His honesty, his candor, his sensitivity, his virtue in the full sense of the word are above all praise. It is not for me to judge his military abilities, but as far as my feeble judgment can discern, his opinion in the council always seemed to me to be the best, though his modesty sometimes kept him from sustaining it, and his predictions have always been fulfilled. In all sincerity, it has been a pleasure for me to give you some idea of the character of my friend, because some people would have tried perhaps to deceive you in this matter.

I have not yet had the honor to see, sir, the officer you recommended to me.[3] I shall try very hard to be of some service to him. I feel it would be wrong to deprive Monsieur des Epiniers of the benefit of being with you, especially since the Canadian expedition has been given up.[4] I can assure you that as your acquaintance grows, so will the good opinion you have of him. You will receive a second letter from me in which I shall take the liberty to inform you of my destination, and in the expectation that I shall have the pleasure of assuring you in person, I beg to persuade you of the most distinguished sentiments with which I have the honor to be, sir, your very humble and obedient servant

THE MIS. DE LAFAYETTE

ALS (NHi: Steuben Papers), translation.

1. Steuben wrote to Lafayette in early February to wish him a "glorious expedition" and to recommend the Baron de Bruno, who had gone to Albany to join Lafayette (ca. February 5, 1778 [NHi: Steuben Papers]). Other letters not found.

2. Steuben's services as a volunteer were accepted in February 1778, and he was at Valley Forge.

3. Bruno.

4. Des Epiniers was Steuben's aide-de-camp.

To [*George Clinton*]

Albany the 16th. march 1778

Sir

I have had the honor to receive a Letter from your excellency where You desire me to send Clols. Wanschoi's and Putnam's regiment to West Point.[1] This on account of the rivers and badness of the roads it will be impossible to comply to before four day's. I hope to get an answer from you by that time, and then the troops which I have ordered to be ready and also the sloops will be sent down by water. Was it possible to send some within two or three days, then Putnam's regiment schould be able to set out immediately—but I understand it wo'nt be practicable so soon.

Give me leave however to represent to your excellency that I receive every day applications from every part of the frontiers for giving to them posts, forts, body of troops able to defend the country against the incursions of the ennemy, indians &c.[2] That I confess is not to be granted but after a deeper examination into the propriety of the measure. However there are some points more interesting to be guarded and the troops now *fit for duty* in this part are not indeed equal to the number of places they could be employed in. It is only a remark of mine which I submit to your judgement.

I was speaking about this matter with Gal. Schuyller who thaught it would be better to keep here Wenschoi's regiment and send Putnam's with the four months militia.[3] I must however advertize your excellency that those 400 militia men when called for return can not make more than hundred and about thirty—the others being yet at home. Clel. Putnam has some part of his regiment in detached posts which will be recalled in and others sent in theyr room. Vanschoy's rgt. was already much complaining of theyr being too dispersed when I propos'd theyr going to Schoary and Cheri-Walley. It seems now to me that under the present circumstances those two posts must be given to some other regiment, as you will perhaps insist on this coming down, and Colonel Hazen's could hold if not both at least one of 'em. A quarter master is gone on to prepare every thing there, and you know it ca'nt go as fast here as it would be possible to expect.

Therefore, Sir, as the rivers and necessary preparations give to us the time of receiving your answer, be so good as to tell me if after considering the scarcity of troops in this part, you think both regiments can be spar'd—then they will be immediately sent down. Other wise if you can do with Putnam's and those of the four month's militia we'l be able to collect, your directions will be also followed, but or all the posts ca'nt be held or the small northen body will be all divided in detachements. West Point seems to me of the greatest importance. I am sorry indeed to hear the fortifications are far from being done, but *late* is better than *never*. I have taken out of the regiments and four months militia every meason and carpenter I have been desired to give and they have been forwarded to you by the Commissioner of the fortifications of North River now at Albany.[4]

I hope that the river will permit soon sending down troops for I am told it is not possible to think of sending them by land. Nothing interesting is come in my hands since my letter about Mjr. Carleton and the gentleman has not been aprehended.[5] I have sent spies to Canada by whom I expect a return of the british forces and theyr intentions.[6]

The commissioners of indian affairs intend to apply to me for the building of a small fort which has been granted to the *Onoyedos* about fifteen miles from Fort Schuyller. I'l send on that purpose a french engeneer the day after to morrow. The wood is already cut, it will be carried by some horses from German Flats, and I intend to apply to the committee of Tryon County to desire theyr sending as workmen to that new little fort those of the four month's militiamen they were ordered but Neglected to furnish. The same engeneer will be directed to examine the fortifications of Fort Schuyller.[7]

Every body wants forts. I have received applications from a committee who wish to have a fort at Chery Walley at the end of those two little lakes. They fear that the Indians or torys could come up the river. They are affraïd too of that settlement of torys betwen the two small lakes I was just now speaking of.[8] There I believe a little excursion could be made by the troops sent at Chery Walley with some militia to take à way theyr arms, or powder or every thing we could look upon as dangerous for us. I beg you would send me your opinion upon those matters.

The people of the nord towards Co'os begs too for a fort—but they furnish materials, workmen, garrison, and even an engeneer—therefore we can let them do.[9] However as Gal. Belay tells now he has thousand militia ready I desire him to send me a return of 'em, and promis'd I will send to examine them. With a pen and some ink it is very easy to recruit. I am told there are some indians friends of ours who came from the *Sault* and are now scattered in the woods. It is represented to me (and particularly by Mr. Deane the indian interpreter) that it schould be a very good scheme to have them settl'd in a certain piece of land upon the frontiers belonging to no body.[10] That I think we owe to do for them on every account but I wish'd to have your opinion upon the matter as I do'nt mean to interfere in raising any dispute and I know that granting lands and permitting settlements is a very delicate point in this country.

With the greatest concern I have seen that the execution of the confiscation ordered by the state has been attended with very improper circumstances.[11] Officer's ladys have been plundered in a very schoking way, and I expect an account of those facts (if they are trüe) which I will send to your excellency.

Do'nt you believe, Sir, that all those Scotchs, british ladys and women, wifes of officers, and known ennemys of the country who are about John's Town and that neighourood, entertaining a correspondance with theyr husbands and friends in the british army, schould be better permitted to go to Canada and Niew York? There is one Mistress MgDonnall with two daughters whom I have half promised passes to, for joining her husband in Canada, and one Mistress Adams who wants to go to Niew York. If your excellency has no objection, I'l gratify theyr desire. We do'nt make war to women and I like better to see our ennemys without than within our country.

There is here, Sir, a particular instance where according to the opinion of Gal. Schuyller, Mjor. Gal. Kalb, and Gal. Connway, I have granted a pass to an officer under Gal. Burgoïgne's convention for going to Canada and even to England where he will consider himself as a prisoner of war till the convention will be agreed betwen Congress and the Court of London. That young gentleman is covered with wounds, he is in a poor condition, and the surgeon has told his arm schould be quiete lost unless he would be allowed to take the baths in England. He is only a lieutenant.[12]

Give me leave, Sir, to tell you my sentiments about the manner in which militia are rais'd in the continent. Substitutes seem to me our ruin. It prevents the continental troops from recruiting. It gives a set of undisciplined rascals, instead of a good body of farmars, men to be depended upon, who if they have not discipline, at least are fired with the love of the country they fight for. Those inconveniences increase every day as much as desertors are scattered in the country. Therefore the army is not fill'd up, and the great object the great advantage of the militia is miss'd. In that four months levée I understand fiew country men are to be found, and indeed I dare not expose them near the frontiers. It will be soon a dishonor to bear arms for the Country—and that duty will be performed by substitutes as a vile one. I have seen a militia man giving sixty dollars for two or three hour's fight to a substitute.[13]

There are prisonners, desertors, running about in the country. Do'nt you think, sir, those men are very dangerous so near the frontiers? Most of 'em are in tory's houses. It seems that the best way would be to send those men towards the southern provinces.

One other remark for the last, Sir. In this Continent every man has a gun, powder and ammunition. Our most noted ennemys have arms in theyr hands, and in the same time we want them they are to be seen in tory houses. Our own soldiers by the most schoking want of discipline and neglect of theyr officers have sold them. Do'nt you think, Sir, it would [not] be a bad plan to have some of 'em seized and pay'd for?

I have received letters from Congress and am happy to find they are pleased with our conduct in stopping *the intended incursion*. Some monney is promised. We are much distressed on that account and this of provisions—but for remediying so many things my hands are tied up on account of General Gates's holding the command of the northen army. Every warrant goes by him, and it is a pity his head quarters are so far—but I am told he will take again the field.

I am yet ignorant of my destination, but do'nt believe it will be to stay in Albany. I expect soon letters from Congress and his excellency Gal. Washington. Every thing the general will think proper for me, I schall take very chearfully, because I am sure he will never think of any thing but what could be agreable for me and useful to the common cause.

With great impatience, sir, I expect your answer, but if the weather would Permit, my expectation wo'nt prevent my sending those of the troops who will be more at hand. I hope you'l be so good as to honor me with your advices and directions about the points I take the liberty to submit to your excellency. With the highest regard I have the honor to be Your excellency's The most obedient servant

THE MIS. DE LAFAYETTE

ALS (PPRF).
1. Clinton wrote to Lafayette on March 13 "to suggest to you, the necessity of imploying" at West Point "Vanschaick's & Colo. Putnam's Regiments now at Albany, or such Part of them as can be spared, & if the same can be done with Propriety & consistent with your Instructions, I doubt not but you will readilly consent to it & give the necessary orders. . . . I am perswaded Congress will approve of almost any Measure that is Calculated to forward the Defences of the River" (*Clinton Papers*, 3:37–38). On March 11 Clinton had told Parsons: "To save Time I will write to the Marquis for Men as it may be long before I can have an answer from Congress on that Subject" (ibid., p. 27).
2. Schuyler wrote to Congress on March 15 from Albany: "Since my return to this place, I have been honoured with a letter from the Legislature of this State, covering petitions from the inhabitants of Schohary, Cherry-V lley, Charlotte River, Delaware and Harper's Field, praying the Legislature for assistance. As it is not in the power of the Commissioners to afford any aid to these exposed settlements, I have communicated the contents of the letter and petitions to the Marquis de la Fayette, that he may take measures to enable the inhabitants to remain on their plantations" (*Collections*

of the New-York Historical Society, 12 [1879]:200–202). See also Vermont Council to [Lafayette], February 28 (*Chittenden Papers*, p. 243), and Cherry Valley Committee to Lafayette, March 31 (*Clinton Papers*, 3:104–105).

3. On January 24, 1778, Congress had recommended that the state of New York call out 400 militiamen to serve for four months under the commanding officer in the northern department (*JCC*, 10:88).

4. Cornelius Wynkoop had been appointed by the state of New York to assist in procuring artificers and materials for the Hudson River fortifications.

5. Lafayette to Clinton, March 3.

6. See Lafayette's orders to Bedel, March 16.

7. The fort was to be built at the main Oneida village of Kanowalohale. On March 21 or 22, Lafayette sent Gouvion to supervise the construction. See Lafayette to the commanding officer at Fort Schuyler, March 21.

8. Unadilla.

9. See Lafayette to Timothy Bedel and to Caleb Willard, both March 16.

10. James Dean was Schuyler's agent among the Indians. Schuyler had written to Bedel on September 11, 1777, about several St. Francis families who wished to settle near Coos, and instructed him: "As it is of importance to secure as many of the Indians to the interest of the American cause as possible, especially such as reside in Canada, you will . . . take measures to remove the . . . Indians to some part of Connecticut River, as near the inhabitants as possible; and, to induce them more readily to come, you will afford them some assistance in provision and ammunition" (*Collections of the New-York Historical Society*, 12 [1879]:189). See also Bedel to Gates, March 14, 1778, requesting instructions concerning the disposition of "the poor Savages now in the woods about Co'os" (*New Hampshire State Papers*, 17:218–219), and Lafayette to Bedel, March 16.

11. On March 6, 1777, the Provincial Convention authorized the appointment of "commissioners of sequestration," who were empowered to confiscate and sell the property of persons who had left to join the British (*Journals of the Provincial Congress, Provincial Convention, Committee of Safety, and Council of Safety of the State of New York, 1775–1777* [Albany, 1842], 1:826). On December 1, 1777, the powers of the commissioners were broadened, authorizing them to enter and search "any houses and places wherein they shall have reason to suspect any goods, chattels or effects of persons gone over to or with the enemy, to be concealed, and to break open any building or dig up any soil for the purpose of seizing and possessing themselves of such goods, chattels and effects" (ibid., p. 1092).

12. William Richardson (Gates to Daniel Jones, June 4, 1778 [NHi: Gates Papers, Box 9]).

13. By the substitute system a man who was called up for militia duty could hire someone else to serve in his place. Washington complained that "the amazing Sums given for Substitutes in the Militia, induces all those, who would otherwise have gone into the Continental service, to prefer a line in which neither duty nor discipline is severe; and in which they have a chance of having the bounty repeated three or four times a year" (Washington to Patrick Henry, November 13, 1777, in Fitzpatrick, *Writings of Washington*, 10:54). On May 22, 1778, Congress resolved to disqualify deserters and prisoners of war from acting as substitutes in the militia (*JCC*, 11:522–523).

To Timothy Bedel

                                                          Albany 16th. March 1778

Sir

I have just wrote an Answer to General Bayley letting him know that altho' our Expedition it cannot be carried on into Execution at this present Moment, yet he is to keep the Thousand Men he mentioned to me in his Letter [1] in the utmost readiness as they may be very Serviceable to the United States as Scouting Parties, in Building the Fort and Garrisoning of it when finished, and in defending the Frontiers of that Quarter. I think Sir you would do well to Engage those Men for the Campaign. You will take Care to inform the Comitees of the Measures we are taking for the Security of the Inhabitants in those parts, and jointly with them you will make every necessary Preparation for the Fort they have desired of me,[2] and you will send to me as soon as possible the Answer of the Engineer to whom I have wrote by you.[3] In all Sir, I expect you will be very particular in your Accounts to me respecting the matter, and let me know the Sentiments of the People also about it. You may assure them that Congress means to use every Step in their Power for their Security and expect in return that they themselves will exert every Nerve in favour of our Common Cause. You will also assure those of the Militia and the Citizens in general who have been employed in the Service of the United States and not received their Pay that we retain the highest Sense of their Service and that those Debts will be soon discharged. I have sent down repeated Expresses on the Subject, and they have given me the Pleasure to know that there will be a sufficiency of Money here [shortly] [4] to satisfy the whole. You will constantly keep out Scouting Parties in order to prevent as much as possible any Spies or Parties of the Enemy from coming among us, and returning again. As I understand there are British Officers (or at least Tories) recruiting in the Country you will take particular Care to discover & apprehend them. You will keep Spies with the Enemy to watch their Motions and learn their Intentions and give particular Accounts of any Intelligence you may receive to the Officer Commanding at Albany.[5] You will receive Advices from me respecting the Settlement proposed in favour of the Indians.[6] I Expect you will send me a most exact Return of the Militia now raised and ready under your Command.[7] I wish it to be Signed by the Commitee in Order that I may be able to send down a true State of the Militia in that Quarter. I believe a General Officer will go to review them in that part.

THE MIS. DE LAFAYETTE

L (NHi: Gates Papers, Box 9), copy in Thomas Hibbard's hand. Lafayette probably enclosed his letter to Caleb Willard, March 16.

1. Neither Bayley's nor Lafayette's letter has been found.

2. For the committees' recommendations for the defense of the Connecticut River frontier, see the Proceedings of Committees of fifteen towns, April 3, 1778 (*New Hampshire State Papers,* 17:223–224).

3. See following letter, and Willard to Lafayette, August 25, 1778 (*New Hampshire State Papers*, 17:264–265).

4. This word appears in other manuscript copies of the letter (e.g., NhHi: Bedel Papers).

5. Bedel to Lafayette and to Gates, both May 14, 1778 (*New Hampshire State Papers*, 17:227–228); Bedel to Schuyler, May 25, 1778 (ibid., pp. 228–229).

6. See Lafayette to Clinton, March 16. Bedel informed Lafayette on May 14 that the Micmacs and St. Francis wished to know what arrangements were to be made for them (*New Hampshire State Papers*, 17:227). No other correspondence between Lafayette and Bedel concerning the Indians has been found.

7. No return of Bedel's Regiment has been found. Stark wrote to Gates on June 21, 1778, that he doubted that Bedel "has half the Number of Men he Returns. . . . He has Drawn for a Regiment Raised last Winter for the Canada Expedition, double pay and Rations, and none of them Ever left their own homes, & Whether any of them was Inlisted or not is Uncertain . . ." (NHi: Gates Papers, Box 9).

To Caleb Willard

Albany 16th. March 1778

Sir

Tho' I have not the pleasure of being acquainted with you as I understand you are among the best of American Engineers and you are recommended to me as such, I desire you wod. proceed immediately to the Place you will be directed by Colo. Bedel towards the Upper Co'os, and point out in that Neighbourhood a proper Ground for Building a Fort which has been requested by the Inhabitants, the Object of that Post is to Cover the Country, protect it against the Incursions of the Indians, or small Parties of the Enemy and defend itself against a small force if Attacked. I wish it could Conveniently contain Two hundred Men of Garrison. You see Sir I don't want expensive or difficult works as you cod. do for works of greater Importance. Now Sir that I hope you understand the Object of this small Fort, I'll desire you to send me the Project the Plan Profiles and all the Dimensions of the Work and every one of his Parts, also an Estimation of the Time, the Money you think wod. be expended. I don't ask a Vague Plan but a Geometrical one were all the Proportions will be Calculated and also for the Profiles. You will put under your Seale the Computation of all the Demensions of that Fort, be so good as to add the Number of Workmen necessary and also how much you think such a number will do in a day. I need not Sir recommend you to any of the Precautions so well known by any one of your Art. In Expecting your Answer [1] I have the Honour to be with great Esteem, Sir, yr. most Obt. Hble. Servt.

The Mis. de Lafayette

L (NHi: Gates Papers, Box 9), copy in Hibbard's hand; probably enclosed in Lafayette to Bedel, March 16.
1. See [Willard] to Lafayette, August 25, 1778 (*New Hampshire State Papers*, 17:264–265). A copy of the plans of the fort at Upper Coos, signed by Willard, is in the Gates Papers (NHi: Box 9); see also Stark to Bedel, May 23, 1778 (*New Hampshire State Papers*, 17:232).

From George Clinton

Poughkeepsie, 18th. March 1778.

Sir,

I am honored with your Letter of the 16th. Instant. With respect to Vanschaak's & Putnam's Regiments I am not authorized to call them from Albany to this Quarter. I only meant by my Letter to submit the Propriety of the Measure to you, as we realy need a greater Number of Troops to carry on the Works for the Defence of the River, with the necessary Expedition than we have at present for this Important Purpose.[1]

I am fully of your Oppinion that if any Troops can be consistently spared from Albany of which you are the best Judge, the four Months Militia will be more useful on Fateigue than in the Field, & therefore they may be better spared for this Service than Van Schaack's Regiment. Genl. Ten Broeck ought to have compleated the four Months Militia to the full Complement as ordered him & you will oblidge me much by reminding him of this.[2]

I am so little acquainted with the Western Frontiers, owing to the Number of New Settlements since I have been in that Part of the Country, that I am not able to advise on the Posts necessary to be taken there. I dare say Genl. Schuyler will at all Times chearfully afford you his advice on that Subject & I know of no Man more capable or in whom you may more confide. I am clear that it is better to remove the Torry Women you mention, than, to suffer them to continue where they now are, & it will afford me Pleasure how soon it is effected. We have always trusted to the Committees to disarm the Tories; we shall soon have Commissioners who will have Power competent for the Purpose.[3] I am Sir with the greatest Respect Your Most Obed't Serv't.[4]

I have the Pleasure to forward to you several Letters which I have this Moment rec'd by Express from his Excellency Genl. Washington.

L (*Clinton Papers*, 3:53–54).
1. Clinton to Lafayette, March 13 (see Lafayette to [Clinton], March 16, note 1).

2. For the four-month militia, see ibid., note 3.

3. On February 5, 1778, the New York legislature had passed an act to create "commissioners for detecting and defeating conspiracies." See *Laws of the State of New-York, Commencing with the First Session . . .* (Poughkeepsie, 1782), pp. 6–7, for a definition of the commissioners' powers.

4. On March 19 Clinton wrote a further response to Lafayette's letter of March 16, in which he approved of Lafayette's grant of a pass to a wounded British officer, but advised Lafayette not to provide a sloop for the officer's transportation. Clinton deferred giving any opinion on a settlement for the Indians without first consulting the state legislature (*Clinton Papers,* 3:54–55).

To the President of Congress

Albany the twentyth march 1778

Dear Sir

I have receiv'd two resolves of Congress, one respecting the furloughs which I will be very happy to put in execution as great many abuses are committed on that respect, the other respecting the fortifications of North River which I will forward the execution of as much as it will be in my power.[1] How much I have been surprised to see that important point in so defenseless condition tho' we were so near the spring of the year it would be useless to say. I confine myself in telling that tho' I had no instructions for it, I thaught it was of the greatest importance to give to that point every assistance I could. I hurrie'd the coming down of the canon by every possible reccommandations to the quarter masters &c. I granted immediately any request from the commissioner now at Albany [2] for carpenters, measons &c. I wrote to the governor and offered to him any services which could depend on me.[3] I expect now an answer from him where I will know if he persists to have two Continental regiments, or if he would not rather take only one and the few militia now met in this place [4]—but I have order'd already the troops to be in readiness and also the sloops. According to the canon being sent down I will send only the answer of Mjor. Stephens, a very valuable officer who commands here the artillery. All what can be done upon this matter, I will consider as my first duty to order as long as I will stay here.

It seems to me, Sir, that by the present time of the year, the only way for getting those canon left behind, will be to have boats built at Fort Edward and Saratoga, bring a part of that canon to Lake George, and from thence down here. Such is at least my present idea I will consult upon and give afterwards orders for. Agreable to the intelligence I owe to Gal. Schuyller that there was at Fort Edward a great plenty of boards unguarded, I'l order a guard to be sent there from Saratoga. Those boards seem to me very precious, as boats, batteaux &c. are of the greatest necessity in this country, and I am far from finding here as many as we ought to have. I have hitherto agreed with Colonel Lewis that he would built as many as he could till farther orders.

view of Ticonderoga from a point on the north shore of Lake Champlain, 1777. Fort Ticonderoga at the upper right; the boats in the foreground are bateaux.

There have been many dissipations made as arms sold by the soldiers &c. and then rgts. left quite unarm'd which I am going to enquire in very strictly. I wish'd too some new regulations would be made about the false returns.[5]

When Gal. Gates left this place, he ordered that as a reward to the troops who had bravely contributed to his succès, a gill of rum schould be given to each soldier in Albany and also to the workmen.

That I dare not alter till I'l have received directions from Congress or the board of war, but beg leave to observe that I have had complaints from the commissary about the scarcity of rum. Inclos'd I send what Mr. Cuyler has delivered for the small Nixon's brigade and corps of artillery for the only month of February.

Inclos'd I have the honor to send to You the copy of a letter I receiv'd from the british surgeon, and this of my answer. That gentleman got leave from Gal. Gates to go to New York, with some disabled men of his hospital, in giving others in exchange *when his accounts would be settl'd.* He came to me much complaining of the commissary of the hospital who, says he, wants to have three times in gold what the rations cost according to the own resolves of Congress settling the rations at ten pences two thirds N.Y.C. As I din't know his engagements and neither instructions neither resolves of Congress have been directed to me on account of the prisonners I would not take upon myself giving a desisive answer. I was yet more adverse to let them go without the accounts schould be settl'd and pay'd, because I would have receiv'd eight days after a very polite letter from Sir Henry Clinton, assuring me that his doctor had no right of taking any engagement.[6] However if Governor Clinton gives me some intelligence, or advices, to grant theyr going, as I think those people schould be much better without than within this town for many reasons, I schall send them.[7] But was he uncertain about the decision then I beg Congress to let me know immediately when, how, after what payment, for which Conditions that people is permitted to go down, and I think the sooner will be the better.

His excellency Gal. Washington will, I believe, mention to Congress that at the request of the commissioners of indian affairs I send Clel. Gouvion and have given proper directions for the building of a small fort which they and myself have thaught very necessary to be grant'd to the Onoyedos. The love of the french blood mix'd with the love of some french *louïs d'or* have engag'd those indians to promise they would come with me.[8]

As I am very certain the Congress of the United States will not propose any thing to me but consistent with my reputation and the sentiment I flatter myself to have obtain'd from 'em, I can assure them by advance, that any post they will give, any disposition they will make with such manners, will be chearfully receiv'd and comply'd to by me with aknowledgement. However I'l beg leave to say that any command whatever honorable it may be, where I would not be so near the danger or occasions of doing some thing, I schall alwaïs look upon as no fit for me.

I never mentionn'd to Congress a long letter I have wrote 4 months ago to France about a project of the East Indias, which I expect the answer of.[9] Was I to succeed in my expectations, it would bring soon that so much desired french war, in spite of some peaceful men, and be of some use to the noble cause of freedom, without bringing the Continent in any expence. With the greatest regard I have the honor to be, Dear Sir, Your most obedient servant

THE MIS. DE LAFAYETTE

There as been a court martial for desertion which I din't approuve of, but as among other men I have found sentenc'd of death, I beg from Congress to be empowered to relieve the man.

ALS (PHi: Dreer Collection), enclosing Dr. John M. Hayes to Lafayette, March 18, and Ebenezer Stevens to Lafayette, March 19 *(Clinton Papers,* 3:55–56, 59–60); Lafayette to Dr. Hayes, March 19 (see note 6); Cuyler's account for rum, February 1778 (not found).

1. The resolution of March 7 restricted the authority to grant furloughs to the commander in chief or the commander of a department; the resolve of March 4 placed the Ticonderoga cannon at Clinton's disposal for use in the Highlands, and instructed the artificers at Albany to assist in stocking the guns *(JCC,* 10:230, 221–222).

2. Wynkoop.

3. Probably Lafayette to Clinton, March 19 (not found).

4. See preceding letter.

5. Richard Varick, deputy mustermaster general for the northern department, complained to Gates on March 23: "Such an Indifference prevails among most officers, about those of their men, who are absent from their Regiments, that they Scarsely take any pains to learn where they are, nor have I reason to Expect a more Exact Return at next Muster, than I had at the last, unless Congress or the Board of War Interfere" (DNA: RG 360, PCC 78, 23:78).

6. Henry Clinton was the British commander at New York. Lafayette wrote to Dr. Hayes on March 19:

I am not entitled to ascertain that the Congress of the United States means to grant the Rations to the British Prisoners at the rates which is given to their Troops as a Bounty, tho it costs much more, but I can assure you, that you will not pay by any means a Farthing more in Gold than we have paid in paper. I am very sorry indeed, that the refusing of our Currency paper in the places now under your power, deprives you of the agreement of purchasing or reimplacing in a way which would perhaps be more convenient for you.

Your proposition of giving pound for pound of equal Quality, seems to be more consistent with the Intentions of the Congress of the United States, [and] therefore, Sir, I think I will be able to agree with you in that point, when I will see or the Powers you are invested with, for taking those engagements and the Time stipulated for their performance, or the proper Security you will be pleased to give. But, Sir, you will easily conceive that I cant give you a desiscive answer, when I do not know yet which have been the particular promises of Genl. Gates about your going to New York. . . .

According to what you have told me in our Conversation, that our Conduct in this place should regulate this of your Generals, I'l only answer that the Time is come, where we have no more Objection to a strict Retaliation on both Sides and on every respect. . . . *[Clinton Papers,* 3:56–58]

7. Clinton responded to Lafayette's letter (of March 19, not found) on March 25:

It is clearly my Oppinion that the British Hospital ought not to be suffered to go to New York on any Account until their exchange shall be properly settled. This can-

not be effected until a final adjustment of their accounts due to the respective
States for necessaries found them be made agreable to the Resolve of Congress of
the 26th. Feb'y, a Copy of which I now inclose you. I begg Leave to suggest to you
the Propriety of removing the Prisoners of War now in Albany & the adjacent
Country to some of the Eastern States as their Continuance in Albany might be an
Inducement to the Enemy to come up the River. [Ibid., pp. 83–84]

8. See also Lafayette to Washington, [March 22,1778].

9. Lafayette to [Maurepas], October 24, 1777. Lafayette had privately told Laurens
of the plan in his letter of December 14.

To Henry Laurens

[Albany,] the twentyhe march 1778

Don't be angry against me, my good friend, and if I have made
blunders you must impute them to my too quick feelings, and forgive
the sinner on account of his repentance. Gal. ⟨Connway⟩[1] came in my
room when your letters were in my hands. As I saw in a moment all
the plan since the Canadian expedition was proposed, my idea took
fire, and my first unreflected motion has been to let him know the
little article of the letter,[2] and see the figure he was cutting in the perusal of it. That is a miss I confess, a great miss, for I schould not
have mentionn'd any thing to him, but I found a kind of entertainement to see how he would take that news from myself. The next
day I aknowledg'd to myself I was in wrong and certainly such an in-
discretion will no more happen. I think it is better to confess the
whole than if I was to aggravate my fault by an ill directed schame.
The Conduct of the gentleman after wards and the protestations he
has done of his innocence have been a proof to every one, that he was
much concerned in the affair in consequence of a plot laid among
them.

The letter by which you desire me not to mention the oppening of
the dispatches directed to the president of Congress is arrived too
late.[3] I di'nt know then it was done by Gal. Gates, and I thaught the
Guilty was the worthy Richard Peters. But now my letters are gone
on, and certainly I will not make an excuse to Mr. Gates because he
has oppened my letters.

Now, my dear Sir, let us speack of Congress. By your last favor I
see they are very far from meaning any disagreament for me, and
therefore I am sorry to have wrote in pretty warm terms. But Consider that by the first intelligence I got from you, it was likely they
would fall upon a plan which every one will look upon as an affront
for me. The only idea of it fired my head, and as even the suspicion

of any uncivil treatement in such occasions will never be suffered by me from any one in the world, I sent immediately down Colonel Armand to let know, not what *I was doing but what I schould do in case such a thing would happen*. I have been too quick perhaps, but such is my temper and that temper of mine ca'nt be altered. I must however confess not to the president of Congress but to Mr. Laurens, that the next day in sending to Gal. Washington an account of my conduct [4] (tho' I had not given up the idea of leaving the american coat) I beg leave to serve near his person as *a stranger* volonteer, to prevent my hurting the cause of freedom by my return in France, and depriving in the same time the army of so many valuable officers, generals and others who want to follow my sort [5] what so ever.[6]

If Gal. Gates, General Lee (let him be exchang'd) Gal. Schuyller, are sent to Albany even previous to my Consent I have no objection to it—but I will not suffer any of my officers being commander in this departement before my refusal. However was I to stay in this part of the continent as I am, I schould certainly decline a command where I am not certain to see the fire of a single gun for the whole campaign. I want only that be proposed to me.

As the affair of Rhode Island seems laid aside and I am not acquainted with that part of the country,[7] I look upon the post of Fish Kill as the only separate command I can wish. Then Gal. Connway could be at Albany under my orders, and myself have an immediate correspondence with Gal. Washington. If that not be the case then I schall take again very chearfully my division and thank Congress for theyr polite offer of the separate command of Albany, if they put myself *à portée* [8] of being satisfied what will be easely done, for I have not the least desire of raising disputes. By far, I love the cause, I love military glory, I want to fight and to fight for you, and so I will do till the last drop of my blood, if necessary the whole campaign unless some unkind [proceedur?] would oblige me to be angry.

As General Gates taking the command, or Putnam holding his post are Yet in the dark, if one or the other happen I will not certainly have any objection to so just a thing—tho' I am fully convinced both would make a great faux pas in trusting upon the fortune of war.

I look upon an expedition against New York as a very eligible plan. There would come many New Yorkers. There you'd see a large number of New England militia who will never go to Gal. Washington's army, and would turn out for an expedition so convenient to 'em on every respect. Such is the idea given to me by every body and principally by Gal. Stark who has been two days in this place and knows very well the minds of the New England militia. New York would be proud to get theyr capitale, New England would entertain the hope of getting some plunder in it. Such a diversion made by troops who wo'nt ever join the grand army schall be of a great use to General Washington for or they'l risk to loose the town, or they will send reinforcements in it from General Howe's. I can only judge of the possibility of the expedition upon a map, and was I directed to it I could get better intelligences—but it seems to me that in making two false attaks towards Long Island and Staten Island to divide theyr forces it would not be impossible to carry King's Bridge.[9] Then the town is oppen'd. We could at least detroy the public stores &c. &c. &c. &c. and were we obliged to leave it, would not it be praticable to fortify King's Bridge on our side? For Fort Washington I do not know enough of it to determine in which way he could be taken, but I think that place could be laid aside, or only invested till after the taking of New York.

Such are the light ideas I dare lay down faster than I can think, but I could make a less imperfect, unreasonable project was I directed to take proper intelligences, and investigate the propriety of the enterprize.

As all the New Yorkers are more exesperated against Gal. Gates than you could ever believe I think those public sentiments would render him very unfit for the command of that part of the Continent.

Tho' I have given proper orders that all the departement schould borrow upon my credit, and I have given warrants even upon Boston for the raising of Colonel Armand's Corps, however monney comes very slow, and I beg you would send reinforcements. I am asham'd some times when I see trifling expenses which ca'nt be pay'd for, and when it comes out from my pocket I ca'nt help laying in telling them that it is given by Congress to me for paying the trifling expenses— that if you please *Entre nous*.

As I am assured the express is a man to be depended upon, I trust him with my dispatches, be so good as to send him or one other back very fast, for I am much tired of seeing those english here about. They are doing nothing but michief and I wish they would be soon out.

As there are a plenty of hessians and british desertors, and even prisoners scattered in the country who may be very dangerous, I have advis'd Governor Clinton to have all that people out of the state.[10] They could be rather sent to New England or down below.

Tell me very candidly my dear Sir, if you have been angry against my *etourderie*.[11] Forgive me, and be certain that my heart better than my head will be yours as long as I leave [live]. With the highest regard I have the honor to be, Dear Sir, Your most obedient servant

THE MIS. DE LAFAYETTE

Thousand compliments to the fair lady and most charming *Miss Ketty*.

Was I to have a separate command the Viscount de Montroy [12] would come as a volonteer, and as I think he is the best man we could get his advices would be very useful to the cause.

I make you my thanks for the monney and will answer to that article by the first opportunity.[13]

ALS (ScHi: Henry Laurens Papers).

1. "Connway" has been canceled out. The cancellation was probably done by Laurens as a discretionary measure.

2. The postscript of Laurens to Lafayette, March 6, intimating that Lafayette and Kalb would be recalled from Albany, and that Conway would assume command there.

3. Laurens to Lafayette, March 7.

4. Armand carried Lafayette's letters to Laurens of March 11 and 12. Lafayette to Washington, March [13?], has not been found. Lafayette had suggested to Washington on February 19 that he would serve only as a volunteer unless he were given some means of erasing the stigma of the abortive expedition. On April 1, 1778, Schuyler reported to Duane that Lafayette "is greatly chagrined at the Conduct of Congress or rather of the board of war towards him. I believe he will quit his rank in the Army and Join Genl. Washington as a Volunteer" (NHi: Duane Papers).

5. Fate.

6. Following this sentence, "but such a thing must not be" was crossed out at the time of writing.

7. A reference to the attack that Spencer was to have led against the British on Rhode Island. On November 28, 1777, Congress ordered an investigation into the failure of the proposed expedition (*JCC*, 9:975). See also Lafayette to Washington, February 23, note 4.

8. Within reach.

9. King's Bridge joined Manhattan Island to the Bronx at the Post Road.

10. Lafayette to Clinton, March 16.

11. Thoughtless act.

12. Mauroy.

13. See Laurens to Lafayette, March 6.

To George Washington

[Albany, March 20, 1778]

Dear General

Alwaïs new instances where I find myself obliged to send to Congress. Was I not so sensible of your excellency's goodness for his officers and particular frienship for me, I schould be afraïd you'd not forgive so many misses tho' unvolontary ones—but such is the case in this particular instance. We have in this place a british hospital, british doctor, british officers, tho' the situation of Albany do'nt seem fit for all this britannic train. The doctor has leave from Gal. Gates to go down to Niew York with his disabled men (on condition of theyr being exchang'd) as soon as he will have settl'd his accounts. Upon those accounts a dispute arises. He wants to pay not what things cost to us but what they are allowed for in the rations of our people—or he will go himself with his men into New York, and from thence send pound for pound of equal quality. This second point I ca'nt grant because his superiors would not acknowledge the authority he had of making the bargain. The first I dare not take upon myself to settle, and therefore I send for an immediate answer from Congress because I am very desirous of seeing that people going home as soon as possible. They already are, and can become much more, inconvenient to us in this place.

I have writen to Governor Clinton for knowing his opinion about sending to Newyork two or three british women, a british officer whose life depends says the surgeon on his going home, and a tory gentleman.[1] I like better to have those people without than within, but however am not of opinion of giving them unlimited passes as a general my precursor [2] has done several times.

General Schuyller and other commissioners of indian affairs having applied to me for granting a small fort to the Onoyedas indians, I send there Clel. Gouvion who will in the same time inspect the fortifications of Fort Schuyller, as I have been prevented from going there myself. The indians have cut theyr wood themselves, some tools, some picquets, and some militia from Tryon County will do the business. ⟨Then I hope I'l be able to get here, and perhaps to bring down to your excellency some scalping gentlemen for dressing the fine hair of the *Howe* actually dancing at Philadelphia.⟩[3]

Colonel Bedel of the militia and Gal. Belay who say they have thousand men, and perhaps have not two hundred, want too to have a fort where they furnish wood, workmen, garrison and engeneer. I have desired him to send me a geometrical plan of his projected fort with its profiles and dimensions.

Gal. Stark has desired me to mention to Congress that he looks upon it as not only an useful but even a necessary thing, that two picquets-forts be built in the month of april one in the neighbourhood of Ognon River, the other in this of Skinburry. I have received one other application from the people of Cherywalley who cry for a fort in theyr country as they are expos'd to the incursions of indians and torys coming up by the back side. This is a long list of forts, but we have the consolation to think that all these fortifications are reduc'd to some picquets. This of the Onoyedos seems [to] Me the most important and so I did not differ giving proper orders for it. The others I hope your excellency will take in consideration, and after mentionning to Congress those of Gal. Stark and this I have granted, give me farther directions.

For the arrangement of the british hospital I think I'l do better to wraït not only to Congress but also to Governor Clinton—and in case the governor schould advise me to let them go in giving proper securitys, then I could take upon myself granting theyr going down.[4]

General Stark has been two days in this town, and seems [to] me very sanguine about a diversion towards Niew York. He says an immense number of militia who would never turn out but for this expedition would join the officer commanding there⟨—but I wo'nt join the [*illegible word*], neither apply my mind to any scheme till I schall know where I am to serve⟩.

I must confess [to] you, my dear general, that I have been too quick upon a hint given to me of Congress recalling me without knowing my sentiments about it—you will have found some resentment in the letters and copys I have sent to your excellency some days ago—but now I am told that Congress far from meaning any disagrement for me, have been polite enough as to expect knowing my sentiments before making any disposition of general officers, I assure you, my dear general, that I will do very chearfully every thing they will propose to me in such a manner.[5] You know too well my heart to be in any doubt but I schall consider myself very happy to serve with you, when this recalling me will not be attended with the ⟨impolite⟩ circumstances I was in right to suspect. I say more—the command at Albany I do'nt look upon as fit for my love of agreable occasions, unless it would be extended below and that I have not any right to demand. In all, my dear general, my mind will be alwaïs super satisfied to be as near you as possible, and I schall look upon any thing you will believe fit for me, as the very best thing I can wish for.

Inclosed I send to your excellency the letter of the british doctor and also my answer.

I have received a resolve of Congress concerning the defense of Hudson's River. It is very extraordinary indeed those precautions come so late, such works schould be done two months ago. Many canons are desired from me and Gal. Gates finds an immense park of artillery in his inkstand, as he had lately found three thousand men, provisions, cloathes &c. &c.[6] You will see in my answer and this of Mjor. Stephens what we can do in this moment.

Inclosed I send to your excellency some petitions and resignations. Besides that there is one Lt. Blak-ley of Clel. James Lewingston rgt. who wo'nt give [up] his commission till the resignation will be accepted, what I beg your leave for.

Farewell, my most dear and beloved general, do'nt forget your northen friend, and be certain that his sentiments for you will only end with his life. I beg you would present my respects to your lady and thousand compliments to the gentlemen of your family. With the greatest respect I have the honor to be Your excellency's the most obedient servant

⟨THE MIS. DE⟩ LAFAYETTE

The Canadian prisonners from Gal. Burgoïgne's army apply every day to me to get leave to return to theyr familys. I send you the copys of my letter to Congress and that of Major Stephens. I have not heard from your excellency since the first letter.

ALS (PEL: Hubbard Collection). The manuscript has been edited in ink, in Lafayette's later hand. The text of significant deletions has been restored in angle brackets.
Enclosures: Dr. Hayes to Lafayette, March 18, and Ebenezer Stevens to Lafayette, March 19 (*Clinton Papers*, 3:55–56, 59–60); Lafayette to Dr. Hayes, March 19 (see Lafayette to Congress, March 20, note 6); Lafayette to Congress, March 20 (the copy sent to Washington is in PEL: Hubbard Collection); miscellaneous petitions (not found).
   1. Lafayette to Clinton, March 16.
   2. Gates.
   3. See Lafayette to Washington, March 22.
   4. See Lafayette to Congress, March 20. Letter to Clinton not found.
   5. See Henry Laurens to Lafayette, March 6, and Lafayette to Congress, March 12.
   6. Acting upon a report by the Board of War, Congress resolved on March 4 that the cannon being brought from Ticonderoga—eight mounted, twenty-three unmounted, and sixty-six pieces of various calibers—should be placed under Clinton's orders. On March 19 Ebenezer Stevens, major of artillery at Albany, had reported to Lafayette that there were twelve mounted, nineteen sound but unmounted, and thirty-three damaged cannon in his park or en route from Ticonderoga. The board's tally probably included the cannon sent to Farmington, Connecticut, in January 1778, which were intended to be used for the defense of the Highlands, but which Stevens did not include in his report to Lafayette (*JCC*, 10:221; *Clinton Papers*, 3:59–60).

From George Washington

Head Quarters 20th. March 1778

In pursuance of a Resolve of Congress of the 13th. inst. a Copy of which is inclosed,[1] I am to desire that you will without loss of time return to Camp, to resume the command of a division of this Army; and that you will communicate a similar order to Major General de Kalb.

By the 2d. Resolve of the same date you will see that I am impowered to remove Hazens or any other Regiment from the Northward to join this Army.[2] I intend no other change for the present than to have Van Schoick's Regiment marched to the Highlands to receive the orders of Major General McDougall,[3] and desire that you will give orders in consequence to the Commanding Officer of that Regiment.

I anticipate the pleasure of seeing you, and with sincere assurances of esteem and regard, remain Dear Sir, Your most obedt. Servt.

G. WASHINGTON

L (DLC: George Washington Papers, Series 4), draft in John Laurens's hand.

1. March 13, 1778, *JCC*, 10:253–254. Henry Laurens had sent Lafayette a note on March 13, informing him that "Congress by a side wind this afternoons meeting were induced, but not without debate, to Resolve that General Washington be authorized to recall Marquis dela Fayette & Baron de Kalb to the Main Army." He wrote because "this may reach you before a Mandate from the General & will afford so much more time to make necessary arrangements for the retrograde journey" (ScHi: Henry Laurens Papers).

2. *JCC*, 10:254.

3. On March 16, 1778, McDougall had been ordered to take command of the Hudson Highlands.

To the Chairman of the Albany Committee

Albany 21st. March [1778]

Sir

Inclosed I have sent you a petition of a certain Mr. Butler who complains that he has been insulted & abused by two officers of our Army.[1] By what I can understand he was the first Agressor, however as he complains loudly I beg you to represent the Matter to the Gentlemen of the Committee; as I do not choose the Military Law should by any means interfere with the civil. I wish you to investigate into the Affair and point out to me how such matters are to be settled.

A few days ago I received Advices from Governor Clinton desiring that two Regiments might be sent him from this place, but upon my representing Matters to him he will be satisfied with Colo. Putnam's Regiment and the four months militia who will be sent down to him in a few days. Now as Col. Putnams Regiment are going away, and Colo. Hazens Officers have never been billitted yet (as has been represented to me by Majr. Taylor) I could wish they might be billitted in the places of Colo. Putnam's. I have also understood that there are many Families in this Town, firm Friends to the Country, having two and three sons in our Army, who have several soldiers billited on them, while there are others who have not a single one. As a private Gentleman I beg leave to recommend to the Committee that they who are acquainted with those Matters will examine into them and if necessary have them agrieved.

I have likewise inclosed to you a letter from Mr. Cruger a Gentleman who wishes to go to New York [2] and who had Genl. Gates permission to do so—and as I am going (by the Advice of Governor Clinton) to send several Tory Ladys from the westward Mrs. McDonald, Mrs. Adams &c. down to New York,[3] if you have no Objections I will suffer Mr. Cruger to take his passage with them. In expecting your Answer, I have the Honour to be, Sir, Your most Obedient Sert.

THE MIS. DE LAFAYETTE

LS (VtU: Wilbur Collection), in Neville's hand.
1. Petition not found.
2. Letter not found.
3. See Lafayette to Clinton, March 16, and Clinton to Lafayette, March 18.

To the Commanding Officer at Fort Schuyler

Albany March 21st. 1778

Sir

Whereas I have at the request of the Commissioners for Indian Affairs granted a small Fort to be built for the Oneidas in their Country about Sixteen or Twenty miles from Fort Shyler, the Bearer hereof, Lieut. Colo. Guvion an Engineer in the continental Service is on his way to give proper Instructions concerning [it] and at the same Time as Colo. Gonsworth [1] is desirous of having the works of Fort Shyler examined I have desired him to do it. I wish you to make any Alteration agreeable to the Advice he may give you. For building this small Fort for the Oneidas which is to be done by some Militia from Tryon County a few Tools will be wanting which you will furnish them with from Fort Shyler as they will be shortly returned. You will also furnish them with provisions, but you may rely on thats being replaced as soon as conveniently may be. I am with Respect, Sir, Your most Obedient Servant

THE MIS. DE LAFAYETTE

LS (NjMoW), in Neville's hand.
1. Colonel Peter Gansevoort was the commanding officer at Fort Schuyler.

To Ebenezer Stevens

Albany March 21st. 1778

Sir

Altho your well kown Activity and Zeal on every occasion might render any advice to you unnecessary, yet I desire to mention a few things to you on our present Circumstances. You have received from Governor Clinton the Resolution of Congress respecting the defence of the North River;[1] the Time is now partly elapsed and swiftly elapsing in which this defence might be necessary. I would have you therefore, Sir, to use every possible exertion in your Power to have the Cannon down; every Assistance that is in my power to afford you, you shall have if requisite; also that of Col. Lewis is at your Service. As it is a matter of the utmost Consequence I wish it to be done with the greatest dispatch and Expedition. I am with sincere Respect, Sir, Your most obedient Servant

THE MIS. DE LAFAYETTE

LS (NHi: Ebenezer Stevens Papers), in Neville's hand.
1. March 4, *JCC*, 10:221–222.

To George Washington

[Albany, March 22, 1778]

Dear General

I can never miss an opportunity of rembembering to your excellency the mighty *Commander in chief of the irruption into Canada,* and I seize with the greatest pleasure the first occasion of telling you how happy I have been to see in your last favor a new assurance of those sentiments of yours so dear to my heart.[1] As soon as I have got intelligence by Gal. Schuyller that you were desirous of having some indians,[2] I have dispatch'd three french men[3] with black belts and yellow guineas to bring down as many as possible. I dare hope theyr love for theyr fathers schall engage some to come with me and I'l bring them to your excellency, for my only actual scheme is to join you, and get clear of many people. I have promis'd to those indians they schould have with 'em french officers if they would and I am bold enough to believe your excellency will not disapprouve any en-

gagement of mine. I schall be very happy to forward the execution of
a business you seem desire, very happy also to see you again, and
present myself to your excellency the assurances of the most profond
respect I have the honor to be with, Your excellency's the most obedient humble servant

THE MIS. DE LAFAYETTE

I am told my division will be six thousand strong—God may grant it!

ALS (DLC: George Washington Papers, Series 4), sent under cover of Schuyler to
Washington, March 22 (ibid.).
    1. Washington to Lafayette, March 10.
    2. At the urging of Washington and the Committee of Conference (Committee of
Conference to Congress, February 20, 1778 [DNA: RG 360, PCC 33, pp. 171–174]),
Congress authorized the employment of 400 Indians in the main army (March 4, JCC,
10:220–221). Washington wrote to the commissioners for Indian affairs in the northern department on March 13, enclosing a copy of this resolution, and requesting their
assistance in engaging 200 Indians. Schuyler responded on March 22: ". . . The Marquis de la Fayette Informs me that he has been promised two or three hundred of
them, when he should require them. A message from him to Invite them down goes
of [f] today, with one of mine to thank them for their offer and to desire that I may be
Informed when they will come" (DLC: George Washington Papers, Series 4). A party of
Indians arrived at Valley Forge on May 14 (Washington to Schuyler, May 15, 1778, in
Fitzpatrick, Writings of Washington, 11:389–392).
    3. Gouvion, Tousard, and possibly Céloron. On March 22, Lafayette ordered Tou-
sard to accompany Gouvion "to help him in building the fort of the Onoyedos, and in
engaging theyr warriors to join me. He will come back to head quarters as soon as he
will be able to have collected a sufficient number of indians to march them to Albany"
(CSmH: Pictorial Field Book of the Revolution; reproduced by permission of The Hunting-
ton Library, San Marino, California).

From the President of Congress

[York,] 24th. March 1778

Sir—

Your Letters of the 11th. & 12th. of this month have been laid
before Congress. They have considered the apprehensions you express, that you & General Kalb are to leave the command of the
Troops in that part of the continent where you now are, to General
Conway, and your request, of permission to go to France, founded
thereon. They wish you to be assured, that they have a very high
sense of your merit and attachment to America. They judge it of advantage to the public service that you and General Kalb be present
with the grand army, but when they came to this determination, had
not yet resolved on a disposition for General Conway, and had no in-

tention to make any injurious to your honour. They expect this declaration, and the disposition since made for General Conway, will make it unnecessary to grant the permission you request.[1]

By order of Congress.[2]

LbC (DNA: RG 360, PCC 13, 1:239).

1. Congress resolved on March 23, 1778, "that General Conway be directed to repair to the army at Peeks Kill, now under the command of General M'Dougal . . ." (*JCC*, 10:280).

2. March 21, 1778, *JCC*, 10:278.

From Henry Laurens

[York,] 24th. March 1778

Sir—

I am honoured with Your Excellency's favor of the 12th. Inst. by the hands of Colo. Armand.

Whatever had been the design, or if it might have been, as Your Excellency charges, intended "deception" of the Board of War I dare again aver, that Congress were not in the project for leaving Genl. Conway in a seperate Command in consequence of recalling Your Excellency & Baron du Kalb from Albany. I have been more than a little astonished by the freedom of speech in treating upon that Gentleman's Character. Severe & harsh sentiments have not only been whispered but loudly sounded in my hearing, & even one Gentleman in whom I know he had reposed the greatest confidence, gave him up by a *mild* declaration that he was *afraid* Genl. Conway was *too indiscreet* a Man to be *trusted* with a Command. Thus are Men deceived in this Rascally World. Poor Conway believes quite a different Creed.[1] I have not the least doubt but that he has wrapped himself secure in the friendship of some, who by fair & soft, personal addresses have tempted him to a confidence, while he is shy of others from whom he has experienced only Candor & plain dealing. God knows what he is, I have not yet fully heard all sides—nor have I very deeply considered what I have heard—but this I will venture to Say to you Dear Marquis, according to the Maxim of an ancient Lawyer "whatsover a Man sowith that shall he reap," if he is *deceitful,* he is paid in this his own Coin. I protest humanity shrinks at hearing Men traduce the Character whom they have taught to place a confidence in them—to hear ferocity, sheer Courage, eminent qualities in the Brute Creation, acknowledged to be the *only* virtues in the mind of a favorite. Is it possible for Men to speak of a friend as they do of a Mastiff? Then steps in, *another Set,* who attempt to strip him even of that specious Virtue. In a word, the General once honoured me by asking for my advice, I gave it honestly, he literally pursued, but indirectly, most effectually contravened it. I have therefore no great encouragement to become *a volunteer* Counsellor, but should my sentiments be again demanded, I would find room for inserting: "be advised by me General & return to France where there is a greater Croud."[2]

Congress have ordered a Letter to be written to Your Excellency which I shall sign by direction & transmit here with,[3] together with a Resolve of yesterday, Ordering Genl. Conway to Peeks Kill under the Command of Major Genl. McDougall.[4] There had been more than a few opinions for Ordering him to York Town.

I trust your Excellency will do Congress the Justice to believe they had never entertained the most remote intention to give you offence, I add & repeat with great pleasure that your Excellency is held by each Individual in the highest Esteem & the House very much relies upon the greatness of your Mind for security against groundless exceptions to any part of their conduct respecting yourself. These indeed are Sentiments not dictated by Congress, but I know they are warranted. However your Excellency may retort, that my declaration in this case will require a little skill to reconcile it, with the total Silence on the Subject of the piracy committed upon the packet of 20th. Febry.[5] Even this most extraordinary conduct cannot be fairly urged as an exception to the professed Esteem & Regard for Marquis dela Fayette, although it may be inconsistent with that Veneration which the Representative of the 13 United States should ever preserve for their own Character if they expect to escape Contempt throughout the Universe. I should have been happy if your Excellency had passed that affair over for reasons which I had assigned but since it has been talked of & since the parties accused are acquainted with the circumstance, I am made very unhappy by a conduct which will endanger us to be exposed to future & greater Insults.[6]

It is impossible to do any thing for the affairs mentioned by Colo. Armand[7] until the arrangement at Camp is completed & tis probable Your Excellency will meet the Committee there.[8] I shall there transmit a Duplicate of Mr. Duplessis Commission & of the Resolve upon which it is founded.[9]

It appears to be more & more the wish & purpose of Gentlemen here to return General Gates to his late Command in the Northern department, & there was lately the appearance of a pretty little attempt to render that Command Independent of all Orders but those of Congress. This will account to you at once for the Silence on that head; how Major General Mc.Dougall may approve of being super-ceded after he shall have gone through the drudgery of Mechanical operations in & about the River is a matter of uncertainty.[10]

With respect to Great Britain, believe me Sir, Administration was greatly shocked by the Account of Mr. Burgoyne's surrender but it does not appear from any hints dropped on their part that they were disposed to terminate the dispute with America by any thing like a Concession to Independence. There may & there possibly will be at-tempts to treat for peace & accomodation some time before the ordi-nary course of opening the Campaign, but I do not expect any thing substantial to follow, but blows. In the mean time the Monied people of England are really alarmed & begin to subscribe for the support of the War. This is a maneuvre which I always dreaded, if the infection spreads our American troubles will not soon be removed. On this side the Water, there is too much ground to fear, some grand exertion, or some injurious sly stroke, will appear against Valley Forge, Wilmington or perhaps York Town before General Washington is sufficiently reinforced to admit of detachments or even of facing the Enemy with his whole present Army.

I most sincerely wished Your Excellency a seperate Command, but since that has not happened, with equal earnestness I wish to hear of Your Excellency's safe arrival at Valley Forge, where possibly this may kiss your hand & upon that presumption Colo. Armand means to take the Camp in his Route.

I dare not detain that Gentleman a moment longer, he is as impa-tient to be gone as he would be if he was going to be Married. He will admit of no delay. He has experienced none from me as an Individ-ual. I have the honour to be with the most sincere Esteem & Regard &cet.

Inclosed are two Letters left here for your Excellency.[11]

LbC (ScHi: Henry Laurens Papers).

1. On June 7, 1778, shortly after he arrived in York, Conway wrote to Gates: "I never had a sufficient idea of Cabals untill I reach'd this place. My reception, you may imagine, was not a warm one. I must except Mr. Sam. Adams, Coll. Richard Henry Lee and a few others who are attach'd to you but who can not oppose the torrent. Before my arrival General Mifflinn had join'd General Washington's army where he com-mands a division. One Mr. Carroll from Maryland upon whose friendshipp I De-pended is one of the hottest of the Cabal" (NHi: Gates Papers, Box 9).

2. Laurens's sentiments were "again demanded" on April 28, 1778, when Congress considered and accepted Conway's resignation (Conway to Congress, April 22, 1778 [DNA: RG 360, PCC 159, pp. 473–476]; JCC, 10:399).

3. Preceding letter.

4. Congress to Conway, March 24, 1778 (DNA: RG 360, PCC 13, 1:239–240).

5. A reference to the Board of War's opening Lafayette's letter to Congress, Febru-ary 20.

6. See Laurens to Lafayette, March 7, and Lafayette to Congress, March 12 and 20.

7. Armand desired commissions for three American officers (Lafayette to Laurens, March 12).

8. The Committee of Conference.

9. Du Plessis had lost his copy of his commission and the resolve of January 19, 1778 (Laurens to Du Plessis, April 28, 1778 [ScHi: Henry Laurens Papers]).

10. On April 15 Gates was directed to take command at Fishkill; McDougall was to return to the main army and resume command of his division (*JCC*, 10:354–355; Washington to McDougall, April 22, in Fitzpatrick, *Writings of Washington*, 11:298). Mc-Dougall wrote to Clinton on May 11: "General Gates is not yet arrived, nor do I learn when tis likely he will. I think I am not well treated by him and Congress" (*Clinton Papers*, 3:294).

11. Not identified.

To George Washington

Albany the 25th. march 1778

Dear General

How happy I have been in receiving your excellency's favor of the tenth present I hope you'l be convinc'd by the knowledge of my tender affection for you. I am very sensible of that goodness which trys to dissipate my fears about that ridiculous canadian expedition. At the present time we know which was the aim of the honorable board, and for which project three or four men have rush'd the country into a great expense, and risked the reputation of our arms, and the life of many hundred men, had the general your deceived friend been as rash and foolish as they seem to have expected. Oh american freedom what schall become of you, if you are in such hands!

I have the pleasure to inform you that a scouting party of twenty men gone from Bennington to Shelbon on Lake Champlain, having taken post there, was attacked in an house by a british officer at the head of forty five men british and indians sent on purpose of taking our party, who after a brave defense sallied out, and routed the enemy. They kill'd five men and took six prisonners and fourteen stand of arms. Among the prisonners two are wounded but four are in condition of being exchang'd for the same number made lately prisonners.[1] General Stark and Lieut. Colonel Safford who gave me that intelligence desire me both to obtain from your excellency that exchange which they seem to have much at heart.

I have receiv'd a letter from the board and a resolve of Congress by which you are direct'd to recall me and the Baron de Kalb whose presence is deem'd absolutely necessary to your army.[2] I believe this of Gal. Connway is absolutely necessary in Albany and he has receiv'd orders to stay there, what I have no objection to as nothing perhaps will be done in this quarter but some disputes of indians and torys. However you know I have wrote to Congress ⟨in order to favor the gentlemen of York with a [short letter of politeness?]⟩ [3] and as soon as theyr leave of staying there will come, I schall let Connway have the command of these few regiments and I schall immediately join my respectable friend. But till I will have receiv'd instructions for leaving this place from yourself I schall stay as powerful commander in chief as if never Congress had resolv'd my presence absolutely necessary for the grand army. [4]

If you mean to recall Hazen's regiment I advize you to take in exchange this of *Ganzewort* of Fort Schuyller, or this of *Wanschoys* of Sconectady because they are much better on every respect. [5] I think your excellency schould order down the arms and ammunition of this quarter without loss of time for *reasons obvious.*

Since your last letter I have given up the idea of Newyork and my only desire is to join you. The only condition [6] I have made in coming here, and the only favor I have asked ⟨to all the protestations of gratefulness⟩ from your commissioners in France, has been not to be under any orders but those of General Washington. I seem to have had an anticipation of our future friendship, and what I have done out of esteem and respect for your excellency's name and reputation, I schould do now out of mere love for General Washington himself.

I am glad to hear Gal. Greene is quarter master general. It is very interesting to have there an honest man and a friend of yours. But I feel the greatest pain not to hear any thing about reinforcements. What can you do, with an handfull of men? ⟨I think those gentlemen below are quite mad⟩—and my poor division whom I was so desirous of instructing, cloathing, managing myself in the winter, whom I was told I schould find six thousand strong for the oppening of the campaign? Do'nt your excellency think that I could recruit a little in General Greene's division now that he is quarter master general? By that promotion I find myself very proud to be the *third* officer of your army. [7]

Inclos'd I have the honor to send a resignation of an officer who *dislikes* the service. [8] With the greatest respect and affection I have the honor to be, Your excellency's the most obedient humble servant

⟨THE MIS. DE⟩ LAFAYETTE

ALS (PEL: Hubbard Collection). The manuscript has been edited in ink, in Lafayette's later hand. The text of significant deletions has been restored in angle brackets.

1. This skirmish occurred at the Pierson house in Shelburne, Vermont, on March 12, 1778.

2. No letter from the Board of War has been found.

3. Probably Lafayette to Congress, March 20.

4. Troup wrote to Gates on March 26: "The Marquis, being fond of Power, is much chagrined with the thought of joining the Southern Army. Tho he has seen the late Resolve of Congress, he will remain here, till it is sanctified with the approbation of Head-Quarters. His delay, in some Measure, fetters the Alertness of General Conway, who wishes to avoid a Dispute, that may only terminate in malicious Invective" (NHi: Gates Papers, Box 9).

5. See also Lafayette to Clinton, March 16. On March 20, Washington requested Lafayette to order Van Schaick's regiment to the Highlands.

6. "Condition" is changed to "request" in Lafayette's later hand.

7. Nathanael Greene was appointed quartermaster general on March 2, 1778 (*JCC*, 10:210). Ordinarily the quartermaster general would have been a staff officer, outside the regular line of promotion, but by the resolution Greene still retained his seniority and a title to command. Lafayette was the third-ranking officer with the main army not because of Greene's appointment but because Sullivan had just been sent to Rhode Island (Washington to Sullivan, March 10, 1778, in Fitzpatrick, *Writings of Washington*, 11:57–58). Lafayette ranked behind Greene and Stirling.

8. Enclosure not found.

From Henry Laurens

[York,] 27th. March 1778

I was honoured this Morning Dear & much Respected Marquis by the receipt of your favor of the 20th.

What branch of any of my Letters, the inadvertent disclosure of which could have occasioned you pain? It is most certain I never intended to communicate & I am persuaded I have not promulged Sentiments inconsistent with the Interests of the public nor derogatory to the honour of my Station; & perfectly sure I am from the integrity of my heart that I have written nothing which can be construed into Slander. It would be indecent to whisper a cross a street & impertinent to read my private correspondences to every Man who calls to see me. But while I am peculiarly careful not to expose what is intrusted to me in the Letters of my friends, I am equally unanxious for the fate of my own. I may safely be so since I cautiously avoid every thing inflammatory, every thing like party whisper & every thing that can spread the present deplorable discord.

If I judge truly, the "little article" which Your Excellency alludes to, is the Postscript of my Letter the 6th. Inst. I read that to General Gates & the fact was public, therefore the intimation can give no offence. In a word permit me to assure Your Excellency that neither the manner nor the matter of the late disclosure affects me with the

Slightest degree of Chagrin, *except my feelings* for the vexation which that circumstance had given you.

Your Excellency's Letter to Congress is Reported & Committed to a select Committee,[1] our business of this nature proceeds slowly therefore I will not detain the Messenger but return him to morrow Morning with this. Such determinations as Congress may make in consequence of the expected Report from Committee will in all probability meet you at Valley Forge. I presume you will commence your retrograde journey soon after the return of the present bearer.

An authentic account from Holland of 25th. October assures us the States have demanded restitution for a Dutch Ship taken in the Channel by an English Man of War under pretences of her being American built—that all the capital Houses in Trade (Hope & Comp. excepted) have united in application for Convoys to their West India Trade & that the number of friends to American Independence increased dailly in that Country.[2]

Yesterday a Gentleman from Virginia imported a piece of intelligence of extraordinary magnitude—which had just arrived from the French West Indies. France Spain Portugal Prussia & Poland have concurred in sentiments to recognize the Independence of the United States. I will not say, this is impossible but have advised the printer to preface the Account by such an apology as will save him hereafter from the charge of forgery.[3]

Your determination Dear Marquis to do nothing which may in any degree injure the American Cause is the fruit of a Noble Heart— indeed were you to retire at this Instant unhappy consequences.

8th. April—Notwithstanding what is said above I have detained this Messenger 13 days from day to day hoping the next would produce Commands from Congress, but the Committee to whom your Letter was referred have not yet Reported. Excuse us good Sir. We are indeed deeply engaged in very important & complicated businesses— but in order to remove an anxiety which this long delay must have occasioned I will not keep this back an hour longer. I think you will soon be at Valley Forge—where Baron Stüben is making great improvements & giving much satisfaction to every Body.[4] Will you Sir be so obliging as to inform Major Du Bois that I have duly presented his addresses to Congress, that these are referred to the B. of W.[5] & that the moment I am furnished with subject I will do my self the honor of writing to him?

LbC (ScHi: Henry Laurens Papers).
1. Lafayette to Congress, March 20, read on March 27 (*JCC,* 10:287).

2. Charles Dumas, American agent at The Hague, to the Committee for Foreign Affairs, October 14, 1777 (Laurens probably confused the date of this letter with that of an enclosure dated September 25) (Wharton, *Diplomatic Correspondence*, 2:407–408).

3. See "Extract of a letter from a gentleman in Martinico to his friend in Alexandria, February 21, 1778," *Virginia Gazette* (ed. Alexander Purdie), March 27. The treaty of alliance with France had been signed on February 6, 1778, but news of it did not reach Congress until May 2.

4. Steuben was acting inspector general at this time.

5. De Bois to Congress, March 10 and 11, 1778 (DNA: RG 360, PCC 78, 2:403–410), requesting $1,000 to pay his return to France. See also April 1, 1778, *JCC*, 10:299.

To Henry Laurens

Albany the 28h. march 1778

Dear Sir

Inclos'd I have the honor to send you by Doctor *Treat* the bills of exchange destinated for the Canadian expedition.[1] I expect every day to hear from Congress and whatever will be theyr decision, I schall go to his excellency's camp. My being so much disappointed once has made me rather cautious and I do'nt want to embark myself in any romantic avanture. The command of Fishkill I no more think of because I hear to day it was given *before my letter was receiv'd* to a vorthy, honest, and good officer who by his being a newyorker can do much better than any other.[2] Therefore, sir, the day after to morrow will see me going down even when I schould not have got any answer from Congress. Its tenor will regulate my being or not being an officer in the army, but it schall not prevent my being near my friend and running everywhere honor and glory will call me.

The doctor bearer of this letter I may give an high character to on account of the good order I have found in the hospitals. With the greatest regard I have the honor to be, dear Sir, Your most obedient servant

THE MIS. DE LAFAYETTE

I am told a general exchange is to take place and wish it be for our advantage.[3]

the 30

I have receiv'd to day the answer of Congress and also the order from Gal. Washington to come down,[4] and schall set out to morrow morning.

ALS (ScHi: Henry Laurens Papers), enclosing bills of exchange.

1. See January 28, 1778, *JCC*, 10:96. Laurens acknowledged the receipt of the "6 sets of Bills of Exchange intended for the Canada Irruption" on April 17 (Laurens to Lafayette [ScHi: Henry Laurens Papers]).

2. McDougall.

3. A reference to the resolution of Congress, February 26, 1778, concerning an exchange of prisoners, which Governor Clinton had sent Lafayette on March 25.

4. Congress to Lafayette, and Laurens to Lafayette, March 24; Washington to Lafayette, March 20.

APPENDIX

FRENCH TEXTS

Significant passages omitted from documents published in Lafayette, *Mémoires,* are printed here in angle brackets.

For the provenance and annotation of these texts, the reader should refer to the translated documents.

Si je confondois, comme il arrive trop souvent, L'entêtement avec la fermeté, je Rougirais de commencer ces memoires que j'ai longtems Refusés, et d'ajouter encore à leur egoïsme, par celui du stile, tandis qu'il eut fallu du moins me couvrir du manteau de la troisieme personne; mais je ne serai point complaisant à demi pour ce tendre et precieux interest qui vaut à ma vie les Honneurs ephemeres d'un journal; il me suffit de penser que ce compte Rendu à quelques amis n'ira jamais plus loin; mon ouvrage a même deux grands avantages sur Beaucoup de livres fameux; c'est que n'aïant Rien à demêler avec le public, il ne lui faut point de preface, et que la dedicace du coeur n'a pas Besoin d'epître.

Il seroit trop poëtique de me placer d'abord dans un autre Hemisphere, et trop minutieux de m'appezantir sur les detaïls de ma naissance qui suivit de près la mort de mon pere à Minden, de mon education en Auvergne auprès de parents tendres et venerés, de ma translation à l'age de onze ans dans un college de Paris, ou je perdis Bientôt ma vertueuse mere, et ou la mort de son pere me Rendit Riche de pauvre que j'etois né, de quelques succès d'ecolier animés par l'amour de la gloire et troublés par celui de la liberté, de mon entrée aux mousquetaires noirs qui ne me sortit de classe que pour les jours de Revüe, enfin de mon Mariage à l'age de seize ans, precedé d'un sejour à L'academie de Versaïlles. J'ai encore moins à vous apprendre sur mon entrée dans le monde, La courte faveur d'une jeune societé ou je faisois nombre, quelques voyages au Regiment de Noaïlles, et le jugement defavorable que m'attira mon silence parce que je ne pensois, et n'entendois gueres de choses qui me parussent meriter d'etre dites. Ce mauvais effet de l'amour propre deguisé, et d'un penchant observateur n'etoit pas adouci par la gaucherie de mes manieres, qui, sans etre deplacées dans les grandes circomstances, ne se plierent jamais aux graces de la cour, ni aux agrements d'un souper de la capitale.

⟨Je vous epargne aussi la confession d'une jeunesse peu edifiante, et même l'Histoire de deux Romans dediés à des Beautés alors celebres, ou ma tête eut plus de part que mon coeur; le premier à peine ebauché se Brisa contre les obstacles de la jalousie que je Heurtai de front; l'autre, ou je voulus d'abord triompher, moins de l'object lui même que d'un Rival, parcourut dans la suite, et malgré les Longues interruptions, tous les periodes possibles; depuis l'estime même jusqu'au sentiment contraire, et se termina enfin par une catastrophe etrangere à moi; il me sera plus doux de parler du tendre et solide attachement que je ne cessai d'epprouver pour la femme que j'ai eu le Bonheur d'epouser.⟩

Vous me demandés l'epoque de mes premiers soupirs vers la gloire et la liberté; je ne m'en rappelle aucune dans ma vie qui soit anterieure à mon entousiasme pour les Anecdotes glorieuses, à mes projets de courir le monde pour chercher de la Reputation; dès l'âge de Huit ans, mon coeur Battit pour cette Hyènne qui fit quelque mal et encore plus de Bruit dans notre voisinage, et l'espoir de la Rencontrer Animoit mes promenades; arrivé au College, je ne fus distrait de l'etude que par le desir d'etudier sans contrainte; je ne méritai gueres d'etre châtié, mais, malgré ma tranquillité ordinaire, il eut été dangereux de le tenter, et j'aime à penser que faisant en Rethorique le portrait du cheval parfait, je sacrifiai un succès au plaisir de peindre celui qui en apperçevant la Verge Renversoit son cavalier; les Relations Republicaines me charmoient, et lorsque mes nouveaux parents me menagerent une place à la cour, je ne Balançai pas à deplaire, pour sauver mon independance; c'est dans cette disposition que j'appris les troubles Americains; ils ne furent Bien connus en Europe qu'en 1776, et la memorable declaration de 4 juïllet y parvint vers la fin de la même Année.

Après s'etre couverte de lauriers et enrichie de conquêtes, après avoir maitrisé toutes les mers, insulté toutes les nations, l'Anglettere avoit tourné son orgueïl contre ses propres colonies; depuis longtems l'Amerique du Nord lui faisoit ombrage; elle voulut joindre aux premiers entraves des vexations nouvelles, et envahir les privileges les plus sacrés; les Americains, attachés à la mere patrie, se Bornerent d'abord à des plaintes; ils n'accuserent que les ministres, et toute la nation s'eleva contre eux; ils furent taxés d'insolence, ensuite de Rébellion, et declarés enfin ennemis; de maniere que l'entêtement du Roy, la passion des ministres, et l'arrogance du peuple Anglais forcerent treize de leurs colonies à se Rendre independantes; jamais si Belle cause n'avoit attiré l'attention des Hommes; c'etoit le dernier combat de la liberté, et sa defaite ne lui laissoit ni azile ni esperance. Oppresseurs et opprimés, tout alloit Recevoir une lecon; ce grand ouvrage devoit s'elever, ou les droits de l'Humanité se perdoïent sous ses Ruines; en même tems les destins de la France et ceux de sa Rivale alloïent se decider; l'Anglettere se voyoit enlever avec les nouveaux etats, un grand commerce tout à son Avantage, un quart de ses sujets augmentans sans cesse par une Rapide multiplication, et l'emigration de toutes les parties de L'Europe, enfin plus que la moitié, et la plus Belle portion du territoire Britannique; mais se Reunissoit-elle à ces treize colonies? C'en etoit fait de nos Antilles et de nos possessions d'Affrique et d'Asie, de notre Commerce Maritime, et par consequent de notre marine, enfin de notre existence politique.

A la premiere connoissance de cette querelle, mon coeur fut enrôlé, et je ne songeai qu'à joindre mes drapeaux; quelques circomstances inutiles à Rapporter m'avoient appris à n'attendre sur cet objet, de ma famille, que des obstacles; je comptai donc sur moi, et osai prendre pour devise à mes armes les mots *Cur non?* afin qu'ils me servissent quelquefois d'encouragement et de Reponse; Silas Deane etoit à Paris, mais on craignoit de le voir, et sa voix etoit couverte par les cris du Lord Stormont; il passoit sous main pour l'Amerique de vieïlles armes qui servirent un peu, et de jeunes officiers Reüssirent mal, le tout expedié pour le compte de M. de Beaumarchais, et quand l'ambassadeur d'Anglettere parloit à notre cour, elle nioit les envois, en ordonnoit le dechargement, et chassoit de ses ports les corsaires Americains. Voulant m'addresser directement à M. Deane, je devins ami de Kalbe allemand à notre service, qui cherchoit de l'emploi chés les *insurgents,* suivant l'expression du tems, et me servit d'interprète. C'est celui que M. de Choiseuïl envoïa visiter les colonies anglaises, et qui à son Retour en obtint de l'argeant, mais point d'audience, tant ce ministre pensoit peu à la Revolution dont quelques personnes lui ont attribué l'Honneur Retrograde. En presentant à M. Deane ma figure à peine agée de dix neuf ans, je parlai plus de mon zele que de mon experience; mais je lui fis valoir le petit eclat de mon depart, et il signa l'arrangement; le secret de cette negociation et de mes preparatifs fut vraiment miraculeux. Famille, amis, ministres, espions francais, espions anglais, tout fut aveuglé. Parmi mes discrets confidents, je dois Beaucoup à M. du Boismartin secretaire du Comte de Broglie, et au Comte de Broglie lui même dont le coeur, après de vains efforts pour m'arrêter, me suivit avec une tendresse paternelle.

On s'occupoit d'expedier un vasisseau lorsqu'il arriva de funestes nouvelles; Newyork, Longisland, les White Plains, le Fort Washington et les Jersays avoïent vu les forces Americaines s'aneantir successivement devant trente trois mille anglais ou allemands; trois mille Hommes Restoïent seuls en armes, et le general Howe les poursuivoit; dès ce moment le credit insurgent s'eteignit; l'envoi d'un Bâtiment devint impossible; les envoïés eux mêmes crurent devoir me temoigner leur decouragement, et me detourner de mon projet; j'allai chés Mr. Deane, et le Remerciant de sa franchise, jusqu'ici, "monsieur", ajoutai-je, "vous n'avés vu que mon zele; il va peutêtre devenir utile; j'achete un Bâtiment qui portera vos officiers; il faut montrer de la confiance, et c'est dans le danger que j'aime à partager votre fortune"; mon projet fut Bien Receu; mais il falloit ensuite trouver de l'argeant, acheter et armer secretement un navire, et tout fut executé avec promptitude.

Nous touchions cependant à l'epoque d'un voyage en Anglettere projetté depuis longtems; je ne pouvois le Refuser sans compromettre mon secret, et en l'acceptant, je couvrois mes preparatifs; ce dernier parti convenoit surtout à MM. Franklin et Deane, car le docteur etoit en France, et quoique je n'allasse pas chés lui, de peur d'y etre Rencontré, nous correspondions par l'entremise de Mr. Carmichaël americain moins connu. J'arrivai donc à Londres avec le Prince de Poix, et vis d'abord l'americain Bancroft, et ensuite Sa Majesté Britannique. A dix neuf ans, on aime peutêtre trop à persifler le tyran qu'on va combattre, à danser chés Lord Germaine, le ministre americain, avec Lord Rawdon qui arrivoit de Newyork, et à Rencontrer à l'Opera ce Clinton que je devois Retrouver à Montmouth; mais en taisant mes intentions, j'affichois mes sentiments; souvent je defendis les Americains, je me Rejouïs de leur succès à Trenton, et mon esprit d'opposition me valut un dejeuner du Lord Shelburne; ⟨sans fermer l'oreïlle aux indiscretions,⟩ je Rejettai l'offre de voir les ports de mer, les embarquements contre les *Rebelles,* et tout ce qui me parut un abus de confiance. C'est au bout de trois semaines, lorsqu'il fallut partir, que refusant à l'ambassadeur mon oncle de le suivre à la cour, je lui confiai la fantasie d'une course à Paris. Il imagina de me dire malade jusqu'à mon retour; je n'aurais pas proposé ce stratageme, mais je ne m'y opposai pas.

Après de cruelles souffrances dans le detroit dont on me consolait par l'idée de leur courte durée, j'arrivai à Paris chez M. de Kalb, me couchai trois jours à Chaïllot, y vis les Americains et quelques amis, et partis pour Bordeaux ou quelques retards inattendus m'arreterent encore; j'en profitai pour envoyer à Paris, d'ou les nouvelles ne furent pas encourageantes. Mais comme mon courrier etait suivi par celui du gouvernement, il n'y avait pas un moment à perdre pour mettre à la voile et les ordres souverains ne purent me joindre qu'au Passage, port espagnol où l'on devait relacher. Les lettres de ma famille furent terribles, et la lettre de cachet peremptoire: "Defense d'aller au continent américain sous peine de desobeissance, injonction d'aller à Marseïlles attendre de nouveaux ordres." Les consequences de l'anathême, les lois de l'etat, la puïssance et la colere du gouvernement ne manquoïent pas de commentaires. Mais la douleur et la grossesse d'une femme cherie, l'idée de ses parents et de ses amis, avoïent plus de pouvoir sur M. de Lafayette. Son vaisseau ne pouvant plus etre arrêté, il Revint à Bordeaux justifier son entreprise, et par une declaration à M. de Fumel il prit sur-lui seul les suites d'une evasion. La cour ne daignant pas se Relâcher, il ecrivit à M. de Maurepas que ce silence etoit un ordre tacite, et cette plaisanterie fut suivie de son depart. Après avoir prit la Route de Marseïlles [il] Revint sur ses pas, et travesti en courier il avoit presque franchi les dangers, lorsqu'à St. Jean de Luz, une jeune fille le Reconnut. Mais un signe la fit taire, et son adroite fidelité detourna les poursuites. C'est ainsi que M. de Lafayette Rejoignit son Bâtiment le 26 Avril 1777, et le même jour, après six mois de travaux et d'impatience, il mit à la voile pour le Continent Americain.

A peine l'effet de la mer diminua-t-il, que M. de Lafayette etudia la langue et le metier qu'il adoptoit. Un lourd Bâtiment, deux mauvais canons, et quelques fusils, n'eussent pas echappé au moindre corsaire. Dans la position de M. de Lafayette, il Resolut de sauter plutôt que de se Rendre; les mesures furent prises avec un Brave Hollandois, nommé Bedaulx, dont la potence etait la sûre alternative. Le Capitaine insista sur une Relâche aux isles, mais on y eut trouvé des lettres de Cachet, et moins de gré que de force on lui fit suivre une Route directe. A 40 Lieues des côtes on fut atteint par un petit Bâtiment. Le Capitaine pâlit, mais l'equipage aimoit M. de Lafayette, les officiers etoïent nombreux; et l'on fit une montre de defense. Par Bonheur c'étoient des Americains, qu'on tâcha vainement d'accompagner. A peine furent-ils perdus de vüe, qu'ils trouverent deux fregattes anglaises, et ce n'est pas la seule fois que pour sauver M. de Lafayette, les elements s'obstinerent à le contrarier. Après sept semaines de Hazards, il eut celui d'arriver en Caroline et de Mouïller devant Georgetown. Remontant en canot la Riviere, il sentit enfin le sol Americain, et son premier mot fut un serment de vaincre ou perir avec cette cause. Debarqué à minuit chés un Major Huger, il y trouva une occasion pour France qui sembloit n'attendre que ses lettres. Plusieurs officiers vinrent à terre, d'autres Resterent à Bord, et tous s'empresserent de gagner Charlestown.

Cette charmante ville est digne de ses Habitants, et tout y annonçoit l'aisance et la delicatesse. Sans trop connoitre M. de Lafayette, le Gouverneur Rutledge, les generaux Howe, Moultrie, et Gasden, s'empresserent à le Bien Recevoir. On lui montra les Nouveaux ouvrages, et cette Batterie que Moultrie defendit si Bien, mais ou les anglais, il faut en convenir, semblent avoir saisi le seul moyen d'echoüer. Beaucoup d'avanturiers, Rebut des isles, voulurent en vain se lier à M. de Lafayette et lui inspirer leurs preventions. Après s'etre procuré des chevaux, il partit avec six officiers pour Philadelphie. Son Bâtiment etoit arrivé, mais ce ne fut plus la même fortune, et lorsqu'il resortoit, il perit sur la Barre de Charlestown. Pour se Rendre au Congrès des Etats Unis, M. de Lafayette fit sur ses chevaux près de neuf cent milles; et c'est par les deux Carolines, la Virginie, les etats de Maryland et Delawar qu'il parvint à la Capitale de Pennsylvanie. En etudiant la langue et les Habitants, il voyoit aussi des productions et des cultures Nouvelles. Les vastes forêts, les fleuves immenses, tout, dans ce païs, pare la nature d'un air de jeunesse et de majesté. Après un mois de Route assés penible, il vit cette Philadelphie maintenant si connüe, et dont, en posant la premiere pierre, Penn sembloit marquer la grandeur future.

Après les Belles Maneuvres de Trenton et Princetown le Gal. Washington etoit Resté dans son camp de Middle Brook. Frustrés dans leur premier espoir, les anglais combinerent une campagne decisive. Dejà Burgoïgne Avançoit avec dix mille Hommes, et les faisoit preceder par ses sauvages et ses proclamations. Tyconderago, fameuse place d'armes fut abandonnée par St. Clair; il se chargea de la Haine publique, mais il sauva le seul corps auquel pouvoient se Rallier les milices. Pendant qu'on les Rassembloit, le Congrès Rappella ses Generaux, les Remplaça par Gates, et força de moyens pour le soutenir. Dans le même tems, la grande Armée Anglaise, dix Huit mille Hommes environ, avoïent fait voile de Newyork, et les deux Howes se Reunissoïent pour une operation secrete. Rhode Island etoit occupé par un corps ennemi, et le Gal. Clinton Resté à Newyork, y preparoit Une expedition. Pour parer à tant de coups, le Gal. Washington Laissant Putnam sur la Riviere du Nord, passa la Delawar avec onze mille Hommes et vint camper à portée de Philadelphie.

C'est dans ces circomstances qu'arriva M. de Lafayette; Mais quoiqu'interessantes pour la Cause, elles etoïent peu favorables aux etrangers. Degoutés par la conduite de plusieurs français, les Americains étoïent Revoltés de leurs pretentions. L'impudence des avanturiers, la Honte des premiers choix, les jalousies de l'armée, les prejugés Nationaux, tout servoit à confondre le zele avec l'interest, les talents avec la charlatannerie. Appüiée sur les promesses de M. Deane, une foule Nombreuse assiegeoit le Congrès, et leur chef etoit M. du Coudray, esprit adroit mais Broüillon, Bon officier, mais vain jusqu'à la folie. Avec M. de Lafayette, Deane envoyoit un autre detachement, et tous les jours il en arrivoit tant, qu'on finissoit par n'ecouter personne. La froideur du premier accueïl avoit tout l'air d'un congé, mais sans etre deconcerté par les deputés qui lui parloient, M. de Lafayette les pria de Rentrer au Congrès et d'y lire le Billet suivant "d'après mes sacrifices, j'aï le droit d'exiger deux graces: l'une est de servir à mes depends, l'autre est de commencer à servir comme volontaire." Un stile aussi nouveau Reveïlla l'attention, on s'occupa des depêches des envoïés, et par une Resolution très flatteuse, M. de Lafayette fut nommé Major General. Parmi les officiers qu'il avoit mené, plusieurs lui etoïent totalement etrangers. Il s'interessa cependant à tous, et ceux qui ne furent pas Receus obtinrent des Gratifications. Quelques mois après, Mr. du Coudray se noïa dans le Schuïllkill, et la perte de cet esprit Brouillon fut peut-être un Heureux Accident.

Les deux Howes ayant paru vers les Caps Delawar, le Gal. Washington vint à Philadelphie, et M. de Lafayette y vit pour la premiere fois ce grand Homme. Quoiqu'entouré d'officiers et de citoïens, la Majesté de sa figure et de sa taïlle ne permettoit pas de le meconnoitre. Un Accueïl affable et noble ne le distinguoit pas moins, et M. de Lafayette le suivit dans ses Reconnoissances. Invité par le General à s'etablir dans sa Maison, il la Regarda dès ce jour comme la sienne, et c'est avec cette simplicité que s'unirent deux amis dont les plus grands interets cimenterent l'attachement et la confiance.

A quelques milles de Philadelphie, l'armée attendoit que les mouvemens ennemis fussent decidés. Le Général en fit la Revüe, et M. de Lafayette y arriva le même jour. Onze mille Hommes environ, mediocrement armés, plus mal vêtus encore, offroïent un spectacle singulier. Dans cet état de Bigarrure, et souvent de nudité, les meïlleurs Vêtements etoïent *des chemises de chasse,* larges vestes de toile grise usitées en Caroline. Quant à la tactique, il suffit de dire, que pour qu'un Regiment en Bataïlle de pied ferme gagnat du terrain sur la droite de son alignement, au lieu de Rompre simplement à droite, la gauche commençoit une eternelle contremarche. Toujours sur deux Rangs, les petits Hommes au premier; l'on n'a jamais observé les Rangs de taïlle. Malgré ces desavantages, on voyoit de Beaux soldats, conduits par des officiers zelés. La vertu tenoit lieu de science, et chaque jour ajoutoit à l'experience et à la discipline. Le Lord Stirling plus Brave que judicieux, un Gal. ⟨Stevens⟩ toujours ivre, Greene dont les talens n'etoïent encore connus que de ses amis, commandoïent en qualité de Majors Generaux. Le General Knox y etoit aussi qui dans le même tems s'etoit fait de libraire, artilleur, avoit formé d'autres officiers, et creoit une artillerie. "Nous devons etre embarassés," dit le Gal. Washington en arrivant, "de nous montrer à un officier qui quitte les troupes francaises." "C'est pour apprendre et non pour enseigner que je suis ici," Repondit M. de Lafayette, et ce ton Reussit parce qu'il n'etoit pas commun aux europeens.

Après avoir menacé la Delawar, la flotte Anglaise avoit encore disparu; pendant plusieurs jours, elle fut l'objet des plaisanteries. Son arrivée dans la Chesapeake les termina, et pour se Rapprocher du debarquement, L'armée patriotique traversa la ville. La tête ornée de Branches vertes, au son des tambours et des fifres, aux yeux de tous les citoïens, ces soldats, malgré leur nudité, offroïent un agreable spectacle. Le general Brilloit à leur tête, et M. de Lafayette etoit à ses cotés. L'armée se porta sur les Hauteurs de Wilmington, et celle des ennemis, debarqua dans Elk River, au fond de la Baïe de Chesapeake. Le jour même qu'elle mit à terre, le General Washington s'exposa très imprudemment; après une longue Reconnoissance, il fut assailli d'un orage, dans une nuit très noire. Entré dans une ferme, fort près des ennemis, sa Repugnance à changer d'avis l'y Retint avec le Gal. Greene et M. de Lafayette. Mais en partant au point de jour, il avoua que le moindre traitre aurait pu le perdre. Quelques jours après, la division de Sullivan joignit l'armée, et al porta treize mille Hommes. Ce Major general⟨, plein de vanité, mais qui ne manquoit pas de talent,⟩ avoit Bien commencé, mais mal fini une espèce de surprise sur Staten Island.

Si dans un plan d'attaque trop etendu, les Anglais commirent de grandes fautes, il faut avoüer que la defense Americaine ne fut pas irreprochable. En se fourrant tête Baissée dans les Bois dont il ne put se degager, Burgoïgne trainoit sur un chemin unique, et ses nombreux cannons, et ses Riches équipages. Sûrs de n'etre pas tournés, les Americains disputoïent tous les pas. Ce genre de guerre attiroit les milices, et Gates se Renforçoit tous les jours. Chaque arbre couvroit un tireur adroit, et les Ressources de la tactique, les talents même des chefs devinrent inutiles. Le corps laissé à Newyork pouvoit, il est vrai, mepriser celui de Putnam, mais trop foible pour aller secourir Burgoïgne, il dependoit dès lors de ses succès au lieu de les assurer. Pendant ce tems, Howe ne songeoit qu'à Philadelphie, et c'est au depends des operations du Nord qu'il la cherchoit par un detour immense. Mais, d'un autre coté, pourquoi le debarquement des anglais fut-il aussi tranquille? Pourquoi, manqua-t-on le moment ou la Riviere d'Elk divisoit leur armée? Pourquoi vit-on dans le sud des tâtonnements, et des inconsequences? C'est que jusqu'à lors les Americains avoïent eu des combats, et non des Batailles. C'est qu'au lieu d'Harrasser une armée, de disputer des gorges, il fallut proteger une capitale ouverte, maneuvrer en plaine, près d'un ennemi qui en les tournant pouvait les perdre. S'il eut suivi l'avis du peuple, le Gal. Washington auroit enfermé dans la ville, et son armée, et les destinées Americaines. Mais en evitant cette folie, il falloit qu'une Bataille dedomagea la Nation; l'Europe même l'attendoit, et quoique créé dictateur pour six mois, le general crut devoir tout soumettre aux ordres du Congrès, aux deliberations des Conseils de guerre.

Après s'etre avancé a *Wilmington,* le général avoit detaché mille Hommes sous *Maxwell* le plus ancien⟨, mais le plus inepte⟩ Brigadier de l'armée. A la premiere marche des Anglais, il fut Battu près de *Christian Bridge* par leur Avant Garde, et pendant ce tems l'armée prenoit à *New Town* une Mediocre position. On y Remua un peu de terre, on y attendit deux jours les ennemis, et dans l'instant ou ils marcherent vers notre droite, un conseil de guerre nocturne porta l'armée sur ⟨les Hauteurs de⟩ *Brandiwine.* Le Ruisseau de ce nom couvroit son front, et le gué de *Chads Ford* placé vers le centre, etoit defendu par des Batteries. C'est dans cette position mal Reconnüe que, d'après une lettre du Congrès on attendit la Bataille. Le 10 7bre au soir, *Howe* S'avança sur deux colonnes, et par un Beau Mouvement, celle de gauche, (8000 Hommes environ sous Lord *Cornwallis* avec les grenadiers et les gardes) se dirigea vers les gués de *Bermingham* placé à trois milles sur notre droite. L'autre colonne continua son chemin et vers neuf Heures du matin, elle parut de l'autre coté du Ruisseau. La liziere du Bois en etoit si près, que la force des ennemis ne pouvoit s'y juger, et le tems se perdit dans une canonnade Reciproque. Le Gal. *Washington* se promenoit le long de ses deux lignes, et y etoit Receu avec ces acclamations qui devroïent annoncer un succès. On eut des avis sur le mouvement de *Cornwallis,* mais ils etoïent confus et contradictoires. Par la conformité de nom entre deux chemins egaux et paralelles, les meïlleurs officiers se tromperent dans leurs Rapports. Les seuls coup de fusil tirés l'avoïent été par Maxwell qui tua du monde aux ennemis, mais fut Repoussé en dejà d'un gué sur notre gauche qu'il avoit passé. Trois mille miliciens ajoutés à l'armée en gardoient de plus eloignés, mais ne prirent point part à l'action. Telle etoit notre situation lorsqu'on scut clairement la marche de Lord Cornwallis vers les gués mal connus de *Bermingham*. Alors on detacha trois divisions, formant environ 5000 Hommes, sous les generaux Sullivan, Stirling, et Stevens. En sa qualité de volontaire, M. de Lafayette avoit toujours accompagné le General; mais la gauche etant tranquille, et les grands coups devant se porter sur la droite, il obtint permission de joindre Sullivan. A son arrivée qui parut agreable aux troupes, il trouva que les ennemis aïant passé le gué, le corps de Sullivan avoit à peine eu le tems de se former sur une ligne en avant d'un Bois clair, et peu d'instants après My Lord Cornwallis deboucha dans le plus Bel ordre. En s'avançant à travers la plaine, sa premiere ligne fit un feu très vif de canon et de Mousqueterie; celui des Americains fut meutrier, mais toute leur droite, et toute leur gauche aïant plié, les generaux, et plusieurs officiers se Reunirent à la division centrale ou etoit M. de Lafayette avec Stirling, et dont 800 Hommes etoient Brillament commandés par Mr. de Conway irlandois au service de France. En debordant cette division de leurs deux ailes, et s'avançant par un terrain ouvert ou ils perdirent Beaucoup, les ennemis Reunissoïent tout leur feu sur le centre. La confusion devint extrême, et c'est en Ralliant les troupes que M. de Lafayette eut la jambe traversée d'une Balle. A cette epoque, tout ce qui Restoit plia, et M. de Lafayette dut à Gimat son aide de camp le Bonheur de Remonter à cheval. Le Gal. Washington arrivoit de loin avec des troupes fraiches, et M. de Lafayette alloit le joindre, lorsque la perte de son sang l'arrêta pour Bander sa Blessure. Encore manqua-t-il etre pris, et les fuïards, les canons, les equipages se jeterent pêle mêle dans le chemin de *Chester*. Ce qui Restoit de jour fut emploïé par le general à Retarder les ennemis; quelques Regiments firent Bien, mais la deroute devint complete. Pendant ce tems, le gué de *Chads* etoit forcé, le canon pris, et le chemin de *Chester* devint la Retraite commune à toute l'armée. Au milieu de cette Horrible confusion, et des tenebres de la nuit, il etoit impossible de se Reconnoitre. Mais à *Chester* douze milles du champ de Bataïlle, on trouva un pont qu'il falloit Bien passer et M. de Lafayette s'occupa d'y arrêter les fuÿards. Il s'y Retablit un peu d'ordre, les generaux, et le commandant en chef arriverent, et M. de Lafayette eut enfin le loisir de se faire panser. C'est à 26 milles de Philadelphie que le sort de la ville s'etoit decidé; chaque coup de canon y etoit entendu, et les deux partis separés en deux Bandes dans les places et tous les endroits publics, attendoïent en silence l'evenement. Enfin un dernier courrier arriva, et les amis de la liberté furent consternés. La perte des Americains fut de mille à douze cent Hommes. Il y en avoit quinze mille environs dans l'armée d'Howe, et leur perte fut si considerable que leurs chirurgiens et ceux des campagnes etant insuffisants, il nous en demanderent pour les prisonniers. Si les ennemis eussent marché à Derby, l'armée etoit coupée et detruite; ils perdirent une nuit precieuse, et c'est peutêtre la plus grande faute d'une guerre ou ils en ont Beaucoup commis.

Transporté par eau à Philadelphie, M. de Lafayette y fut entouré de citoïens qu'interessoïent sa jeunesse et sa situation. Le même soir, le depart du

Congrès fut decidé; une multitude d'Habitants quitta ses foïers; les familles entieres abandonnant tout, et ne comptant plus sur Rien, se Refugioient vers les Montagnes. Un Bateau porta M. de Lafayette à Bristol; il y Revit le Congrès fugitif qui ne se Rassembla que derriere la Susquehana; et lui même fut conduit à Bethleem, etablissement morave, où la douce Relligion de ce peuple de frères, la communauté de Biens, d'education, et d'interets dans cette grande et innocente famille, contrastoient avec les scenes de Carnage, et les Convulsions de la guerre civile.

Après la deroute de Brandiwine, les deux armées maneuvrerent le long du Schuïlkill; le Gal. Washington se tint toujours au dessus des ennemis, Hors de leur portée, et l'occasion de le couper ne se Retrouva plus. Waïne Brigadier Americain fut detaché pour observer les Anglais; mais surpris dans la nuit près le *White Horse* par le Gal. Grey, il y perdit une grande partie de son Corps. Enfin Howe passa le *Schuïlkill* à *Swedes Ford,* et Lord Cornwallis entra dans *Philadelphie.*

Malgré l'independance des nouveaux etats, tout portoit alors l'empreinte d'une guerre civile. Les noms de *Whigg* et *tory* distinguoient les Republicains et les Royalistes; l'armée Anglaise s'appelloit encore *troupes Reglées:* en nommant le *Roy,* l'on entendoit le souverain Britannique. La fureur des partis divisoit les provinces, les villes, les familles; on a vu des freres officiers dans les deux armées, se Rencontrant dans la maison paternelle, sauter à leurs armes pour se combattre. Tandis que dans leur orgueïlleuse Rage les Anglais se livroïent à toutes les Horreurs de la licence et de la cruauté; tandis que la discipline trainoit à leur suite ces Allemands vendus qui ne savoïent que tuer, piller, et Brûler des maisons; on voïoit dans la même armée des Regiments Americains qui foulant aux pieds leurs freres, asservissoïent leur patrie devastée. Chaque Canton en Renfermoit un Bien plus grand nombre, dont l'unique objet etoit de nuire aux amis de la liberté, d'avertir ceux du despotisme. A ces torys inveterés, il faut joindre tous ceux que la crainte, l'interest, ou leur Relligion eloignoit de la guerre. Si les presbiteriens enfants de Cromwell et Fairfax Haïssoient la Royauté, les Anglicans qu'elle forma etoïent plus divisés. Les quakers ⟨, jesuites plebeïens,⟩ abhorroïent le carnage mais y servoient de guides aux troupes Royales. Les insurrections n'etoïent pas Rares; près des postes ennemis, les fermiers se fusilloïent, et les voleurs même etoïent encouragés. En voyageant dans le païs les chefs *Rebelles* couroïent des Risques; on s'annoncoit dans une maison pour loger dans une autre; on s'y Barricadoit, et l'on ne s'endormoit qu'environné d'armes. Au milieu de ces troubles, M. de Lafayette n'etoit dejà plus un etranger; jamais adoption ne fut si complete, et tandis que dans les Conseïls de guerre, il fremissoit de penser que sa voix de vingt ans pouvoit decider le sort des deux mondes, il etoit egalement initié dans ces deliberations ou Rassurant les Whigs, intimidant les torys, soutenant une monnoïe ideale, Redoublant de fermeté dans le malheur, les chefs de la Revolution la conduisoïent à travers tant d'obstacles.

Renfermé dans son lit pour six semaines, M. de Lafayette y souffrit de sa Blessure, et plus encore de son inaction. Les Bons frères moraves l'aimoïent, et gemissoïent de sa folie guerriere; c'est en ecoutant leurs sermons qu'il projettoit d'embraser l'Europe et l'Asie. Ne pouvant plus qu'ecrire, il ecrivit au commandant de la Martinique, et lui proposa, sous pavillon Americain, un coup de main sur les isles Anglaises. Il ecrivit à M. de Maurepas, et s'offrit à conduire des Americains à l'Isle de France, où il eut concerté avec des particuliers l'attaque des comptoirs anglais. D'aprés ce qu'on a su depuis, le projet de l'Inde eut Reussi; mais il fut Rejetté à Versaïlles, et l'on ne Repondoit pas alors à M. de Lafayette. Bouïllé, plus ardent, adopta tout, mais il fallut une permission, et ces lenteurs conduisirent à l'epoque de la guerre que M. de Lafayette souhaittoit ammener. Pendant son sejour à *Bethleem,* les Anglais se Retranchoïent à *Philadelphie,* et les deux Rivieres qui embrassent la ville etoïent jointes par une chaine d'abbatis et de Bonnes Redoutes couvertes en partie par une inondation. A *German Town* cinq milles en avant de leurs lignes, campoit une portion de leur armée; elle fut attaquée le 4 octobre par le General Washington, et quoique sa colonne de gauche fut Retardée par une Ridicule preseance de divisions, egarée par un Brouïllard epais, quoique l'avant garde de la droite, sous Conway, attaqua de front ce qu'elle devait prendre en flanc, les ennemis ne furent pas moins surpris, Battus, et le General avec son aile victorieuse traversa le camp tout tendu des Anglais. Tout alloït Bien jusques là, mais le faux mouvement de la colonne gauche, et plus encore l'attaque d'une maison de pierre qu'il eut fallu tourner, donnerent aux ennemis le tems de se Rallier; Howe songeoit à la Retraite, mais Cornwallis accourut avec un Renfort. Les Americains Repasserent à travers le Camp Anglais, et l'action finit par leur defaite generale. On perdit Beaucoup des deux cotés; les generaux Agnew anglais, et Nash américain furent tués. Ceux-ci avoïent quelques dragons sous Pulawsky, confederé polonais, qui seul avoit Refusé sa grace, intrepide et vertueux chevalier, devot et libertin, meïlleur capitaine que general, il vouloit etre polonais partout, et M. de Lafayette, après avoir contribué à sa Reception, travaïlloit souvent à ses Raccomodements.

N'attendant pas que sa Blessure fût fermée, M. de Lafayette avoit joint le quartier general à 25 milles de Philadelphie. Repliés dans leurs lignes, les ennemis attaquoïent les forts *Mifflin* sur une isle, et *Red Bank* sur la Rive gauche de la Delaware. Des chevaux de frise protegés par ces forts et quelques galeres arretoïent la flotte, les Magazins, et les detachements Renvoïés de la Cheseapeake. Parmi les Rencontres de petits partis, on distingua la surprise d'un corps de milices au *Crooked Billet* ou les anglais Brûlerent les Blessés dans une grange. Telle etoit la situation du Sud, lorsqu'on y apprit la Capitulation de Burgoïgne.

En quittant le Canada, ce general avoit esperé une division sur sa droite; mais St. Leger echoua devant le fort *Schuyller,* et lui même en s'avançant vers Albany paroit avoir perdu Bien du tems; à ses troupes Continentales, Gates joignoit de Nombreuses milices; tout citoïen etant armé, et milicien, un signal d'alarme les Rassembloit, ou Bien un ordre de l'etat les faisoit Marcher. Mais si cette croizade etoit un peu Volontaire, le sejour au camp l'etoit encore plus, et leur discipline Repondoit à leur formation. Les continentaux au contraire appartenoïent au treize etats, dont chacun fournissoit des Regiments; les soldats y etoïent engagés pour la guerre, ou pour trois ans, seconde alternative vicieuse, mais qu'exigea la jalousie Republicaine. Ces troupes Reglées avoïent

une ordonnance militaire, une discipline assés dure, et les officiers de chaque
etat Rouloïent ensemble pour l'avancement; dans une position Retranchée, au
milieu des Bois, la droite à la Rivière du Nord et sur le chemin d'Albany,
Gates Reunissoit seize mille Hommes, et cette invasion, en menaçant la Nouvelle Anglettere, avoit appellé ses Braves milices. Dejà elles s'etoïent essaïées à
Bennington, ou Stark avoit entouré et detruit un detachement de Burgoïgne.
Parvenus à trois milles de Gates, et ne pouvant le tourner sans abandonner
equipages et canons, les ennemis tenterent deux fois de le forcer. Mais à
peine marchoïent-ils, qu'Arnold etoit sur eux avec sa division, et dans ces Bois
farcis de tireurs, ils ne purent arriver jusqu'aux Retranchements. A la seconde
affaire, Arnold eut la jambe fracassée; Lincoln, l'autre Major General, fut
egalement Blessé. Quatre mille Hommes embarqués à Newyork avoïent, il est
vrai, Remonté L'Hudson, et tandisque Vaughan Brûloit inutilement *Osopus,*
Clinton avoit pris tous les forts qui defendoïent la Riviere. Ils furent peu
gênés par le vieux Putnam, lui qui dans les premiers troubles avoit detellé sa
charüe pour porter à l'armée plus de zele que de talents; mais cette diversion
etoit trop foible, et dans un Billet qu'un espion surpris Avala, mais qu'une
doze d'emetique lui fit Rendre, on voit que Clinton Reconnoit son insuffisance. Abandonné des sauvages, Regrettant ses meïlleurs soldats et Frazer
son meïlleur General, Reduit à cinq mille Hommes qui manquoïent de vivres,
Burgoïgne voulut, mais trop tard, se Retirer; sa communication n'etoit plus
libre, et c'est à Saratoga, quelques milles en arriere de son camp, qu'il signa la
fameuse Convention. Une Brillante troupe dorée sortit avec Burgoïgne; ils
Rencontrerent Gates et ses officiers tous vetus de gris; aprés un Repas frugal,
les deux Generaux virent defiler l'armée vaincüe, et suivant l'assertion d'un
membre du parlement, *cinq mille Hommes traverserent le païs Rebelle pour prendre
leurs quartiers d'Hiver auprès de Boston.* Alors Clinton Redescendit à *Newyork,* et
les milices Retournerent dans leurs foïers. Le merite de Gates consiste dans le
choix d'une position; le malheur de Burgoïgne dans la nature d'un païs presque desert et impraticable. Si les ennemis du premier, critiquerent les termes
de la convention, M. de Lafayette s'empressa de celebrer sa gloire. Mais il le
Blama, de s'etre Rendu independant de son general, de Retenir ensuite les
troupes qu'il devoit lui envoïer. Pour les Ravoir, on fut obligé de depêcher
Hamilton, aide de camp intime du general, jeune Homme plein d'esprit et de
talents, dont les conseïls avoïent une grande et juste preponderance.

Les forts de la *Delawar* tenoïent toujours, et celui de *Red Bank* avec quatre
cent Hommes fut attaqué l'epée à la main par seize cent Hessois. L'ouvrage
aïant été Reduit par Mauduit jeune français, les ennemis s'engagerent entre
l'ancien et le Nouveau Retranchement. Ils y furent Repoussés en perdant 700
Hommes, et le Comte d'Onop leur chef, dont le dernier mot fut: *je meurs vic-
time de mon Ambition et de L'avarice de mon souverain.* Ce fort etoit commandé
par un vieux et Respectable Colonel Greene, qui trois ans après fut massacré
par des Anglais auxquels il s'etoit Rendu, tandis que, le couvrant de son
corps, un fidele negre perit Heroïquement. Le fort *Mifflin,* battu par terre et
par eau, ne se defendoit pas moins; dejà *L'Augusta* vaisseau de ligne Anglais
avoit sauté; une fregatte y perit aussi, et le Colonel Smith ne pensoit pas à se
Rendre. Mais l'isle fut tournée par un passage inconnu, et l'ouvrage etant pris

à Revers on fut obligé de l'evacüer. Lord Cornwallis et cinq mille Hommes s'etant portés dans les *Jersays,* il fallut aussi quitter *Red Bank* qu'on fit sauter, et le Gal. Greene passant la Rivière à Trenton fut opposé à nombre egal au detachement de Cornwallis.

Quoique sa Blessure fut encore assés ouverte pour ne pas mettre de Botte, M. de Lafayette accompagna Greene jusqu'à *Mount Holly,* et se detachant pour Reconnoitre, il trouva les ennemis le 25 9bre. à Glocester vis à vis Philadelphie. Le produit de leur fourrage passoit la Riviere, et pour s'en assurer M. de Lafayette s'avança sur la langue de terre de Sandy Point. Imprudence qui lui auroit couté cher, si ceux qui pouvoïent le tüer, n'eussent trop compté sur les dragons qui auroïent du le prendre. Après avoir un peu calmé l'emotion de ses guides, il se trouva vers quatre Heures à deux milles du camp Anglais vis à vis un poste de 400 Hessois avec du canon. N'aïant avec lui que trois cent cinquante Hommes la plupart militiens, il attaqua Brusquement les ennemis qui plierent; Lord Cornwallis s'y postant avec ses grenadiers, crut dans ces Bois avoir affaire au corps de Greene, et se laissa pousser jusqu'auprès de Glocester avec perte d'une soixantaine d'Hommes. Greene arriva dans la nuit, mais il ne voulut pas attaquer, et Lord Cornwallis aïant passé la Riviere, le detachement Americain Rejoignit l'armée dans sa Position de *White Marsh* à douze milles de Philadelphie. Depuis un mois elle y occupoit d'excellentes Hauteurs, et le juste coup d'oeüil du General avoit deviné ce camp à travers un Bois presque impenetrable.

Le petit succès de *Glocester* plut à l'armée et surtout aux milices; il fut Resolu par le Congres, *qu'il leur seroit extremement Agreable de voir le marquis de Lafayette à la tête d'une division.* Changeant alors son etat de volontaire, il Remplaça ⟨le vieux Buveur⟩ Stevens dans le commandement des virginiens. La jonction de Cornwallis etant l'ouvrage de quelques Heures, et celle de Greene Exigeant plusieurs Marches, on ne sait pourquoi le Gal. Howe lui donna le tems d'arriver, et ne porta son armée que le 5 decembre à *Chesnut Hill* trois milles de *White Marsh.* Après avoir tâté la droite qui lui en imposa, il menaça l'extremité gauche, et cette aile suivant Son mouvement, se prolongea sur le Retour des Hauteurs. Il y eut quelques coups tirés entre les chasseurs Anglais et les *Riflemen* Carabiniers fort adroits, Habitants des frontieres sauvages. Ne pouvant attaquer cette position, et ne voulant pas la tourner franchement, Howe Revint le quatrieme jour à Philadelphie. Malgré les Renforts du Nord, les Americains etoïent Reduits à neuf mille, et l'arriere saison acceleroit leur deperissement. La protection du païs couta cher à l'armée, et le 15 decembre enfin ou marcha vers Swed's Ford, ou, par Hazard Lord Cornwallis fourrageoït sur l'autre Rive. M. de Lafayette etant de jour, il Reconnoissoit une position, quand son escorte et les ennemis se fusillerent. L'incertitude etant mutuelle, Lord Cornwallis et le Gal. Washington suspendirent leur marche, et le premier s'etant Retiré pendant la nuit, l'armée passa le Schuïlkill et se Retrancha dans la position de Valley Forge à vingt deux milles de Philadelphie. C'est là que disposant avec art les troncs de petits arbres, on vit s'elever en peu de jours une ville de Bois, et toute l'armée s'y arrangea de tristes quartiers d'Hiver. Un petit corps fut detaché à Wilmington, et s'y fortifia sous les ordres du Brigr. Smallwood.

Malgré les succès du Nord, la situation des Americains ne fut jamais si critique. Un papier monnoïe, sans fondement solide, sans aucun mélange d'especes, etoit Contrefait par les ennemis, discredité par leurs partisans. On craignoit d'etablir des taxes, on Pouvoit encore moins les lever; Revolté contre les impôts Anglais, le peuple s'etonnoit d'en païer de plus chers, et la force manquoit aux gouvernements. D'un autre Coté Newyork et Philadelphie Regorgoïent d'or et de marchandises; la menace de mort n'arrêtoit point une communication trop facile. En Refusant les taxes, depreciant le papier, nourrissant l'ennemi, on arrivoit surement à la fortune; les privations et la misere ne tomboïent que sur les Bons Citoïens; chaque proclamation Anglaise etoit soutenüe par leurs seductions, leurs Richesses, et l'intrigue des Torys. Tandis qu'à Newyork une Nombreuse Garnison vivoit somptueusement, quelques centaines d'Hommes mal vêtus, mal Nourris erroïent sur les Bords de l'Hudson. Nouvellement Recrutée d'Europe, Abondament fournie de tout, l'armée de Philadelphie Comptoit dix Huit mille Hommes; celle de Valley Forge fut successivement Reduite à cinq milles, et deux marches sur le Beau chemin de *Lancaster* ou etoïent la chaine des magazins, en etablissant les Anglais en arriere de notre flanc droit, eussent Rendu intenable notre position, dont cependant on n'avoit aucun moyen de sortir. Habits, chapeaux, chemises, souliers, tout manquoit aux malheureux soldats; leurs pieds et leurs jambes Noircissoïent en Gelant, et souvent il a fallu les couper. Faute d'argeant, on n'avoit ni vivres, ni moïens de transport; les Colonels furent toujours Reduits à deux, quelquefois à une Ration. Les Provisions de l'armée manquoïent des jours entiers, et la patiente vertu des officiers et soldats fut un miracle continuel à chaque instant Renouvellé. Mais le tableau de leur misere arrêtoit les engagements, il devint presque impossible de Recruter, il etoit aisé de deserter sur les derrieres du païs. Le feu sacré de la liberté Brûloit toujours, et la majorité des citoïens abhorroit la tyrannie Britannique. Mais le triomphe du nord, et la tranquillité du sud avoïent endormi les deux tiers du continent; le Reste etoit Harassé par deux armées, et dans cette Revolution la plus grande difficulté fut toujours, Que pour Cacher le mal aux ennemis, il falloit le Cacher au peuple, qu'en Eveïllant l'un, on Avertissoit les autres, et qu'un coup mortel eut frappé les endroits foibles, avant que la lenteur democratique y eut apporté le Remede. C'est pourquoi dans cette guerre, la force de l'armée ne cessa d'etre un mistere profond; on evitoit d'en instruire le Congrès; les Generaux eux mêmes etoïent souvent trompés. La Confiance du Gal. Washington eut toujours des Bornes; pour M. de Lafayette, elle fut illimitée parceque pour lui seul elle partoit du coeur. Plus la situation etoit critique, plus la discipline devint necessaire; dans ses visites de nuit, au milieu des neiges, M. de Lafayette fit casser les officiers Negligeants. Son costume, sa table, ses moeurs, tout etoit Americain; mais il fut encore plus simple, plus frugal, plus austere qu'aucun autre; elevé mollement, il changea tout à coup de vie, et son temperament se plia aux privations comme aux fatigues. ⟨Sur toutes les affaires,⟩ il avoit pris le droit d'ecrire librement au Congrès. Ou quelquefois imitant la prudence du General, il donnoit son opinion à quelques membres de ce corps ou d'une assemblée d'etat, afin qu'adoptée par eux, elle fut ainsi soumise aux deliberations.

Outre les difficultés qu'on a depeintes, et qui durerent toute la guerre, l'Hiver de *Valley Forge* en Rappelle encore de plus facheuses. A *York Town* derriere la *Susquehana*, le Congrès se partageoit en deux factions, Qui malgré leur distinction de *l'est* et du *sud* n'en divisoient pas moins les membres d'un même etat. Aux voeux de leurs concitoïens, les deputés substituoïent leurs propres intrigues. Plusieurs gens impartiaux s'etant eloignés, quelques etats n'avoïent pas de Representants, ou n'en avoïent qu'un seul; cet esprit de parti fut tel, que trois ans après le Congrès s'en Ressentoit encore. Un grand interest cependant Reveïlloit le patriotisme, et quand Burgoïgne declara son traité Rompu, l'on sut Bien arrêter le depart de ses troups, dont tout, à commençer par le peu de vivres des transports, annonçoit maladroitement l'intention. Mais de toutes ces divisions, il pensa Resulter le plus grand des maux, la perte du seul Homme qui put Conduire la Revolution.

⟨Ennivré de son triomphe,⟩ Gates etoit à York Town, et ⟨ce vieux general⟩ en imposoit par son ton, ses promesses, et les Connoissances europeennes. Parmi les deputés qui s'unirent à lui, on distingua les *Lees* Virginiens, ennemis des Washingtons, et les deux Adams ⟨Republicains Rigides, mais plus Habiles à detruire qu'à Conserver⟩. Mifflin Quartier Maitre General, l'aida de ses talents, et de sa Brillante eloquence. Il leur falloit un enfant perdu, et ils prirent Conway qui se crut un chef de parti. Vanter Gates, etoit pour une partie du Continent et des troupes, l'occasion de parler d'eux mêmes. Le peuple s'attache aux generaux Heureux, et le commandant en chef ne l'avoit pas été. Sa personne imprimoit le Respect et même l'amour; mais Greene, Hamilton, Knox, ses meïlleurs amis etoïent dechirés, et les torys fomentoïent ces dispositions. La presidence du Bureau de guerre, crée pour Gates, Restraignit les pouvoirs du General. Ce degoust ne fut pas le seul; un committé du Congrès vint au Camp et l'on osa proposer l'attaque de Philadelphie. Il est singulier que pour les plus, fins, Gates ne fut pas l'objet de l'intrigue. Quoique Bon officier, ⟨il n'avoit ni le talent, ni l'esprit, ni la force de tête necessaire. Ecrasé sous le fardeau,⟩ il eut fait place au fameux general *Lee* alors prisonnier des anglais, dont le premier soin eut été de leur vendre et ses amis et toute L'Amerique.

Attaché au General, et plus encore à la Cause, M. de Lafayette ne Balança pas, et malgré les caresses de l'autre parti, tint à celui dont on prevoïoit la Ruine. Tous les jours il voyoit son ami, lui ecrivoit souvent, et lui parloit ou d'ameliorations dans l'armée, ou de sa situation particuliere. Aïant fait venir sa femme au camp, le General portoit dans la societé ce noble Calme d'une ame forte et vertueuse. "Je n'ai pas Recherché cette place," disoit-il à M. de Lafayette; "si je deplais au peuple je m'en irai, mais jusques là, je Resisterai à l'intrigue." Le 22 janvier il fut Resolu par le Congrès qu'on entreroit en Canada, et le choix tomba sur M. de Lafayette avec les Gaux. Conway et Stark. Esperant ennivrer, et Conduire un Commandant si jeune, le Bureau de guerre, sans consulter le general, lui manda d'aller attendre ses instructions à *Albany.* Mais après avoir persuadé le Comité du Congrès au Camp, M. de Lafayette courut à York Town, et y declara "qu'il lui falloit des ordres detaïllés, un etat des moyens, la securité de ne pas tromper les Canadiens, une augmentation de generaux, des grades pour plusieurs français, penetrés,"

ajoutoit-il, "des devoirs et de l'avantage d'un tel nom, enfin la Condition premiere de n'etre pas, Comme Gates, independant du Gal. Washington." Ce fut
chés Gates même qu'il Brava son parti, et leur fit porter en Rougissant la
santé de leur General. Dans le Congrès, ou Laurens, president, le servit Bien,
on accorda ce qu'il exigeoit. Les instructions du Bureau de guerre promirent
2500 Hommes Reunis à *Albany,* un gros Corps de milices à *Coos,* deux millions
en papier, quelque argeant monnäie, et tous les moyens de traverser sur la
glace le lac *Champlain,* d'ou après avoir Brûlé la flotille Anglaise, il tomberoit à
Mont Real, et y agiroit suivant les circomstances.

Repassant alors, non sans danger, la *Susquehana* qui Rouloit d'enormes
glaçons, M. de Lafayette partit pour *Albany* et malgré l'embarras des glaces et
des neiges, il fit lestement cette Route de 400 milles. En voyageant ainsi sur
ses chevaux, il voyoit les moeurs pures des Habitants, leur vie partriarchale,
leur esprit Republicain. Livrées à leur menage, les femmes en goutent, en
procurent toutes les douceurs. C'est aux filles qu'on parle amour, et leur
coqueterie est aimable autant que decente. Dans les mariages de Hazard
qu'on fait à Paris, la fidelité des femmes Repugne souvent à la nature, à la
Raison, et même aux principes de la justice. En Amerique on epouse son
amant, et ce seroit en avoir deux à la fois, que de Rompre un Traité Valide,
parceque les deux partis savent à quoi, et Comment ils s'engagent. Au milieu
de leurs familles, les Hommes travaïllent à leurs affaires, et se Reunissent
entre eux pour agiter celles de l'etat. C'est en Büvant qu'on politique, et le patriotisme echauffe plus que les plus fortes liqueurs. Tandisque des enfants
pleuroïent du nom de torys; des vieïllards prioïent le ciel de leur laisser voir la
fin de cette guerre. Dans ses Courses, aussi Repetées que Rapides, M. de
Lafayette se mêlant à toutes les classes des citoïens, ne fut pas inutile à la
Bonne Cause, à l'interest francais, au parti du General Washington.

Arrivé à Albany, M. de Lafayette eut Bien à decompter. Au lieu de 2500
Hommes, il n'y en avoit pas 1200. Les milices de Stark n'etoïent pas même
Averties. Habits, vivres, Magazins, traineaux, Raquettes, tout etoit insuffisant
pour cette expedition Glaciale. En s'y preparant mieux, en nommant plustôt
le general, on auroit probablement Reussi. Dejà quelques Canadiens Re-
muoïent, et dès ce moment ils s'interesserent à M. de Lafayette. Mais pour
avoir ce qui manquoit, il falloit deux mois, et vers le milieu de mars le lac
commence à degeler. General à Vingt ans d'une petite armée, chargé d'une
operation importante et singuliere, autorisé par les ordres du Congrès, animé
par l'attente de l'Amerique, et Bientôt celle de l'Europe, M. de Lafayette avoit
Bien des motifs pour s'avanturer. Mais d'un autre coté, ses moyens etoïent
foibles, le tems trop court, les ennemis Bien disposés, et le Lieutenant General
Carleton lui preparoit un autre *Saratoga.* Forcé sur le champ à decider, il
ecrivit Moderement au Congrès, et, en gemissant, abandonna l'expedition. A
la même epoque, le Congrés un peu moins Confiant envöioit de ces conseïls in-
certains, qui arrivant trop tard, ne servent qu'à compromettre le general, et à
justifier le gouvernement. Mais la prudence de M. de Lafayette fut ensuite
applaudie par eux et par le peuple at jusqu'à l'ouverture de la Campagne, il
commanda ce departement. Il y trouva cet intrepide Arnold que sa Blessure

Retenoit encore, et qui depuis . . . Il s'y lia aussi très intimement avec Schuyller, predecesseur de Gates, disgracié Comme St. Clair, mais qui servoit encore
la cause, et par son esprit superieur, et par son existence dans cette partie du
continent, et par la confiance de l'etat de Newyork dont il est citoïen.

Si le Canada n'envoïoit plus d'armée offensive, tous les sauvages etoïent
soudoïés, et sous la protection de partis Anglais, les Hurons, les Iroquois,
devastoïent cette frontiere. Quelques colifichets, un Barril de Rum leur met-
toïent le casse tête en main, et fondant sur les villages, ils Brûloïent les maisons, detruisoïent les Recoltes, massacroïent tout sans distinction d'age ni de
sexe et Recevoïent au Retour le prix des chevelures sanglantes. Une jeune
Americaine, que son amant officier Anglais attendoit pour l'epouser, fut tuée
par les sauvages qu'il lui avoit envoyés pour escorte. Deux Americains furent
mangés par les Senecas, et le Clel: Butler etoit un des convives. C'est ainsi leur
disoit-on en Buvant dans les conseïls, c'est ainsi qu'il faut Boire le sang des
Rebelles. Ne pouvant garder une si vaste entendüe, M. de Lafayette faisoit
preparer partout des quartiers, annonçoit des troupes à tous les comtés, et ce
stratagème arrêta les Sauvages qui n'attaquent gueres ou ils prevoïent Beaucoup de Resistance. Mais il tint ensemble les troupes d'Albany, les satisfit un
peu sur leur païe, approvisiona les forts jusques là Negligés, et prevint un
complot dont on n'a jamais Bien su les detaïls. Il trouva dans George Clinton
gouverneur de l'etat de Newyork un Cooperateur ferme et eclairé. Bientôt
après, Schuyller et Duane, chargés des affaires sauvages indiquerent une assemblée Generale à *Johnstown* sur la Riviere *Mowack*. Reveïllant leur Ancien
Amour pour les français, M. de Lafayette fut en traineaux s'y montrer à ces
Nations que les Anglais avoïent tâché de prevenir contre lui. 500 Hommes,
femmes, et enfants, Barriolés de couleurs et de plumes, avec leurs oreïlles
decoupées, leurs néz chargés de joïaux, et leurs corps presque nuds marqués
de figures diverses, assistoïent à ces conseïls, et leurs vieïllards, en fumant, y
parloïent fort Bien sur la politique. La Balance des pouvoirs seroit leur objet,
si l'ivresse du Rum, comme en Europe celle de l'ambition ne les en detournoit
souvent. Adopté par eux, M. de Lafayette en Receut le nom de *Kayeheawla*
que portoit jadis un de leurs guerriers, et sous lequel il est connu de tous les
sauvages. Quelques louïs en guise de medaïlles, quelques ettoffes de l'etat de
Newyork, ne Brilloïent pas auprès des presens d'Anglettere. On fit un traité,
quelques uns l'observerent, le mal fut au moins suspendu; les Onoïdas, et
Tuscaroras, nos seuls vrais amis demanderent un fort, et M. de Lafayette leur
laissa M. de Gouvion officier français dont l'esprit, les talents, et la vertu for-
ment un assemblage Rare. Quand on voulut des sauvages à l'armée, quand on
eut affaire à ces nations, il fallut Recourir au credit de M. de Lafayette dont
ils Respectoïent *les colliers et les paroles.*

A son Retour, M. de Lafayette trouva la formule d'un serment Nouveau
que suivant le Rite Relligieux d'un chacun, tout officier civil et militaire devoit
prêter. "Une Reconnoissance de l'independance liberté et souveraineté des
Etats Unis, une eternelle Renonciation à George Trois, ses successeurs, ses
aïant Cause, et tout Roy d'Anglettere, une promesse de defendre les dits etats
contre le dit George Trois." Ce furent jurées en ses mains dans tout le departement du Nord.

Agreement with Silas Deane

Paris ce Sept Xbre. 1776

Le desir que Monsieur le Marquis de la Fayette marque, de servir dans les troupes des Etats Unis de L'Amérique Septentrionale, et L'interet qu'il prend a la justice de leur cause, luy faisant Souhaiter des occasions de se distinguer a la guerre, et de s'y rendre utile autant qu'il sera en luy; Mais ne pouvant se flater d'obtenir L'agrément de sa famille pour servir en Pays étranger et passer les mers, qu'autant qu'il y iroit comme Officier Général. J'ay crû ne pouvoir mieux servir mon Pays et mes commettants qu'en luy accordant au nom du tres honorable Congrès, le grade de Major général que je supplie les états de luy confirmer, ratifier et en faire Expédier la Commission pour tenir et prendre rang a compter de ce jour, avec les officiers Généraux du meme grade. Sa haute naissance, ses alliances, Les grandes dignités que sa famille possède en cette Cour, ses biens considérables en ce Royaume, son mérite personnel, sa réputation, son desinteressement, et surtout son zèle pour la liberté de nos Provinces, m'ont seuls pû engager a luy faire la promesse dudit grade de major general, au nom desdits Etats Unis. En foy de quoy j'ay signé le present, fait a Paris ce Sept Xbre. mil Sept cent Soixante-Seize.

Aux conditions cy dessus, je m'offre et promet de partir quand et comme Monsieur Deane le jugera a propos, pour servir Lesd. Etats avec tout le zele possible sans aucune pension ny traitement particulier, me reservant seulement la Liberté de revenir en Europe, Lorsque ma famille ou mon Roy me rapelleront. Fait a Paris ce Sept Xbre. 1776.

LE MIS. DE LAFAYETTE

Etats des Officiers d'Infanterie et de Troupes Legères destinés à servir dans les armees des Etats generaux de L'Amerique Septentrionale

Sçavoir

Noms des Officiers	Grades en dattes de leur Engagemts.
Mrs. Le Marquis de Lafayette	Major General du sept Decembre 1776
Le Baron de Kalb	Major General du 7 Novembre
Delesser	Colonel du premier Decemr.
de Valfort	Colonel du d. jour 1er. Xbre.
de Fayols	Lieut. Colonel du Vingt Novembre
de Franval	Lieut. Colonel du premier Decemr.

Sçavoir (continued)

Noms des Officiers	Grades en dattes de leur Engagemts.
de Bois Martin	Major du sept Novemr.
de Gimat	Major du premier Decemr.
de Vrigny	Capt. d'une Compie. franche de premier Decemr.
de Bedaulx Capitaine	Capitaine du premier Decemr.
de la Colombe	Lieutenant do.
Candon	Lieutenant du sept Novembre 1776

Les dits Grades et les appointements que le tres honorable Congrès y attachera à commencer aux Epoques marquées au present Etat ont été arretes d'accord Entre nous soussignés Silas Deane Esqre. en qualité de Deputé des d. Etats Generaux Americains d'une part, Le Marquis de La Fayette et le Baron de Kalb d'autre part, fait double a Paris ce septieme Decembre mil sept cent soixante seize.

DE KALB
LE MIS. DE LAFAYETTE
SILAS DEANE

To William Carmichael

[Paris, février 1777]

Je suis bien reconnoissant, monsieur, de la lettre que vous avés bien voulu m'ecrire. Je compte bien sur l'amitié que vous m'avés temoignée pour le succès de notre affaire. J'irois vous voir demain si je ne craignois pas d'aller trop souvent chés Mr. Deane et d'y trouver du monde. Je serois enchanté de vous recevoir chés moi si vous en aviés le tems. J'y serai demain à cinq heures après midi, si vous me faites le plaisir de me venir voir nous causerons sur nos affaires. Je voudrois bien que vous fussiés persuadé monsieur, du tendre attachement avec lequel je vous prie de me croire, votre très h. serviteur

LE MIS. DE LAFAYETTE

To William Carmichael

[Paris, 11 février 1777]
ce mardi à trois he[ures]

Je ne pars que dimanche pour l'Anglettere, monsieur, ainsi j'aurai le tems de voir monsieur Franklin et monsieur Deane. Il m'est impossible d'accepter le rendés vous d'aujourdhui parceque la reine donne un bal auquel je suis obligé de me trouver. Si je pouvois vous voir demain entre six et sept heures du soir, je viendrois vous prendre comme l'autre jour dans ma voiture, et nous parlerions de nos affaires. Je vous annonce avec grand plaisir, monsieur, que je viens d'acheter mon vaisseau, et que dans un mois au plustost j'espere pouvoir aller porter dans votre patrie le zele qui m'anime pour leur bonheur, leur gloire, et leur liberté. Tous vos concitoïens me sont chers, et je n'en trouverai jamais auxquels je sois plus tendrement attaché qu'à vous.

LE MARQUIS DE LAFAYETTE

Si vous ne me faites pas de reponse, ce sera marque que vous m'attendrés demain.

To Adrienne de Noailles de Lafayette

[Calais] ce 20 fevrier 1777

Nous voilà arrivés à Calais sans accident, non cher coeur, prets à nous embarquer demain, et à voir cette fameuse ville de Londres. Il m'en coutera pour quitter le rivage, je quitte tous les gens que j'aime, je vous quitte, mon cher coeur, et en verité sans savoir pourquoi. Mais le sort en est jetté, il faut bien y aller. Nous sommes venus tres doucement, nous avons [cassé?], parceque c'est attaché à mon sort, et nous sommes arrivés ici dans la douce esperance d'y passer cinq ou six jours, cependant demain nous pouvons passer fort legerement, et nous en serons quittes pour etre malades quatre ou cinq heures. Je vous prie, mon coeur de faire donner de mes nouvelles à mes tantes, je vous ecrirai de Londres dès que j'y serai, et j'espere y avoir bientôt une lettre de vous. Ecrivés moi exactement c'est me faire un grand plaisir. Adieu, cher coeur, dans quelque pays que j'aïlle je vous aimerai toujours bien tendrement, je voudrois que vous pussiés connoitre combien cette assurance est sincere et combien votre sentiment fait à mon bonheur.

To Adrienne de Noailles de Lafayette

[Londres] ce 25 fevrier [1777]

Nous voici arrivés à Londres, mon cher coeur, et ce n'est pas sans peine. Le tems que nous avons resté à Calais a été bien ennuïeux, enfin nous sommes parvenus ici hier. Je vous ecris de chés le Mis. de Noaïlles, qui nous a receu avec un grand empressement. Nous n'avons encore vu que quelques hommes ce matin, nous venons de diner chés notre ambassadeur, et nous partons pour l'opera; ensuite nous sommes priés à souper, au bal, nous verrons cette nuit toutes ces dames. Je trouve encore que Paris vaut bien mieux que Londres, quoique nous y soyons receus fort agreablement. J'ai une grande impatience de voir toutes ces jeunes femmes, et la fameuse duchesse de Devonshire. C'est le soir que nous faisons notre entrée. J'ai bien envie que le prince se conduise bien, il pretend que j'ai toujours peur qu'il ne dise quelque sottise. Adieu, cher coeur, je suis si pressé que je n'ai que le tems de vous dire que je vous aime de tout mon coeur.

To Adrienne de Noailles de Lafayette

[Londres] ce 28 [février 1777]

Pour le coup, mon cher coeur, me voilà comme ces messieurs. Londres est une ville charmante, on m'y comble de bontés, et je n'ai que le tems de m'y amuser. Tous les hommes sont honnêtes et aimables. Pour nous, toutes les femmes sont jolies, et d'une societé agreable. Les plaisirs sont plus vifs qu'a Paris, on danse toute la nuit, et j'aime le bal ici, peut-etre parceque ma danse est plus au niveau de tout le monde, car il y a de bonnes figures dans ma nouvelle patrie. Le Mis. de Noäilles est charmant, plein d'attention pour nous. Il est fort consideré à Londres, et tient un fort bon etat. Il est vrai que je suis disposé à voir tout en beau. Je suis deja dans la societé de Londres presque comme dans celle de Paris. La poste est arrivée aujourdhui, j'esperois recevoir de vos nouvelles et j'ai vu avec chagrin qu'il n'y en avoit pas. Je me flatte d'etre plus heureux le premier courier; adieu, mon cher coeur, je n'ai que le tems de vous dire un mot; j'ai mille choses à faire ce soir, terminées par un bal, car ici nous ne nous couchons jamais avant cinq heures.

To Adrienne de Noailles de Lafayette

[Londres, mars 1777]

J'ai été bien faché, mon cher coeur, de ne pas recevoir de vos nouvelles depuis deux couriers; heureusement je sais que vous n'etes pas malade et seulement paressesseuse, parceque nous en avons eu de la vicomtesse et de nos autres amis qui ne parlent point de vous. Les plaisirs de Londres vont toujours fort vite, et je suis ettonné de leur vivacité, moi qui ne suis pas accoutumé à une vie bien retirée. D'abords de sortir du diner à sept heures et demie, et de souper entre deux et trois heures me paroit une fort mauvaise habitude. Je m'amuse fort bien ici, il y a des femmes vraiment charmantes, des hommes fort aimables et pleins de bontés pour nous, et quand on peut sortir les premieres de leurs [precieuses] assemblées et les hommes de leur clobs, pour les mettre en societé [illegible] ils sont très aimables. Le terme de votre exil à Versaïlles approche et je vous en fais mon compliment, dites à Mr. le duc d'Ayen que je n'ai pas un instant à moi jusqu'à présent, que j'aurai l'honneur de lui ecrire au premier moment, et de lui parler de Mr. de La Rochette. Je le trouve si aimable que souvent pendant que Mr. de Poix va faire sa cour aux dames je m'enferme avec lui pour causer, et je suis parfaitement heureux. Mille respects à Mde. d'Ayen mille compliments à mes soeurs ne m'oubliés pas non plus, mon cher coeur, auprès de mon grand pere, de mes tantes, de Mde. d'Abos. Je desire bien apprendre que celle-ci est presentée. Adieu, cher coeur, je suis obligé d'ecrire à la volée, le peu de sejour que je ferai peut-etre à Londres, me rend le tems plus precieux que si j'y passois quatre mois comme mes predecesseurs. Si j'avois besoin de nouvelles preuves pour me convaincre combien je vous aime tendrement, ce seroit la peine que j'ai epprouvé en ne recevant pas de vos lettres, lorsque j'en avois de tous mes amis. *Bonjour.*

To Adrienne de Noailles de Lafayette

Londres ce 7 mars [1777]

Enfin, mon cher coeur, j'ai receu de vos nouvelles et avec un grand plaisir, j'en attends encore aujourd hui, et quelque soit le mouvement de Londres, je pense toujours avec impatience aux jours de couriers, et je suis bien heureux quand ils arrivent. Nous dansons, nous soupons, nous veïllons toujours beaucoup, et nos occupations n'ont gueres été relatives qu'à la société. Aujourdhui cependant je me suis promené avec Mr. de La Rochette (qui je ne peux plus quitter) dans le port de Londres et plusieurs endroits remarquables de cette ville. Demain ou après demain nous allons à Porsmouth munis des plus ample reccommandations pour tout voir; ainsi je pourai bien etre un ou deux couriers sans vous ecrire. On continüe à nous combler de bontés dans ce païsci, et nous y sommes le plus agreablement du monde. Mr. de Poix est le grand arbitre des modes et coiffe toutes ces dames, ces dames seulement. Nous attendons avec bien de l'empressement l'ami Etienne qui arrive lentement avec le duc d'Orset. Cependant il faut esperer qu'à la fin on en aura quelques nouvelles. Les Anglois croïent beaucoup à la guerre, ou pour mieux dire la devinent. Il est vrai qu'il ne faut pas etre bien malin pour la prevoir au moins dans quelquetems; ici cependant je n'ai pas l'air d'en etre persuadé. Je dine aujourdhui chés un homme que je n'avois connu que courant les champs avec Melle. Grandi et que j'ai été ettonné de retrouver ici possesseur d'une femme et d'une maison belle au moins si elle n'est pas bonne au lieu que sa femme n'est ni l'un ni l'autre à ce qu'on dit. En tout je suis fort ennuïé d'etre obligé d'y aller, et ma mauvaise humeur en est d'autant plus grande que je suis forcé de prendre congé de vous. Il est cinq he. 1/4 dans ce païs-ci c'est l'heure ou l'on commence à demander si son carosse est arrivé. Je vais faire depecher le prince qui est toujours à cheval, et fort occupé d'en acheter. Adieu, mon coeur, mille respects à Mde. d'Ayen mille tendres compliments à la vicomtesse, à mes soeurs; je suis toujours faché quand je vous quitte même par ecrit, et c'est à la fatalité de mon etoile qui veut que je courre toujours, que je dois m'en prendre quand je ne vous vois pas la sixieme partie de ce que je vous verrois avec un vrai plaisir. Mais vous connoissés mon coeur ou du moins sa franchise, et vous me croirés, j'espere, toujours, quand je vous assurerai qu'il vous aime pour la vie du sentiment le plus solide et le plus tendre.

Embrassés vingt fois pour moi notre chere Henriette.

Ne m'oubliés pas auprès de monsieur votre pere. Je n'ai encore vu que des plumes comme à Paris et j'attends pour lui ecrire de pouvoir lui rendre compte de quelque promenade plus interessante.

J'espere vous ecrire encore une fois avant mon petit voyage.

To the Duc d'Ayen

ce 9 mars [1777] à Londres

Vous allés etre ettonné, mon cher papa, de ce que je vais vous mander; il m'en a plus couté que je ne puis vous exprimer pour ne pas vous consulter. Mon respect, ma tendresse, ma confiance en vous doivent vous en assurer. Mais ma parole y etoit engagée, et vous ne m'auriés pas estimé si j'y avois manqué; au lieu que la demarche que je fais, vous donnera j'espere bonne opinion, au moins de ma bonne volonté. J'ai trouvé une occasion unique de me distinguer et d'apprendre mon metier. Je suis officier general dans l'armée des Etats Unis de l'Amerique. Mon zele pour leur cause, et mon franchise ont gagné leur confiance. De mon coté j'ai fait tout ce que j'ai pu pour eux, et leurs interest me seront toujours plus chers que les miens; enfin, mon cher papa, dans ce moment-ci je suis à Londres attendant toujours des nouvelles de mes amis. Dès que j'en aurai, je partirai d'ici et sans m'arrêter à Paris j'irai m'embarquer sur un vaisseau que j'ai fretté, et qui m'appartient. Mes compagnons de voyage sont Mr. le baron de Kalb officier de la plus grande distinction brigadier des armées du roi, et major general au service des Etats Unis ainsi que moi, avec quelques officiers excellens qui veulent bien partager mes avantures. Je suis au comble de ma joïe d'avoir trouvé une si belle occasion de faire quelque chose et de m'instruire. Je sais bien que je fais des sacrifices enormes, qu'il m'en coutera plus qu'a personne pour quitter ma famille, mes amis, vous, mon cher papa, parceque je les aime plus tendrement qu'on n'a jamais aimé. Mais ce voyage n'est pas bien long, on en fait tous les jours de plus considerables pour son seul plaisir, et d'äilleurs j'espere en revenir plus digne de tout ce qui aura la bonté de me regretter. Adieu, mon cher papa, j'espere vous revoir bientôt. Conservés moi votre tendresse, j'ai bien envie de la meriter, et je la merite deja par celle que je sens pour vous, et le respect que conservera toute sa vie. Votre tendre fils

LAFAYETTE

[Paris, 16 mars 1777]

J'arrive un instant à Paris, mon cher papa, ne prenant que le tems de vous dire adieu. Je voulois ecrire à mon oncle et à Mde. de Lusignem mais je suis si pressé que je vous prie de vous charger de mes hommages.

To Adrienne de Noailles de Lafayette

[Paris, 16 mars 1777]

Je suis trop coupable, pour me justifier, je suis trop cruellement puni pour ne pas meriter mon pardon. Si j'avois cru sentir mes sacrifices d'une maniere aussi affreuse, je ne serois pas a present le plus malheureux des hommes. Mais ma parole est donnée, et je mourrois plutôt que d'y manquer. Mr. le duc d'Ayen vous expliquera mes folies. Ne m'en sachés pas mauvais gré. Croiés que je suis cruellement dechiré. Je n'avois jamais compris combien je vous amois—mais je reviendrai bientôt, dès que mes engagemens seront acquissés. Adieu, adieu ecrivés moy souvent, tous les jours. Embrassés notre chere Henriette. Et encore, vous êtes grosse, tout ajoute a mon tourment; si vous saviés tout ce qu'il m'en coute vous plaindriés plus que vous ne Serés surement; pour ajouter a mon malheur les gens que j'aime vont croire que je suis bien content de partir. Au reste, c'est un voyage, pas plus long que celui de Mr. Votre pere en Italie. Je vous reponds qu'il sera court. Adieu, j'ai reservé cette lettre pour la derniere, je finis mes adieux, par vous; on va m'entrainer bien loin, j'ai une peine horrible a m'arracher d'ici, et je n'ai pas le courage de vous parler plus longtems d'un homme qui vous aime de tout son coeur, et qui se reproche cruellement le tems qu'il va passer sans vous voir.

L.

Act of Embarkation

a Bordx. Le 22 Mars 1777

J'attes que Sr. Gilbert du Moitie Chevalier de Chavaillac age de 20 ans taille haute, cheveux blond; Jean Simon Camus de la Villedieu en Franche Comté a la Suite de Mr le Chevalier age de 32 ans taille moyène cheveux blonds, Michel Moteau de Saclay pres Paris age de 27 ans taille moyenne Cheveux Blond a la meme Suite, Francois Aman-Rogé de Nantes, age de 20 ans taille moyenne Cheveux blonds a la Suite de Mr. le baron de Canne, et Antoine Redon de Sarlat, age de 22 ans, taille moyenne cheveux Chateins, sont anciens Catholiques lesquels desirent s'embarquer sur la Victoire, Cape. Lebourcier, pour aller au Cap, ou ils vont pour affaires.

Gilbert Du Motier

J. S. Camus

To the Comte de Broglie

a Bordeaux Ce 23 Mars 1777

J'ai l'honneur de vous prevenir M. le Comte, que je pars pour le Pays que vous savez et pour cette Aventure que vous ne me conseillez pas de risquer. Vous serez etonné de ma demarche, mais il m'etoit impossible de faire autrement, et la Preuve de cette Verité est, que je ne me suis pas rendu à vos avis. Je n'ai pas même voulu vous en redemander parceque avec la meillure Volonté du Monde, le Destin m'avoit empeché malgré moi de les suivre. Vous auriez combattu mes Desirs, j'avois dejà assez d'Obstacles à lever. A present il y a d'autant moins de Danger à vous faire ma Confidence, que ma Lettre partira pour Paris dans le Moment que je partirai pour Philadelphie, et alors il seroit inutile, de me faire sentir les Inconvenients d'une Demarche dejà faite, pour parler le Language commun d'une Folie dejà consommée. J'espere même que vous voudrez bien m'aider et encourager une Enterprise que vous ne pouvez plus empêcher. Moi du mon Coté je tacherai de justifier cette Legereté (j'admets le terme) et d'acquierir des Connoissances et des moyens de me distinguer.

To William Carmichael

[Bordeaux, 3 avril 1777]

Je suis retenu par ordre du roi, mon cher ami, j'envoïe un courier pour en obtenir La revocation. En attendant j'ai mis le vaisseau et les autres officiers hors de danger. Je suis bien malheureux que ma bonne volonté pour vous ait un si mauvais succès. Je suis si pressé que je n'ai pas le tems de vous en dire davantage. Faites part de mes regrets à monsieur Deane. Adieu, la force pourra m'empecher de vous rendre les services que je voudrois, mais comme elle n'agit pas sur les coeurs, on ne m'empechera pas d'etre toute ma vie votre frere et votre ami.

Le Mquis. de Lafayette

To Adrienne de Noailles de Lafayette

a bord de La victoire ce 19 avril [1777] a St. Sebastien

Ah, mon cher coeur, ils ont donc cru, que La crainte, feroit plus d'effet sur moy que Le sentiment; c'est Bien mal me connoitre; et puisqu'on m'arrache a vous, puisqu'on m'oblige de ne pas vous voire d'un an, puisqu'on ne veux qu'abattre ma fierte, sans interesser mon coeur; au moins cette cruelle absence sera employée d'une maniere digne de moy. La seule idée qui put me retenir, etoit La douce consolation de vous embrasser, de vous etre rendu, et a tous les gens que j'aime. J'ai fait valoir ces motifs, j'ai demandé quinze jours, seulement quinze jours pour etre avec vous, a St. Germain, ou l'on voudroit; on m'a refusé; je refuse aussi, et ayant a choisir entre l'esclavage que tout le monde s'est cru en droit de m'imposer, et La Liberté qui m'appelloit a La gloire, je suis parti.

Mon voyage ne sera pas plus long, peutetre moins, vous aures encore plus souvent de mes nouvelles. Mille vaisseaux vous en porteront a tous momens, je ne m'exposerai point, je me menagerai, je penserai que vous m'aimés, vous pouves etre bien tranquille. C'est plutot en philosophe qu'en militaire que je verrai tout ce pays la. . . .

J'ai ete reçu ici avec des transports de joye bien-flatteurs, j'y suis aimé au dela de mes esperances; mais que je suis loin de bonheur; mon coeur est dechiré, c'est demain le moment cruel du depart; je vous ecris La veille pour etre plus sur que ma lettre sera raisonnable. Si vous ne me mandés pas, que vous m'aimés toujours, que vous me pardonnés, que vous aurés bien soin de votre santé, je serai au desespoir. Je vous jure par tout ce que l'honneur, a de plus sacré, par mon sentiment pour vous, que mon plus grand regret en partant, est de vous quitter, que ma plus grande inquietude est pour vous. Rendés moy moins malheureux, en m'ecrivant bien vîte. Adieu, je reviendrai peutetre plutôt que Mr. Le duc d'Ayen. Aimés moy toujours, meme dans ce moment ou je ne le merite que par ma douleur de vous quitter, et par ma vive tendresse.

Embrassés notre Henriette; ayés bien soin de notre autre enfant; j'espere etre bientôt reuni a toute ma famille. Ecrivés moy tout de suite, mon adresse est Mjor. Gal. . . . Il faut aller avec Mde. d'Ayen, vous faire ecrire ches Mr. Deane. C'est un homme du plus grand merite, le plus honête homme du monde, et mon ami. Il se chargera de votre 1ere. lettre. Pour les autres le mis. de Coigny vous donnera l'adresse.

Adieu, encore une fois, ne doutés pas d'un sentiment, que je sens mieux que jamais dans ce cruel moment. Rien ne me paroit, meme des inconveniens, auprès du chagrin de vous quitter.

L.

To William Carmichael

à bords de La Victoire ce 19 avril [1777]

Voici, monsieur, la derniere lettre que vous recevrés de moi en françois; mais je n'ose pas encore vous écrire dans votre langue; et je veux me servir de celle dont je connois le mieux les expressions, pour vous temoigner combien je suis heureux de me retrouver ici. La crainte de faire quelque tort à mes amis m'avoit forcé à un cruel·sacrifice; dès qu'elle a cessé je n'ai pas perdu un instant, et pars plein de joïe, d'esperances, et de zele pour notre cause commune. On m'a dit que milord [S]tormont avoit pris un peu d'humeur de mon depart. En tout cette affaire a produit tout l'eclat que je desirois, et à present que tout le monde a les yeux sur nous, je tacherai de justifier cette celebrité. J'ose vous repondre de n'etre pas pris par les anglois, et j'espere que vous pouvés etre tranquille.

Tous les officiers que j'emmene m'ont receu avec une amitié qui est d'un heureux augure. Le nombre est augmenté par Mr. de Montroy qui m'est arrivé de votre part. Je vous remercie bien sincerement de m'avoir donné Mr. Brice. Je l'aime tendrement, il est cheri de tout le monde. Nous serons toujours ensemble comme vous avés paru le desirer. J'ai été aussi bien content de la connoissance de Mr. Bedaulx. Il m'a prié de demander qu'il fut toujours employé avec moi. J'espere que vous aurés la bonté de Nous reccommander encore dans vos lettres. La seule grace que je desire c'est qu'on me fournisse toutes les occasions possibles, d'employer ma fortune, mes peines, toutes les ressourses de mon imagination et de verser mon sang pour mes freres et mes amis. L'unique recompense que je demande après le succès c'est d'obtenir de nouveaux moyens de leur etre utile.

Soïés bien rassuré sur tout ce qui regarde ma famille, et même cet ordre que j'ai receu. Une fois parti, tout le monde sera de mon avis, une fois vainqueur, tout le monde applaudira à mon entreprise. C'est de vos reccommandations que j'attends les moyens de faire un effet aussi avantageux pour nous tous. Je desire etre né aussi bon general que je suis né bon americain, et je n'oublierai rien pour justifier votre amitié et l'estime publique. Je souhaitte aussi que ce soit une maniere de vous prouver le tendre et eternel attachement avec lequel j'ai l'honneur d'etre, monsieur, votre très humble et très obeïssant serviteur

Le Mis. de Lafayette

Si par hazard vous aviés jamais Quelque besoin de mes amis, je leur ai mandé que je ne connoitrois leur sentiment qu'en proportion des soins qu'il mettroïent à vous etre utiles.

Memoir by the Vicomte de Mauroy[E]

J'etois Capitaine D'infanterie depuis quinze ans, lors qu'en 1772 j'obtins le Brevet de lieut. Col. Quelques jours ensuite on me mit en activité en me faisant passer a la lieutenance Colonel des grenadiers Royaux du Comté de Bourgogne, Régiment dont Mr. le mis. Demauroy etoit alors Colonel.

Monsieur Le Cte. de St. Germain Reforma le Regiment, et la foulle d'officiers que tant de Réformes laissoient sans Employ, ne permit ny a mr. de St. Germain ny aux ministres qui luy succedoient de me Remplacer.

Ce fut dans ces circonstances qu'on me proposa de passer en Amérique, et que Mr. *Deanes* Envoyé en France par les 13 provinces unies, nous accepta, le mis. de la Fayette, Le Bon. de *Kalb,* et moy, pour servir a l'Armée Continentale—avec le grade de géneral major.

Je n'etois pas dans le Cas de Choisir, et quoi qu'il me fut facile de prévoir dès lors tous les Désagrémens qu'il me faudroit Essuyer. Je pensai du moins qu'on me tiendroit Compte de ma Bonne volonté, et que le moins favorable Evenement au quel je Dusse m'attendre, étoit de me voir Remplacé immédiatement a mon Retour en France.

Je Recus un Brevét de Brigadier pour les Colonies, et des lettres de service pour St. Domingue; alors je me livrai au plus flateur Espoir, le nom de mon maitre etoit bien fait pour me Rassurer et dans cet instant même ou tout m'announce que le Brevét etoit illusoire, il m'est impossible de Concevoir Comment un nom aussi Réspectable que celuy de *Louis* ne Constate pas irrévocablement l'Etat de celuy qui a l'honneur de l'offrir Comme preuve de son Existence.

Quoi qu'il en soit je me mis en Route le 10 Avril 1777. Je me Rendis a *Bordeaux* et fus a six lieues de la, joindre le mis. de la Fayette.

Ce seigneur, d'après les Rumeurs publiques sur son Compte, et les ordres dit on, du ministre avoit pris le party de feindre l'abandon total de son projet. Il avoit pris la Route d'Italie, mais il s'Etoit arrêsté en chemin pour attendre ou de nouvelles instances de la part de sa famille, ou les sentimens Réflechis, du public. J'arrivai en même tems que son Courier, nous primes un chemin détourné pour Eviter Bordeaux, et nous gagnames *Le Passage* [premier] port d'Espagne, ou nous trouvames La Victoire, Batiment de 250 tonnaux, et nous mimes a la voile Le 20 avril, sans moyens pour nous Déffendre si l'on vouloit nous intercepter, sans autre préliminaire que notre Dévoüement a la fortune.

Mes Compagnons de voyage etoient dans un Enthousiasme Risible, et je n'avois Certainement pas formé le projét de les En guérir; mais le mis. de la Fayette m'avoit vraiment intéressé; sa jeunesse, cette ardante Envie de se Distinguer, son nom, sa fortune, les plaisirs qu'il sacrifioit a la gloire, sa Constance a lutter Contre tous les obstacles, et le Bonheur qu'il avoit Eprouvé en les surmontant tous, m'attachèrent fortement a ses succès. Tandis que tout ce qui l'Environnoit s'occupoit du soin de Bercer ses plus Douces Esperances, je voulus par mes objections le tenir préparé Contre les Désagrémens qu'il Eprouveroit peut ètre, et qui feroient sur luy une impression trop Douloureuse, s'il la Recevoit au moment ou son imagination se trouveroit le plus Exaltée sur le chapitre des Americains.

"Eh! quoy," me Disoit il un jour, "vous nes Croyés pas que le peuple soit une par l'Amour dē la vertue, de la liberté? Vous ne Croyés pas que ce soit des gens simples, Bons, hospitaliers, qui préferent la Bienfaisance a tous nòs vains plaisirs, et la mort a l'Esclavage?"

Si les sauvages du nouveau Continent, luy Répondis-je, s'Etoient Reunis pour vivre en societé, que quelqu'homme de génie avec de la vertu, des talens, et de la Constance, nouveau *Timoléon* eut donné des lois a l'Amerique Sept., un tel peuple pourroit nous offrir le tableau Riant que vous venés de me tracer, mais C'etoient des hommes déja Civilisés, (et qui ne l'avoient point eté par de tels philosophes) qui sont venus porter sur un sol sauvage, les vües, les préjugés de leur métropole Respective.

Le fanatisme, l'insatiable desir d'accumuler, et la misère, voila les trois sources d'ou Découle malheureusement presque sans interruption, cette foule d'Emigrans qui le fer a la main, vont abbatre sous un ciel nouveau pour eux, des forêts aussi Anciennes que le monde, arrosent une terre encore vierge du sang de ses sauvages habitans, et fertilisent par des milliers de Cadavres Epars, des Champs qu'ils ont Conquis par le Crime. Dans ce tableau qui n'est que trop fidèle, voyés vous moins d'horreurs, que ne vous en offriroit celuy que vous estes a même de faire du Continent que nous quittons? Je vois que vous allés m'objecter les *Quakers* et le Bonheur qu'au moins la Pensilvanie doit nous offrir, mais—outre que cette mannière de l'envisager, tourne au Desavantage des autres provinces—C'est qu'il est de fait que les pretendus Bonnes gens, se prèstent a Regrèt aux projets de tous leurs voisins, qu'ils ne Désirent saintement que la paix et l'abondance, et qu'enfin toute puissance leur est Egalle, puis que par leur Constitution vraiment monnachale, nulle puissance ne peut les lier. Voila sur quoy je me fonde pour vous avoüer ingenuement que je m'attens a ne trouver en Amérique, que des hommes faits Comme ceux de notre Continent; je pense qu'en Raison de leurs préjuges, nous autres francois nous devons etre detestés par eux, tandis que Comme gens qui venons leur offrir des lumières superieures aux leurs, nous Blèsserons leur orgueil en général, et nous Exciterons l'Envie en particulier. Cependant Rassurés vous, la politique vous accueillera, je ne connois pas les Ressources de mr. de *Kalb,* et Comme les miennes sont nulles, je serois Complettement la Dupe de tout cecy, si je ne Retirois pas du moins d'un pareil voyage, le fruit qui est toujours sous la main de celui qui Regarde de sang froid. . . .

To Adrienne de Noailles de Lafayette

A bords de La Victoire ce 30 Mai [1777]

C'est de bien loin que je vous ecris, mon cher coeur, et à ce cruel eloignement je joins l'incertitude encore plus affreuse du tems ou je pourrai savoir des vos nouvelles. J'espere cependant en avoir bientôt; parmi tant d'autres raisons qui me font desirer d'arriver, aucune ne me donne autant d'impatience que celle là. Que de craintes, que de troubles, j'ai à joindre au chagrin dejà si vif de me separer de tout ce que j'ai de plus cher. Comment aurés vous pris mon second depart? M'en aurés vous moins aimé? M'aurés vous pardonné? Aurés vous songé que dans tous les cas il falloit etre separé de vous, errant en Italie, et trainant une vie sans gloire au milieu des personnes les plus opposées et à mes projets, et à ma façon de penser. Toutes ces reflexions ne m'ont pas empeché d'epprouver un mouvement affreux dans ces terribles moments qui me separoïent du rivage. Vos regrets, ceux de mes amis, ⟨votre grossesse,⟩ Henriette, tout s'est representé à mon ame d'une maniere dechirante. C'est bien alors que je ne me trouvois plus d'excuse. Si vous saviés tout ce que j'ai souffert, mon cher coeur, les tristes journées que j'ai passées en fuïant tout ce que j'aime au monde. Joindrai-je à ce malheur celui d'apprendre que vous ne me pardonnés pas? En verité, mon coeur, je serois trop à plaindre. Mais je ne vous parle pas de moi, de ma santé, et je sais que ces detaïls vous interessent.

Je suis depuis ma derniere lettre dans le plus ennuïeux des païs; la mer est si triste, et nous nous attristons je crois mutuellement elle et moi. Je devrois etre arrivé, mais les vents m'ont cruellement contrarié; et je ne me verrai pas avant huit ou dix jours à Charlestown. C'est là que je compte debarquer et ce sera un grand plaisir pour moi. Une fois arrivé j'aurai tous less jours l'esperance de recevoir des nouvelles de France, j'apprendrai tant de choses interessantes et sur ce que je vais trouver, et surtout sur ce que j'ai laissé avec tant de regret! Pourvû que j'apprenne que vous vous portés bien, que vous m'aimés toujours, et qu'un certain nombre d'amis sont dans le même cas, je serai d'une philosophie parfaite sur tout le reste de quelque espece et de quelque païs qu'ils puissent etre. Mais aussi si mon coeur etoit attaqué dans un endroit bien sensible; si vous, mon cher coeur, vous ne m'aimiés plus tant je serois trop malheureux. Mais je ne dois pas le craindre, n'est ce pas mon cher coeur? J'ai été bien malade dans les premiers tems de mon voyage, et j'aurois pu me donner la consolation des mechants qui est de souffrir en nombreuse compagnie. Je me suis traité à ma maniere, et j'ai été plutôt gueri que les autres. A present je suis à peu près comme à terre. Une fois arrivé je suis sur d'avoir acquis l'assurance d'une santé parfaite pour bien longtems. N'allés pas croire, mon cher coeur, que je courre des dangers reels dans les occupations que je vais avoir. Le poste d'officier general a toujours été regardé comme un brevet d'immortalité. C'est un service differend de celui que j'aurois fait en France, comme colonel par exemple. Dans ce grade là on n'est que pour le conseïl. Demandés le à tous les officiers generaux françois dont le nombre est d'autant plus grand qu'une fois arrivés là ils ne courrent plus aucun risque et par consequent ne font pas place à d'autres comme dans les autres services. La preuve que je ne veux pas vous tromper c'est que je vous avoüerai qu'a present nous courrons quelques dangers parceque nous risquons d'etre attaqués par des vaisseaux anglois et que le mien n'est pas de force à se defendre. Mais une fois arrivé je suis en sureté parfaite. Vous voyés que je vous dit tout, mon cher coeur, ainsi ayés y confiance et ne soyés pas inquiette sans sujet. Je ne vous ferai pas de journal de mon voyage; ici les jours se suivent, et qui pis est se ressemblent. Toujours le ciel, toujours l'eau, et puis le lendemain c'est la même chose. En verité les gens qui font des volumes sur une traversée maritime doivent etre de cruels bavards. Car moi j'ai eu des vents contraires comme un autre, j'ai fait un très long voyage comme un autre, j'ai essuïé des orages, j'ai vu des vaisseaux et ils etoïent beaucoup plus interessants pour moi que pour tout autre. Eh bien je n'ai rien remarqué qui valut la peine d'etre ecrit, ou qui ne l'eut été par tout le monde.

A present, mon cher coeur, parlons de choses plus importantes: parlons de vous, de la chere Henriette, de son frere, ou sa soeur. Henriette est si aimable qu'elle donne le goust des filles. Quelque soit notre nouvel enfant, je le recevrai avec une joïe bien vive. Ne perdés pas un moment pour hâter mon bonheur en m'apprenant sa naissance. Je ne sais pas si c'est parceque je suis deux fois pere, mais je me sens pere plus que jamais. Mr. Deane, et mon ami

Mr. Carmichall vous fourniront des moyens. Je suis bien sur qu'ils ne ne-gligeront rien pour me rendre heureux le plutôt possible ⟨, parcequ'ils sont vraiment mes amis⟩. Ecrivés, envoyés même un homme sur. Un homme qui vous auroit vu me feroit tant de plaisir à interroger, Landrin par exemple . . . enfin comme vous le jugerés à propos. Vous ne connoissés pas, mon cher coeur, mon sentiment aussi vif, aussi tendre qu'il est si vous croyés pouvoir negliger quelque chose qui ait rapport à vous. Vous recevrés bien tard de mes nouvelles cette fois-ci. Mais quand je serai etabli vous en aurés souvent et de bien plus fraiches. Il n'y a pas grande difference entre les lettres d'Amerique et celles de Sicile. Je vous avoüe que j'ai furieusement cette Sicile sur le coeur. Je me suis cru si près de vous revoir. Mais brisons court à l'article Sicile. Adieu mon cher coeur; je vous ecrirai de Charlestown; je vous ecrirai avant d'y ar-river. Bonsoir *pour aujourdhui.*

                                                                                      ce 7 juin
     Je suis encore dans cette triste plaine, mon cher coeur, et c'est sans nulle comparaison ce qu'on peut faire de plus ennüeux. Pour me consoler un peu je pense à vous, à mes amis. Je pense au plaisir de vous retrouver, mon coeur; quel charmant moment quand j'arriverai, que je viendrai vous embrasser tout de suite sans etre attendu. Vous serés peut-etre avec nos enfants. J'ai, même à penser à cet heureux instant, un plaisir delicieux. Ne croyés pas qu'il soit eloigné. Il me paroitra bien long surement, mais dans le fait il ne le sera pas autant que vous allés vous imaginer. Sans pouvoir decider ni le jour ni même le mois sans voir par moi même l'etat des choses, cet exil prescrit jusqu'au mois de janvier par Mr. le duc d'Ayen me paroissoit si immense, que cer-tainement je ne prendrai pas sur moi de m'en ordonner un bien long. Vous avoüerés, mon coeur, que l'occupation et l'existence que je vais avoir sont bien differentes de celles qu'on me gardoit dans ce futile voyage. Defenseur de cette liberté que j'idolatre, libre moi même plus que personne, en venant comme ami offrir mes secours à cette republique si interessante, je n'y porte que ma franchise, et ma bonne volonté. Nulle ambition, nul interest par-ticulier. En travaïllant pour ma gloire, je travaïlle pour leur bonheur. J'espere qu'en ma faveur vous deviendrés bonne americaine. Au reste c'est un sen-timent fait pour les coeurs vertueux. Le bonheur de l'Amerique est in-timement lié au bonheur de toute l'humanité; elle va devenir le respectable et sur azile, de la vertu, de l'honneteté, de la tolerance, de l'egalité, et d'une tranquille liberté.
     Nous avons de tems en tems quelques petites alertes, mais avec un peu d'adresse et de bonne fortune, je suis bien sur de passer sans inconvenient. J'en serai d'autant plus charmé que je deviens tous les jours excessivement raisonable. Vous savés que le vicomte est sujet à repeter *que les voyages forment les jeunes gens.* S'il ne le disoit qu'une fois tous les matins et une fois tous les soirs en verité ce ne seroit pas trop, car je sens de plus en plus la justesse de cette sentence. Je ne sais ou il est ce pauvre vicomte, non plus que le prince, non plus que tous mes amis. C'est pourtant une cruelle chose que cette igno-rance. Toutes les fois que vous pourrés rencontrer dans un coin quelqu'un que j'aime, dites lui mille et dix mille choses pour moi. Embrassés bien tendre-

ment mes cheres soeurs, dites leur qu'elles se souviennent de moi, et qu'elles m'aiment. Faites bien mes compliments à Melle. Marin. Je vous reccommande aussi, mon cher coeur, ce pauvre Abbé Fayon. Quant à Mr. le marechal de Noaïlles, dites lui que je ne lui ecris pas de peur de l'ennuyer, et parceque je n'ai à lui apprendre que mon arrivée. Que j'attends ses commissions pour des arbres, ou plantes, ou ce qu'il voudra de moi, et que je voudrois bien que mon exactitude put etre une preuve de mon sentiment pour lui. Presentés aussi mes hommages à Mde. la duchesse de la Tremoïlle, et dites lui que je lui fais les mêmes offres qu'à Mr. le marechal de Noaïlles pour elle ou pour la belle fille qui a un fort beau jardin. Faites aussi savoir à mon vieux ami Deplaces que je suis en bonne santé. Quant à mes tantes, à Mde. d'Ayen, à la vicomtesse je leur ecris.

Voilà mes petites commissions, mon cher coeur; j'ai ecrit aussi en Sicile. On voit aujourdhui plusieurs especes d'oiseaux qui annoncent que nous ne sommes pas bien loin de la terre. L'esperance d'y arriver est bien douce car la vie de ce païs-ci est bien ennüeuse. Heureusement que ma bonne santé me permet de m'occuper un peu; je me partage entre les livres militaires et les livres anglois. J'ai fait quelques progrès dans cette langue qui va m'etre si necessaire. Adieu, mon coeur, la nuit ne me permet pas de continuer, car j'ai interdit toute lumiere dans mon vaisseau depuis quelques jours. Voyés comme je suis prudent. Adieu, donc, si mes doigts sont un peu conduits par mon coeur, je n'ai pas besoin d'y voir clair, pour vous dire que je vous aime, et que je vous aimerai toute ma vie.

ce 15 juin chés le major Hugey

J'arrive, mon cher coeur, en fort bonne santé dans la maison d'un officier americain, et par le plus grand bonheur du monde un vaisseau francois met à la voile. Jugés comme j'en suis aise. ⟨Je n'ai que le tems de fermer ma lettre.⟩ Je vais ce soir à Charlestown, je vous y ecrirai. Il n'y a point de nouvelles interessantes. La campagne est ouverte, mais on ne se bat pas, très peu du moins. Les manieres de ce monde-ci sont simples, honnêtes, et dignes en tout du pays ou tout retentit du beau nom de *liberté*. Je comptois ecrire à Mde. d'Ayen mais c'est impossible. Adieu, adieu, mon cher coeur. De Charlestown je me rendrai par terre à Philadelphie et à l'armée. N'est-il pas vrai, mon coeur, que vous m'aimerés toujours.

To Adrienne de Noailles de Lafayette

ce 19 juin [1777] à Charlestown

Si j'ai été pressé, mon cher coeur, de finir ma derniere lettre ecrite il y cinq ou six jours j'espere au moins que le capitaine americain (que je croyois françois) vous l'aura fait tenir dans le moins de temps possible. Cette lettre disoit que je suis arrivé à bon port dans ce païs-ci, après avoir été un peu malade dans les premieres semaines, que j'etois actuellement chés un officier fort obligeant dans la maison duquel j'avois debarqué, que j'avois voulu aller tout droit, que mon voyage avoit duré près de deux mois; cette lettre parloit de tout ce qui interesse le plus mon coeur, du regret de vous avoir quitté, de votre grossesse, de nos chers enfants. Elle disoit aussi que je me porte à merveilles. Je vous en fais l'extrait, mon cher coeur, parceque messieurs les anglois pourroïent bien s'amuser à la prendre en chemin. Cependant je compte assés sur mon etoile pour esperer qu'elle vous parviendra. Cette etoile vient de me servir de maniere à ettonner tout ce qui est ici; comptés y un peu, mon coeur, et soyés sure qu'elle doit vous tranquilliser entierement. J'ai debarqué après m'etre promené plusieurs jours le long d'une côte qui fourmille de vaisseaux ennemis. Quand je suis arrivé ici tout le monde m'a dit que mon vaisseau etoit pris surement parceque deux fregates angloises bloquoïent le port. J'ai même envoïé et par terre et par mer des ordres au capitaine de mettre les hommes à terre et bruler le navire s'il etoit tems encore, eh bien par un bonheur inconcevable un coup de vent ayante eloigné pour un instant les fregates, mon vaisseau est arrivé en plein midi sans rencontrer ami ni ennemi. J'ai trouvé à Charlestown un officier general actuellement de service, le *General Howe,* le president des etats doit arriver ce soir de la campagne, tous les gens avec qui j'ai voulu faire connoissance ici m'ont comblé de politesses et d'attentions (et ce ne sont pas des politesses d'Europe). Je ne peux que me loüer de la reception que j'ai eu ici quoique je n'ai pas jugé à propos d'entrer dans aucun detaïl ni sur mes arrangements, ni sur mes projets. Je veux voir auparavant le Congrès. J'espere partir dans deux jours pour Philadelphie, c'est une route par terre de plus de deux cent cinquante lieües; nous nous separerons en petites troupes, j'ai dejà acheté des chevaux et de petites voitures pour me transporter. Il se trouve actuellement ici des vaisseaux francois et americains qui sortent ensemble demain matin dans un instant ou ils ne verront pas les fregates. D'aïlleurs ils sont nombreux, armés et m'ont promis de se bien defendre contre de petits corsaires qu'ils rencontreront surement. Je partagerai mes lettres sur les differends navires en cas qu'il arrive quelque chose à un d'eux.

Je vais à present vous parler du pays, mon cher coeur, et de ses habitans. Ils sont aussi aimables que mon entousiasme avoit pu se le figurer. La simplicité de manieres, le desir d'obliger, l'amour de la patrie et de la liberté, une douce egalité regne ici parmi tout le monde. L'homme le plus riche et le plus pauvre sont de niveau, et quoiqu'il y ait des fortunes immenses dans ce pays, je defie qu'il se trouve la moindre difference entre leurs manieres respectives les uns pour les autres. J'ai commencé par la vie de campagne chés le major Hugey, à present me voici à la ville. Tout y ressemble assés à la façon angloise excepté qu'il y a plus de simplicité, d'egalité, de cordialité, et de douceur chés eux qu'en Anglettere. La ville de Charlestown est une des plus jolies, des mieux baties, et des plus agreablement peuplées que j'ai jamais vu. Les femmes americaines sont fort jolies, fort simples, et d'une propreté charmante. Elle regne ici partout avec la plus grande recherche, bien plus même qu'en Anglettere. Ce qui m'enchante ici c'est que tous les citoyens sont freres; il n'y a en Amerique ni pauvres ni même ce qu'on appelle païsan. Chaque particulier a un bien honnête, ⟨un nombre considerable de negres,⟩ et tous les mêmes droits que le plus puissant proprietaire du pays. Les auberges sont bien differentes d'Europe. Le maitre et la maitresse se mettent à table avec vous, font les honneurs d'un bon repas, et en partant vous payés sans marchander. Quand on ne veut pas aller dans une auberge on trouve des maisons de campagne ou il suffit d'etre bon americain pour etre receu avec les attentions qu'on auroit en Europe pour son ami.

Quant à ma reception particuliere j'ai epprouvé la plus agreable possible de tout le monde; il suffit d'etre venu avec moi pour etre acceüillé de la maniere la plus satisfaisante ⟨et avec tout l'empressement imaginable⟩. Je viens d'etre cinq heures à un grand diner donné par un particulier de cette ville à mon intention. Les generaux Howe et Mutrey, et plusieurs officiers de ma caravanne y etoïent, nous avons bu des santés, et barbouïllé de l'anglois—jusqu'à present je commence à parler un peu. Demain je ferai ma visite et menerai tous ces messieurs chés Mr. le president des etats, et je travaïllerai à mes arrangements de depart; après demain les generaux qui commandent ici me meneront voir la ville et tous ses environs et ensuite je partirai pour l'armée. Il faut que je ferme et que j'envoye ma lettre tout de suite parceque le vaisseau ira ce soir à l'entrée du port pour decamper demain à cinq heures. Comme tous les bâtimens courent des dangers je partage mes lettres sur tous. J'ecris à MM. de Coïgni, de Poix, de Noaïlles, de Segur, et à Mde. d'Ayen. S'il y en a quelqu'une qui reste en chemin donnés leur de mes nouvelles.

D'aprés l'agreable existence que j'ai dans ce pays-ci, mon cher coeur, la simpathie qui me met aussi à mon aise avec les habitans que si je les connoissois depuis vingt ans, la ressemblance de leur maniere de penser et de la mienne, mon amour pour la gloire et pour la liberté, on doit croire que je suis bien heureux. Mais vous me manqués, mon cher coeur, mes amis me manquent, et il n'y a pas de bonheur pour moi loin de vous et d'eux. Je vous demande, mon cher coeur, si vous m'aimés toujours, mais je me le demande bien plus souvent à moi même et mon coeur me repond toujours qu'ouï. J'espere qu'il ne me trompe pas. J'attends de vos nouvelles avec une impatience inexprimable; j'espere en trouver à Philadelphie. Toute ma crainte est que ce corsaire qui devoit m'en porter ne soit pris en voyage. Quoique j'imagine avoir fort deplu aux anglois en prenant la liberté de partir en depit d'eux pour arriver à leur barbe, j'avoüe, mon cher coeur, qu'ils ne seront pas en reste avec moi s'ils attrappent ce vaisseau, ma chere esperance, sur lequel je compte tant pour avoir de vos lettres. Ecrivés en souvent, s'il vous plait, et de longues. Vous ne connoissés pas assés toute la joïe que j'aurai à les recevoir. Embrassés bien Henriette; puis je dire, mon cher coeur, embrassés bien nos enfants? Ces pauvres enfans ont un pere qui court les champs, mais un bon et honnête homme dans le fonds, un bon pere qui aime bien sa famille, et un bon mari aussi car il aime sa femme de tout son coeur. Faites bien mes compliments *à vos amies* et aux miens, je dirais aussi à mes amies avec la permission de la comtesse Auguste et de Mde. de Fronsac. Ce qui j'entends par *mes amis* vous savés bien que c'est la chere societé; societé de la cour autrefois et qui par le laps des tems est devenüe societé de l'epée de bois; nous autres republicains nous trouvons qu'elle en vaut bien mieux. Celle-ci vous sera rendüe par un capitaine francois qui je crois ira vous la remettre lui même. Mais je vous confie, mon cher coeur, que je me prepare encore une bonne affaire pour demain, c'est de vous ecrire par un americain qui part aussi mais plus tard. Adieu donc, mon cher coeur, je finis faute de papier, faute de tems, et si je ne vous repete pas dix mille fois que je vous aime ce n'est pas faute de sentiment, mais bien faute de modestie parceque j'ai la confiance d'esperer que je vous en ai persuadée. Il est fort avant dans la nuit, il fait une chaleur affreuse, et je suis devoré de moucherons qui vous couvrent de grosses ampoules mais les meïlleurs païs ont comme vous voyés leurs inconvenients. Adieu mon coeur adieu.

To the Duc de Mouchy

[Charleston, 22 juin 1777]

Vos bontés pour moi, mon cher oncle, me font esperer, que vous voudrez bien prendre part à mon bonheur et à mon arrivée en Amérique. J'ai pris mon second parti un peu lentement; mais, si j'ai mal fait, la contrition est encore à venir, & je mettrai cette faute au nombre de ces pêches, qui font tant de plaisir à commettre. J'ai échappé assez heureusement aux attentions des Frégates Angloises, qui avoient bien voulu m'attendre sur cette Côte. Il est impossible d'être reçu avec plus d'empressement, de cordialité, & d'une manière plus agréable que je ne l'ai été par le Peuple Américain, & par tous les gens en place dans ce Pays. M. [Restarges], qui vous remettra cette Lettre, pourra vous en rendre compte. Il est chargé d'affaires pour Paris, pour les intérêts de notre République. Il est établi depuis longtems dans le Pays, et peut être [regardé] comme naturalisé. Puis-je compter assez sur vos bontés, MON CHER ONCLE; pour espérer, que votre reception à Bordeaux pour un Américain, & les services, que vous voudrez bien lui faire rendre en ce qui concerne ses affaires, m'acquitteront un peu de tous ceux que je reçois de tout le monde dans ce Pays. Je vous recommande bien particulièrement nos intérêts dans tout ce qui regarde votre Département. Adieu, MON CHER ONCLE, je ne veux pas plus longtems vous détourner de vos affaires. Conservez-moi vos bontés: je veux tâcher de les mériter: Le prix, que j'y mets, égale la tendresse & le respect, avec lesquels j'ai l'honneur d'être, &c.

LA FAYETTE

To Adrienne de Noailles de Lafayette

Petersburg ce 17 juillet [1777]

Je suis bien heureux, mon cher coeur, (si le mot de bonheur est fait pour moi tant que je serai loin de tout ce que j'aime). Voici un vaisseau prêt à partir pour France, et je pourrai vous dire avant d'arriver à Philadelphie que je vous aime, mon coeur, et que vous pouvés etre bien tranquille sur ma santé. J'ai soutenu la fatigue du voyage sans m'en appercevoir. Il a été bien long, et bien ennuïeux par terre, quoiqu'il le fut encore davantage quand j'etois dans mon triste vaisseau. Je suis à present à huit journées de Philadelphie et dans le beau Païs de la Virginie. Toutes les fatigues sont passées, et je crains bien que celles de la guerre ne soïent bien legeres s'il est vrai que le General Howe est parti de New York pour aller je ne sais ou. Mais toutes les nouvelles sont si incertaines que j'attends mon arrivée pour fixer mon opinion. C'est là, mon coeur, que je vous ecrirai une longue lettre. Vous devés en avoir receu quatre de moi si elles ne sont pas tombées entre les mains des anglois. Je n'ai pas encore receu de vos nouvelles, mon cher coeur, et mon impatience d'arriver à Philadelphie pour en avoir ne peut se comparer à rien. Jugés, mon coeur, de l'etat de mon ame, après cette immensité de tems sans recevoir deux lignes d'aucun de mes amis. Enfin j'espere que cela finira, car je ne peux pas vivre dans une telle incertitude. J'ai entrepris une tâche en verité trop forte pour mon coeur. Il n'etoit pas né pour tant souffrir.

Vous aurés appris le commencement de mon voyage; vous savés que j'etois parti brillamment en carosse, vous saurés à present que nous sommes tous à cheval après avoir brisé les voitures selon ma louable coutume, et j'espere vous ecrire dans peu de jours que nous sommes arrivés à pied. Il y a un peu de fatigue, mais quoique plusieurs de mes compagnons en aïent beaucoup souffert je ne m'en suis pas du tout apperceu. Peut-etre le capitaine qui porte ma lettre ira vous faire une visite alors je vous prie de le bien recevoir.

J'ose à peine penser au temps de vos couches, mon cher coeur, et cependant j'y pense à tous les moments de ma journée. Je ne m'en occupe pas sans un tremblement, une crainte affreuse—en verité mon coeur, je suis bien malheureux d'etre si loin de vous—quand vous ne m'aimeriés pas vous devriés me plaindre; mais vous m'aimés, et nous nous aimerons toujours, mon cher coeur, toujours nous serons heureux l'un par l'autre. Ce petit billet est bien raccourci en comparaison des volumes que je vous ai envoyés, mais vous en recevrés un autre sous peu de jours.

Plus je m'avance vers le nord plus j'aime et ce païs et ses habitants. Il n'y a pas de politesses de prevenances que je n'en epprouve quoique plusieurs sachent à peine qui je suis. Mais je vous manderai tout cela plus au long à Philadelphie, je n'ai ici que le tems de vous prier mon cher coeur de ne pas oublier un malheureux qui a païé bien cher le tort de vous quitter et qui n'avoit jamais si bien senti combien il vous aime.

Mes respects à Mde. d'Ayen, mes tendres compliments à ma soeur. Faites savoir à Mons. de Coïgni et à Mr. de Poix que je me porte bien s'il arrive malheur à des lettres que j'enverrai par une autre occasion qu'on m'a dit ou je vous ecrirai encore un mot mais je n'en suis pas si sur que de celleci.

To Adrienne de Noailles de Lafayette

[Annapolis] le 23 juillet 1777

Je tombe toujours, mon cher coeur, sur des occasions qui vont partir; mais pour celle-ci elle est si pressée que je n'ai qu'un demi quart d'heure à moi. Le vaisseau est à la voile, et je ne peux vous mander autre chose que mon heureuse arrivée à Annapolis à quarante lieües de Philadelphie. Je ne vous dirai pas comment elle est car en descendant de cheval je m'arme d'une petite broche trempée dans de l'encre blanche. Vous avés du recevoir cinq lettres de moi à moins que le roi George n'en ait receu quelqu'une. La derniere a été expediée il y a trois jours. Je vous y rendois compte de ma bonne santé qui n'a pas été alterée un moment, de mon impatience d'arriver à Philadelphie. J'apprends ici une mauvaise nouvelle. Ticonderoga le poste le plus fort d'Amerique a été forcé par les ennemis. C'est bien facheux. Il faudra tacher de reparer cela. En revanche nos troupes ont pris un officier general anglois près de New York. Je suis tous les jours plus malheureux de vous avoir quittée, mon cher coeur, j'espere recevoir de vos nouvelles à Philadelphie, et cette esperance tient une grande place dans l'impatience que j'ai d'y etre arrivé. Adieu, mon coeur, je suis si pressé que je ne sais pas ce que je vous mande, mais je sais bien, mon cher coeur, que je vous aime plus tendrement que jamais, qu'il falloit le chagrin de cette separation pour me convaincre à quel point vous m'etiés chere, et que je donnerois la moitié de mon sang pour obtenir le plaisir de vous embrasser une fois, de vous dire une fois moi même combien je vous aime.

Mes respects à Mde. d'Ayen, mille compliments à la vicomtesse à mes soeurs à tous mes amis je n'ai le tems d'ecrire qu'à vous. Ah mon coeur si vous saviés combien je vous regrette, combien je souffre d'etre loin de vous, et tout ce que me dit mon coeur en verité vous me trouveriés un peu digne d'etre aimé. Il ne me reste plus de place pour mon Henriette, dirai-je pour mes chers enfans, embrassés, mon cher coeur, embrassés cent mille fois, je serai toujours de moitié.

[*Addressed to:* Mde. la Mise. de Lafayette de la part d'un fils tendre qui embrasse sa maman de tout son coeur, en lui presentant des hommages bien respectueux mais encore plus tendres.]

Journal of a Campaign in America by Du Rousseau de de Fayolle[E]

Le 12, nous aperçûmes la terre à neuf heures du matin. Nous eûmes l'espoir d'entrer ce jour-là dans un port, mais notre espérance fut vaine. Nous louvoyâmes tout le jour et toute la nuit sans pouvoir arriver à rien.

La nuit du 13, nous eûmes des vents contraires, nous regagnâmes le large et dans le jour nous revînmes à la terre et mouillâmes à portée d'un petit port appelé Georgeston.

M. le marquis de Lafayette et M. de Kalb descendirent pour prendre des connaissances; le navire mouilla et attendit jusqu'au lendemain 14 à midi le retour de ces messieurs, qui nous dirent que nous n'aurions aucune ressource pour rejoindre Charleston à moins que d'aller à pied et par des chemins affreux. Alors il y en eut la moitié qui se décidèrent à prendre leur parti par terre.

Je fus du nombre de ceux qui restèrent à bord. Je n'en fis pas mieux, quoique nous soyons arrivés à bon port, mais c'est le plus grand de tous les hasards, les Anglais ayant croisé avec une attention particulière devant le port de Charleston, où nous sommes entrés le 18 à dix heures du matin. Notre ressource était d'échouer si nous eussions été poursuivis, mais c'eût été une mauvaise affaire. Enfin, après cinquante-six jours de traversée, non compris notre séjour du Passage, nous sommes arrivés très heureusement à Charleston, port dans la Caroline. Il nous reste encore plus de deux cent lieues à faire pour rejoindre Philadelphie, mais nous les ferons comme nous pourrons, par terre et à grands frais, car tout est d'une cherté affreuse.

La ville de Charleston est assez jolie: les rues y sont large et alignées, les maisons de même, quelques-unes bâties en briques, les autres en bois, toutes couvertes de cette dernière espèce. L'entrée du port de Charleston est fort difficile à cause d'une barre sur laquelle à basse mer il n'y a pas d'eau, et à haute, et cela dans les plus grandes marées, un vaisseau prenant plus de dix-sept pieds d'eau ne peut point entrer. Le nôtre, qui n'en prend que 13, a touché trois fois; à la verité la marée descendait. A la suite de cette barre, sont deux forts battant la rivière par son travers; les batteries en sont parfaitement bien faites. Le premier s'appelle le fort Moultrie, nom de celui qui l'a si vaillamment défendu l'année 1776, le 28 de juin, que les Anglais tentèrent par une forte marée de passer la barre et entrer dans le port de Charleston. Trois frégates réussirent, mais s'échouèrent vis-à-vis le fort, ne connaissant pas la rivière. Elles furent foudroyées par le feu de ce fort; depuis cette époque, ils n'ont fait aucune tentative.

Plus loin est le fort Johnson, devant lequel il faut encore que les vaisseaux passent pour aller à la ville; il y a deux batteries l'une sur l'autre, et en tout il est composé d'une vingtaine. L'on travaille à présent à faire des batteries le long de la rivière pour défendre le port et par conséquent l'entrée de la ville qui, du côté de la terre, n'a aucune espèce de fortification.

Partie de Charleston le 26 juin pour aller à Philadelphie, notre caravane était composée de 6 officers et 4 domestiques ou charretiers, ce qui faisait 10 personnes, traînés par 2 chariots attelés chacun de quatre chevaux. Le chariot dans lequel j'étais a perdu le troisième ou quatrième jour un cheval de limon; il est mort dans une heure de tranchées sur la route. Nous avons été obligés d'en racheter un autre qui nous a coûté fort cher, mais qui s'est trouvé bon.

Nous avons éprouvé des chaleurs abominables dans la Caroline du Sud, et pour nous refaire, à la fin de nos journées, des logements affreux et de l'eau exécrable. Aussi un des nôtres est-il tombé malade à Charlotte, seconde petite ville que nous avons rencontrée. C'est un des plus mauvais endroits que l'on puisse imaginer. Nous y avons cependant trouvé un docteur qui a eu grand soin du malade; il l'a pris chez lui ainsi que nous, et je n'ai quitté sa maison que quand j'ai eu laissé l'officer malade hors de danger. Nous avons acheté dans ce même Charlotte deux autres chevaux pour ajouter aux quatre premiers qui étaient trop chargés, et afin de pouvoir rattraper le temps que la maladie nous a fait perdre.

L'autre chariot a suivi sa route; il aura au moins quinze jours d'avance. Pour moi, je suis parti le 19 juillet à cheval pour arriver plus vite à Philadelphie et faire avoir des secours pécunieux au chariot qui arrivera longtemps après moi. Les espèces commencent à nous manquer par les emplettes et séjours que nous avons été obligés de faire.

Ce qu'il y a de certain jusqu'à présent, rien n'est flatteur pour nous, n'ayant trouvé de secours qu'à force d'argent, et en total des gens fort peu officieux. Tous les hommes bien bâtis et alertes, mais les femmes bien maussades. Je ne sais si l'avenir sera plus agréable, mais il n'est rien de ce que l'on nous a dit en France. Ils sont désunis pour la cause commune et je ne crois pas qu'ils fassent jamais rien de merveilleux. La vanité les poignarde; ils veulent être tous officers et non soldats, et ne valent pas mieux dans l'un que dans l'autre. Il faut voir jusqu'au bout pour être plus sûr de son jugement.

Je compte être à Philadelphie, s'il ne m'arrive point d'accident, du 8 ou 15 d'août. Je laisse notre chariot avec cinq chevaux bons et frais, ce qui me fait espérer qu'il arrivera à bien.

Arrivé à Philadelphie le 6 août après avoir éprouvé dans ma route des chaleurs très fortes et trouvé de fort mauvais chemins; mais à cheval on se sauve de partout. Ma route a été très heureuse et sans événement, quoique je l'aie faite tout seul et que j'aie traversé six cents milles de pays dont la plus grande partie est tout bois. Cependant la différence des provinces est très grande, et celle de Virginie, qui a deux cents lieues de large sur près de trois cents lieues de long, est celle du continent qui fournit le plus et qui est la plus riche et la mieux cultivée. Celle de Maryland est belle aussi, mais je n'en ai vu que 30 ou quarante milles au plus. Celle de Pensylvanie est plus ancienne, par conséquent plus cultivée, mais je ne la crois pas plus riche que la Virginie.

Philadelphie, capitale de la Pensylvanie, est une belle et grande ville, mais triste par la largeur de ses rues et le peu d'élévation des maisons, qui sont cependant assez bien bâties, toutes en briques et couvertes en bois. Elle paraît riche, mais la guerre y a fait de grands changements.

Notre réception dans cette ville par le Congrès n'a pas été ce que nous attendions, mais, au contraire, on ne peut rien de plus malhonnête. Elle a même été au point de nous faire pressentir que l'on était fort étonné de nous voir. Aussi désirons-nous pour la plus grande partie nous en retourner en France. M. le marquis de Lafayette, après avoir eu lieu particulièrement de s'en plaindre, d'après les démarches généreuses et honnêtes qu'il a faites en leur faveur, en a obtenu enfin le grade de général-major. Cela a produit l'effet qu'ils en attendaient, et il est devenu, comme ci-devant, leur zélé partisan, malgré la mauvaise composition de tout ce qui intéresse les progrès qu'il veuille faire tant en civil qu'en guerre. Il est impossible de trouver rien qui ait l'air plus désordonné que tout ce qui a rapport à la guerre. Leur armée est misérable dans tous les points, et encore plus pour la composition des officers, dont on ne peut se faire un idée. Il n'y existe aucune espèce de discipline; mais ce qu'il y a encore de plus contre eux c'est une ignorance et une fausse vanité, qui ne leur permettra pas de résister aux forces du général anglais s'il veut faire quelque tentative pour conquérir leur pays, ce qui est la chose la plus facile. Il est même incroyable qu'il y ait fallu jusqu'à présent pour réussir. C'est sans doute politique de sa part.

Ce qu'il y a de certain, je n'envie point du tout combattre pour leur liberté, attendu qu'il n'y a pour les honnêtes gens que du déshonneur ou la mort à gagner. L'on ne peut compter sur rien quand l'on se porte en avant. Cet esprit de liberté, qui les fait agir dans ce moment-là, produit un tout autre effet sur eux, et bien loin de chercher à seconder les bonnes intentions que l'on peut avoir, ils disent qu'ils ne veulent point y aller et qu'ils préfèrent s'en retourner, ce qu'ils font tout de suite. D'ailleurs, quand il pleut très décidément, ils ne marchent point. Ce serait à ne point finir en rendant leurs ridicules.

Parti de Philadelphie le 14 septembre 1777 pour me rendre à Boston, je n'ai quitté cette ville qu'après avoir reçu mon congé du Congrès et la lettre d'échange sur Paris pour payer mon retour en France.

Memoir by the Chevalier Dubuysson

Je ne parlerai point de notre traversée. Mille petites avantures longues a raconter, interessantes pour nous dans leurs tems, le seroit peu aujourdhui pour ceux qui me liront. Il doit sufir de dire que le vaiseaux achété par le mis. de La Fayette est parti de Bordeaux le 26 mars, et est arivé a Charles-town le 20 juin. Les causes d'une aussi longue traversée sont notre sejour forcé sur la cote d'Espagne pour attendre le mis. de La Fayette et Mr. de Mauroy, des longs calmes, et des vents souvents contraires. La mauvaise administration des vivres, aiant été distribué avec profusion dans les commencemens, nous a forcé a beaucoup de frugalité dans les derniers jours de notre voiage.

Notre desir etoit darriver droit au port de Charles-touun: mais les courants et la Crainte de tomber entre les mains des anglois nous ont fait aborder 25 lieues plus haut. Apres avoir pris langue, le mis. de La Fayette, le bon. de Kalb, 6 officiers et 2 domestiques y dessindirent. Les autres resterent dans le vaiseaux qui n'ariva que 4 jours apres a Charles-touun. Nous y fumes par terre a pied, naiant put trouver que 3 chevaux. Quelques de nous etoient en bottes: mais ne pouvant marcher ainsi, ils furent obligés de les jetter, et dachever la route nus-pieds, maniere de voiager peu comode sur un sable brulant, et dans des bois. J'en ai eü pendant quinze jours les jambes aussi grosses que les cuisses. [Nous] avions preferé de nous charger d'armes plustot que de linges, pour nous defendre des negres-maraus. Aussi arivames nous apres trois jours de marche a Charles-touun, fort comme des guex et des

brigans. Nous fumes reçeu en consequence; et montrés au droit par la populace du païs lorsque nous nous dimes des officiers francois uniquement con-
duis par le desir de la gloire, et de Defendre leur liberté, et traité d'avanturiers, même par les françois, qui sont en grand nombre a Charles-touun. La
pluspart de ces françois sont des officiers perdus de dettes, plusieurs chassés
de leurs corp. Les colonies francoises en fournisent baucoup. Les gouveneurs
les purgent le plus qu'ils peuvent de tous les mauvais sujets, qui arivant de
Françe, en leur donnant des letres de recomandation pour les genereaux
anglo-ameriquains. Les premiers ont été fort bien reçeu: mais leur conduite
aiant fait conaitre ce qu'ils etoient, on n'a plus de foy aujourdhui aux lettres
de recomandation, et l'on fait en Amerique fort peü de cas des gens qui les
apportent. En tout les françois y·sont bien peü paié des sacrifices, qu'ils font
pour un peuple qui leur en sçai peü de grés, et qui le merite aussi peü.

   Le lendemain de notre arivé le vaisseau du mis. de La Fayette entra triom-
phant dans le port, et fit une revolution sur les esprit en notre faveur. Nous
somes alors parfaitement acceuillés; les officiers françois qui avoient été les
premiers a se moquer de nous vinrent en foule faire bassement la cour au
marquis de La Fayette, et chercherent a se rallier a lui.

   La populaçe de Charles-touun ainsi que celle de toute cette partie du continent deteste les françois et l'accable d'invectives. Il n'en est pas de même de la
bonne compagnie. Nous en fumes parfaitement acceuillés, et fetés par tout.
Nous avons passé huit jours en fête et gala. Nous en avons eu une dans un
fort a 6 mille de la ville des plus manifiques. On y rendés au marquis les honneurs que l'on auroit put rendre a un marechal de France, ou au protecteur
de la liberté.

   Ce fort est curieux par sa construction—j'en apporterai un plan—par 80
pieçes de cannon prises aux françois sur le vaiseaux le Foudroÿant, et par la
vigoureuse defense qu'il a fait l'année derniere: mais plus encore par un reve-
tement interieur et exterieur de palmier couchés les uns sur les autres; et liés
fortement. Cet arbre est si sepongieux, que le boulet sy arrestré, et entre dans
le bois sans faire d'eclat. Le troü se referme de lui même: de sorte que les
anglois l'on rendü plus fort en le battant, etant aujourdhui comme fraisé de
boulets.

   Nous avions contés partire le 25 juin: mais il se presente un obstacles très
imprevüe. Le marquis avoit sur son vaisaux une riche Cargaison. Il setoit
anoncé pour Vandre le tout. Il avoit trouvée de 3 a 4 cent pour cent de profit
sur cette some considerable. Il esperois tous nous obliger. Nous contions en
avoir assée pour passer au moins 2 ou 3 ans avec aissance dans ce payis cy;
mais quelle fut notre surprise quand le Capitaine du vaissaux aporta au marquis un biliet de 40000# signée de luy au profit de l'armateur, par lequel La
Fayette Consant que le vaissaux et toutes sa Cargaison retourne en France
pour y aître vandü, et que sur le produit l'armateur preleve les 40000# a luy
düe, et 35 pour Cent, 25 dassurance, et 10 de Comissions. Le marquis auroit
signée a Bordaux sans examin tout ce que luy auroit demandée, luy qui luy
offeroit de seconder son amour pour la gloire; mais a Charltoune son Carac-
taire obligant soufrit Crüelément davoir été ainsi volé; nous fumes tres
heureux de trouver a gros interest 36 mille livre a Empruntér. Avec cette

some nous fimes nos Equipages et nous préparames a partire pour Philadelphye.

Nous nous partagames en trois bandes. 6 de nous achetere 2 Charios
7000#. Cette premiere depance a été plus chers que la notre: mais il leurs en
a néenmoins bien moin Coutés qua nous pour arivér. Il ont eu lagremens de
porter avec eux tous leurs Equipages sans aitre volés comme nous. Trois de
nous ont été par eau sans craindre d'etrepris par les anglois. La Fayette, Le
baron de Kalb et ceux de nous qui avions debarqués avec eux avons loué 4
chariost 5700 pour nous conduire avec nos equipages. L'aide de camp du
marquis se chargea d'etre notre guide, quoiqu'il n'eut aucune idée du païं.
Voila quel fut l'ordre de marche en sortant de Charles-touun. La marche etoit
ouverte par un des gens du marquis vetus en hussard. La voiture du marquis
etoit une espece de sofa decouvert porté par 4 resort avec un avante-train. A
coté de sa voiture il avoit un domestique a cheval faisant les fonctions
d'ecuier. Le baron de Kalb etoit dans la même voiture. Les deux colonels con-
silers de La Fayette suivoient dans une seconde voiture a deux roués. La
seconde etoit celles des aides de camp. La 4eme. pour les equipages et la
marche etoit fermé par un negre a cheval.

Je suprimerai le detail des avantures de notre route comme celui de notre
traversée, quoiqu'elle renferme plusieurs remarques et quelques evenements
assce interessant et curieux. Je me reserve de les dire moi même.

Des le quatrieme jour une partie de nos voitures etoient en poussiere.
Plusieurs de nos cheveaux, qui etoient presque tous vieux et pensif, etoient
crevis ou esetopés. Nous avons été obligé d'en acheter d'autres en route. Ces
depenses ont consomés tous nos fonds. Nous avons été obligés de laisser en
route partie de nos equipages, et partie nous a été vollé. Nous avons faits une
grande partie du chemain a pied, couchants souvent dans les bois, mourant de
faim, arassés de cheau, plusieurs de nous avec la fiebvre et la disenterie: enfin
apres 32 jours de marche nous sommes arivés a Philadelphie, dans un etat encore plus piteuse que lors de notre entrés a Charles-touun. Je crois pouvoir
dire qu'il ny a pas de campagne en Europe plus dure que ce voiage. Les
peines ny sont jammais continuelles. Elles sont même compensées par bien des
plaisirs: au lieu que dans ce voiage nos meaux s'augmentoient chacque jour,
et n'avoient d'autres soulagement que l'espoir d'ariver enfin a Philadelphie.
L'idée flateusse que nous nous étions faite de la reception qu'on nous feroit
nous soutenoit; et nous auroit je puis le dire avec verité fait braver les tra-
veaux les plus rudes avec le même zele et la même quieté, que l'on m'a veü
lorsque je me suis decidé au parti que j'ai pris. Nous etions tous animés du
même esprit. Le zele de La Fayette auroit enflamé celui, qui en auroit eü
moins que lui.

Nous arivames le 27 juilliet au matin. Apres nous etre un peü decrossés
nous fumes chez le president du Congres, a qui nous remîmes nos letres de
recomandation et d'affaire, et nos capitulations. Il nous renvoia au sieur
Mouse membre du congress. Celui-ci nous donna rendez-vous pour le lendemain a la porte du congress. Pendant ce temps nos papiers furent lüs et ex-
aminés. Nous fumes exats le lendemain. On nous fit attendre fort long-tems:
enfin paru le Sr. Mouse avec un autre membre. Il nous dit: "Monsieur parle

fort bien français. Il est chargé d'expedier tout ceux de votre nation. Ainsi c'est a lui a qui vous aures d'or-én-avant affaire." Il rentra; et le dit Sieur nous reçeu dans la rüe ou il nous laissee apres nous nous avoir traite en tres bon francois comme des avanturiers. Il termine son harangue en nous disant: messieurs aves-vous veü les pouvoirs de Mr. Dain? Nous l'avions chargé de nous envoier quatre ingenieurs francois. Au lieu de cela il nous a envoie le sieur Du Coudray avec des pretendüs ingenieurs qui ne le sont pas, et des ar-tillieurs qui n'ont pas servis. Nous avons chargés Mr. Francquelin de nous en-voier ces 4 ingenieurs. Ils nous sont arivés. Les officiers françois sont bien appres a venir nous servir sans que nous les demendions. L'année derniere il est vrai nous avions besoin d'officier; mais cette année nous en avon baucoup, et de tous experimentés.

Tel fut notre premier reception du Congres. Nous ne scavions que'a pen-ser. Il est impossible d'etre plus stupefoit que nous le fumes. Mrs. de La Fayette, de Kalb et de Mauroy suivis de 10 officiers avec des recomendation semblables aux notres, au moins toleré, s'il n'etoient pas avoué ouvertement par le gouvernement de Françe, pouvoient-ils s'attendre a une pareil recep-tion? Le baron de Kalb entre autres connüs dans le païe et même du Congress.

Nous primes le parti d'attendre et de chercher la motif de cet affront avant de nous en plaindre. Nous l'attribuames avec raison a la mauvaise conduite de nos compatriotes qui nous avoient devancés. Nous apprimes effectivement l'inconduite de plusieurs, et le discredit que leur conduite avoit donné aux letres de recomandation, qu'ils avoient aporté en venant de nos colonies; et qu'a cela se joignoient plusieurs autres raisons. La conduite faible d'un Mr. de Fermois a la poste de Ticonderago—ce Mr. de Fermoix est françois et a le grade de brigadier-major—le mepris de tous les officiers de la brigade de Mr. de Bore, pour leur chef, aussi françois; le zele outré et quelque fois temeraire et indiscret d'un marquis de La Voirie qui a levé ici a ses frais un regnt., tous sert ici a faire detester les francois: car ceux qui ont une tres bonne conduite y contribuent comme ceux dont je viens de parler. Mr. de Canoite brigadier-major est detesté des officiers de sa brigade et jalousé de tous les genereaux même de Varsignton, parcequils fait servir sa brigade, et qu'au lieu de la lais-ser oisive dans le camp, il la fait manoeuvre et l'instruit lui même.

Mais ce qui je crois nous a fait le plus de tort, aiant revolte tout le Congress c'est Mr. Ducoudrai. Il est arivé ici avec un ton de Seigneur, se donnont pour en etre un, et pour brigadier en Françe, se disant conseiller des ministres de Françe et ami de tous les prinçes et ducs, dont il montre des lettres. Il a presenté au Congress une capitulation signée du Sr. Dain, par la quelle il doit avoir le grade de general-major, et etre comandant en chef de l'artillerie et du genie et de tous les forts faits et a faire, avec pouvoir de nommer, faire, defendre, pourvoir aux emplois &c. sans etre teneü a rendre de compte qu'au general et au Congress, avec des apointemens de 36000, et une promesse du 300000# apres la guerre finnies. Il a poussé l'impudence jusqu'a dire et ecrire au Congress, que c'est a ses solicitations vives et pressantes qu'ils devoient les secours envoiés par la Françe.

Le Congress n'osoit ny refuser, ny accorder ses enormes demendes; lorsque les quatres ingenieurs envoiés par Mr. Fanquelin sont arivés, on leur a confronté en plain Congress Mr. Ducoudrai. Il l'ont demasqué, et prouvé qu'il en imposoit en tout, jusque sur son etat, etant chef de brigade d'artilerie et non Brigadier, et fils d'un marchand de vin de Rennes. Du Coudrai a donné un memoire, ou il invective tous les francois, même le mis. de La Fayette a qui il a escrit une letre fort malhonête.

D'apres ces eclaircisemens, sur les motif de la conduite du Congres a notre egard, nous les adressames un memoire pour demander d'etre plaçés, ou defraiés et renvoiés. La Faiette, le Baron et Mr. de Mauroy firent sentir qu'ils n'etoient pas faits pour etre traité comme les aventuriers, qui s'etoient presentés et confondus avec eux. Le Congres leur envoia le Sr. Lauvelle le même qui nous avoit si mal reçeu. Il etoit acompagné d'un autre membre plus polli et plus adroit; ils firent des espeçes d'excuses a La Fayette. Le second membre dont je viens de parler avoit vraisemblablement ordre de sonder La Fayette. Il le vit en particulier, lui promet mons et merveille, et sçu de lui tout ce qu'il vouloit scavoir. Dans une seconde conference avec La Faÿette, il lui fit consentir a accepter du Congress le grade de general-major, mais seulement de ce jour, sans egard a la capitulation, et sans aucun apointemens ny commandement, et en lui faisant prometre quil n'auroit jamais aucun pretention a commandent une division. Deux heures apres avoir fait cette promesse, on lui envoia son ruban avec une letre du Congress par la quelle on lui dit que "par consideration pour son nom, ses grandes alliances, et veü les sacrifices qu'il avoit fait par amour pour la liberté, le Congress vouloit bien le nommer de ce jour general major, bien entendu qu'il n'auroit aucune pretention a aucuns comandements, apointemens, ny pension, atachés a ce grade. On le mena sur le champ au general Waginton, qui lui fit milles amitites, l'engagea a prendre un logement ches lui, et a accepter sa table pour toute la campagne: enfin on l'ebloui si fort qu'il nous oublia un instant; mais je lui rend justice. Il a un trop excellent coeur pour que cet oubli put etre long. Il fit l'impossible pour nous faire plaçer, mais en vain, car il est sans credit; et s'il eu teneü bon. de Kalb auroit été general-major, et nous aurions tous été placés. On n'a donné au marquis le grade de general major que par egard pour son nom, et non pour sa persone, parsque ce grade sera sans fonxion. La même cause nous auroit fait tout plaçer selon la capitulation s'il ne fut obstiné a faire cause comune avec nous. Il a été tres faché d'avoir accepté le ruban. Il a voulu le renvoier. Mais on la engage par des promesses a les garder, et on lui a envoié un chariot a 4 cheveaux pour faire cesser ses plaintes. La Fayette a été emmené sur le champ au camp. Quand a nous on nous a laissé a Philadelphie, et le Congress nous a envoié en papier 18000# pour paie nos dettes, sans nous faire aucunes autres reponses.

Lorsqu'il a parü decidé, que nous nous en retournerions tous, exepté le marquis et son aide de camp, je fis un memoire particulier, pour etre presente au general, et un pour le Congress. Par ces memoires je disois qu'etant venüs avec La Faÿette, etant son parent, du même regnt. que lui, recomandé par les mêmes persones que lui, je dois dire en France pour y justifier mon retour que La Fayette n'a pas même ici le credit d'y faire placer le seul officier pour le quel il s'interesse. J'envoiai ces memoires a La Fayette au camp pour les signer. Il vint le lendemain me trouver a Philadelphie. Il me promet que je serois plaçe major d'un regnt. de cavalerie, si je voulois attendre et rester avec lui. C'etoit tout ce que je demandois. Je consenti volontier a rester. Il me remercia de ne pas l'abandonner, et me promit qu'il alloit traveiller pour moy. Au bout de quelque tems ne voiant rien venir, je parlai de mes esperances a un membre du Congress chez le quel je loge. Il m'avoua que le marquis s'abusoit, s'il croÿoit me faire plaçer, qu'il etoit decidé que l'on ne vouloit aucun francois, et que le general Warsington loin de donner une division a La Fayette, comme il me l'avoit dit, se plaignoit de lui au president du Congrèss, disant qu'il le tourmentoit pour avoir un division, qu'il ne scavoit comment s'en defaire, que le Congres en etoit tres mecontant, le Mis. aiant promi par ecrit de ne jamais demender de division.

Quand je vis que je n'avois plus despoir d'etre placé, je me decidai avec douleur a revenir avec mes commarades et le baron de Kalb, des que nous aurions obtenu nos derniers demandes pour notre retour. Mais auparavant je voulüs au moins voir l'armée, et en demander la permission au Congrais offrant de servir comme volontaire, ne demendant que dun ration pour vivre jusqu'au moment de nôtre depart. On m'a refusé cette graçe, en me repondant que si je venois a faire quelque action qui merita recompense je demendrois encore a etre placé, ce qu'on ne vouloit pas faire pour aucun francois.

En entreprenant un aussi long voiage l'ambition n'etoit pas mon seul but. J'etois desolé d'etre venüs pres du theatre de la guerre sans pouvoir la faire, et sans prendre aucunes des conoisances que j'etois venüs chercher. Je me decidai a aller au camp malgré le refus que nous avoit fait. Je pris une chemise dans ma poche, un fusil et une bayonnette, et j'ai offrit mes services a Mr. Canoite brigadier-major qui passe pour avoir la brigade la mieux instruite et la plus diciplinée. Il me reçeu a merveille. Il me donna un matelat dans sa tante et me permit de faire le service de volontaire dans sa brigade. J'ai fait ce metier pendant quelques tems, et j'ai pris quelques idées du service et des troupes ameriquaines. La manoeuvre quelle executent le mieux, ou pour ainsi dire la seule quelle executent c'est de faire un decharge tres juste derriere des foines (c'est-a-dire des bruieres de 5 pied de heaut qui sont extremement comunes et entourent les champs defrichés). Un regnt. se place derriere une de ces foines, attend l'ennemi derriere, etant bien couvert. Il passe les fusils a travers, ajuste bien, et apres avoir tiré leur coup il decampe, et sote avec toute la legereté possible plusieurs foines, et va a un quart de lieu de la attendre l'ennemi derriere encore quelques foines. Si l'ennemi parvit on repette la même manoeuvre plusieurs fois. Comme je n'ai trouve a ce genre de service rien dasses instructif, pour le faire long-tems comme simple volontaire, et que mes camarades etoient tous a Philadelphie dont il doivent partir incessament, je suis revenü les joindre.

Les forces ameriquaines sont de 25 mille hommes de troupes pretendües reglées et de 50000 hommes de milices. Les premiers sont mal vetues, et tres incompletes. La moitié des officers toujour absants, sous pretexte de faire des recreües. Les milices sont baucoup plus belles et tres completes. Les causes de la diference de ces deux especes de troupes sont que le Congres ne donne que 200 dengagement a un homme pour faire toute la guere dans les troupes reglées, et que les milices ne sont qu'un service de 4 mois, au bout de quel

tems elles sont remplacées par d'autres, que tout le monde est teneü a ce service, et que les gens riches s'en dispense en donnant jusqua onze cent livres a
celui qui le fait a leur place. Le Congress et Wasington ont dit a l'un, "tu seras
soldat," a l'autre, "je te fais lieutenant, capitaine, colonel, ou tambour, ou general." Ils ont dit a celui la, "tu defendra aussi la liberté commune, et pour cela
tu servira [à] l'armée, ou tu sera chargé des magazines," a cet autre, "tu par-
ticipera aussi a la même gloire en suivant l'armée comme vivandier,
boulanger, boucher, &c." Ils ont criés a tout liberté, et tout a marche a ce cri,
et s'est crü du coeur et un peuple de heros, tant qu'ils n'ont pas veü de
danger. Mais alors les poltrons, et c'est le grand nombre, ont dit, "Nous con-
senterons a defendre notre liberté, et celle de nos compatriotes, mais comme
il faut des chantiers et des fourniseurs des vivres, nous preferons d'etre chan-
tier du general, au grade de lieutenant, car l'un meure de faim, et l'autre vit
bien cependant tous les deux servent pour la même cause. Je prefere ont-ils
dit etre vivandier, fourniseur des vivres &c. a etre capitaine. Tout deux tra-
veillant pour la même cause, mais l'un s'enrichit sans rien craindre, et l'autre a
souvent grand paur sans s'enrichir. Quel fond peut-on faire sur des troupes
dont foila l'esprit?

Il seroit superflu d'entraire icy dans des details sur les Causes de cette
guere. Tout le monde les sai en Europe. Mais Ce qu'on ignore peut estre,
Cest quelle finiroit aujourd'huy, si l'Angletaire consantoit a labolition de 30
million de dettes qu'il luy etoit düe par l'Amerique, et dont le signal de bancroute a été la levée de l'etandard de Revolte, on dit assée publiquement icy
que la paix ne tiens qua cette Condition, et a une promesse d'estre soutenue
dans une pareil bancroute vis a vis les puissances de l'Europe.

La paix est desirée par beaucoup de gens. Les quakres, qui sont dans cette
province la plus grands nombres d'habitans, sont presque tous royalistes, et
favorisent autant qu'il peuvent l'arivée d'Hauve a Phidalphye. On les y a forces
par les vexations que le Congrès leurs a fait Eprouvér, et en les excluans de
toutes les charges du gouevernemen sous pretence qu'ils ne se battent pas. Il
fournissent sous main des vivres a l'armée enemies. Les habitans de ce païes
ayant peu de plaisir se fons un habitude invincible de leux dont ils peuvent
jouires, de sorte que la prevations du thé, des vins de Maders, de quelques
Epices &c. est beaucoup plus grande pour eux quelle ne seroit pour un Euro-
péen, et leurs fais desirer la paix. Beaucoup de gens qui ons leurs parenes et
amis dans l'armée Englaise la desire Egalement. Cette guere doit donc aitre
regardée plustot Comme une guere civile, que come la revolte d'un peuples
qui cherches a secouer le joug de son souverain. Et d'après cella on augura
avec vraisemblance quelle ne peut estre de longue durée.

Nous venons enfin d'aracher aujourd'huy 15 daoust une reponse positive
du Congrès. Il est decidé a nous renvoyer tous, exceptés La Fayette, en
payant notre retoure. Nous avions donés nos demandes, qui consitent primo
de nous defraiyer de tout, secondo, un passport du général Englois, ou la permission de passer a l'armée Engloise dela En Engletaire et en France, tersio,
un Certificat, come quoi Mr. Daine leurs Envoyée en France na pas de pouvoir pour envoyer des officiers françois ni faire de Capitulation avec eux. Le
Congrès a tous acordés, a la resserve de la permission de passer a l'armée

Engloise. Ainsi nous songons tous a notre départ, que nous ferions même sur le Cham, si nos Equipages n'etois pas dispersai en plusieurs endrois. Je Crains bien que nous ne soyons obligées pour les retrouver de retourner a Charlestouune, ou nous en avons une partis ou bien de les abandoner. Dans tous les Cas nous esperons aitre en France avant la fin du mois de janvier.

Extrais de la lettre qui acompagnée ce memoire

le 12 Septembre [1777]

Rien de changés a notre situations, Et nous partons sans avoir pu obtenir d'employe ni persuader le marquis de La Fayette de revenir avec nous. Il a été Blessée le 11 aoust d'une balcs a la jambe mais il en ai totalement retablie, il sest Comportes dans cette affaire avec la plus grande valeure.

Les affaires prenent une fort mauvaise tournure en Amerique. Vous pouvés doner ces nouvelles pour très vraix. Le général Hauve a debarqué le 10 juliette, a 18 lieues de Philadelphye, avec 12 mille homes, 5 cens chevaux, et 50 pieces de canons. Vasginton posté a 8 lieu de luy, et a 10 de Philadelphye, avec près de 25 mille homes, luy a laisse faire son débarquement, et c'est luy même fortifiés dans un point inataquable. Hauve la laissé faire ne voulant point l'ataquer, mais prandre Philadelphy au bout de 15 jours. Les troupes etant reposées il a fait une marche forcés pandant tout une nuit, et est venue se poster a la même hauteur de Philadelphy, que les Ameriquins sur leurs droites. Ce mouvemens a obligué Vasginton a quiter son camp, et il y a eu une escarmouche assée vive. Le 11 aoust a 9 heures du matin les Anglois on fait une fausse ataque par la droite, ayant masqué leurs front, par un feu considérable d'artilerie. Vasginton, y ayant porté les forces, les anglois se sont developés sur leurs gauche avec beaucoup d'ordre, et prontitude, et ont culbuté tout ce qu'ils ont rencontré. Les seules divisions de milord Setirlin, et de Mr. de Canoite ont teneus quelques tems. Le mis. de La Fayette s'est porté a cette derniere, ou etoient quelques francois. Il a mis pied a terre, et a fait l'impossible par la faire charger, la bajonete au bout du fusil. Les francois metoient eux même a chacque homme la bajonette au bout le deur fusil; et La Fayette les poussoit par le dos pour charger. Mais les Ameriquoins peu fait a ce genre de combat n'ont jamais voulu mordre, et bientot cette brigade a fui comme le reste de l'armée, qui a été se rallier a quatre lieues de la. C'est la ou La Fayette a été blessé.

On a dit hier 11 septembre, que l'armée de Varsington vouloit avoir sa revanche, mais on ogure quelle sera batüe encore une fois, et il y a aparier qu'avant 6 jours Houe sera maïtre de Philadelphie. Notre depart a été retardé par l'attente de nos equipages. Si nous les avions put avoir il y a long-tems que nous serions parti. Depuis deux mois le baron de Kalb et moy sommes avec deux chemises, et un seul habit tout dechiré, mais bien portant; et malgré mes meaux fort contant d'avoir fait ce voiage. Mon infortune constante m'a accoutume a soufrir patiament, et a scavoir trouver des momens de plaisirs au millieu des peines et de l'infortune. J'ai adressé des copies du memoire que je vous envoi a Mr. le comte de Broglie et a mon oncle il y a 15 jours. Mais comme les letres que nous ecrivons en Europe y arivent dificilement, il seroit possible qu'ils ne les eussent pas reçeus. En ce cas je vous prirois de leur en faire passer des copies.

Request for Verification of Appointments for Valfort and Lesser

[Philadelphie, environ 29 juillet 1777]

Les Sieurs De Lessers et De Valfort, colonels au Service de France, réclament la Justice des personnes qui sont chargées de les entendre, pour être employés en qualité de Brigadiers Généraux, dans les armées des Etats Unis D'Amérique.

Monsieur Deane, envoyé des êtats en France, n'a d'abord établis ces deux officiers que comme colonels, sur L'etat addressé au Congrès; prétendant qu'il craignois de trop multiplier les officiers Généraux en Amerique. Ces arrangemens Se faisant a L'instant précis du Départ; Les Srs. De Lessert et De Valfort n'ont point crû devoir insister, étant assuré que les Militaires avoüés de leur Gouvernement, qui aveient Jusqu'ici offert leurs Services aux Etats Unis, avoient obtenu un Grade audessus de celui dont ils étoient pourvus en France.

Le Bar. de Kalb
Le Marquis de Lafayette

To Adrienne de Noailles de Lafayette

ce 12 7bre. [1777] Philadelphie

Je vous ecris deux mots, mon cher coeur, par des officiers francois de mes amis qui etoïent venus avec moi et qui n'ayant pas été placés s'en retournent en France. Je commence par vous dire que je me porte bien parceque je veux finir par vous dire que nous nous sommes battus hier tout de bon, et nous n'avons pas été les plus forts. Nos americains après avoir tenu ferme pendant assés longtems ont fini par etre mis en deroute. En tachant de les rallier messieurs les anglois m'ont gratifié d'un coup de fusil qui m'a un peu blessé à la jambe, mais cela n'est rien, mon cher coeur, la balle n'a touché ni os ni nerf et j'en suis quitte pour etre couché sur le dos pour quelque tems, ce qui me met de fort mauvaise humeur. J'espere, mon cher coeur, que vous ne serés pas inquiette, c'est au contraire une raison de l'etre moins parceque me voilà hors de combat pour quelque tems, etant dans l'intention de me bien menager. Soyés en bien persuadée, mon cher coeur; cette affaire aura, je crains, de bien facheuses suites pour l'Amerique, il faudra tacher de reparer si nous pouvons. Vous devés avoir receu bien des lettres de moi à moins que les anglois n'en veuïllent à mes epitres autant qu'à mes jambes. Je n'en ai encore receu qu'une de vous et je soupire après des nouvelles. Adieu, on me defend d'ecrire plus longtems, depuis plusieurs jours je n'ai pas eu celui de dormir, la derniere nuit a été emploïée à notre retraite, et à mon voyage ici ou je suis fort bien soigné. Faites savoir à mes amis que je me porte bien, mille tendres respects à Mde. d'Ayen, mille compliments à ma vicomtesse et à mes soeurs; ces officiers partiront bientôt, ils vous verront, qu'ils sont heureux! Bonsoir mon cher coeur je vous aime plus que jamais.

To Adrienne de Noailles de Lafayette

[Bethlehem] ce 1er. octobre 1777

Je vous ai ecrit, mon cher coeur, le 12 septembre; c'est que ce douze est le lendemain du onze, et pour ce onze là j'ai une petite histoire à vous raconter. A la voir du beau coté je pourrais vous dire que des reflexions sages m'ont engagé a rester quelques semaines dans mon lit à l'abri des dangers. Mais il faut vous avouer que j'y ai été invité par une très legere blessure à la jambe, que j'ai attrappé je ne sais comment car je ne m'exposois pas en verité. C'etoit la premiere affaire ou je me trouvois, ainsi voyés comme elles son rares; c'est la derniere de la campagne, du moins la derniere grande bataïlle suivant toute apparence. Et s'il y avoit quelque autre chose vous voyés bien que je n'y serois pas. En consequence, mon cher coeur, vous pouvés etre bien tranquille. J'ai du plaisir à vous rassurer; en vous disant de ne pas craindre pour moi je me dis à moi même que vous m'aimés, et cette petite conversation avec mon coeur lui plait fort; car il vous aime plus tendrement qu'il n'a jamais fait.

Je n'eus rien de plus pressé que de vous ecrire le lendemain de cette af-faire; je vous disois bien que ce n'est rien et j'avois raison. Tout ce que je crains c'est que vous ne l'ayés pas receüe; comme en même tems le general Howe donne au roi son maitre des detaïls un peu bouffis de ses exploits d'Amerique, s'il m'a mandé blessé, il pourroit bien me mander tué aussi; cela ne coute rien, mais j'espere que mes amis et vous surtout mon cher coeur n'ajouterés jamais foi aux rapports de gens qui avoïent bien osé faire imprimer l'année passée que le Gnl. Washington et tous les officiers generaux de son armée etant ensemble sur un batteau, la barque avoit chaviré et tout le monde etoit noyé. Mais parlons donc de cette blessure; elle passe dans les chairs, ne touche ni os ni nerf. Les chirurgiens sont ettonnés de la prompti-tude avec laquelle elle guerit, ils tombent en extase toutes les fois qu'ils me pansent, et pretendent que c'est la plus belle chose du monde. Moi je trouve que c'est une chose fort sale, fort ennuyeuse, et assés douloureuse, cela de-pend des gouts. Mais dans le fonds si un homme se faisoit blesser pour se divertir, il viendroit regarder comme je suis, pour l'etre de même. Voilà mon cher coeur, l'histoire de ce que j'appelle pompeusement ma blessure pour me donner des airs et me rendre interessant.

A present comme femme d'un officier gral. americain il faut que je vous fasse votre leçon. On vous dira ils ont été battus, vous repondrés c'est vrai, mais entre deux armées *egales en nombre,* et en plaine, de vieux soldats ont de l'avantage sur des neufs, d'ailleurs ils ont eu le plaisir de tuer beaucoup mais beaucoup plus de monde aux ennemis qu'ils n'en ont perdu; aprés cela on ajoutera c'est fort bon, mais Philadelphie est pris, la capitale de l'Amerique, le boulevard de la liberté. Vous repartirés poliment vous etes des imbecilles; Philadelphie est une triste ville, ouverte de tous cotés, dont le port etoit dejà fermé, que la residence du Congress a rendu fameuse je ne sais pourquoi, ⟨elle est plein d'une vilaine espece de peuple, de sots quakers qui ne sont bons qu'a aller dans une chambre avec de grands chapeaux sur leur tête quelque tems qu'il fasse, et là attendre le St. Esprit en silence, jusqu'à ce que l'un d'eux s'en-nuïant de ne pas le voir arriver se leve et dit en pleurant beaucoup de bêtises. Voilà ce que c'est que ce peuple de Philadelphie qui d'ailleurs ne se bat point,⟩ voilà ce que c'est que cette fameuse ville, laquelle par parenthese nous leur ferons bien rendre tôt ou tard. S'ils continuent à vous pousser de questions vous les enverrés promener en termes que vous dira le vte. de Noaïlles par-ceque je ne veux pas perdre le tems de vous ecrire à vous parler politique.

J'ai conservé votre lettre pour la derniere dans l'esperance que je recevrois de vos nouvelles, que je pourrois y repondre, et que je vous en donnerois le plus tard possible de ma santé. Mais on me dit que si je n'envoïe pas sur le champ à vingt cinq lieües ou est le Congress mon capitaine sera parti, et adieu l'occasion de vous ecrire. C'est cela qui occasione un griffonage plus bar-bouillé encore qu'à l'ordinaire. Au reste si je vous ecrivois autrement qu'un chat c'est alors qu'il faudroit demander pardon pour la nouveauté du fait. Pensés, mon cher coeur, que je n'ai pas encore receu de vos nouvelles qu'une fois par le cte. de Pulaski. J'ai un guignon affreux, et j'en suis cruellement malheureux. Jugés quelle horreur d'etre loin de tout ce que j'aime dans une incertitude si desesperante. Il n'y a pas moyen de la supporter. Et encore, je le sens, je ne merite pas d'etre plaint; pourquoi ai-je été enragé à venir ici? J'en suis bien puni. Je suis trop sensible, mon coeur pour faire de ces tours de force. Vous me plaindrés j'espere; si vous saivés tout ce que je souffre surtout dans ce moment ou des nouvelles de vous sont si interessantes. Je n'y pense pans sans fremir. On m'a dit qu'un paquet de France etoit arrivé. J'ai depeché des exprès sur tous les chemins et dans tous les coins, j'ai envoyé au Congrès un officier. Je l'attends tous les jours; vous sentés avec quelle impatience. Mon chirurgien l'attend aussi avec ardeur, parceque cette inquietude me fait bouïller le sang qu'il veut tranquilliser. Mon dieu, mon cher coeur, si j'apprends de bonnes nouvelles de vous, de tout ce que j'aime, si ces char-mantes lettres arrivent aujourdhui que je puis etre heureux! Mais aussi avec quel trouble je vais les ouvrir!

Soyés tranquille, mon cher coeur, sur le soin de ma blessure. Tous les doc-teurs de l'Amerique sont en l'air pour moi. J'ai un ami qui leur a parlé de façon à ce que je fus bien soigné. C'est le general Washington. Cet homme re-spectable dont j'admirois les talents, les vertus, que je venere a mesure que je le connois davantage a bien voulu etre mon ami intime; son interest tendre pour moi a eu bientôt gagné mon coeur. Je suis etabli chés lui, nous vivons comme deux freres bien unis dans une intimité et une confiance reciproque. Cette union me rend le plus heureux possible dans ce païs-ci. Quand il m'a envoyé son premier chirurgien il lui a dit de me soigner comme si j'etois son fils parce qu'il m'aimoit de même. Ayant appris que je voulois rejoindre l'armée de trop bonne heure, il m'a ecrit une lettre pleine de tendresse pour m'engager à me bien guerir. Je vous fais tous ces detaïls, mon cher coeur, pour que vous soyés tranquille sur les soins qu'on prend de moi. Parmi les officiers francois qui tous m'ont temoigné beaucoup d'interest j'ai Mr. de Gimat mon aide de camp qui depuis avant la bataïlle a toujours été comme mon ombre, et m'a donné toujours toutes les marques possibles d'attachement. Ainsi, mon coeur, soïés bien rassurée sur cet article pour à present et pour l'avenir.

Tous les etrangers qui sont à l'armée (car je ne parle seulement pas de ceux qui n'ont pas d'emploi et qui rendront à leur retour en France des comptes de l'Amerique très peu justes parceque l'homme piqué et l'homme qui se venge ne sont pas de bonne foi) tous les autres etrangers dis-je employés ici sont mecontents, se plaignent, sont detestans, et detestés; ils ne comprennent pas comment je suis aimé seul d'etranger en Amerique; moi je ne comprens pas comment ils y sont si haïs. Pour ma part au des disputes et des dissenssions ordinaires dans toutes les armées surtout quand il y a des officiers d'autres nations, moi qui suis un bon homme, je suis assés heureux pour etre aimé par tout le monde etranger ou americain, je les aime tous. J'espere meriter leur estime, et nous sommes fort contents mutuellement les uns des autres. Je suis à present dans la solitude de Bethleem dont l'abbé Reynal parle tant. Cet etablissement est vraiment touchant, et fort interessant. Ils menent une vie douce et tranquille; nous causerons de tout cela à mon retour; et je compte bien ennuïer les gens que j'aime vous toute la premiere par consequent de la relation de mes voyages. Car vous savés que je suis un bavard.

Soyés le je vous en prie, mon cher coeur, dans tout ce que vous dirés pour moi à Henriette, ma pauvre petite Henriette; embrassés la mille fois, parlés lui de moi, mais ne lui dites pas tout le mal que je merite. Ma punition sera de n'etre pas recconnu par elle en arrivant; voilà la penitence que m'imposera Henriette. A-t-elle une soeur ou un frere? Le choix m'est egal, mon coeur, pourvû que j'aie une seconde fois le plaisir d'etre pere et que je l'apprenne bientôt. Si j'ai un fils, je lui dirai de bien connoitre son coeur, et s'il a un coeur tendre, s'il a une femme qu'il aime comme je vous aime, alors je l'avertirai de ne pas se livrer à un entousiasme qui l'eloigne de l'objet de son sentiment, parcequ'ensuite ce sentiment vient vous donner d'affreuses inquietudes.

⟨Que ne puis-je vous dire, mon cher coeur, je pars tel jour pour la France? Je puis au moins vous assurer de partir le plutôt possible. Je ne serai ici qu'autant que je croirai y etre retenu par les loix de mon honneur. J'ai tant d'envie de vous revoir, que je crois, dieu me pardonne, que si je pouvois j'irois demain moi même à Paris quitte à retourner ensuite en Amerique si je m'y croïois obligé. Mais non j'irai bientôt j'espere, si bientôt est un terme dont mon impatience puisse se servir quand je compte par mois, et ce sera pour tout à fait.⟩

J'ecris par une autre occasion à d'autres differentes personnes, mais je vous ecris aussi à vous. Je pense que celle-ci arrivera plutôt. Si par hazard le vaisseau arrive et que l'autre se perde, j'ai donné au vicomte la liste des lettres que j'ecrivois par lui, j'y ai oublié mes tantes, donnés leur de mes nouvelles dès que vous recevrés celle ci. Je n'ai gueres fait de duplicata que pour vous, parceque je vous ecris dans toutes les occasions. Faites aussi savoir de mes nouvelles à Mr. Margelay, l'abbé Fayon et Desplaces. Mille tendresses à mes soeurs, je leur permets de me mepriser comme un infame deserteur mais il faut qu'elles m'aiment en même tems. Mes respects à Mde. la ctesse. Auguste et Mde. de Fronsac; si la lettre de mon grandpere ne lui parvient pas presentés lui aussi mes tendres hommages. Adieu, adieu, mon cher coeur, aimés moi toujours; je vous aime si tendrement.

Faites mes compliments au docteur Francklin et à Mr. Deane. Je voulois leur ecrire mais le tems me manque.

To Monsieur Duboismartin

Au camp de *White Marsh* ce 23 octobre 1777

Voici, monsieur, une triste mais sure occasion de vous ecrire, et je ne la laisserai pas echapper. Mr. de Valfort me quitte, ou pour mieux dire il ne peut pas rester et l'etat affreux de sa santé l'oblige à retourner en France quand j'avois le plus de besoin de lui et d'assurance d'obtenir ce qu'il demandoit. Il connoit toutes mes affaires. Je lui ai communiqué toutes mes idées, ainsi il pourra vous donner bien au long de mes nouvelles que l'amitié que je vous connois pour moi vous fera surement demander. Mais je veux cependant vous dire moi même combien je vous suis tendrement attaché, ce sentiment, monsieur, que je conserverai toute ma vie pour vous n'avoit pas besoin ni des peines que je vous ai données, ni des marques d'interest que j'ai receües de vous, ni enfin de toutes mes obligations, pour etre bien vif et bien sincere.

J'ai ecrit a Monsieur le cte. de Broglie depuis ma blessure une fois par un vaisseau devant partir de Charlestown; je lui ecris à present par un paquetbot envoyé par le Congress. Je tache d'y faire passer Mr. de Valfort. En cas que par hazard cela ne se pût pas je joins ici la lettre que j'ecris à Mr. de Maurepas. J'en envoïe la copie faite par Mr. de Gimat à qui j'ai donné avec toute justice une entiere confiance. Vous y verrés des idées bien extraordinaires, bien folles, bien ridicules peut-etre, mais vivement tourmenté par l'envie de faire quelque chose pour ma vanité et l'utilité de ma patrie dans ce pays-là, je n'ai pas pu me refuser de soumettre mon plan à votre jugement et celui de Mr. le cte. de Broglie. Si vous ne le trouviés pas deraisonable voulés vous bien faire parvenir mon epitre au premier ministre actuellement en exercice de quelque qualité et païs qu'il puisse etre, car qui sait ce que Mr. de Maurepas est peut-etre devenu? Je ne m'etendrai pas sur les raisons qui me rendent amoureux de mon projet, vos connoissances etendues sur les Indes vous fairoïent paroitre mes raisonnements bien pitoïables. Faites je vous prie seulement reflexion qu'il me faut tout au plus 1 contre 4 de probabilités pour entreprendre et que jusqu'ici les hazards ne m'ont pas été defavorables. Vous vous souvenés bien de l'entreprise de Mr. d'Estaing, elle eut du succès; d'aïlleurs un espece de ouï du ministre me mettroit à couvert des inconvenients en grande partie. Je ne vous en dirai pas davantage, monsieur, jugés moi, *indulgés moi* et servés moi dans mon entreprise si elle est entreprenable. Au moins envoyés la lettre par Mr. de Valfort si elle est envoyable. Il ne faut pas je crois qu'il ait l'air d'en savoir le contenu et pour Monsieur le cte. de Broglie il jugera s'il est utile qu'il paroisse s'en mêler ou s'il vaut mieux qu'il ignore aussi. Je compte tant sur ses bontés, ma confiance est si entiere, que j'ose ne pas douter qu'il ne s'interesse à moi dans cette affaire comme dans l'autre.

Croiriés vous que je joins au present ridicule celui d'ecrire serieusement à Mr. de Bouïllé pour tacher de l'engager à fermer les yeux sur une expedition dont le foyer seroit son isle? Elle ne me prendroit pas en tout deux mois de cet hiver. Je voudrois armer quelques vaisseaux avec des commissions du congrès, prendre quelques hommes dans les etats de mon cousin le gouverneur, et tomber sur quelques petites isles angloises dont les negres päieroïent les fraix de l'entreprise. Mais cela est comme l'Asie dans les espaces imaginaires. Pour cette Asie, si j'y vais que vos conseïls me seront utiles!

Vous aurés vu monieur votre frere, je suis plus faché encore pour moi que pour lui qu'il ne soit pas resté. Je n'entrerai pas sur ce sujet dans des detaïls que je vous ai jejà rebattus ainsi qu'à Mr. le cte. de Broglie. Je me contenterai de vous repeter que plusieurs membres du congrès ont eu bien des torts. Du Coudrai leur avoit tourné la tête. Mais il y en a qui sont des gens de vertu et de merite. Au reste dans toutes les accusations et les torts j'espere que l'on excepte toujours le General Washington mon ami, et mon ami intime, comme j'aime à les choisir j'ose dire que c'est faire son éloge que de lui donner ce titre.

Si toutes les divisions de notre armée etoïent commandées par des officers generaux francois comme j'ai l'honneur d'en connoitre beaucoup, je ne me donnerois pas les airs d'en prendre une. Mais la disproportion n'etant pas la même et d'aïlleurs ayant envie de faire quelque chose pour m'occuper et m'essaïer je serai fort aise à present que le Gral. Washington m'en donne une. Les occasions de bien faire sont rares (quand je saurois en profiter) pour un etranger. Cette qualité fait toujours jalouser ou ettouffer ce qu'il pourroit faire de bien dans tous les païs du monde, c'est au moins ce que disent les francois employés ici qui crient comme des diables. Moi qui n'ais pas à me plaindre je ne peux pas crier, je puis même me vanter d'etre parfaitement avec tout le monde, et l'amitié du gral. me donne tout l'agrement possible, tant que je serai comme cela j'aurois mauvaise grace à me fâcher.

Je veux aussi vous prevenir sur l'erreur qui nous faisant trois fois plus forts que l'ennemi diminüe toujours par consequent l'honneur du succès et augmente le desagrement de la défaite. Je vais m'amuser à guerroyer tout cet hiver. Il n'y a pas moyen de quitter l'Amerique en si beau chemin et dans une crise interessante. Si mon projet me faisoit rappeler je ne perdrois pas de tems. Dans tous les cas, faites moi le plaisir de me mander ce que vous penseriés sur mon retour, sur le bon ou mauvais effet qu'il pourroit faire &c. Les circonstances etant variables à l'infini je desire avoir des conseïls pour me conduire dans toutes suivant les [differentes] faces. Cependant selon toute apparence je ferai ici la campagne prochaine si je ne reçois pas de nouvelles. Celle de la guerre me decideroit à partir tout de suite fut-ce à la nage. Helàs, monsieur, si l'on fait une descente en Anglettere pour dieu ne me le laissés pas ignorer.

Si vous n'etes pas trop ennuyé ou endormi, Mr. de Valfort vous dira le reste. Vous comprenés par le tendre attachement et l'amitié qui m'unit à lui combien je desire que Mr. le cte. de Broglie s'interesse à ses affaires. Adieu, monsieur, je vous embrasse de tout mon coeur.

LAFAYETTE

Mille compliments, je vous prie, à monsieur votre frere et á nos compagnons de voyage. Ma lettre n'a surement pas le sens commun mais l'on fait derriere moi un plan de campagne qui me casse la tête parceque les deux disputants ont des voix fort claires et fort bruïantes.

To [the Comte de Maurepas]

au camp de White Marsh en Pensilvanie
le 24 octobre 1777

Monsieur

Vous aves été ennuyé bien malgré moi par la part qu'on vous fit prendre à mes premiers projets, vous allés l'etre encore malgré vous par l'attention que j'ose vous demander pour les nouveaux: ils pourroient se trouver aussi peu dignes que les autres d'occuper des moments precieux; mais à present comme alors ma bonne volonté (fût elle mal dirigée) me servira d'excuse. Mon age en fut une aussi peut-être. Tout ce que je demande aujourdhui, c'est qu'il ne vous empêche pas de considerer ce que mes idées pourroïent avoir de raisonable.

Je ne me permets pas d'approfondir quels secours recoit la belle cause que nous defendons ici, mais mon amour pour ma patrie me fait considerer avec plaisir sous combien de points de vüe les chagrins de famille de l'Anglettere peuvent lui etre avantageux. Il en est un surtout qui dans tous les cas et *à tout evenement* me paroit presenter une utilité d'autant plus grande qu'il seroit suivi avec plus de moyens, et je sens que c'est lui en ôter dejà un que de me proposer pour l'execution. Je parle d'une expedition plus ou moins considerable aux Indes Orientales.

Sans me donner des airs de prophete sur les affaires presentes, mais persuadé bonnement que nuire à l'Anglettere c'est servir (oserois je dire c'est venger) ma patrie, je crois cette idée faite pour mettre en activité les ressources quelqu'onques de tout individu qui a l'honneur d'etre françois. Je suis venu ici sans permission, j'y sers sans autre approbation que celle du silence, je pourrois me permettre encore un petit voyage sans autorisation. Si le succès en est douteux, j'ai l'avantage de ne risquer que moi, et qui m'empeche alors d'etre entreprenant? Pour peu que je reûssis la flamme du moindre etablissement anglois, dût-elle fondre une partie de ma fortune, satisfairoit mon coeur en echauffant mes esperances pour une occasion plus propice.

Guidé par les legeres connoissances dont mon ignorance a pu s'eclairer, voici, monsieur, comment je pourrois tenter cette entreprise. Une patente americaine qui me mettroit en regle, les minces secours dont elle pourroit etre soutenüe, ceux que me fourniroïent aux isles francoises ou les speculations de quelques negotians ou la bonne volonté de quelques compagnons de voyage, telles sont les foibles ressources qui me conduiroïent pacifiquement à l'Isle de France. C'est là que je trouverois, je crois, et des armateurs pour m'aider, et des hommes pour me suivre, assés au moins pour aller attendre les vaisseaux qui reviennent de la Chine comme une source de nouveaux moyens, assés peut être pour descendre sur un ou deux de leurs comptoirs et les ruiner avant qu'ils fussent secourus. Avec des forces que je n'ose pas esperer, surtout avec des talents que je suis encore bien plus loin d'acquerir, ne pourroit on pas tirer quelque parti, et de la jalousie des differends nababs, et de la haine des marattes, et de la venalité des cipaïes, et de la mollesse des anglois, ne pourroit-on pas emploïer utilement la foule de francois dispersés sur cette côte? Pour moi dans tous les cas la crainte de compromettre ma patrie m'empecheroit de me glorifier de ce nom, à peu près comme dans certaines provinces la noblesse depose quelquefois ses marques d'honneur pour les reprendre un jour.

Quoique nullement aveuglé sur mon imprudence, j'eusse hazardé seul ce voyage, si la crainte de nuire aux interests que je veux servir faute de les bien connoitre, ou de faire tort à quelque expedition mieux concertée, n'eut arrêté tous mes desirs. Car j'ai la vanité de croire qu'un projet à peu près pareïl pourroit etre un jour executé plus en grand par des mains plus habiles. Il peut l'etre au moins d'une maniere qui me paroit presque certaine, si je pouvois esperer du gouvernement, non pas un ordre, non pas des secours, pas cependant une simple indifference, mais un je ne sais quoi, pour lequel aucune langue ne me fournit une expression assés delicate. Alors un ordre du roi qui daigneroit me *rendre pour un tems à ma famille et à mes amis* sans *me defendre de revenir m'avertiroit de* me munir de commissions continentales de l'Amerique; alors quelques instructions, quelques preparatifs en France precederoïent ce pretendu retour, et me conduiroïent droit aux Indes Orientales; *alors cette même discretion qui* fût peut-etre autrefois un tort, devenant un devoir sacré, serviroit à cacher ma vraïe destination, et surtout l'espece d'approbation qu'elle pourroit obtenir.

Telles sont, monsieur, les idées que, tout penétré de mon incapacité et du defaut de ma jeunesse, j'ai cependant la presomption de soumettre à votre jugement, et (si elles pouvoïent vous plaire) aux differentes modifications dont vous les croiriés susceptibles. Je suis sur au moins qu'elles ne le sont pas de ridicule, parcequ'elles partent d'un motif trop respectable, l'amour de la patrie. Je ne demande que l'honneur de la servir sous un autre pavillon, et j'aime à voir ses interests unis à ceux des republicains pour lesquels je combats en desirant qu'il me soit bientôt permis de faire la guerre sous les drapeaux francois. Alors une commission de grenadier dans l'armée du roi me flatteroit plus que tous les grades des armées etrangeres.

Je me reproche trop, monsieur, de vous presenter etourdiment des projets d'Asie, pour vous tracer encore maladroitement des descriptions d'Amerique ornées de mes reflexions dont vous n'avés que faire et qu'on ne me demande pas. D'ailleurs le zele qui m'a conduit ici, et principallement l'amitié qui m'unit au general en chef me feroïent soupçonner d'une partialité dont je crois cependant etre exempt. Je me reserverai seulement l'honneur de vous parler à mon retour des officiers de merite que l'amour de leur metier à fait venir dans ce continent. Tout ce qui est françois, monsieur, a la droit d'avoir confiance en vous. C'est à ce titre que je vous demande votre indulgence, j'en ai un second dans le respect avec lequel j'ai l'honneur d'etre, monsieur, Votre très humble et très obeïssant serviteur

LAFAYETTE

Cette lettre vous parviendra, monsieur, d'une maniere trop sure peut-etre, si elle vous ennuye. Je la confie à Monsieur de Valfort Capitaine au rgt. d'Aunis avec brevet de colonel dans nos isles, que ses talents, sa reputation, et sa vertu rendoïent interessant à ce païs-ci, que le desir du Gral. Washington y auroit retenu si sa santé ne l'obligoit absolument de retourner en France. J'attendrai ici vos ordres (qui ne parviennent pas dans les ports americains sans difficulté) ou j'irai les chercher suivant les circonstances, n'en ayant pas receu depuis mon arrivée qui puissent me diriger.

To Adrienne de Noailles de Lafayette

Ce 29 octobre [1777] au camp près White Marsh

Je vous envoïe une lettre toute ouverte, mon cher coeur, dans la personne de Mr. de Valfort, mon ami et que je vous prie de traiter comme tel; il vous dira bien au long de mes nouvelles, mais moi je veux vous dire ici combien je vous aime. J'ai trop de plaisir a epprouver ce sentiment pour n'en avoir pas à vous le repéter, mille fois si je pourrois ⟨, mais le malheureux sort qui m'attache ici s'y oppose bien cruellement⟩. Je n'ai d'autres ressources, mon cher coeur, que d'ecrire, et de recrire encore, sans esperance que mes lettres puissent vous parvenir, et cherchant à me consoler par le plaisir de m'entretenir avec vous du chagrin, du tourment mortel de ne pas recevoir un mot de France. Il est impossible de vous exprimer à quel point mon coeur en est inquieté, dechiré souvent; quand je le pourvois je ne l'essaïerois pas pour ne pas mêler du noir aux plus doux instants de mon ⟨triste⟩ exil, ceux ou je puis vous parler de ma tendresse. ⟨Quel moyen de vous l'exprimer! Quand me sera-t-il permi de lui demander pardon, de lui jurer moi même de l'aimer toujours!⟩ Au moins me plaignés vous, comprenés vous combien je souffre, combien je suis puni ⟨d'une demarche inconsiderée que j'ai hazardée sans connoitre les forces

de mon coeur? Il n'est pas capable de supporter une telle separation de tout
ce qu'il aime). Au moins si je savois ce que vous faites, ou vous etes, je le
saurois bien tard mais enfin je ne serois pas separé de vous comme si j'etois
mort. J'attends des lettres avec une avidité que rien ne peut distraire. On me
promet qu'il en arrivera bientôt mais puis-je m'y fier? Ne negligés pas une occasion de m'ecrire, mon cher coeur, si mon bonheur vous interesse encore.
Repetés moi que vous m'aimés, moins je merite votre sentiment plus les assurances que vous m'en donnerés sont pour moi une consolation necessaire.

Vous devés avoir receu tant de nouvelles de ma legere blessure que des repetitions deviennent inutiles. D'ailleurs si vous avés cru que ce fut quelque
chose Monsieur de Valfort pourra vous desabuser. Dans très peu de tems je
ne serai plus boiteux du tout. ⟨D'hors en avant je n'aurai plus besoin de me
montrer ni de m'exposer et je vous reponds d'etre bien sage. D'ailleurs à
present la guerre va se faire par petits detachements ou je n'aurai que faire.
L'ami que je vous adresse m'est tendrement attaché, il est obligè de me quitter
et cette separation est douloureuse pour nous deux. Un coeur brisé par de
grandes seccousses en est plus sensible aux chagrins legers. La perte d'un
homme pour qui j'ai de la confiance me rappelle cruellement les pertes affreuses que j'ai faites de tout ce qui m'est cher. J'ai fait une grande etourderie,
mon cher coeur, et l'agrement avec lequel je sers ici est une bien mince consolation pour un si grand malheur. Faites bien des honnetetés à Mr. de Valfort,
je lui ai promis que vous le recevriés bien, et je compte beaucoup le voir en
France parcequ'a beaucoup de connoissances il joint le meïlleur coeur et la
plus haute vertu.⟩

⟨Il est arrivé un accident à mes finances; Mr. de Valfort vous l'expliquera; je
crois cependant qu'il y a encore du remede; je fais ici le moins de depense que
je peux et cependant j'en fais beaucoup. La cherté abominable des plus petites
choses, le discredit du papier en sont la cause. L'article le plus fort après mon
voyage de Charlestown ici est les six semaines que j'ai demeuré blessé à Bethlehem, et vous sentés que j'avois pas de depenses de plaisir à y faire. En general on ne peut pas dire que l'amour du plaisir m'entraine dans ces contrées
ou l'on ne pense que politique ou l'on ne s'occupe que des horreurs d'une
espece de guerre civile. Ma tête s'est fort remise sur l'article de l'argeant et je
vous reponds que je ne cherche que l'absolu necessaire—il est piquant qu'il
m'en ait couté si cher pour me rendre malheureux moi même. Comme
mon navire est assuré j'espere que tout n'est pas perdu, la lettre d'assurance
etant partie avant la perte; du moins on dit que c'est la loi des negotians.⟩

N'est-il pas affreux, mon cher coeur, de penser que c'est par le public par
des papiers anglois, des gazettes venant de l'ennemi que je sais de vos nouvelles. Dans un article assés inutile sur mon arrivée ici ils finissent par parler de
vous, de votre grossesse de vos couches. de cet objet de mes craintes, de mes
esperances, de mon tremblement, de ma joïe. Quel bonheur en effet pour
moi si j'apprenois que je suis pere une seconde fois, que vous vous portés
bien, que mes deux enfans, que leur mere se preparent à faire ma felicité
pour toute ma vie. Ce païs-ci est charmant pour l'amour paternel maternel et
filial—il y est poussé à une passion à des soins vraiment touchans. La nouvelle
de vos couches y sera receue avec joïe surtout à l'armée, et surtout par celui qui

la commande. ⟨Tout mon ami qu'il est que j'ai d'impatience de lui dire bonsoir! Que j'aimerois à courir bien vîte les risques d'etre pris et de satisfaire
messieurs les anglois! Mais je ne peux pas savoir encore quel jour j'aurai le
bonheur de vous embrasser, quoique je puisse vous promettre de partir dès
que je croirai pouvoir en honneur quitter l'armée ou je sers. Cette armée a encore quelques choses à faire, si nous etions à proportion aussi fort que l'etoit
Gates vis à vis le general Jean Burgoïgne nous pourrions jouïr le même tour à
Mr. Howe, ensuite nous predroins. New York bien vîte et dans quinze jours
je mettrois à la voïle. Ce n'est pas pourtant que je compte voir la fin de cette
guerre en Amerique—Dieu m'en preserve; dès que je pourrai deserter hon-
nêtement je suis à vous, mon cher coeur, et vous me verrés arriver (si les circonstances s'arrangent comme je desire) plutôt que l'on ne pense. Si l'on
trouve que je n'y reste pas assés longems, je les enverrai essaïer un petit
voyage d'un an ou dix huit mois loin de tout ce qu'ils aiment pour voir comment ils l'en trouvent—ce n'est ni le beau ni le mauvais tems qui decidera mon
retour—je ne quitterai pas la guerre pour le bal, et ce n'est pas pour ces
genres de plaisirs que j'abandonnerai une armée combattant pour la liberté,
et contre les anglois. Mais je retournerai pour vous voir, pour voir mes amis,
je retournerai parceque je n'aurai plus la patience de rester, et tous les mois
me seront bons, à l'exception que le plutôt me plaira toujours davantage.⟩

Je vais trouver ma pauvre petite Henriette bien gentille quand je reviendrai, j'espere qu'elle me fera un beau sermon ⟨sur ma sotte levée de boucliers⟩
et elle me parlera avec toute la franchise de l'amitié. Car ma fille sera toujours, j'espere, la meïlleure de mes amies. Je ne veux etre pere que pour
aimer, et l'amour paternel s'arrangera à merveïlles avec l'amitié. Embrassés-la,
mon coeur, dirai-je embrassés les pour moi? Mais je ne veux pas m'appesan-
tir sur tout ce que je souffre de cette incertitude, je sais que vous partagés des
peines de mon coeur, et je ne veux pas vous affliger. J'ai ecrit la derniere fois
à Mde. d'Ayen, depuis ma blessure j'ai ecrit à tout le monde. Mais ces lettres
sont peut-etre perdües; cela n'est pas ma faute, je peux rendre un peu de mal
à ces vilains preneurs de lettres, quand ils sont sur terre, mais en pleine mer je
n'ai que la consolation du foible, qui est de maudire de bon coeur ceux dont
on ne peut pas encore se venger. Mille tendres respects à Mde. votre mere,
mille amitiés à mes soeurs. Ne m'oubliés pas auprès de Mr. le mal. de
Noaïlles, de vos parentes paternels et maternels. J'ai reçeu quatre sottes lignes
du mal. de Mouchy qui ne me dit pas un mot de vous. J'ai juré après lui dans
toutes les langues. Adieu, mon coeur, adieu, interrogés Mr. de Valfort mon
bien et honnête ami. Le papier me manque c'est une terrible chose que d'etre
reduit à ecrire quand on aime autant que je vous aime mon cher coeur, et que
je vous aimerai jusqu'au dernier soupir.

Je n'ai pas laissé passer une occasion, pas la plus indirecte sans vous ecrire.
Faites en autant, mon cher coeur, si vous m'aimés, et je serois bien ingrat,
bien insensible si j'en doutois.

To Adrienne de Noailles de Lafayette

Ce 6 novembre au camp de White Marsh 1777

Vous recevrés peut-etre cette lettre, mon cher coeur, dans cinq ou six ans, car je vous ecris par une occasion à crochet dont je n'ai pas grande idée; voyés un peu le tour que va faire ma lettre—un officier de l'armée la porte au Fort Pitt à 300 milles sur les derrieres du continent, ensuite elle sera embarquée sur le grand fleuve de l'Ohio à travers des païs habités uniquement par des sauvages; une fois arrivée à la Nouvelle Orleans un petit bâtiment la transportera aux isles espagnoles; ensuite un vaisseau de cette nation la prendra (dieu sait quand) lorsqu'il retournera en Europe. Mais elle sera encore bien loin de vous, et ce n'est qu'après avoir eté crassée par les sales mains de tous les Maitres de poste espagnols qu'il lui sera permis de passer les Pirenées; elle pourra bien aussi etre decachetée et recachetée cinq ou six fois avant de parvenir en vos mains. Alors elle sera une preuve à mon cher coeur que je ne neglige pas une occasion même la plus eloignée de lui donner de mes nouvelles, et de lui repeter combien je l'aime. Cependant ce n'est gueres que pour mon propre satisfaction que je vous le dis ici avec un nouveau plaisir; j'espere avoir celle de jeter moi même la presente au feu à son arrivée attendu que je serai là et que ma presence rendra ce chiffon de papier fort inutile. Cette idée est bien douce à mon coeur; je m'y livre avec transport; qu'il est charmant de prevoir les moments ou nous serons ensemble, mais qu'il est cruel aussi, mon cher coeur, de penser que mon sentiment ne peut encore se nourrir que d'illusions, et que la realité de mon bonheur est à deux mille lieües de moi, à travers des mers immenses, et ces coquins de vaisseaux anglois. Ils me rendent bien malheureux ces vilains vaisseaux; une seule lettre de vous, une seule, mon cher coeur, m'est encore parvenüe. Les autres sont egarés, prises, au fond de la mer selon toute apparance. Je ne puis m'en prendre qu'aux ennemis, de cette affreuse privation, car vous, surement vous ne negligés pas de m'ecrire par tous les ports, par tous les paquets du docteur Franklin et Mr. Deane. Cependant des vaisseaux sont arrivés j'ai dépeché des exprès dans tous les coins du continent, et toutes mes esperances ont été frustrés. Apparement vous n'etiés pas bien instruite—je vous en prie, mon coeur, informés vous avec attention des moyens de me faire parvenir quelques lettres. La privation en est si cruelle; je suis si malheureux d'etre separé de tout ce que j'aime! Tout coupable que je suis de mon propre malheur vous me plaindriés bien si vous saviés tout ce que mon coeur souffre ⟨d'etre si loin de vous et de tout ce qui peut m'etre cher⟩.

A quoi bon vous mander des nouvelles dans une lettre destinée à voyager des années, qui vous arrivera peut-etre en morceaux, et qui representera l'antiquité même. Toutes mes autres depêches vous ont instruit de reste des evenements de la campagne. La bataïlle de Brandiwine ou j'ai laissé habilement un petit morceau de jambe, la prise de possession de Philadelphie si loin d'avoir les inconvenients dont on est persuadé en Europe, une attaque de

poste à Germain Town ou je n'etois pas parceque j'etois blessé tout fraiche-
ment et que n'a pas reussi, la reddition du Gral. Bourgoïgne avec ciq mille
hommes, de ce même Bourgoïgne qui vouloit nous avaler tout ce printems, et
se trouve en automne fait prisonnier de guerre par notre armée du nord,
enfin notre position actuelle à quatre lieues vis à vis les uns des autres, le Gral.
Howe etabli à Philadelphie, faisant tous ses efforts pour prendre certains forts
qui ne se rendent point et y ayant deja perdu un gros et un petit vaisseau,
vous voilà, mon cher coeur, toute aussi instruite que si vous etiés General en
chef d'une des deux armées. J'ajouterai seulement ici que cette blessure du 11
7bre dont je vous ai parlé dejà mille fois est presque entierement guerie,
quoique je boite encore un peu, mais dans peu de jours il n'y paroitra plus ou
pas grand chose. Mais tous ces detaïls, mon cher coeur, vous auront été faits
bien au long par mon ami Mr. de Valfort à qui j'ai donné une lettre pour
vous, et dans les rapports duquel vous pouvés avoir la plus entiere confiance.
Je viens d'apprendre qu'il est parti non sur un paquetbot comme je croïois
mais à bords d'une bonne fregate de 35 canons ainsi il y auroit du malheur s'il
etoit pris. Entre lui et l'epitre que je lui ai confié il y a cinq ou six jours vous
saurés tout ce que votre bonté pour moi peut vous faire desirer d'apprendre.
Je voudrois bien que vous sussiés aussi le jour precis de mon retour, car j'ai
bien de l'impatience de le fixer moi même et de pouvoir vous dire dans la joie
de mon coeur tel jour je pars pour vous joindre, pour retrouver le bonheur
⟨que j'ai eu la bêtise de perdre⟩.

Un petit monsieur bleu, parement citron et veste blanche, allemand de nation, venant solliciter ici du service qu'il n'obtiendra pas, et baragouïnant le
francois, m'a dit qu'il etoit parti au mois d'aoust. Il m'a parlé politique, il m'a
parlé ministre, il a boulversé l'Europe en general et toutes les cours en particulier, mais il ne savoit pas un mot de ce qui pouvoit interesser mon coeur.
Je l'ai tourné de tous les cotés, je lui ai nommé cinquante noms, il me disoit
toujours, *moi pas connoitre ces seigneurs-la.* ⟨Enfin je lui ai demande˙ s'il avoit lu
les gazettes, et s'il y avoit quelque nouvelle de societé; il m'a dit que ouï, que
tout le monde se portoit bien, qu'il n'y avoit rien de nouveau. C'est ainsi qu'a
fini son interrogatoire et je n'en ai pas été plus savant—qu'il est cruel d'en etre
reduit-là.⟩

Je vous ai fait de grands raisonements par Mr. de Valfort sur mes finances
⟨ou vous verrés combien je suis devenu raisonable, mais si je les repetois ici
vous trouveriés que mon redoublement de raison vous donne un redoublement d'ennui fort mal à propos⟩. L'accident arrivé à mon vaisseau m'a fort
affligé parceque ce vaisseau alloit à l'arrangement de mes affaires comme un
charme. Mais il n'est plus, et je me reprocherois bien de l'avoir renvoïé si je
n'avois pas eté forcé d'en faire une close de mes arrangements en consequence de ma minorité. Tout est ici d'une cherté incroïable, nous avons la
consolation des mechans en pensant que la disette de tout est bien plus
grande à Philadelphie. A la guerre on se console de ce qu'on peut souffrir et
en faisant quatre fois pis à son ennemi. D'aïlleurs nous sommes ici dans
l'abondance de nourriture, et j'apprends avec plaisir que messieurs les anglois
commencement à n'etre pas de même.

N'allés pas vous aviser d'etre à present inquiette sur moi, tout est fini pour

les grands coups il y auroit à present tout au plus de petites affaires en minia-
ture qui ne me regardent pas—ainsi je suis aussi en sureté dans le camp qu'au
milieu de Paris; ⟨toute la difference est que je n'y suis pas si heureux. Cepen-
dant⟩ si tout l'agrement possible en servant ici, si l'amitié de l'armée en gros et
en detaïl, si une union tendre avec le plus respectable le plus admirable des
hommes le Gral. Washington, soutenüe d'une confiance reciproque, si le sentiment de tous les americains dont je puis desirer d'etre aimé, si tout cela suf-
fisoit à mon bonheur je n'aurois rien à souhaitter, mais que mon coeur est loin
d'etre tranquille! Que vous seriés attendrie mon cher coeur, si vous saviés et
tout ce qu'il sent, et combien il vous aime!

Nous sommes à present dans une saison qui me fait esperer quelques lettres; que m'apprendront elles? Que dois-je craindre, que dois-j'esperer? Ah,
mon cher coeur, qu'il est cruel de gemir de cette affreuse incertitude dans
une circonstance si interessante à mon bonheur. Ai-je deux enfants? Un second objet de ma tendresse est-il joint à ma chere Henriette? Embrassés la
mille fois pour moi ma chere petite fille, *embrassés les* mon cher coeur, bien
tendrement, j'espere qu'ils connoitront un jour combien je les aime.

Mille respects à Mde. d'Ayen, mille choses tendres à la vicomtesse à mes
soeurs. Dites en aussi un million à tous mes amis. Chargés vous de mes hommages pour tout le monde. Adieu, mon coeur, aïés soin de votre santé,
donnés moi des nouvelles bien detaïllées, croïés que je vous aime plus que
jamais, que je vous regarde comme le premier objet de ma tendresse et la plus
sure assurance de mon bonheur. Les sentiments gravés dans un coeur qui est
tout à vous y seront conservés jusqu'à son dernier soupir. M'aimerés vous
toujours, mon cher coeur, j'ose l'esperer, et que nous nous rendrons heureux
mutuellement par une affection aussi tendre qu'eternelle. Adieu, adieu; qu'il
me seroït doux de vous embrasser à present de vous dire moi même mon cher
coeur je t'aime plus que je n'ai jamais aimé et c'est pour toute ma vie.

Baron de Kalb to Pierre de Saint-Paul[E]

A l'armée des Etats Unis de l'Amérique, le 7 novembre 1777

Si depuis longtems je n'ay pas eu l'honneur de vous écrire, Monsieur, ce
n'est pas que j'aye oublié ny que je puisse jamais oublier les marques de bonté
et d'amitié donc vous m'avez honoré de tout tems, et donc je vous demande
avec instance la continuation pour moy et pour ma famille, surtout si elle etoit
privée de me revoir pendant quelque tems par mon acceptation d'une commission de Major Genéral dans l'armée Continentale. N'attribuez mon silence
qu'à l'incertitude ou le Congrès a laissé pendant long tems les officiers francois arrivés avec moy ou en même tems s'ils seroient employés ou non, le
refus qu'il a fait enfin de tous ceux qui ne parlent pas la langue du Pays et
l'incertitude si je devois (presque seul de ma band) accepter ou refuser le
Grade qui m'etoit offert par une voix unanime du Congrès. Je craignois d'un
coté d'etre blamé en France de n'avoir pas suivy le sort de ceux qui y retur-

nent, et de l'autre d'etre taxé d'inconsequence pour avoir entrepris un voyage long et penible sans remplir l'objet pour lequel je l'ay fait, pouvant rester meme avec distinction par les sollicitations qui m'en ont été faites. Je suis donc convenu avec le Congrès, et cela par ecrit, qu'en servant je me reserverais la faculté de quitter leur service si la party de rester icy étoit désapprouvée en France, soit par les ministres, soit par mes amis, de même que si par desagrément ou autrement je croirois avoir des raisons de m'en retourner. Ces conditions m'etant accordées et l'assurance donnée du commandement d'une Division, j'ay été à l'armée pour scavoir si le General Washington, ny aucun des officiers generaux Americains aux quels mon arrivée pouvoit fait tort, ny avoient point d'objection à faire. J'y restay trois semaines, et sur l'assurance du Chef que mon service [ne] pouvoit etre qu'agreable à l'armée je fis mon equipage et je viens de rejoindre au camp de White Mash a 13 milles de Philadelphia. Le Congrès croyoit que mon refus d'abord provenoit de mécontentment d'avoir donné la préference sur moy a M. le marquis de la Fayette auquel ils avoient donné le grad de Major General sans appointment et sans commandment, et m'offroit d'antidater ma commission à la sienne, mais j'ay refusé cet article et n'ay voulu l'avoir que de même datte (elles sont de 31 Juillet) a fin qu'il soit en mon pouvoir de luy laisser prendre rang sur moy de s'etre trouvé à la Bataille de Brandywine pres Wilmington, Lorsqu'on ne m'avoit pas encore formellement engagé a rester. L'amitié dont il m'honore depuis que j'ay fait sa connaissance, et celle que je luy ay voué fondées sur ses qualités personnelles, m'engagent a cette déférence pour luy. Personne ne merite mieux que luy la consideration dont il jouit icy. C'est un Prodige pour son age, il est plein de valeur, d'Esprit, de jugement, de bon procedés, de sentiments de Générosité et de Zele pour la cause de Liberté de ce Continent. Sa Blessure va très bien. Il vient de rejoindre l'armée pour ne pas perdre d'occasions de gloire et de danger. J'ay appris que sa famille a été persuadée que j'ay eu part au party qu'il a pris de venir en Amérique. Je dois me justifier de cette imputation, supposé qu'elle ait eu lieu, et je serois bien aise de la faire par votre moyen, si vous avez occasion d'en parler, ou s'il en a jamais été question vis a vis les ministres, ou de vous, Monsieur. Je vais donc vous faire le détail de ce que j'ay scu en fait sur cela. M. le Vte. de Noailles et M. le Mis. de la Fayette me sont venus voir au commencement de [novem]bre 1776 (Je n'avois pas l'honneur de les connoitre avant) pour me dire que M. le Duc D'Ayen consentoit à ce qu'ils proposassent tous deux à M. Deane leurs services pour l'Amérique, si on leur accordoit le Grade d'Officiers Generaux, me firent quelqu'honnetetés sur ce qu'ils avoient appris de mon arrangement avec l'agent Américain et de la plaisir qu'ils aur[oien]t de servir dans la même armée que moy, et finirent par me prier de les presenter quelque jour a M. Deane, ce que je promis de faire à leur commodité. Au bout de quelques jours M. le Viscomte de Noailles m'écrit qu'il a abandonné le projet de passer en Amérique. M. le Marquis de la Fayette, au contraire, est revenu plusieurs fois, je l'ay presenté a M. Deane et luy ay servi d'interprète pour sa proposition, toujours disant que M. le [Duc] D'Ayen le desiroit et y consentoit. Nous nous voyons tous les jours. Il venoit chez moy ouvertment et sans le moindre mystère, ne devant pas en soupconne j'allois de même chez luy a l'hôtel de Noail-

les, et l'on me faisoit entrer sans difficulté, lors même que Madame de la
Fayette étoit avec luy. Je n'aurois donc jamais du imaginer que toutes ses
demarches se faisoient a l'inseu de sa famille. A la fin du même mois de
[novem]bre il signa sa convention avec M. Deane (il est vray que c'est moy qui
a leur requisition l'ay fait et écrit). Je partis de Paris le 8 Xbre pour m'embarquer au Havre. Je pris congé de M. de la Fayette, il me dis, jusqu'au revoir
en Amérique. Mon embarquement n'ayant pu avoir lieu, je revins à Paris et
pendant un tems il n'etoit plus question de ce voyage. Au mois de fevrier
1777 M. Deane reprit son Projet de me faire partir, et M. le Marquis de la
Fayette voulant etre de la partie, et craignant des delais trop longs pur son
impatience, il proposa d'armer un vaisseau à ses propres dépens, ce qu'il fit
sans que je m'en sois melé le moins du monde (car j'eusse tout aussi bien attendu le vaisseau que M. Deane vouloit faire armer pour moy). Il fournit
[illegible word] qu'il en a chargé de l'argent, le fait partir pour Bordeaux, et luy
même part pour Londres avec M. le Prince de Poix, pour icy rester qui jusq'a
la reception des nouvelles de son vaisseau dez qu'il seroit prêt a metter à la
voile. Je luy ecrivais sur cela a l'adresse de M. le Mis. de Noailles, Ambassadeur en Angleterre, d'apres les lettres que j'avois recu de Bordeaux. Il
revint le 13 ou 14 Mars à Paris, ou plutot à Chaillot (sur prétexte d'eviter une
scene d'attendrissement et d'afflictions à Madame de la Fayette) et nous partimes ensembles de chez moy (ou il s'est rendû le jour même, sa voiture y
ayant été envoyée deux jours avant) le 16 Mars à midy. Mon etonnement fut
extrême, lorsqu'en arrivant à Bordeaux, il me confessa que son depart, aussy
bien que son projet de servir l'Amérique etoit ignoré de toute sa famille, et
qu'il alloit envoyer un courier à Paris pour apprendre l'effet que ses lettres
laissées pour les en instruite auroient produit. Son courier revint le 25 au
matin avec des lettres effrayantes de ses amis, sur la colere du Roy, et surtout
de celle de M. le Duc D'Ayen. Mon avis etoit qu'il abandonna son projet, qu'il
returna sur le champ à Paris, et qu'il chargea ses armateurs du soin de son
vaisseau. Mais tout ce que je pû gaigner fut de relâcher dans une autre Port
ou il put recevoir la confirmation des Ordres du Roy, que les lettres de ses
amis luy annoncoient et l'on convint du Port de St. Sebastian en Espagne, ou
il recu un Courier de M. le Comte de Fumel, commandant à Bordeaux, sur
quoy je l'ay persuadé de se rendre aux ordres de Sa Mté. et au voux de sa
famille. Il partit donc sous la condition expresse que je ne [illegible word] pas
remettre à la voile que je n'eusse recu de ses nouvelles, parcequ'il feroit les
derniers efforts pour avoir la permission de partir. Je ne pus me refuser à
une demande si raisonnable, d'autant plus que le vaisseau luy appartenoit en
propre. [. . .] qu'on permettoit tacitement son entreprise et nous partimes
aussytôt le 20 avril. Quant à ses affaires d'argent et de depenses je ne m'en
suis mêlé que pour luy conseiller l'oeconomie et si j'ay endorsé à Charlestown
les lettres de change de 28000 l. qu'il a tirées sur son homme d'affaires à Paris
ce n'etoit que parce que sans cela il n'auroit pû toucher (à cause de son age)
de l'argent. Le correspondent de M. Raimbaux ne voulant pas luy en fournir
à compte de la cargaison de son vaisseau, qu'il n'eut auparavant la main levée
de l'armateur de Bordeaux conformement à un acte passé entre M. le Marquis et luy. Le tout a été recu par luy et il en a disposé comme il l'a jugé à

propos. Quoiq'il soit riche, je desirois pour luy qu'il donnoit dans des occasions moins carriere à sa Generosité et a sa liberalité. Je n'ay pas manqué de luy en parler souvent. Le peu d'emplettes qu'il m'avoit prié de luy faire, nos frais de voyage en commun de Paris à Bordeaux et ceux de Charlestown à Philadelphie, avec ce que je luy ay remis quelque fois ou payé pour luy a été compté et compensé par un compte definitif fait double entre nous le 1 7bre. dernier par lequel il me redevoit 388 l. 18 s. en espèce dont il m'a fourny un Billet à mon ordre sur son homme d'affaires et trente piestres ou Dollars en Papiers monnoye qu'il m'a payé. Ces details font ma lettre plus longue que je n'aurois voulû et je crains que cela ne vous ennuye, mais je desirois vous faire voir ma conduite dans cette affaire. Je ne vous parleray pas du mécontentement que M. le Vte. de Mauroy, M. de Lesser du Regt. d'Aunis, M. le Cher. de Fayolle du Regt. de Brie et d'autres qui s'en retournent, feront peutêtre paroitre de ce que j'ay accepté du service, pendant qu'on n'a pas voulu leur en offrir, et dont ils paroissoient même ne pas se soucier. Ils ne pourront pas dire néanmoins que je ne me sois pas employé vivement à leur faire accorder le remboursement de leur frais et les moyens pour leur retour. Comme je ne doute pas que quelques uns n'imaginent que j'aye négligé leurs intérrets pour ne songer qu'a moy et qu'ils feront peutêtre une espece de plainte de moy à M. le Ct. de Broglie, j'ay prié M. de Valfort du Regt. d'Aunis de dire sur cela tout ce qu'il scait, et il scait mieux que Personne ce que s'est passé et ce que j'ay fait. C'est un homme d'honneur et de bon sens qui voudra bien me rendre justice à cet égard. Je n'en diray pas d'avantage si non que je n'ay aucun reproche à me faire.

Je vais finir ma lettre par vous dire quelques nouvelles d'icy de notre guerre, et des bons et mauvais succès. . . .

To [Denis du Bouchet]

au camp de Whitemarsh ce premier decembre [1777]
Je suis bien faché, monsieur, que votre santé vous oblige à nous quitter; il est toujours fort agreable de se trouver en pays etranger avec des compatriotes qui Sy conduisent comme vous; croyés qu'à ce sentiment general je joins un interest bien particulier; j'ai appris avec un grand plaisir combien vous etiés aimé et estimé dans l'armée ou vous serviés; et je vous assure que j'aurois été bien charmé de faire la campagne avec vous dans celle-ci. Je ne profite pas des offres obligeantes que vous me faites pour La France; nous avons malheureusement une occasion plus près de nous dans Mr. de Cannway que nous allons, je crains, perdre entierement; j'attends de ses nouvelles tous les jours. Je me rappelle avec grand plaisir, monsieur, d'avoir été au college avec Mr. votre frere, et je vous prie de lui faire mille compliments quand vous le verrés. Je desire bien que vous ne soyés pas pris en mer, mais en cas de malheur, je vous prie de vous souvenir que vous trouverés dans l'armée du General Washington des amis fort disposés à vous servir. J'espere que

vous voudrés bien ne pas douter du sincere attachement avec lequel j'ai l'honneur d'etre, monsieur, votre très humble et obeïssant serviteur

LE MQUIS. DE LAFAYETTE

Mille tendres compliments je vous prie au General Gates. Dites aussi au Graux. Arnold et Lincoln combien j'ai envie de faire connoissance avec eux.

To the Duc d'Ayen

Au camp du Golphe en Pensilvanie
ce 16 decembre 1777

Cette lettre-ci, si jamais elle arrive, vous trouvera du moins en France; c'est toujours quelques risques d'evités; quoique cependant je ne doive jamais me flatter beaucoup; je n'ecris jamais un mot pour l'Europe sans m'attendrir d'avance sur le sort qui l'attend, et je travaïlle certainement plus pour Lord Howe que pour aucun de mes amis. Heureusement voici la mauvaise saison; les vaisseaux anglois seront obligés de quitter leur maudite croisiere, alors il m'arrivera des lettres, il en partira d'ici sur lesquelles je pourrai compter avec quelque certitude; cela me rendra bien heureux, et cela m'evitera de vous rendre bien ennuyé par la repetition de choses que je voulois vous faire savoir, mais dont je ne voudrois pas vous faire souvenir à chaque fois. J'attends avec bien de l'impatience des nouvelles de votre voyage; je compte principallement sur les bontés de Mde. de Lafayette pour en obtenir quelque detail; elle doit bien connoitre tout l'interest que je mets à en avoir. Mr. le mal. de Noaïlles me dit en general que les lettres qu'il recoit d'Italie l'assurent que tout les voÿageurs sont en bonne santé, et se trouvent fort bien de leur expedition; c'est aussi par lui que j'ai appris les couches de Mde. de Lafayette; il ne m'en parle pas comme de l'evenement du monde le plus heureux; mais mon inquietude etoit trop grande pour faire de distinction de sexe, et la bonte qu'il a eu de m'ecrire, de me faire savoir toutes ces nouvelles, m'a fait cent fois plus de plaisir qu'il n'a pu l'imaginer en me mandant que je n'avois qu'une fille. Voilà la rüe St. Honoré decredités pour jamais, tandisque l'autre hôtel de Noaïlles a acquis un nouveau lustre par la naissance d'Adrien. C'est vraiment un bien vilain procedé de faire ce tort. Là à une maison ou j'ai receu tout de bontés. Vous devés dans ce moment-ci vous geler sur les grands chemins de France; ceux de Pensilvanie deviennent aussi fort froids, et je tache en vain de me persuader que la difference de latitude devroit nous donner un hiver charmant en comparaison de Paris. On m'annonce même qu'il sera plus rigoureux. Nous sommes destinés à le passer sous des huttes à vingt milles de Philadelphie tant pour couvrir le pays, que pour profiter des circonstances, et en même tems etre plus à même d'instruire les troupes en les tenant plus rassemblées. Peut-etre eut-il beaucoup mieux valu de prendre tranquillement de vrais quartiers d'hiver, mais des raisons politiques ont engagé la Gal. Washington a se decider pour ce parti mitoïen.

Je voudrois bien etre assés habile pour vous rendre des evenements militaires de ce pays-ci un compte qui put vous satisfaire; mais outre mon insuffisance, des raisons Que vous sentirés bien m'empechent de risquer dans une lettre à travers des vaisseaux anglois, ce qui pourroit expliquer bien des choses si j'avois le bonheur d'en causer avec vous. Cependant je vais tacher de vous repeter encore une fois ce qui s'est passe d'interessant dans cette campagne; ma gazette à la quelle je n'ajoute pas de remarques et qui en vaut bien mieux, sera toujours preferable à celles d'Europe, parcequ'enfin l'homme qui voit dut-il ne pas bien voir est toujours plus digne de foi que celui qui ne voit rien du tout. Quant aux gazettes dont les anglois nous inondent elles sont tout au plus faites pour amuser les porteurs de chaise de Londres à coté d'un pot de porter, encore faut-il avoir deja bu quelque coup pour en mecconnoitre la mauvaise foi. Il me paroit que le plan du ministere anglois etoit de couper en long cette partie de l'Amerique qui s'etend depuis la Baye de Chesepeak jusqu'à Ticonderoga, le Gal. Howe avoit ordre de se rendre à Philadelphie par Elk, Bourgoïgne de descendre à Albany, et Clinton de remonter de Niew York par la Riviere du Nord. Le trois generaux devoïent par ce moyen se donner la main, on auroit receu ou fait semblant de recevoir les soumissions des provinces pretendues conquises, on ne nous laissoit pour quartier d'hiver que les derrieres du pays et pour ressource unique les quatre etats du sud; peutetre aussi une entreprise sur Charlestown etoit-elle projettée, ainsi voilà l'Amerique presque soumise dans le cabinet du roi d'Anglettere; heureusement la providence a permis quelques alterations dans l'execution de ce beau projet, pour exercer encore quelquetems la constance britannique.

En arrivant à l'armée au mois d'aoust j'ai été bien ettonné de ne point trouver d'ennemis. Après quelques marches en Jersay ou il ne s'etoit rien passé, le Gal. Howe s'etoit embarqué à New York; nous etions campé assés près de Philadelphie, et on attendoit leur descente du coté de Chester lorsqu'on apprit qu'ils etoïent à l'embouchure de la Riviere d'Elke. Le Gal. Washington alla au devant d'eux et après avoir pris plusieurs positions il se determina à les attendre au ruisseau de Brandiwine sur de fort bonnes hauteurs; le 11 septembre les anglois vinrent nous attaquer et pendant qu'ils nous amusoïent par leur canon et beaucoup de mouvements vis-à-vis nous ils firent filer la plus nombreuse partie de leurs troupes, avec toute l'elite de l'armée et tous les grenadiers commandés par le Gal. Howe lui même et Lord Cornwalis pour passer un gué à 4 milles sur notre droite. Dès que le Gal. Washington eut connu ce mouvement il detacha pour aller au devant d'eux toute son aile droite. De maudits avis qui avoïent toute l'apparence de la verité et qui detruisoïent les premiers rapports la firent arrêter longtems dans sa marche, et quand elle arriva les ennemis etoïent passés. Alors il fallut combattre en plaine contre des troupes superieures en nombre; aussi après avoir soutenu quelque tems un feu très vif et tué de leur coté beaucoup de monde aux anglois les americains plierent ⟨de tous cotés⟩. Une partie fut ralliée et ramenée, c'est la que je fus blessé; enfin pour couper court tout alla mal de tous les cotés, et le Gal. Washington fut battu par cette raison qu'il ne pouvoit pas gagner la premiere bataïlle generale qui ait été donnée dans cette guerre. On se rassembla à Chester. Ayant été transporté loin de l'armée je n'en suivis pas les differends mouvements. Le Gal. Howe profita du desordre ou une pluïe affreus avoit mis notre armée, pour passer le Schullchill, il se rendit à Philadelphie pour en prendre possession et prit poste entre la ville et Germain Town. Le Gal. Washington l'attaqua le 4 octobre et l'on peut dire que Notre general battit le leur quoique leurs troupes aïent repoussé les notres puisqu'il le surprit, et chassa même les anglois pendant long tems mais enfin leur experience triompha encore de la nouveauté de nos officiers et de nos soldats. Quelque tems auparavant un brigadier americain detaché de l'autre coté de la riviere avoit été attaqué la nuit dans son camp et avoit perdu ⟨assés⟩ de monde. Voilà tout ce qu'il y avoit eu d'interessant de ce coté là quand je revins au camp après avoir été six semaines au lit sans etre parvenu à fermer ma blessure. Dans ce tems-là nous receumes de bonnes nouvelles du Gral. Bourgoïgne. La premiere fois que je joignis l'armée pendant que le Gal. Howe etoit sur l'eau on m'apprit que les americains avoïent evacué precipitament Ticonderoga, en y laissant une grande quantité de canons [et] de munitions de toutes especes ⟨sans prendre le tems de les detruire⟩. Ce succès ⟨inattendu⟩ enfla l'orgueïl du Gal. Bourgoïgne ⟨et alors il pensa serieusement à executer sa commission⟩. Il produisit au public une pompeuse et ridicule proclamation qu'il a bien payée depuis. Son premier pas fut d'envoyer un detachement qui fut reppoussé; il ne se rebuta pas et s'avanca ⟨etourdiment⟩ au milieu de bois immenses, dans un pays ou il n'y a qu'un chemin. Le Gal. Gates avoit sous ses ordres quinze à seize mille hommes. On se battoit en tirant des coups de fusil derriere les arbres. Vainqueur ou vaincu Bourgoïgne s'affoiblissoit, et chaque quart de lieüe lui coutoit beaucoup de monde. Enfin entouré de toutes parts, mourant de faim, il a été obligé de faire une convention en vertu de laquelle il a été conduit par les milices de la Nouvelle Angleterre dans cette même *province* de Mashashuchet ou il avoit promis à Londres de prendre ses quartiers d'hiver. Il doit delà etre conduit avec ce qui lui restera de ses cinq mille hommes en Anglettere au depens du roi son maitre. Ticonderoga a été depuis evacué par les anglois.

Le Gal. Clinton qui⟨, avec sa permission,⟩ etoit parti un peu tard de New York, après avoir pris et detruit le Fort Montgommery sur la Riviere du Nord tachoit d'arriver sur les derrieres de Gates; mais ayant entendu parler de la convention il reprit le même chemin par lequel il etoit venu. S'il s'y etoit pris plutôt les affaires du Gal. Gates etoïent assés mauvaises.

Lorsque ma blessure après six semaines m'a permis de joindre l'armée, je l'ai trouvée à quinze milles de Philadelphie; des renforts du nord nous etoïent arrivés; le Gal. Howe etoit fort gené dans sa ville par deux forts, l'un sur la côte de Jersay, l'autre sur la petite Isle de Mud que vous trouverés sur votre carte au dessous du Schulchill. Ces deux forts defendoïent les chevaux de frise de la Delaware; ils ont soutenu fort longtems tous les efforts des troupes angloises de terre et de mer. Il y avoit deux jeunes françois qui y faisoïent le service d'ingenieurs et y ont acquis beaucoup d'honneur, MMs. de Fleury du rgt. de Rouergue, et de Mauduit du Plessis qui y commandoit en même tems l'artillerie ou il est officier en France. Des hessois commandés par le comte d'Onop sont venus attaquer celui ou etoit le dernier, et ont été reppoussés avec une perte considerable; le cte. d'Onop y fut pris et blessé mortellement.

Ces forts après une resistence vigoureuse ont été evacués. Lord Cornwallis passa alors dans le Jersay avec cinq mille hommes; un pareïl nombre de nos troupes y etoïent sous un de nos majors generaux. N'etant encore que volontaire j'allai m'y promener, et m'etant trouvé par hazard avec un detachement qui etoit près de l'ennemi, la bonne conduite de mes soldats justifia une attaque imprudente. Tout le monde nous a dit que my lord y avoit été blessé; il repassa ensuite la riviere, et nous en fimes autant. Toute l'armée etant rassemblée quelques jours après à White Marsh à treize milles de Philadelphie, toute celle du Gal. Howe vint nous attaquer; mais après avoir regardé notre position de tous les cotés, ils jugerent plus prudent de s'en aller pendant la nuit après quatre jours d'incertitude. Alors nous poursuivimes le projet de passer de ce coté-ci du Schullchill, et après avoir été arreté sur l'autre bords parceque nous trouvames sur celui-ci une partie de l'armée ennemie (quoique cela se soit borné a quelques coups de canon) ils nous laisserent le passage libre pour le lendemain, et nous allons etre tous sous des huttes pout tout l'hiver.

C'est-là que l'armée americaine va tacher de se vêtir parcequ'elle est nüe de toute nudité, de se former parcequ'elle a très grand besoin d'instruction, et de se recruter parcequ'elle est très foible mais les treize etats vont s'executer et nous envoyer du monde; ma division sera j'espere une des plus forte, je ferai mon possible pour qu'elle soit la meïlleure sur tous les points. La situation presente des ennemis n'est pas desagreable. L'armée de Bourgoïgne est nourrie au depens de la republique, et le peu qu'ils en pourront retirer (car plusieurs se perdront en chemin) sera remplacé sur le champs par d'autres troupes; Clinton est fort tranquille à New York avec une nombreuse garnison; le Gal. Howe fait sa cour aux belles ⟨dont il est fort amateur⟩ dans Philadelphie. La liberté qu'ils se permettent de voler et piller amis comme ennemis le met fort à son aise; ses vaisseaux viennent à present jusqu'à la ville, pas cependant sans danger; et sans Compter le vaisseau de 64 canons et la fregate brulées devant les forts, sans compter tous ceux que j'espere que la glaçe nous vaudra, plusieurs perissent tous les jours dans le passage difficile ou ils sont obligés de se risquer.

La perte de Philadelphie est bien loin d'avoir l'importance qu'on lui donne en Europe⟨; cette ville la moins disposée de toutes pour la liberté ne merite pas le nom dont on l'honore en France de la capitale de l'Amerique. C'est une triste cité habitée principallement par d'ennuïeux Quakers, dont l'honneteté n'est pas aussi recconnue que dans le livre de l'abbé Reynal. Tout ce qu'il y a d'honnêtes gens se sont retirés du coté de Lancaster⟩. Si la difference de circomstances, de païs, de proportion dans les deux armées n'etoit pas aussi manifeste, les succès du Gal. Gates seroïent bien surprenans à coté des evenements de cette partie-ci vu la prodigieuse superiorité de merite du Gal. Washington sur l'autre. Notre general est un homme vraiment fait pour cette revolution qui ne pourroit s'accomplir sans lui; je le vois de plus près qu'aucun homme au monde et je le vois digne de l'adoration de son pays. Sa tendre amitié et son entiere confiance en moi sur tous les objects militaires et politiques grands et petits qui le concernent, me mettent à portée de juger tout ce qu'il a à faire, à concilier, et à vaincre. J'admire tous les jours davantage la beauté de son charactere et de son ame. Quelques etrangers piqués de n'etre pas placés quoique cela ne depende en aucune façon de lui, quelques uns dont il n'a pas voulu servir les projets ambitieux, quelques jaloux cabaleurs ⟨peut-etre⟩ voudroïent ternir sa reputation, mais son nom sera reveré dans tous les siecles par tous les amateurs de la liberté et de l'humanité, et quoique je dus faire les honneurs de mon ami, je crois que le rôle qu'il joüe me donne le droit de faire connoitre combien je le respecte et l'admire. Il y a bien des choses interessantes que je ne peux pas ecrire, que je vous dirai un jour, sur lesquelles je vous prie de suspendre votre jugement et qui redoubleront votre estime pour lui.

L'Amerique attend avec impatience que nous nous declarions pour elle; et un jour, j'espere, la France se determinera à humilier l'insolente Angletterre. Cette consideration, et les demarches que l'Amerique me pariot decidée à faire me donnent de grandes esperances pour le glorieux etablissement de l'independance. ⟨Degagé du premier moment d'entousiasme⟩ je ne nous vois pas aussi forts que je le croyois ⟨en Europe⟩, mais cependant nous pouvons nous battre, nous le ferons, j'espere, avec quelque succès, et avec le secours de la France nous gagnerons avec depends la cause presente que je cheris parcequ'elle est juste, parcequ'elle honore l'humanité, parcequ'elle interesse ma patrie, ⟨parcequ'elle nuit à l'Angletterre,⟩ et parceque mes amis et moi y sommes engagés fort avant. La campagne prochaine sera interessante; on dit que les anglois nous envoïent des hanovriens, quelque tems auparavant c'etoit bien pis, on nous menaçoit des russes. Une petite menace de la France diminuera le nombre de ces renforts; plus je vois les anglois de près, plus je m'apperçois qu'il faut leur parler haut.

Après vous avoir ennuyé des affaires publiques vous ne pouvés pas vous dispenser d'etre ennuyé des miennes. Il est impossible d'etre tous les jours plus agreablément en pays etranger que je le suis ici. Je n'ai qu'à loüer, et j'ai lieu d'etre tous les jours plus satisfait de la conduite du Congress pour moi quoique mes occupations militaires ne m'en aient laissé connoitre que très peu de membres; ceux là surtout me comblent d'honnetetés et de soins. Le nouveau president Mr. Laurens un des hommes les plus respectables d'Amerique est mon ami le plus particulier; quant à l'armée j'ai eu le bonheur d'obtenir l'amitie de tout le monde⟨, et je puis me flatter qu'il est impossible de pouvoir desirer d'y etre plus agreablement que j'y suis⟩. On ne pert pas une occasion de m'en donner des preuves. J'ai passé tout le'été sans prendre de division comme vous savés que c'etoit mon projet. J'ai passé tout ce tems-là chés le Gal. Washington comme j'aurois pu etre chés un ami de vingt ans; depuis mon retour du Jersay il m'a dit de choisir de plusieurs brigades la division que me conviendroit le mieux. J'en ai pris une toute composée de virginiens. Elle est foible à present, même en proportion de la foiblesse de l'armée, elle est fort nüe; mais l'on me fait esperer du drap dont je ferai des habits, et des recrües dont il me faudroit faire des soldats à peu près dans le même tems. Mais par malheur l'un est plus difficile que l'autre même par des gens plus habiles que moi. Le metier que je fais ici si j'avois dejà assés d'acquitt pour le bien faire seroit fort utile à mon instruction. Le Mjor. Gal. remplace le lieutenant general et marechal de camp, dans leurs positions les plus interessantes; ainsi j'aurois de quoi employer bien du merite et de l'experience si la providence, et mon extrait de baptême m'avoient donné lieu de me vanter de l'un et de l'autre. Je lis, j'etudie, j'examine, j'ecoute, je pense, et de tout cela je tache d'en former une idée ou je fourre le plus de sens commun que je peux; je ne parlerai pas beaucoup de peur de dire des sottises, j'hazarderai encore moins de peur d'en faire, car je ne suis pas disposé à abuser de la confiance qu'on daigne me temoigner. Telle est le plan de conduite que j'ai suivi et suivrai jusqu'ici. Mais lorsque j'ai quelques idées dont je crois qu'en les rectifiant on peut faire quelque chose, je me presse d'en faire part à un grand juge qui veut bien me faire croire qu'elles lui plaisent. D'un autre coté quand ce coeur me dira qu'il se presente une occasion favorable, je ne pourrai pas lui refuser d'en courir les risques. Mais je ne crois pas que la gloriole d'un succès doive faire hazarder le salut d'une armée ou d'une de ses parties qui n'est pas faite, ni calculée pour l'offensive. Si j'osois risquer une maxime avec quelque assurance de ne pas dire une bêtise, je m'avanturerois à ajouter que quelques forces que nous ayons, il faut nous en tenir à un plan purement defensif exceptés pourtant dans le moment ou nous sommes forcés à une action, parceque j'ai cru m'appercevoir que les troupes angloises seroïent plus ettonnées d'une attaque brusque que d'une resistance ferme.

⟨Quant à mon retour en France, il m'a paru que c'etoit votre opinion ainsi que celle de tous les gens qui ont de la bonté pour moi qu'il me falloit faire ici plus d'une campagne. Cette opinion sera ma loi, et d'aïlleurs comme la campagne presente n'a point eu de fin, et que même Nous sommes à present dans une demie situation qui ne peut pas s'appeller un quartier d'hiver, je me crois en conscience, autant que par deference pour tous les avis que je respecte le plus, obligé de rester encore quelquetems ici.⟩

Cette lettre vous sera remise par le fameux Adams dont le nom vous est surement connu; comme je ne me suis jamais permis de quitter l'armée je n'ai pas pu le voir. Il a desiré que je le reccommanda en France, et surtout à vous. Puis-j'esperer que vous aurés la bonté de le bien recevoir et même de lui donner quelques connoissances sur les affaires presentes. J'ai imaginé que vous ne seriés pas faché de causer avec un homme dont le merite est si connu. Il desire ardemment de reussir à obtenir l'estime de notre nation. C'est un de ses amis qui m'a dit tout cela.

To Adrienne de Noailles de Lafayette

au camp près de Valley Forge ce 22 decembre [1777]

Je me trouve bien attrappé, mon cher coeur; j'avois reservé votre lettre pour la derniere, comptant avoir bien le tems d'ecrire, et la personne qui doit porter ma lettre a Mr. Adams, vient de me mander qu'il est obligé de partir sur le champ. J'avois deja prepare une longue epître pour Mr. Le duc d'Ayen, une pour le prince, une pour mon grandpere; et a present je n'ai que le tems de vous dire bonjour, et vais vous ecrire plus au long par une autre occasion, qui arrivera peutêtre plutôt. J'ai reçu la nouvelle de votre heureux accouchement, et j'en ai ete comblée de la joye la plus pure, et la plus vive. Je n'ai jamais ete si heureux de ma vie que dans le moment ou la nouvelle m'en est arrivée. Je n'ai pas reçu de lettres de vous a ce sujet, mais l'on me mande qu'il y en a darrivées dans cinq ou six ports d'Amerique. Vous jugés avec quelle impatience je les attends. Je vous ai ecrit depuis que j'ai appris vos couches, et vous deves avoir recu ma lettre. Celle-ci vous sera remise par le fameux Mr. Adams, auquel je vous prie de faire toutes les politesses possibles. Comme j'ai toujours ete a larmée, je n'ai pas été a portée de le connoître beaucoup, mais je sais, qu'il a autant d'esprit que de merite, et la plus grande modestie. J'espere que les honetêtés que vous et mes amis lui feront, et les connoissances que vous lui procurerés, revaudront un peu toutes celles que jeprouve ici. Mr. le duc d'Ayen, et surtout le prince, vous diront plus au long les details qui me concernent, et moy, mon cher coeur, je vais me contenter de vous repeter ici avec un plaisir toujours nouveau, que je vous aime avec une tendresse inexprimable, que je vous aime plus que jamais, et que j'espere que nous serons heureux toute notre vie, par notre sentiment mutuel. J'embrasse mille et mille fois, nos deux cheres filles, dites leur que leur papa les aime a la folie, ainsi que leur charmante mere. Croïés, que je ne perdrai pas un moment pour vous rejoindre, aussitôt que je le pourrai. Adieu, adieu je vous embrasse dix millions de fois.

Mille tendres respects a Mde. la dsse. d'Ayen à Mr. le mal. de Noailles &c. Adieu, adieu, aimés moy toujours.

J'espere que Mr. Adams vous parlera beaucoup de mon tendre, et charmant ami, le grand et respectable, Gal. Washington.

L.

To Adrienne de Noailles de Lafayette

Au camp pres Valley Forge ce 6 janvier [1778]

Quelle datte, mon cher coeur, et quel pays pour ecrire au mois de janvier; mon etoile est bien singuliere; c'est dans un camp, c'est au milieu des bois, c'est à quinze cent lieues de vous que je me vois enchainé au milieu de l'hiver ⟨tandisque depuis deux mois je devrois etre avec vous, tandisque, mon coeur, tous mes desirs, et le bon sens même me forcoïent à partir. Mais un sentiment delicat plus fort que la raison, et que vous comprendrés mieux que je ne puis vous l'exprimer m'a toujours retenu ici de jour en jour. Nous autres françois nous sommes faits de tout tems un point d'honneur de ne pas quitter une campagne avant la conclusion. Celle-ci n'a pas eu de fin, et je me suis vu entrainé insensiblement jusqu'à ce moment ici ou je suis ettonné et presque effraïé de me retrouver dans les deserts d'Amerique⟩. Il n'y a pas encore bien longtems que nous n'etions separés des ennemis que par une petite riviere; à present même nous en sommes à 7 lieues, et c'est là que l'armée americaine passera l'hiver sous de petites barraques qui ne sont gueres plus gaïes qu'un cachot. Je ne sais s'il conviendra au Gal. Howe de venir visiter notre nouvelle ville; nous tacherions de lui en faire les honneurs, et le porteur de cette lettre vous dira quel est l'agreable sejour que je prefere au bonheur d'etre avec vous, avec tous mes amis, au milieu de tous les plaisirs possibles. De bonne foi, mon cher coeur, croïés vous qu'il ne faïlle pas de fortes raisons pour se determiner à ce sacrifice. Tout me disoit de partir, l'honneur m'a dit de rester, et vraiment quand vous connoitrés en detaïl les circomstances ou je me trouve, ou se trouve l'armée, mon ami qui la commande, toute la cause americaine, vous me pardonnerés, mon cher coeur, vous m'excuserés même, et j'ose presque dire que vous m'approuverés. Que j'aurai de plaisir à vous dire moi même toutes mes raisons, à vous demander en vous embrassant un pardon que je suis sur alors d'obtenir. Mais ne me condamnés pas avant de m'avoir entendu; outre la raison que je vous ai dejà dit j'en ai une autre que je ne voudrois pas raconter à tout le monde parceque cela auroit l'air de me donner un ridicule importance. Ma presence est necessaire dans ce moment-ci à la cause americaine plus que vous ne le pourriés penser. Tant d'etrangers qui n'ont pas été employés ou dont on n'a pas ensuite voulu servir l'ambition ont fait des cabales puissantes. Ils ont essayé par toutes sortes de pieges de me degouter et de cette revolution et de celui qui en est le chef; ils ont repandu tant qu'ils ont pu que je quittois le continent. D'un autre coté les anglois l'ont dit hautement, leur haine pour moi paroit augmenter par mon sejour. Je ne puis pas en conscience donner raison à tout ce monde là. Si je pars beaucoup de francois utiles ici suivront mon exemple. Le Gal. Washington seroit vraiment malheureux si je lui parlois de partir. Sa confiance en moi est plus grande que je n'ose l'avoüer à cause de mon age. Dans la place qu'il occupe on est entouré de flatteurs ou d'ennemis secrets. Il trouve en moi un ami sur dans le sein duquel il peut epancher son coeur et qui lui dira toujours la verité. Il n'y a pas de jour qu'il n'ait de grandes conversations avec moi ou m'ecrive de longues lettres, et il veut bien me consulter sur les points les plus interessans. Il y a dans ce moment-ici une circomstance particuliere ou ma presence ne lui est pas inutile; ce n'est pas le moment de parler de depart. J'ai aussi dans le moment present avec le president du Congress qui après le Gal. est mon meïlleur ami dans ce païs-ci une correspondance interessante. ⟨J'ai envie que cette revolution reussisse.⟩ L'abaissement de l'⟨insolente⟩ Anglettere, l'avantage de ma patrie, le bonheur de l'humanité qui est interessé à ce qu'il y ait dans le monde un peuple entierement libre, et les fraix que moi et mes amis avons fait pour cette cause, tout m'engagoit à ne pas la quitter dans un moment ou mon absence lui auroit fait tort. D'aïlleurs après un petit succès dans le Jersay le Gal. par le voeu unanime du Congress m'a engagé à prendre une division de l'armée, et à former à ma guise autant que mes foibles moyens le pourroïent permettre; je ne devois pas repondre à ces marques de confiance en lui demandant ses commissions pour l'Europe. Telles sont, mon cher coeur, une partie des raisons que je vous confie sous le secret; je vous en ajouterai moi même bien d'autres que je ne puis pas hazarder dans une lettre⟨; ne croïés pas que mon sejour ici entraine la necessité de faire la campagne prochaine. Mille circonstances peuvent me donner l'occasion de partir bientôt, et soïés sur, mon coeur, que je decamperai aussitôt que je pourrai hon-nêtement m'echapper. Vous devés sentir que ce n'est pas pour mon plaisir que je demeure enterré dans ce triste gîte tandisque tous les bonheurs possibles m'attendent à Paris au milieu de tous mes amis, dans les bras d'une charmante femme que j'aime plus que jamais. Si vous pouviés lire un moment dans mon coeur, je n'aurois pas besoin d'excuses, et pour peu que ma tendresse vous interesse j'ose dire que vous seriés contente des sentiments que vous y liriés⟩.

Cette lettre-ci vous sera remise par un honnête monsieur francois qui est venu de cent milles pour prendre mes commissions. ⟨J'en suis penetré de recconnoissance; recevés le bien, mon cher coeur, il repart peu aprés son arrivée pour ce pays-ci. Profités en pour m'ecrire; et quoique votre lettre puisse bien me trouver parti depuis longtems, ecrivés toujours en cas que je sois assés malheureux que d'etre encore ici, pour adoucir un peu l'ennui et le chagrin de mon exil.⟩ Je vous ai ecrit il y a peu de jours par le fameux Mr. Adams ⟨que je vous ai reccommendé. J'espere que vous le recevrés bien⟩; il vous facilitera les occasions de me donner de vos nouvelles. Vous en aurés receu auparavant que je vous envoyai dès que j'eus appris vos couches. Que cet evenement m'a rendu heureux mon cher coeur! J'aime à vous en parler dans toutes mes lettres parceque j'aime à m'en occuper à tous moments. Quel plaisir j'aurai à embrasser mes deux pauvres petites filles, et à leur faire demander mon pardon à leur mere. Vous ne me croyés pas assés insensible, mon cher coeur, et en même tems assés ridicule pour que le sexe de notre nouvel enfant ait diminué en rien la joïe de sa naissance. Notre caducité n'est pas au point de nous empecher d'en avoir encore un autre sans miracle. Celui-là, il faudra absolument que ce soit un garçon. Au reste, si c'est pour le nom qu'il falloit etre faché, je declare que j'ai formé le projet de vivre assés longtems pour le porter bien des années moi même avant d'etre obligé d'en faire part à un nouvel etre. C'est à Mr. le Mal. de Noaïlles que je dois cette nouvelle. J'ai une bien vive impatience d'en recevoir de vous. J'eus l'autre jour une lettre de Desplaces qui m'en annonce une anterieure; mais la fantaisie des vents et des flots, sans compter la rencontre des anglois derangent bien souvent l'ordre de mes correspondances. J'ai eu plusieurs jours d'inquietudes sur le compte du Vte. de Coïgni qu'on me mandois qui alloit plus mal; mais cette lettre de Desplaces qui ne me parle point de lui, et qui me dit que tout le monde va bien m'a rassuré; j'en ai receu aussi quelques autres qui ne me disent pas un mot de sa santé. Je vous en prie quand vous m'ecrirés, mon cher coeur, envoyés moi bien des detaïls sur tous les gens que j'aime et même toute la societé. C'est une chose bien extraordinaire que je n'aie pas encore entendu parler des couches de Mde. de Fronsac. Dites lui mille choses aussi tendres que respectueuses pour moi ainsi qu'à la Ctesse. Auguste. Si ces dames n'entrent pas dans les raisons qui me forcent malgré moi de rester ici ⟨de jour en jour⟩, elles doivent me juger un etre bien ridicule, surtout etant à portée de voir mon cher coeur, de quelle charmante femme je me separe. Mais cette même idée doit leur faire sentir ⟨que si je reste, si je sacrifie le plaisir à l'ennui, le bonheur au chagrin, la vie des plus aimables societés, à la triste vie d'un sauvage, si enfin, mon cher coeur, je suis loin de vous au lieu d'en etre près, c'est⟩ que j'ai d'invincibles motifs pour m'y determiner. ⟨On n'ira pas imagner, je pense, que c'est pour me divertir que je m'enterre dans ces bois deserts.⟩ Plusieurs officers generaux font venir leurs femmes au camp, je suis bien envieux non pas de leur femmes ⟨qui sont assés maussades⟩, mais du bonheur qu'ils ont d'etre à portée de les voir. Le Gal. Washington va aussi se determiner à envoyer chercher la sienne, qui est une personne honnête, respectable, et qui aime son epoux à la folie. Mons. les anglois ⟨ont pris je crois le parti de se servir des femmes des autres au defaut des leurs,⟩ il leur est arrivé de plus un renfort de trois cent demoiselles de Newyork; et nous leur avons pris un autre vaisseau pleine de chastes epouses d'officiers qui venoïent rejoindre leur maris; elles avoïent grand peur qu'on ne voulut leur garder ⟨tout l'hiver⟩ pour ⟨l'usage⟩ des armées americaines.

Vous apprendrés par le porteur de cette lettre que ma santé est très bonne, que ma blessure est guerie, et que le changement de pays ne m'a fait aucun effet. ⟨Le Blanc et Baptiste ne sont pas si heureux: ce dernier a pensé mourir et j'en aurois été bien faché car c'est un brave garçon.⟩ Ne pensés vous pas, mon cher coeur, qu'après mon retour nous serons assès raisonables pour nous etablir dans notre maison, y etre heureux ensemble, y recevoir nos amis, y etablir une douce liberté, et lire les gazettes des païs etrangeres sans avoir la curiosité d'aller voir nous même ce qui s'y passe. J'aime à faire des châteaux en France de bonheur et de plaisirs. Vous y etes toujours de moitié, mon cher coeur, et une fois que nous serons reunis rien ne pourra plus nous separer, et nous empêcher de gouter ensemble, et l'un par l'autre, la douceur d'aimer, et la plus delicieuse, la plus tranquille felicité. Adieu, mon coeur, je voudrois bien que ce plan put commencer dès aujourdhui. Ne vous conviendra-t-il pas mon cher coeur? Presentés mes plus tendres respects à Mde. d'Ayen, embrassés mille fois la vicomtesse et mes soeurs. ⟨Faites aussi mes compliments à l'abbé Fayon et Mlle. Marin. Mille respects à mon grand pere; je lui ai ecrit l'autre jour, et je lui recrirai encore si on me donne le tems.⟩ Adieu, adieu, mon très cher coeur, aimés moi toujours, et n'oubliés pas un instant, le malheureux exilé qui pense toujours à toi avec une nouvelle tendresse.

To Adrienne de Noailles de Lafayette

Ce 3 fevrier [1778] at York

Je ne me reprocherai jamais, mon cher coeur, de laisser passer une occasion de vous ecrire, et j'en trouve une par Mr. du Bouchet qui a le bonheur de s'embarquer pour France. ⟨Que je l'envie mon cher coeur! Je me hais souvent moi même, et me mets en colere contre ma folle tête qui ma' embarqué dans une affaire dont je ne peux plus me retirer. Dans ce moment même on me fait General en chef d'une armée dans le Nord destinée à une expedition du coté du Canada. Quelque flatteuse que soit cette place et quelque agreable qu'il fut de reuissir, vû les immenses difficultés, je vous assure, mon cher coeur, que j'aimerois bien mieux partir pour France. Ce qu'on appelle dans les troupes *la maladie du païs* commence à me gagner et j'en epprouve de

tristes simptômes. Les mêmes choses qui m'auroient tourné la tête à mon arrivée ne me font plus aucun plaisir. L'amour de mon metier et un peu d'envie
d'etre quelque chose dans la ligne des militaires (ce n'est pas des rangs que je
parle) joint à mon amitié pour le Gal. Washington et un respectable president
actuellement à la tête du Congress, j'ajouterai les avances que j'ai dejà fait
pour cette cause americaine, telles sont les raisons qui m'ont poussé si avant
dans l'hiver, et me font actuellement accepter un commandement que j'aurois
bien troqué contre celui d'un petit vaisseau allant en France. Je suis triste,
mon cher coeur, et je suis malheureux. Dans le même tems Qu'il me faut faire
un visage riant aux gens auxquels je ne peux pas devoiler mon coeur et repondre aux dix milles affaires dont je suis occupé, mon ame gemit en secret,
et je suis tout seul à me plaindre moimême. Cette lettre vous sera remise par
le beau frere d'un des officiers generaux envoïés sous moi; c'est un jeune
homme aussi estimable par ses nobles sentiments et sa conduite qu'il est par sa
bravoure, et son merite. Il servoit dans le nord sous le Gal. Gates qui en fait
grandeur et tout le monde m'en dit du bien. Recevés le bien, mon cher coeur,
temoignés lui quelque interest, et parlés de lui avec quelque instance à Mr. de
Causan son colonel quand vous le trouverés chés Mde. de Fresnet.⟩

⟨Quoique de soit pour moi, mon cher coeur, un des plus vifs plaisirs dont je
puisse jouïr ici que celui de vous ecrire, mon coeur se serre en vous disant que
c'est un autre que moi qui est destiné à vous donner de mes nouvelles. Si je
suis triste dans ce païs-ci il n'y a pas moyen de faire partager mes sentiments à
tous les etrangers qui m'entourent et alors je ne peux pas m'empecher d'etre
maussade dans les rares occasions que je trouve de pancher mon coeur. J'aimerois mieux dans les fonds que vous me crussiés entierement heureux et
content parceque cela vous eviteroit de souffrir de ma peine mais, mon cher
coeur, je vous mentirois si je vous disois que mon ame est satisfaite loin de
vous et de tout ce que j'aime. Le premier moment d'entousiasme peut empêcher de regardes derriere soi pour quelques instants, mais ensuite, mon
coeur, j'epprouve que lorsqu'on porte une ame sensible on n'est pas longtems
à se repentir d'une demarche inconsiderée.⟩

Vous aurés receu dejà plusieurs lettres ou je vous parle de la naissance de
notre nouvel enfant et de la joïe que ce charmant evenement m'a causé. Si je
pensois que vous avés soupçonné ce contentement d'avoir souffert quelque
diminution par ceque notre Anastasie n'est qu'une fille, en verité, mon coeur,
je serois si en colere contre vous que je ne vous aimerois plus qu'un peu pour
quelques instants. Ah mon coeur quel delicieux plaisir de vous embrasser
tous! Quelle consolation de pouvoir pleurer avec mes autres amis celui que j'ai
perdu.

Je ne vous ferai pas de long detaïls sur la marque de confiance dont
l'Amerique m'honore. Il vous suffira de savoir que le Canada est opprimé par
les anglois⟨, et (entre nous) qu'il n'a pas eu lieu d'etre content des americains⟩.
Tout cet immense païs est en possession des ennemis, ils y ont une flotte, des
troupes et des forts. Moi je vais me rendre avec le titre de Gal. en chef de l'armée du nord et A la tête d'environ mille hommes, pour voir si l'on peut faire
quelque mal aux anglois dans ces contrées; l'idée de rendre toute la Nouvelle
France libre et de la delivrer d'un joug pesant est trop brillante pour s'y ar-

rêter. Alors mon armée augmenteroit immensement et seroit augmentée par des françois. ⟨Il y a un grand nombre d'officiers françois qui m'y suivent, et je me trouve bien glorieux d'etre à leur tête.⟩ J'entreprens un terrible ouvrage, surtout ayant peu de moyens. Quant à ceux de mon propre merite ils sont bien nuls pour une telle place, et ce n'est pas à vingt ans qu'on est fait pour etre à la tête d'une armée, chargé de tous les immenses detaïls qui roulent sur un general, et ayant sous mes ordres directs une grande etendüe de pays.

Le nombre de troupes que j'aurai sous moi qui seroit peu de chose en Europe est considerable en Amerique. Ce qui me fait le plus de plaisir dans tout cela c'est que de façon ou d'autre ⟨cela sera plus court que si j'avois resté dans l'armée du Gal. Washington, et⟩ je serai plustôt en etat de vous joindre. ⟨Je languis après cet heureux moment,⟩ qu'il seroit charmant de faire bien vite mes affaires avec les anglois de la haut ⟨et de decamper tout de suite pour ma bonne patrie⟩. Je pars dans l'instant pour Albany et de là à un autre endroit a peu près cent cinquante lieües d'ici, et delà je commencerai à travaïller. Ce mois-ci n'est pas agreable pour voyager; je ferai une partie de la course en traineaux. Une fois arrivé la haut je ne marcherai que sur des glaçes.

Je n'ecris à aucun de mes amis par cette occasion. J'ai une immensité d'affaires, et il y a une infinité de choses politiques et militaires à arranger, il y a tant de choses à reparer, tant de nouveaux obstacles à lever, qu'en verité il me faudroit quarante ans d'experience et des talents superieurs pour ne pas en sortir avec desagrement. Au moins je ferai de mon mieux, et ne pus-je reussir qu'à occuper leur attention dans le nord quand je ne leur ferois pas d'autre mal c'est toujours un grand service à rendre, et ma petite armée ne seroit pas inutile. Faites moi le plaisir de dire au prince ⟨au Vte. et à tous mes amis de mes nouvelles. Assurés le prince⟩ que son chetif capitaine tout general en chef qu'il est n'en sait gueres plus long qu'il n'en savoit au poligone, et qu'il ne sait trop, a moins que le hazard ou son bon ange ne l'inspire, comment justifier la confiance qu'on lui temoigne. Mille tendres respects a Mde. d'Ayen; mille assurances de ma tendre amitié à la vicomtesse à toutes mes soeurs. Ne m'oubliés pas auprés de vos amies, de Mr. votre pere, Mde. de Tessé, Mr. le Mal. de Noaïlles &c. Adieu, Adieu, mon cher coeur, embrassés nos chers enfans, j'embrasse leur charmante mere une million de fois; quand me retrouverai-je dans ses bras!

To the Baron von Steuben

Albany ce douze mars 1778

Monsieur

J'ai receu avec bien de la recconnoissance les lettres que vous m'avés fait l'honneur de m'ecrire; elles me sont arrivées dans le même tems à peu près, et j'attendois pour repondre à la premiere de pouvoir vous dire quelque chose de certain sur l'expedition dont on m'a fait l'honneur de me charger. Le vif desir que j'ai de meriter l'estime d'un homme tel que vous, et ma vive sensibilité pour les lettres obligeantes qui j'ai receu de vous, me font mettre le plus grand prix à connoitre votre opinion sur cette affaire. Je suis un bien jeune soldat, monsieur, et par consequent plus sujet que personne à me tromper, mais j'ose dire que la necessité a dicté la conduite que j'ai tenu par cette seule raison qu'il n'y avoit rien autre chose à faire. Je ne trouve pas plus du tiers des troupes qui m'etoïent promises et je les trouve prêtes à faire eclater leur mecontentement pour l'horrible negligence qu'on a mis à les payer; point d'argeant, point d'habits, ni voitures, ni provisions, ni magazins de prêts, le tems nous faisoit la loi, et comme celui de se procurer même la moitié de ce qui etoit necessaire, m'auroit mené plus loin que la saison ou le lac est passable, j'ai mieux aimé m'arrêter à tems, que d'exposer les armes americaines à une honte certaine par une entreprise mal combinée. Le detaïl de ce qui vient de m'arriver paroitroit extraordinaire en Europe, mais dans un pays jeune il faut prendre patience, et se prêter aux circomstances. Le Congress a approuvé dans sa reponse la conduite que j'ai été forcé de tenir.

Je ne sais pas encore, monsieur, dans quelle partie de ce continent je suis destiné à servir. Je me croirai bien heureux d'avoir l'occasion de faire connoissance avec vous, de la cultiver, et de meriter votre amitié et votre estime. Quoique je risque de perdre beaucoup de la trop bonne opinion que mes amis ont bien voulu vous donner de moi, je vous assure que mes craintes sur cet article cederont de beaucoup au plaisir que j'aurai de vous voir, et à l'avantage que j'espere tirer de vos conseïls si je peux obtenir que vous vouliés bien me les accorder.

Permettés moi, monsieur, de vous faire mon compliment sur ce que vous etes à portée de voir le general Washington. Ce grand homme ne peut trouver d'ennemis que dans ceux de sa patrie, et encore toute ame noble et sensible ne pourra pas s'empêcher d'aimer les excellentes qualités de son coeur. Je crois le connoitre aussi bien que personne, et telle est exactement l'idée que j'ai de lui. Son honneteté, sa franchise, sa sensibilité, sa virtu autant que l'idée de ce mot peut l'etendre sont au dessus de tout eloge. Ce n'est pas à moi à juger ses talents militaires, mais autant que mes tres foibles lumieres peuvent s'etendre son avis dans le conseïl m'a toujours paru le meilleur quoique sa modestie l'empêcha quelquefois de le soutenir, et ses predictions ont toujours été accomplies. J'ai été bien aise de vous donner une idée du caractere de mon ami avec toute la sincerité du mien, parceque quelques personnes auroïent peut-etre cherché à vous tromper sur cet article.

Je n'ai pas encore eu l'honneur de voir, monsieur, l'officier que vous m'annoncés. Je serai bien empressé de pouvoir lui etre de quelque utilité. Je sens que ce seroit faire grand tort à monsieur des Epiniers que de le priver de l'avantage d'etre avec vous, surtout aprés que l'expedition du Canada est arrêtée. Je puis vous repondre que la bonne opinion que vous avés de lui augmentera à mesure que vous le connoitrés d'avantage. Vous recevrés une seconde lettre de moi ou je prendrai la liberté de vous faire part de ma destination, et en attendant que j'ai le plaisir de vous en assurer moimême je vous prie d'etre persuadé des sentiments les plus distingués avec lesquels j'ai l'honneur d'etre, monsieur, Votre très humble et obeïssant serviteur

Le Mis. de Lafayette

INDEX

compiled by Joseph L. Narun

Note on the Index

This index is designed to complement the volume's annotation. The Table of Contents and the List of Illustrations are not indexed.

Significant textual variants, printed in parentheses, immediately follow the accepted orthography. Cross references from variants to the main entries are supplied. Places are indexed under their eighteenth-century names.

French names are indexed according to the form most common in the documents. Names incorporating "la" are indexed under La. Given-name preferences are printed in small capitals.

Entries and subentries adhere to letter-by-letter alphabetization; mentions are provided as the last subentry. All documentary references appear at the head of the subentries; letters to and from Lafayette precede third-party letters. The official correspondence of the presidents of Congress is indexed under both Congress and the names of the officeholders. Italicized page numbers denote documents that are not directly quoted in the volume. Receipts, recommendations, testimonials, and the like are considered letters for the purposes of the Index. Page references are given in preference to annotation references except in the case of letters.

Aahquagee (Onoquaga, now Colesville), N.Y., Indian village, 324

Abos, Marie de Guérin, marquise d' (Mlle de Chavaniac) (1756–1778), L's first cousin (*see* Genealogical Chart, xliv–xlv), 26

Adams, Mrs., loyalist, 356, 374

Adams, John (1735–1826), member of Congress (from Massachusetts), American commissioner to France (from November 28, 1777):
letter from, 278
letters to, 226–227, *278;* from Thaxter, 195n
as commissioner to France, 179; and Conway Cabal, 171; and L, 187, 197–198, 278; L on, 198, 227; on G. Washington, 326, 327n; mentioned, 194, 196, 224, 228n, 278

Adams, Samuel (1722–1803), member of Congress (from Massachusetts), cousin of John:
letter to, from Lovell, 187n
and Conway Cabal, 171; mentioned, 379n

Additional Continental Regiments. *See* Jackson, Henry; Lee, William Raymond; Warner, Seth.

Agnew, James (? –1777), British brigadier general, 97, 120, 121n

Aguesseau. *See* Daguesseau.

Albany, N.Y.: American garrison at, 247; American troop strength at, 269; British foreign agents at, 341; British hospital at, 369; British prisoners at, 366n; and Canadian expedition, 245, 293; chain of command at, 298n; conspiracy at, 328, 345; L's arrival at, 246, 288, 299; L on his command at, 351,

371; L pays for debts at, 326; L's and Kalb's recall from, 369n, 377; munitions at, 326, 365n; mentioned, 317n, 329, 330n, 363

Albany Committee of Correspondence:
letters from, 303–304, *306;* to G. Clinton, 331n
letters to, 293–294, 330–331, 373–374
and Canadian expedition, 293–294, 303–304; and conspiracy, 328, 345; powers and functions of, 294n, 303

Albert de Luynes, Duc d'. *See* Luynes, Louis-Joseph-Charles-Amable.

Alexander, Catherine (Kitty), daughter of William, 283, 286, 369

Alexander, William (Lord Stirling) (1726–1783), American major general:
letter from, *205;* to G. Washington, 206n
at Brandywine, 84, 94, 95, 101n; and Conway Cabal, 206n; mentioned, 91, 240n–241n, 283n, 285, 287, 299, 382n

America, United States of: abundance of food in, 11, 144, 184; and Brandywine aftermath, 110; capital punishment in, 329, 365; climate in, 64, 76, 106, 173–175, 226, 245; democracy in, 170; Hudson River's importance to, 329, 341; L on virtues of people in, 55, 60; L's opinion of, 11, 58–59, 64, 138, 223, 350; peace rumors in, 346, 348; post time from, 58; postal service in, 179, 324, 339–341; profiteering and high cost of goods in, 144, 169–170; regional differences and factions in, 71, 213; roads in, 71, 283, 285, 354; social life and customs of, 61–63, 66, 71, 75, 82,

*Lafayette in the Age of
the American Revolution*

Designed by R. E. Rosenbaum.
Composed by Vail-Ballou Press, Inc.,
in 10 point VIP Baskerville, 2 points leaded,
with display lines in Helvetica.
Printed offset by Vail-Ballou Press on
Warren's Old Style, 50 pound basis.
Bound by Vail-Ballou Press
in Joanna book cloth
with Multicolor endpapers,
and stamped in All Purpose foil.
Jackets printed by Simpson/Milligan Printing Co.

Library of Congress Cataloging in Publication Data
(For library cataloging purposes only)

Lafayette, Marie Joseph Paul Yves Roch Gilbert du
    Motier, marquis de, 1757–1834.
    Lafayette in the age of the American Revolution.

    (His The papers of the Marquis de Lafayette)
    "French texts": v. 1, p.
    Bibliography: v. 1, p.
    Includes index.
    CONTENTS: v. 1. December 7, 1776–March 30, 1778.
    1. Lafayette, Marie Joseph Paul Yves Roch Gilbert du Motier, marquis de,
1757–1834.   2. United States—History—Revolution, 1776–1783—Sources.   3. United
States—History—Confederation, 1783–1789—Sources.   4. Generals—United States—
Correspondence.   5. Generals—France—Correspondence.   I. Idzerda,   Stanley   J.
II. Title.   III. Series: Lafayette, Marie Joseph Paul Yves Roch Gilbert du Motier,
marquis de, 1757–1834. The papers of the Marquis de Lafayette.
E207.L2A4   1977   944.04'092'4   [B]   76-50268
ISBN 0-8014-1031-2 (v. 1)